Dassel-Cokato Jr. Sr. High School Library
Independent District 466

Y0-DKD-826

EIGHT
AMERICAN ETHNIC PLAYS

Eight American Ethnic Plays

EDITED BY

FRANCIS GRIFFITH

JOSEPH MERSAND

CHARLES SCRIBNER'S SONS
New York

Copyright © 1974 Charles Scribner's Sons

Library of Congress Cataloging in
Publication Data

Griffith, Francis J   comp.
 Eight American ethnic plays.
 CONTENTS: Alfred, W. Hogan's goat.—Van Druten, J. I remember mama.—Rose, R. Dino. [etc.]
 1. Minorities—United States—Drama. 2. American drama—20th century. I. Mersand, Joseph E., 1907-   joint comp. II. Title.
PS627.M5G7   812'.5'40803   73-5191
ISBN 0-684-13653-8 (pbk.)

This book published simultaneously in the
United States of America and in Canada—
Copyright under the Berne Convention

All rights reserved. No part of this book
may be reproduced in any form without the
permission of Charles Scribner's Sons.

1 3 5 7 9 11 13 15 17 19 V|P 20 18 16 14 12 10 8 6 4 2

Printed in the United States of America

Contents

Introduction	vii
The Irish in the United States	1
Hogan's Goat by WILLIAM ALFRED	5
The Scandinavians in the United States	79
I Remember Mama by JOHN VAN DRUTEN	83
The Italians in the United States	131
Dino by REGINALD ROSE	135
The Jews in the United States	159
The Tenth Man by PADDY CHAYEFSKY	163
The Blacks in the United States	215
A Raisin in the Sun by LORRAINE HANSBERRY	221
Day of Absence by DOUGLAS TURNER WARD	275
The Puerto Ricans in the United States	299
The Oxcart by RENÉ MARQUÉS	303
The Mexicans in the United States	367
Wetback Run by THEODORE APSTEIN	371

Introduction

One of the most significant phenomena in recent years in both secondary and higher education is the interest in ethnic studies. Hundreds of colleges have established programs in Black Studies, Puerto Rican Studies, Jewish Studies, Chicano Studies, Scandinavian Studies, and many other areas. Thousands of students are discovering new aspects of their cultural heritage and developing new pride in that heritage. Whereas earlier in the century assimilation and acceptance of exclusively American cultural values were stressed in the educational programs, today many leaders and educators are realizing that retaining one's cultural heritage is an important means of enriching our nation's cultural, moral, and intellectual values.

The general interest shown by various ethnic groups in their national and cultural heritage has certainly not been limited to study in educational institutions. Witness the success in the 1970s of such films as *The Emigrants* (dialogue in Swedish), the many films and television programs by and about Black Americans, and the many programs of ethnic content, such as *Realidades* on New York's Channel 13, the National Educational Television Station, or the *Eternal Light* produced by the Jewish Theological Seminary—all testify to the increasing demand for programs of multiethnic and multicultural orientation. This trend will continue and should indeed be encouraged.

Our own anthology is an attempt to provide the student with a number of plays of multiethnic and multicultural orientation. Each play was chosen first because of its intrinsically high level of literary quality. Each attempts, in one way or another, to represent the subtle process by which a group or an individual blends his own ethnic identity with his adopted American culture. Sometimes it is a conscious struggle as in *A Raisin in the Sun*; sometimes an almost unconscious accommodation as in *The Tenth Man*. *Wetback Run* depicts a failure in one sense; *I Remember Mama* a triumph. Dino's ethnicity is inferred rather than explicitly stated; Matthew Stanton's is part of his every action. But each play illuminates, either positively or negatively, some aspect of the delicate process by which the multiethnic culture of America is enriched.

Each play is prefaced by a brief but compact essay about the ethnic group dealt with in the play, indicating something about the history of that group in

America, its problems and trials, as well as its contributions and achievements. Bibliographies follow each essay containing suggestions for further reading about the group, as well as titles of other plays. Following each play is a series of questions designed to provide stimulus for class discussion and to prompt individual reflection on the part of the students.

It is our sincere hope that readers of this anthology not only will enjoy each play in its own right, but will go on to develop a respect and admiration for cultures other than their own. We trust that through such respect and understanding will arise a greater love for our national values of tolerance, understanding of others, and working for the common good.

We should like to express our appreciation to the scores of individuals who have assisted us in hunting down appropriate plays and bibliographical references. Among those who have been most helpful are: Professor Nils Hasselmo of the University of Minnesota and Dr. Dorothy Burton Skardal of Oslo for their advice on Scandinavian plays; Mrs. Carlotta Cardenas Dwyer of SUNY at Stony Brook, Professor Mary Escudero of Arizona State University, Professor Garrett Ballard of North Texas State University, Dr. Rogelio H. Villa of the Department of Education, State of Minnesota, William C. de Lannoy of the San Diego City Schools, and Professor Donald F. Castro for Chicano plays; Professor Anthony Roy Mangione for his rich bibliography of ethnic literature in America; Paul Myers, curator of the Lincoln Center Library and Museum of the Performing Arts and Robert H. Land, Chief of the museum's Research Department, General Reference and Bibliography Division, and Stanley Richards, play anthologist *par excellence*, who helped us in many ways.

To our wives, Kathryn and Estelle, we wish to express our profound appreciation for their encouragement and assistance in this project over many years.

We wish to thank also our editor at Charles Scribner's Sons, Edward J. Cutler, who was extremely helpful in establishing criteria and guidelines and assisted us in the many aspects of editorial supervision that make the difference between just another play anthology and what we trust is an exciting and significant one.

New York
May 1973

Francis Griffith
Joseph Mersand

EIGHT
AMERICAN ETHNIC PLAYS

The Irish in the United States

A potato blight caused one of the great migrations of history. In 1845 a disease struck the potato plants of Ireland. Almost overnight the fields became a mass of putrefying vegetation. The blight devastated the crops in 1846, 1847, and 1848.

The crop failure was a major calamity. The poor were most affected. The potato, cheap and easily obtainable, had long been the chief staple of their diet. Without money to spend on meat or other food, they were driven to wander from place to place begging for something to eat. More than a million died of starvation. The English government gave little aid—and gave it too late.

In desperation the Irish fled their country. Within eight years 2 million emigrated to other lands, mainly to the United States. The emigration continued for fifty years after the famine until more than 4.5 million had departed from their native land, causing the population to drop from 8.5 million to less than 4 million.

The famine years brought on increased poverty and unemployment. In the west of Ireland alone, more than a fourth of the population was unemployed. This condition provided increased incentive for seeking a new life elsewhere. It also insured that most immigrants were pitiably poor—a fact that was to influence their beginnings in America greatly.

Oppression was another cause of their emigration. During the eighteenth century the Irish, most of whom were Catholics, were harshly treated under English law. They were denied the right to an education, prohibited from entering the legal profession, denied the privilege of serving on juries, forbidden to hold many civil offices, and restricted in the practice of their religion. They could not hold property valued at more than five pounds. Intermarriage between Catholics and Protestants was forbidden under penalty of fine and imprisonment.

By the nineteenth century many of the restrictions on Catholics had been withdrawn, but the Irish were further rankled by restrictive land laws, absentee landlordism, and excessively high rents, which kept the peasantry impoverished and prevented them from buying land of their own. Added to this was Britain's denial of self-government to Ireland. Repeated rebellions to secure independence were cruelly put down.

Famine, poverty, and oppression, then, were the main causes of the Irish migration. The first arrivals in America sent back word of the opportunities in their new homeland, urged their friends and relatives to join them, and often included passage money with their letters. The emigrants traveled across the Atlantic in over-crowded, dirty, and vermin-infested "coffin ships". Four persons slept in a space 6′ × 6′. The emigrants had to supply their own bedding and food and do their own cooking. In mid-century the crossing took five weeks. Epidemics often broke out and many died en route from disease. On one ship, the *Virginius*, which carried 476 passengers, there were 267 deaths; other vessels had rates almost as high.

When the Irish arrived in the United States, they were not always welcome. They were despised because they were poor and consequently considered inferior. Their religion was strange to most Americans and therefore regarded with suspicion and fear. A common line in newspaper want ads was "No Irish need apply." Since they were simple, trusting, and often illiterate, they were gulled and tricked by sharpers, loan sharks, thieves, and confidence men. Although most were originally farmers, they congregated in the coastal cities where the ships docked because they did not have the train fare to go elsewhere. They began as unskilled laborers, cutting the country's canals, laying its railroad tracks, constructing its roads, unloading its ships, and mining its coal.

They pulled themselves up by their own bootstraps. With their flair for politics, they began to play a role in government, starting at the ward or district level and continuing into citywide, state, and national affairs. They became councilmen, mayors, governors, congressmen, and senators. Ultimately, a descendant of an immigrant who had come to this country during the famine years became president, John F. Kennedy.

Many descendants of Irish immigrants became famous churchmen. The first United States cardinal was John Cardinal McCloskey, the son of a Brooklyn shipping clerk who came to this country in the 1800s. John J. Hughes, the first archbishop of New York, was Irish born, and James Cardinal Gibbons of Baltimore and Francis Cardinal Spellman of New York were sons of Irish immigrants.

The Irish have played a prominent part in every war in which the United States has been engaged. At least half of George Washington's army was Irish, according to testimony in the British House of Commons in 1779. The father of the American navy, Commodore John Barry, was Irish born. Civil War generals Phil Kearney, Philip H. Sheridan, George G. Meade, and Thomas Francis Meagher were Irish-Americans. General Anthony McAuliffe, who replied "Nuts!" to the German surrender demands at Bastogne during World War II, was of Irish background.

Education has always been a major concern of the Irish in America. They founded the extensive parochial school system as a reaction against the Protestant practices that permeated public schools in the nineteenth century: the King James version of the Bible was read daily, the Protestant version of the Lord's Prayer was recited, and Protestant hymns were sung. To protect their children's faith, the Irish workers contributed their pennies and dimes in Sunday collections and managed to establish hundreds of schools in which their religion was taught.

Hunter College in New York City was named after Thomas Hunter, an Irish immigrant who amassed a fortune and donated it to establish free higher education. William Barton Rogers, the son of an Irishman, founded the

Massachusetts Institute of Technology. The Irish also were prime movers in founding the universities of Notre Dame, Georgetown, and Holy Cross.

The *Dictionary of American Biography* lists five hundred famous Americans who were born in Ireland and thousands of others who trace their ancestry to Ireland. Dr. Tom Dooley achieved fame in medicine for his selfless efforts on behalf of thousands of ill and suffering Vietnamese. Among Supreme Court Justices of Irish lineage are Pierce Butler, Frank Murphy, and William J. Brennan, Jr. In sports, John L. Sullivan, James J. Corbett, and Gene Tunney were heavyweight boxing champions of the world; John J. McGraw became manager of the New York Giants at twenty-seven and led the team to ten National League pennants before he retired. The world of art as well has been inhabited by Irish-Americans. Augustus Saint-Gaudens, the sculptor, was born in Dublin, as was Victor Herbert, the composer, whose melodies are beloved by all. Louis Sullivan, architect, and Georgia O'Keefe, painter, had Irish backgrounds, as did Eugene O'Neill, playright, Helen Hayes, actress, and Pat O'Brien, actor.

Hogan's Goat reveals some of the distinctive traits of the Irish in America. Here, as elsewhere, they are shown as clannish, devoutly religious, imaginative, poetic, eloquent, kind and generous, supportive of one another, high-minded, intellectual, and skilled in the devious ways of politics. At the same time the play frankly exposes their faults. Their actions are often impetuous and their sorrow for a rash act is sudden. Like all of us, no matter what our national origin, the Irish are a bundle of contradictions.

Suggested Reading

Books about the Irish

Considine, Bob. *It's the Irish.* New York: Doubleday and Company, 1961. In a delightful style Bob Considine tells the fascinating saga of the ancestors of the 20 million Americans of Irish descent in the United States today, their coming to America, and what they have done here up to now.

Wittke, Carl. *The Irish in America.* New York: Teachers College Press, 1968. This pamphlet, a student's guide to localized history, sets forth concisely the causes of Irish immigration, the cultural contributions of the Irish, the part they have played in various labor movements, and their complete Americanization.

Woodham-Smith, Cecil. *The Great Hunger.* New York: Harper and Row, 1962. An English historian describes in a balanced and dispassionate way the conditions during the famine years in Ireland and their effects on history. It is an enthralling record of suffering, courage, blundering stupidity, good intentions, tragedy, and hope.

Plays about the Irish

Murphy, Thomas. *A Whistle in the Dark.* New York: Samuel French, Inc., 1971.

O'Neill, Eugene. *A Touch of the Poet.* New Haven: Yale University Press, 1957.

O'Neill, Eugene. *Long Day's Journey into Night.* New Haven: Yale University Press, 1956.

Hogan's Goat

In *Hogan's Goat* the congeniality and optimism traditionally associated with the Irish, their flair for poetic expression, and their mercurial disposition are shown in almost every scene. The characters are adept in politics, religious, sociable, loyal, ambitious, fluent, sensitive to the plight of those in need, contentious, and rash. Mayor Edward Quinn, who has climbed rung by rung up the political ladder, is generous to his supporters and expects them in turn to be loyal to him. When Matthew Stanton, the protagonist, shows himself disloyal by breaking with Quinn and seeking the mayoralty, Quinn uses questionable means to retain his position. Stanton, like Quinn, has a capacity for political maneuvering and a lust for power. His eloquence, youth, and personable appearance attract voters, but his fatal flaw is his self-love which blinds him to his moral obligations and the sensitivities of others. Father Coyne is close to his parishioners and aware of their shortcomings. His wise and firm counsel acts as a restraint on their impetuousness. All are devoted to their religion except Stanton who has broken from it for selfish reasons. He is cast in sharp contrast to Ann Mulcahy, the priest's housekeeper, whose devotion and selflessness approach saintliness.

Hogan's Goat is a poetic play, a relatively rare form of dramatic expression in modern times. Shakespeare and his contemporaries wrote in verse but since Shakespeare's time most playwrights have written in prose. A few modern writers have attempted verse plays, some with conspicuous success. Maxwell Anderson's *Winterset*, T. S. Eliot's *Murder in the Cathedral*, and Archibald McLeish's *J.B.* are among the handful of poetic dramas written for the contemporary stage.

Hogan's Goat is written in unrhymed or blank verse. Each line has five stressed syllables. Each stressed syllable is usually preceded by an unstressed syllable:

I néver meánt to dó this tó you, Mátt.
I dídn't knów. I néver meánt to dó it.

The combination of an unstressed and stressed syllable is called an iambic foot. Since there are five feet in each line, the verse is called iambic pentameter, from a Greek word meaning five feet.

Shakespeare was the first dramatist to use blank verse successfully in English and no one since has used it with greater mastery. Why did he use blank verse? The Greek and Roman epics had been written in unrhymed verse, so that the form carried with it a certain classical quality and prestige. Moreover, he was trying to present extraordinary rather than ordinary events and blank verse was more appropriate for this purpose than prose. Super-ordinary and romantic events required a more than ordinary mode of expression. Rhymed verse would not do because it was restrictive and lacking in variety. Blank verse was adaptable and rhythmic; it provided great freedom and variety of expression.

In *Hogan's Goat* William Alfred daringly attempts to use blank verse in a realistic rather than a romantic setting, and carries it off successfully. The vigor and imagery of the play's poetic expression is striking. The poetry has a conversational flow. It sounds like ordinary conversation heightened by intense feeling; there is an absence of artificiality and rhetoric. Since the drama is realistic, the verse is appropriately earthy at times:

> There's a bit of skunk in all of us, you know.
> We stink when we're afraid or hurt. Ned's both.

There are also moments of high emotion when the verse is charged and glowing:

> She was ten years my senior. But, oh, Kate,
> To look at her downstairs, you'd never know
> What once she was! Her hair was bronze and silver
> Like pear trees in full bloom, her eyes were opal,
> Her skin was like new milk, and her blue veins
> Trembled in the shimmer of her full straight neck
> Like threads of violets from her hair
> And filliped by the breeze.

The play was unanimously acclaimed by dramatic critics. Walter Kerr wrote in *The New York Tribune*: "The play ... stands as plainly, as simply, as possessively on the stage as though it had been born there and continued to claim the address." Writing of Mr Alfred's style, Harold Taubman said in *The New York Times*: "He is not afraid to strike for the vivid image: he can compose lines that shimmer with poetry. There are moments, long passages, when his phrases surge with freshly felt and sharply etched emotion. There are other places where he is capable of capturing a humorous or ironic thought with lusty earthiness." A drama critic of the *Virginia Quarterly Review* wrote:

> As poetry no less than drama *Hogan's Goat* is a marvellous achievement and readers ordinarily interested in poetry will find this one of those rare plays which allow them to make common cause with theater goers and raise a unanimous cheer for a playwright who sacrifices no dramatic value to the cause of poetry, a poet who sacrifices no poetic value to the cause of drama.

In *Hogan's Goat* much of the action has taken place before the play begins and, as in an Ibsen drama, is revealed as it progresses, keeping the reader in a constant state of suspense. The incidents grow out of individual failings and strengths; they are the natural outcomes of combinations of vices and virtues. The ultimate tragedy, inevitable yet unexpected, leaves us shaken and aware of our own pettinesses as we witness a man who, basically good, brings about his own destruction by his over-vaunting ambition and blind self-love.

WILLIAM ALFRED, born in Brooklyn in 1922 and educated at Brooklyn College and Harvard University, is presently a professor of English at Harvard. Verse is his dramatic metier. He has written one other poetic drama, *Agamemmon*, and is currently at work on two more. He has stated his goal simply: "I would like a theater that belongs to the whole people. By that I mean a theater where you can have complicated things talked about and yet not in complicated ways." In *Hogan's Goat*—a play with universal appeal, dealing with common people in ordinary surroundings—William Alfred achieves this goal. The motives of the characters are complex, yet they are presented uncomplicatedly. Consequently, all can understand and sympathize with these human beings enmeshed in a web of fate.

Hogan's Goat

BY

WILLIAM ALFRED

CHARACTERS

MATTHEW STANTON, *leader of the Sixth Ward of Brooklyn.*
KATHLEEN STANTON, *his wife.*
EDWARD QUINN, *Mayor of Brooklyn.*
FATHER STANISLAUS COYNE, *Pastor of St. Mary Star of the Sea.*
JAMES "PALSY" MURPHY, *Boss of the city of Brooklyn.*
JOHN "BLACK JACK" HAGGERTY, *Assistant Ward Leader.*
MARIA HAGGERTY, *his wife, the Stanton's janitor.*
JOSEPHINE FINN, *Maria Haggerty's niece.*
PETEY BOYLE, *a hanger-on of Stanton's.*
BESSIE LEGG, *a back-room girl.*
ANN MULCAHY, *Father Coyne's housekeeper.*
BOYLAN, *a policeman.*
BILL, *a hanger-on of Quinn's.*
A PRIEST, A DECKHAND, A DOCTOR, VARIOUS CONSTITUENTS.

SCENES

The action of the play takes place in Brooklyn, in 1890.

Hogan's Goat by William Alfred, reprinted with the permission of Farrar, Straus & Giroux, Inc., copyright © 1958, 1966 by William Alfred.
NOTE: All rights, including professional, amateur, dramatic, motion picture, recitation, lecturing, public-reading, radio and television broadcasting, are strictly reserved and no portion of this play may be performed without express written permission. Inquiries about such rights should be addressed to the author's dramatic agent, Miss Toby Cole, 234 West 44th Street, Suite 700, Sardi Building, New York, New York 10036.

Hogan's Goat

ACT ONE

SCENE 1

Ten o'clock, the evening of Thursday, April 28, 1890. The parlor of Matthew Stanton's flat on the second floor of his house on Fifth Place, Brooklyn. The set is on two levels, the lower level containing the kitchen of the Haggertys, which is blacked out. To Stage Right there is a steep, narrow staircase. Enter MATTHEW STANTON, *carrying a bottle of champagne. He is a handsome, auburn-haired man in his late thirties, dressed carefully in a four-buttoned suit of good serge, and a soft black hat. He bounds up the stairs and into his flat, and throws his hat on a chair and hides the bottle of champagne behind the sofa. The furnishings of the room are in period: the chairs are tufted and fringed, the mantelpiece covered with a lambrequin, the window heavily draped.*

STANTON.
Katie? Katie! Where the devil are you?
Come on out in the parlor.
  (*Enter* KATHLEEN STANTON, *closing the door behind her. She is tall and slim and dressed in a black broadcloth suit which brings out the redness of her hair and the whiteness of her skin.*)
  KATHLEEN.
I wish you wouldn't take those stairs so fast;
They're wicked: you could catch your foot and fall—
I had a bit of headache and lay down.
Why, Mattie darling, what's the matter with you?
You're gray as wasps' nests.
  STANTON.
              I'm to be the mayor!
No more that plug who runs the Court Café
And owes his ear to every deadbeat sport
With a favor in mind and ten cents for a ball,
But mayor of Brooklyn, and you the mayor's lady.
They caught Ned Quinn with his red fist in the till,
The Party of Reform, I mean, and we
"Are going to beat their game with restitution
And self-reform." Say something, can't you, Kate!
  (KATHLEEN *sits down heavily, and puts her hand to her temple.*)
  KATHLEEN.
Oh, Mattie, Mattie.

STANTON.
                    Jesus! Are you crying?
I've what I wanted since I landed here
Twelve years ago, and she breaks into tears.
KATHLEEN.
It's that I'm—
STANTON.
                    What? You're what?
KATHLEEN.
                              Afraid.
STANTON.
                                   Kathleen,
Now please don't let's go into that again.
KATHLEEN.
Would you have me tell you lies?
STANTON.
                         I'd have you brave.
(KATHLEEN *rises angrily, and strides towards the bedroom.*)
Where are you going, Kate? To have a sulk?
Wait now, I'll fix a sugar teat for you,
Unless, of course, you'd rather suck your thumb,
Brooding in your room—
KATHLEEN.
                    I have the name!
As well to have the game!
STANTON.
                    It's riddles, is it?
KATHLEEN.
Riddles be damned! You think me idiotic;
I might as well fulfill your good opinion—
    (STANTON *walks towards her.*)
Come near me, and I'll smash your face for you.
    (STANTON *embraces her.*)
STANTON.
You're terrible fierce, you are. I wet me pants.
KATHLEEN.
You clown, you'll spring my hairpins. Mattie, stop.
STANTON.
Are these the hands are going to smash my face?
They're weak as white silk fans . . . I'm sorry, Kate:
You made me mad. And you know why?
KATHLEEN.
                              I do.
You're as afraid as I.
STANTON.
         I am, I am.
You know me like the lashes of your eye—
KATHLEEN.
That's more than you know me, for if you did,
You'd see what these three years have done to me—

(STANTON *breaks away from her.*)
Now it's my turn to ask you where you're going.
 KATHLEEN.
I begged you not to bring that up again.
What can I do?
 KATHLEEN.
     You can tell Father Coyne,
And ask him to apply for dispensation,
And we can be remarried secretly.
 STANTON.
Now?
 KATHLEEN.
  Yes, Matt, now. Before it is too late.
We aren't married.
 STANTON.
     What was that in London,
The drunkard's pledge I took?
 KATHLEEN.
      We're Catholics, Matt.
Since when can Catholics make a valid marriage
In a city hall? You have to tell the priest—
 STANTON.
Shall I tell him now? Do you take me for a fool
To throw away the mayor's chair for that?
 KATHLEEN.
I slink to Sunday Mass like a pavement nymph.
It's three years now since I made my Easter Duty,
Three years of telling Father Coyne that we
Receive at Easter Mass in the Cathedral,
Mortal Sin on Mortal Sin, Matt. If I died,
I'd go to Hell—
 STANTON.
    I think the woman's crazy!
 KATHLEEN.
Don't you believe in God?
 STANTON.
     Of course, I do.
And more, my dear, than you who think that He
Would crush you as a man would crush a fly
Because of some mere technical mistake—
 KATHLEEN.
Mere technical mistake? It's that now, is it?
A blasphemous marriage, three years' fornication,
And now presumption—Technical mistake!
  (KATHLEEN *takes a cigarette out of a box on the table and lights it.*)
 STANTON.
I wish you wouldn't smoke them cigarettes.
High-toned though it may be in France and England,
It's a whore's habit here. (*Pause.*)

KATHLEEN.
             "Those cigarettes."
Don't try to hurt me, Matt. You know you can,
As I know I can you.
    STANTON.
             What do you want!
    KATHLEEN.
I want to be your wife without disgrace.
I want my honor back. I want to live
Without the need to lie. I want you to keep faith.

    STANTON.
Not now! Not now!
    KATHLEEN.
             You've said that for three years.
What is it you're afraid of?
    STANTON.
             Losing out.
You do not know these people as I do.
They turn upon the ones they make most of.
They would on me, if given half a chance.
And if it got around that we were married
In an English City Hall, lose out we would.

    KATHLEEN.
Matt, losing out? What profit for a man
To gain the world, and lose his soul?

    STANTON.
             His soul!
That's Sunday school! That's convent folderol,
Like making half-grown girls bathe in their drawers
To put the shame of their own beauty in them,
And break their lives to bear the Church's bit.
We are not priests and nuns, but men and women.
The world religious give up is our world,
The only world we have. We have to win it
To do the bit of good we all must do;
And how are we to win the world unless
We keep the tricky rules its games are run by?
Our faith is no mere monastery faith.
It runs as fast as feeling to embrace
Whatever good it sees. And if the good
Is overgrown with bad, it still believes
God sets no traps, the bad will be cut down,
And the good push through its flowering to fruit.
Forget your convent school. Remember, Katie,
What the old women in the drowned boreens
Would say when cloudbursts beat their fields to slime,
And the potatoes blackened on their stalks
Like flesh gone proud. "Bad times is right," they'd say,
"But God is good: apples will grow again."

What sin have we committed? Marriage, Kate?
Is that a sin?
KATHLEEN.
    It is with us.
STANTON.
        Because
You feel it so. It isn't. It's but prudence.
What is they should make a scandal of us?
KATHLEEN.
Could we be worse off than we are?
STANTON.
        Kathleen!
KATHLEEN.
Could we be worse off than we are, I said?
STANTON.
Could we! We could. You don't know poverty.
You don't know what it is to do without,
Not fine clothes only, or a handsome house,
But men's respect. I do. I have been poor.
"Mattie, will you run down to the corner,
And buy me some cigars" or "Mattie, get
This gentleman a cab." Nine years, I served
Ned Quinn and Agnes Hogan, day by day,
Buying my freedom like a Roman slave.
Will you ask me to put liberty at stake
To ease your scrupulous conscience? If you do,
You're not the woman that I took you for
When I married you. Have you no courage, Kate?
KATHLEEN.
Will you lecture me on courage? Do you dare?
When every time I walk those stairs to the street
I walk to what I know is an enemy camp.
I was not raised like you. And no offense,
Please, Mattie, no offense. I miss my home.
Whore's habit it may be to smoke, as you say,
But it brings back the talk we used to have
About old friends, new books, the Lord knows what,
On our first floor in Baggot Street in Dublin.
This following you think so much about,
We live in Mortal Sin for fear you'll lose it,
I never knew the likes of them to talk to,
Person to person. They were cooks and maids,
Or peasants at the country houses, Matt.
All they can find to talk of, servants' talk,
Serfs' talk, eternal tearing down.
I'm like a woman banished and cut off.
I've you and May in the flat downstairs. That's all.
Don't tell me I don't know what poverty is.
What bankruptcy is worse than loneliness.
They say the sense of exile is the worst

Of all the pains that torture poor damned souls.
It is that sense I live with every day.
   STANTON.
Are you the only exile of us all?
You slept your crossing through in a rosewood berth
With the swells a hundred feet below your portholes,
And ate off china on a linen cloth,
With the air around you fresh as the first of May.
I slept six deep in a bunk short as a coffin
Between a poisoned pup of a seasick boy
And a slaughtered pig of a snorer from Kildare,
Who wrestled elephants the wild nights through,
And sweated sour milk. I wolfed my meals,
Green water, and salt beef, and wooden biscuits,
On my hunkers like an ape, in a four-foot aisle
As choked as the one door of a burning school.
I crossed in mid-December: seven weeks
Of driving rain that kept the hatches battened
In a hold so low of beam a man my height
Could never lift his head. And I couldn't wash.
Water was low; the place was like an icehouse;
And girls were thick as field mice in a haystack
In the bunk across. I would have died of shame,
When I stood in the landing shed of this "promised land,"
As naked as the day I first saw light,
Defiled with my own waste like a dying cat,
And a lousy red beard on me like a tinker's,
While a bitch of a doctor, with his nails too long,
Dared tell me: "In Amurrica, we bathe!"
I'd have died with shame, had I sailed here to die.
I swallowed pride and rage, and made a vow
The time would come when I could spit both out
In the face of the likes of him. I made a vow
I'd fight my way to power if it killed me,
Not only for myself, but for our kind,
For the men behind me, laughing out of fear,
At their own shame as well as mine, for the women,
Behind the board partition, frightened dumb
With worry they'd be sent back home to starve
Because they'd dirty feet. I was born again.
It came to me as brutal as the cold
That makes us flinch the day the midwife takes
Our wet heels in her fist, and punches breath
Into our dangling carcasses: Get power!
Without it, there can be no decency,
No virtue and no grace. I have kept my vow.
The mayor's chair is mine but for the running.
Will you have me lose it for your convent scruples? (*Pause.*)
   KATHLEEN.
You never told me that about your landing.

STANTON.
There's many things I never told you, Kate.
I was afraid you'd hold me cheap.
KATHLEEN.
                    Oh, Mattie,
Don't you know me yet?
STANTON.
                    Stand by me.
Stand by me, Kate. The next four days count hard.
By Sunday next, I'll have won all or lost.
KATHLEEN.
What's Sunday next?
STANTON.
            The Clambake for Quinn's birthday:
We're to make things up between us and make the announcement
On the steamer voyage to Seagate Sunday evening.
Stand by me, Kate. As sure as God's my judge
The minute I get into City Hall
The first thing I will do is call the priest,
And ask him to make peace with God for us.
Stand by me, Kate.
KATHLEEN.
            I will though it costs my life.
(STANTON *kisses her.*)
STANTON.
God stand between us and all harm! There now!
I've wiped those words from your lips.—Oh, where's my mind!
I've brought champagne, and it's as warm as tears.
Go get the glasses.
    (KATHLEEN *takes two glasses down from a cupboard.* STANTON *opens
    the champagne and pours it. They touch glasses.*)
            Let the past be damned,
The dead bury the dead. The future's ours.

CURTAIN

ACT ONE

SCENE 2

Eleven o'clock the same night. The back room of Stanton's Saloon, The Court Café. To Stage Left, glass-paned double doors cut the room off from the bar, from which a hum of VOICES can be heard. To Stage Right, the Ladies' Entrance. Next to it, a square piano with a pot of dead fern on it. Around the room, squat round tables and bent iron chairs. Stage Center, around one of the tables, with whiskeys in front of them, three people. At the head, JOHN "BLACK JACK" HAGGERTY, *in his late sixties, wearing his Sunday clothes, his hair parted in the middle and swagged over his eyebrows in dove's wings, his handlebar mustache repeating the design. Both hair and mustache are dyed an improbable black. To* HAGGERTY'S *left,* PETEY BOYLE, *a young tough in his twenties, his heavy hair parted in the middle and combed oilily back, the teeth marks of the comb still in it. His rachitic frame is wiry as a weed; and he is dressed in a Salvation Army suit that droops in the seat, balloons at the knees and elbows. Next to* BOYLE, *but facing the audience,* BESSIE LEGG, *a blond girl in her late twenties or early thirties, her hair in a pompadour under a Floradora hat that looks like an ostrich nest, a long feather boa on, together with many strands of glass beads, and rings on every finger but her thumbs, all cheap. Her doll's face is a bit crumpled, but there is no petulance in it, merely jocose self-indulgence. There is a crepe-paper shamrock tacked to the piano, and four sprung tapes of green and gold crepe paper run from the corners of the room and belly over the table in a haphazardly celebrative way.*

HAGGERTY.
That Walsh from Albany was no man's fool.
The first thing that he asked about was Ag Hogan,
And then about Matt's temper, you know, the time
He nearly broke Tim Costigan in two
For calling him Hogan's Goat. But at last we cleared Matt.
    BOYLE.
Bess, Black Jack thinks the nomination'll stand!
    HAGGERTY.
Stop your tormenting, Petey. Of course, it will.
Amn't I Assistant Leader of this Ward
And head of the Matthew Stanton Association?
And isn't Palsy Murphy Boss of Brooklyn
And head of the Edward Quinn Association?
Walsh said that Father Coyne and the both of us
Would constitute a due and legal caucus;
And he's the representative of the Party,
He ought to know.
    BESSIE.
                Yeah? When does Quinn find out?
    HAGGERTY.
Tomorrow morning. It has to be told him fast.
We're to break the news Matt's nominated Sunday
At the Clambake for Quinn's birthday down in Seagate.
    BOYLE.
Is both Associations going on this Clambake?
    HAGGERTY.
Yes. Murphy's got the job of telling Quinn
And getting him to make things up with Matt.
    BOYLE.
That's a moonlight voyage we'll all be seeing stars.
It'll make the riot on the *Harvest Queen,*
When that Alderman knifed that guy in '87,

Look like a slapping match in St. Mary's schoolyard.
Quinn ain't never giving up to no Stanton
In no four days.
> BESSIE.
>> Dust off your steel derby,
> Or your head will be all lumps like a bag of marbles.
>> BOYLE.
> You tell him, kid. I'll hold the baby.
>> HAGGERTY.
>>> Lord!
> What a pair of lochremauns! That's why Murphy's Boss:
> He could talk a Hindu out of a tiger's mouth.
> He'll find some cosy way to break the news,
> And Quinn will purr like a kitten.

(Enter MARIA HAGGERTY through the Ladies' Entrance. She is a tall, raw-boned woman in her late sixties, with loose-stranded iron-gray hair pulled back around a center part in a tight bun. She wears a rusty black toque, and a long black woolen coat with a frayed hem, and is carrying a large handbag, which she sets down on the floor as she settles wearily into the chair to Stage Right of HAGGERTY, her husband.)

> MARIA.
>> Ah, there you are!
> How are you, Mrs. Legg? How are you, Petey?
> I thought you might be waiting here for Matt,
> When Josie told me. Why is it so secret?
>> HAGGERTY.
> It won't be secret long with Josie Finn
> Trumpeting it from here to Fulton Ferry
> Like an elephant in heat. Quinn doesn't know yet.
> That's why it's so secret.
>> MARIA.
>>> What's that you're drinking?
>> HAGGERTY.
> Whiskey and water, May.
>> MARIA.
>>> Give Ma a swallow.
>> HAGGERTY.
> Great God in Heaven, drink it all, why don't you!
> We're met to celebrate Matt Stanton's luck.
> Corner-boy Boyle and Bessie the balloon brain
> See trouble in store undreamed by Albany,
> And my wife drags in here with a puss on her
> Like a lead-horse on a hearse. What's the matter with you?
>> MARIA.
> I'm sure I'm glad for Matt's sake. He's worked hard,
> And he's been good, giving us the flat and all.
> But in a way, you know, Ned Quinn is right:
> Matt's hard on people, harder than he should be.
> He's a lot to answer for before he dies.

BESSIE.
You mean Ag Hogan?
MARIA.
                Yes, I do.
BESSIE.
                        Poor girl.
When I was there this morning, she looked awful.
MARIA.
She'll never live to comb out a gray head.
I've just now come from giving her her tea,
In that coffin of a furnished room in Smith Street.
I looked at the cheesecloth curtains hung on strings;
And I thought of all those velvet-muffled windows,
Those carpets red as blood and deep as snow,
Those tables glistening underneath the lamps
Like rosy gold, in her big house in Seagate.
And I said to myself, if it weren't for Agnes Hogan,
Matt would be a grocery clerk at Nolan's,
And not the owner of The Court Café.
And candidate for mayor; and there she lies,
Flat on her back with two beanbags of buckshot
On her shriveled breasts, to chain her to the mattress,
As if she could move, her eyes in a black stare
At the white paint peeling off that iron bedstead,
Like scabs of a rash; and he never once comes near her,
For fear, I suppose, they'd call him Hogan's Goat,
And his missis might find out about their high jinks.
And yet if Matt were any kind of man,
Wouldn't he go and take her in his arms,
And say, "You hurt me bad three years ago;
But I hurt you as bad. Forgive and forget."
Maybe it's because the girl's my niece,
But I think I'd feel the same if she were not.

   HAGGERTY.
Be that as may be, what has passed between them
Is their affair. It isn't ours to judge,
Especially after all Matt's done for us—
And you'll set this one thinking how Tom Legg
Left her in the lurch in Baltic Street,
And spraying us all like a drainpipe in a downpour,
If you keep up that way. Sure, what's past is past.
What can't be remedied must be endured.

   BESSIE.
Say, listen here, Napoleon the Turd,
Legg never found me in no bed with no one,
Like Matt done Ag, if that's what you're implying.

   HAGGERTY.
How could he, when he worked in the subway nights,
And was so blind he couldn't tie his shoes

Without his nose to the eyelets, his rump in the air,
Like a startled ostrich.
>BESSIE.
                         Say that again, I dare you!
>HAGGERTY.
No matter now. It served what it was meant to:
Better glares than tears—
> (*A loud* SHOUT *from the bar.* APPLAUSE, CHEERS *and* SINGING. *Enter* STANTON *from the bar with a* CROWD *around him, singing. The* FOUR *at the table join in.*)
>EVERYBODY.
He'll make a jolly good mayor!
He'll make a jolly good mayor!
He'll make a jolly good mayor!
Which nobody can deny!
>HAGGERTY.
Speech, Mattie, speech!
>STANTON.
                    Thanks all! What will I say!
It's me who should be singing songs to you,
Not you to me. And I don't know how you've learned
That I'm to run for mayor. It's a secret.
Ask the man who told you if it isn't,
Jack Haggerty—(*Applause.*)
                    When I returned from England
Three years ago with my new wife, I thought
My chances to get back into the Party
Were gone for good. Yet in those three short years
You stuck by me so fast, the Party made me
Leader of the Ward in which the mayor
I had a falling-out with lives; and now
You're bent on giving me his place.
Ned Quinn—
> (BOOING *and* HISSING. PETEY BOYLE *jumps on a table, puts one fist on his hip, throws his head back insolently, and sings, in a nasal imitation of John McCormack. Enter* FATHER COYNE, *unnoticed, through the Ladies' Entrance, wearing his biretta and an old black overcoat shorter than his cassock.*)
>BOYLE.
Is it Ned Quinn you mean?   (*Repeat.*)
Says the Shan Van Vocht,*
He's in Fogarty's shebeen
Drinking bourbon with some quean,   (*Repeat.*)
Says the Shan Van Vocht.
Let him drink it to the dregs,   (*Repeat.*)
Says the Shan Van Vocht.

---

* *Shan Van Vocht*: literally, "the poor old woman," the title of a 1798 ballad often called the Irish *Marseillaise*. Since Ireland could not be referred to by name in eighteenth-century poems and songs, poets and balladeers referred to their country under such titles as "the poor old woman," "dark Rosaleen," and "the dear dark head."—Eds.

For the goose that lays gold eggs
Lays no more for hollow legs, (*Repeat.*)
Says the Shan Van Vocht.
    (*APPLAUSE and LAUGHTER.* BOYLE *motions for silence and sings.*)
    BOYLE.
Go and tell that swindler!
    (BOYLE *points to* HAGGERTY.)
    HAGGERTY.
Go and tell that swindler!
    (HAGGERTY *points to* BESSIE.)
    BESSIE.
Go and tell that swindler!
    BOYLE.
What the Shan Van Vocht has said!
    (BOYLE *apes a choir director.*)
    EVERYBODY.
What the Shan Van Vocht has said!
    (*LAUGHTER and APPLAUSE.* FATHER COYNE *angrily jostles his way to Stage Center, the* PEOPLE *shamefacedly making way for him.*)
    FATHER COYNE.
For shame! For shame! Have you no charity?
Don't turn upon the man, but on his sin.
    HAGGERTY.
Father! Sit down. I thought you'd be in bed.
    FATHER COYNE.
I couldn't sleep. I thought I'd come by here
And have a word with Matt alone.
    BOYLE.
                      A word or a drink?
    FATHER COYNE.
What's that you say, Pete Boyle? Speak up, why don't you,
And show them how malicious you can be,
And you so drunk!
    BOYLE.
                  I didn't mean no harm.
    FATHER COYNE.
You meant no harm! You're all of you alike.
You talk to preen your wit or flex your pride,
Not to lay bare your hearts or tell God's truth.
Words have more force than blows. They can destroy.
Would you punch an old man's face to test your arm?
Answer me, Pete Boyle.
    BOYLE.
                  You know I wouldn't.
    FATHER COYNE.
You did as much to me.
    BOYLE.
                I'm sorry, Father.

FATHER COYNE.
I hope you are, my son. Don't look so pious,
The rest of you. You're just as bad as him,
Dancing around the ruin of Quinn's name
Like a pack of savages. Do you know the story
The Rabbis set down centuries ago
Beside the part in Exodus where the Jews
Are shown exulting over the drowned troops
Of Pharaoh on the shores of the Red Sea?
The angels, says the story, joined their voices
With those of the men below. And God cried out:
"What reason is there to hold jubilee?
The men of Egypt are my children too!"
The men of Egypt were God's enemies,
And Edward Quinn's your friend, may God forgive you!
STANTON.
That kind of justice is too heavenly
For us on earth. If we condone Ned Quinn,
Don't we condone corruption with him, Father?
FATHER COYNE.
You know, don't you, a man can commit theft,
And yet not be a thief by nature, Matt?
Corruption sometimes saps the choicest men;
Sometimes it is disordered sweetness drives
A man to act contrary to what's right.
Collusion can arise from faithfulness,
And graft from bankrupt generosity.
You know I'd never ask you to condone that.
But once he's made the city restitution,
The loss of office is enough chastisement
For Edward Quinn. You must not banish him.
What purpose would it serve to break a man
Who's slaved for Church and people thirty years?
STANTON.
What purpose would it serve? 'Twould end corruption.
Corruption, Father, may be, as you say,
Disordered sweetness sometimes, but in men
Who govern others, can we risk disorder
To save the heart it works its ferment on?
A man may cut away the seething bruise
That festers in good fruit or even flesh.
The heart's corruption poisons surgery.
The pulse of it is rapid. It pollutes
Like ratbite, and like ratbite spawns
Plagues to charge whole graveyards.
Isolate its carriers fast, I say. Disown them,
Before they can infect us with the pox
We came across the ocean to avoid,
Liberty gone blind, the death of honor!—
Would you have the big men of this city say

That they were right in keeping us cheap labor,
Because we are not fit for nobler service,
We dirty what we touch? Say that they will,
And with full right, unless we dare cut free
From these enfeebling politics of pity,
And rule the city right. Ned Quinn must go—
    (*APPLAUSE.*)
    HAGGERTY.
Hurray for Stanton! The man is right, God bless him.
What answer, Father, can you make to that?
    FATHER COYNE.
What answer, Black Jack, but the same old answer?
Judge not, Matt Stanton, lest yourself be judged;
Beware, Matt Stanton, lest in pointing out
The mote within your neighbor's watering eye,
You overlook the beam that blinds your own.
    STANTON.
I meant no disrespect. Forgive me, Father.
    FATHER COYNE.
Do not delude yourself it is offense
Has made me quote the Scripture to you, man.
I dare not take offense. My task is love.
I have no passion save the one for souls.
Salus suprema lex,* remember that,
Salvation is the law that must come first.
My cure includes both you and Edward Quinn.
Because it does, I have to warn you, Matt,
Do not mistake vindictiveness for justice.
I hope you take my meaning. Do you?
    STANTON.
                           Yes.
I'll make no move against Ned Quinn, I promise,
Unless he moves against me first.
    FATHER COYNE.
                        Good, Matt.
    STANTON.
For your penance, Petey, draw the priest a beer.
    FATHER COYNE.
I won't tonight, Matt, thank you. I've a matter
I'd like to talk to you about alone.
    STANTON.
Sure, Father—Out, the lot of you, to the bar.
The drinks are on the house.
    HAGGERTY.
Stanton abu,† boys.
    BOYLE.
Let the Jickies and the Prods,
Says the Shan Van Vocht,

---

* *Salus suprema lex*: the salvation (of souls) is the supreme law.—Eds.
† *abu*: an Irish word meaning "forever."—Eds.

Look down on us like gods,
Says the Shan Van Vocht.
We've got Stanton, damn the odds,
Says the Shan Van Vocht.
    (*Exit* EVERYBODY *cheering. Pause.*)
    FATHER COYNE.
It's no good being delicate. If I tried,
I'd put your eye out, Matt, or break your bones.
I'll just come out and say it: go see Ag.
    STANTON.
Agnes Hogan, Father?
    FATHER COYNE.
                    Agnes Hogan.
What other Ag would I mean?
    STANTON.
                    I can't do that.
    FATHER COYNE.
You can't or you won't?
    STANTON.
               One knock at Aggie's door,
And Josie Finn would be scissoring down Fifth Place
With the wind in tatters around her, and at Kate's ear
Before the latch was lifted. It would all come out—
    FATHER COYNE.
It should have come out long since. Ag's dying, Matt.
Tell Kate about her, and go.
    STANTON.
                 Whose fault she's dying?
Did you ever know her stop when the thirst was on her?
Who poured that whiskey down her fourteen months
Until the lungs were tattered in her breast?
Who landed her in Saranac? (*Pause.*)
                    She was always like that.
Whiskey, or clothes, or diamonds . . . or men!
You can say what you want of Joe Finn and her tongue,
If it wasn't for her, I'd never have found out
I was the goat for fair.

    FATHER COYNE.
              Ag was fully clothed.
And so was Quinn.
    STANTON.
               You didn't see them, Father.
They were leg in leg when Josie brought me in.
Asleep, I grant you, but his ham of a hand
Was tangled in the fullness of her hair—

    FATHER COYNE.
You told me that long since. What's done is done.
Don't let the woman die unreconciled.
Tell Kate, and go to see her.

STANTON.
                        Yes, but—
FATHER COYNE.
                               What?
What can I know of love, a celibate,
Numb as a broomstick in my varnished parlor,
With my frightened curate jumping at each word,
And Ann Mulcahy to do my housekeeping
Without a whimper of complaint? What can I know?
Putting aside the fact that priesthood's marriage
To a Partner Who is always right, I know
If you don't tell Kate, there are others will,
Before the ink is dry on the campaign posters,
And that would be disastrous—
STANTON.
                            Tell her what!
FATHER COYNE.
Don't take that tone with me.
STANTON.
                          I lived with her?
Shall I tell my wife I serviced Ag three years?
FATHER COYNE.
If you're trying to shock me, Matt, you're being simple.
For forty years, no Saturday's gone by,
I have not sat alone from three to nine
In my confessional, and heard men spill
Far blacker things than that. Man, use your reason!
STANTON.
I loved Ag, and kept faith.
FATHER COYNE.
                      Who says you didn't?
STANTON.
I loved her and kept faith. I did my part.
She played me false with Quinn.
FATHER COYNE.
                          If you loved her, Matt,
How is it that you didn't marry her,
Before she, how did you put it, played you false? (*Pause.*)
STANTON.
Not to give you a short answer, Father,
But don't you think that's my affair?
FATHER COYNE.
                            No, Matt.
STANTON.
It's not the kind of thing you talk to priests of.
FATHER COYNE.
You're trying to make me angry, aren't you?
Since *you* won't tell *me* why, let me tell you.
You only wanted Ag for fun and games;
You didn't want her on your neck for life.

You thought she'd spoil your chances, didn't you?
Your chances for the mayor's chair? You thought,
If you married her, they'd call you Hogan's Goat
To the day you died. Your heart rejoiced when you found
The both of them in bed—
    STANTON.
                     Are you finished, Father?
    FATHER COYNE.
No, Matt. I'm not. Do you know why you're fuming?
Because you're a good man, and you feel ashamed,
Because I'm saying what you tell yourself:
Whatever wrong was done was on both sides.
The woman made you what you are today;
The woman's dying. Hogan's Goat, or not,
Pocket your pride, and tell your wife about her.
Go talk with Ag, and let her die in peace,
Or else you'll be her goat in the Bible sense,
With all her sins on your head, and the world a desert.
Do you think I like to say such things to you?
I'm trying to help you, Matt.
    STANTON.
                     I had the right
To show her no one plays Matt Stanton false
More than one time!
    FATHER COYNE.
                  If you'd the right, my son,
Why are you screaming at me?
    STANTON.
                     Because you'd have me
Destroy this new life I've been three years building,
Not only for myself but for my kind,
By dragging my poor wife to the room in my heart
Where my dead loves are waked. (*Pause.*)
    FATHER COYNE.
                   Tell Kathleen, Matt.
Maybe it's that which stands between you, son,
And stiffens both your backs against each other.
    STANTON.
Who dares to say that something stands between us?
That's a pack of lies!
    FATHER COYNE.
            Is it? Tell Katie, Matt—
(BOYLE *bursts through the bar door.*)
    BOYLE.
It's Aggie Hogan, Father.
She's dying; and she won't confess to your curate.
They want you.
    FATHER COYNE.
         Mattie?

STANTON.
                    Sacred Heart of Jesus!
  FATHER COYNE.
Will you come with me?
  STANTON.
                    I will, Father. I will.
  (*Exit all* THREE *through the Ladies' Entrance.*)

                    CURTAIN

ACT ONE

SCENE 3

Midnight the same night. The all-night Printers' Church in the News-paper Row of Brooklyn on lower Fulton Street. STANTON *kneels on a prie-dieu with a framed baize curtain atop it.* FATHER MALONEY *sits on the other side of the prie-dieu, hearing his Confession.*

  STANTON.
Bless me, Father. I have sinned. Three years.
It is three years since I made my last Confession.
I accuse myself of lying many times.
  FATHER MALONEY.
How many times?
  STANTON.
                    God knows!
  FATHER MALONEY.
                         With a mind to harm?
  STANTON.
God knows!
  FATHER MALONEY.
            Take hold of yourself. What ails you!
  STANTON.
I did a woman wrong. Tonight she died.
Tomorrow is her wake.
  FATHER MALONEY.
                 What kind of wrong
Is it you did her?
  STANTON.
            I . . .
  FATHER MALONEY.
                 What kind of wrong?
  STANTON.
I lived with her three years before I married.
They pulled the sheet over her face an hour ago.
The hem of it gave. It was gray as a buried rag.

She wouldn't have the priest. She lay there sweating,
And they around her with their lighted candles.
She glowered and said, "If such love was a sin,
I'd rather not make peace with God at all."
They pressed her hard. She shook and shook her head.
She kept on shaking it until she died—
Absolve her through me!

FATHER MALONEY.
      You know I can't do that.

STANTON.
What can you do then!

FATHER MALONEY.
      Absolve *you* from *your* sin.

STANTON.
Her sin is mine. Absolve the both of us.

FATHER MALONEY.
Why did you leave this woman?

STANTON.
      She played me false.
I found her in the one bed with a man—
She stood on the wide porch with her hair down, crying.
I walked away. I heard her screaming at me.
She told me, go, yes go, but not to come back. Never.
She'd rip the clothes she bought me into threads
And throw them in the fire. She'd burn my letters,
And every bit of paper that I'd put my name to.
And she did . . . I'm sure she did. She was wild by nature.
But tonight . . . when I came back . . . she stretched out her hands
Like a falling child . . .

FATHER MALONEY.
      Go on.

STANTON.
      And I turned away—
I cannot rest with thinking of her face
And that black look of stubborn joy on it.

FATHER MALONEY.
Well for you, you can't rest. She died in the Devil's arms
In a glory of joy at the filthy shame to her flesh
You visited on her, and like all the rest,
You come to a strange priest outside your parish
In the mistaken hope he will not judge you,
But give you comfort when you need correction.
What about this other one you took up with
When you threw the dead one over?—

STANTON.
      Jesus, Father!

FATHER MALONEY.
Don't take the name of the Lord in vain to me!

STANTON.
I don't know why I came here in the first place.

FATHER MALONEY.
You came here for forgiveness—
   STANTON.
                           From the likes of you!
For thirty years I've put up with your kind.
Since my First Communion. Saturday Confession!
Spayed mutts of men, born with no spice of pride,
Living off the pennies of the poor,
Huddled in their fat in basement booths,
Calling the true vaulting of the heart
Towards its desire filth and deviation,
Dragging me, and all unlike you down—
   FATHER MALONEY.
Whatever a noble creature like yourself
May think of me, I'm here to do God's work;
And since that begins with dragging you down to the earth
We all have come from and must all return to,
Drag you down I will. God lifts none but the humble—
   STANTON.
The pride steams off you like the stink of cancer,
And you sit there and preach humility!
   FATHER MALONEY.
Take care! I will deny you absolution.
   STANTON.
What harm! Who can absolve us but ourselves!
I am what I am. What I have done, I'd cause for.
It was seeing what life did to her unmanned me;
It was looking in her eyes as they guttered out
That drove me here like a scared kid from the bogs
Who takes the clouds that bruise the light for demons.
But thanks to the words from the open grave of your mouth
I see that fear for the wind in fog that it is
And it is killed for good. I'm my own man now.
I can say that for the first time in my life.
I'm free of her; and I'm free of you and yours.
Come what come may to me, from this day forward,
I'll not fall to my knees for man or God.
   (STANTON *rises, and quickly strides out.* FATHER MALONEY *rises.*)
   FATHER MALONEY.
Will you dare to turn your back on the living God!

CURTAIN

ACT ONE

SCENE 4

Ten o'clock, Friday morning, April 29, 1890. The back room of Fogarty's Saloon. JAMES "PALSY" MURPHY *sits at a chair pushed well*

> back from a table, apprehensively holding a sheaf of papers in his hand. He is a florid, rather stout man in his late fifties, with black hair en brosse, graying at the temples. MAYOR EDWARD QUINN stands facing MURPHY like a statue of a lawyer in a park. He is a tall, husky, big-boned man in his seventies, bald, but with hair growing out of his ears. He is dressed in rumpled morning clothes.

QUINN.
Does Matthew Stanton think he can oust me
By hole-in-corner meetings in school halls,
With craw thumpers and Sunday-pass-the-plates,
Black Jack the plug and the ga-ga Parish Priest
Both nodding yes to everything he says
Like slobbering dummies?—What is it that he said?
    MURPHY.
Do you want to hear?
    QUINN.
               Would I ask, James, if I didn't?
    MURPHY.
Listen then. I have . . . full notes on it.
I took down everything that Stanton said.
    QUINN.
Read it. Read it. Do you want applause?
    MURPHY.
No, Ned: attention. Here: "My dear old friends,
When Father Coyne asked me to speak to you,
He said it was about Ag Hogan's bills,
A gathering to help raise funds to pay them.
I never thought the purpose of this meeting
Would be political"—
    QUINN.
               "I never thought
The purpose of this meeting"—Father Coyne!
I roofed his sieve of a church and glazed it too;
And put a tight new furnace in its cellar.
There's not a priest you can trust!
    MURPHY.
Will you listen, Ned!
    QUINN.
               I'm listening. Go on.
    MURPHY.
"The Party of Reform"—
    QUINN.
"The Party of Reform"! Ah, yes, reform!
A Lutheran lawyer with a flytrap mouth
And a four-bit practice of litigious Swedes
In a closet rank as rats down by the river!
A lecherous broker with a swivel eye
You wouldn't trust with Grandma in a hack!
A tear-drawers arm in arm with a gaping bollocks!

MURPHY.
Will you quit your interrupting!
QUINN.
      Read on. Read on.

MURPHY.
"The Party of Reform has in its hands
Sworn affidavits on the city books"—
QUINN.
Got by collusion and by audits forged
As the certificates above their parents' beds!—
MURPHY.
"The Party of Reform has in its hands
Sworn affidavits on the city books,
Drawn up from careful audit, and declaring
A hidden deficit of fifteen thousand"—
QUINN.
Of fifteen thousand! The unfortunates!
They couldn't even get that business right.
It's twenty thousand, Palsy, if it's a cent! (*Glum pause.*)
I'm in the treasury for twenty thousand. (*Pause.*)
MURPHY.
"You say they will expose us to the public,
Unless we guarantee that Edward Quinn
Resigns as candidate in the next election"—
QUINN.
See, that's Matt's game. He's out to get my job;
But he's not the guts to grab it like a man.
Will you listen to the cagey way he puts it:
"*You* say *they* will expose *us* to the public!"
As sneaky as a rat in a hotel kitchen.
Don't you see the cunning of it, James? The craft?
It's not my job he wants, but to save the Party!
And all I did for him. I made him, James.
I picked him up when he first came to me,
Twelve years ago, when he was twenty-five
And lost his job for beating up that grocer.
He'd no knees in his pants; his coat was slick
With grease as a butcher's thumb. He was skin and bones.
I was sitting here in Fogarty's back room,
With poor Ag Hogan codding me, when he
Burst in the door, and asked me for my help.
"I'll do anything that's honest, Mr Quinn,"
Is what he says. He had that crooked grin—
It reminded me of Patrick that's long dead,
Patrick, my poor brother—
MURPHY.
     Go on, now, Ned!
Leave out the soft-soap. He'd a crooked grin
You knew would serve you well among the women—

QUINN.
I should have said, "Go now, and scare the crows,
Raggedy-arse Keho; that's all you're good for!"
But, no, there was that grin; and Ag said, "Take him."
She loved him, the poor slob, from the day she saw him,
Fat good it did her. "You can put him on
With Judge Muldooney," says she; "take him, Ned,
God will bless us for it . . ." (*Pause.*)
                         Aggie's dead, James. Dead.
   MURPHY.
Yes, Ned. She is.
   QUINN.
               Did Stanton get to see her? (*Pause.*)
Did he?
   MURPHY.
     Yes.
   QUINN.
              She wouldn't let me in. (*Pause.*)
   MURPHY.
I'm sorry, Ned.
   QUINN.
            And Stanton's high-toned wife?
What did she say when she found out about them?
   MURPHY.
She didn't, Ned. She knows that Ag helped Matt,
But nothing else.
   QUINN.
             Ah, nothing else? I see.
Where was I, Palsy?
   MURPHY.
           "All I done for him,"
Fifth book, tenth chapter—
   QUINN.
              Go to hell, James Murphy.
You think it's funny, do you? I'll give you fun.
If it's jail for me, you know, it's jail for you.
No hundred-dollar suits and fancy feeds
With tarts in Rector's drinking cold champagne
From glasses bright as ice with hollow stems,
But tea from yellowed cups and mulligan
Foul as the odds and ends they make it from.
   MURPHY.
Sure, they'll send us puddings.
   QUINN.
               Are you mad, or what?
I tell you, I'm in danger. I'm in danger.
Don't shake your head. They're spoiling for the kill.
It's in their blood.
   MURPHY.
      Whose blood?

QUINN.
                              Whose blood but our own.
They turn upon the strong, and pull them down,
And not from virtue, James, but vicious pride.
They want to hold their heads up in this city,
Among the members of the Epworth League,
The Church of Ethical Culture and the Elks,
That's why they're taking sides with Ole Olson,
Or whatever the hell his name is, and that whore
From Wall Street in the clean pince-nez. For thirty years
I've kept their heads above the water, James,
By fair means or by foul. Now they've reached the shore
They'd rather not remember how they got there.
They want to disown me. They're a faithless lot,
And Matthew Stanton is the worst of all—
Read on, why don't you? What's the matter with you? (*Pause.*)
    MURPHY.
"I would not stand in this school hall before you
If Edward Quinn had not, in his full power,
Made of me what I am. I cannot think,
Since you have shared his generosity
As long as I, that you are asking me
To help you pull him down"—
    QUINN.
                    Good Jesus, James!
    MURPHY.
"The way to cope with the Party of Reform's
To raise the funds to make Quinn's deficit up.
I pledge three thousand dollars, and I ask
Each and every one of you who can
To give as much as possible. Ned Quinn
Must not live out his final days in jail
Because he was too kindly to be wise"—
    QUINN.
I want no handouts from the likes of him.
Will he pity me?
    MURPHY.
            What's that?
    QUINN.
                    You heard me, James.
Will he pity me? Does he think I need his pity!
I made him, and I can unmake him too,
And make another in his place. I'm old,
I'm far too old to live on charity
From a greenhorn that I picked up in a barroom
To run my sweetheart's errands. Don't you see, James?
He took Ag from me first; that's how he started.
He ran her roadhouse for her. "He was handsome!
He'd skin like milk, and eyes like stars in winter!"
And he was young and shrewd! She taught him manners:

What clothes to wear, what cutlery to begin with,
What twaddle he must speak when introduced
To the state bigwigs down from Albany.
He told her that he loved her. She ditched me.
I'm twenty years her senior. Then that day,
That famous Labor Day three years ago,
We'd a drink or two, you know, for old times' sake,
And we passed out, and that bitch Josie Finn
Found out about us, and brought Matt in on us,
Our arms around each other like two children.
And he spat on poor Ag's carpet, called her a whore,
Me a degenerate. Three years ago,
The very year he married this Kathleen,
The Lord knows who, James, from the Christ knows where,
In some cosy hocus-pocus there in London,
To show Ag he could do without her. He never spoke
To Ag at all until he found her done for,
Dying lung by lung. He'd never speak to me at all
If I were not in trouble.
Don't you see the triumph of it, Palsy Murphy!
He takes his vengeance in a show of mercy.
He weeps as he destroys! He's a crocodile—
MURPHY.
Ned, I . . .
QUINN.
   Ned what?
MURPHY.
      I hope you won't be hurt.
We on the Party board agree with Matt.
We feel the time has come for some new blood—
QUINN.
"We on the Party board agree with Matt"!
Now it comes out at last! It all comes out!
You and your pack of lies, your trumped-up story,
Pretending to be reading what he said
When you can't read a thing that hasn't pictures.
Did you think me such a boob I wouldn't know
What you and Walsh were up to here last night?
It made the rounds of the Ward by half past nine! (*Pause.*)
Bismarck the diplomat! You goddamned fool,
Pouring that vat of soft-soap over me!
"Because he was too kindly to be wise"!
They'll soon be making you the editor
Of *The Messenger of the Sacred Heart*.
MURPHY.
      Now, Ned—
QUINN.
"Now, Ned." "Now, Ned." Shut up, or I'll drink your blood.
The only thing rang true in what you said
Was Stanton's offer to be noble to me. (*Pause.*)

MURPHY.
I wanted to break it easy. Matt made no offer.
The Party it is will cover you on the books.
But on one condition, Ned: you must resign.
QUINN.
I must resign. We'll see who backs out first.
I didn't stay the mayor of this city
For thirty years by taking orders, James.
You tell the Party board I'll rot in prison
Before I'll let Matt Stanton take my place.
You tell the Party board I'll meet the debits
The Party of Reform found in the books.
You tell the Party board they'd best not cross me.
Don't look as if you think this all is blather.
There's not a one of you I can't get at,
You least of all. Remember that, James Murphy.
How long, do you think, that knowing what I know
About your money, James, and how you got it,
The Jesuit Fathers at St. Francis Xavier's,
With all their bon-ton notions of clean hands,
Would let your boys play soldier in their yard?
Don't glare like that at me. You tell the board
What I have said. I meant it, every word.
MURPHY.
The Party will disown you!
QUINN.
                Let them try!
I'll grease the palm of every squarehead deadbeat
From Greenwood Cemetery to the Narrows
Who'll stagger to the polls for three months' rent,
I'll buy the blackface vote off all the fences
Down Fulton Street from Hudson Avenue.
I'll vote from every plot in Holy Cross
With an Irish headstone on it. I'll win this fight—
MURPHY.
I'll telegraph to Albany. I warn you!
QUINN.
Damn Albany! Get out of here. Get out!
    (*Exit* MURPHY *Stage Left.* QUINN *walks over to the bar door to Stage Right.*)
Hey, Bill.
    (*Enter* BILL, *a wiry bowlegged man about seventy who has the look of a drunk.*)
                Go down to one-o-seventy Luqueer Street,
And get me Josie Finn—On second thought,
Best wait till noon and collar me some schoolboy
To run the errand for me. If they saw you,
They'd know 'twas I that wanted her. And yes!
Send to Fitzsimmons and Rooney for a wreath,
A hundred-dollar wreath, and have them spell

This message out in them gold-paper letters
On a silk-gauze band: "For Agnes Mary Hogan,
Gone but not forgotten." Look alive!

CURTAIN

ACT ONE

SCENE 5

Eight o'clock the same evening. The Haggertys' kitchen, beneath the Stantons' parlor in the double set. The kitchen table and chairs are of cheap oak, varnished and revarnished until they look charred and blistered. The chairs are unmatched, and of the "Queen Anne" style, jerry-built replicas of a bad idea of eighteenth-century furniture, with die-embossed designs on the back, their seats repaired with pressed cardboard. Behind the table stands the big coal cooking stove, jammed into the chimney. The mantelpiece is covered with newspaper cut into daggers of rough lace and filled with every kind of souvenir you could think of, yellowing letters, bills, clippings stuck behind the grimy ornaments. To Stage Right of the stove, an entrance into the three remaining rooms of the flat, an opening hung with a single portiere of heavy, warped, faded brown velour on greasy wooden rings. Through that opening, from time to time, as the scene progresses, can be heard the sound of PEOPLE *saying the Rosary. The door of the flat, giving on the hall and the stairs to the Stantons' flat, is ajar; and leaned against it glitters Edward Quinn's appalling flower piece. Seated to Stage Left of the table is* JOSIE FINN, *a tall, rather handsome woman in her late thirties, with her black hair in a loose bun. Opposite her sits* ANN MULCAHY, *a small, plump woman with a face like a withered apple, red hair gone white, and fine searching eyes. Between them, its back to the audience, stands an empty chair. They have cups in front of them, and are waiting for the kettle to boil for the tea.*

ANN.
I'm sure Matt will have luck for burying Ag
And letting Maisie hold the wake downstairs here
In his own house for all that past between them.
    (JOSIE *nods disconsolately. Enter* PETEY BOYLE, *swaying slightly, his hat in his hands.*)
BOYLE.
I'm sorry for your trouble, Mrs Finn.
    JOSIE.
My trouble, Petey. Trouble it is for fair.
That's Aggie Hogan that's laid out in there,
My dead aunt's daughter, that I haven't talked to
For, Mother of God, I think it's three long years
September.

BOYLE.
          If you come to crow about it,
My ass on you then, kid—
   JOSIE.
                Sir, you presume!
John Haggerty!
   (BOYLE *scurries through the portiere to the sanctuary of the coffin.*)
   ANN.
Now don't be calling Jack. It will cause trouble.
Poor Petey Boyle was always ignorant.
He meant no harm by talking to you dirty,
Josie dear.
   JOSIE.
         It's not his talking dirty
Made me mad. What kind of creature must he take me for,
To come to crow at my own cousin's wake!—
You know, Ag wouldn't see me at the last?
   ANN.
Nor would she have the priest. She was crazed with pain,
In fever tantrums, don't you know, half dead.
She hardly knew what she was doing.
   JOSIE.
Ann, you're a saint.
   ANN.
             Now, Josie, praise is poison,
Though I thank you for the kindness that's behind it.
   JOSIE.
How can you live, remembering what you've done,
Unless you are a saint, or a half brute,
Like Quinn in there!
   ANN.
            By doing what you must;
And begging for the grace to forgive yourself
As well as others when you don't do right.
You just reminded me: I hope Ned's going soon.
It's getting on towards eight; and Matt's expected down.
   JOSIE.
Oh, Quinn knows that. Sure, Quinn knows everything:
Whose money's stained, and how, and whose is not;
Who's in whose bed, and who is not, and why;
Who has a shame to hide that he can use
To coat his nest with slime against the wind!
   ANN.
There's a bit of skunk in all of us, you know.
We stink when we're afraid or hurt. Ned's both.
   JOSIE.
Pray for me, Ann Mulcahy. I've made a vow
On my dead mother's grave to guard my tongue
And keep my temper.

ANN.
                    God in Heaven help you.
JOSIE.
It's up to me, not Him.
ANN.
                        Ah, don't say that.
Sure, that's presumption.
JOSIE.
                       Then I won't say that.
But thinking back on things I've said and done,
And my knees all bunions, kneeling out novenas,
If you think that God and all His holy angels
Can shut my mouth once anger oils the hinges,
You're more a fool than ever I took you for
When first I met you—
      (*Enter* FATHER COYNE, *dressed in the same rusty black coat and frayed biretta.*)
FATHER COYNE.
                    Here in the nick of time!
Who's calling my lost parish's one saint
A fool to her face!
JOSIE.
                   Good evening to you, Father.
FATHER COYNE.
Good evening, Mrs. Finn. I'm glad to see
Your three hard years of war with the deceased
Has ended in some show of gallantry.
What was the fight about? Do you recall?
JOSIE.
You well know that I do. But what's been has been.
She'd have done the same for me.
FATHER COYNE.
                         I'm sure she would:
For where would be the harm in that, I ask you?
There'd be small danger of much conversation
To thaw your icy hearts—
ANN.
                   Please, Father Coyne—
FATHER COYNE.
Dear God, forgive me. I forgot you, Ann.
It's like me to fly out at Mrs. Finn
With the one soul left here I could scandalize
From Dwight Street to the steps of City Hall.
I'll be as gracious as St. Francis Sales
To make it up to you, Ann—Now, Mrs. Finn,
And how have you been ever since?
JOSIE.
                        Since when?
FATHER COYNE.
Since Easter Sunday three long years ago,

The last time that I saw you in my church!
JOSIE.
There's other churches!
FATHER COYNE.
      Yes, but not this parish;
And that's where you belong—
 (ANN *touches* FATHER COYNE *on the sleeve and looks into his eyes.*)
        I'm a sinful man.
Pray for me, Ann Mulcahy. I'll begin the beads,
Before I throw my forty years of prayer
Into the pits of Hell to best a slanderer.
Will you come with me?
ANN.
      In a minute, Father.
The kettle's on the boil.
 (*Exit* FATHER COYNE *through the portiere. Pause.*)
JOSIE.
     I have the name;
As well to have the game!
ANN.
      He meant no harm.
He's torn apart with trying to talk sense
To poor Ag dying; and he struck at you
Because you brought the days back Ag was well. (*Pause.*)
Will you wet the tea, while I go in and ask
If Ned Quinn can't be hurried just a bit.
I'm destroyed with worrying that Matt will come.
 (*Exit* ANN. *Sound of* ROSARY. JOSIE *rises, and brews the tea in a large earthenware pot. Enter* QUINN *quietly through the portiere. Sound of* ROSARY. JOSIE *looks up from the stove, directly at him, then away. Most of their conversation is carried on with averted faces.*)
QUINN.
Why have they put that wedding ring on Ag? (*Pause.*)
JOSIE.
She asked them to. She said it was her mother's. (*Pause.*)
QUINN.
What harm would there be in it, I'd like to know!
JOSIE.
You'd like to know? You know damned well what harm.
I told you no this afternoon. I meant it.
Am I your cat's-paw, do you think, Ned Quinn,
To pull your poisoned chestnuts from the fire
And feed them to your foes? I told you. No.
QUINN.
You didn't think that way the day you led him
Into the room where her that's dead in there
Lay in my arms as guiltless as a baby
In a fit of drunken warmth she took for love!
JOSIE.
More shame to me I didn't think that way!

She was my own blood, and she loved the man;
And I tried to get between them, and broke her heart.
It's all my fault that she lies dead in there,
No one's but mine. And she was good to me,
And I betrayed her—Ned, she wouldn't see me.
She wouldn't let me in the room at the last.
They say she'd not confess her life with Matt;
They say she would not call that life a sin. (*Pause.*)
I'll never interfere that way again.
If it were not for me, they'd have been married,
And there'd have been no sin. Has Ag gone to Hell?
Do you think that, Ned? For that would be my fault.
Have I destroyed her life forever, Ned,
In this world and the next? (*Pause.*)

QUINN.

                               You're talking blather.
Ach, God's more merciful than Father Coyne,
Be sure of that, or we'd have been roasted black,
The whole damned lot of us, long since. (*Pause.*)

                                                   Come on.
Wouldn't you like to make it up to Ag, Jo?
Do something for her dead? That's all I'm asking.
Shouldn't Matt pay for what he did to her?
All that you'd need to say's a single sentence,
When the Lady Duchess Kathleen Kakiak
Descends in visitation: "Mrs. Stanton,
Sure, God will bless you for your charity."
"My charity?" she'll ask. You'll say, "You know,
Ag having lived with Matt three years and all."
That's all you'd have to say.

JOSIE.

                                 What am I, Ned,
That you take me for a fool and villain both?
Don't talk to me about your broken heart,
And how you feel you owe poor Ag revenge!
If she had wanted that, would she have died
Without the sacraments to spare Matt pain?
I know you want to drive Matt from the running
And that you'd stop at nothing short of murder
For one more term as lord of City Hall.
Best give it up, Ned. Fast. It will destroy you.

QUINN.
Give what up, Jo?

JOSIE.

                          Your pride. Your murderous pride.

QUINN.
I don't know what you mean by that at all.
They're out to get me, Jo. I have to fight.
They telephoned today at half past three:
"Albany says resign or they'll destroy you!"

I had to send a letter to that bastard
Throwing in the sponge. But I'm not through yet;
And I'll win out. I always have before.
But if I go down, I won't go down alone.
You may call that pride, if you like. I call it honor.
 JOSIE.
No, Ned. Not honor, I know. Pride kept me from her.
I'd not admit the wrong was on my side,
And her with the blood of her heart on her shaking chin
In that icebox of a hallroom down in Smith Street,
The wall at her nose. Oh, Sacred Heart of Jesus,
I should have flung myself on the oilcloth floor
And not got up until she gave me pardon.
She'd have laughed at me, and called me a young whale,
Or some such nonsense. She'll never laugh again . . .
What must Matt feel?
 QUINN.
                    Good riddance to bad rubbish
Is what he feels!
 JOSIE.
                You never knew Matt, Ned,
If you think that.
 QUINN.
                I knew him well enough!—
You're still in love with him—
 JOSIE.
                            What's that to you!
 QUINN.
And him with the worst word in his mouth for you,
As he always has had!
 JOSIE.
                I don't believe you, Ned.
 QUINN.
Ah, well. Ah, well. No one believes me now.
Stanton's your god; and that's just as it should be.
You're traitors all, as fickle as the sunlight
On April Fools' Day. But there'll come a time
You'll say Ned Quinn was right.
 JOSIE.
                            What kind of thing
Is it he says of me?
 QUINN.
                No matter, now.
You'd not believe me if I told it you.
 JOSIE.
What does he say? (*Pause.*)
 QUINN.
                    For one thing that you're two-faced,
And well enough, since the face that you were born with's
Like a madman's arse.

JOSIE.
                    You son of a bitch, Ned Quinn,
That sounds like you, not him.
    QUINN.
                           Have it your own way.
I'm old, you know; I'm all dustmice upstairs.
It's hard for me to lay my mind on recollections.
Yet it seems to me I can recall a toast
Matt drank his birthday night at Villepigue's
Two weeks before we had that fight in Seagate . . .
He stood there fingering that green silk tie
That you embroidered those gold shamrocks on—
    JOSIE.
How do you know that I gave Matt that tie?
    QUINN.
He told me when he gave the tie to Petey—
    JOSIE.
You made that up! (*Pause.*)
    QUINN.
                    He lifted up his glass,
And laughed, and said: "Confusion to the devil
That's bent Jo Finn as fast around my neck
As a coop around a barrel; and her legs as loose
As her lying tongue—
    JOSIE.
                  God's curse on you for that!

    QUINN.
God's curse on me? I'm only telling truth.
Come to your senses, woman. He played me false.
And Ag. And her he's married to, Kathleen.
What makes you think you are the bright exception?
    JOSIE.
Because I know him for a good man, Ned.
And not a poisonous old woman of a thief,
Destroying names to keep himself in office—
    QUINN.
A thief, am I! I'll get what I want without you;
And when Stanton plays you false, don't whine to me.
        (*Enter* KATHLEEN, STANTON, *and* MURPHY. MURPHY *is carrying a case of liquor, which he sets on the chair nearest him, his eyes fixed on* QUINN *and* STANTON *confronting each other.*)
    STANTON.
I will not play her false, nor will I you . . .
I got your letter; and I thank you for it.
I'm sorry that my winning means your loss.
        (*Pause.* QUINN *glares at* STANTON, *then he takes a step towards the door.*)
    MURPHY.
Wait, Ned!

STANTON.
    I swear, I'll see you through this trouble.
I want to be your friend again. Shake hands.
Come on, man. And what better place than here.
I'm sure Ag would have wanted it. Come on—
  QUINN.
Good God! The goat can talk. When Ag was living, though,
You rarely met the livestock in the house!
    (STANTON *hurls himself at* QUINN, *and takes him by the throat.*
    KATHLEEN *screams.* JOSIE *and* MURPHY *rush to get between them.*)
  STANTON.
I'll kill him!
  MURPHY.
        Hold him back. Go on, Ned. Go.
Remember Ag, Matt. Please. No disrespect.
    (MURPHY *is holding* STANTON'S *arms.* QUINN, *disengaging himself
    from* JOSIE, *blackly looks* STANTON *up and down, and spits in his face.
    It takes both* MURPHY *and* KATHLEEN *to hold* STANTON *back.* QUINN
    watches the struggle. Exit QUINN *slowly.* JOSIE *fetches a rag, and hands
    it to* STANTON. *He wipes the spittle off his face and coat.*)
  JOSIE.
Pay him no heed, Matt. Sure, what need have you
To care what a thief thinks who's been found out—
  STANTON.
I'll thank you to keep out of this, Jo Finn.
You always were a one for interfering.
  JOSIE.
Why take things out on me? It was he spit at you.
  KATHLEEN.
Mattie, Mattie, are you crazed or what?
You've hurt the woman's feelings.
  STANTON.
               Kate, come ahead.
Where are the Haggertys?
  JOSIE.
              Inside with the rest.
Inside in the parlor.
    (STANTON *takes* KATHLEEN *by the arm, but she holds back.*)
  KATHLEEN.
           Matt, beg her pardon.

  STANTON.
For what? For what? Don't waste your sympathy
On that one. And stay clear of her as can be:
She has a wicked tongue. Watch out for her—
  KATHLEEN.
The woman heard you!—
  STANTON.
             Devil a bit I care!
Will you come into the parlor!

KATHLEEN.
                    Matt, she's crying.
(STANTON *strides over towards* JOSIE, *awkward with remorse.*)
STANTON.
Josie—
　　JOSIE.
        Never mind. I heard you, Matt.
　　STANTON.
                              The devil
Take you then, for your big ears!
　　JOSIE.
                    The devil take me, Matt.
　　KATHLEEN.
Please, Mrs. Finn—
　　JOSIE.
              Go in now to the wake,
And let me be!
            (*Pause.* MURPHY *shakes his head, and motioning* KATHLEEN *towards the portiere, holds it up for her. Exit* KATHLEEN, STANTON, *and* MURPHY. JOSIE *walks to the table and picks up the rag which* STANTON *used to wipe the spittle off himself. In a spasm of rage, she tears it in two and throws it on the floor. Enter* MARIA HAGGERTY.)

　　MARIA.
What's this that Mrs. Stanton's after saying
About a fight between her man and you?
　　JOSIE.
I'm not the kind that would demean myself
By having words with the likes of him, Maria.
　　MARIA.
The likes of him? What is this all about?
I've never heard you talk that way of Matt.
　　JOSIE.
I never found him out until just now.
He treated me like dirt. And who is he
To be so high and mighty—Hogan's Goat,
A fancy boy made good! Ag's fancy boy!
　　MARIA.
You shut your mouth, or I will shut it for you.
Matt's broken up because of Aggie's death;
That's why he lost his temper. That and Quinn,
Bad luck be with the day I let him in here.
I'll not have you make trouble for Matt, Jo.
I want you to come into the parlor now
And take Matt's hand.
　　JOSIE.
                It's he should take my hand.
　　MARIA.
Will you come in, if he comes out to you first?
            (*Enter* KATHLEEN *softly behind* MARIA.)

JOSIE.
I'll make no promises.
>*(Pause.* KATHLEEN *puts her black-gloved hand on* MARIA's *shoulder.*
>MARIA *starts, and acknowledges her with nervous heartiness.)*

MARIA.
              Why, Mrs. Stanton!
KATHLEEN.
I'd like to talk to Mrs. Finn alone. *(Pause.)*
Maria? Just a moment or two. Alone.
>*(Exit* MARIA *reluctantly.)*

Mrs. Finn, please. Matthew meant no harm . . .
He has a dreadful temper. You know that.
And he's like a scalded cat since yesterday
When he got the news that Agnes Hogan died. *(Pause.)*
He told me just how much she'd meant to him
When he was starting out on his career.
You know that better, maybe, than myself—
JOSIE.
He told you that, did he! Did he tell you how
He lived with her three years in a state of sin
In a love nest of a roadhouse down in Seagate?
And the devil take the talk! Did he tell you, too,
She drank herself consumptive for his sake
Because he threw her over three years since,
When he'd got all he wanted from her, missis,
And married you—
>(KATHLEEN *gasps and runs out the door.* JOSIE *looks straight ahead into the air before her face, brings both hands to her forehead with a slap, and sits swaying in her chair.)*

CURTAIN

END OF ACT ONE

ACT TWO

SCENE 1

Eleven o'clock the same evening. The Stantons' flat. Before the Curtain rises, the sound of a SCUFFLE and a CRY. KATHLEEN *stands, tight with fury, a large silver hand mirror, which she has just struck* STANTON *with, in her hand.* STANTON *sits on the edge of the couch, a handkerchief to his forehead, which is bleeding slightly.* KATHLEEN *turns her gaze from* STANTON *to the floor. With that sudden recession of energy which follows drunken violence, she sways and slumps, the hand with the mirror in it hanging slackly at her side. She kicks at the fragments of the mirror with the toe of her shoe, as if she were puzzled by them. She is very drunk, but on brandy; that is, her mind is sharper than it would seem to be.*

KATHLEEN.
The mirror's broken.
  STANTON.
       Yes. That means bad luck.
  KATHLEEN.
I know it does. But now I can see plain,
Just as it says in First Corinthians:
When I was a child, I saw as a child does,
Saw what I loved as in a mirror darkly,
But now I see his face—
  STANTON.
      This night of all nights!
When I have Quinn's note resigning in my hand!
The bitch of a Josie Finn with her snake's tongue!—
Where have you been till now? Where did you get it?
  KATHLEEN.
Did I get what, Matt?
  STANTON.
      The drink that's crazed you.
  KATHLEEN.
In your own back room with a woman named Miss Legg.
Miss Bessie Legg. She'd yards and yards of beads on,
And a hat like a berry patch attacked by magpies,
And a fancy neckpiece like twelve Persian cats
All tied together. You'd think she'd blow away
At the first breeze with all those feathers on her.
  STANTON.
How could you do a thing like that to me?
Get paralyzed for everyone to gawk at,
And with the district whore?
  KATHLEEN.
      She's that, is she?
Birds of a feather flock together, Matt,
And whore will meet with whore. That's what I am.
We aren't married. We aren't. You know that.
Isn't it the same as you and Agnes?
  STANTON.
      Jesus, Katie! (*Pause.*)
  KATHLEEN.
Are you hurt bad, Matt?
  STANTON.
      It's nice of you to ask.
  (KATHLEEN *flies at him.*)
  KATHLEEN.
You son of a bitch, I'll kill you.

(STANTON *pinions her arms. She drops the mirror. What began as battle ends as embrace.*)

Mattie, Mattie.

STANTON.
Oh, Katie, what's the matter with us both!

KATHLEEN.
What can a woman say when she learns the man
She left her country and her God to marry
Has married her to show his cast-off mistress
That he can do without her, or even worse,
Only to earn his good name back again?

STANTON.
I married you because I love you, Kate.

KATHLEEN.
Then why was I the one soul in this city
Who didn't know of you and Agnes? Why?

STANTON.
I didn't want to hurt you.

KATHLEEN.
     Well, you have—
How do I know you won't abandon me
If I don't get you what you want from life?

STANTON.
Don't say such things.

KATHLEEN.
    No wonder they seemed strange,
Your what-d'ya-callem's, your constituents:
They none of them could look me in the face
For fear they might let on. Didn't Bessie Legg
Tell me she thought the only reason Agnes Hogan
Went to bed with Quinn was to prove to herself
That there was someone loved her, when she saw
Your feelings for her dying like wet coal,
And realized she'd lost you? How do I know
The same thing will not happen to myself;
And people won't be saying a year from now,
Kate went the same way as the poor dead whore?

STANTON.
Kate. Don't call her that.

KATHLEEN.
     Why not? Don't they?

STANTON.
They don't. And don't you call her out of name.
You never knew her. And the talk you've heard
Has been about her as she was in public,
Stripping the heavy diamonds off her fingers
To keep the party going one more hour.
I knew what lay behind it. It was mine:
Her will to fullness. She contained a man
As the wind does, the first giddy days of spring,

When your coat blows open, and your blood beats hard,
As clear as ice, and warm as a chimney wall.
'Twas she first gave me heart to dare be free.
All threats turned promise when she talked to you.
With her on your arm, you saw your life before you
Like breast-high wheat in the soft dazzle of August.
She had a way of cupping her long hands
Around my bulldog's mug, as if I were
Some fancy fruit she'd bought beyond her means,
And laughing with delight. She put nothing on
She did not feel, and felt with flesh and soul.
I don't believe she knew what shame might be.
You could not resist her. *I* could not. I tried.
I was twenty-five years old, when first I met her.
I'd never . . .
  KATHLEEN.
     What?
    STANTON.
        I was what you'd call a virgin . . .
  KATHLEEN.
The saints preserve us!
    STANTON.
        Yes, it's funny now;
It wasn't funny then. (*Pause.*)
        It was she wooed me.
It seemed—Lord knows, I don't—unnatural.
She was ten years my senior. But, oh, Kate,
To look at her downstairs, you'd never know
What once she was! Her hair was bronze and silver
Like pear trees in full bloom, her eyes were opal,
Her skin was like new milk, and her blue veins
Trembled in the shimmer of her full straight neck
Like threads of violets fallen from her hair
And filliped by the breeze. She bought me presents:
A handmade vest of black brocaded silk,
A blond Malacca cane with a silver head
Cast like an antique statue, the Lord knows what,
There were so many of them. And she'd cock
That angel's head of hers, and tell me:
"You look like such a slob, Matt, I took pity
And bought you something nice. You can pay me back . . .
Some day." (*Pause.*)
      I took them not to hurt her, Kate;
And when she asked me would I work for her,
Would I run the gaming rooms in Seagate for her,
And keep her out of trouble, I said yes;
And when she asked me would I be her man,
I'd have said yes, but I could scarcely breathe
Between the want and fear of her. I nodded—
I never knew a man say no to her
Until I did myself that Labor Day

I found her in the one bed with Ned Quinn.
I looked her in the eyes, and I said, "No!
I'll play the fancy boy to you no more." (*Pause.*)
That's what I was, Kathleen, Ag's fancy boy,
I was Hogan's Goat to everyone, Ag's stud.
All my high hopes for power and for office
Fell down around my ears like a spavined roof
When I first heard them call me that—And, Kate,
When it comes to feelings, there was my side too:
I might have been some tethered brute in the yard
The way she acted. That last year she seemed bent
On driving home to me she was all I had,
Without her, I was nothing—Even after Newark,
She never changed—

    KATHLEEN.
                      What happened in Newark?—

    STANTON.
                                              Nothing!
I don't know why I brought it up in the first place.
We had a fight. I left her. I went to Newark.
She followed me. We made it up. That's all.
Let's not talk about it. It brings things back.

    KATHLEEN.
You loved her, didn't you? You love her still.

    STANTON.
Ag's dead, Kathleen. How can you love a corpse?
And in my heart she's been that these three years—
Part of me lay dead as a horse in the street
In that house in Seagate, till I met you in London.
It was as if God had sent me down an angel
To bring me back from the grave. That's why I asked you
To marry me in that London City Hall
Without the eight weeks' wait to cry the banns,
And come back with me right away. I was afraid,
I was afraid I'd lose you, if I left
And waited here for you till the banns were cried—
I swear to you, on my dead mother's grave,
As soon as the election's past, we'll marry
Right in St. Mary's Church, and damn the gossip! (*Pause.*)
I didn't tell you—

    KATHLEEN.
                Why?—

    STANTON.
                     I was ashamed
That I was ever young. I wanted you
To think I knew my way around from birth.

    KATHLEEN.
Lord help us!

    STANTON.
             And somehow, even more, I was ashamed

That I had let her woo me like a girl,
And I could not resist her or say no
For three long years. It was that slavery
I was ashamed of most—
    KATHLEEN.
                      That slavery,
My dear, is love—
    STANTON.
                      What is it you just said?
    KATHLEEN.
I'm terrible drunk.
    STANTON.
                      Sure, don't I know that!
And if you weren't, Kate, you'd be a widow.
You'd have brained me good and proper with that mirror,
If your eye had not been blurred—
    KATHLEEN.
                      But I see plain!
    STANTON.
Come, Katie, let me help you into bed—
    KATHLEEN.
You never came to look for me, did you?
    STANTON.
I did. I couldn't find you.
    KATHLEEN.
                      Tell the truth!
You were too proud. You sat up here and waited.
You knew I would come back like a hungry cat,
Like Agnes Hogan! Call to her, why don't you?
She'll stiffen in the coffin at your voice
And drag herself up those dark stairs outside
On her bare feet! They never put shoes on them.
She's back to where she was before in Ireland:
The dirt will clog her toes!
    STANTON.
                      Oh, Jesus, Katie!
    KATHLEEN.
Don't you understand me, Mattie?
    STANTON.
                      Come on now, Kate.
The fire's sunk. You'll catch your death of cold,
If you keep up this way. Kate, come on to bed.
    KATHLEEN.
No, never!
    STANTON.
                Katie, Katie, what's the matter!
    KATHLEEN.
I looked at her downstairs. I feel afraid.
They say death visits three before it's done.
I looked at her sewn lips, her spotted hand

With the wedding ring you never gave her on it.
They said it was her mother's. Poor Aggie, Matt!
Poor you and me!
> (*Pause.* STANTON *covers his face with his hands and falls to the couch.* KATHLEEN *suddenly throws herself on her knees, and embraces him around the waist.*)

      I don't want liberty!
Don't leave me, Mattie, please. I feel afraid.
> (STANTON *uncovers his face, cups the back of her head in his hand, and kisses her temples.*)

STANTON.
Toc-sha-shin-inish, my darling. Don't be talking—
KATHLEEN.
It isn't God I want, it's you—
STANTON.
      Sh. Sh.
KATHLEEN.
I wanted to go away, Matt; but I couldn't.
Those things you said about you and Ag Hogan,
About resenting how you felt for her,
They go for me—Oh, Matt, we're like twin children:
The pride is in our blood—I'd like to kill you,
Or die myself. Do you understand me, Matt!
Don't let me. I am sick with shame. I love you—
> (STANTON *kisses her on the mouth, lifts her to her feet, and helps her towards the bedroom.*)

STANTON.
You're crying drunk—
KATHLEEN.
    In vino veritas:
There's truth in drink.
STANTON.
     God! Now she's quoting Latin,
And me so ignorant that all I know
Is that I'm cold and want my wife beside me
Before I can feel warm again or rest.
Ag's dead, Kate, dead.
But, Katie, we're alive.
Come with me out of the cold. Ag's gone for good.

      CURTAIN

ACT TWO

SCENE 2

Midnight the same night. The back room of Stanton's Saloon. Stanton for Mayor *is spelled out in gold-paper letters hanging from the crepe-paper streamers.*

BESSIE LEGG *sits at a table, looking downcast and bewildered, an empty glass before her, her back to the Ladies' Entrance. The door to the Ladies' Entrance swiftly opens a crack.* BILL *sticks his head in and withdraws it. The door swiftly closes.* BESSIE *cranes round, sees nothing, and returns to her glum daydream. Enter* QUINN *and* BILL *through the Ladies' Entrance.*

BESSIE.
Watch what the hell you're doing!
Creeping up on parties like the Blackhand!
Good Christ, it's you! What are you doing here?
You want to start a riot?
QUINN.
Go easy, Bessie,
Or you'll have them in here. I'll tell you what to do.
Go get two doubles; and tell them at the bar
You'd like to be alone in here awhile,
You have a customer.
(QUINN *puts a ten-dollar bill on the table in front of her.*)
BESSIE.
I'm through with that.
QUINN.
I'm through with that, says she, and her stairs in splinters
From the armies charging up and down them nights!
Don't sit there that way with your mouth sprung open
Like a busted letter box. Go get the drinks.
(QUINN *moves out of sight of the bar. Exit* BESSIE, *opening and closing the door as if it were mined.*)
Keep watch outside now, Bill. Give the door a kick
If you see that bastard coming. If the trunk is there,
And the box is in it, I'll pass you out the key.
(*Exit* BILL *through the Ladies' Entrance.* QUINN *walks around the room as if examining it before taking it over. KICK at the bar door.* QUINN *starts, looks towards the Ladies' Entrance, then back at the bar door. When he sees that someone is opening the door for* BESSIE, *he draws back into the shadows. Enter* BESSIE *with two double whiskeys in her hand.*)
BESSIE.
When I say private, I mean private, Percy.
Didn't your mother teach you manners—Thanks for nothing!
Pinching a person when a person's helpless!
Shut the door or you'll get a bourbon eyewash.
(*As the bar door shuts behind her, a* MALE VOICE *chants in falsetto.*)
MALE VOICE.
Remember St. Peter's,
Remember St. Paul's,
Remember the goil
You kissed in the hall!
BESSIE.
Honest, if there ain't more snots than noses,

I'm the Mother Superior at Good Shepherd's!
Here's your lousy drinks.
>   (BESSIE *sets the doubles before herself and* QUINN *as she sits down. She pushes the change from the ten across the table.* QUINN *smiles, and pushes it back to her.*)

That was a ten-spot.
Them drinks were forty cents.
>   (QUINN *smiles again, shakes his head, and motions her to take the money. She does, with a shamefaced smile. They lift their glasses to each other and drink.*)

QUINN.
How are you since? . . .
BESSIE.
You didn't come here for no dish of tea.
QUINN.
As a matter of fact, I'd like to ask a favor;
And I missed you at the wake. That's why I came.
BESSIE.
You didn't miss me, kid. I didn't go.
Dead people make me nervous. What's this favor?
QUINN.
I hear you've been spelling out May Haggerty
Looking after Ag this past year, Bessie.
I wonder did Ag still have a cowhide trunk?
BESSIE.
A yellow leather trunk? She did.
QUINN.
Where is it?
BESSIE.
It's around the corner in her room in Smith Street,
The Haggertys didn't have time to cart it home.
QUINN.
There's something in it that I'd like to have,
For a keepsake, don't you know. Have you the key?
BESSIE.
The key to Ag's room? Yeah.
QUINN.
Good. Give it here.
BESSIE.
What's in this trunk you want?
QUINN.
An onyx brooch.
It was my poor old mother's. I gave it Ag
When I first met her.
BESSIE.
She ain't got that now.
I seen that tin box that she kept her things in
Two days ago. That's where May got the ring
They're burying Ag in. That was all there was,
That and some old papers—

QUINN.
                    I'd like to see those too.
BESSIE.
Why?
QUINN.
    Why! To make sure that there are no receipts there
To fall into wrong hands.
BESSIE.
                    You go ask Maisie.
I got no right to give no key to you.
Those things are hers now.
QUINN.
                    Lord! I can't do that.
She'd go ask Matt; and then I'd never get them!
BESSIE.
I thought you wanted that thing that was your mother's.
QUINN.
I do. That onyx ring.
BESSIE.
                    You said a brooch.
There's something in that box that'll cause trouble.
I'm going to take and give the key to Matt.
QUINN.
I wouldn't do that, child, if I were you.
Remember what you told them in the bar,
You wanted to be alone in here awhile,
You had a customer? Shall I call the cop,
What's this his name is, Boylan's on this beat,
And have you up on lewd solicitation?
Would you like a three months' course in sewing mailbags
In the Women's Prison? Bessie, smarten up.
Hand me the key.
        (BESSIE *rummages in her bag, then throws the key and the change from
        the drinks on the table. She rises, and walks towards the bar door.*)
                    Where do you think you're going?
BESSIE.
Ain't you finished with me yet?
QUINN.
                    Sit down, my dear.
You'll not leave here till the box is in my hands.
You'd be up the street and at Matt's ear in no time
Like a wasp at a pear. Sit down when I tell you to.
        (BESSIE *sits down.* QUINN *opens the door to the Ladies' Entrance. Sound
        of* RUNNING FEET. QUINN *closes the door, returns to the table, and
        sits down. He pushes the change from the drinks back to* BESSIE.)
Would you like another drink while we're waiting, Bessie?—
BESSIE.
I wouldn't drink with you if I had the jimjams
And every crack in the wall had a rat's snout in it.

QUINN.
I know how my morality must offend
A fine upstanding woman like yourself—
> (BESSIE *throws her whiskey in* QUINN's *face, looks terrified, then bursts into tears. With great coolness,* QUINN *pulls a large silk handkerchief out of his pocket, and blots his face and clothing.*)

You always were a great one for the crying.
BESSIE.
I guess I done some bum things in my life
But this is the first time that I ever ratted.
QUINN.
Ratted, my dear? I don't know what you mean.
I told you all I wanted was old receipts.
> (*Sound of* RUNNING. BILL *runs through the Ladies' Entrance and hands* QUINN *a tin box.* QUINN *motions* BILL *back out to keep watch. Exit* BILL. QUINN *puts the box on the floor and kicks it. It opens. He puts the box on the table.*)

I gave that box to Ag myself. The lock
Was always window dressing. For how could I know
When there might be something here I'd like to see.
Will you look at this? A bundle of scorched letters:
Matt Stanton, Esq., Care of the Gen PO,
Newark, New Jersey. That's where Mattie went
When he slipped Ag's tether in Seagate. And look, the necktie
That Josie made for Matt, and a dried camellia,
And a pair of busted garnet rosaries.
And this, dear God in Heaven, look at this,
A letter with no salutation on it
In poor Ag's pothook script. It has no date.
"You're dead to me, because I'm dead myself.
I have been since you left me. If you think
I mean to cause you trouble for what you've done,
You never knew me. You've made your dirty bed.
Lie in it now till you feel the filth in your bones.
I—" No more. No more!—Ag always was too proud.
She never sent it.
BESSIE.
              Put them things all back.
They don't belong to you.
QUINN.
              Wait now. Wait now.
There's a trick to this false bottom. There it goes.
If it's not the kind of receipt I knew would be here!
It's charred. She meant to burn it. But you can read it.
BESSIE.
Give me them things.
QUINN.
           I only want this, Bessie.
(QUINN *puts the paper in his pocket.*)
I'm through now. We can part. Don't worry, child.

I'm putting these things in the box, and Bill will return it
And lock the trunk and room behind him. But mark me.
You're not to say a thing of this to Stanton.
He's a worse suspicious nature than your own;
And we've got to come, you know, to a meeting of minds
At the Clambake on my birthday Sunday, Bessie,
Stanton and I. It would only throw him off
If he heard I had been going through Ag's things.
We wouldn't want that, Bessie; would we, child,
Any more than you'd want that stretch in jail.
I hope you take my meaning—I must leave you, Bessie.
    (QUINN *rises with the box under his arm, and moves towards the Ladies' Entrance.*)
    BESSIE.
I hope you rot in Hell!
    QUINN.
               You must love me, child,
That you should want my company forever.
    (*Exit* QUINN. *Sound of a HACK rolling off.* BESSIE *grabs the money off the table and crumples it up in her hands. She looks at the door and at the money. She puts the money in her bag and bursts out crying.*)

CURTAIN

ACT TWO

SCENE 3

Twilight, the evening of Sunday, May 1, 1890. The stern of a Coney Island steamer bound for Seagate. The lower deck is overhung with an upper, upon which people pass from time to time. There are two oval portraits, one of STANTON, *the other of* QUINN, *suspended from the railings of the upper deck, above entrances to Stage Right and Stage Left. Between them, there is a large shield printed in bold Pontiac reading* For the Public Good. *The shield and portraits are hung over swagged bunting. On the lower deck, to Stage Right, there is a table with a cluster of carpet-seated folding chairs around it. Set off a little from them, its back to the table, there is a carpet-seated armchair.*
    HAGGERTY, BOYLE, *and* ANN MULCAHY *are seated at the table.* HAGGERTY *is wearing a green-and-gold sash with* The Matthew Stanton Association *printed on it. Enter* MARIA HAGGERTY *with a large, loaded tea tray, which she sets on the table. She pours and passes the tea.*

    MARIA.
One hour more, and we'll be into Seagate.
That's what the deckhand says. I'm glad of that.

Two hours more of sailing, I declare to God,
And the babies all would be drunk in their carriages.
    HAGGERTY.
Where's missis, May? Will I bring her tea to her?
    MARIA.
No. Let her sleep. She's dozed off in Matt's stateroom.
The brandy must have killed the queasiness.
    ANN.
Wasn't that a grand speech Ned Quinn made
Before Matt came, on the pier at Fulton Street,
When he said he was glad he'd arranged the Clambake late,
So that he could begin his voyage into the evening,
His loyal supporters at his side to the end.
    BOYLE.
I'm coming. I'm coming.
And my belly's full of gin.
I hear their drunken voices calling
Old Ned Quinn.
    HAGGERTY.
Don't dance on Quinn's grave, Petey. It's unlucky.
We're not through this night yet.
    MARIA.
                        True for you there, Jack!
They've yet to make the bad blood up between them.
Father Coyne's been in Quinn's stateroom this past hour,
And Palsy's been at Matt in the Saloon Bar.
Quinn wants Mattie to come to *him*; and Matt
Won't move an inch towards him till Quinn begs his pardon
For spitting in his face at Aggie's wake.
    HAGGERTY.
Woman, shut up. No call to worry that much.
If you knew politics as well as I do,
You'd see they'll both bow down to a higher law
Before this night is out.
    BOYLE.
            St. Albany,
Pray for us.
    HAGGERTY.
               Stop your blaspheming, Petey.
I don't mean Albany, but the public good—
    (*Enter* BESSIE LEGG, *Stage Right, in a rush.*)
    BESSIE.
Oh, Petey. Petey. Come to the front of the boat.
You can see the electra light from Coney there,
And that hotel they built like a elephant.
Why don't youse all come. God, it's beautiful.
    (*Exit* BOYLE *and* BESSIE, *the* HAGGERTYS *and* ANN, *Stage Right.*)
    BOYLE.
I asked me mother for fifty cents,
To see the elephant jump the fence.

He jumped so high, he touched the sky,
And never come down till the Fourt' of July.

The Fourt' of July when he crashed to earth
He landed near my fat Aunt Gert.
She says you lumpy pig-eyed skunk
Stay off that sauce if you get that drunk.
>(*Sound of their LAUGHTER fading. Enter* QUINN *and* BILL, *with* FATHER COYNE *following, Stage Left.*)

FATHER COYNE.
You'll meet with him here then?
QUINN.
Yes, Father, I will.
I'll meet with him anywhere. But he'll come to me.
FATHER COYNE.
I'll go and get him.
>(*Exit* FATHER COYNE, *Stage Left.* QUINN *stands back and looks at the shield and posters.*)

QUINN.
Look at that now, Billy.
Brooklyn, how are you! For the public good!
A whore for a mayor and a spoiled nun for his lady!
We mustn't let that happen, must we now?—
Play lose me, Billy. Here's the lot of them.
>(*Exit* BILL, *Stage Right. Enter* FATHER COYNE, *followed by* MURPHY *and* STANTON. STANTON *walks forward, keeping his eyes straight ahead.* QUINN *rakes all three of them with his eyes, then averts his gaze from* STANTON. QUINN, *to* MURPHY.)

If it isn't the Lord Beaconsfield of Brooklyn
With the ten thumbs of his fine Italian hands
Done up in ice-cream gloves.
>(*He turns suddenly to* STANTON.)

How are you since?—

STANTON.
I'll speak no word until he begs my pardon.
I told you, Father. Has he grown so old and silly
He thinks men can do harm without amends!
FATHER COYNE.
Do you want him to get down on his knees to you!
He's lost enough already. Leave him his pride.
MURPHY.
The food in the mouth of the voters is at stake,
It's bread and lard for lunch for thousands, thousands,
If this election's lost; and it will be lost
Unless you join your hands and pull together.
QUINN.
For all that's passed between us, I'll shake his hand,
If he will mine.
MURPHY.
Come on now, Matt. Come on.

QUINN.
When he gets as old as I am, he'll understand
It was death I spat at that night at the wake,
And wish he'd come to terms with an old man's rage.
> *(Pause.* STANTON *suddenly grabs* QUINN's *hand.* QUINN *gives him a clumsy bear hug, his face appearing over* STANTON's *shoulder.)*

STANTON.
Go on now, Ned. You're not that old. You've years.
There's years of use in you.
QUINN.
              Matt boy.
MURPHY.
They say that when a man shakes hands with his foe,
A suffering soul shoots out of Purgatory
Straight into Heaven, like a lark from a cage.

FATHER COYNE.
What Council was it, Palsy, declared that dogma?
QUINN.
Sister Mary Asafoetida Doyle,
His fourth-grade teacher.
MURPHY.
             To the Saloon Bar!
Drinks for all comers, and on the Party too!
> (MURPHY *and* FATHER COYNE *move towards the exit, Stage Left, with* QUINN *and* STANTON *a few paces behind them.)*

QUINN.
You know, Matt, if you left the landing to me,
I could drive it home to all what terms we're on,
And make the kind of an occasion of it
Your missis would remember all her life.
With both the bands of our Associations
Thundering and ringing out below us
And all the voters stamping and applauding,
I'd like to take your wife and you by the hand
And bring you down. A little taste of glory
Has never done a creature any harm—

STANTON.
That's just the thing, maybe, might pick her up.
The water made her qualmish and she lay down—
You've never met Kathleen to talk to, have you?
Come down with me now, and I will introduce you.
> *(Exit* FATHER COYNE *and* MURPHY, QUINN *and* STANTON, *Stage Left. Pause. Enter* KATHLEEN *slowly, Stage Right. She is dressed in a black traveling suit and is wearing a large black hat. She stands looking at the wake of the steamer a moment, moves the armchair into the shadows, and sits in it, her back to the soft bustle of* VOICES *coming towards her. Pause. Enter the* HAGGERTYS, ANN MULCAHY, BOYLE, *and* BESSIE. *They do not notice* KATHLEEN. MARIA *is carrying yet another large pot of tea, and herding* HAGGERTY *before her.)*

HAGGERTY.
You'll have my kidneys burst with all that tea.
MARIA.
Never mind. You've a night of drink before you.
Keep moving, bullhead.
HAGGERTY.
                    Have a little respect.
BESSIE.
Didn't I tell youse it was beautiful!
ANN.
Going back to Seagate's a bit sad
With poor Ag in the ground just yesterday.
BESSIE.
Yeah. Ain't it. Yeah. I wish it was Coney instead.
The shoot-the-chutes—
BOYLE.
                    The tunnel of love.
BESSIE.
                              Oh, Petey.
ANN.
Will you ever forget the Clambake Aggie gave us
Three years ago, on that lovely stretch of beach!
We'd pails of clams and oysters, steamed and fresh,
And pounds of butter in round wooden tubs,
And crabs and lobsters bigger than our heads,
Chickens and potatoes, roasted corn—
BOYLE.
And wagonloads of beer.
HAGGERTY.
                    And good beer too.
ANN.
And all day long the men with accordeens
Went weaving in and out us on the sand
Till the stars were thick and near us in the sky.
MARIA.
And Aggie, God have mercy on her soul,
Got skittish when they freshened up the fires,
And danced a jig on three kegs roped together,
With all them little bells she used to sew
Into the hems of her dresses ringing thin
Like birds at dawn. (*Pause.*)
HAGGERTY.
                    She nearly broke her arse.
MARIA.
John Haggerty!
HAGGERTY.
            She did! Don't look at me so stark.
One keghead gave, and she went on her ear.
She showed us everything she had that time,
The clocks of her stockings to her knicker buttons,

Acres and acres of somersaulting drawers.
Amn't I right, Pete boy?
BOYLE.
                    You're right as rain.
BESSIE.
You was too young to notice.
   (BOYLE *pulls the lower eyelid of his left eye down with his left forefinger.*)
BOYLE.
                    Do you see green?—
That was the night Matt found Ag playing tigress
To Tiger Quinn.
MARIA.
                    You shut your mouth, Pete Boyle.
BOYLE.
He said she broke her ass!
HAGGERTY.
                    That wasn't gossip.
It was a simple statement of pure fact,
To use the lawyer's parlance.
MARIA.
                    The lawyer's parlance!
Drink your tea, you omadhaun.* You're drunk.
Shut up and drink your tea.
HAGGERTY.
                    "Ah, man! Proud man!
Dressed in a little brief authority"†—
   (MARIA *gives him what she'd call "one look."*)
I'm drinking it fast as I can! My mouth's destroyed!
BESSIE.
You should see Pete jigging. He's the best there is.
He learned me how.
BOYLE.
                    Get up and we'll show them, kid.
HAGGERTY.
They'll show us, will they! Stand up to me there, woman,
And show them how we won the branch and bottle
On the pounded clay of every Kerry crossroads.
   (MARIA *and* HAGGERTY *begin the jig with* BOYLE *and* BESSIE *doing a little shuffle all their own.* ANN *remains seated, helpless with shamefaced laughter.* KATHLEEN *rises and, standing half in the shadows, watches them with a shy smile. They are too engrossed to notice her.*)
BOYLE.
He gave it to Maisie;
It near drove her crazy,
The leg of the duck!
The leg of the duck!

---

* *omadhaun*: an Irish word meaning a fool or simpleton.—Eds.
† "Ah, man! Proud man! Dressed in a little brief authority." The quotation is from Shakespeare's *Measure for Measure*, II, ii, 117.—Eds.

(*Enter* STANTON, *searching for* KATHLEEN. *He looks amused; but when he sees* KATHLEEN, *his face blackens.*)
I gave it to Bessie;
She says it was messy,
The leg of the duck!
The leg of the duck!
    STANTON.
What kind of song is that in front of my wife?
    HAGGERTY.
We didn't see her, Matt.
    STANTON.
                   Are you blind or what!
You, you narrow-back plug, with your mouth of slime,
You can slather this one all that you've a mind to,
But there are others born with a little shame!—
I'd be amazed at you two, May and Jack,
If I'd not noticed the liberties you've been taking
These past few months. There'll be an end to that.
    HAGGERTY.
All right. All right. There'll be an end to that . . .
Come, May and Ann, we'd best go inside now.
    BOYLE.
Wait; we'll come too. I'll lug these things for you.
    (*All* FOUR *move towards the exit to Stage Right.*)
    KATHLEEN.
Maria, dear, come back in a few minutes.
I need you. Please. I'm not myself at all.
    MARIA.
Yes, ma'am. Yes, ma'am.
    (*Exit* BOYLE *and* BESSIE, HAGGERTY *and* MARIA.)
    KATHLEEN.
      Beg their pardon, Mattie.
They didn't see me; and what harm if they did,
They were only dancing.
    STANTON.
                Things have changed now, Kate.
You have to demand respect, or you won't get it.
From this day on, they're to learn their place and keep it.
We're with them, but not of them.—Kate, I've won!
Quinn and I made it up and he wants to meet you.
    KATHLEEN.
If that's what winning means, God help us both.
    STANTON.
What's the matter with you?
    KATHLEEN.
                    It's being aboard a ship,
It's that, I suppose. When I watch the wake of the boat
Spread out like a pigeon's tail with the wind going through it,
I think of all that's left behind or canceled,
And the heart of me feels pillaged in my breast.

The farther away I go from what is past,
The more I stiffen with the sense of danger.
I look around me at all, and want to hold it:
May dancing there with her back straight as a bowstring
Despite the tug of age on all her bones,
And the dazzle of Jack's eyes as they browsed her face,
And Ann Mulcahy helpless with pure joy,
And that dusty weed of a boy and Bessie Legg,
Playing their little games like aging children.
There's not a thing that is not riches, Mattie,
And it all goes from us, darling, like those days
On the boat from England, glazed with salt and sunshine,
We melted first into light like flame and candle,
It all goes from us. Hold me, Mattie, hold me.
Don't thrust me from you as you just did them.
    STANTON.
Katie, I'd sooner hack the hands from my wrists
Than thrust you from me. As for what's been lost,
God in Heaven be with the days I lay
Like a bee in a lily with the ocean's glitter
Live gold on the stateroom panels. They were good.
But what's ahead, you'll not believe till you see it.
We've won! We've won, Kate! Quinn's arranged our landing:
You'll be breathing music like the saints in Heaven
As you walk ashore. But let him tell it you.
    (STANTON *kisses her.*)
What is that? Brandy, that I smell on you?
    KATHLEEN.
I took a glass or two for the seasickness.
    STANTON.
Promise me on your dead parents' grave,
You'll drink no more from this time forward, Kate.
There's no sight worse on earth than a drunken woman.
I know it to my shame, from her that's dead. (*Pause.*)
    KATHLEEN.
... I promise, Mattie.
    (STANTON *kisses her hand.*)
    STANTON.
               There now. I'll get the mayor.
    (*Exit* STANTON, *Stage Left.* BESSIE *emerges from the shadows, Stage Right, and hurries over to* KATHLEEN.)
    BESSIE.
You mind if I sit down? Remember me?
    KATHLEEN.
Of course, I do, Miss Legg. Please do sit down.
I'm pleased to see you.
    BESSIE.
            It isn't Miss. It's Mrs.
    KATHLEEN.
Yes. Mrs. Legg. Of course.

BESSIE.
                        Was he that mad
Just for that dirty song that Petey sung,
Or was it something that Quinn said to him
That he took out on us? You know what I mean.
    KATHLEEN.
No, I don't, Miss Legg. I don't know what you mean.
    BESSIE.
Not Miss. It's Mrs.
    KATHLEEN.
                    What would the mayor say?
Matt's just gone in to get him. They're friends now.
    BESSIE.
They're friends now. Yeah. They're friends.
    KATHLEEN.
                                What is it, please?
    BESSIE.
Oh, he hurted my feelings, see, the way he talked,
And I got nervous. I'm a nervous girl.
That, and you know, what you said up my flat that night,
About there was some mix-up in the marriage.
It sounded so romantic when you said it,
"The man I left my God and country to marry."
I couldn't make it out. You was awful . . . you know.
    KATHLEEN.
If I said that, I was awful drunk indeed.
You didn't believe me, did you, Mrs. Legg?
    BESSIE.
Oh, no. Oh, no. But I don't know where you was
Before I went and took you up my flat.
I thought that maybe Quinn got wind of it—
    KATHLEEN.
I hope you've not repeated what I said.
You haven't, have you?
        (BESSIE *rises*.)
    BESSIE.
                    Excuse me. I'll be going.
    KATHLEEN.
Now don't be that way.
    BESSIE.
                    What do you think I am,
Some kind of rat . . . I thought you was a sport.
You're like the rest . . . Oh, I seen you looking round
When I brought you back up my flat that night.
It's not my fault the place is such a mess.
I only rent it, see? It isn't mine.
And we only just got in when you passed out—
I mean, fell off to sleep . . . I didn't like
To make no noise . . . It's hard to keep things nice.
There was a time I had things beautiful.

When Legg was living with me, Legg, you know,
My husband . . . I passed the flat we used to have
On Baltic Street and Court the other day.
We lived in it two years. I kept it spotless . . .
The windows all were dirty when I passed,
The windows of the flat we used to have,
I mean. All dirty . . . It nearly broke my heart.
I had a lovely home. I used to have . . .
Canary bird. Piano. Everything—
It's not my fault Legg left. Where he is, Christ knows.
Maybe he's dead. I hope to God he is,
May God forgive me, but I hope he is!
(BESSIE *burst into tears.* KATHLEEN *rises and comforts her. Enter* BOYLE, *Stage Right.*)
KATHLEEN.
Oh, Bessie, Bessie, God in Heaven help us.
BOYLE.
Who turned on the hydrants?
BESSIE.
                        Hello, Petey.
Buy me a drink or something, will you, ha?
BOYLE.
Sure, kid, sure.
(BOYLE *walks to the exit, Stage Right.* KATHLEEN *and* BESSIE *look at one another.*)
KATHLEEN.
           Goodbye.
BOYLE.
                You coming, Little Eva?
(*Exit* BOYLE. BESSIE *walks to the exit, then turns to* KATHLEEN *again.*)
BESSIE.
Don't worry, missis. Don't. There ain't no call.
There ain't no one can hurt you. You're a lady.
(*Exit* BESSIE. KATHLEEN *walks to the rail and looks at the wake of the steamer. Sound of a SHIP'S BELL. Enter* MARIA *with a water glass of brandy.*)
DECKHAND.
Seagate. Seagate. In ten minutes. Seagate.
MARIA.
I brought you this.
KATHLEEN.
             I won't. I promised Matt—
MARIA.
House devil and street saint, sure, he's worse than Quinn!
He's down there now with Quinn playing king of England.
He traipses up to me in the Saloon Bar
And takes my hand and thrusts ten dollars in it.
He's not dead yet! There'll come a time he'll see
There are some things in the world you can't take back.
If I could get a job, we'd move. We would—

(KATHLEEN *presses her fist to her mouth and sinks into the armchair.*)
Good Jesus, Mrs. Stanton, what's the matter!
Promise or no, best have a drop of this.
    (KATHLEEN *downs half the glass of brandy.*)
    KATHLEEN.
Promise or no.
    MARIA.
               You'll feel the good of that.
    (*Pause. Sound of SHIP'S BELL and of the PADDLE churning water for the turn inshore.*)
    KATHLEEN.
Do you know what I am thinking about, Maria?
How it is this time of year back home in Ireland.
The foxglove has come out in the boreens,
And the seals are barking on the mossy rocks
Below Mount Brandon. On this very day,
They'll dress the loveliest girl in all the village
In a wedding gown, and lead her to the church
To put a crown of roses on the Virgin.
And all the children in Communion clothes,
White suits and dresses, smilax wreaths, pearl prayer books,
Will stand around her as she climbs the ladder,
And sing that song that always makes me cry:
Daughter of a mighty Father,
Maiden, patron of the May,
Angel forms around thee gather,
Macula non est in te.
Macula non est in te: Never spot was found in thee.
    (KATHLEEN *breaks into tears.*)
    MARIA.
Oh, Mrs. Stanton.
    KATHLEEN.
               What's the matter with me?
My ears are ringing like a field of weeds,
Noontime in August, when the sun's raw fire.
    MARIA.
I wonder is it flashes.
    KATHLEEN.
               At my age!
    MARIA.
More likely kicks. Are you all together, missis.
    KATHLEEN.
Am I what, Maria?
    MARIA.
               Have you missed your term?
Don't bite your lip and blush. You're not a nun.
    KATHLEEN.
No, I've not missed my term.
    (*Enter* QUINN, *Stage Left. He stands looking over at* MARIA *and* KATHLEEN, *unnoticed by them at first.*)

MARIA.
       Then it's the dead.
KATHLEEN.
The dead?
 MARIA.
    The dead. Who do you know needs prayers?
They say that's how the dead call on the living,
By whining in their blood.
 KATHLEEN.
       Poor Agnes Hogan,
The Lord have mercy on her and preserve her . . .
  (KATHLEEN *notices* QUINN.)
Don't look so troubled, May. I'm better now.
You know there's a bottle of that Worth perfume
Down in the stateroom in my reticule.
Would you bring it to me, dear, with a handkerchief.
  (*Exit* MARIA, *Stage Right.* QUINN *walks over to* KATHLEEN.)
 QUINN.
Good evening to you, Mrs. Stanton. May I?
 KATHLEEN.
Please do, Your Honor.
  (QUINN *sits down.*)
 QUINN.
      Matt's stuck in the bar,
Buying drinks for all the upright voters,
So I came up alone. It would fill your eye
To see him there. You'd think he trusted them!
 KATHLEEN.
God forbid he shouldn't trust them, Mayor.
 QUINN.
If you think, my dear, not trusting people's a sin,
You'd best get out of politics.
 KATHLEEN.
        It's the worst sin.
Without trust, there's no faith or hope or love.
 QUINN.
That kind of talk is like a penny cream puff,
All wind and whey, and deadly when it sours.
Trust no one. No one. Let no man too close.
They are as quick to fury as to love.
Once give them purchase, they will pull you down,
And for a sigh let slip, for a ruptured smile.
They're a pack of wicked mutts that go for shadows.
There is no reason in their ugliness,
No justice in their rage. Trust no one, missis.
 KATHLEEN.
Who are "they"? Is it my husband, Mayor,
Or old John Haggerty or Mister Murphy?
From what you say, you think the people devils
Who've honored you as mayor of this city

For thirty years. Do you really think them that?
    QUINN.
I do . . . And Stanton is the worst of all!—
    KATHLEEN.
Do you think I'll sit and listen to your slander!
    QUINN.
"Do you think this? Do you think this?" Or "Don't you?"
"Faith and hope and love," and I mustn't slander—
You're awful pious for a woman living
With your husband in a state of Mortal Sin;
And a Mortal Sin it is for a Catholic woman
To marry a man outside the Catholic Church.
I don't know much religion, but I know that,
As, I might add, do all our holy voters. (*Pause.*)
    KATHLEEN.
I suppose you must have got that from Miss Legg.
    QUINN.
No, my dear. From England. Where you did it.
I've known it years. I hoped I'd not have to use it,
But need is need. And it's not Miss. It's Mrs.
    KATHLEEN.
You rejoice when people go wrong, don't you, Mayor!
    QUINN.
We've no time now to talk morality.
We'll wait for Stanton, then go get Father Coyne
And the rest, and walk down to my stateroom
And arrange what we will say. I've bought off those accountants,
Paid back that little sum from the funds I borrowed,
And the books are doctored. All that now remains is
To find a way to break the joyous news
That I will run again. I think Matt should do it!
    KATHLEEN.
If you're a man who'd ruin two reputations
To gain your ends, what have you done with your life?
    QUINN.
What I have done with my life is my affair!
Do you think I'll let that bastard have my office?
I loved the woman that he took from me,
And I let her go with him, but I kept my office.
And I heard them here in Seagate making sport
Of all I'd done for them, but I kept mum,
And I kept my office. And I watched the poor bitch die
While he grew high and mighty, but I kept my office.
Keep my office I will to the day I die,
And God help those who try to take it.
    KATHLEEN.   Make sense.
The scandal about the funds is a public fact;
But you and Mrs. Legg are the only ones
Who know about the marriage. Spare my husband.

Spare him, Mayor. God will bless you for it.
>QUINN.

Sure, that's what Aggie said when she pleaded for him,
The first time that she met him, the poor slob,
Did God bless her, missis?

>KATHLEEN.
>>They'll never let you run!

They'll gang up with the Party of Reform
And crucify you.

>QUINN.
>>We'll see about that, missis.

Do you think I'll let them turn their backs on me
And turn their backs on me for the likes of him,
A narrow-back pimp, who rose to where he is
On the broken heart of the woman that I loved!

>KATHLEEN.

Pour all the venom you want into my ears!
The Party will stand by us! They'll stand by us.
They'll cover us on the marriage. And they should!
For though we were not married in the Church,
May God forgive us, we are man and wife! (*Pause.*)

>QUINN.

I wouldn't be too sure of that now, missis.

>KATHLEEN.

What do you mean by that, you lying devil?
>>(QUINN *pulls a scorched paper out of his pocket, and throws it into* KATHLEEN's *lap.*)

>QUINN.

I'm a lying devil, am I! Look at that!
Look at it, why don't you. Are you blind!
How can you be his wife when he married Ag
In the Sacred Heart in Newark in '86!
>>(*Repeated sound of SHIP'S BELL. People are gathering, preparing to get off. Sound of winches, lowering gangplank.* KATHLEEN *sits as if shot, the paper in her hands.*)

>DECKHAND.

Seagate! Seagate! Everybody off.

>KATHLEEN.

All gone. All gone.
>>(KATHLEEN *rises suddenly, the paper in her hand, swaying with shock, as if drunk. The disembarking passengers look curiously at her.*)
>>God damn the day I met him.

God damn this mouth that spoke him fair, these eyes
That flooded my blood with his face. God damn this flesh
That kindled in his arms, and this heart that told me,
Say yes, say yes, to everything he asked.
It would have been better had I not been born.
>>(QUINN *grabs the paper out of* KATHLEEN's *hand and puts it back into his pocket fast.*)

QUINN.
For God's sake, missis. Don't take on this way.
We have to keep this quiet. There's people watching.
>   (QUINN *runs to the table and fetches the half-finished glass of brandy.*
>   KATHLEEN, *still swaying, her arms at her side, automatically accepts the glass from him and, as if by reflex, presses it to her breast. She does not see the people who are staring at her. Enter* STANTON *with* MURPHY *and* FATHER COYNE, *a group of voters around him.*)

STANTON.
It isn't in the courts reform must work
But in each striving heart . . .
>   (STANTON *sees the people staring at* KATHLEEN *and* QUINN. *He breaks away from those around him and hurries over to her. He speaks in a steely whisper.*)

Look at you. Look at you, for the love of Jesus.
In front of all these people. You're owl-eyed drunk,
With the bands about to fife us off the boat!
I'll get Maria to help you sober up.
Quinn and I will walk ashore together.
You are not fit for decent men to be seen with!
>   (KATHLEEN *smashes the glass to the floor. She speaks in a ringing voice.*)

KATHLEEN.
Did you think that—
Did you think that when you lied to me in London,
And I let you marry me in the City Hall,
Because you said you couldn't wait for the banns,
You wanted me so much! Did you think that
When you had me in the bed in sacrilege
Above the corpse of your true-wedded wife,
Ag Hogan!
>   (*Hostile reaction from the* CROWD. *The sound of the* BANDS *suddenly blares out.*)

CURTAIN

ACT TWO

SCENE 4

> *Very late the same night. The double set. There is a dim light in the hall by the Haggertys' door; and the light in Stanton's flat is on full. There are two trunks in the parlor, one already locked, the other open.* KATHLEEN *moves in and out of the bedroom, packing. Enter* FATHER COYNE *and* MURPHY, *the* HAGGERTYS, BOYLE, *and* BESSIE. *The* HAGGERTYS *and* BOYLE *are laden down with baskets and pillows done up in steamer blankets, and have the tired, apprehensive look of new immigrants.* HAGGERTY *sets down his basket and unlocks the door.*

MARIA.
Open it, can't you! He may be right behind us.
And I'll not stand in the one hall with him!—
We'll be out of here before the week is done,
If I have to beg to do it—
            FATHER COYNE.
                        Now, Maria—
MARIA.
Now Maria, Father? Are we saints!
If he got on his knees to me, I'd not forgive him!
            MURPHY.
It's grand of you to let us wait here for him.
You must be tired.
            (HAGGERTY *opens the door.*)
            MARIA.
                        I'll not close an eye
Until I'm out from underneath this roof!
            HAGGERTY.
Come in the parlor, Father. I'll light the fire.
You're famished with the cold. May, bring the whiskey.
Come in now, Pete. Come in all.
            (MARIA, FATHER COYNE, MURPHY, BOYLE, *and* BESSIE *pass through the portiere, followed by* HAGGERTY. *Pause.* KATHLEEN *moves in and out of the parlor, packing. Enter* STANTON. *He runs lightly up the stairs and into the parlor. He looks at the trunks and falls into a chair. Enter* KATHLEEN, *with some clothes. She sees him, averts her gaze, and puts the clothes into the trunk.*)
            STANTON.
Where do you think you're going!
            (KATHLEEN *passes back into the bedroom for more clothes and returns with them.*)
                        Answer me!
            KATHLEEN.
I'm going home.
            STANTON.
                        Your home is here with me.
            KATHLEEN.
You haven't even the grace to beg my pardon!
How can you look me in the face again!
            STANTON.
It's I should ask that question. It's all over.
They gave the nomination back to Quinn.
He brought me to the pitch of hope and betrayed me.
And you stood by and let him do it to me!
            KATHLEEN.
It ill becomes you, man, to talk betrayals.
Can you tell me whom you've known you've not betrayed!—
You killed Ag Hogan. But you won't kill me!
            STANTON.
I had the right to leave her. She played me false—

KATHLEEN.
Had you the right to marry me? The right
To cut me off from all that I hold holy?
　　　STANTON.
Would "all that you hold holy," our precious Church,
Have granted me a divorce from Agnes Hogan,
An adulteress!—
　　　KATHLEEN.
　　　　　　　　What kind of man are you!
That woman died without the Sacraments
Because in her last fever she was afraid
If she confessed her sins she might betray you.
She died cut off from God to spare you harm.
And you have the worst word in your mouth for her.
Do you know why? Because you're no good, man.
You waited for your chance to throw her over.
You saw that with her you'd be nothing. Nothing.
You had to be the mayor of this city
And she was in the way. You married me
To make yourself respectable again.
That's the only reason.

　　　STANTON.
　　　　　　　　I loved . . . I loved you, Kate.
Kathleen, I've nothing left.
I need you.
　　　KATHLEEN.
　　　　　　　Yes. To patch your kick-down fences.
But I have my pride too!—
　　　STANTON.
　　　　　　　　　　Go then, God damn you!
Do you think I'll kneel on the floor and beg your help!
I never begged for help from man or God,
And I won't now. You'll not drive me to my knees!
　　　KATHLEEN.
To sit and tell me you have nothing left!
No more do I! You've taken it out of me
By demanding more than anyone can give.
That's what evil is,
The starvation of a heart with nothing in it
To make the world around it nothing too.
You never begged from man or God! You took!
You've taken all your life without return!
You never gave yourself to a single soul
For all your noble talk.—Even in bed
You stole me blind!—
　　　STANTON.
　　　　　　　　Get out of here! Get out!
You're not a woman. You're a would-be nun!
You were from the beginning.

KATHLEEN.
                    God help you, Matt.
    (KATHLEEN *closes and locks the second trunk, and puts on her hat.*)
I'll book my passage quickly as I can.
There's nothing in those trunks your money bought me.
Leave May the key. The Express will call for them.
I put the jewelry in the velvet box
In the top drawer of the bureau by the window;
And left the dresses and the sable coat
Hanging in your wardrobe. And that perfume
You bought me's on the vanity.
    (KATHLEEN *walks out the door to the head of the stairs.*)
                    Don't look so black.
You're free now, Matt. That's what you always wanted.
Marry if you like.
    (KATHLEEN *almost breaks down.*)
                I'm not your wife. I never was.
    STANTON.
You mean to leave me here alone!
    KATHLEEN.
                                I'm sorry, man;
But that's the way we all are, but for God.
    (STANTON *rushes out the door and grabs* KATHLEEN.)
    STANTON.
You'll not leave me! I'll see to that!
    (*BLACKOUT.* KATHLEEN *screams and hits the bottom of the stairs.* MARIA *rushes into the kitchen with a kerosene lamp in her hand, followed by* HAGGERTY, FATHER COYNE, MURPHY, BOYLE, *and* BESSIE. BOYLE *is carrying a glass of whiskey.* HAGGERTY *flings open the door, revealing* KATHLEEN *at the foot of the stairs in a heap, and* STANTON *halfway down the flight in a near faint.*)
    HAGGERTY.
Good Jesus, May! How did it happen, man?
Give me your whiskey, Pete. Poor Mrs. Stanton.
    KATHLEEN.
Ah, Jack. And May. And is that the Father there?
Amn't I a shame and a disgrace
To get so legless drunk I fall downstairs
Like an unwatched child—
    STANTON.
                Oh, Katie. Katie, Katie.
Are you hurt bad.
    KATHLEEN.
            Sh!
    HAGGERTY.
                Petey, go get Boylan on the beat,
And tell him to get a doctor that's still up,
There's been an accident—
    KATHLEEN.
                That's right. That's right.

I caught my heel on the baluster and fell.
>BOYLE.
I seen a man fall off a hoist through a hold
On Pier Sixteen down in the Erie Basin.
His head was bent that way. Her neck is broke—
>HAGGERTY.
Don't stand there nattering. Go get the doctor.
>(*Exit* BOYLE, *running.*)
>MURPHY.
I'd best go too. I've a thing to do, I must.
>(STANTON *takes* KATHLEEN *from* HAGGERTY *and cradles her in his arms.*)
>STANTON.
Will you get away from her so I can hold her!
>HAGGERTY.
Be careful with her—
>STANTON.
>>Katie, you were right.
I've taken without returning all my life.
And I'd the face to call Ned Quinn corrupt!
The harm I've done and called it good! The harm!
I saw that harm in Aggie Hogan's face,
And now I see it in yours. Can you forgive me?
>KATHLEEN.
Hush now, Matt darling. Toc-sha-shin-inish:
Let others talk. We'll keep our own safe counsel.
There's been shame enough already without more—
Do you know what stopped my breath up on the landing?
I love you still. I thought of us on the boat from England.
There's few have been as happy as we were—
Is that the Father there? I want the Father.
>(*Enter* BOYLE *with the* POLICEMAN, BOYLAN, *and a* DOCTOR.)
>FATHER COYNE.
Here I am, child. Here I am right beside you.
>(FATHER COYNE *leans over* KATHLEEN, *putting on his stole as he does so.*)
>KATHLEEN.
Oh . . . my God . . . I am . . . heartily sorry
For . . . having . . . offended Thee—
>(STANTON *pulls* KATHLEEN *away from the priest in a tight embrace.*)
>STANTON.
You're not to die!
>KATHLEEN.
>>The boat from England, Mattie . . .
>(STANTON *kisses her on the mouth, and hugs her to him, his hand on the back of her head.*)
>STANTON.
Yes, we'll have that again. I'll make it up to you.
I'll make it up. We'll go back home to Ireland.
I'll give The Court Café to Jack to run,

And we'll go home, and take a high-stooped house
In one of them good squares, I mean, those squares . . .
>   (STANTON *loosens his embrace to look in* KATHLEEN's *face. Her head falls to the side.*)

Why don't you answer me? Don't turn away!—
Where in the name of Jesus Christ's the doctor?
>   (*The* DOCTOR *kneels and puts his ear to* KATHLEEN's *chest. He rises with a negative shudder of his head to* HAGGERTY. FATHER COYNE *motions* BOYLAN *and the* DOCTOR *out with his head. Exit* BOTH. *Pause.*)

HAGGERTY.
She's dead, you know, Matt boy.

STANTON.
>   You're lying, man!
Do you think I have no feeling in my flesh!
She's warm as a newborn child. We're going home—
>   (STANTON *loosesns his embrace again.* KATHLEEN's *hair comes down.*)

I've sprung her hairpins on her—God in heaven,
I was making love to nothing. She is dead.

FATHER COYNE.
Get up please, son; let me finish giving her
Conditional absolution—
>   (STANTON *tightens his embrace on* KATHLEEN *again and glares at the priest like a cornered animal.*)

STANTON.
>   Absolve *her*, Father!
Absolve your God, why don't you, He did this!
When she found out the marriage was no good,
She packed her trunks upstairs. She meant to leave me.
She never died in drink! She never fell!
I flung her down the stairs to keep her here.
I thought she'd sprain her ankle—Don't come near me.
I'll spit in your face if you come near me, Father—

FATHER COYNE.
Go easy, son. Go easy.

HAGGERTY.
>   Get up now, Matt.

FATHER COYNE.
Yes, Matt. You have to follow Boylan to the precinct.
When there's a question of murder, it's the law.
>   (STANTON *relinquishes* KATHLEEN *to* FATHER COYNE, *and rises.* STANTON *turns his back on his dead wife and the priest as if in mortal offense.*)

STANTON.
Maria, lay my wife out on the bed
With some degree of decency, and spill
That bottle of the Worth perfume she loved
Over that bedspread that she was so proud of,
And sit with her until the coroner comes . . .
I will not have her stink, or lie alone—

(*With great difficulty*, STANTON *brings himself to turn and look at his wife and the priest.*)

With all her sins on my head, and the world a desert.

(STANTON *throws his arms out in a begging embrace and falls on his knees. Enter* MURPHY *and* QUINN, *unnoticed by* STANTON.)

Maisie, Jack. And Petey. Bessie, Father,
Help me, for the love of Jesus, help me.
Dear God in Heaven, help me and forgive me.

(*The* HAGGERTYS *rush to him and grasp his hands.* HAGGERTY *raises him, and relinquishes him to* FATHER COYNE.)

MURPHY.
God have mercy on her. Our election's lost.

(STANTON *wheels around. His eyes meet with* QUINN's.)

QUINN.
I never meant to do this to you, Matt.
I didn't know. I never meant to do it.
I only meant to look out for my good.
I'm nobody. I'm no one, if I'm not the mayor.
I'm nothing, Matt. I'm nobody. I'm nothing—

(STANTON *rakes* QUINN's *face with a blind man's stare. Exit* STANTON.)

FATHER COYNE.
Why are you standing round like imbeciles!
Carry her up the stairs, and lay her out
As Mattie asked you to.

(HAGGERTY *and* BOYLE *lift* KATHLEEN, *and start up the stairs with her.* MARIA *follows, her mouth in the crook of her elbow, shaking with tears.* QUINN *and* MURPHY, BESSIE *and* FATHER COYNE *look on from below.*)

Well you may cry!
Cry for us all while you're at it. Cry for us all!

CURTAIN

Topics for Further Study

1. One critic has said of *Hogan's Goat* that it is "a turbulent, melodramatic tale of cynicism, corruption, and pride, the by-products of political lusting in Brooklyn in the 1890s." Point out instances of cynicism, corruption, and pride in the play and show how each incident is the result of political ambition.

2. In his *Poetics* the Greek philosopher Aristotle wrote that tragedy purified its beholders by purging their emotions through pity and terror, a conception that is referred to as his theory of *catharsis*.
Hogan's Goat is a tragedy. By referring to incidents, show how the play might arouse pity and terror. Discuss whether you think the Aristotelian theory of catharsis applies to it.

3. Aristotle also wrote that incidents which arouse pity and fear have the greatest effect on the mind when they occur unexpectedly and at the same time causally, that is, when they are unanticipated yet follow in the logical sequence of things. Select a major incident in *Hogan's Goat* and show how it occurred both by accident and design.

4. In every great tragedy the protagonist or main character has a fatal flaw, a defect which eventually brings about his downfall. By referring to the final scene and to other portions of the play, show how Matthew Stanton's tragic flaw is that he never really loved anyone but himself.

5. "Father Coyne is the voice of reason and love." Cite passages that justify this statement.

6. Every character is sharply etched. Compare or contrast the following:
        Bessie Legg and Ann Mulcahy
        Matthew Stanton and Edward Quinn
        Kathleen Stanton and Josephine Finn

7. Why did Matthew Stanton keep his marriage with Agnes Hogan secret?

8. Read aloud several striking lines of poetry, particularly lines with unusual images or turns of phrase. For example:

> . . . Josie Finn would be scissoring down Fifth Place
> With the wind in tatters around her.

> The pride steams off you like the stink of cancer.

> And he's like a scalded cat since yesterday
> When he got news that Agnes Hogan died.

> Numb as a broomstick in my varnished parlor.

What is the effect of such lines upon the realism and emotional impact of the drama? Would this play be more effective if written in prose? Justify your answer.

9. What traits often considered characteristic of the Irish are shown by the characters in the play? Refer to specific episodes and lines.

The Scandinavians in the United States

The first Scandinavians to come to America were Swedes who founded a colony in the Delaware River Valley in 1638. In 1655 the Dutch took over the colony, but the Swedish farmers were permitted to keep their land. Scandinavians from Denmark and Norway came in small numbers until the mid-nineteenth century. But by the time of the Civil War in America, the pressure of population upon the limited agricultural resources of the Scandinavian countries had reached an acute stage. In Denmark if a man had enough land to support a horse and two or three cows he was considered independent and prosperous; a tenant farmer in Sweden or Norway earning fifty or a hundred dollars a year was considered fortunate indeed. It seemed that the time was ripe for another Viking migration—this time not to devastate the coastal cities of England or to grab the fair land of Normandy, but to inhabit by legal means and with hard work the great prairies of virgin soil beyond the Mississippi River.

As Scandinavians came and settled in central United States—mostly in Wisconsin and Minnesota—they wrote to their families back home, describing the favorable agricultural conditions. With the end of the Civil War, there ensued such an enormous exodus that the Scandinavian governments were frightened. Within a single generation Norway lost a larger percentage of her population to America than any other Old World country except Ireland. One-third of Denmark's Icelandic population crossed the Atlantic. Before half a century had passed, Scandinavians in the United States equaled one-quarter of the combined populations of Denmark, Norway, and Sweden.

The Scandinavians were eminently qualified to settle in the upper Mississippi country and to establish prosperous communities there. They were skilled in agricultural pursuits and in forestry, since the vast majority of immigrants were from the hard-stricken agricultural areas in their native lands. Since they had been accustomed from birth to the harsh winters in the northern climates, they were not affected by the inclemencies of their new country. An industrious, God-fearing, and family-conscious people, they worked very hard to wrest a living from the soil, to make their farms prosper, and to give their children the educational advantages which they had not been given in their homeland. They founded their own institutions of higher learning such as St. Olaf College in Minnesota and Augustana College in Illinois, which placed strong emphasis on

Scandinavian studies long before ethnic studies became fashionable. They published newspapers, magazines, and books in their native languages. They wanted their children to learn English and to attend the public schools, but they also tried to make provisions for them to learn the language of their forefathers and prepared special grammars and workbooks for that purpose. They even had plays in the original languages and for a time there was a flourishing Scandinavian theater in the United States. At festival time native costumes were brought out of the cedar chests, the Old World dances were performed, and the old songs sung. The younger generation was not permitted to forget so easily their rich Scandinavian heritage.

Before the building of railroads, the Scandinavian pioneers advanced with cart and horse or even on foot to Western Minnesota, to the Dakotas, and upward into the Red River Valley. By 1870 there were more than 2,000 farmers in the valley. Then, as more and more of their kinsmen arrived, they spread out in all directions, taking advantage of every opportunity to develop the resources at hand. Though the vast majority tilled the soil, farming was not their only occupation. As lumberjacks, they cut and hewed timber for houses and barns. They worked on flat boats carrying hay and grain to market. They established tiny trading posts here and there in the forests and on the plains.

Many books, both fiction and nonfiction, have attempted to describe some of the hardships of the Scandinavian pioneers. Among those outstanding are Johan Bojer's *The Emigrants* (1928), dealing with Norwegian pioneers struggling in the Dakota wilderness; Ole Rolvaag's *Giants in the Earth* (1927), also concerned with the hardships of Norwegians in a South Dakota settlement; Willa Cather's *O Pioneers!* (1913), about the struggles of Swedish and Bohemian settlers to make a good living in Nebraska in the 1880s, and her *Song of the Lark* (1915), the story of the daughter of a Swedish minister who escapes from the small town environment in Colorado and becomes a famous opera star. Another striking picture is afforded in Sophus Keith Winter's *Take All to Nebraska* (1936), about a Danish family trying to make a living in Nebraska in the early 1900s amidst hardships imposed by the land, the hostile elements, unscrupulous landlords, and moneylenders as well.

As the children of the pioneers grew up, they did not all remain on the ancestral farm. Many studied in institutions of higher learning and went on to join the ranks of doctors, lawyers, legislators, teachers, and scientists. Charles Lindbergh, Sr., for example, was a newspaper editor and congressman, while his more distinguished son, Charles Lindbergh, Jr., became a world famous pilot. Ole Rolvaag was a professor of Norwegian literature and a great novelist at St. Olaf College in Minnesota, while his son served as governor of Minnesota. Today the sons and the grandsons of the pioneers who settled in the Great Plains in the 1880s have themselves sired sons and daughters who have distinguished themselves in countless vocations.

I Remember Mama represents a Norwegian family living in San Francisco in the early 1900s. Their generation of immigrants are no longer exclusively agricultural pioneers. Mama represents the true pioneer spirit in her determination to keep her family living within their income, in her hopes for a better life for her children, in her close family relationships with her relatives, and in her own integrity and personal worth. In this respect she does not differ from millions of other immigrant mothers who came here with little more than a hope and a prayer and who lived to see that hope realized.

Suggested Reading

Books about the Scandinavians

Blegen, Theodore. *Norwegian Migration to America.* Northfield, Minnesota: Norwegian-American Historical Association, 1931–1940. 2 vols.
Janson, Ebrance. *The Background of Swedish Immigration 1840–1930.* Chicago: University of Chicago Press, 1931.
Stephenson, George N. *The Religious Aspects of Swedish Immigration.* Minneapolis: University of Minnesota Press, 1932.

Fiction about the Scandinavians

Because there are so few plays about Scandinavians in America in English, the following list of a few outstanding novels is appended for further reading.
Bjorn, Thyra Ferre. *Papa's Wife.* New York: Holt, Rinehart and Winston, 1955.
Cather, Willa. *O Pioneers!* Boston: Houghton Mifflin, 1913.
Kaup, Elizabeth D. *Not for the Meek.* New York: Macmillan, 1941.
Rolvaag, Ole. *Giants in the Earth.* New York: Harpers, 1927.
Schlytter, Leslie Evan. *The Tall Brothers.* New York: D. Appleton-Century, 1941.

I Remember Mama

John van Druten's *I Remember Mama* is based on a series of seventeen sketches by Kathryn Forbes (the pen-name of Mrs. Kathryn Anderson McLean), published in 1943 as *Mama's Bank Account*. The sketches, based on the experiences of the author's maternal grandmother, an immigrant Norwegian, won wide recognition for the humor, warmth, and deep sympathy with which they sought to recreate the struggles, heartaches, and triumphs of Mama's closely knit family in San Francisco in 1910. Each episode deals with Mama's heroic efforts to keep her family together in the face of illness, prejudice, strikes, and hard life in general. In that paragon of virtue and devotion readers saw a mother or grandmother with similar qualities whom they had known and similarly loved and respected. It may also have been the horrible nightmare of 1943, when the United States entered World War II, that led so many people to respond to and appreciate the escapades of Mama and her family.

John van Druten, already a successful playwright with several hits to his credit, adapted the sketches for the stage, and his play, now entitled *I Remember Mama*, was one of the hits of the 1944–1945 Broadway season. Burns Mantle included it in his annual collection of the year's ten best plays. Directed by the playwright himself, it was produced by Rodgers and Hammerstein, whose *Oklahoma* was then making stage history. Audiences were particularly pleased with the unusual and boldly imaginative staging, which made use of such techniques and mechanical devices as narrative asides, traveler curtains, and revolving stages, allowing instantaneous scene changes.

Many of those who had read the original sketches were delighted with the skill and artistry with which John van Druten turned them into a play, judiciously omitting what was nonessential and highlighting the more dramatic episodes. The result was so successful that in 1948 it was made into a movie starring Irene Dunne and Barbara Bel Geddes, which is still occasionally shown on television today. A television series also called *I Remember Mama* ran from 1949 to 1957.

The keynotes of this saga of a San Francisco Norwegian family in 1910 are simplicity, sincerity, struggle, and eventual success. What makes *I Remember Mama* truly stand out is the warmth, tenderness, and fortitude of its principal characters. The love and respect that Mama and Papa had for one another were models for their children. Theirs was the story of millions of other immigrants who came to America with little more than the clothes on their backs. but with faith that could move mountains. Striving for an education was characteristic of these immigrants; and there was no limit to the sacrifices that both parents and children made to achieve their educational goals, although their plans were often disrupted or abandoned completely in the face of perpetual hardship and financial crisis. It was an era when hard work was expected from all, when luxuries were few and far between, and when the book was respected as a source of entertainment, wisdom, and consolation. Today's student, brought up on television, radio, and movies, might do well to reflect on the simple satisfactions derived from Mr. Hyde's nightly reading to the family of *A Tale of Two Cities*. In an era of rampant crime, drug addiction, and dissatisfaction with institutions, *I Remember Mama* brings us back to a more halcyon era and a more livable one.

JOHN VAN DRUTEN was born in London in 1901 and trained for the law at University College, London. He taught law and legal history for a time at the University College in Wales, but his true love was the theater, and his work soon showed great promise both in England and in the United States. In addition to *I Remember Mama*, he is remembered for such comedies as *Bell, Book and Candle* (1949) and *The Voice of the Turtle* (1943). His first great hit was the serious play *Young Woodley* (1925), which, though denied a licence in London, was produced in America with considerable success. Many of his plays were filmed and were as successful on the screen as on the stage. Among his more notable successes are: *There's Always Juliet* (1931), *The Distaff Side* (1932), *Old Acquaintance* (1940), *The Mermaids Singing* (1945), *The Druid Circle* (1947), *Bell, Book and Candle* (1950), and *I Am a Camera* (1951), based on a series of short stories by Christopher Isherwood, which eventually were transformed twenty years later into the musical *Cabaret* and later into the highly acclaimed film of the same name.

Van Druten's *Playwright at Work* (1953) is most illuminating for those who wish to know some of the trials and tribulations of first writing and then directing a play successfully. Seldom has a dramatist opened the inner workings of his mind and heart so completely to his readers. The charm and wit which characterized so many of his plays are revealed in page after page. His autobiography, *The Way to the Present* (1938), also makes fascinating reading. On December 19, 1957, after devoting more than three decades to the theater, John van Druten died.

I Remember Mama

BY

JOHN van DRUTEN

CHARACTERS

KATRIN	DR. JOHNSON
MAMA	ARNE
PAPA	A NURSE
DAGMAR	ANOTHER NURSE
CHRISTINE	SODA CLERK
MR. HYDE	MADELINE
NELS	DOROTHY SCHILLER
AUNT TRINA	FLORENCE DANA MOOREHEAD
AUNT SIGRID	BELL-BOY
AUNT JENNY	SCRUBWOMAN
UNCLE CHRIS	NURSES
A WOMAN	DOCTORS
MR. THORKELSON	HOTEL GUESTS

I Remember Mama, copyright 1944, 1945, 1952 by John van Druten; renewed 1972, 1973 by Carter Lodge, executor of the estate of John van Druten. Reprinted by permission of Harcourt, Brace, Jovanovich, Inc.

CAUTION: Professionals and amateurs are hereby warned that *I Remember Mama*, being fully protected by copyright, is subject to royalty. All rights, including professional, amateur, motion picture, radio broadcasting, television, recitation, public reading, and rights of translation into foreign languages, are strictly reserved. All inquiries should be addressed to the author's agents, International Famous Agency, 1301 Avenue of the Americas, New York, New York 10019, except that in the case of amateur rights, inquiries should be addressed to the Dramatists Play Service, Inc., 440 Park Avenue South, New York, New York 10016.

I Remember Mama

ACT ONE

The period of the play is around 1910.
On either side of the stage, down front, are two small turntables, left and right, on which the shorter front scenes are played against very simplified backgrounds. As each scene finishes the lights dim and the table revolves out, leaving an unobstructed view of the main stage. The main stage is raised by two steps, above which traveler curtains open and close.
When the curtain rises, KATRIN, *in a spotlight, is seated at a desk on the right turntable, facing the audience. She is writing and smoking a cigarette.* KATRIN *is somewhere in her early twenties. She should be played by an actress who is small in stature, and capable of looking sufficiently a child not to break the illusion in subsequent scenes. She is a blonde. Her hair, when we see her first, is in a modern "up" style, capable of being easily loosened to fall to shoulder length for the childhood scenes. She wears a very short dress, the skirt of which is concealed for the prologue by the desk behind which she is seated.*
KATRIN *writes in silence for a few moments, then puts down her pen, takes up her manuscript, and begins to read aloud what she has written.*

KATRIN. (*Reading.*) "For as long as I could remember, the house on Steiner Street had been home. Papa and Mama had both been born in Norway, but they came to San Francisco because Mama's sisters were here. All of us were born here. Nels, the oldest and the only boy—my sister Christine—and the littlest sister, Dagmar." (*She puts down her manuscript and looks out front.*) It's funny, but when I look back, I always see Nels and Christine and myself looking almost as we do today. I guess that's because the people you see all the time stay the same age in your head. Dagmar's different. She was always the baby—so I see her as a baby. Even Mama —it's funny, but I always see Mama as around forty. She couldn't always have been forty. (*She puts out her cigarette, picks up her manuscript and starts to read again.*) "Besides us, there was our boarder, Mr. Hyde. Mr. Hyde was an Englishman who had once been an actor, and Mama was very impressed by his flowery talk and courtly manners. He used to read aloud to us in the evenings. But first and foremost, I remember Mama." (*The light dims down, leaving* KATRIN *only faintly visible. Lights come up on the main stage, revealing the house on Steiner Street—a kitchen room. It has a black flat, with a dresser, holding china. On either side of the dresser is a door, one to the pantry, one to the rest of the house. The left wall is a short one. It is the wall of the house, and contains a door upstage leading into the street, being presumably the back door of the house, but the one most commonly used as the entry-door. Beyond it the street is visible, with a single lamp-post at left, just outside the house. Behind the room rises the house itself with upper windows lighted, and behind it a painted backdrop of the San Francisco hills, houses, and telegraph posts. The furniture of the kitchen is simple. A central table, with two chairs above it, armchairs at either end, and a low bench below it. Against the right wall, a large stove, below it another armchair. The window is below the door in the left wall and has a low Norwegian chest under it.* KATRIN'S VOICE *continuing in the half-dark, as the scene is revealed.*) "I remember that every Saturday night Mama would sit down by the kitchen table and count out the money Papa had brought home in the little envelope."

(*By now the tableau is revealed in full, and the light on* KATRIN *dwindles further. The picture is as she described.* MAMA—*looking around forty—is in the armchair right of the table, emptying the envelope of its silver dollars and smaller coins.* PAPA—*looking a little older than* MAMA—*stands above her. His English throughout is better than hers, with less accent.*)

MAMA. You call the children, Lars. Is good they should know about money.

(PAPA *goes to door back and calls.*)

PAPA. Children! Nels—Christine—Katrin!

CHILDREN'S VOICES. (*Off, answering.*) Coming, Papa!

MAMA. You call loud for Katrin. She is in her study, maybe.

PAPA. She is where?

MAMA. Katrin make the old attic under the roof into a study.

PAPA. (*Amused.*) So? (*Shouting.*) Katrin! Katrin!

KATRIN. (*Still at her desk, down front.*) Yes, Papa, I heard.

PAPA. (*Returning to the room.*) A study now, huh? What does Katrin study?

MAMA. I think Katrin wants to be author.

PAPA. Author?

MAMA. Stories she will write. For the magazines. And books, too, maybe, one day.

PAPA. (*Taking out his pipe.*) Is good pay to be author?

MAMA. I don't know. For magazines, I think maybe yes. For books, I think no.

PAPA. Then she becomes writer for magazines.

MAMA. Maybe. But I like she writes books. Like the ones Mr. Hyde reads us. (DAGMAR *enters from the pantry. She is a plump child of about eight and carries an alley cat in her arms.*) Dagmar, you bring that cat in again?

DAGMAR. Sure, she's my Elizabeth—my beautiful Elizabeth! (*She crosses to the chest under the window, and sits, nursing the cat.*)

PAPA. Poor Elizabeth looks as if she had been in fight again.

DAGMAR. Not poor Elizabeth. *Brave* Elizabeth. Elizabeth's a Viking cat. She fights for her honor!

PAPA. (*Exchanging an amused glance with* MAMA.) And just what is a cat's honor, little one?

DAGMAR. The honor of being the bravest cat in San Francisco. (CHRISTINE *comes in. She, like* KATRIN, *should be played by a small young actress, but not a child. Her hair is to her shoulders—her dress short—her age indeterminate. Actually, she is about 13 at this time. She is the cool, aloof, matter-of-fact one of the family. She carries a box of crayons, scissors and a picture book.*) Aren't you, Elizabeth?

CHRISTINE. (*Sitting above the table and starting to color the picture-book with the crayons.*) That disgusting cat!

DAGMAR. She's not disgusting. She's beautiful. Beautiful as the dawn!

CHRISTINE. And when have *you* ever seen the dawn?

DAGMAR. I haven't seen it, but Mr. Hyde read to us about it. (MR. HYDE *comes in from back door. He is a slightly seedy, long-haired man in his fifties. Rather of the old-fashioned English "laddie" actor type. He wears a very shabby long overcoat, with a deplorable fur collar, and carries his hat. His accent is English.*) Didn't you, Mr. Hyde? Didn't you read to us about the dawn?

MR. HYDE. I did, my child of joy. The dawn, the rosy-finger-tipped Aurora . . .

DAGMAR. When can I get to *see* the dawn, Mama?

MAMA. Any morning you get up early.

DAGMAR. Is there a dawn every morning?

MAMA. Sure.

DAGMAR. (*Incredulous.*) It's all that beautiful, and it happens every *morning?* Why didn't anyone *tell* me?

MR. HYDE. My child, that is what the poets are for. To tell you of *all* the beautiful things that are happening every day, and that no one sees until they tell them. (*He starts for the door.*)

MAMA. You go out, Mr. Hyde?

MR. HYDE. For a few moments only, dear Madam. To buy myself a modicum of that tawny weed, tobacco, that I lust after, as Ben Jonson says. I shall be back in time for our nightly reading. (*He goes out and disappears down the street.*)

MAMA. (*Who has gone to the back door, calls with a good deal of sharpness and firmness.*) Nels! Katrin! You do not hear Papa call you?

NELS. (*From off, upstairs.*) Coming, Mama!

KATRIN. (*At her desk.*) Yes, Mama. I'm coming. (*She rises. In her few moments in the dark, she has loosened her hair to her shoulders, and we see that her skirt is short as she walks from her desk, and up the steps into the set. As soon as she has left it, the turntable revolves out. Immediately after her.* NELS *comes in. He is a tall, strapping young fellow—old enough to look 18 or 19, or 15 or 16, according to his dress, or demeanour. Now, he is about 15.* KATRIN, *to* CHRISTINE.) Move over. (*She shares* CHRISTINE'S *chair at the table with her.*)

PAPA. So now all are here.

MAMA. Come, then. (CHRISTINE, NELS *and* KATRIN *gather around the table.* DAGMAR *remains crooning to* ELIZABETH, *but rises and stands behind* PAPA. *Sorting coins.*) First, for the landlord. (*She makes a pile of silver dollars. It gets pushed down the table from one member of the family to the next, each speaking as he passes it.* PAPA *comes last.*)

NELS. (*Passing it on.*) For the landlord.

KATRIN. (*Doing likewise.*) For the landlord.

CHRISTINE. (*Passing it to* PAPA.) The landlord.

PAPA. For the landlord. (*He dumps the pile at his end of the table, writing on a piece of paper, which he wraps around the pile.*)

MAMA. (*Who has been sorting.*) For the grocer.

(*The business is repeated. During this repeat,* DAGMAR'S *crooning to the cat becomes audible, contrapuntally to the repetitions of "For the grocer."*)

DAGMAR. (*In a crescendo.*) In all the United States no cat was as brave as Elizabeth. (*Fortissimo.*) In all the *world* no cat was as brave as Elizabeth!

MAMA. (*Gently.*) Hush, Dagmar. Quietly. You put Elizabeth back into the pantry.

DAGMAR. (*In a loud stage whisper, as she crosses to pantry.*) In Heaven or HELL no cat was as brave as Elizabeth! (*She goes out with the cat.*)

MAMA. For Katrin's shoes to be half-soled. (*She passes a half dollar.*)

NELS. Katrin's shoes.

KATRIN. (*Proudly.*) *My* shoes!

CHRISTINE. (*Contemptuously.*) Katrin's old shoes.

PAPA. Katrin's shoes.

CHRISTINE. (*Rising and coming to* MAMA.) Mama, Teacher says this week I'll need a new notebook.

MAMA. How much it will be?

CHRISTINE. A dime.

MAMA. (*Giving her a dime.*) For the notebook. You don't lose it.

CHRISTINE. I won't lose it. (*She wraps it in her handkerchief.*)

MAMA. You take care when you blow your nose.

CHRISTINE. I'll take care. (*She returns to her seat.*)

PAPA. Is all, Mama?

MAMA. Is all for this week. Is good. We do not have to go to the Bank. (*She starts to gather up the few remaining coins.* KATRIN *leaves the group, comes and sits on steps, front.*)

NELS. (*Rising.*) Mama.... (*She looks up, catching an urgency in his tone.* PAPA *suspends smoking for a moment.*) Mama, I'll be graduating from grammar school next month. Could I ... could I go on to High, do you think?

MAMA. (*Pleased.*) You want to go to High School?

NELS. I'd like to... if you think I could.

MAMA. Is good.

(PAPA *nods approvingly.*)

NELS. (*Awkwardly.*) It... it'll cost a little money. I've got it all written down. (*Producing a piece of paper from his pocket.*) Carfare, clothes, notebooks, things I'll really need. I figured it out with Cy Nichols. He went to High last year.

(PAPA *rises and comes behind* MAMA *to look at the paper* NELS *puts before them.*)

MAMA. Get the *Little* Bank, Christine.

(CHRISTINE *gets a small box from the dresser.*)

KATRIN. (*From the steps—herself again, in the present—looking out front.*) The Little Bank! That was the most important thing in the whole house. It was a box we used to keep for emergencies—like the time when Dagmar had croup and Papa had to go and get medicine to put in the steam kettle. I can *smell* that medicine now! The things that came out of the Little Bank! Mama was always going to buy herself a warm coat out of it, when there was enough, only there never was.

(*Meanwhile,* MAMA *has been counting the contents.*)

NELS. (*Anxiously.*) Is there enough, Mama?

MAMA. (*Shaking her head.*) Is not much in the Little Bank right now. We give to the dentist, you remember? And for your roller-skates?

NELS. (*His face falling.*) I know. And there's your warm coat you've been saving for.

MAMA. The coat I can get another time. But even so... (*She shakes her head.*)

CHRISTINE. You mean Nels can't go to High?

MAMA. Is not enough here. We do not want to have to go to the Bank, do we?

NELS. No, Mama, no. I'll work in Dillon's grocery after school.

(MAMA *writes a figure on the paper and starts to count on her fingers,* PAPA *looks over, and does the sum in his head.*)

PAPA. Is not enough.

MAMA. (*Finishing on her fingers against her collarbone.*) No, is not enough.

PAPA. (*Taking his pipe out of his mouth and looking at it a long time.*) I give up tobacco.

(MAMA *looks at him, almost speaks, then just touches his sleeve, writes another figure and starts on her fingers again.*)

CHRISTINE. I'll mind the Maxwell children Friday nights. Katrin can help me.

(MAMA *writes another figure.* PAPA *looks over—calculates again, nods with satisfaction.*)

MAMA. (*Triumphantly.*) Is good! Is enough!

NELS. Gee! (*He moves beside* PAPA *and starts to play with a wire puzzle.*)

MAMA. We do not have to go to the Bank.

(DAGMAR *returns, without the cat.*)

DAGMAR. (*Hearing the last line.*) Where is the Bank?

CHRISTINE. (*Leaving the table, cutting out the picture which she colored.*) Downtown.

DAGMAR. What's it look like?

CHRISTINE. Just a building.

DAGMAR. (*Sitting on the bench, below the table.*) Like a prison?

CHRISTINE. (*Sharply.*) No, nothing like a prison.

DAGMAR. Well, then, why does Mama always say "We don't want to go to the Bank"?

CHRISTINE. Because... well, because no one ever wants to go to the Bank.

DAGMAR. Why not?

CHRISTINE. Because if we went to the Bank all the time, there'd be no money left there. And then if we couldn't pay our rent, they'd turn us out like Mrs. Jensen down the street.

DAGMAR. You mean, it's like saving some of your candy for tomorrow?

MAMA. (*Busy with coffee and cups at the stove and the dresser.*) Yes, my Dagmar. Is exactly like saving your candy.

DAGMAR. But if... if all the other people go to the Bank, then there won't be any money left for us, either.

NELS. (*Kindly.*) It isn't like that, Dagmar. Everyone can only get so much.

DAGMAR. How much?

NELS. However much you've got there... put away. You see, it's *our* money that we put there, to keep safe.

DAGMAR. When did we put it there?

NELS. I... I don't know when. A long time back, I guess. Wasn't it, Mama?

MAMA. Is enough about the Bank.

DAGMAR. How much money have we got in the Bank?

NELS. I don't know. How much, Mama?

MAMA. Enough. (*During the last speeches* AUNT TRINA *appears from the wings. She is a timid, mouselike little woman of about 40, with some prettiness about her. She wears her hat and coat, and a pathetic feather boa. She comes up the street and knocks on the house door.* MAMA, *hearing the knock.*) Was the door?

CHRISTINE. (*Quickly moving.*) If it's the aunts, I'm going to my boodwar.

KATRIN. (*Rising, entering the scene.*) And I'm going to my study.

MAMA. (*Stopping them.*) You cannot run away. We must be polite to the aunts. (*She opens the door.*) Why, is Trina!

PAPA. Trina, and all by herself!

MAMA. Say good evening to Aunt Trina, children.

CHILDREN. (*Together.*) Good evening, Aunt Trina.

TRINA. Good evening, children. How well they all look. (*She comes above the table.*)

MAMA. You have a feather boa. Is new. (*Inspecting it.*) Beautiful.

TRINA. (*Simpering a little.*) It was a present.

MAMA. (*Smiling.*) A present! Look, Lars. Trina has a present.

PAPA. (*Feeling it.*) Is fine. (*He puts* TRINA's *hat, coat and boa on the chest under the window.*)

MAMA. Jenny and Sigrid don't come with you, Trina?

TRINA. (*Embarrassed.*) No, I... I didn't tell them I was coming. I want to talk to you, Marta.

MAMA. (*Smiling.*) So? Sit then, and we talk. (*She puts her in* PAPA's *chair at the left of the table.*)

TRINA. (*Nervously agitated.*) Could we talk alone?

MAMA. Alone?

TRINA. If you wouldn't mind.

MAMA. Children, you leave us alone a little. I call you. Dagmar, you go with Katrin.

KATRIN. (*Protesting.*) Oh, but, Mama...

MAMA. (*Firmly.*) Katrin, you take Dagmar!

KATRIN. Yes, Mama. (*Pushing* DAGMAR, *resentfully.*) Come on.

(*The* CHILDREN *go out back.*)

MAMA. Now—what is it, Trina?

TRINA. (*Looking down, embarrassed.*) Marta...

MAMA. (*Helpfully.*) Yes?

TRINA. Oh, no, I can't say it.

MAMA. (*Anxiously.*) Trina, what is it?

TRINA. It's... something very personal.

MAMA. You want Lars should go outside?

TRINA. Would you mind, Lars? Just for a minute?

PAPA. (*Good-humoredly.*) No, I go. I know what women's secrets are. (*Teasing.*) As your Uncle Chris say— "Vomen! Pff!"

MAMA. You have your pipe, Lars? Is fine night. (PAPA *takes out his pipe—then lays it down.*) What is it?

PAPA. I forget. I give up tobacco.

MAMA. Is still some tobacco in your pouch? (PAPA *nods.*) Then you do not give up tobacco till you have finish. You give up *more* tobacco—not the tobacco you already have.

PAPA. Is not right, Marta. (*He pats her, takes his pipe, and goes out, standing outside the house, under the lamp-post, and looking up at the stars, smoking.*)

MAMA. So, Trina. Now. What is it?

TRINA. Marta... I want to get married.

MAMA. You mean... you want to get married, or there is someone you want to marry?

TRINA. There's someone I want to marry.

MAMA. Does *he* want to marry *you*?

TRINA. (*Sitting on bench.*) He says he does.

MAMA. (*Delighted.*) Trina! Is wonderful! (*She sits beside her.*)

TRINA. (*Crying a little.*) *I* think it is.

MAMA. Who is?

TRINA. Mr. Thorkelson.

MAMA. From the Funeral Parlor? (TRINA *nods.* MAMA *nods, speculatively, but with less enthusiasm.*)

TRINA. I know he isn't very handsome or . . . or tall. I know it isn't what most people would think a very nice profession, but . . .

MAMA. You love him, Trina. (TRINA *nods ecstatically.*) Then is good. (*She pats* TRINA's *hand.*)

TRINA. Marta, will you . . . will you help me tell the others?

MAMA. Oh . . . Jenny and Sigrid . . . they do not know?

TRINA. No. I was afraid they'd laugh at me. But if *you* tell them . . .

MAMA. Jenny will not like you tell me first.

TRINA. (*Desperately.*) I can't help that. You've got to tell them not to laugh at me. If they laugh at me, I'll . . . I'll kill myself.

MAMA. (*With decision.*) Jenny and Sigrid will not laugh. I promise you, Trina.

TRINA. Oh, thank you, Marta. And . . . Uncle Chris?

MAMA. (*With some seriousness.*) Ah!

TRINA. Will you talk to him?

MAMA. It is Mr. Thorkelson who must talk to Uncle Chris. Always it is the husband who must talk to the head of the family.

TRINA. Yes. I know, but . . . well, Uncle Chris is so very frightening. He's so big and black, and he shouts so. And Mr. Thorkelson is (*Gesturing a very small man.*) . . . well, kind of timid, really.

MAMA. (*Gently.*) But Trina, if he is to be your husband, he must learn not to be timid. You do not want husband should be timid. *You* are timid. It not good when *both* are timid. (*Then firmly.*) No! Jenny and Sigrid I speak to, but Mr. Thorkelson must go to Uncle Chris.

PAPA. (*Re-enters the house.*) Marta, Trina, I do not want to interrupt your talk, but Jenny and Sigrid are coming.

TRINA. (*Alarmed.*) Oh, dear! (*She rises, quickly.*)

PAPA. I see them get off the cable-car. They came up the hill.

TRINA. (*In a flurry.*) I'd better go to your room for a minute. (*She starts for the door, turns back, gets her things from the chest, and runs out, carrying them. Meanwhile,* MAMA *has been whispering the news to* PAPA.)

MAMA. The coffee is ready—I get more cups.

(*During the above,* AUNTS JENNY *and* SIGRID *have entered.* JENNY *is a domineering woman in her fifties,* SIGRID, *whining and complaining.*)

SIGRID. (*In the street.*) Wait, Jenny, I must get my breath. This hill kills me every time I climb it.

JENNY. You climbed bigger hills than that in the old country.

SIGRID. I was a *girl* in the old country.

(*They march to the door and knock* —SIGRID *following* JENNY.)

MAMA. (*Opening the door to them.*) Jenny. Sigrid. Is surprise. (*To* SIGRID.) Where's Ole?

SIGRID. Working. He's always working. I never see anything of him at all.

MAMA. (*Crossing to the stove for coffee-pot.*) Is good to work.

SIGRID. It's good to see your husband once in a while, too. (*Sits near table.*)

JENNY. (*No nonsense about her.*) Has Trina been here?

MAMA. Trina?

JENNY. She's gone somewhere. And she doesn't know anyone but *you.* . . .

MAMA. That is what *you* think.

JENNY. What do you mean by that?

MAMA. Give Lars your coat. I give you some coffee. Then we talk about Trina.

SIGRID. (*As* PAPA *helps with coats.*) She *has* been here?

MAMA. Yes, she has been here. (*Pouring coffee and passing cups.*)

JENNY. What did Trina want?
MAMA. She want to talk to me.
JENNY. What about?
MAMA. Marriage.
SIGRID. What?
MAMA. (*Pouring calmly.*) Marriage. (*Passing* SIGRID'S *cup.*) Trina wants to get married.
JENNY. (*Seated left of table.*) That's no news. Of course she wants to get married. Every old maid wants to get married. (*She rolls up her veil.*)
MAMA. There is someone who wants to marry Trina.
JENNY. Who'd want to marry Trina?
MAMA. Mr. Thorkelson.
SIGRID. Peter Thorkelson? Little Peter? (*She gestures a midget.*)
MAMA. He is not so little.
SIGRID. He's hardly bigger than my Arne—and Arne is not ten yet.
MAMA. So he is hardly bigger than your Arne. Does every husband have to be big man?
JENNY. Trina's making it up. That happens with old maids when they get to Trina's age.
MAMA. (*Firmly.*) No, Jenny—it is true. Mr. Thorkelson wants to marry Trina.
JENNY. (*Changing her tactics slightly.*) Mr. Thorkelson. She'd be the laughing stock. (*She laughs, rising and moving left.*)
MAMA. (*Moving to her.*) Jenny, Trina is here. She will come in in a minute. This is serious for her. You will not laugh at her.
JENNY. I shall do what I please.
MAMA. No, Jenny, you will not.
JENNY. And why won't I?
MAMA. Because I will not let you.
JENNY. And how will you stop me?
MAMA. If you laugh at Trina, I will tell her of the time before your wedding when your husband try to run away.
SIGRID. (*Rising, intrigued.*) What is that?
JENNY. Who told you that?
MAMA. I know.
SIGRID. (*Intrigued—stealing around and below the table.*) Erik . . . tried to run away?
JENNY. It's not true.

MAMA. Then you do not mind if I tell Trina.
JENNY. Uncle Chris told you.
SIGRID. (*Tenaciously.*) Tried to run away?
MAMA. It does not matter, Sigrid. Jenny will not laugh at Trina now. Nor will you! For if *you* laugh at her, I will tell her of your wedding night with Ole, when you cry all the time, and he send you back to Mother.
PAPA. (*With sudden enjoyment.*) This I do *not* know!
MAMA. (*Reprovingly.*) Is no need you should know. I do not tell these stories for spite—only so they do not laugh at Trina. Call her, Lars. You like more coffee, Jenny? Sigrid?
(PAPA *goes to the back door, calls,* "*Trina.*" MAMA *pours coffee for* JENNY. MR. HYDE *reappears and lets himself into the house. The* AUNTS *rise, standing in line with* MAMA.)
MR. HYDE. (*Seeing company.*) Oh, I beg your pardon. I was not aware . . .
MAMA. Mr. Hyde, these are my sisters.
MR. HYDE. Enchanted, ladies, Madame, Madame. The Three Graces. (*He bows.* SIGRID *giggles coyly. He goes to the back door.*) You will excuse me?
MAMA. Sure, Mr. Hyde.
MR. HYDE. I shall be in my room. (*He goes out.*)
JENNY. (*Moving to table again.*) So that's your famous boarder. Has he paid you his rent yet? Three months he's been here, hasn't he?
MAMA. (*At the other side of table.*) Is hard to ask. Surely he will pay soon.
JENNY. (*With a snort.*) Surely he won't! If I ran my boarding house the way you run this place . . .
PAPA. Maybe your boarders wouldn't always leave you.
JENNY. If Marta thinks she's going to get the warm coat she's always talking about out of *that* one . . .
MAMA. Jenny, Mr. Hyde is a gentleman. He reads to us aloud. Wonderful books . . . Longfellow, and Charles Dickens, and

Fenimore Kipling. (TRINA *steals back.* MAMA, *seeing her hesitant in the doorway.*) Come in, Trina. The coffee is getting cold. (*She pours a cup. There is a silence.*) I tell them.

JENNY. Why did you come to Marta first?

PAPA. (*Beside her.*) She thought Marta would understand.

JENNY. Aren't Sigrid and I married women, too?

PAPA. You have been married longer than Marta. She think maybe you forget.

JENNY. What sort of a living does Mr. Thorkelson make?

TRINA. (*On bench near table.*) I . . . I haven't asked.

SIGRID. (*At right of table.*) Can he keep you?

TRINA. I don't think he would have asked me to marry him if he couldn't.

JENNY. Maybe he thinks you are going to keep *him.*

MAMA. (*Warningly.*) Jenny!

SIGRID. Maybe he thinks Trina will have a dowry like the girls at home.

TRINA. Well, why shouldn't I? You all had dowries. . . .

JENNY. We were married in Norway. And our parents were alive. Where would your dowry come from, I'd like to know?

TRINA. Uncle Chris. He's head of the family.

JENNY. And who will ask him?

TRINA. He won't need asking. When Mr. Thorkelson goes to see him . . .

JENNY. Uncle Chris will eat him!

SIGRID. (*Giggling maliciously.*) Little Peter and Uncle Chris!

MAMA. (*With meaning.*) Maybe Uncle Chris will tell him some family stories. He knows many, does Uncle Chris.

(*The* AUNTS *put down their cups, discomfited.*)

JENNY. (*To change the subject.*) Where are the children? Aren't we going to see them before we go?

PAPA. Of course. I'll call them. (*He goes to the door and does so, shouting.*) Children! Your aunts are *leaving!*

CHILDREN'S VOICES. (*Eagerly shouting back.*) Coming, Papa!

JENNY. You come with us, Trina?

MAMA. I think maybe Trina like to stay here and listen to Mr. Hyde read to us. You like, Trina?

TRINA. Well, if I wouldn't be in the way. I asked Mr. Thorkelson to call for me here. He'll see me home. I'll help you with the coffee things. (*She takes the tray of coffee cups and goes into the pantry.*)

(KATRIN *returns from her study. She carries her diary.* DAGMAR *follows her, and behind them,* CHRISTINE.)

KATRIN *and* DAGMAR. (*Curtseying.*) Good evening, Aunt Sigrid. Good evening, Aunt Jenny.

(CHRISTINE *sketches a perfunctory curtsey without speaking.*)

JENNY. Where have *you* all been hiding yourselves?

DAGMAR. (*Going into the pantry.*) We've been in Christine's boodwar.

JENNY. Her *what?*

MAMA. Christine makes the little closet into a boudoir. I give her those bead portieres, Jenny, that you lend us when we come from the old country.

SIGRID. And what does she do there?

CHRISTINE. (*Impertinently.*) What people usually do in boudoirs.

MAMA. Christine, that is rude. It is her little place to herself.

(NELS *enters.*)

NELS. Hello, Aunt Sigrid. Hello, Aunt Jenny.

SIGRID. (*Shaking hands.*) Good evening, Nels. My, how tall he is getting!

MAMA. (*Proudly.*) Yes, is almost as tall as his Papa.

(NELS *sits on the chest under the windows.*)

SIGRID. He looks to me as if he was outgrowing his strength. Dagmar was looking pale, too. (DAGMAR *returns now, carrying the cat again.* SIGRID, *jumping.*) Goodness, what a horrid-looking cat.

DAGMAR. She's not. She's beautiful.

PAPA. Is her new friend. She goes with Dagmar everywhere.

CHRISTINE. (*Seated, above table.*) She does. First thing you know, she'll have the cat sleeping with her.

DAGMAR. (*Eagerly.*) Oh, Mama, can I? Can I, Mama? (*She comes to the bench and sits.*)

JENNY. Certainly not. Don't you know a cat draws breath from a sleeping child? You wouldn't want to wake up some morning *smothered*, would you?

DAGMAR. I wouldn't care. Elizabeth can have *all* my breath! (*She blows into the cat's face.*) There!

JENNY. (*Putting on gloves.*) Elizabeth—what a very silly name for a cat.

NELS. (*Rising.*) It's a very silly name for *that* cat. It's a Tom.

MAMA. Nels, how you know?

NELS: I looked!

DAGMAR: How can you tell?

NELS: You can.

DAGMAR. But how?

MAMA (*Quickly warning.*) Nels, you do not say how!

NELS (*To* DAGMAR.) So you'd better think up another name for him.

DAGMAR. I won't. He's Elizabeth. And he's going to *stay* Elizabeth.

PAPA. We could call him *Uncle* Elizabeth!

DAGMAR. (*Laughing delightedly.*) Uncle Elizabeth! Do you hear, Elizabeth? You're called *Uncle* Elizabeth now!

JENNY. Such foolishness! Well, good-by, all. Marta. Lars.

(*Good-bys are exchanged all around, the* CHILDREN *curtseying formally.*)

MAMA. Good-by, Jenny. Good-by, Sigrid. Nels, you go tell Mr. Hyde we are ready for the reading.

(NELS *goes off. The* AUNTS *leave and* MAMA *stands in the doorway, waving good-by.*)

SIGRID. (*As they go.*) Well, I never thought we'd live to see Trina get married.

JENNY. She's not married yet. She's got Uncle Chris to deal with first.

(*They disappear into wings.*)

MAMA. (*Returning to the room and calling into the pantry.*) Trina, they have gone. Dagmar, you put Elizabeth out for the night now.

DAGMAR. (*Correcting her.*) *Uncle* Elizabeth!

MAMA. *Uncle* Elizabeth. (DAGMAR *goes out into the pantry with the cat.* TRINA *comes in as* MR. HYDE *and* NELS *return.*) Mr. Hyde, this is my sister Trina.

MR. HYDE. (*Bowing.*) Enchanted!

MAMA. (*Seating herself at the table.*) Mr. Hyde reads to us "The Tales From Two Cities." Is beautiful story. But sad.

TRINA. (*Brightly.*) I like sad stories. (*She gets out her handkerchief.*)

(*The whole family group themselves around the table,* MAMA *near the table in her old chair—*PAPA *behind her.* TRINA *at one side behind table,* NELS *on the other side behind table.* DAGMAR *returning and seating herself on the floor in front of* MAMA. MR. HYDE *takes the armchair at left of table.* CHRISTINE *sits on the floor in front of table.* KATRIN *is on the steps.*)

MR. HYDE. Tonight, I would like to finish it.

MAMA. Is good.

MR. HYDE. Are you ready?

CHILDREN. Yes, please, Mr. Hyde.

MR. HYDE. I will go on from where we left off. (*He starts to read.*) "In the black prison of the Conciergerie, the doomed of the day awaited their fate. They were in number as the weeks of the year. Fifty-two were to roll that afternoon on the life-tide of the City to the boundless, everlasting sea. . . ."

(*The lights dim down slowly, leaving spots on* KATRIN *and* MR. HYDE *only.*)

KATRIN. I don't think I shall ever forget that night. It was almost midnight when he came to the end, and none of us had noticed.

MR. HYDE. (*Reading from the last page.*) "It is a far, far better thing that I do than I have ever done; it is a far, far better rest that I go to than I have ever known." (*He closes the book.*) "The End."

(*The turntable revolves in again.* KATRIN *rises from the step and crosses to her desk on the turntable.*)

KATRIN. I wrote in my diary that night before I went to bed. (*She reads aloud from it.*) "Tonight Mr. Hyde finished *The Tale of Two Cities*. The closing chapters are indeed superb. How beautiful a thing is self-sacrifice. I wish there were someone *I* could die for." (*She sits looking out front.*) Mr. Hyde read us all kinds of books. He thrilled us with *Treasure Island* and terrified us with "The Hound of the Baskervilles." I can still remember the horror in his voice as he read. . . .

MR. HYDE. (*Still on the main stage in his spot, reading.*) "Dr. Mortimer looked strangely at us for an instant, and his voice sank almost to a whisper as he answered: 'Mr. Holmes, they were the footprints of a gigantic *hound*!'" (*He closes the book.*) We will continue tomorrow night. If you are interested.

KATRIN. (*Looking out front.*) If we were interested! You couldn't have kept us from it. It meant a lot to Mama, too, because Nels stopped going nights to the street corner to hang about with the neighborhood boys. The night they got into trouble for breaking into Mr. Dillon's store, Nels was home with us. And sometimes Mr. Hyde read us poetry. "The Lady of the Lake" . . . and the "Rime of the Ancient Mariner."

MR. HYDE. (*Reading.*)
  "About, about, in reel and rout
  The death-fires danced at night.
  The water, like a witch's oils,
  Burnt green and blue and white."
  (*His spot goes out, and the traveler curtains close on the kitchen scene.*)

KATRIN. There were many nights I couldn't sleep for the way he had set my imagination dancing. (*Reading from her diary again.*) "What a wonderful thing is literature, transporting us to realms unknown." (*To herself.*) And all the time my schoolteacher kept telling me that I ought to write about things I knew. I did write a piece for her once about Uncle Chris, and she said it wasn't nice to write like that about a member of one's own family. Papa called Mama's Uncle Chris a black Norwegian, because of his dark hair and fierce mustache, but there were others in the family who claimed that he was black in a different way. The aunts, for example.

(*Spot goes up on turntable, representing* JENNY's *kitchen.* JENNY *and* TRINA *are discovered.* JENNY *is rolling pastry.* TRINA *is crocheting.*)

JENNY. Black! I'll say he's black. Black in his heart. Cursing and swearing. . . .

TRINA. Marta says that's only because it hurts him to walk.

JENNY. Rubbish. I know all about his limp and the accident back in the old country—but has anyone ever heard him complain? Marta's always making excuses for him.

TRINA. I know . . . but he *is* good to the children. All those oranges he's always sending them. . . .

JENNY. Oranges! What good is oranges? Turn 'em yellow. They're the only things he's ever been known to give away, anyway. He's got other uses for his money.

TRINA. What you mean?

JENNY. Bottles! And that woman he lives with!

TRINA. He *says* she's his housekeeper.

JENNY. Well, he couldn't very well come right out and call her what she is, could he? Though *I* will one of these days. And to his face, too.

(SIGRID *comes through the curtains. She crosses to* JENNY *and* TRINA.)

SIGRID. Jenny. Trina. What do you think? What do you think Uncle Chris has done now?

TRINA. What?

JENNY. Tell us.

SIGRID. You know my little Arne's knee—that fall he had two months ago? The man at the drugstore said it was only a bruise, but today it was hurting him again, so I left him home when I went to do the marketing. I asked Mrs. Schultz next door to keep an eye on him, and who should turn up, not ten minutes after I'd gone, but Uncle Chris. And what do you think?

JENNY. Well, tell us, if you're going to. Don't keep *asking* us.

SIGRID. He took one look at Arne's knee, bundled him into that rattletrap old automobile of his, and rushed him straight off to the hospital. I've just come from there... and what do you think? They've operated! They've got him in plaster of Paris!

JENNY. Without consulting you?

SIGRID. It seems the doctor is a friend of his... that's why he did it. No, this time he's gone too far. To put a child of Arne's age through all that pain. They wouldn't even let me *see* Arne. I'm going to tell Uncle Chris exactly what I think of him...

JENNY. That's right.

SIGRID. I'm going to tell him right now. (*Weakening a little.*) Come with me, Jenny.

JENNY. Well, I... No, I can't leave my baking.

SIGRID. You must, Jenny. We must stand together. You come, too, Trina, and ask about your dowry. *Make* him give it to you.

TRINA. Oh, but... Marta said Mr. Thorkelson should do that....

JENNY. Well, then, go and get Mr. Thorkelson. Go down to the mortuary and get him now. Sigrid is right. We girls have got to stand together!

(*Blackout. Turntable revolves out.*)

KATRIN. (*At her desk.*) Nobody knew where Uncle Chris lived. That was part of the mystery about him. He used to roam up and down the state buying up farms and ranches that had gone to pieces, and bullying them back into prosperity. Then he'd sell at a profit and move on again. Two or three times a year he'd descend on the city in his automobile and come roaring and stamping into our house.

(*Her light dims. The sound of a very old and noisy Ford car changing gears is heard in the distance. A grinding and screaming as it comes to a standstill. Then* UNCLE CHRIS' VOICE, *shouting.*)

UNCLE CHRIS' VOICE. Marta! Lars! Children—vere are you?

(*The curtains part on the kitchen again. Outside in the street is* UNCLE CHRIS' *car—an antique model. A woman is seated beside the empty driver's seat.* UNCLE CHRIS *is knocking on the house door. He is an elderly, powerful, swarthy man with a limp. In the kitchen,* NELS *and* CHRISTINE *are cowering.*)

UNCLE CHRIS. Marta! Lars!

CHRISTINE. (*Scared.*) It's Uncle Chris.

NELS. (*Equally so.*) I know.

CHRISTINE. What'll we do?

UNCLE CHRIS. Is nobody home? Hey, there—is nobody home? (*Banging on the door.*) Hey—someone—answer the door. (*He tries the door handle, it opens and he strides, limpingly, in. He has a strong accent, and uses the Norwegian pronunciation of the children's names.*) So, vat is—you do not answer the door? You do not hear me calling? (*The* CHILDREN *cower silently.*) I say, you do not hear me calling? I do not call loud enough?

CHRISTINE. Y-yes, Uncle Chris.

UNCLE CHRIS. Which yes? Yes, you do not hear me—or yes I do not call loud enough?

NELS. We heard you, Uncle Chris.

UNCLE CHRIS. Then why you do not come?

NELS. We... we were just going to.

(KATRIN *has left her desk and come up the steps.*)

UNCLE CHRIS. Let me look at you. You too, Katrinë, do not stand there—come and let me look at you. (*They line up as though for inspection. He thumps* NELS *between the shoulder blades.*) Stand tall! (*They all straighten up.*) Umhum. By the dresser, where the marks are. (NELS *goes to the wall by the dresser.* UNCLE CHRIS *compares his mark with the previous one—and makes a new one on the wall, writing by it.*) Two inches. Two inches in... (*Examining the date.*) six months. Is good. Christinë. (CHRISTINE *replaces* NELS.) Show me your teeth. (*She does so.*) You brush them goot? (*She nods.*) Nils, there is a box of oranges in the automobile. You fetch them in. (NELS *goes out.* UNCLE CHRIS *measurers* CHRISTINE.) Where is the little von? Dagmar?

KATRIN. She's sick, Uncle Chris.

UNCLE CHRIS. (*Arrested.*) Sick? What is the matter with her?

KATRIN. It's her ear. She's had an earache for two days. Bad earache. Mama sent for the doctor.

UNCLE CHRIS. Goot doctor? What he say?

KATRIN. He's in there now. (*She points off. Meanwhile* CHRISTINE *has remained standing by the wall, afraid to move.*)

UNCLE CHRIS. I go in. (*He starts to the door, but* MAMA *and* DR. JOHNSON *come into the room as he does so. During this* NELS *has gone to the car, and with nervous smiles at the woman seated by the driver's seat, has heaved out a huge box of oranges. He returns with the oranges during the ensuing scene.*)

MAMA. (*Greeting him.*) Uncle Chris.

UNCLE CHRIS. How is with Dagmar?

MAMA. Is bad. Doctor, this is my uncle, Mr. Halvorsen.

DOCTOR. How do you do, sir? (*He goes for his hat and bag which are on the bench in front of the window.*)

UNCLE CHRIS. What is with the child?

DOCTOR. We must get her to a hospital. At once. We'll have to operate.

MAMA. Operate?

DOCTOR. I'm afraid so.

MAMA. Can wait? Until my husband comes home from work?

DOCTOR. I'm afraid not. Her best chance is for us to operate immediately.

MAMA. (*After a second.*) We go. (*She goes to the dresser for the Little Bank.*)

UNCLE CHRIS. (*Who has watched her decision with approval, turns to the doctor, moving to him.*) What is with the child?

DOCTOR. I'm afraid it's a mastoid.

UNCLE CHRIS. Ah . . . then you operate immediately.

DOCTOR. (*Resenting this.*) That's what I said.

UNCLE CHRIS. Immediately!

MAMA. (*Who has poured the contents of the Little Bank onto the table.*) Doctor . . . is enough?

DOCTOR. (*At table.*) I was thinking of the County Hospital.

MAMA. No. No. We pay. Is enough?

KATRIN. If there isn't, we can go to the Bank.

CHRISTINE. We've got a bank account.

MAMA. Is enough without we go to the Bank, Doctor? My husband is carpenter. Make good money.

UNCLE CHRIS. If there is need of money, *I* pay.

DOCTOR. (*Mainly in dislike of* UNCLE CHRIS.) It'll be all right. We'll take her to the clinic. You pay what you can afford.

UNCLE CHRIS. Goot. Goot. I have a patient there already. My nephew, Arne. They operate this morning on his knee.

DOCTOR. Are you a physician, sir?

UNCLE CHRIS. I am better physician than most doctors. Nils, there, my other nephew, he become doctor when he grow up.

(NELS, *who has just returned, looks up, surprised.*)

DOCTOR. (*Chilly.*) Oh, indeed . . . very interesting. Well, now, if you will have the child at the clinic in . . . shall we say an hour's time. . . .

UNCLE CHRIS. (*Striding in front of table.*) The child will be at the clinic in *ten minutes'* time. I haf my automobile.

DOCTOR. I can hardly make arrangements in ten minutes.

UNCLE CHRIS. (*At table.*) *I* make arrangements. I know doctors.

MAMA. Uncle Chris, Dr. Johnson arrange. He is good doctor.

DOCTOR. (*Ironically.*) Thank you, Madam.

MAMA. You go, Doctor. We come.

DOCTOR. Very well, in an hour, then. And Dagmar will be well taken care of, I promise you. I will do the operation myself.

UNCLE CHRIS. I watch.

DOCTOR. You will do no such thing, sir.

UNCLE CHRIS. Always I watch operations. I am head of family.

DOCTOR. I allow no one to attend my operations.

UNCLE CHRIS. Are so bad?

DOCTOR. (*To* MAMA.) Mrs. Hanson, if I am to undertake this operation and the care of your child, it must be on the strict understanding that this gentleman does not come near either me or my patient.

MAMA. Yes, Doctor, I talk to him. . . . You go to hospital now, please.

DOCTOR. Very well. But you understand . . . nowhere near me, or I withdraw from the case. (*He goes*.)

UNCLE CHRIS. I go see Dagmar.

MAMA. (*Stopping him above table*.) Wait. Uncle Chris, is kind of you, but Dagmar is sick. You frighten her.

UNCLE CHRIS. I frighten her?

MAMA. Yes, Uncle Chris. You frighten everyone. . . .

UNCLE CHRIS. (*Amazed*.) I?

MAMA. Everyone but me. Even the girls . . . Jenny, Sigrid, Trina . . . they are frightened of you.

UNCLE CHRIS. The girls! Vomen! Pff!

MAMA. And the children, too. So Nels and I get Dagmar. You drive us to hospital in your automobile, but you do not frighten Dagmar. And you leave doctor alone. Dr. Johnson is *fine* doctor. You come with me, Nels. You carry Dagmar.

(NELS *and* MAMA *go out*. UNCLE CHRIS *stands in amazement and puzzlement. The* TWO GIRLS *watch him, hardly daring to move*.)

UNCLE CHRIS. (*Coming to table*.) Is true? I frighten you? Christinë . . . Katrinë . . . you are frightened of me? Come, I ask you. Tell me the truth. You are frightened of me?

KATRIN. (*Tremulously*.) A . . . a little, Uncle Chris.

UNCLE CHRIS. (*On bench*.) No? And you, Christinë?

CHRISTINE. Y . . . yes, Uncle Chris.

UNCLE CHRIS. But Nils . . . Nils is a boy . . . he is not frightened?

CHRISTINE. Not . . . not as much as we are. . . .

UNCLE CHRIS. But he is frightened?

CHRISTINE. Yes, Uncle Chris.

UNCLE CHRIS. (*With a roar*.) But why? What is there to be frightened off? I am your Uncle Chris . . . why do I frighten you?

CHRISTINE. I don't know.

UNCLE CHRIS. But that is bad. Very bad. The aunts, yes, I like to frighten them. (*The* GIRLS *giggle*.) That makes you laugh. (*He crosses to them*.) You do not like the aunts? Come, tell me. You do not like the aunts? Say!

KATRIN. Not . . . very much, Uncle Chris.

UNCLE CHRIS. And which do you not like the most? Jenny . . . Sigrid . . . Trina. . . . Tell me—huh?

KATRIN. I think I like Aunt Jenny least. She's so . . . so bossy.

CHRISTINE. I can't stand Aunt Sigrid. Always whining and complaining.

UNCLE CHRIS. (*With a great roar of laughter*.) Is good. Jenny, bossy. Sigrid, whining. Is true! But your Mama, she is different. And she cook goot. The aunts, they cannot cook at all. Only you do not tell your Mama we have talked of them so. It is a secret, for us. Then you cannot be frightened of me any more . . . when we have secret. I tell you my secret, too. *I* do not like the aunts. And so that they do not bother me, I frighten them and shout at them. You I do not shout at if you are goot children, and clean your teeth goot, and eat your oranges. (*He takes out a snuffbox and partakes of its contents*.)

(*As he says "You I do not shout at," the posse of* AUNTS *appears, in outdoor clothes, accompanied by* MR. THORKELSON, *a terrified little man. They come in at the left and start up to the house*.)

SIGRID. (*Stopping in the street*.) Jenny. Do you see what I see? A woman, in his automobile.

JENNY. How shameful!

SIGRID. Ought we to bow?

JENNY. Bow? To a woman like that? We cut her. That's what we do. I'll show you. (*She strides to the front door, ignoring the woman in the car, and enters the house. The others follow.* JENNY, *entering.*) Uncle Chris, Sigrid has something to say to you.

SIGRID. (*With false bravery.*) Uncle Chris, you took Arne to the hospital. . . .

UNCLE CHRIS. (*At table.*) Yes, I take Arne to the hospital. And now we take Dagmar to the hospital, so you do not clutter up the place.

JENNY. (*On the other side of table.*) What's the matter with Dagmar?

CHRISTINE. It's her ear. Dr. Johnson's going to operate.

SIGRID. (*Catching her favorite word.*) Operate? This is some more of Uncle Chris' doing. Did you hear what he did to Arne?

UNCLE CHRIS. (*Turning to her.*) Sigrid, you are a whining old fool, and you get out of here. . . .

SIGRID. (*Deflating.*) We'd better go, Jenny. . . .

JENNY. (*Stoutly.*) No . . . there has been enough of these high-handed goings-on. . . .

UNCLE CHRIS. And you, Jenny . . . you are a bossy old fool, and you get out of here, too, and we take Dagmar to hospital. (NELS *enters, carrying* DAGMAR *in his arms, wrapped in a blanket.*) You got her goot, Nils?

NELS. Sure, Uncle Chris.

UNCLE CHRIS. We go.

JENNY. (*Getting between him and the door.*) No! You are going to hear me out. (*Weakening.*) That is, you are going to hear Sigrid out. . . .

UNCLE CHRIS. If you do not get out of the way of the door before I count three, I trow you out. And Sigrid, too, as big as she is. Von. . . . (SIGRID *moves.*) Two. . . . (JENNY *moves. He looks back at the children with a wink and a smile.*) Is goot! You put her in back of the car, Nils.

(NELS *goes out carrying* DAGMAR, *and lifts her into the car.* UNCLE CHRIS *follows and starts cranking.*)

TRINA. (*Running to the door after him, with* MR. THORKELSON.) But, Uncle Chris, I want to introduce Mr. Thorkelson. . . .

(*But* UNCLE CHRIS *ignores her, continuing to crank. She returns crestfallen into the room with* MR. THORKELSON. MAMA *re-enters, wearing hat and coat and carrying a cheap little overnight case.*)

MAMA. Jenny . . . Trina, we go to hospital. (*She goes to* KATRIN *and* CHRISTINE.) You will be good children until Mama comes home?

THE GIRLS. Sure, Mama.

UNCLE CHRIS. (*Calling from the car.*) Marta, we go!

MAMA. (*Calling back.*) I come! (*She turns to the children again.*) There is milk in the cooler, and fruit and cookies for your lunch.

CHRISTINE. We'll be all right, Mama. Don't worry.

MAMA. I go now. (*She starts for the door.*)

SIGRID. (*Stopping her.*) Marta!

MAMA. What is it?

SIGRID. You *can't* go in his automobile.

MAMA. Why not?

UNCLE CHRIS. (*Calling again.*) Marta, we go!

MAMA. I come!

SIGRID. Because . . . because *she's* in it. The . . . the woman!

MAMA. So it will kill me, or Dagmar, if we sit in the automobile with her? I have see her. She looks nice woman. (*Calling off, as she goes.*) I come!

UNCLE CHRIS. We go! (MAMA *climbs into the rear of the car, which backs noisly off during the next speeches.*)

MR. THORKELSON. (*In a low whisper to* TRINA.) Is that woman his wife?

TRINA. (*Nervously.*) Yes. . . .

MR. THORKELSON. Yes?

TRINA. (*Whispering back, loudly.*) No!

JENNY. (*To the* GIRLS.) Don't stand there gaping like that, girls. (*She shoos them into the pantry.*) Go away! Go away! (*The* GIRLS *go.* JENNY *turns and sees the disappearing car through the open door.*) Oh! They've gone! We go after them! Sigrid, you lead the way! (*She gives* SIGRID *a push and the four go out, with* JENNY *dragging* MR. THORKELSON, and TRINA *following. Blackout. The travelers close.*)

(*Spot on turntable, representing a kind of closet room. Roller skates hanging on the wall.* KATRIN *is seated on the floor and* CHRISTINE *on a small kitchen stepladder with glasses of milk, and cookies on plates.*)

KATRIN. How long have they been gone now?

CHRISTINE. About three hours. And I wish you wouldn't keep asking that.

KATRIN. How long do operations take? I heard Aunt Sigrid telling about Mrs. Bergman who was five hours on the table.

CHRISTINE. Aunt Sigrid's friends always have everything worse than anyone else. And it gets worse each time she tells it, too.

(KATRIN *smiles—drinks some milk and eats a cookie.*)

KATRIN. (*With a certain melancholy enjoyment.*) The house feels lonesome, doesn't it—without Mama? It's like in a book. "The sisters sat huddled in the empty house, waiting for the verdict that was to spell life or death to the little family."

CHRISTINE. Oh, don't talk such nonsense.

KATRIN. It's not nonsense.

CHRISTINE. It is, too. In the first place, we're not a little family. We're a big one. And who said anything about life or death, anyway? Always trying to make everything so dramatic!

KATRIN. Well, it *is* dramatic.

CHRISTINE. It's not. It's just . . . well, worrying. But you don't have to make a tragedy out of it.

(*Pause.*)

KATRIN. You're not eating anything.

CHRISTINE. I know that.

KATRIN. You're not drinking your milk, either. Aren't you hungry?

CHRISTINE. No. And you wouldn't be, either, if you'd any feeling for Mama and Dagmar, instead of just heartlessly sitting there eating and enjoying making a story out of it.

KATRIN. Oh, Chris, I'm not heartless. I do have feeling for them. I can't help it if it goes into words like that. Everything always does with me. But it doesn't mean I don't feel it. And I think we *ought* to eat. I think Mama would want us to.

(*Pause.* CHRISTINE *hesitates a moment, then takes a bite of a cookie. They both eat in silence. The light dims on them, and the turntable revolves out. The travelers part on the hospital corridor. A wall runs diagonally up from the front of the main stage towards the back. In front of this is a bench, on which* MAMA *and* NELS *are sitting, holding hands, looking off. Below the bench is the elevator, and above the bench, set back a little, is a closet for brooms and mops, etc. The reception desk, at which a nurse is sitting, is towards the front. The wall goes up into darkness, and behind the nurse's desk is darkness. As the curtains open, there is a hubbub down by the nurse's desk, where the* AUNTS *are haranguing* UNCLE CHRIS. MR. THORKELSON *stands slightly behind them.*)

SIGRID. But, Uncle Chris, I tell you I must see him!

UNCLE CHRIS. (*Storming.*) You don't understand English? No visitors for twenty-four hours.

SIGRID. But *you've* seen him.

UNCLE CHRIS. I am not visitor. I am exception.

SIGRID. Well, then, his mother should be an exception, too. I'll see the doctor.

UNCLE CHRIS. *I* have seen doctor. I have told him you are not goot for Arne.

SIGRID. Not good for my own son. . . .

UNCLE CHRIS. Not good at all. You cry over him. I go now. (*He starts to do so, but* JENNY *pushes* TRINA *forward.*)

TRINA. (*With desperate courage.*) Uncle Chris . . . Uncle Chris . . . I *must* speak to you.

UNCLE CHRIS. I have business.

TRINA. But, Uncle Chris . . . I want to get married.

UNCLE CHRIS. Well, then, *get* married. *He starts off again.*)

TRINA. No, wait, I . . . I want to marry Mr. Thorkelson. Here. (*She produces him from behind her.*) Peter, this is Uncle Chris. Uncle Chris, this is Mr. Thorkelson.

UNCLE CHRIS. (*Staring at him.*) So?

MR. THORKELSON. How are you, sir?

UNCLE CHRIS. Busy. (*He turns again.*)

TRINA. Please, Uncle Chris . . .

UNCLE CHRIS. What is? You want to marry him? All right, marry him. I have other things to think about.

TRINA. (*Eagerly.*) Then . . . then you give your permission?

UNCLE CHRIS. Yes, I give my permission. If you want to be a fool, I cannot stop you.

TRINA. (*Gratefully.*) Oh, thank you, Uncle Chris.

UNCLE CHRIS. So. Is all?

TRINA. (*Anxious to escape.*) Yes, I think is all.

JENNY. (*Firmly.*) No!!

UNCLE CHRIS. No? (MR. THORKELSON *is pushed forward again.*)

MR. THORKELSON. Well, there . . . there was a little something else. You see, Trina mentioned . . . well, in the old country it was always usual . . . and after all, we do all come from the old country. . . .

UNCLE CHRIS. What is it? What you want?

MR. THORKELSON. Well, it's a question of Trina's . . . well, not to mince matters . . . her dowry.

UNCLE CHRIS. (*Shouting.*) Her what?

MR. THORKELSON. (*Very faintly.*) Her dowry . . .

UNCLE CHRIS. Ah. Her dowry. Trina wants a dowry. She is forty-two years old. . . .

TRINA. (*Interrupting.*) No, Uncle Chris. . . .

UNCLE CHRIS. (*Without pausing.*) And it is not enough she gets husband. She must have dowry.

NURSE. (*Who has been trying to interrupt, now bangs on her desk and moves towards them.*) Please! Would you mind going and discussing your family matters somewhere else? This is a hospital, not a marriage bureau.

UNCLE CHRIS. (*After glaring at the* NURSE, *turns to* MR. THORKELSON.) You come into waiting room. I talk to you about dowry. (*He strides off into the darkness behind the* NURSE'S *desk.* MR. THORKELSON, *with an appealing look back at* TRINA, *follows him. The* AUNTS *now remember* MAMA, *sitting on the bench, and cross to her.*)

JENNY. Did you hear that, Marta?

MAMA. (*Out of a trance.*) What?

JENNY. Uncle Chris.

MAMA. No, I do not hear. I wait for doctor. Is two hours since they take Dagmar to operating room. More.

SIGRID. Two hours? That's nothing! When Mrs. Bergman had her gall bladder removed she was *six* hours on the table.

MAMA. Sigrid, I do not want to hear about Mrs. Bergman. I do not want to hear about anything. I wait for doctor. Please, you go away now. You come this evening.

TRINA. But, Marta, you can't stay here all by yourself.

MAMA. I have Nels. Please, Trina . . . I wait for doctor . . . you go now.

JENNY. We go.

TRINA. Oh, but I must wait for Peter and Uncle Chris. . . .

JENNY. We'll go next door and have some coffee. Sigrid, do you have money?

SIGRID. Yes, I . . . I have a little.

JENNY. Good. Then I treat you. We'll be next door if you want us, Marta.

(MAMA *nods without looking at them, her eyes still fixed on the elevator door. The* AUNTS *leave, going down the steps from the stage as though they were the hospital steps, and for a moment the stage is quiet. Then a scrubwoman enters, carrying a mop and pail, which she puts into the closet, and then leaves. The elevator door opens and a doctor in white coat comes out, followed by an orderly, carrying a tray of dressings. They disappear behind the desk.* MAMA *rises, agitatedly, looking after them.*)

(*Then* DR. JOHNSON *returns, carrying his hat and bag. He sees* MAMA *and crosses to her.*)

DOCTOR. Oh, Mrs. Hanson....

MAMA. Doctor....

DOCTOR. Well, Dagmar's fine. She came through it beautifully. She's back in bed now, sleeping off the anesthetic.

MAMA. Thank you, Doctor. (*She shakes hands with him.*)

DOCTOR. You're very welcome.

MAMA. Is good of you, Doctor. (*She shakes hands with him again.*) Where is she? I go to her now.

DOCTOR. Oh, I'm sorry, but I'm afraid that's against the rules. You shall see her tomorrow.

MAMA. Tomorrow? But, Doctor, she is so little. When she wakes she will be frightened.

DOCTOR. The nurse will take care of her. Excellent care. You needn't worry. You see, for the first twenty-four hours, clinic patients aren't allowed to see visitors. The wards must be kept quiet.

MAMA. I will not make a sound.

DOCTOR. I'm very sorry. Tomorrow. And now... (*He glances at his watch.*) Good afternoon. (*He puts on his hat and goes out, down the steps and off.* MAMA *stands still a moment, looking after him.*)

MAMA. Come, Nels. We go find Dagmar.

NELS. But, Mama, the doctor said...

MAMA. We find Dagmar. (*She looks vaguely around her. Then goes to the* NURSE'S *desk.*) You tell me, please, where I can find my daughter?

NURSE. What name?

MAMA. Dagmar.

NELS. Dagmar Hanson.

NURSE. (*Looking at her record book.*) Hanson, Ward A. Along there. (*She points upstage.* MAMA *starts to go up.*) Oh, just a moment. (MAMA *returns.*) When did she come in?

MAMA. This morning. They just finish operation.

NURSE. Oh, well, then, I'm afraid you can't see her today. No visitors for the first twenty-four hours.

MAMA. Am not visitor. I am her Mama.

NURSE. I'm sorry, but it's against the rules.

MAMA. Just for one minute. Please.

NURSE. I'm sorry, but it's against the rules.

(MAMA *stands staring.* NELS *touches her arm. She looks at him, nods, trying to smile, then turns and walks out with him.*)

MAMA. We must think of some way.

NELS. Mama, they'll let you see her tomorrow. They said so.

MAMA. If I don't see her today how will I know that all is well with her? What can I tell Papa when he comes home from work?

NELS. The nurses will look after her, Mama. Would you like to come next door for some coffee?

MAMA. (*Shaking her head.*) We go home. We have coffee at home. But I must see Dagmar today. (*She plods off with* NELS.)

(*The travelers close. Spot goes up on turntable.* UNCLE CHRIS *and* MR. THORKELSON *are seated on a bench and chair, as in a waiting room. A table with a potted plant is between them. A clock on the wall points to 2:30.*)

UNCLE CHRIS. (*On bench.*) Well, it comes then to this. You love my niece, Trina? (MR. THORKELSON, *very scared, gulps and nods.*) You want to marry her? (MR. THORKELSON *nods again.*) You are in position to support her? (MR. THORKELSON *nods again.*) Why, then, you want dowry? (*No answer. He shouts.*) What for you want dowry?

MR. THORKELSON. Well... well, it would be a nice help. And it is customary.

UNCLE CHRIS. Is not customary. Who give dowries? Parents. Why? Because they are so glad they will not have to support their daughters any more, they pay money. I do not support Trina. I do not care if Trina gets married. Why then should I pay to have her married?

MR. THORKELSON. I never thought of it like that.

UNCLE CHRIS. Is insult to girl to pay dowry. If I do not give dowry, will you still marry Trina?

MR. THORKELSON. I . . . I don't know.

UNCLE CHRIS. You don't know? You don't know? You think I let Trina marry a man who will not take her without dowry?

MR. THORKELSON. No, I suppose you wouldn't.

UNCLE CHRIS. What kind of man would that be? I ask you, what kind of man would that be?

MR. THORKELSON. (*Fascinated—helpless.*) Well, not a very nice kind of man.

UNCLE CHRIS. And are you that kind of man?

MR. THORKELSON. I . . . I don't think so.

UNCLE CHRIS. (*Conclusively.*) Then you don't want dowry!!

MR. THORKELSON. (*Giving up.*) No, I . . . I guess I don't.

UNCLE CHRIS. (*Slapping his back.*) Goot. Goot. You are goot man. I like you. I give you my blessing. And I send you vedding present. I send you box of oranges!

(*While he is boisterously shaking* MR. THORKELSON'S *hand, blackout. Turntable revolves out. The curtain opens on the kitchen. It is empty.* MAMA *and* NELS *come up the hill and let themselves into the house. There is silence as they take off their hats and coats.*)

MAMA. (*After a moment.*) Where are the girls?

NELS. I guess they're upstairs. (*Goes to back door and calls.*) Chris! Katrin!

GIRLS' VOICES. Coming!

NELS. Shall I make you some coffee? (MAMA *shakes her head.*) You said you'd have coffee when you got home.

MAMA. Later. First I must think.

NELS. Mama, please don't worry like that. Dagmar's all right. You know she's all right.

(*The* GIRLS *come in.*)

CHRISTINE. (*Trying to be casual.*) Well, Mama, everything all right?

MAMA. (*Nodding.*) Is all right. You have eaten?

KATRIN. Yes, Mama.

MAMA. You drink your milk?

CHRISTINE. Yes, Mama.

MAMA. Is good.

CHRISTINE. (*Seeing her face.*) Mama, something's the matter.

KATRIN. (*Overdramatically.*) Mama, Dagmar's not—? She isn't—? Mama!

MAMA. No, Dagmar is fine. The doctor say she is fine. (*She rises.*) What is time?

NELS. It's three o'clock.

MAMA. Three hours till Papa come home. (*She looks around and then goes slowly into the pantry.*)

KATRIN. Nels, what is it? There *is* something the matter.

NELS. They wouldn't let Mama see Dagmar. It's a rule of the hospital.

CHRISTINE. But Dagmar's all right?

NELS. Oh, yes, she's all right.

CHRISTINE. (*Impatiently.*) Well, then . . . !

NELS. But Mama's very upset. She started talking to me in Norwegian in the street-car.

KATRIN. (*Emotionally.*) What can we do?

CHRISTINE. (*Coldly.*) You can't do anything. When *will* they let her see Dagmar?

NELS. Tomorrow.

CHRISTINE. Well, then, we'll just have to wait till tomorrow.

KATRIN. Chris, how can you be so callous? Can't you see that Mama's heart is breaking?

CHRISTINE. No. I can't. And you can't, either. People's hearts don't break.

KATRIN. They do, too.

CHRISTINE. Only in books. (MAMA *comes back, she wears an apron, and carries a scrub brush and a bucket of hot water.*) Why, Mama, what are you going to do?

MAMA. (*Coming down to the table.*) I scrub the floor. (*She gets down on her knees, facing front.*)

CHRISTINE. But you scrubbed it yesterday.

MAMA. I scrub it again. (*She starts to do so.*)

KATRIN. But, Mama . . .

MAMA. (*Bending low.*) Comes a time when you've got to get down on your knees.

KATRIN. (*To* CHRISTINE.) Now do you believe me?

(CHRISTINE, *suddenly unendurably moved, turns and rushes from the room.*)

NELS. Mama, don't. Please don't. You must be tired.

KATRIN. (*Strangely.*) Let her alone, Nels. (*They stand in silence watching* MAMA *scrub. Suddenly she stops.*) What is it, Mama? What is it?

MAMA. (*Sitting back on her haunches.*) I tink of something! (*Slowly.*) I tink I tink of something!

(*The lights dim and the curtains close on the kitchen. From the front* UNCLE CHRIS' VOICE *singing. The lights slowly come up on the turntable, showing* ARNE [*a child of about nine*] *in a hospital bed, with* UNCLE CHRIS *beside him.*)

UNCLE CHRIS. (*Singing.*)

"Ten t'ousand Svedes vent t'rough de veeds
    At de battle of Coppen-hagen.
Ten t'ousand Svedes vent t'rough de veeds
    Chasing vun Nor-ve-gan!"

ARNE. Uncle Chris!

UNCLE CHRIS. Yes, Arne?

ARNE. Uncle Chris, does it *have* to hurt like this?

UNCLE CHRIS. If you vant it to be vell, and not to valk alvays like Uncle Chris, it does . . . for a little. Is very bad?

ARNE. It is . . . kinda . . . Oo—oo . . . !

UNCLE CHRIS. Arne, don't you know any svear vords?

ARNE. W-what?

UNCLE CHRIS. Don't you know any svear vords?

ARNE. N-no, Uncle Chris. Not real ones.

UNCLE CHRIS. Then I tell you two fine vons to use when pain is bad. Are "Damn" and "Damittohell." You say them?

ARNE. N-now?

UNCLE CHRIS. No, not now. When pain comes again. You say them then. They help plenty. I know. I haf pain, too. I say them all the time. And if pain is *very* bad, you say, *God*damittohell. But only if is *very* bad. Is bad now?

ARNE. No, it's . . . it's a little better.

UNCLE CHRIS. You sleep some now, maybe?

ARNE. I'll try. Will . . . will you stay here, Uncle Chris?

UNCLE CHRIS. Sure. Sure. I stay here. You are not frightened of Uncle Chris?

ARNE. No. Not any more.

UNCLE CHRIS. Goot. Goot. You like I sing some more?

ARNE. If you wouldn't mind. But maybe something a little . . . well, quieter.

UNCLE CHRIS. (*Tenderly.*) Sure. Sure. (*He begins quietly to sing a Norwegian lullaby, in the midst,* ARNE *cries out.*)

ARNE. Oo—oo . . . Oh, *damn.* Damn Damittohell!

UNCLE CHRIS. (*Delighted.*) Goot! It helps—eh?

ARNE. (*With pleased surprise.*) Yes—yes.

UNCLE CHRIS. Then you sleep some! (*He fixes* ARNE'S *pillows for him, and resumes the lullaby, seated on his chair beside the bed. After another verse, he leans over, assuring himself that the child is asleep, and then very quietly, without interrupting his singing, takes a flask from his pocket and lifts it to his lips, as the light dims. The table revolves out.*)

(*The curtains part on the hospital corridor again. There is a different* NURSE *now at the reception desk, talking on the telephone as* MAMA *and* KATRIN *come in and go up the steps.*)

MAMA. (*As they come up, in an undertone.*) Is not the same nurse. Katrin, you take my hat and coat. (*She takes them off, revealing that she still wears her apron.*)

KATRIN. But, Mama, won't they . . .

MAMA. (*Interrupting, finger to lips.*) Ssh! You let me go ahead. You wait on bench for me. (*She goes to the closet door above the bench and opens it.* KATRIN *stares after her in trepidation.* MAMA *takes out a damp mop and pail, and gets down on her knees by the nurse's desk, starting to clean the floor. The* NURSE *looks up.*)

MAMA *catches her eye, brightly.*) Very dirty floors.

NURSE. Yes, I'm glad they've finally decided to clean them. Aren't you working late?

MAMA. (*Quickly, lowering her head.*) Floors need cleaning. (*She pushes her way, crawling on hands and knees, up behind the desk, and disappears up the corridor, still scrubbing.* KATRIN *steals to the bench, where she sits, still clutching* MAMA'S *hat and coat, looking interestedly around her. The light dims, leaving her in a single spot, as she starts to talk to herself.*)

KATRIN. (*To herself.*) "The Hospital" . . . A poem by Katrin Hanson. (*She starts to improvise.*)

"She waited, fearful, in the hall,
And held her bated breath."

Breath — yes, that'll rhyme with death. (*She repeats the first two lines.*)

"She waited fearful in the hall
And held her bated breath.
She trembled at the least footfall,
And kept her mind on death."

(*She gets a piece of paper and pencil from her pocket and begins to scribble, as a* NURSE *comes out of the elevator, carrying some charts, which she takes to the desk, and then goes out.* KATRIN *goes on with her poem.*)

"Ah, God, 'twas agony to wait.
To wait and watch and wonder. . . ."

Wonder — under — bunder — funder — sunder. Sunder! (*Nods to herself and goes on again.*)

"To wait and watch and wonder,
About her infant sister's fate.
If Death life's bonds would sunder."

(*Then to herself again, looking front.*) That's beautiful. Yes, but it isn't true. Dagmar isn't dying. It's funny — I don't want her to die — and yet when Mama said she was all right I was almost — well, almost disappointed. It wasn't exciting any more. Maybe Christine's right, and I haven't any heart. How awful! "The girl without a heart." That'd be a nice title for a story. "The girl without a heart sat in the hospital corridor. . . ."

(*The lights come up again as* UNCLE CHRIS *appears, behind the desk. He wears his hat and is more than a little drunk. He sees* KATRIN.)

UNCLE CHRIS. Katrinë! What you do here? (*He sits on the bench beside her.*)

KATRIN. (*Nervously.*) I'm waiting for Mama.

UNCLE CHRIS. Where is she?

KATRIN. (*Scared.*) I . . . I don't know.

UNCLE CHRIS. What you mean . . . you don't know?

KATRIN. (*Whispering.*) I think . . . I think she's seeing Dagmar.

UNCLE CHRIS. (*Shaking his head.*) Is first day. They do not allow visitors first day.

KATRIN. (*Trying to make him aware of the* NURSE.) I know. But I think that's where she is.

UNCLE CHRIS. Where *is* Dagmar?

KATRIN. I don't know.

(UNCLE CHRIS *rises and goes to the* NURSE *at the desk.*)

UNCLE CHRIS. In what room is my great-niece, Dagmar Hanson?

NURSE. (*Looking at her book.*) Hanson . . . Hanson . . . when did she come in?

UNCLE CHRIS. This morning.

NURSE. Oh, yes. Were you wanting to see her?

UNCLE CHRIS. What room is she in?

NURSE. I asked were you wanting to see her.

UNCLE CHRIS. And *I* ask what room she is in.

NURSE. We don't allow visitors the first day.

UNCLE CHRIS. Have I said I vant to visit her? I ask what room she is in.

NURSE. Are you by any chance, Mr. . . . (*Looking at her book.*) Halvorsen?

UNCLE CHRIS. (*Proudly, and correcting her pronunciation.*) Christopher Halvorsen.

NURSE. Did you say you were her uncle?

UNCLE CHRIS. Her great-uncle.

NURSE. Well, then, I'm afraid I can't tell you anything about her.

UNCLE CHRIS. Why not?
NURSE. Orders.
UNCLE CHRIS. Whose orders?
NURSE. Dr. Johnson's. There's a special note here. Patient's uncle, Mr. Halvorsen not to be admitted or given information under any circumstances.
UNCLE CHRIS. (*After a moment's angry stupefaction.*) Goddamittohell! (*He strides away, taking out his flask, and shaking it, only to find it empty.*)
(MAMA *returns, carrying the mop and pail, walking now and smiling triumphantly.*)
MAMA. (*To the* NURSE.) Thank you. (*She replaces the mop and pail in the closet, and then sees* UNCLE CHRIS. *Crossing to him.*) Uncle Chris, Dagmar is fine!
UNCLE CHRIS. (*Amazed.*) You see her?
MAMA. Sure, Uncle Chris, I see her.
UNCLE CHRIS. (*Reiterating, incredulous.*) You see Dagmar?
MAMA. Sure. (*She takes her hat from* KATRIN *and starts to put it on.*) Is fine hospital. But such floors! A mop is never good. Floors should be scrubbed with a brush. We go home. Uncle Chris, you come with us? I make coffee.
UNCLE CHRIS. (*Joining them in a little group on the steps.*) Pah! Vot good is coffee? I go get drunk.
MAMA. (*Reprovingly.*) Uncle Chris!
UNCLE CHRIS. Marta, you are a fine woman. Fine. But I go get drink. I get drunk.
MAMA. (*Quickly aside to* KATRIN.) His leg hurts him.

UNCLE CHRIS. And you do not make excuses for me! I get drunk because I like it.
MAMA. (*Conciliating him.*) Sure, Uncle Chris.
UNCLE CHRIS. (*Shouting.*) I like it! (*Then, with a change.*) No, is not true. You know is not true. I do not like to get drunk at all. But I do not like to come home with you, either. (*Growing slightly maudlin.*) You have family. Is fine thing. You do not know how fine. Katrinë, one day when you grow up, maybe you know what a fine thing family is. I haf no family.
KATRIN. (*On the lower step.*) But, Uncle Chris, Mama's always said you were the head of the family.
UNCLE CHRIS. Sure. Sure. I am head of the family, but I haf no family. So I go get drunk. You understand, Marta?
MAMA. Sure, Uncle Chris. You go get drunk. (*Sharply.*) But don't you feel sorry for yourself! (UNCLE CHRIS *glares at her a moment, then strides down the steps, boisterously singing his song of "Ten Thousand Swedes."* MAMA *watches him go, then takes her coat from* KATRIN.) Is fine man. Has fine ideas about family. (KATRIN *helps her on with her coat.*) I can tell Papa now that Dagmar is fine. She wake while I am with her. I explain rules to her. She will not expect us now until tomorrow afternoon.
KATRIN. You won't try and see her again before that?
MAMA. (*Gravely.*) No. That would be against the rules! Come. We go home.

(*They go off.*)

ACT TWO

SCENE: *Opening, exactly as in Act One.* KATRIN *at her desk*

KATRIN. (*Reading.*) "It wasn't very often that I could get Mama to talk—about herself, or her life in the old country, or what she felt about things. You had to catch her unawares, or when she had nothing to do, which was very, very seldom. I don't think I can ever remember seeing Mama unoccupied." (*Laying down the manuscript and looking out front.*) I do remember one occasion, though. It was the day before Dagmar came home from the hospital. And as we left, Mama suggested treating me to an ice cream soda. (*She rises, gets her hat from beside her—a schoolgirl hat—puts it on and crosses while she speaks the next lines.*) She had never done such a thing before, and I remember how proud it made me feel—just to sit and talk to her quietly like a grown-up person. It was a kind of special *treat*-moment in my life that I'll always remember—quite apart from the soda, which was *wonderful*. (MAMA *has come from between the curtains, and starts down the steps.*)

MAMA. Katrin, you like we go next door, and I treat you to an ice-cream soda?

KATRIN. (*Young now, and overcome.*) Mama—do you mean it?

MAMA. Sure. We celebrate. We celebrate that Dagmar is well, and coming home again. (*They cross to the turntable, which represents a drugstore, with a table and two chairs at which they seat themselves.* MAMA *is at the left of table.*) What you like to have, Katrin?

KATRIN. (*With desperate earnestness.*) I think a chocolate . . . no, a strawberry . . . no, a chocolate soda.

MAMA. (*Smiling.*) You are sure?

KATRIN. (*Gravely.*) I think so. But, Mama, can we *afford* it?

MAMA: I think this once we can afford it.
(*The* SODA CLERK *appears.*)

SODA CLERK. What's it going to be, ladies?

MAMA. A chocolate ice-cream soda, please—and a cup of coffee.
(*The* SODA CLERK *goes.*)

KATRIN. Mama, he called us "ladies"! (MAMA *smiles.*) Why aren't you having a soda, too?

MAMA. Better I like coffee.

KATRIN. When can I drink coffee?

MAMA. When you are grown up.

KATRIN. When I'm eighteen?

MAMA. Maybe before that.

KATRIN. When I graduate?

MAMA. Maybe. I don't know. Comes the day you are grown up, Papa and I will know.

KATRIN. Is coffee really nicer than a soda?

MAMA. When you are grown up, it is.

KATRIN. Did you used to like sodas better . . . before you were grown up?

MAMA. We didn't have sodas before I was grown up. It was in the old country.

KATRIN. (*Incredulous.*) You mean they don't have sodas in Norway?

MAMA. Now, maybe. Now I think they have many things from America. But not when I was a little girl.
(*The* SODA CLERK *brings the soda and the coffee.*)

SODA CLERK. There you are, folks. (*He sets them down and departs.*)

KATRIN. (*After a good pull at the soda.*) Mama, do you ever want to go back to the old country?

MAMA. I like to go back once to look, maybe. To see the mountains and the fjords. I like to show them once to you all. When Dagmar is big, maybe we all go back once . . . one summer . . . like tourists. But that is how it would be. I would be tourist there now. There is no one I would know any more. And maybe we see the little house where Papa and I live when we first marry. And . . . (*her eyes grow misty and reminiscent*) something else I would look at.

KATRIN. What is that? (MAMA *does not answer.*) What would you look at, Mama?

MAMA. Katrin, you do not know you have brother? Besides Nels?

KATRIN. No! A brother? In Norway? Mama. . . .

MAMA. He is my first baby. I am eighteen when he is born.

KATRIN. Is he there now?

MAMA. (*Simply.*) He is dead.

KATRIN. (*Disappointed.*) Oh. I thought you meant . . . I thought you meant a real brother. A long-lost one, like in stories. When did he die?

MAMA. When he is two years old. It is his grave I would like to see again. (*She is suddenly near tears. biting her lip and stirring her coffee violently, spilling some. She gets her handkerchief from her pocketbook, dabs at her skirt, then briefly at her nose, then she returns the handkerchief and turns to* KATRIN *again.*)

Matter-of-factly.) Is good, your ice-cream soda?

KATRIN. (*More interested now in* MAMA *than in it.*) Yes. Mama . . . have you had a very *hard* life?

MAMA. (*Surprised.*) Hard? No. No life is easy all the time. It is not meant to be. (*She pours the spilled coffee back from the saucer into her cup.*)

KATRIN. But . . . rich people . . . aren't *their* lives easy?

MAMA. I don't know, Katrin. I have never known rich people. But I see them sometimes in stores and in the streets, and they do not *look* as if they were easy.

KATRIN. Wouldn't you like to be rich?

MAMA. I would like to be rich the way I would like to be ten feet high. Would be good for some things—bad for others.

KATRIN. But didn't you come to America to *get* rich?

MAMA. (*Shocked.*) No. We come to America because they are all here—all the others. Is good for families to be together.

KATRIN. And did you like it right away?

MAMA. Right away. When we get off the ferry boat and I see San Francisco and all the family, I say: "Is like Norway," only it is better than Norway. And then you are all born here, and I become American citizen. But not to get rich.

KATRIN. *I* want to be rich. Rich and famous. I'd buy you your warm coat. When are you going to get that coat, Mama?

MAMA. Soon now, maybe—when we pay the doctor, and Mr. Hyde pay his rent. I think now I *must* ask him. I ask him tomorrow, after Dagmar comes home.

KATRIN. When I'm rich and famous, I'll buy you lovely clothes. White satin gowns with long trains to them. And jewelry. I'll buy you a pearl necklace.

MAMA. We talk too much! (*She signs to the* SODA CLERK.) Come, finish your soda. We must go home. (*The* SODA CLERK *comes.*) How much it is, please?

SODA CLERK. Fifteen cents.

MAMA. Here are two dimes. You keep the nickel. And thank you. Was good coffee. (*They start out and up the steps towards the curtains.*) Tomorrow Dagmar will be home again. And, Katrin, you see Uncle Elizabeth is there. This afternoon again she was asking for him. You keep Uncle Elizabeth in the house all day until she comes home.

(*They disappear behind the curtains. After a second, the howls of a cat in pain are heard from behind the curtains—low at first, then rising to a heart-rending volume, and then diminishing again as the curtains part on the kitchen once more.* MAMA, PAPA, *and* DAGMAR *are entering the house.*)

DAGMAR. (*Standing on threshold, transfixed.*) It's Uncle Elizabeth, welcoming me home! That's his song of welcome. Where is he, Mama? (*She looks around for the source of the howls.*)

MAMA. He is in the pantry . . . (*As* DAGMAR *starts to rush thither.*) But wait . . . wait a minute, Dagmar. I must tell you. Uncle Elizabeth is . . . sick.

DAGMAR. Sick? What's the matter with him?

PAPA. He has been in fight. Last night. He come home this morning very sick indeed.

(DAGMAR *starts for the pantry door, as* NELS *comes out.*)

MAMA. Nels, how is Uncle Elizabeth? Nels has been doctoring him.

NELS. He's pretty bad, Mama. I've dressed all his wounds again with boric acid, but . . . (*As* DAGMAR *tries to get past him.*) I wouldn't go and see him now, baby.

DAGMAR. I've got to. He's my cat. I haven't seen him in a whole month. More. (*She runs into the pantry and disappears.*)

MAMA. Nels, what you think?

NELS. I think we ought to have had him put away before she came home.

MAMA. But she would have been so unhappy if he was not here *at all.*

NELS. She'll be unhappier still if he dies.

(*Another howl is heard from the pantry, and then* DAGMAR *comes rushing back.*)

DAGMAR. Mama, what happened to him? What happened to him? Oh, Mama . . . when I tried to pick him up, his bandage slipped over his eye. It was bleeding. Oh, Mama, it looked awful. Oh . . . (*She starts to cry.*)

MAMA. (*Fondling her.*) He looks like that all over. Nels, you go see to his eye again. (*Wearily,* NELS *returns to the pantry.*) Listen, Dagmar . . . *Lille Ven* . . . would it not be better for the poor thing to go quietly to sleep?

DAGMAR. You mean—go to sleep and never wake up again? (MAMA *nods gently.*) No.

PAPA. I think he die, anyway. Nels try to make him well. But I do not think he can.

DAGMAR. Mama can. Mama can do everything. (*Another howl from offstage. She clutches* MAMA *agonizedly.*) Make him live, Mama. Make him well again. *Please!*

MAMA. We see. Let us see how he gets through the night. And now, Dagmar, you must go to bed. I bring you your supper.

DAGMAR. But you will fix Uncle Elizabeth? You promise, Mama?

MAMA. I promise I try. Go now. (DAGMAR *goes out.*) I must fix her supper. (*She starts for the pantry. Howls again. She and* PAPA *stand and look at each other.* NELS *comes out.*)

NELS. Mama, it's just cruelty, keeping that cat alive.

MAMA. I know.

PAPA. (*As another howl, the loudest yet, emerges.*) You say we see how the cat get through the night. I ask you how do *we* get through the night? Is no use, Marta. We must put the cat to sleep. Nels, you go to the drugstore, and get something. Some chloroform, maybe. (*He gives him a coin.*)

NELS. How much shall I get?

PAPA. You ask the man. You tell him it is for a cat. He knows. (NELS *goes out and down the street. Looking at* MAMA's *face.*) Is best. Is the only thing.

MAMA. I know. But poor Dagmar. It is sad homecoming for her. And she has been so good in hospital. Never once she cry. (*She pulls herself together.*) I get her supper. (*Another howl from off stage.*) And I take the cat outside. Right outside, where we . . . where *Dagmar* cannot hear him. (*She goes into the pantry.* PAPA *takes a folded newspaper from his pocket, puts on his glasses and starts to read. The back door opens gently and* MR. HYDE *peeps out. He wears his hat and coat and carries his suitcase and a letter.* PAPA *has his back to him.* MR. HYDE *lays the letter on the dresser and then starts to tiptoe across to the door. Then* PAPA *sees him.*)

PAPA. You go out, Mr. Hyde?

MR. HYDE. (*Pretending surprise.*) Oh . . . Oh, I did not see you, Mr. Hanson. (*He puts down the suitcase.*) I did not know you were back. As a matter of fact, I . . . I was about to leave this letter for you. (*He fetches it.*) The fact is . . . I . . . I have been called away.

PAPA. So?

MR. HYDE. A letter I received this morning necessitates my departure. My immediate departure.

PAPA. I am sorry. (MAMA *returns with a tray, on which are milk, bread, butter, and jelly.*) Mama, Mr. Hyde says he goes away.

MAMA. (*Coming to the table with the tray.*) Is true?

MR. HYDE. Alas, dear Madam, yes. 'Tis true, 'tis pity. And pity 'tis, 'tis true. You will find here . . . (*he presents the letter*) my check for all I owe you, and a note expressing my profoundest thanks for all your most kind hospitality. You will say good-by to the children for me? (*He bows, as* MAMA *takes the letter.*)

MAMA. (*Distressed.*) Sure. Sure.

MR. HYDE. (*Bowing again.*) Madam, my deepest gratitude. (*He kisses her hand.* MAMA *looks astonished. He bows to* PAPA.) Sir—my sincerest admiration! (*He opens the street door.*) It has been a privilege. Ave atque vale! Hail and farewell! (*He makes a gesture and goes.*)

MAMA. Was wonderful man! Is too bad. (*She opens the letter, takes out the check.*)

PAPA. How much is check for?

MAMA. Hundred ten dollar! Is four months.

PAPA. Good. Good.

MAMA. Is wonderful. Now we pay doctor everything.

PAPA. And you buy your warm coat. With fur now, maybe.

MAMA. (*Sadly.*) But there will be no more reading. You take the check, Lars. You get the money?

PAPA. (*Taking it.*) Sure. I get it. What does he say in his letter?

MAMA. You read it while I fix supper for Dagmar. (*She starts to butter the bread, and spread jelly, while* PAPA *reads.*)

PAPA. (*Reading.*) "Dear Friends, I find myself compelled to take a somewhat hasty departure from this house of happiness...."

MAMA. Is beautiful letter.

PAPA. (*Continuing.*) "I am leaving you my library for the children...."

MAMA. He leaves his books?

PAPA. He says so.

MAMA. But is wonderful. Go see, Lars. See if they are in his room.

(PAPA *lays down the letter and goes out.* NELS *and* CHRISTINE *appear, coming up to the house.* CHRISTINE *carries schoolbooks.*)

CHRISTINE. I'm sure it was him, Nels. Carrying his suitcase, and getting on the cable car. I'm sure he's going away.

NELS. Well, I hope he's paid Mama.

(*They open the street door.*)

CHRISTINE. (*Bursting in.*) Mama, I saw Mr. Hyde getting on the cable car.

MAMA. I know. He leave.

CHRISTINE. Did he pay you?

MAMA. Sure, he pay me. Hundred ten dollar....

NELS. Gee....

MAMA. (*Smiling.*) Is good.

CHRISTINE. Are you going to put it in the Bank?

MAMA. We need it right away. (PAPA *returns, staggering under an armload of books.*)

Mr. Hyde leaves his books, too. For you.

NELS. Say! (PAPA *stacks them on the table.* NELS *and* CHRISTINE *rush to them, reading the titles.*) The Pickwick Papers, The Complete Shakespeare ...

CHRISTINE. *Alice in Wonderland, The Oxford Book of Verse* ...

NELS. *The Last of the Mohicans, Ivanhoe* ...

CHRISTINE. We were right in the middle of that.

MAMA. Nels can finish it. He can read to us now in the evenings. He has fine voice, too, like Mr. Hyde. (NELS *flushes with pleasure.*) Is wonderful. So much we can learn. (*She finishes the supper-making.*) Christine, you take the butter back to the cooler for me, and the yelly, too. (CHRISTINE *does so.*) I go up to Dagmar now. (*She lifts the tray, then pauses.*) You get it, Nels?

NELS. What? ... Oh.... (*Taking a druggist's small bottle from his pocket.*) Here.

MAMA. You put it down. After I come back, we do it. You know how?

NELS. Why, no, Mama, I ...

MAMA. You do not ask?

NELS. No, I ... I thought Papa ...

MAMA. You know, Lars?

PAPA. No, I don't *know* ... but it cannot be difficult. If you *hold* the cat ...

MAMA. And watch him die? No! I think better you get rags ... and a big sponge, to soak up the chloroform. You put it in the box with him, and cover him over. You get them ready out there.

NELS. Sure, Mama.

MAMA. I bring some blankets.

(NELS *goes off to the pantry, as* CHRISTINE *comes back. Again* MAMA *lifts the tray and starts for the door. But there is a knock on the street door from* AUNT JENNY, *who has come to the house in a state of some excitement.*)

MAMA. (*Agitated.*) So much goes on! See who it is, Christine.

CHRISTINE. (*Peeping.*) It's Aunt Jenny. (*She opens the door.*)

MAMA. Jenny....

JENNY. (*Breathless.*) Marta ... has he gone?

MAMA. (*Above table,*) Who?
JENNY. (*Near table.*) Your boarder ... Mr. Hyde....
MAMA. Yes, he has gone. Why?
JENNY. Did he pay you?
MAMA. Sure he pay me.
JENNY. How?
MAMA. He give me a check. Lars has it right there.
JENNY. (*With meaning.*) A check!
MAMA. Jenny, what is it? Christine, you give Dagmar her supper. I come soon. (CHRISTINE *takes the tray from her and goes out.*) What is it, Jenny? How do you know that Mr. Hyde has gone?
JENNY. I was at Mr. Kruper's down the street ... you know, the restaurant and bakery ... and he told me Mr. Hyde was there today having his lunch, and when he left he asked if he would cash a check for him. For fifty dollars. (*She pauses.*)
PAPA. Well, go on.
JENNY. Your fine Mr. Hyde didn't expect Mr. Kruper to take it to the bank until tomorrow, but he did. And what do you think? Mr. Hyde hasn't even an *account* at that bank! (NELS *returns and stands in the pantry doorway.*)
MAMA. I don't understand.
PAPA. (*Taking the check from his pocket.*) You mean the check is no good?
JENNY. No good at all. (*Triumphantly.*) Your Mr. Hyde was a crook, just as I always thought he was, for all his reading and fine ways. Mr. Kruper said he'd been cashing them all over the neighborhood. (MAMA *stands quite still, without answering.*) How much did he owe you? Plenty, I'll bet. (*Still no answer.*) Eh? Marta, I said I bet he owed you plenty. Didn't he?
MAMA. (*Looks around, first at* NELS *and then down at the books on the table. She touches them.*) No. No, he owed us nothing. (*She takes the check from* PAPA, *tearing it.*) Nothing.
JENNY. (*Persistently.*) How much was that check for? (*She reaches her hand for it.*)
MAMA. (*Evading her.*) It does not matter. He pay with better things than money. (*She goes to the stove, where she throws the check, watching it burn.*)

JENNY. I told you right in the beginning that you shouldn't trust him. But you were so sure ... just like you always are. Mr. Hyde was a gentleman. A gentleman! I bet it must have been a hundred dollars that he rooked you of. Wasn't it?
MAMA. (*Returning to the table.*) Jenny, I cannot talk now. Maybe you don't have things to do. I have.
JENNY. (*Sneeringly.*) What? What have *you* got to do that's so important?
MAMA. (*Taking up the medicine bottle, fiercely.*) I have to chloroform a cat!
(JENNY *steps back in momentary alarm, almost as though* MAMA *were referring to her, as she goes out into the pantry with the medicine bottle, not so very unlike Lady Macbeth with the daggers. Blackout and curtains close. After a moment, the curtains part again on the kitchen, the next morning. The books have been taken off the table, and* MAMA *is setting the breakfast dishes, with* PAPA *helping her.* DAGMAR *comes bursting into the room.*)
DAGMAR. Good morning, Mama. 'Morning, Papa. Is Uncle Elizabeth all better?
MAMA. Dagmar, there is something I must tell you.
DAGMAR. I want to see Uncle Elizabeth first. (*She runs into the pantry.* MAMA *turns helplessly to* PAPA.)
MAMA. Do something! Tell her!
PAPA. If we just let her think the cat die ... by itself. ...
MAMA. No. We cannot tell her lies.
(PAPA *goes to the pantry door, opening it.*)
DAGMAR. (*Heard in pantry, off.*) What a funny, funny smell. Good morning, my darling, my darling Elizabeth. (MAMA *and* PAPA *stand stricken.* DAGMAR *comes in, carrying the cat, wrapped in an old shirt, with its head covered. She comes over to table.*) My goodness, you put enough blankets on him! Did you think he'd catch cold?
MAMA. (*Horror-stricken.*) Dagmar, you must not ... (*She stops at the sight of the cat, whose tail is twitching, quite obviously alive.*)

Dagmar, let me see . . . Let me see the cat! (*She goes over to her, below table front, and uncovers the cat's head.*)

DAGMAR. (*Overjoyed.*) He's well. Oh, Mama, I *knew* you'd fix him.

MAMA. (*Appalled.*) But, Dagmar, I didn't, I . . .

DAGMAR. (*Ignoring her.*) I'm going to take him right up and show him to Nels. (*She runs off, calling.*) Nels! Nels! Uncle Elizabeth's well again!

MAMA. (*Turning to* PAPA.) Is a miracle! (*She sits, dumfounded, on the bench in front of the table.*)

PAPA. (*Beside her, shrugging.*) You cannot have used enough chloroform. You just give him good sleep, and that cures him. We rechristen the cat, Lazarus!

MAMA. But, Lars, we must tell her. Is not *good* to let her grow up believing I can fix *everything*!

PAPA. Is best thing in the world for her to believe. (*He chuckles.*) Besides, I know *exactly* how she feels. (*He lays his hand on hers.*)

MAMA. (*Turning with embarrassment from his demonstrativeness and slapping his hand.*) We finish getting breakfast. (*She turns back to the table.*)

(*The curtains close. Lights go up down front.* KATRIN *and* CHRISTINE *enter from the wings, in school clothes, wearing hats.* CHRISTINE *carries schoolbooks in a strap.* KATRIN *is reciting.*)

KATRIN.
"The quality of mercy is not strained,
  It droppeth as the gentle rain from heaven
  Upon the place beneath: it is twice blest;
  It blesseth him that gives, and him that takes. . . ."

(*She dries up.*) ". . . him that takes. It blesseth him that gives and him that takes. . . ." (*She turns to* CHRISTINE.) What comes after that?

CHRISTINE. I don't know. And I don't care.

KATRIN. Why, Chris!

CHRISTINE. I don't. It's all I've heard for weeks. The school play, and your graduation, and going on to High. And never a thought of what's happening at home.

KATRIN. What do you mean?

CHRISTINE. You see—you don't even know!

KATRIN. Oh, you mean the strike?

CHRISTINE. Yes, I mean the strike. Papa hasn't worked for four whole weeks, and a lot you care. Why, I don't believe you even know what they're striking *for*. Do you? All you and your friends can talk about is the presents you're going to get. You make me ashamed of being a girl.

(*Two girls,* MADELINE *and* DOROTHY, *come through the curtains, talking.*)

MADELINE. (*To* DOROTHY.) Thyra Walsh's family's going to add seven pearls to the necklace they started for her when she was a baby. Oh, hello, Katrin! Did you hear about Thyra's graduation present?

KATRIN. (*Not very happily.*) Yes, I heard.

MADELINE. I'm getting an onyx ring, with a diamond in it.

KATRIN. A real diamond?

MADELINE. Yes, of course. A *small* diamond.

DOROTHY. What are *you* getting?

KATRIN. Well . . . well, they haven't actually told me, but I think . . . I think I'm going to get that pink celluloid dresser set in your father's drugstore.

DOROTHY. You mean that one in the window?

KATRIN. (*To* MADELINE.) It's got a brush and comb and mirror . . . and a hair-receiver. It's genuine celluloid!

DOROTHY. I wanted Father to give it to me, out of stock, but he said it was too expensive. Father's an awful tightwad. They're giving me a bangle.

MADELINE. Oh, there's the streetcar. We've got to fly. 'By, Katrin. 'By, Christine. See you tomorrow. Come on, Dorothy.

(*The* TWO GIRLS *rush off.*)

CHRISTINE. Who said you were going to get the dresser set?
KATRIN. Nobody's said so . . . for certain. But I've sort of hinted, and . . .
CHRISTINE. (*Going up the steps.*) Well, you're not going to get it.
KATRIN. How do you know?
CHRISTINE. (*Turning up back. Still on steps.*) Because I know what you *are* getting. I heard Mama tell Aunt Jenny. Aunt Jenny said you were too young to appreciate it.
KATRIN. What is it?
CHRISTINE. Mama's giving you her brooch. Her *solje.*
KATRIN. You mean that old silver thing she wears that belonged to Grandmother? What would I want an old thing like that for?
CHRISTINE. It's an heirloom. Mama thinks a lot of it.
KATRIN. Well, then, she ought to keep it. You don't really mean that's *all* they're going to give me?
CHRISTINE. What more do you want?
KATRIN. I want the dresser set. My goodness, if Mama doesn't realize what's a suitable present . . . why, it's practically the most important time in a girl's life, when she graduates.
CHRISTINE. And you say you're not selfish!
KATRIN. It's not selfishness.
CHRISTINE. Well, I don't know what else you'd call it. With Papa not working, we need every penny we can lay our hands on. Even the Little Bank's empty. But you'll devil Mama into giving you the dresser set somehow. So why talk about it? I'm going home. (*She turns and goes through the curtains.*)
   (KATRIN *stands alone with a set and stubborn mouth, and then sits on the steps.*)
KATRIN. Christine was right. I got the dresser set. They gave it to me just before supper on graduation night. Papa could not attend the exercises because there was a strike meeting to decide about going back to work. I was so excited that night I could hardly eat, and the present took the last remnants of my appetite clean away.
   (*The curtains part on the kitchen.* PAPA, MAMA, *and* DAGMAR *at table, with coffee.* CHRISTINE *is clearing dishes.*)
CHRISTINE. I'll just stack the dishes now, Mama. We'll wash them when we come home. (*She carries them into the pantry.*)
PAPA. (*At table. Holding up a cube of sugar.*) Who wants coffee-sugar? (*He dips it in his coffee.*) Dagmar? (*He hands it to her.*) Katrin? (*She rises from the steps, coming into the scene for the sugar.*)
MAMA. (*At other side of table.*) You get your coat, Katrin; you need it.
   (KATRIN *goes out.*)
DAGMAR. (*Behind table.*) Aunt Jenny says if we drank black coffee like you do at our age, it would turn our complexions dark. I'd like to be a black Norwegian. Like Uncle Chris. Can I, Papa?
PAPA. I like you better blonde. Like Mama.
DAGMAR. When do you get old enough for your complexion *not* to turn dark? When can we drink coffee?
PAPA. One day, when you are grown up.
   (JENNY *and* TRINA *have come to the door.* JENNY *knocks.*)
MAMA. There are Jenny and Trina. (*She goes to the door.*) Is good. We can start now. (*She opens the door.* JENNY *and* TRINA *come in.*)
JENNY. Well, are you all ready? Is Katrin very excited?
PAPA. (*Nodding.*) She ate no supper.
   (MAMA *has started to put on her hat, and to put on* DAGMAR's *hat and coat for her.* CHRISTINE *comes back from the pantry.* PAPA *gives her a dipped cube of sugar.*)
JENNY. Is that *black* coffee you dipped that sugar in? Lars, you shouldn't. It's not good for them. It'll . . .
PAPA. (*Finishing for her.*) Turn their complexions black. I know. Well, maybe it is all right if we have *one* colored daughter.

JENNY. Lars, really!
(KATRIN *returns with her coat.*)
KATRIN. Aunt Jenny, did you see my graduation present? (*She gets it from a chair.* CHRISTINE *gives her a disgusted look, and goes out.* KATRIN *displays the dresser set above the table.*) Look! It's got a hair-receiver.
JENNY. (*At left of table.*) But I thought . . . Marta, I though you were going to give her . . .
MAMA. No, you were right, Jenny. She is too young to appreciate that. She like something more gay . . . more modern.
JENNY. H'm. Well, it's very pretty, I suppose, but . . . (*She looks up as* MAMA *puts on her coat.*) You're not wearing your *solje*!
MAMA. (*Quickly.*) No. I do not wear it tonight. Come, Trina, we shall be late.
TRINA. (*Behind table.*) Oh, but Peter isn't here yet.
MAMA. Katrin has her costume to put on. He can follow. Or do you like to wait for Peter?
TRINA. I think . . . if you don't mind . . .
MAMA. You can stay with Lars. He does not have to go yet.
JENNY. I hope Katrin knows her part.
PAPA. Sure she knows it. *I* know it, too.
TRINA. It's too bad he can't see Katrin's debut as an actress.
MAMA. You will be back before us, Lars?
PAPA. (*Nodding.*) I think the meeting will not last long.
MAMA. Is good. We go now. (*She goes out with* JENNY *and* DAGMAR. CHRISTINE *and* NELS *return and follow, waiting outside for* KATRIN, *while the others go ahead.* KATRIN *puts on her hat and coat and picks up the dresser set.*)
PAPA. (*To* TRINA.) You like we play a game of checkers while we wait?
TRINA. (*Sitting at table.*) Oh, I haven't played checkers in years.
PAPA. Then I beat you. (*He rises to get the checker set.* KATRIN *kisses him.*)
KATRIN. Good-by, Papa.
PAPA. Good-by, daughter. I think of you.
KATRIN. I'll see you there, Aunt Trina.

TRINA. Good luck!
PAPA. I get the checkers.
(KATRIN *goes out.* PAPA *gets the checkers set from a cupboard under the dresser, brings it to the table and sets it up during the ensuing scene, which is played outside in the street.*)
CHRISTINE. (*Contemptuously.*) Oh, bringing your cheap trash with you to show off?
KATRIN. It's not trash. It's beautiful. You're just jealous.
CHRISTINE. I told you you'd devil Mama into giving it to you.
KATRIN. I didn't. I didn't devil her at all. I just showed it to her in Mr. Schiller's window. . . .
CHRISTINE. And made her go and sell her brooch that her very own mother gave her.
KATRIN. What?
NELS. Chris . . . you weren't supposed to tell that!
CHRISTINE. I don't care. I think she ought to know.
KATRIN. Is that true? Did Mama—Nels—?
NELS. Well, yes, as a matter of fact, she did. Now, come on.
KATRIN. No, no, I don't believe it. I'm going to ask Papa.
NELS. You haven't time.
KATRIN. I don't care. (*She rushes back to the house and dashes into the kitchen.* CHRISTINE *goes off and* NELS *follows her.*) Papa—Papa—Christine says— Papa, did Mama sell her brooch to give me this?
PAPA. (*Above table.*) Christine should not have told you that.
KATRIN. It's true, then?
PAPA. She did not sell it. She traded it to Mr. Schiller for your present.
KATRIN. (*Near tears.*) Oh, but she shouldn't . . . I never meant . . .
PAPA. (*Taking her by the shoulders.*) Look, Katrin. You wanted the present. Mama wanted your happiness; she wanted it more than she wanted the brooch.
KATRIN. But I never meant her to do that. (*Crying.*) She *loved* it so. It was all she had of Grandmother's.

PAPA. She always meant it for you, Katrin. And you must not cry. You have your play to act.

KATRIN. (*Sobbing.*) I don't want to act in it now.

PAPA. But you must. Your audience is waiting.

KATRIN. (*As before.*) I don't care.

PAPA. But you must care. Tonight you are not Katrin any longer. You are an actress. And an actress must act, whatever she is feeling. There is a saying—what is it—

TRINA. (*Brightly.*) The mails must go through!

PAPA. No, no. The show must go on. So stop your crying, and go and act your play. We talk of this later. Afterwards.

KATRIN. (*Pulling herself together.*) All right, I'll go. (*Sniffing a good deal, she picks up the dresser set and goes back to the street and off.* PAPA *and* TRINA *exchange glances, and then settle down to their checkers.*)

PAPA. Now we play.

(*The lights fade and the curtains close. Spot up on turntable. The two girls from the earlier scene are dressing in costumes for* The Merchant of Venice *before a plank dressing table.*)

DOROTHY. I'm getting worried about Katrin. If anything's happened to her . . .

MADELINE. (*Pulling up her tights.*) I'll forget my lines. I know I will. I'll look out and see Miss Forrester sitting there, and forget every single line. (KATRIN *rushes in. She carries the dresser set, places it on the dressing table.*) We thought you'd had an accident, or something. . . .

KATRIN. Dorothy, is your father here tonight?

DOROTHY. He's going to be. Why?

KATRIN. I want to speak to him. (*As she pulls off her hat and coat.*) Will you tell him . . . please . . . not to go away without speaking to me? After. After the exercises.

DOROTHY. What on earth do you want to speak to Father for?

KATRIN. I've got something to say to him. Something to ask him. It's important. *Very* important.

MADELINE. Is that the dresser set? (*Picking it up.*) Can I look at it a minute?

KATRIN. (*Snatching it from her, violently.*) No!

MADELINE. Why, what's the matter? I only wanted to look at it.

KATRIN. (*Emotionally.*) You can't. You're not to touch it. Dorothy, you take it and put it where I can't see it. (*She thrusts it at her.*) Go on . . . Take it! Take it! Take it!!

(*Blackout. Curtains part on the kitchen.* MAMA *and* PAPA *in conclave at the table with cups of coffee.*)

MAMA. (*Behind table.*) I am worried about her, Lars. When it is over, I see her talking with Mr. Schiller—and then she goes to take off her costume and Nels tells me that he will bring her home. But it is long time, and is late for her to be out. And in the play, Lars, she was not good. I have heard her practice it here, and she was good, but tonight, no. It was as if . . . as if she was thinking of something else all the time.

PAPA. (*At table.*) I think maybe she was.

MAMA. But what? What can be worrying her?

PAPA. Marta . . . tonight, after you leave, Katrin found out about your brooch.

MAMA. My brooch? But how? Who told her?

PAPA. Christine.

MAMA. (*Angry.*) Why?

PAPA. I do not know.

MAMA. (*Rising with a sternness we have not seen before, and calling.*) Christine! Christine!

CHRISTINE. (*Emerging from the pantry, wiping a dish.*) Were you calling me, Mama?

MAMA. Yes. Christine, did you tell Katrin tonight about my brooch?

CHRISTINE. (*Frightened, but firm.*) Yes.

MAMA. (*Level with her.*) Why did you?

CHRISTINE. Because I hated the smug way she was acting over that dresser set.

MAMA. Is no excuse. You make her unhappy. You make her not good in the play.

CHRISTINE. Well, she made *you* unhappy, giving up your brooch for her selfishness.

MAMA. (*Moving towards her, behind table.*) Is not your business. I choose to give my brooch. Is not for you to judge. And you know I do not want you to tell. I am angry with you, Christine.

CHRISTINE. I'm sorry. But I'm not sorry I told. (*She goes back to the pantry with a set, obstinate face.*)

PAPA. Christine is the stubborn one. (NELS *and* KATRIN *have approached the house outside. They stop and look at each other in the lamplight.* KATRIN *looks scared. Then* NELS *pats her, and she goes in,* NELS *following.* MAMA *looks up inquiringly and searchingly into* KATRIN'S *face.* KATRIN *turns away, taking off her hat and coat, and taking something from her pocket.*)

NELS. What happened at the meeting, Papa?

PAPA. We go back to work tomorrow.

NELS. Gee, that's bully. Isn't it, Mama?

MAMA. (*Seated again, at table, absently.*) Yes, is good.

KATRIN. (*Coming to* MAMA.) Mama . . . here's your brooch. (*She gives it to her.*) I'm sorry I was so bad in the play. I'll go and help Christine with the dishes. (*She turns and goes into the pantry.*)

MAMA. (*Unwrapping the brooch from tissue paper.*) Mr. Schiller give it back to her?

NELS. (*Behind table.*) We went to his house to get it. He didn't want to. He was planning to give it to his wife for her birthday. But Katrin begged and begged him. She even offered to go and work in his store during her vacation if he'd give it back.

PAPA. (*Impressed.*) So? So?

MAMA. And what did Mr. Schiller say?

NELS. He said that wasn't necessary. But he gave her a job all the same. She's going to work for him, afternoons, for three dollars a week.

MAMA. And the dresser set—she gave that back?

NELS. Yes. She was awful upset, Mama. It was kinda hard for her to do. She's a good kid. Well, I'll say good night. I've got to be up early.

PAPA. Good night, Nels.

NELS. Good night, Papa. (*He goes out back.*)

MAMA. Good night, Nels.

PAPA. Nels is the kind one. (*He starts to refill* MAMA'S *coffee cup. She stops him, putting her hand over her cup.*) No?

MAMA. (*Rising and calling.*) Katrin! Katrin!

KATRIN. (*Coming to the pantry door.*) Yes, Mama?

MAMA. (*Sitting at table.*) Come here. (KATRIN *comes to her.* MAMA *holds out the brooch.*) You put this on.

KATRIN. No . . . it's yours.

MAMA. It is your graduation present. I put it on for you. (*She pins the brooch on* KATRIN'S *dress.*)

KATRIN. (*Near tears.*) I'll wear it always. I'll keep it forever.

MAMA. Christine should not have told told you.

KATRIN. (*Moving away.*) I'm glad she did. Now.

PAPA. And I am glad, too. (*He dips a lump of sugar and holds it out to her.*) Katrin?

KATRIN. (*Tearful again, shakes her head.*) I'm sorry, Papa. I . . . I don't feel like it. (*She crosses in front of the table and sits on the chest under the window, with her back to the room.*)

PAPA. So? So? (*He goes to the dresser.*)

MAMA. What do you want, Lars? (*He does not answer, but takes a cup and saucer, comes to the table and pours a cup of coffee, indicating* KATRIN *with his head.* MAMA *nods, pleased, then checks his pouring and fills up the cup from the cream pitcher which she empties in so doing.* PAPA *puts in sugar and moves to* KATRIN.)

PAPA. Katrin. (*She turns. He holds out the cup.*)

KATRIN. (*Incredulous.*) For me?

PAPA. For our grown-up daughter.

(MAMA *nods, standing arm in arm with* PAPA. KATRIN *takes the cup, lifts it—then her emotion overcomes her. She thrusts it at* PAPA *and rushes from the room.*) Katrin is the dramatic one! Is too bad. Her first cup of coffee, and she does not drink it.

MAMA. It would not have been good for her, so late at night.

PAPA. (*Smiling.*) And you, Marta, you are the practical one.

MAMA. You drink the coffee, Lars. We do not want to waste it. (*She pushes it across to him.*)

(*Lights dim. Curtains close. Light up on turntable, representing the parlour of* JENNY's *house. A telephone on a table, at which* TRINA *is discovered, talking.*)

TRINA. (*Into phone.*) Yes, Peter. Yes, Peter. I know, Peter, but we don't know where he is. It's so long since we heard from him. He's sure to turn up soon. Yes, I know, Peter. I know, but . . . ((*Subsiding obediently.*) Yes, Peter. Yes, Peter. (*Sentimentally.*) Oh, Peter, you know I do. Good-by, Peter. (*She hangs up, and turns, to see* JENNY, *who has come in behind her, eating a piece of toast and jam.*)

JENNY. What was all that about?

TRINA. Peter says we shouldn't wait any longer to hear from Uncle Chris. He says we should send the wedding invitations out right away. He was quite insistent about it. Peter can be very masterful sometimes . . . when he's alone with *me*!

(*The telephone rings again.* JENNY *answers it, putting down the toast, which* TRINA *takes up and nibbles at during the scene.*)

JENNY. This is Mrs. Stenborg's boarding house. Mrs. Stenborg speaking. Oh, yes, Marta . . . what is it? (*She listens.*)

(*Spot up on opposite turntable, disclosing* MAMA *standing at a wall telephone booth. She wears hat and coat, and has an opened telegram in her hand.*)

MAMA. Jenny, is Uncle Chris. I have a telegram. It says if we want to see him again we should come without delay.

JENNY. Where is he?

MAMA. (*Consulting the telegram.*) It comes from a place called Ukiah. Nels says it is up north from San Francisco.

JENNY. Who is the telegram from?

MAMA. It does not say.

JENNY. That . . . woman?

MAMA. I don't know, Jenny. I think maybe.

JENNY. I won't go. (SIGRID *comes in through the curtains, dressed in hat and coat, carrying string marketing bags, full of vegetables.* JENNY *speaks to her, whisperingly, aside.*) It's Uncle Chris. Marta says he's dying. (*Then, back into phone.*) Why was the telegram sent to* you*? I'm the eldest.

MAMA. Jenny, is not the time to think of who is eldest. Uncle Chris is dying.

JENNY. *I* don't believe it. He's too mean to die. Ever. (NELS *comes to booth from wings and hands* MAMA *a slip of paper.*) I'm not going.

MAMA. Jenny, I cannot stop to argue. There is a train at eleven o'clock. It takes four hours. You call Sigrid.

JENNY. Sigrid is here now.

MAMA. Good. Then you tell her.

JENNY. What do you say the name of the place is?

MAMA. Ukiah. (*Spelling in Norwegian.*) U—K—I—A—H

JENNY. I won't go.

MAMA. That *you* decide. (*She hangs up. Her spot goes out.*)

SIGRID. Uncle Chris dying!

JENNY. The wages of sin.

TRINA. Oh, he's old. Maybe it is time for him to go.

JENNY. Four hours by train, and maybe have to stay all night. All that expense to watch a wicked old man die of the D.T.'s.

SIGRID. I know, but . . . there is his will. . . .

JENNY. Huh, even supposing he's anything to leave—you know who he'd leave it *to*, don't you?

SIGRID. Yes. But all the same he's dying now, and blood is thicker than water. Especially when it's Norwegian. I'm going. I shall take Arne with me. Uncle Chris was always fond of children.

TRINA. I agree with Sigrid. I think we should go.

JENNY. Well, *you* can't go, anyway.

TRINA. Why not?

JENNY. Because of that woman. You can't meet a woman like that.

TRINA. Why not? If you two can . . .

SIGRID. We're married women.

TRINA. I'm engaged!

JENNY. That's not the same thing.

SIGRID. Not the same thing at all!

TRINA. Nonsense. I've never met a woman like that. Maybe I'll never get another chance. Besides, if he's going to change his will, there's still my dowry, remember. Do you think we should take Peter?

JENNY. Peter Thorkelson? Whatever for?

TRINA. Well, after all, I mean . . . I mean, his profession . . .

JENNY. Trina, you always were a fool. Anyone would know the last person a dying man wants to see is an undertaker!

(*Blackout. Turntable revolves out. Spot up on* KATRIN. *She wears her schoolgirl hat.*)

KATRIN. When Mama said I was to go with her, I was excited and I was frightened. It was exciting to take sandwiches for the train, almost as though we were going on a picnic. But I was scared at the idea of seeing death, though I told myself that if I was going to be a writer, I had to experience everything. But all the same, I hoped it would be all over when we got there. (*She starts to walk up the steps.*) It was afternoon when we arrived. We asked at the station for the Halvorsen ranch, and it seemed to me that the man looked at us strangely. Uncle Chris was obviously considered an odd character. The ranch was about three miles from the town: a derelict, rambling old place. There was long grass, and tall trees, and a smell of honeysuckle. We made quite a cavalcade, walking up from the gate. (*The procession comes in behind* KATRIN. MAMA, JENNY, TRINA, SIGRID *and* ARNE.) The woman came out on the steps to meet us.

(*The procession starts moving upwards. The* WOMAN *comes through the curtains, down one step. The* AUNTS *freeze in their tracks.* MAMA *goes forward to her.*)

MAMA. How is he? Is he—?

WOMAN. (*With grave self-possession.*) Come in, won't you? (*She holds the curtains slightly aside.* MAMA *goes in.* KATRIN *follows, looking curiously at the* WOMAN. *The* AUNTS *walk stiffly past her,* SIGRID *clutching* ARNE *and shielding him from contact with the* WOMAN. *They disappear behind the curtains. The* WOMAN *stands a moment, looking off into the distance. Then she goes in behind the curtains, too.*)

(*The curtains draw apart, revealing* UNCLE CHRIS' *bedroom. It is simple, and shabby. The door to the room is at the back. In the wall at left is a window, with curtains, drawn aside now. In front of it, a washstand. The afternoon sunlight comes through the window, falling onto the big double bed, in which* UNCLE CHRIS *is propped up on pillows. Beside him, on a small table, is a pitcher of water. He has a glass in his hand.* MAMA *stands to his right,* JENNY *to the left. The others are ranged below the window. The* WOMAN *is not present.*)

UNCLE CHRIS. (*Handing* MAMA *the empty glass.*) I want more. You give me more. Is still some in the bottle.

MAMA. Uncle Chris, that will not help now.

UNCLE CHRIS. It always help. (*With a glance at* JENNY.) Now especially.

JENNY. (*Firmly.*) Uncle Chris, I don't think you realize . . .

UNCLE CHRIS. What I don't realize? That I am dying? Why else do I think you come here? Why else do I think you stand there, watching me? (*He sits upright.*) Get out. Get out. I don't want you here. Get out!

JENNY. Oh, very well. Very well. We'll

be outside on the porch, if you want us. (*She starts toward the door.*)

UNCLE CHRIS. That is where I want you—on the porch! (JENNY *goes out.* TRINA *follows.* SIGRID *is about to go, too, when* UNCLE CHRIS *stops her.*) Wait. That is Arne. Come here, Arne. (ARNE, *propelled by* SIGRID, *advances toward the bed.*) How is your knee?

ARNE. It's fine, Uncle Chris.

UNCLE CHRIS. Not hurt any more? You don't use svear vords any more?

ARNE. N-no, Uncle Chris.

UNCLE CHRIS. You walk goot? Quite goot? Let me see you walk. Walk around the room. (ARNE *does so.*) Fast. Fast. Run! Run! (ARNE *does so.*) Is goot.

SIGRID. (*Encouraged and advancing.*) Uncle Chris, Arne has always been so fond of you. . . .

UNCLE CHRIS. (*Shouting.*) I tell you all to get out. Except Marta. (*As* KATRIN *edges with the* AUNTS *to the door.*) And Katrinë. Katrinë and I haf secret. You remember, Katrinë?

KATRIN. Yes, Uncle Chris.

MAMA. Uncle Chris, you must lie down again.

UNCLE CHRIS. Then you give me drink.

MAMA. No, Uncle Chris.

UNCLE CHRIS. We cannot waste what is left in the bottle. You do not drink it . . . who will drink it when I am gone? What harm can it do . . . now? I die, anyway. . . . You give it to me. (MAMA *goes to the washstand, pours him a drink of whisky and water, and takes it to him, sitting on the bed beside him. He drinks, then turns to her, leaning back against her arm and the pillows.*) Marta, I haf never made a will. Was never enough money. But you sell this ranch. It will not bring moch. I have not had it long enough. And there is mortgage. Big mortgage. But it leave a little. Maybe two, three hundred dollars. You give to Yessie.

MAMA. Yessie?

UNCLE CHRIS. Yessie Brown. My housekeeper. No, why I call her that to you? You understand. She is my vowan. Twelve years she has been my voman. My wife, only I cannot marry her. She has husband alive somewhere. She was trained nurse, but she get sick and I bring her to the country to get well again. There will be no money for *you*, Marta. Always I wanted there should be money to make Nils doctor. But there were other things . . . quick things. And now there is no time to make more. There is no money, but you make Nils doctor, all the same. You like?

MAMA. Sure, Uncle Chris. It is what Lars and I have always wanted for him. To help people who suffer. . . .

UNCLE CHRIS. Is the greatest thing in the world. It is to have a little of God in you. Always I wanted to be doctor myself. Is the only thing I have ever wanted. Nils must do it for me.

MAMA. He will, Uncle Chris.

UNCLE CHRIS. Is goot. (*He strokes her hand.*) You are the goot one. I am glad you come, *Lille Ven.* (*He moves his head restlessly.*) Where is Yessie?

MAMA. I think she wait outside.

UNCLE CHRIS. You do not mind if she is here?

MAMA. Of course not, Uncle Chris.

UNCLE CHRIS. You call her. I like you both here. (MAMA *goes, with a quick glance at* KATRIN, *who has been standing, forgotten, listening intently.* UNCLE CHRIS *signs to* KATRIN *to come closer. She sits on the chair beside the bed.*) Katrinë, your Mama write me you drink coffee now? (*She nods. He looks at her affectionately.*) Katrinë, who will be written. . . . You are not frightened of me now?

KATRIN. No, Uncle Chris.

UNCLE CHRIS. One day maybe you write story about Uncle Chris. If you remember.

KATRIN. (*Whispering.*) I'll remember.

(MAMA *returns with the* WOMAN. *They come to his bed, standing on either side of it.*)

UNCLE CHRIS. (*Obviously exhausted and in pain.*) I like you both stay with me . . . now, I think best now maybe Katrinë go away

Good-by, Katrinë. (*Then he repeats it in Norwegian.*) Farvell, Katrinë.

KATRIN. Good-by, Uncle Chris.

UNCLE CHRIS. You say it in Norwegian, like I do.

KATRIN. (*In Norwegian.*) Farvell, Onkel Chris. (*She slips out, in tears.*)

UNCLE CHRIS. Yessie! Maybe I should introduce you to each other. Yessie, this is my niece, Marta. The only von of my nieces I can stand. Marta, this is Yessie, who have give me much happiness. . . .

(*The* TWO WOMEN *shake hands across the bed.*)

MAMA. I am very glad to meet you.

JESSIE. I am, too.

UNCLE CHRIS. (*As they shake.*) Is goot. And now you give me von more drink. You have drink with me . . . both of you. That way we finish the bottle. Yes?

(JESSIE *and* MAMA *look at each other.*)

MAMA. Sure, Uncle Chris.

UNCLE CHRIS. Goot. Yessie, you get best glasses. (*With a chuckle to* MAMA.) Yessie does not like to drink, but this is special occasion. (JESSIE *gets three glasses from a wall shelf.*) What is the time?

MAMA. It is about half-past four, Uncle Chris.

UNCLE CHRIS. The sun come around this side the house in afternoon. You draw the curtain a little maybe. Is strong for my eyes. (MAMA *goes over and draws the curtain over the window. The stage darkens.* JESSIE *pours three drinks, filling two of the glasses with water. She is about to put water in the third when* UNCLE CHRIS *stops her.*) No, no, I take it without water. Always the last drink without water. Is Norwegian custom. (*To* MAMA, *with a smile.*) True? (JESSIE *sits on the bed beside him, about to feed his drink to him, but he pushes her aside.*) No. No, I do not need you feed it to me. I can drink myself. (*He takes the glass from her.*) Give Marta her glass. (JESSIE *hands a glass to* MAMA. *The* TWO WOMEN *stand on either side of the bed, holding their glasses.*) So. . . . Skoal!

JESSIE. (*Clinking glasses with him.*) Skoal.

MAMA. (*Doing likewise.*) Skoal.

(*They all three drink. Slow dim to blackout. Curtains close. Spot up on turntable. A porch with a bench, and a chair, on which the three* AUNTS *are sitting.* JENNY *is dozing in the chair.*)

SIGRID. (*Flicking her handkerchief.*) These gnats are awful. I'm being simply eaten alive.

TRINA. Gnats are always worse around sunset. (*She catches one.*)

JENNY. (*Rousing herself.*) I should never have let you talk me into coming. To be insulted like that . . . turned out of his room . . . and then expected to sit here hour after hour without as much as a cup of coffee. . . .

SIGRID. I'd make coffee if I knew where the kitchen was.

JENNY. *Her* kitchen? It would poison me. (*Rising.*) No, I'm going home. Are you coming, Trina?

TRINA. Oh, I think we ought to wait a little longer. After all, you can't *hurry* these things. . . . I mean . . . (*She breaks off in confusion at what she has said.*)

JENNY. (*To* SIGRID.) And all your talk about his will. A lot of chance we got to say a word!

TRINA. Maybe Marta's been talking to him.

(MAMA *comes from between the curtains.*)

JENNY. Well?

MAMA. Uncle Chris has . . . gone.

(*There is a silence.*)

JENNY. (*More gently than is her wont.*) Did he . . . say anything about a will?

MAMA. There is no will.

JENNY. Well, then, that means . . . we're his nearest relatives. . . .

MAMA. There is no money, either.

SIGRID. How do you know?

MAMA. He told me. (*She brings out a small notebook that she is carrying.*)

JENNY. What's that?

MAMA. Is an account of how he spent the money.

JENNY. Bills from a liquor store.

MAMA. No, Jenny. No. I read it to you. (JENNY *sits again.*) You know how Uncle Chris was lame . . . how he walked always with limp. It was his one thought . . . lame people. He would have liked to be doctor and help them. Instead, he helps them other ways. I read you the last page. . . . (*She reads from the notebook.*) "Joseph Spinelli. Four years old. Tubercular left leg. Three hundred thirty-seven dollars, eighteen cents." (*Pause.*) "Walks now. Esta Jensen. Nine years. Club-foot. Two hundred seventeen dollars, fifty cents. Walks now." (*Then, reading very slowly.*) "Arne Solfeldt. . . ."

SIGRID. (*Startled.*) *My* Arne?

MAMA. (*Reading on.*) "Nine years. Fractured kneecap. Four hundred forty-two dollars, sixteen cents."

(KATRIN *and* ARNE *come running in.*)

ARNE. (*Calling as he comes running across.*) Mother . . . Mother . . . Are we going to eat soon? (*He stops, awed by the solemnity of the group, and by* MAMA, *who puts out her hand gently, to silence him.*) What is it? Is Uncle Chris . . . ?

MAMA. (*To the* AUNTS.) It does not tell the end about Arne. I like to write "Walks now." Yes?

SIGRID. (*Very subdued.*) Yes.

MAMA. (*Taking a pencil from the book.*) Maybe even . . . "runs"? (SIGRID *nods, moist-eyed.* TRINA *is crying.* MAMA *writes in the book, and then closes it.*) So. Is finished. Is all. (*She touches* JENNY *on the shoulder.*) It was good.

JENNY. (*After a gulping movement.*) I go and make some coffee.

(*The woman,* JESSIE, *appears from between the curtains on the steps.*)

JESSIE. You can go in and see him now if you want. (JENNY *looks back, half-hesitant, at the others. Then she nods and goes in.* TRINA *follows her, mopping her eyes.* SIGRID *puts her arm suddenly around* ARNE *in a spasm of maternal affection, and they, too, go in.* MAMA, KATRIN *and* JESSIE *are left alone.* KATRIN *stands apart,* MAMA *and* JESSIE *are in front of the curtains.*) I'm moving down to the hotel for tonight . . . so that you can all stay. (*She is about to go back, when* MAMA *stops her.*)

MAMA. Wait. What will you do now . . . after he is buried? You have money? (JESSIE *shakes her head.*) Where you live?

JESSIE. I'll find a room somewhere. I'll probably go back to nursing.

MAMA. You like to come to San Francisco for a little? To our house? We have room. Plenty room.

JESSIE. (*Touched, moving to* MAMA.) That's very kind of you, but . . .

MAMA. I like to have you. You come for a little as our guest. When you get work you can be our boarder.

JESSIE. (*Awkwardly grateful.*) I don't know why you should bother. . . .

MAMA. (*Touching her.*) You were good to Uncle Chris. (JESSIE *grasps her hand, deeply moved, then turns and goes quickly back through the curtains.* MAMA *turns to* KATRIN.) Katrin, you come and see him?

KATRIN. (*Scared.*) See him? You mean . . .

MAMA. I like you see him. You need not be frightened. He looks . . . happy and at peace. I like you to know what death looks like. Then you are not frightened of it, ever.

KATRIN. Will you come with me?

MAMA. Sure. (*She stretches out her hand, puts her arm around her, and then leads her gently in through the curtains.*)

(*Spot up on turntable, representing a park bench against a hedge.* TRINA *and* MR. THORKELSON, *in outdoor clothes, are seated together.* TRINA *is cooing over a baby carriage.*)

TRINA. Who's the most beautiful Norwegian baby in San Francisco? Who's going to be three months old tomorrow? Little Christopher Thorkelson! (*To* MR. THORKELSON.) Do you know, Peter, I think he's even beginning to *look* a little like Uncle Chris! Quite apart from his black curls—and those, of course, he gets from *you.* (*To baby again.*) He's going to grow up to be a black Norwegian, isn't he, just like his daddy and his Uncle Chris? (*Settling down beside* MR. THORKEL-

SON.) I think there's something about his mouth . . . a sort of . . . well . . . *firmness.* Of course, it's *your* mouth, too. But then I've always thought you had quite a lot of Uncle Chris about you. (*She looks back at the baby.*) Look—he's asleep!

MR. THORKELSON. Trina, do you know what next Thursday is?

TRINA. (*Nodding, smiling.*) Our anniversary.

MR. THORKELSON. What would you think of our giving a little party?

TRINA. A party?

MR. THORKELSON. Oh, quite a modest one. Nothing showy or ostentatious—but, after all, we have been married a year, and with your having been in mourning and the baby coming so soon and everything, we've not been able to entertain. I think it's time you . . . took your place in society.

TRINA. (*Scared.*) What . . . sort of a party?

MR. THORKELSON. An evening party. (*Proudly.*) A soirée! I should say about ten people . . . some of the Norwegian colony . . . and Lars and Marta, of course. . . .

TRINA. (*Beginning to count on her fingers.*) And Jenny and Sigrid. . . .

MR. THORKELSON. Oh . . . I . . . I hadn't thought of asking Jenny and Sigrid.

TRINA. Oh, we'd have to. We couldn't leave them out.

MR. THORKELSON. Trina, I hope you won't be offended if I say that I have never really felt . . . well, altogether comfortable with Jenny and Sigrid. They have always made me feel that they didn't think I was . . . well . . . *worthy* of you. Of course, I know I'm not, but . . . well . . . one doesn't like to be reminded of it . . . *all* the time.

TRINA. (*Taking his hand.*) Oh, Peter.

MR. THORKELSON. But you're quite right. We must ask them. Now, as to the matter of refreshments . . . what would you suggest?

TRINA. (*Flustered.*) Oh, I don't know. I . . . what would you say to . . . ice cream and cookies for the ladies . . . and coffee, of course . . . and . . . perhaps port wine for the gentlemen?

MR. THORKELSON. (*Anxiously.*) Port wine?

TRINA. Just a little. You could bring it in already poured out, in *little* glasses. Jenny and Sigrid can help me serve the ice cream.

MR. THORKELSON. (*Firmly.*) No. If Jenny and Sigrid come, they come as guests, like everyone else. You shall have someone in to help you in the kitchen.

TRINA. You mean a waitress? (MR. THORKELSON *nods, beaming.*) Oh, but none of us have *ever* . . . do you really think . . . I mean . . . you did say we shouldn't be ostentatious. . . .

MR. THORKELSON. (*Nervously, rising and starting to pace up and down.*) Trina, there's something I would like to say. I've never been very good at expressing myself or my . . . well . . . *deeper* feelings—but I want you to know that I'm not only very fond of you, but very . . . well . . . very *proud* of you as well, and I want you to have the best of everything, as far as it's in my power to give it to you. (*He sits again—then, as a climax.*) I want you to have a waitress!

TRINA. (*Overcome.*) Yes, Peter. (*They hold hands.*)

(*The lights fade and the turntable revolves out. Curtains part on kitchen, slightly changed, smartened and refurnished now.* MAMA *and* PAPA *seated as usual.* MAMA *is darning.* DAGMAR, *looking a little older, is seated on the chest, reading a solid-looking book.* NELS *enters from back door, carrying a newspaper. He wears long trousers now, and looks about seventeen.*)

NELS. (*Hitting* PAPA *playfully on the head with the paper.*) Hello! Here's your evening paper, Papa.

(PAPA *puts down the morning paper he is reading and takes the evening one from* NELS.)

PAPA. (*At table.*) Is there any news?

NELS. No. (*He takes out a package of cigarettes with elaborate unconcern.* MAMA

I REMEMBER MAMA

watches with disapproval. Then, as he is about to light his cigarette, he stops, remembering something.) Oh, I forgot. There's a letter for Katrin. I picked it up on the mat as I came in. (*Going to back door and calling.*) Katrin! Katrin! There's a letter for you.

KATRIN. (*Answering from off stage.*) Coming!

MAMA. (*At table.*) Nels, you know who the letter is from?

NELS. Why, no, Mama. (*Hands it to her.*) It looks like her own handwriting.

MAMA. (*Gravely inspecting it.*) Is bad.

PAPA. Why is bad?

MAMA. She gets too many like that. I think they are stories she send to the magazines.

DAGMAR. (*Closing her book loudly, rising.*) Well, I'll go and see if I have any puppies yet. (*Crosses below the table and then turns.*) Mama, I've just decided something.

MAMA. What have you decided?

DAGMAR. If Nels is going to be a doctor, when I grow up, I'm going to be a— (*looking at the book title, and stumbling over the word*)—vet-vet-veterinarian.

MAMA. And what is that?

DAGMAR. A doctor for animals.

MAMA. Is good. Is good.

DAGMAR. There are far more animals in the world than there are human beings, and far more human doctors than animal ones. It isn't fair. (*She goes to the pantry door.*) I suppose we couldn't have a horse, could we? (*This only produces a concerted laugh from the family. She turns, sadly.*) No. . . . I was afraid we couldn't. (*She goes into the pantry.*)

(KATRIN *comes in. She wears a slightly more adult dress than before. Her hair is up and she looks about eighteen.*)

KATRIN. Where's the letter?

MAMA. (*Handing it to her.*) Here.

(KATRIN *takes it, nervously. She looks at the envelope, and her face falls. She opens it, pulls out a manuscript and a rejection slip, looks at it a moment, and then replaces both in the envelope. The others watch her covertly. Then she looks up, with determination.*)

KATRIN. (*Above table.*) Mama . . . Papa . . . I want to say something.

PAPA. What is it?

KATRIN. I'm not going to go to college.

PAPA. Why not?

KATRIN. Because it would be a waste of time and money. The only point in my going to college was to be a writer. Well, I'm not going to be one, so . . .

MAMA. Katrin, is it your letter that makes you say this? It is a story come back again?

KATRIN. Again is right. This is the tenth time. I made this one a test. It's the best I've ever written, or ever shall write. I know that. Well, it's no good.

NELS. What kind of story is it?

KATRIN. Oh . . . it's a story about a painter, who's a genius, and he goes blind.

NELS. Sounds like *The Light That Failed*.

KATRIN. Well, what's wrong with that?

NELS. (*Quickly.*) Nothing. Nothing!

KATRIN. (*Moving down.*) Besides, it's not like that. My painter gets better. He has an operation and recovers his sight, and paints better than ever before.

MAMA. Is good.

KATRIN. (*Bitterly unhappy.*) No, it isn't. It's rotten. But it's the best I can do.

MAMA. You have asked your teachers about this?

KATRIN. Teachers don't know anything about writing. They just know about literature.

MAMA. If there was someone we could ask . . . for advice . . . to tell us . . . tell us if your stories are good.

KATRIN. Yes. Well, there isn't. And they're *not*.

PAPA. (*Looking at the evening paper.*) There is something here in the paper about a lady writer. I just noticed the headline. Wait. (*He looks back for it and reads.*) "Woman writer tells key to literary success."

KATRIN. Who?

PAPA. A lady called Florence Dana

Moorhead. It gives her picture. A fat lady. You have heard of her?

KATRIN. Yes, of course. Everyone has. She's terribly successful. She's here on a lecture tour.

MAMA. What does she say is the secret?

PAPA. You read it, Katrin. (*He hands her the paper.*)

KATRIN. (*Grabbing the first part.*) "Florence Dana Moorhead, celebrated novelist and short story writer . . . blah-blah-blah . . . interviewed today in her suite at the Fairmont . . . blah-blah-blah . . . pronounced sincerity the essential quality for success as a writer." (*Throwing aside the paper.*) A lot of help that is.

MAMA. Katrin, this lady . . . maybe if you sent her your stories, *she* could tell you what is wrong with them?

KATRIN. (*Wearily.*) Oh, Mama, don't be silly.

MAMA. Why is silly?

KATRIN. (*Behind table.*) Well, in the first place because she's a very important person . . . a celebrity . . . and she'd never read them. And in the second, because . . . you seem to think writing's like . . . well, like cooking, or something. That all you have to have is the recipe. It takes a lot more than that. You have to have a gift for it.

MAMA. You have to have a gift for cooking too. But there are things you can learn, if you have the gift.

KATRIN. Well, that's the whole point. I haven't. I *know* . . . now. So, if you've finished with the morning paper, Papa, I'll take the want ad section, and see if I can find myself a job. (*She takes the morning paper and goes out.*)

MAMA. Is bad. Nels, what you think?

NELS. I don't know, Mama. Her stories seem all right to me, but I don't know.

MAMA. It would be good to know. Nels, this lady in the paper . . . what else does she say?

NELS. (*Taking up the paper.*) Not much. The rest seems to be about *her* and her home. Let's see . . . (*He reads—walking down.*) "Apart from literature, Mrs. Moorhead's main interest in life is gastronomy."

MAMA. The stars?

NELS. No—eating. "A brilliant cook herself, she says that she would as soon turn out a good soufflé as a short story, or find a new recipe as she would a first edition."

MAMA. (*Reaching for the paper.*) I see her picture? (*She looks at it.*) Is kind face. (*Pause while she reads a moment. Then she looks up and asks.*) What is first edition?

(*Blackout. Lights up on turntable, representing the lobby of the Fairmont Hotel. A couch against a column with a palm behind it. An orchestra plays softly in the background.* MAMA *is discovered seated on the couch, waiting patiently. She wears a hat and a suit, and clutches a newspaper and a bundle of manuscripts. A couple of guests come through the curtains and cross, disappearing into the wings.* MAMA *watches them. Then* FLORENCE DANA MOORHEAD *enters through the curtains. She is a stout, dressy, good-natured, middle-aged woman. A* BELLBOY *comes from the right, paging her.*)

BELLBOY. Miss Moorhead?

F. D. MOORHEAD. Yes?

BELLBOY. Telegram.

F. D. MOORHEAD. Oh, . . . Thank you. (*She tips him, and he goes.* MAMA *rises and moves towards her.*)

MAMA. Please . . . Please . . . Miss Moorhead . . . Miss Moorhead.

F. D. MOORHEAD. (*Looking up from her telegram, on the steps.*) Were you calling me?

MAMA. Yes. You are . . . Miss Florence Dana Moorhead?

F. D. MOORHEAD. Yes.

MAMA. Please . . . might I speak to you for a moment?

F. D. MOORHEAD. Yes—what's it about?

MAMA. I read in the paper what you say about writing.

F. D. MOORHEAD. (*With a vague social smile.*) Oh, yes?

MAMA. My daughter, Katrin, wants to be writer.

F. D. MOORHEAD. *(Who has heard that one before.)* Oh, really? *(She glances at her watch on her bosom.)*

MAMA. I bring her stories.

F. D. MOORHEAD. Look, I'm afraid I'm in rather a hurry. I'm leaving San Francisco this evening. . . .

MAMA. I wait two hours here for you to come in. Please, if I may talk to you for one, two minutes. That is all.

F. D. MOORHEAD. *(Kindly.)* Of course, but I think I'd better tell you that if you want me to read your daughter's stories, it's no use. I'm very sorry, but I've had to make a rule never to read anyone's unpublished material.

MAMA. *(Nods—then after a pause.)* It said in the paper you like to collect recipes . . . for eating.

F. D. MOORHEAD. Yes, I do. I've written several books on cooking.

MAMA. I, too, am interested in gastronomy. I am good cook. Norwegian. I make good Norwegian dishes. Lutefisk. And Kjötboller. That is meat balls with cream sauce.

F. D. MOORHEAD. Yes, I know. I've eaten them in Christiania.

MAMA. I have a special recipe for Kjötboller . . . my mother give me. She was the best cook I ever knew. Never have I told this recipe, not even to my sisters, because they are not good cooks.

F. D. MOORHEAD. *(Amused.)* Oh?

MAMA. But . . . if you let me talk to you . . . I give it to you. I promise it is good recipe.

F. D. MOORHEAD. *(Vastly tickled now.)* Well, that seems fair enough. Let's sit down. *(They move to the couch and sit.)* Now, your daughter wants to write, you say? How old is she?

MAMA. She is eighteen. Just.

F. D. MOORHEAD. *Does* she write, or does she just . . . *want* to write?

MAMA. Oh, she write all the time. Maybe she should not be author, but it is hard to give up something that has meant so much.

F. D. MOORHEAD. I agree, but . . .

MAMA. I bring her stories. I bring twelve.

F. D. MOORHEAD. *(Aghast.)* Twelve!

MAMA. But if you could read maybe just one . . . To know if someone is good cook, you do not need to eat a whole dinner.

F. D. MOORHEAD. You're very persuasive. How is it your daughter did not come herself?

MAMA. She was too unhappy. And too scared . . . of you. Because you are celebrity. But I see your picture in the paper. . . .

F. D. MOORHEAD. That frightful picture!

MAMA. Is the picture of woman who like to eat good. . . .

F. D. MOORHEAD. *(With a rueful smile.)* It certainly is. Now, tell me about the Kjötboller.

MAMA. When you make the meat balls you drop them in boiling stock. Not water. That is one of the secrets.

F. D. MOORHEAD. Ah!

MAMA. And the cream sauce. That is another secret. It is half *sour* cream, added at the last.

F. D. MOORHEAD. That sounds marvelous.

MAMA. You must grind the meat six times. I could write it out for you. And . . . *(Tentatively.)* while I write, you could read?

F. D. MOORHEAD. *(With a laugh.)* All right. You win. Come upstairs to my apartment. *(She rises.)*

MAMA. Is kind of you. *(They start out.)* Maybe if you would read *two* stories, I could write the recipe for Lutefisk as well. You know Lutefisk . . . ?

(They have disappeared into the wings, and the turntable revolves out. KATRIN *is at her desk.)*

KATRIN. When Mama came back, I was sitting with my diary, which I called my Journal now, writing a Tragic Farewell to my Art. It was very seldom that Mama came to the attic, thinking that a writer needed privacy, and I was surprised to see her standing in the doorway. *(She looks up.* MAMA *is standing on the steps.)* Mama!

MAMA. You are busy, Katrin?

KATRIN. (*Jumping up.*) No, of course not. Come in.

MAMA. (*Coming down.*) I like to talk to you.

KATRIN. Yes, of course.

MAMA. (*Seating herself at the desk.*) You are writing?

KATRIN. (*On the steps.*) No. I told you, that's all over.

MAMA. That is what I want to talk to you about.

KATRIN. It's all right, Mama. Really, it's all right. I was planning to tear up all my stories this afternoon, only I couldn't find half of them.

MAMA. They are here.

KATRIN. Did *you* take them? What for?

MAMA. Katrin, I have been to see Miss Moorhead.

KATRIN. Who's Miss . . . ? You don't mean Florence Dana Moorhead? (MAMA *nods.*) You don't mean . . . (*She comes down to her.*) Mama, you don't mean you took her my stories?

MAMA. She read five of them. I was two hours with her. We have glass of sherry. Two glass of sherry.

KATRIN. What . . . did she say about them?

MAMA. (*Quietly.*) She say they are not good.

KATRIN. (*Turning away.*) Well, I knew that. It was hardly worth your going to all that trouble just to be told that.

MAMA. She say more. Will you listen, Katrin?

KATRIN. (*Trying to be gracious.*) Sure. Sure. I'll listen.

MAMA. I will try and remember. She say you write now only because of what you have read in other books, and that no one can write good until they have felt what they write about. That for years she write bad stories about people in the olden times, until one day she remember something that happen in her own town . . . something that only she could know and understand . . . and she feels she must tell it . . . and that is how she write her first good story. She say you must write more of things you know. . . .

KATRIN. That's what my teacher always told me at school.

MAMA. Maybe your teacher was right. I do not know if I explain good what Miss Moorhead means, but while she talks I think I understand. Your story about the painter who is blind . . . that is because . . . forgive me if I speak plain, my Katrin, but it is important to you . . . because you are the dramatic one, as Papa has said . . . and you think it would feel good to be a painter and be blind and not complain. But never have you imagined how it would really be. Is true?

KATRIN. (*Subdued.*) Yes, I . . . guess it's true.

MAMA. But she says you are to go on writing. That you have the gift. (KATRIN *turns back to her, suddenly aglow.*) And that when you have written story that is real and true . . . then you send it to someone whose name she give me. (*She fumbles for a piece of paper.*) It is her . . . agent . . . and say she recommend you. Here. No, that is recipe she give me for goulash as her grandmother make it . . . here . . . (*She hands over the paper.*) It helps, Katrin, what I have told you?

KATRIN. (*Subdued again.*) Yes, I . . . I guess it helps. Some. But what have *I* got to write about? I haven't seen anything, or been anywhere.

MAMA. Could you write about San Francisco, maybe? Is fine city. Miss Moorhead write about her home town.

KATRIN. Yes, I know. But you've got to have a central character or something. She writes about her grandfather . . . he was a wonderful old man.

MAMA. Could you maybe write about Papa?

KATRIN. Papa?

MAMA. Papa is fine man. Is wonderful man.

KATRIN. Yes, I know, but . . .

MAMA. (*Rising.*) I must go fix supper. Is late. Papa will be home. (*She goes up the steps to the curtains, and then turns back.*) I like you should write about Papa. (*She goes inside.*)

KATRIN. (*Going back to her seat behind the desk.*) Papa. Yes, but what's he ever done? What's ever happened to him? What's ever happened to *any* of us? Except always being poor and having illness, like the time when Dagmar went to hospital and Mama . . . (*The idea hits her like a flash.*) Oh . . . Oh . . . (*Pause—then she becomes the* KATRIN *of today.*) And that was how it was born . . . suddenly in a flash . . . the story of "Mama and the Hospital" . . . the first of all the stories. I wrote it . . . oh, quite soon after that. I didn't tell Mama or any of them. But I sent it to Miss Moorhead's agent. It was a long time before I heard anything . . . and then one evening the letter came. (*She takes an envelope from the desk in front of her.*) For a moment I couldn't believe it. Then I went rushing into the kitchen, shouting. . . . (*She rises from the desk, taking some papers with her, and rushes upstairs, crying, "Mama, Mama." The curtains have parted on the kitchen—and the family tableau—* MAMA, PAPA, CHRISTINE, *and* NELS. DAGMAR *is not present.* KATRIN *comes rushing in, up the steps. The turntable revolves out as soon as she has left it.*) Mama . . . Mama . . . I've sold a story!

MAMA. (*At table.*) A story?

KATRIN. Yes, I got a letter from the agent . . . with a check for . . . (*gasping*) five hundred dollars!

NELS. (*On the chest.*) No kidding? (*He rises.*)

MAMA. Katrin . . . is true?

KATRIN. Here it is. Here's the letter. Maybe I haven't read it right. (*She hands the letter.* PAPA *and* MAMA *huddle and gloat over it.*)

CHRISTINE. (*Behind* MAMA's *chair.*) What will you *do* with five hundred dollars?

KATRIN. I don't know. I'll buy Mama her warm coat, I know that.

CHRISTINE. Coats don't cost five hundred dollars.

KATRIN. I know. We'll put the rest in the Bank.

NELS. (*Kidding.*) Quick. Before they change their mind, and stop the check.

KATRIN. Will you, Mama? Will you take it to the Bank downtown tomorrow? (MAMA *looks vague.*) What is it?

MAMA. I do not know how.

NELS. Just give it to the man and tell him to put it in your account, like you always do.

(MAMA *looks up at* PAPA.)

PAPA. You tell them . . . now.

CHRISTINE. Tell us what?

MAMA. (*Desperately.*) Is no bank account! (*She rises, feeling hemmed in by them—sits on bench.*) Never in my life have I been inside a bank.

CHRISTINE. But you always told us . . .

KATRIN. Mama, you've always said . . .

MAMA. I know. But it was not true. I tell a lie.

KATRIN. But why, Mama? Why did you pretend?

MAMA. Is not good for little ones to be afraid . . . to not feel secure. (*Rising again.*) But now . . . with five hundred dollar . . . I think I can tell.

KATRIN. (*Going to her, emotionally.*) Mama!

MAMA. (*Stopping her, quickly.*) You read us the story. You have it there?

KATRIN. Yes.

MAMA. Then read.

KATRIN. Now?

MAMA. Yes. No—wait. Dagmar must hear. (*She opens pantry door and calls.*) Dagmar.

DAGMAR. (*Off.*) Yes, Mama?

MAMA. (*Calling.*) Come here, I want you.

DAGMAR. (*Off.*) What is it?

MAMA. I want you. No, you leave the rabbits! (*She comes back.*) What is it called . . . the story?

KATRIN. (*Seating herself in the chair that* MR. HYDE *took in the opening scene.*) It's called "Mama and the Hospital."

PAPA. (*Delighted.*) You write about Mama?

KATRIN. Yes.

MAMA. But I thought . . . I thought you

say . . . I tell you . . . (*She gestures at* PAPA, *behind his back.*)

KATRIN. I know, Mama, but . . . well, that's how it came out.

(DAGMAR *comes in.*)

DAGMAR. What is it? What do you want?

MAMA. Katrin write story for magazine. They pay her five hundred dollar to print it.

DAGMAR. (*Completely uninterested.*) Oh. (*She starts back for the pantry.*)

MAMA. (*Stopping her.*) She read it to us. I want you should listen. (DAGMAR *sits on the floor at* MAMA'*s feet.*) You are ready, Katrin?

KATRIN. Sure.

MAMA. Then read.

(*The group around the table is now a duplicate of the grouping around* MR. HYDE *in the first scene, with* KATRIN *in his place.* CHRISTINE *is in* TRINA'*s chair.*)

KATRIN. (*Reading.*) "For as long as I could remember, the house on Steiner Street had been home. All of us were born there. Nels, the oldest and the only boy . . ." (NELS *looks up, astonished to be in the story*) "my sister, Christine . . ." (CHRISTINE *does likewise*) "and the littlest sister, Dagmar. . . ."

DAGMAR. Am I in the story?

MAMA. Hush, Dagmar. We are all in the story.

KATRIN. "But first and foremost, I remember Mama." (*The lights begin to dim and the curtain slowly to fall. As it descends, we hear her voice continuing.*) "I remember that every Saturday night Mama would sit down by the kitchen table and count out the money Papa had brought home in the little envelope. . . ."

(*By now, the curtain is down.*)

Topics for Further Study

1. Which episode do you find most revealing of the character of Mama? Of Old Chris? Of Katrin?
2. Aside from Mama, who, in your opinion, is the most interesting character? Why?
3. Which of the family's traits do you think are peculiar to the Norwegian-American family? Which of the family's traits are universal, characteristic of all families?
4. Do you approve of Mama's way of getting to see Dagmar in the hospital?
5. Is Chris's death scene sad or amusing?
6. What do the subplots (Trina's marriage and Uncle Chris's story) contribute to the main plot?
7. How does Katrin reveal her literary gifts?
8. Is the flashback method in this play helpful and effective?
9. If there is a central theme in this play, what do you believe it to be?
10. Consult *The New York Critics Reviews* for 1944 to discover what the critics thought of the original production and discuss your findings with the class.
11. Read *Mama's Bank Account* and compare it with *I Remember Mama* with respect to:
    (a) emotional effect upon you
    (b) interest sustained
    (c) vividness of portrayals
    (d) beauty of language
    Present your comparison orally or in a written report.
12. Discuss in an essay of about 250 words one of the following:
    (a) Mothers were stronger in those days.
    (b) Those who read together stay together.
    (c) No education is worthwhile unless one works hard.
    (d) The love of parents for each other is reflected in the children.

The Italians in the United States

Italians discovered America twice, first at the end of the fifteenth century and again at the end of the nineteenth. For four hundred years after Columbus only a trickle of immigrants came here from Italy. Not until 1881 did the mass migration begin.

Between 1881 and 1911 eleven million people, a quarter of the Italian population, emigrated. Many went to South America, Africa, Britain, Canada, and Australia. Four million went to the United States. "The land literally hemorrhaged peasants," comments a modern historian.

Most of the immigrants were from southern Italy, one of the poorest regions of Europe. Eighty per cent of them were males between eighteen and forty-five, and nearly all were unskilled laborers. Their number swelled rapidly from 12,254 in 1881 to 285,731 in 1907. By 1921 they were the second most numerous foreign group, outnumbered only by the German-Americans.

What impelled them to emigrate? There was no work for them at home and America's expanding industrial system had an urgent need for workers. The cost of passage was cheap, thirty dollars. Steamship agents fanned throughout the land recruiting passengers with tales of high salaries to be earned in America. Friends and relatives sent back glowing accounts of the riches to be had for the asking and many of their letters contained passage money.

Italian middlemen, called *padroni* or bosses, met the immigrants when they arrived and took them to cheap rooming houses where they slept as many as fifteen in a room. They worked for the *padroni* as rag pickers and in such pick-and-shovel occupations as sewer-diggers and subway-diggers. In return for sheltering them and providing employment, the *padroni* took a share of their wages. The typical daily wage of a digger was one dollar, of which the *padroni* took sixty cents. Since the laborers were illiterate or only semiliterate and could not speak English, and since most of them had never lived in a city and were unfamiliar with American ways, they were almost helpless in the hands of their exploiters. Usually a couple of years passed before they acquired enough confidence to break away from the *padroni*.

The Italians of New York City congregated in the Lower East Side of Manhattan, an area which soon became known as Little Italy, where the population density was 290,000 persons per square mile. They lived in dark and run-down tenements, sometimes as many as ten in a small room, with few beds and chairs and no partitions. A third of all the babies born died within the first year of life. Conditions in the slums of Philadelphia, Boston, and Chicago were similar.

They clung to one another because of their ignorance of English and the prejudice they encountered from native Americans who looked on them as inferior and contemptuously referred to them as Dagoes, Wops, and Guineas. Americans also regarded them as criminals, although statistics show that they were no more criminal than any other immigrant group.

Actually most were law-abiding and ambitious, fighting to work their way out of poverty. Although they were extremely poor, they rarely sought relief from public agencies. Indeed, out of their meager earnings they managed to remit money to their poverty-stricken relatives in the old country. It is estimated that by World War I they had sent back nearly $750 million.

Their children went to school and attended regularly. Soon these same children, because of their superior education, began to look down on their parents and their Italian background. They knew little about Italy; they were concerned only with life in the United States and becoming assimilated into the stream of American culture. Some second generation Italians abandoned their Italian names because they were ashamed of their cultural background or because they wished to avoid discrimination. The gap between the two generations began to widen.

But the gap was only temporary. The pendulum soon began to swing the other way. Third and fourth generation Italians began to feel more certain of their status and to take more pride in Italian traditions and culture. Thousands began to study Italian in schools and colleges. Organizations dedicated to preserving the Italian-American heritage sprang up. Today the descendants of Italian immigrants are completely Americanized, but at the same time they proudly assert their ethnicity. They take pride in the accomplishments of their forebears and are renewing Italian customs.

Family attachment is traditionally strong among Italian-Americans. The family, here as in Italy, is a closely-knit unit whose members are bound together by filial affection and respect. Parents, sons, daughters, and other relatives are supportive of one another in adversity and happy at one another's successes. The family's strength lies in its inner cohesion. Every member is expected to do what is right, not only for himself but for the family as a whole.

Italian-Americans are bound together by religious ties, perhaps not so much by theological beliefs as by a common religious tradition and by love for their fellow man. Their appreciation of music and art, their joy in singing and dancing, and the pleasure they take in flowers and gardening are too well known to need mention. These esthetic delights are rooted in their culture.

Italian-born Americans and their descendants have achieved prominence in many fields. Enrico Fermi, who won the Nobel Prize for physics in 1938, fled to this country from Mussolini's Fascist regime and led the team of scientists which produced the world's first sustaining nuclear reaction on December 2, 1942, the achievement which opened up the atomic age. In 1904 Amadeo Giannini, an immigrant, founded the Bank of Italy, which later became the Bank of America, one of the largest banking institutions in the world. Ralph D. DeNunzio became president of the New York Stock Exchange at 39. In 1970 Lee Iacocca became president of Ford Motors at 46. John J. Riccardo, the son of an Italian immigrant, is president of Chrysler.

In government there have been many prominent Americans of Italian descent: for example, John A. Volpe, former governor of Massachusetts and a presidential cabinet member; Senator John O. Pastore of Rhode Island; and Fiorello H. LaGuardia, mayor of New York City in the 1930s.

Singers Vic Damone and Frank Sinatra, baseball players Joe DiMaggio and Phil Rizzuto, publisher Generoso Pope, and distinguished scholars Gaetano Salvemini, professor of history at Harvard University, and Antonio Borgese, professor of Romance languages at the University of Chicago, have achieved eminence in their respective fields.

Americans listen to Italian music, view Italian films, drive Italian cars, wear Italian clothes, drink Italian wines, and eat Italian food. Pizza pie is almost as American as the hot dog, and spaghetti, lasagna, and ravioli are completely Americanized. Truly, Italian culture has enriched America in many large and small ways.

Suggested Reading

Books about the Italians

Amfitheatrof, Eric. *The Children of Columbus.* Boston: Little, Brown, 1973. An absorbing account of the proud and sometimes tragic history of the Italian-Americans, beginning with the first explorers and continuing to the present day. The author describes how the Italian-Americans differ from other ethnic groups and among themselves. "It is a book about people both humble and famous, whose accomplishments form a central chapter in the history of our nation."

DeConde, Alexander. *Half-Bitter, Half-Sweet.* New York: Scribners, 1971. Professor DeConde objectively deals with Italian-American political, social, and cultural relations from the seventeenth century to the present, and discusses the Italian contribution to American life.

Kennedy, John F. *A Nation of Immigrants.* New York: Popular Library, 1964. President Kennedy tells in concise fashion the struggles of successive waves of immigrants against great odds and argues for a revision of our immigration laws. He writes as he spoke—with eloquence and conviction.

Plays about the Italians

Chayevsky, Paddy. *Marty.* New York: McGraw-Hill, 1968.
Miller, Arthur. *A View from the Bridge.* New York: Viking, 1957.
Odets, Clifford. *Golden Boy.* New York: Atheneum Press, 1965.

Dino

D*ino* was first presented as a TV play on the CBS network on January 2, 1956, and was so successful that it was adapted into a three-act stage play and, later, into a motion picture with Sal Mineo in the title role.

At the outset Dino, the chief character, resents almost everybody, except his younger brother. He is antagonistic toward his parole officer, his psychotherapist, his peers, and his parents, particularly his father. "The story," said one critic, "is handled with simplicity and sincerity." Another remarked that "*Dino* is as succinct, simple, and fragmentary as its title." A third pointed out that it squarely examines the anguish of loneliness. The play is a tense psychological drama, depending not so much on plot, but rather on the intense, often emotion-packed exchanges between the characters. Particularly fascinating are the psychotherapist's analytical interviews with Dino. As the play ends Dino is on his way to resolving his problems. He has searched for and found a solution.

Dino is an ethnic play dealing with the problems of an Italian family in a big city, but neither Dino nor his parents are typical Italian-Americans. Since Mr. and Mrs. Falcaro do not speak with an Italian accent, it may be assumed that they were born in this country, the descendants of Italian immigrants, and that Dino, their son, is a third generation Italian-American. The play does not deal with the problems of Italian immigrants but with the problems of succeeding generations of Italians who are so caught up with the struggle for existence that they have lost sight of their obligations to one another. The Falcaros seem to have lost touch with the traditions and values of their Italian culture. Their family life is not cohesive; the influences that unite many Italian families are missing. They do not plan or do things together, and they seem lost and lonely in a metropolis. Reginald Rose confronts these problems honestly in his highly sympathetic treatment of the family.

REGINALD ROSE was born in New York City in 1920 and educated at the College of the City of New York. After serving in the army, he turned to television writing and soon earned national recognition for his work. He wrote the TV series *The Defenders*, which was one of the most popular dramatic series on the air. Among other TV plays which won him critical acclaim were *Twelve Angry Men*, *Black Monday*, and *Thunder on Sycamore Street*. Several of his TV scripts have been made into films. Relatively few playwrights have won an Emmy award for distinguished television achievement. Reginald Rose has won three!

Dino

BY

REGINALD ROSE

CHARACTERS

DINO FALCARO	TONY FALCARO
MR. MANDEL	DANNY
MR. SHERIDAN	STEVE
MR. FIELDS	GIRL
SHIRLEY WALLACE	BOY'S VOICE
MR. FALCARO	EXTRAS
MRS. FALCARO	

TIME   The present

PLACE   A New York City Settlement House

SCENES

1 Settlement House Lobby
2 Small Office
3 Small Section of Street
4 Dino's Living Room
  Dino's Bedroom
  Dino's Hall
5 Gymnasium

Dino by Reginald Rose. Copyright 1956 by Reginald Rose. Reprinted by permission of International Famous Agency.

CAUTION: Amateur performing rights are controlled by the Dramatist Publishing Company, 86 East Randolph Street, Chicago, Illinois 60601. Inquiries on all other rights should be referred to the author's agent, Bridget Aschenberg, International Famous Agency, 1301 Avenue of the Americas, New York, N.Y. 10019.

Dino

ACT ONE

The scene is the cluttered lobby of the James Street Settlement House. It is 4:30 P.M. of a winter day. Jammed into the lobby are some wooden benches, a large bulletin board, a drinking fountain, a battered trophy case, a bronze wall plaque, a floor directory. On one side, we see old-fashioned frosted glass doors leading to the street. On them is lettered James Street Community House. *Near the entrance is a narrow staircase. This lobby has the look of two brownstones, knocked together. It needs a painting badly. It is dingy-looking, although brightly lighted. It is much too small to serve as a lobby, and yet it also serves as a filing room. Along one wall are a number of files. Standing at the files, patiently filing papers, is* SHIRLEY WALLACE, *a very plain, short, bespectacled, extremely shy sixteen-year-old girl.* SHIRLEY *can always be found after school hours, working at the files in the lobby, watching silently the busy comings and goings of everyone. No one speaks to her much, nor she to anyone. Among the teenagers she is something of a joke. The lobby is busy. People of all ages move through it. Two elderly people enter from the street, smiling, and nod to a middle-aged man on his way out. A group of ten-year-old boys comes tearing down the stairs and around through the lobby, clutching towels, running like mad, screeching. One boy flings his towel at another as* MR. FIELDS *crosses through the lobby.* MR. FIELDS, *director of the settlement house, is a shaggy, benevolent man in his early fifties. He stops.*

MR. FIELDS. (*Not too severely.*) Let's hold down the noise here.
(*A young man in a sweat shirt and exercise pants comes down the stairs and after the boys. He carries a basketball.* MR. FIELDS *looks at him as he crosses the lobby. The boys scamper off, somewhat subdued. We hear a shrill screech off.*)
BOY'S VOICE. Hey, cut it out, stinkhead!
(*There is a loud laugh, and the young man plunges after the boys.* MR. FIELDS *watches him, smiles. The camera pans with him, then stops at the water fountain as he continues off, after nodding to a group of teenagers standing near the fountain. The camera holds them for a moment: three boys and a girl, all laughing* uproariously *at some joke. Two of the boys wear jackets lettered "Golden Arrows." The girl wears a sweater and jeans. These are tough-looking youngsters of sixteen or seventeen. One of them,* DANNY, *smacks another one on the back.*)
DANNY. Man, I flipped! I'm tellin' ya.
(STEVE, *the boy who was smacked, laughs again.*)
STEVE. My old lady did that once. She walked right into the class and asked Mr. MacNamara how come I flunked shop. Mr. MacNamara! I thought he was gonna saw her in half!
(*They laugh again, and the camera pans from them across the lobby as people of all ages, on all kinds of projects, pass through. These include*

138

a boy with a checkerboard, two young women carrying a sewing machine, a man carrying a stack of books. The place is noisy, bustling with activity as always. The camera holds the entrance now. The door opens, and two teenage girls enter and cross the lobby. The door opens again, and a man and a boy enter. The man, in his late thirties, is plainly dressed, rugged looking, and, we will learn, a tough guy with rare understanding of juvenile problems. His name is MR. MANDEL. *The boy is* DINO FALCARO. *He is perhaps seventeen, dark, slender, fairly good looking. But he is an intensely hostile boy, who alternates between unpredictable violence and extreme withdrawal. His is a brooding face, mirroring an inner agony which is almost frightful to behold. He never smiles, never laughs, has never learned how to give of himself. His fight is a fight to the death against the world, yet his fear is that he may win it. Handling* DINO, *we will learn, is like holding a handful of acid. As* DINO *and* MR. MANDEL *cross toward a bench in the lobby, we hear one of the two girls, who entered just ahead of them, speak.)*

GIRL. (*Off.*) I'm gonna try that arts and crafts class today. This girl Mary Waddyecallit, y'know her? Well, she made this gorgeous bracelet in about two hours. It's silver or something. I'm telling you it's really gorgeous.
(*Her voice trails off.* DINO *and* MR. MANDEL *reach the bench. The camera dollies with them.*)

MR. MANDEL. Have a seat, Dino.
(DINO *looks at him and then sits down. His face is blank.* MR. MANDEL *watches him for a second, as if to make sure he'll stay there, and then he crosses the lobby. The camera dollies back.* DINO *sits amidst the activity, a dark, lonely, hostile figure, looking blankly at the floor. It is important to note that never is he the arrogant,* tough, out-spoken prototype of the motion picture juvenile delinquent. He is silent, instead, withdrawn almost to the point of danger, and when he does burst into violence, it shows no planned direction. He is almost impossible to reach, because no one in all his life has ever tried.* MR. MANDEL *stops at the water fountain for a drink. The camera now includes the group of teenagers at the water fountain. They are just getting ready to split up.*)

STEVE. Hey, I'm goin' to the gym to shoot baskets.

DANNY. See ya, Daddio.
(STEVE *turns to leave, and then spots* DINO. *He turns back to* DANNY *and taps his arm.*)

STEVE. (*Low.*) Hey.
(DANNY *looks at him. He gestures toward* DINO. DANNY *turns and looks, with awe.*)

DANNY. (*Whispering.*) Willya look at him!
(*All four of them look, silent now. And* MR. MANDEL *observes this whole business.* DINO *looks slowly up at them. They turn quickly away. Anger shows in his face for a moment, and then it goes blank again. He stares ahead as the camera dollies to him for a big close-up, then cuts to the door of an office just off the lobby.* MR. MANDEL *is knocking on it.*)

MR. SHERIDAN. (*From the inside.*) Come in.
(MR. MANDEL *opens the door. We see the interior of a very small office, files, a desk, a bookcase, three or four chairs. This is the office of* MR. SHERIDAN, *one of the case-workers at the settlement house.* MR. SHERIDAN *is seated at the desk. In his middle or late thirties, he is a man of strength and compassion whose whole adult life has been devoted to dealing with disturbed kids and their equally disturbed parents. He has a deep understanding of these kids' problems, and a firm but gentle manner, which has brought him much success in solving them. He is overworked, underpaid, but happy with his accomplishments. Standing at the window, which looks out on the*

street, is MR. FIELDS. *From time to time we see someone pass by in the street.* MR. SHERIDAN *looks at the door as* MR. MANDEL *enters, stands up, and speaks.*) Hello, Frank.

MR. MANDEL. (*Coming over to him, shaking hands; both smiling.*) How goes it?

MR. SHERIDAN. Over my head, as usual. Say, have you met our Director, Mr. Fields? (MR. MANDEL *and* MR. FIELDS *turn to each other.*) This is Mr. Mandel of the Youth Board.

MR. FIELDS. Nice to meet you, Mr. Mandel.

MR. MANDEL. Same here.

(*They shake hands.*)

MR. SHERIDAN. (*Grinning.*) Sit down, Frank. I don't know if I should say it's good to see you, or not. What've you got this time?

MR. MANDEL. Dino Falcaro.

(*He sits down.* MR. SHERIDAN *sits on the edge of his desk.*)

MR. SHERIDAN. Dino Falcaro. That sounds familiar. Who is he?

(MR. FIELDS *looks at his watch.*)

MR. MANDEL. He's a kid from the neighborhood.

MR. FIELDS. (*Interrupting.*) Excuse me a minute. (*To* MR. SHERIDAN.) If you don't need me, Larry . . . (MR. SHERIDAN *shakes his head.*) Good. (*To* MR. MANDEL.) I'm supposed to judge a Hobby show upstairs. Those kids'll destroy me if I'm late. Good seeing you, Mr. Mandel.

MR. MANDEL. Thanks.

(MR. FIELDS *hurries out with a wave at* MR. SHERIDAN. *The door closes.*)

MR. SHERIDAN. That's the busiest man I've ever known in my whole life.

MR. MANDEL. Except you.

MR. SHERIDAN. (*Grinning.*) What about this boy—what's his name?

MR. MANDEL. Dino Falcaro. He lives right over here at 321 Morris Street. Mother, father, both work. One brother age thirteen. Dino's gonna be seventeen next month. (*He lights a cigarette.*) I brought him home from the Parkinson State Reformatory this morning. Four years. (MR. SHERIDAN *shows concern.*) He was sent there when he was twelve and a half for participating in a murder. (MR. SHERIDAN *grimaces. This is obviously painful to him.*)

MR. SHERIDAN. Twelve and a half!

MR. MANDEL. It happens; I don't have to tell you. Three kids broke into a warehouse. The others were fifteen or sixteen years old. An old night watchman surprised them. They beat his head in.

MR. SHERIDAN. (*Stopping him.*) Okay.

MR. MANDEL. Yeah. It's pretty terrible.

MR. SHERIDAN. You his parole officer? (MR. MANDEL *nods.*) What's he like?

MR. MANDEL. I only met him this morning. He's been quiet. But he looks like he's on fire. Y'know what I mean?

MR. SHERIDAN. Parkinson's a pretty lousy place.

MR. MANDEL. He turned around and spit at the gate when we walked out. It's the only emotion he showed. Just turned around and spit.

MR. SHERIDAN. What d'you want me to do, Frank?

MR. MANDEL. See him. He needs help.

MR. SHERIDAN. What kid around here doesn't?

MR. MANDEL. This kid killed somebody.

MR. SHERIDAN. I've got nine hours a day, six days a week. All filled. They want to bring in their mothers and fathers for psychotherapy, too.

MR. MANDEL. See him: he'll do it again.

MR. SHERIDAN. What about the Youth Board?

MR. MANDEL. The case-workers have waiting lists a mile long. It'll be a year. Listen, he lives right in the neighborhood.

MR. SHERIDAN. Frank, I wouldn't kid you; I'm drained. I've got more than I can handle. Starting in a half hour, I've got three borderline schizos in a row. One of them is nine years old.

MR. MANDEL. I picked him up at the school this morning and rode him into the city. I took him to his house. Four years in a reformatory, and when he gets home there's nobody there. Just a note. The mother and father'll be home at 6:30.

They wouldn't even take a day off to meet him.

MR. SHERIDAN. Listen, I can't . . .

MR. MANDEL. (*Interrupting.*) A minute ago I saw some kids, from one of these gangs you've got, coming here staring at him like he was a freak. He didn't know what to do. He's gonna explode. Larry, see him. Please. (MR. SHERIDAN *looks squarely at* MR. MANDEL, *a tough guy pleading with compassion for someone he doesn't even know.* MR. SHERIDAN *shakes his head.*)

MR. SHERIDAN. (*Almost sadly.*) You're trying to kill me.

(MR. MANDEL *looks at him for a minute, smiles, then gets up and goes to the door. He opens it, looks out. The camera holds* MR. SHERIDAN. *He sighs wearily, looks at a pile of papers on his desk, shoves them aside. Then he looks up at the door. The camera cuts to the door as* DINO *enters.* MR. MANDEL *closes the door.* DINO *stands inside, not looking at either of the two men. It is almost as if he is daring them to reach him. His face is blank.*)

MR. MANDEL. Dino, this is Mr. Sheridan.

MR. SHERIDAN. Hello, Dino.

(DINO *turns briefly in his direction, and then away.*)

MR. MANDEL. Mr. Sheridan is a caseworker here. He wants to talk with you to see if he can help you. (DINO *looks at* MR. MANDEL *as if to say,* "That's impossible.") If he wants to make other appointments with you, I'd like you to keep 'em. Right? (DINO *looks around the room.* MR. MANDEL *looks at* MR. SHERIDAN. MR. SHERIDAN *nods at him.*) Okay, Dino, I'll see you in a few days. You're reporting to me once a week; you know that. If you need anything in the meantime, call me. (*He pats* DINO *on the shoulder, then speaks to* MR. SHERIDAN.) So long, Larry.

MR. SHERIDAN. So long. (MR. MANDEL *opens the door, and turns back to* MR. SHERIDAN. *He mouths the word,* "Thanks," *and exits.* DINO *stands awkwardly in the room.* MR. SHERIDAN'S *attitude during this next scene is one of absolute calm, and warmth, no matter how* DINO *behaves. Now* MR. SHERIDAN *looks at him.* DINO *stands just where he was, waiting.*) Would you like to sit down? (*He indicates the chair at the side of his desk.* DINO *looks at it, and then walks over to it and sits down. He faces* MR. SHERIDAN *now.* MR. SHERIDAN *watches him.*) You can take off your jacket if you want. (DINO *doesn't answer, but begins to toy swiftly with a paper weight on the desk.*) I don't blame you. It's kinda cool in here. Our heating plant's not exactly the greatest. (MR. SHERIDAN *looks him over for a moment.*) Have you seen your brother yet?

(DINO *looks at him sharply.*)

DINO. No.

(DINO *looks away again.*)

MR. SHERIDAN. If you don't want me to ask you a lot of questions, I don't have to.

(DINO *doesn't answer.* MR. SHERIDAN *looks him over. A head goes by outside the window.* DINO, *spotting it out of the corner of his eye, leaps suddenly to his feet, races to the window, and lowers the Venetian blind violently. He turns to face* MR. SHERIDAN, *who sits calmly there.*)

DINO. (*Through his teeth.*) You're a psychiatrist, right?

MR. SHERIDAN. (*Calmly.*) It's sort of like that. We call it caseworker. I'm sorry about the blind. I usually have it drawn. I don't like to have people looking in here either.

(DINO *turns away, faces the blind. He stares at it, his back to* MR. SHERIDAN. *There is a pause.*)

DINO. I don't wanna sit near you.

MR. SHERIDAN. That's okay.

(*There is another pause.* DINO *begins tensely to twist the Venetian blind cord in his hands, keeping his back to* MR. SHERIDAN.)

DINO. How long am I supposed to stay here?

MR. SHERIDAN. It doesn't have to be any special time.

DINO. (*To the Venetian blind.*) You wanna know what I'm thinking, right?

MR. SHERIDAN. If you want me to.

DINO. (*Angry.*) What d'ya mean if *I* want! I want nothin'! I wanna outa here. (MR. SHERIDAN *doesn't answer.* DINO *walks away from the window, keeping his back to* MR. SHERIDAN. *He walks to the door. There is a pause.*) Suppose I walk right out this door...!

MR. SHERIDAN. Well, you can come back tomorrow if you like.

DINO. That dirty stinkin' Mr. Mandel...

(*There is a pause.* DINO *keeps his back to* MR. SHERIDAN, *then explodes.*) Well, say something! What d'ya want outa me?

MR. SHERIDAN. Well, I don't want anything out of you, Dino. I want to help you to feel better. That's all.

DINO (*Angry.*) So why dontcha give me a rubdown? (*He waits to see if there is any effect. There is not.*) Feel better!

MR. SHERIDAN. I mean to feel not so angry. Maybe to feel not so (*Carefully.*) mixed up about things...

DINO. (*Sharply.*) What things?

MR. SHERIDAN. Yourself. Who you are.

DINO. (*Wildly.*) Who I am! That's the stuff! I'm telling you, you're just like the psychiatrist at Parkinson. I saw him one time. He's an idiot!

MR. SHERIDAN. (*Calmly.*) Why don't you sit down and be comfortable, Dino?

(DINO *turns around and looks at him for the first time since he got up.*)

DINO. Why dontcha sock me?

MR. SHERIDAN. Well, you haven't done anything to me. Why should I?

(DINO *looks steadily at him. There is a pause.*)

DINO. (*Too loud.*) Well, why dontcha ask me a question?

MR. SHERIDAN. What's your brother's name?

DINO. Tony! Why dontcha ask me if I dream at night? I know you guys!

MR. SHERIDAN. Do you dream at night?

DINO. (*Triumphantly.*) Never in my whole life!

(*Now he can slowly walk over to the chair and sit down.* MR. SHERIDAN *waits patiently.* DINO *begins to toy with the paper weight again.*)

MR. SHERIDAN. I see quite a few boys regularly, Dino. I try to help them learn how to get along better.... A lot of them are very angry with me at first. I can understand that. (DINO *pretends not to be listening. He toys with the paper weight.*) Well, here's what we do; we just sit and talk. Very often, after a while they feel a lot happier. Sometimes it takes a while before they recognize that they really need help. It's not an easy thing. (DINO *still is not listening.*) I think I can help you, Dino. We can meet three or four times a week for a while and see.

(DINO *toys furiously with the weight.*)

DINO. (*Dully.*) What's wrong with me?

MR. SHERIDAN. (*Stopped by this one.*) Well, I don't think that means anything right now. We all have problems. Some of us are just able to handle them better than others. I don't think you...

DINO. (*Interrupting.*) This guy at Parkinson used to wake up every night screaming and yelling from bad dreams! A real psycho! One night they ganged him.

MR. SHERIDAN. (*Pointedly.*) This guy?

DINO. (*Looking at him tensely.*) Some guy.

MR. SHERIDAN. It's not the easiest thing in the world being in a place like that when you're twelve and a half.

DINO. No? It's like every place else.

MR. SHERIDAN. Like home?

DINO. It's all split up into big guys and little guys. The little guys do what the big guys tell 'em or they get their skulls busted. (*A pause.*) Just like home. (MR. SHERIDAN *sits there, watching him quietly. There is a long pause.*) So what d'ya want me to say?

MR. SHERIDAN. Anything you like.

DINO. I don't wanna say nothin'. (*They sit silently for a while. Suddenly* DINO *shouts.*) You wanna fiddle with me, why dontcha give me an operation or something? Stop lookin' at me! (MR. SHERIDAN *sits calmly there.* DINO *looks at him. Then suddenly he gets up and flings the paper weight at the window. It strikes the Venetian blind with a crash.* MR.

SHERIDAN *sits calmly there.* DINO *watches him.*) I'm not stayin' in here. You can't make me. (*He heads swiftly for the door. At the door, he stops.*) And if those kids out there stare at me, I'm gonna wipe up the lobby with 'em.

(*He flings the door open.*)

MR. SHERIDAN, (*Calmly.*) I'll see you at four fifteen tomorrow afternoon, Dino.

(DINO *exits and slams the door.* MR. SHERIDAN *looks calmly after him. Then he turns to the papers on his desk. The camera cuts to the lobby.* DINO *walks fast, ploughing through the same ten-year-old boys who had run through the lobby throwing towels. They are crossing the lobby on their way back from gym. He scatters them aside. Several of them shout "Hey you!" at him.* SHIRLEY WALLACE, *at the files, pauses in her work and looks at him, and wonders about him. He exits. The camera cuts to the steps outside.* DINO *walks down and stands at the foot of the steps. It is dark out. The camera moves in close, on his face, which is smoldering with rage and frustration. In the background, we hear a sudden burst of laughter. He shuts his eyes, and then turns and walks swiftly out. Behind him, where his head had been on camera, is the window of* MR. SHERIDAN'S *office.* MR. SHERIDAN *stands at it, watching him. Fade out.*)

Fade to the outside of the door to DINO's apartment. This is in a rickety tenement hallway, dark, mean, cramped. We hear the sound of running water from inside, and the clanking of pots and pans. We hear DINO's footsteps coming up the stairs. From inside, we hear the rather shrill voice of MRS. FALCARO. There is no Italian accent, but rather a tough Brooklynese inflection to her voice.

MRS. FALCARO. Shut off the water!

(*There is a pause, during which time* DINO *walks in and stands in front of the door.*)

TONY. (*Angry.*) What are you yelling all the time!

MRS. FALCARO. Don't you talk back . . . (*She cuts off her sentence, as* DINO *knocks.*) Who is it?

(DINO *turns the knob and opens the door. We see* DINO *big, in the foreground, and in the room, turned to look at him, are* TONY *and* MRS. FALCARO, *standing in the middle of the floor; and* MR. FALCARO, *seated in an armchair.* MRS. FALCARO *is in her mid-forties.* MR. FALCARO, *who speaks with a slight Italian accent, is a bit older. Both are factory laborers, both unattractive, poorly dressed. Both live only to struggle forever against unbeatable odds. Their lack of parental ability is reflected in the asocial drives of their children, drives which they are totally unequipped to direct properly. With* DINO, *their attitudes are nearly similar. They were secretly relieved that he had spent four years in reform school, that they had not had to cope with him, that his fate was out of their hands. Yet with this relief there was guilt for their rejecting attitudes. And their guilt will now make them even more rejecting of* DINO. *All they really want is to have this young tiger off their hands, where they can forget about his ability to remind them of their total inadequacy. They all stare at him now, as he stands in the doorway.* TONY, *aged thirteen, and trying to be a miniature* DINO, *speaks first.*)

TONY. Dino. Hey, Dino!

(DINO *enters the room, trying to control himself, trying to behave. He feels a stranger. He looks around the room. What he sees is not pleasant: a small drab, poorly furnished room, a window looking onto a court. Off to the right we can see part of a kitchen. A long dark hall leads off left.*)

DINO. (*Low.*) Hey, Tony. (TONY *smiles*

shyly. DINO *walks over to his mother. His father stands up.*) Hello, Mom.

MRS. FALCARO. Hello, Dino. (*There is a pause.*) Say "Hello" to your father!

(DINO *turns to* MR. FALCARO.)

DINO. Hello, Pop.

MR. FALCARO. (*Slowly.*) Hello, Dino. How are you?

DINO. Okay.

(*They stand there awkwardly.*)

MRS. FALCARO. How do you feel?

DINO. Okay.

MRS. FALCARO. Did you get my note? (*He nods.*) I couldn't take time off from work. There's a real rush on. Spring stuff! Your father has a lot of work, too.

(*The camera cuts to close-up of* DINO. *His face is blank.*)

DINO. Okay. (*Camera cuts to longer shot of the family group.* DINO *looks at* TONY. TONY *smiles tentatively. There is a pause.*) Tony got big.

MRS. FALCARO. (*Nodding.*) I'm glad you're home, Dino. (*But she says it without conviction.*) I guess you're too big to kiss.

(DINO'S *expression doesn't change. He would like to be kissed. There is a pause.*)

DINO. (*Looking around.*) Everything looks the same.

MR. FALCARO. That's right.

(*They all stand there, awkwardly.* MRS. FALCARO *fusses with her apron. There is a bubbling noise from the kitchen. Gratefully, she turns in that direction.*)

MRS. FALCARO. I gotta fix supper.

(*She flees into the kitchen.* MR. FALCARO *stands there. He and* DINO *look at each other.*)

MR. FALCARO. Your mama and me...We hope you're gonna behave now. (DINO'S *face tenses.* MR. FALCARO *turns to the kitchen. Then he stops.*) We didn't see you in a long time. It was hard to get up there all the time.

DINO. I know.

MR. FALCARO. I got a bad leg.

(*He looks at* DINO *for a minute, and then goes uneasily into the kitchen.*

DINO *and* TONY *are in the room alone. They stand facing each other, awkward, uncertain.*)

TONY. (*Whispering.*) Hey, Dino.

DINO. Hey, Tony.

(*And suddenly they are in each other's arms, hugging each other tight, and we know that the only defenses they have against life and their parents are each other. They step back, all awkwardness gone.*)

TONY. Wow, Dino, I'm pretty glad.

DINO. Yeah. Hey, what're you, thirteen?

TONY. Goin' on fourteen.

DINO. Boy!

TONY. Hey, come on in here. (*He turns down the hall,* DINO *following, and enters a tiny bedroom, sparsely furnished, drab-looking. He pulls the light cord. A ceiling light goes on. He turns to* DINO.) Your old room, Dino. (DINO *looks around.* TONY *sits down on the bed.* DINO *goes to the dresser, looks in the mirror. He feels the dresser with his hands.*) I'm sleepin' here. You want it?

(DINO *looks at him in the mirror.*)

DINO. Nah, I'll sleep in the living room.

TONY. You could have it.

DINO. Nah. Thanks.

(*There is a pause.*)

TONY. So what did you do all the time?

DINO. (*Shrugging.*) You know. Nothin'! A lotta standin' in line, work in the kitchen. Stuff like that.

(*He walks over and sits on the bed.* TONY *slaps his knee.*)

TONY. I missed you. I'm tellin' you. What a time...

DINO. (*Nodding.*) So what's goin' on?

TONY. Oh, a lot of stuff.

DINO. What about the old man?

TONY. The same. Yellin' all the time. Mad. I never see him, hardly.

DINO. What d'ya do?

TONY. (*Shrugging.*) Just hang around. Sometimes I go to school. (*Proudly.*) Listen, Dino, we got a gang. The Silk Hats. Real great guys, I'm tellin' you. Like, we had a rumble with the Little Counts, y'know from Pearl Street. (*He pauses dramatically.*) We wiped 'em up.

DINO. (*Almost grinning.*) No kiddin'.

TONY. Right on their turf! (*Laughing.*) Wow, what a ball! I'm the youngest in the gang. Most of 'em're sixteen. (DINO *socks* TONY *affectionately on the arm.* TONY *appraises* DINO *for a moment.*) All the guys are talkin' about you, Dino. They want to meet you, y'know?

DINO. Come on . . .

TONY. Honest. They heard all about you and everything. (*Another dramatic pause.*) They want you to join. You could be the leader. (DINO *looks at* TONY *hard.*) They asked me to ask you. I mean it! Because you're more experienced. (*He jumps up and goes to his closet, opens it and takes out a gang jacket. On the back of it is lettered* SILK HATS, *and there is a picture of a silk hat sewn near the lettering.*) We got jackets and everything, Dino. How do you like it?

DINO. It looks nice.

TONY. (*Proud.*) We're one of the only gangs around here that didn't join the settlement house. Most of 'em did. What a chicken deal! Ping-pong tournaments!

DINO. You got real big, Tony.

TONY. Yeah. Dino, we even got a job planned. The night after tomorrow night. We're gonna knock off this gas station on Darrow Street. We're all gonna wear crazy masks. We cased it and everything. It's the easiest, Dino. One of our guys has a heat. He made it himself! It shoots great. Dino, you could lead the whole thing. I'm supposed to tell 'em okay tomorrow night. (*A pause.*) Well, what d'ya say? (DINO *doesn't answer.*) They really want you.

MRS. FALCARO. (*Calling, off.*) Supper's on the table in here.

TONY. (*Low.*) You're very big with them.

MRS. FALCARO. (*Yelling.*) Tony!

TONY. (*Yelling.*) All right! (*He looks wisely at* DINO.) The Silk Hats!

(*Then he exits, leaving* DINO *to think about it.* DINO *sits there blankly. Fade out.*)

ACT TWO

The scene is again the lobby of the settlement house. It is about 4:10 P.M. the following afternoon. Again there is much activity in the lobby. Ignoring it all, sitting frozen-faced on the bench, is DINO. *He doesn't move, barely blinks, as people of all ages mill by him: the same people as in the opening of the first act, but engaged on different projects. The younger kids come in singly, instead of in a group. Someone walks through with a ladder. A boy walks through, batting a ping-pong ball in the air. A group of teenage girls stands chatting in the center of the lobby. An elderly man sweeps up.* SHIRLEY WALLACE *enters from an office, carrying a filing basket loaded with papers. She passes* DINO, *and some of the papers slide off the top, falling in his lap. He jumps.*

SHIRLEY. Sorry. (*The papers slide to the floor.* DINO *sits there.* SHIRLEY *bends down and begins picking them up, right at his feet.*) That was very clumsy of me. (*He pretends not to notice her. She looks up into his face sympathetically, feeling somehow his misery, yet too shy to say anything to him. As she squats there, a teenage girl from the group, chatting in the center of the lobby, calls out to her.*)

GIRL. Hey, Shoil, you're a poil!

(SHIRLEY *looks up, smiling, happy to have been addressed.*)

SHIRLEY. (*Hopefully.*) Hi!

(*The girl, who spoke to her, giggles. The others join, and then all start ad libbing with each other, ignoring* SHIRLEY. *Her smile fades, and she continues to pick up papers. She finishes, and walks over to the files.* DINO *sits there, motionless. The camera cuts to the entrance. The door opens and the three teenage boys, who appeared in the first act, enter now.* DANNY *is in the lead, softly singing a rock and roll number.* STEVE *and the other boy grin.*)

DANNY. (*Singing.*)
One o'clock, two o'clock, three o'clock, rock!
Four o'clock, five o'clock, six o'clock, rock!
Seven o'clock, eight o'clock, nine o'clock, hey ...
(*And as the three of them pass* DINO, DANNY *continues in the same rhythm.*)
Dig the crazy killer, men, twelve o'clock, rock!
(DINO *tenses as they walk by, his face alive with rage. None of them looks at him.* DANNY *continues, singing softly.*)
We're gonna rock around the clock tonight.

STEVE. (*Simultaneously to the third boy.*) He's waitin' for the skull doctor.
(DINO *springs at them, wild, animal-like, piles into them, throwing punches in all directions. They shout in amazement. The four of them are a flailing mass in a split second, and at this point, no more than a second after* DINO *has launched himself at them, there is a strong arm around his chest, and* MR. SHERIDAN *is shouting firmly.*)

MR. SHERIDAN. Stop it! (DINO *makes one last desperate effort.*) Stop it, Dino! (*He stops, his eyes bulging with rage.* MR. SHERIDAN *speaks to the other boys.*) Get away from him!
(*They step back.*)

DANNY. (*Outraged.*) Boy, I'm telling ya, I was walkin' in here ...

MR. SHERIDAN. (*To* DINO.) Come on! (*He starts to walk* DINO *towards his office, ignoring the other boys.*)

STEVE. What a flip!

DANNY. Didja see that? Man!

(MR. SHERIDAN, *ignoring them, reaches his office, his arm around* DINO. *He stops at the door, looks at* DINO.)

MR. SHERIDAN. (*Calm.*) It's four-fifteen. You're right on time, Dino.
(DINO *looks back. The camera cuts to the three boys, standing there, staring at him, then to the office door, as* MR. SHERIDAN *opens it. They enter. He guides* DINO *over to the chair alongside the desk.* DINO *is still shaking. He gently sits* DINO *down, stands over him for a moment, then sits down at the desk. He waits, watching* DINO.)

DINO. (*Passionately.*) I could kill 'em! (MR. SHERIDAN *doesn't say anything.* DINO *darts a look at the window; the blinds are drawn. He looks at the desk; the paper weight is right at his hand. He picks it up and starts to toy with it. He speaks to himself.*) Knock off their dirty heads! Slice 'em in the face with a hatchet! (MR. SHERIDAN *doesn't answer.*) Didja see 'em? They almost fell apart, they were so scared! (DINO *gives* MR. SHERIDAN *a look.* MR. SHERIDAN *watches him calmly.* DINO *speaks with hostility.*) What—are you just gonna sit there again, waitin' for me to say somethin'?

MR. SHERIDAN. That's what it is, Dino: just talking—learning about yourself.

DINO. I know about myself. You think I'm gonna stay here for an hour with you lookin' at me?

MR. SHERIDAN. It's hard.
(DINO *looks at* MR. SHERIDAN *speculatively.*)

DINO. (*Relaxing a bit.*) Boy, I raised a stink in here yesterday, didn't I?

MR. SHERIDAN. A little bit. It's all right. In here you can act the way you really feel. If you want to be angry, or yell, or curse, or cry—it's okay.

DINO. (*Interrupting.*) Cry? You think I'm gonna cry?

MR. SHERIDAN. You might.

DINO. Hey, what arm do you take it in? Cry! (MR. SHERIDAN *sits there calmly.* DINO *looks down at the floor. There is a pause. He toys with the paper weight.*) How come I threw this thing?

MR. SHERIDAN. Well, why do you think you did?

DINO. I was sore. Everybody throws things when they get sore.

MR. SHERIDAN. Do they?

DINO. Sure they do! Why don't you answer me once? What are ya all the time makin' me answer my own questions?

MR. SHERIDAN. Well, it's more important to find out how *you* feel about them than how I do.

(*There is a momentary pause.*)

DINO. (*Softly.*) Do you think I'm—nuts?

MR. SHERIDAN. (*Carefully.*) I think you have problems.

DINO. What kinda problems?

MR. SHERIDAN. I've only seen you for a few minutes, Dino. Don't ask me that yet.

(DINO *abruptly gets up and walks over to the window. He stands with his back to* MR. SHERIDAN.)

DINO. (*Bitterly.*) Waitin' for the skull doctor! (*He whirls around.*) I'm telling ya I could kill him! Why do I have to come in here? You think I can't get along?

MR. SHERIDAN. Can you?

DINO. Sure! You just bust everybody before they bust you.

MR. SHERIDAN. (*Slowly.*) Well, how can you be sure they *want* to "bust" you?

DINO. Because I got experience with that.

MR. SHERIDAN. Maybe some people want to like you.

DINO. (*Angrily.*) What for? What's there to like? If they're scared of me, that's the best!

MR. SHERIDAN. Well, how do you get them to be scared of you, Dino?

DINO. Be stronger. Tougher. Braver. Belt 'em around! Then they respect you. When I was little, that's what they did to me.

MR. SHERIDAN. Who's they?

DINO. What's a matter with you? Everybody!

MR. SHERIDAN. Who was the first?

DINO. How do I know? My father! So what?

MR. SHERIDAN. Do you respect him?

(DINO *whirls around, facing* MR. SHERIDAN.)

DINO. No!

(*And then he realizes the point that* MR. SHERIDAN *has made.*)

MR. SHERIDAN. Well, how do you feel about him?

DINO. (*Shouting.*) None of your business! (*There is silence for a moment. Then* DINO *strides swiftly to the door.* MR. SHERIDAN *waits calmly.* DINO's *hand goes to the knob. Then he doesn't move. He speaks to the door.*) Like in the warehouse, that time when the watchman came out and the other guys ganged him, I was hiding behind a crate. I was so scared. But when he was down on the floor, I ran over and took a smack at him, and I felt good all of a sudden. (*He turns around to* MR. SHERIDAN.) I don't know why! (MR. SHERIDAN *doesn't say anything.* DINO *is angry.*) I don't know why I said that.... Stop lookin' at me!

(MR. SHERIDAN *looks squarely at* DINO. DINO *lowers his head and walks slowly over to the chair. He slumps down in it, looking at the floor.*)

MR. SHERIDAN. What did you feel like afterwards?

DINO. (*Low.*) What do I know?

MR. SHERIDAN. How did you feel when they caught you?

DINO. Glad. (*Then he looks up.*) What kinda thing is this? I never said that to anyone.... You sit there like an idiot. Why dontcha get excited once?

MR. SHERIDAN. That wouldn't help you, would it?

DINO. (*Loud.*) Yes!

MR. SHERIDAN. No, it wouldn't. Life isn't all people getting excited and yelling and throwing things. You know that.

DINO. (*Low.*) That's just words. What do *you* know about it?

MR. SHERIDAN. Well, it's my business, Dino. (DINO *looks up at him.*) Why do you want me to yell at you?

DINO. Because then I know where I stand. You're mixin' me up.—You and that stinkin' Mandel. I'd like to punch him in the mouth.

MR. SHERIDAN. Why?

DINO. Because!

MR. SHERIDAN. And me, too?

DINO. (*Loud.*) Yes!

MR. SHERIDAN. Dino, that doesn't make me angry. A lot of people have feelings like that. Sometimes they feel that way about a person because they're afraid that person won't like them, so they figure they'd better not like that person first. It protects them from the pain of being rejected. They become the ones who do the rejecting. Then, as you say, they at least know where they stand. Only sometimes they end up rejecting society completely . . .

DINO. (*Low.*) So what!

MR. SHERIDAN. Everybody wants to be liked. Even you, Dino.

DINO. That's what you think!

MR. SHERIDAN. (*Carefully.*) Those kids out there might like you, if you'd let 'em. They're having a dance here tomorrow night. You could go, if you wanted to.

DINO. Lemme alone.

MR. SHERIDAN. You know the boy who said that thing about waiting for the skull doctor? (*A pause.*) He comes in here, too. (DINO *looks at him, surprised.*) That's right. It's nothing to be ashamed of.

DINO. Listen, will you shut up! (MR. SHERIDAN *does. They sit silently there for a moment.*) I don't care if you like me or not. (MR. SHERIDAN *doesn't answer.*) I'm not goin' to any chicken dances. (MR. SHERIDAN *doesn't answer.* DINO *gets up fast.*) I'd like to bust this place apart! (MR. SHERIDAN *waits calmly.*) I got a headache. My head is killin' me. I'm gettin' outa here.

(*He heads for the door, opens it.*)

MR. SHERIDAN. Dino. (*He turns.*) Same time tomorrow. (DINO *exits, slamming the door.* MR. SHERIDAN *sits there for a minute. Then he gets up and goes to the window. He raises the blinds. It is dark out. He stands there for a minute. There is a knock on the door. He turns.*) Come in.

(MR. FIELDS *pokes his head in.*)

MR. FIELDS. I'm not breaking in on anything, am I?

MR. SHERIDAN. No. Come on in.

(MR. FIELDS *does so.*)

MR. FIELDS. I just saw the Falcaro boy leaving.

MR. SHERIDAN. Yeah. He made an excuse about having a headache. He can't stand more than ten minutes of this at a time.

MR. FIELDS. (*Sitting down.*) What's he like?

MR. SHERIDAN. Rough. There are obvious distortions; I don't know how serious they are yet. If he doesn't take this therapy, God knows what he'll do; he's liable to kill someone. I don't know if I can get to him, though. If there's not some progress very quickly, even illusory progress, he'll stop coming.

MR. FIELDS. Well, what about that Youth Board fellow?

MR. SHERIDAN. Mandel? He can keep him coming here for a little while, probably, but he has no authority to force him to come. If the boy decides to stop . . .

(*He shrugs.*)

MR. FIELDS. (*Getting up.*) Well—it's your problem, Larry. They're all tough.

(*He starts to exit.*)

MR. SHERIDAN. Mr. Fields. (MR. FIELDS *turns questioningly.*) I'd like to see if I can persuade him to go to the dance tomorrow night.

MR. FIELDS. What for?

MR. SHERIDAN. Well, he's never been with kids his own age who're enjoying themselves doing something socially acceptable. He doesn't even know what it's like to be accepted in a social situation.

MR. FIELDS. Are you sure you know what you're doing?

MR. SHERIDAN. (*After a pause.*) No, I'm not.

MR. FIELDS. We can't force these kids to be nice to him. Supposing he's not accepted!

MR. SHERIDAN. He's liable to tear the place to shreds.

MR. FIELDS. That's right.

MR. SHERIDAN. It's a chance I'd like to take, if I can get him to go. Maybe someone'll make a positive move toward him.

MR. FIELDS. If no one does, it'll just prove to him that his antisocial attitudes are valid.

MR. SHERIDAN. I said it was a chance.

(MR. FIELDS *looks at* MR. SHERIDAN *for a moment.*)

MR. FIELDS. Okay. If you think you've got something to gain, Larry. It's up to you.

(MR. FIELDS *leaves, as* MR. SHERIDAN *goes back to the window, and stands there staring. Fade out.*)

The scene changes to DINO's *living room.* DINO *is lying on the couch, staring at the ceiling. No one else is home. He lies there for a moment, and then hears a key in the lock. The door opens and* MR. FALCARO *enters, carrying a newspaper and some paper bags. He flips on the ceiling light, and then looks at* DINO, *as* DINO *sits up.*

MR. FALCARO. (*Coldly.*) Hello, Dino.

DINO. Hello.

(DINO *sits on the couch as* MR. FALCARO *takes off his coat and hat, and lays his packages on a table.* MR. FALCARO *shoots him a look as he lays the packages down.*)

MR. FALCARO. What were you doing?

DINO. Laying down.

MR. FALCARO. So where you been today?

DINO. Around.

MR. FALCARO. I had some tough day, I'm telling you. (*He takes the packages into the kitchen, and comes out again.*) Anybody home?

DINO. No.

(*He passes* DINO, *steps in front of him and looks down at him.*)

MR. FALCARO. Some man visits me at the factory today. Right in fronta everybody. He's your parole officer. (DINO *looks sharply at him. His whole body seems to tense.*) He's checkin' up on *me.* (MR. FALCARO *walks over to the armchair and sits down with his paper.* DINO *watches him.*) Everyone in the whole place's lookin' at me. Great, hah? (DINO *doesn't answer.*) So you know what he told me? He says you goin' to the Settlement House seein' that waddyecallim—head doctor. (*He points to his head.* DINO *doesn't answer.*) That's for crazy people, right? (DINO *doesn't answer.*) So what're you goin' there for? It's not enough people see me talkin' with a parole officer? (DINO *gets up and starts to walk toward the kitchen.*) Listen! I don't want you goin' there no more! (DINO *stops.* MR. FALCARO *is turned around in his chair.*) There's no crazy people in this house! (DINO *grits his teeth and enters the kitchen. The camera holds* MR. FALCARO *watching him. We hear the water running for a minute.* MR. FALCARO *watches.* DINO *comes out of the kitchen, wiping his mouth with his hand.*) What time is it?

DINO. I don't know.

(*He watches* DINO *cross the room. As* DINO *gets to the couch,* MR. FALCARO *speaks.*)

MR. FALCARO. What does he say to you, that doctor?

DINO. (*Tense.*) Nothin'.

MR. FALCARO. (*Not believing.*) Yeah? (*A pause.*) What does he say about me?

DINO. (*Fast.*) He says you're a stink . . . (*He breaks the word off in the middle, and stands there throttling his rage, his fists clenched, his face black with hatred.* MR. FALCARO *stares at him, then he turns back to his paper.*)

MR. FALCARO. Well, you're not goin' there no more!

(DINO *turns around, walks to the chair and plants himself in front of* MR. FALCARO *suddenly.* MR. FALCARO *looks up.*)

DINO. (*Tensely.*) You can't tell me! (MR. FALCARO *throws the paper down.* DINO *bends over him, furiously.*) You can't tell me nothin'!—Where I go, what I do, nothin'!

(MR. FALCARO *shoves him away.*)

MR. FALCARO. (*Angry.*) Get away!

DINO. I been outa this house four years. Big guys knockin' me on the head every day except Sunday. Sunday they sat with their folks! *(Screaming.)* Where were you?

MR. FALCARO. Hey, shut up!

DINO. You can't tell me what to do!

MR. FALCARO. I said, "Shut up!" *(He stands up.)*

DINO. It kills you to have me home, don't it?

(MR. FALCARO advances on him.)

MR. FALCARO. I'm warnin' you, Dino!

DINO. Come on, let's get it over with! You're not tellin' me nothin' any more! *(MR. FALCARO advances. He is face to face with DINO.)* Why dontcha hit me? Just like old times—a smack across the face. You been doin' it since I was old enough to stand up. Go ahead, be happy! Smack me!

MR. FALCARO. *(Advancing.)* You bet I'm gonna smack you. Talkin' to me like that. I'm your father.

DINO. *(Shouting.)* And you wish you weren't, dontcha? Dontcha? *(MR. FALCARO reaches him and cracks him across the face.)* Dontcha? *(He cracks him again.)* Dontcha? *(He cracks him again.)* Go ahead, have a ball! *(He cracks him again.)* You can't tell me nothin', you dirty . . . *(He cracks DINO again. The door opens. TONY enters. MR. FALCARO turns to him. DINO shouts.)* Come on! Come on! Come on, father! The punching bag is home again. Take another shot!

MR. FALCARO. *(To TONY.)* He's crazy . . . *(He looks at DINO, then at TONY. Amazed.)* I tell you. He's crazy.

(He exits down the hall. TONY closes the door. DINO stands there.)

TONY. *(Low.)* Hey, Dino!

DINO. *(Dazed.)* What?

TONY. What happened?

DINO. Nothin'.

(TONY walks over to him.)

TONY. You all right? *(DINO doesn't answer. He just stands there. TONY takes his arm and leads him to the chair. He sits him down. DINO holds TONY's arm, and shakes.)* What's a'matter?

(Finally DINO gets control.)

DINO. Nothin'. It's okay. *(Then he tries to smile. Speaks softly.)* Hey, Tony!

TONY. *(Mystified.)* Hey! *(TONY stands over him.)* Listen, you sure you're okay? You're acting funny.

DINO. I'm okay.

(TONY surveys him for a minute.)

TONY. I'm supposed to tell the guys tonight.

DINO. What?

TONY. The guys—about the job tomorrow night. If you're gonna run the deal. They wanta know, Dino. *(There is no answer.)* They want you to do it. So what'll I say?

(There is a pause.)

DINO. *(Blankly.)* Okay.

TONY. *(Grinning.)* Crazy! *(He squats down in front of the chair.)* Boy, that's great! Now listen: tomorrow morning you have to go over and look at it. *(DINO looks at him.)* I'll take you. *(DINO nods. TONY socks him on the arm, and grins.)* Crazy!

(He continues to grin at DINO, who stares back at him, blankly. Fade out.)

ACT THREE

The scene is again the lobby of the Settlement House. It is about 4:30 the following afternoon. The lobby is just as active as it had been the previous afternoons. SHIRLEY WALLACE *is filing as usual, yet watching everything that goes on. Two teenage girls, ad libbing to each other, head for the door. One of them opens it at precisely the same time that* DINO *opens it from the outside. He walks rudely between the girls, not noticing that they are there. They turn to look at him, annoyed.* SHIRLEY

WALLACE *sees him coming. She tries to smile at him, but he walks right by her, and to the door of* MR. SHERIDAN'S *office. He opens the door swiftly, enters, closes it.* MR. SHERIDAN, *seated at his desk, looks up and smiles.*

MR. SHERIDAN. Hello, Dino.
(DINO *stands at the door, hands in his jacket pockets.*)
DINO. I'm not comin' back here no more. (MR. SHERIDAN *shows no surprise, but sits and waits.* DINO *is angry.*) So why don't you say somethin' when I say somethin'? I said I'm not comin' back here no more. So what about it?
MR. SHERIDAN. I think you need to come here, Dino.
DINO. I need nothin'.
(*He paces to the window. The blinds are lowered.*)
MR. SHERIDAN. (*Carefully.*) Did something happen last night, Dino?
DINO. (*Fast.*) No!
MR. SHERIDAN. Well, what are you so angry about? Nothing's happened in here yet. You haven't even taken off your jacket. (*There is a pause.* DINO *turns away from* MR. SHERIDAN, *who speaks quietly.*) How's your brother?
DINO. (*Still angry.*) What do you care?
MR. SHERIDAN. I thought maybe you were angry at *him*.
DINO. (*Loud.*) No, I'm not, genius! (*There is a pause.* MR. SHERIDAN *waits. Finally* DINO *turns to* MR. SHERIDAN.) I'm angry at you!
MR SHERIDAN. Why?
DINO. (*Loud.*) Because you're sittin' there with your face hangin' out, waitin' for me to say stuff I don't wanna say.
MR. SHERIDAN. Why don't you want to say it?
DINO. (*Shouting.*) Because! (*There is a pause.*) MR. SHERIDAN *waits.*) I don't know. (MR. SHERIDAN *waits. Slowly* DINO *walks over to the desk and sits down. He picks up the paper weight and toys with it. When he finally speaks his voice is strained, low, tormented. This is sheer torture for him. He begins to squirm in the chair halfway through his lines, becoming more and more anxious as he speaks. He faces the floor most of the time.*) Like it's everybody's business. Why don't you mind *your* business? Makin' me come in here. What do you want to know so much for? (*He looks at* MR. SHERIDAN.) It's too hot in here. (*He looks down at the floor, getting no response.*) Stinkin' little room. Like sittin' in jail! I wasn't gonna come here at all. I just came to tell you that, and that's all you're gettin' outa me. (*He looks up at* MR. SHERIDAN.) What're ya lookin' at? Stop fatherin' me! (*Then he realizes his slip.*) Stop *botherin'* me! (MR. SHERIDAN *doesn't respond.* DINO *looks down at the floor.*) I made him smack me last night. So what! That's all he wants, anyway. He can't hurt me; he could never hurt me in my whole life.
MR. SHERIDAN. (*Softly.*) Who?
DINO. (*Low.*) You know who. My old man.
MR. SHERIDAN. (*Softly.*) He never hurt you?
DINO. (*Speaking to himself.*) Never! Because I'm tough. He can smack me forever. I'm too tough. (*There is a pause.*) Even when I was little—I never cried. I'm tellin' ya. He could knock out my teeth. Anything!—I wouldn't cry. (*Another pause.*) What'd he want to hit me all the time for?—The dirty bum! On my birthday once. The dirty lousy bum. I yelled at him because he forgot to give me a present. A million other times. When I was little—wow, I was scared! Like there was nothin' in the world but him, like a giant. He never did nothin' for me. So I never cried for him. And I never will. (*His voice goes lower and lower, and he turns and twists, staring at the floor. It is as though* MR. SHERIDAN *is no longer there.*) I don't remember anyone kissed me, ever. So what? All they wanted was me outa there. Him and my mother. So I get outa there. Boy, that's what they wanted! So I got into reform school. How come nobody ever kissed me? They wanted me outa there. (*His voice begins to break.*) That dirty, rotten bum! He

never took me anywhere. He never fooled around with me, or gave me bear hugs. Nothin'. He didn't want me. He didn't want to see me. Just to hit. But I never cried! I never cried! I never cried! (*And suddenly he is in tears, sobbing violently, head down on the desk, close to hysteria, crying out the pain as if he will never stop.* MR. SHERIDAN *watches him quietly. Slowly his sobbing begins to stop. Finally, after a long while, he raises his head. He is much too ashamed to look at* MR. SHERIDAN. MR. SHERIDAN *hands him a kleenex. He brushes it away.*)

MR. SHERIDAN. (*Gently.*) Most people cry in here. It's a very normal, natural thing to do, Dino. (DINO *turns away in shame.*) I think you were crying for all the times you wanted to cry when you were small. Tears make people feel better sometimes; they're nothing to be ashamed of.

(DINO *finally manages to look at* MR. SHERIDAN.)

DINO. (*Angry.*) You made me ...

MR. SHERIDAN. No one made you, Dino; you just couldn't help it. Like maybe your father just can't help being the way he is, or your mother. Because just the way their emotional problems helped make you what you are, so did their parents' problems affect them, and their's them. This is the way it is, Dino. No one's really to blame. So many people just aren't equipped to be people. Just, no matter how sad and unfair it seems, don't blame your mother and father too much. They have a very hard time, just trying to stay alive and well and reasonably unafraid. Don't expect too much from them. They just haven't got it to give. Maybe after a while you'll understand that, and adjust to it. I hope so, Dino.

(*During these lines* DINO *has been staring at the wall, but he's listened. Now he stands up and walks to the window.*)

DINO. (*Still shaken.*) I want to go now.

MR. SHERIDAN. Whenever you like.

DINO. And I'm not comin' back. I'm not goin' through that again.

MR. SHERIDAN. (*Gently.*) It's hard. Getting face to face with yourself is one of the toughest things you'll ever do, Dino. But it's worth it.

DINO. I don't want to listen to you. I'm gettin' out of here!

(*He strides to the door, and opens it.*)

MR. SHERIDAN. Same time tomorrow, Dino.

DINO. (*Angry.*) I said I'm not comin' back! Are you deaf or something?

(*He exits, slamming the door, and almost bumping into* SHIRLEY WALLACE, *who is walking down the hall carrying a waste-basket filled with papers. She steps back. They look at each other for a minute. Then his hand goes to his tear-stained face, and he walks swiftly away. The camera dollies with him to the front door. He pushes it open violently.* MR. MANDEL *stands outside, just ready to open the door.* DINO *races past him, not seeing him.* MR. MANDEL *starts to say,* "Hi," *but stops, realizing that* DINO *doesn't want him to. He watches as* DINO *exits, and then he enters the lobby. He heads for* MR. SHERIDAN'S *office. We see him knock on the door, and hear* MR. SHERIDAN *say,* "Come in," *before the fade out.*)

DINO'S *bedroom. He lies on the bed in the dark. There is no one home. A clock on the dresser says 8:20. He smokes a cigarette. We hear a key in the lock. The front door opens and closes. We hear a few footsteps. Then we hear* TONY, *off.*

TONY. Dino. (DINO *doesn't answer.*) Hey, Dino!

DINO. (*With an effort.*) In here.

(*The camera cuts to* TONY, *walking down the hall of a darkened apartment to the bedroom. He looks in the door. The room is dark.*)

TONY. Dino?

DINO. I'm on the bed.

TONY. What've ya got all the lights out for?

DINO. Nothin'!

TONY. What, did I wake ya up or somethin'?

DINO. No.

(TONY, *slightly mystified, enters the room.*)

TONY. Everybody's out, right?

DINO. That's right.

TONY. So what're ya lyin' here for?

DINO. I feel like it.

TONY. Oh. (*He looks at the clock. It's twenty after eight.*) I just came home to remind ya about tonight. We're meetin' at quarter after eleven, Dino.

DINO. Okay.

TONY. On the corner of First and Darrow. That's where you said, right?

DINO. Right. I know all about it.

TONY. Well, I didn't see you all day, so I figured I better remind you. I'm goin' to the movies now. You wanta come?

DINO. No.

TONY. (*With concern.*) Dino, don't you feel good? I mean, because of how you're actin'.

DINO. I'm okay.

TONY. (*Embarrassed.*) I was waitin' so long for you to get back home. Boy, four years! So I hope you're okay . . . (*There is a pause.*) I'll see ya eleven-fifteen.

DINO. Eleven-fifteen, Tony.

(TONY *takes a long look at the bed and then exits. We hear the front door close.* DINO *puffs on his cigarette. Then he gets up, turns on the light, and puts his cigarette out. He goes to the mirror and looks in it. He looks closely at his eyes to see if they are still red from crying. Then, suddenly, he hears the doorbell ring. He heads for the front door. He reaches the door, opens it.* MR. MANDEL *is outside.* DINO *stares at him darkly.* MR. MANDEL *smiles.*)

MR. MANDEL. Hello, Dino. (DINO *steps back from the door.*) Mind if I come in? (DINO *doesn't answer.* MR. MANDEL *enters.* DINO *closes the door and stands there.* MR. MANDEL *walks into the living room.* DINO *watches him.* MR. MANDEL *turns around and looks at* DINO.) I'm not checking up or anything, Dino.

DINO. No? So what'd you come up for?

MR. MANDEL. I was just passing by.

(*He stands in the living room and* DINO *enters and sits down.* DINO *stares at him insolently.*)

DINO. Well, what d'ya want? I'm pretty busy here.

MR. MANDEL. Nothing. Just to say, "Hello."

DINO. So you said that!

(*There is a pause.* MR. MANDEL *still stands.* DINO *watches him.*)

MR. MANDEL. How's it going, Dino?

DINO. (*Fast.*) Fabulous.

MR. MANDEL. I saw Mr. Sheridan a little while ago.

DINO. (*Furious.*) That's none 'a your business! Who do you think you are, stickin' your big nose in there about me?

MR. MANDEL. (*Calmly.*) It wasn't about you. He's an old friend of mine. I just dropped in.

DINO. Yeah! So what'd he tell you? The whole thing, right? What I did, and everything.

(*He waits, almost in physical pain.*)

MR. MANDEL. He tells nothing. What goes on in there is between you and him.

DINO. Yeah, I'll bet.

MR. MANDEL. (*A little tough.*) I'm not kiddin' you. I couldn't wring it outa him with a crowbar.

DINO. (*Low.*) So what d'ya want?

MR. MANDEL. I just wanted to give you something.

(DINO *watches incredulously as* MR. MANDEL *brings a small package out of his coat pocket. He hands it to* DINO.)

DINO. What's this?

MR. MANDEL. From me to you, Dino.

DINO. What for?

(MR. MANDEL *looks him over carefully.*)

MR. MANDEL. All he told me was, maybe you were gonna take in that dance at the settlement house tonight . . .

DINO. (*Fast.*) He told you wrong.

MR. MANDEL. And I was thinking about one time when I was, I don't know, sixteen, seventeen, and I was goin' to my first dance. I was scared to death. So my old man slipped me a bottle of shaving lotion, and he grinned at me and told me, "Have a ball, son."

DINO. Listen . . .

MR. MANDEL. (*Giving* DINO *a long look, speaks softly.*) Have a ball, son.

(*Then he turns and exits.* DINO *stares after him, holding the tissue-wrapped package. Then, slowly he opens it. It is a bottle of shaving lotion. He unscrews the cap and smells it. Then, slowly, he pours some in his hands, and rubs them together. He smells them. Then he closes his eyes. Fade out.*)

The gymnasium at the Settlement House is garishly decorated with streamers. A record player in one corner blasts out a rock 'n roll tune. Teenagers dance uninhibitedly. DANNY *and* STEVE *are there, as are four or five other teenage boys, and an equal number of girls.* MR. FIELDS *is off in one corner, watching. A small table at one side holds bottles of coke, paper cups, and candy.* SHIRLEY WALLACE *stands at the table alone, drinking a coke, watching the dancing shyly. The dancing goes on for a few moments.* MR. FIELDS *watches, amused. The camera moves in on him.* DANNY *and a girl dance close by.* DANNY *calls out over his shoulder.*

DANNY. (*Grinning.*) Hey, Mr. Fields, whyntcha grab a girl and go?

MR. FIELDS. (*Smiling.*) No, thanks, I don't "dig" this kind of music.

(DANNY *laughs and dances by.*)

DANNY. We'll play ya a waltz.

(*The music blasts on.* MR. FIELDS *grins. Then he turns toward the door, and we see his expression change.* DINO *stands there. He has made an effort to dress up, but he looks patched together, shabby. He stands uncertainly, his face dark. The dancers dance gaily by. One girl notices* DINO, *and nudges her partner. He looks. Then some of the others look, and in a short moment, a buzz has passed over the floor. Everyone has looked, turned away, and seems to be dancing faster and wilder than ever. Now no one looks at the doorway.* DINO *stands there, tensely. Then he takes a few steps into the gym. He stands there, ready to be triggered into action, and the dancers go by him. Then suddenly the record stops, the dancers stop gyrating, and* DANNY *and* STEVE *and their girls, laughing at some secret joke, walk toward the record player. On the way by,* DANNY *bumps into* DINO, *seemingly without having noticed him. But the four of them are by, before* DINO *can do anything. He stands there, seething inside, unconsciously clenching his fists. The room is alive with ad lib conversation, laughing. One boy, near* DINO, *teaches a girl a new step without benefit of music. Everyone seems to have someone to be with. All but* DINO. *He stands alone in the middle of the floor, not knowing which way to turn, and no one pays attention to him, or even acknowledges that he is there. The music starts again, and the dancing starts, and suddenly, frustratingly,* DINO *finds himself in the way of the dancers. He turns now, angry, helpless, rejected, and walks swiftly toward the door, trying to thread his way through several dancing couples. The camera cuts to* MR. FIELDS, *watching him, helpless to do anything about it.* DINO *reaches the door. Then in an agony of frustration he turns, rage on his face, and faces the dancers. He opens his mouth as if to shout at them in anger, and we hear* SHIRLEY WALLACE'S *voice, very small, hesitant, shy.*)

SHIRLEY. (*Off.*) Wouldja like to dance? (*He turns, and we see that* SHIRLEY *is to one side of him, looking hopefully at him, afraid that he may reject an offer which has taken a great deal of courage for her to make. He looks at* her, and she at him, for a long moment. She sees a dark, wild, angry face. He sees a frightened one, hiding behind eyeglasses, a bad hairdo and a trembling mouth. She tries to smile.)

DINO. Okay.
(*He walks over to her stiffly, and together, silently, they walk to the dance floor. She holds out her hands and they begin slowly to dance. They dance very badly together. They are the object of many quick, amused glances as they struggle by, dancing out of tempo. But* DINO's *face, set in anger, gradually relaxes a bit, and little by little they become inured to the stares and smothered giggles of the others. They move closer to each other.* SHIRLEY, *without looking at him, speaks softly.*)

SHIRLEY. My name is Shirley. (*He nods. They dance.*) What's yours?
DINO. (*Stiffly.*) Dino.
SHIRLEY. (*Repeating.*) Dino.
(*They move closer together. Then* DINO *stumbles. He stops dancing.* DANNY *whirls by with his girl, grinning.*)
DINO. (*Slowly.*) I don't dance so good.
SHIRLEY. Me neither. (*She shrugs.*) So what? I like it.
(*They start again, close to each other, and after a moment we can almost see a smile on* DINO's *face. She looks at him, and finally she closes her eyes. We are close on them. She puts her face next to his. From the background, we hear* STEVE's *voice.*)
STEVE. Crazy, man, crazy!
(DINO *pulls his face away from* SHIRLEY's *slightly. She looks at him.*)
SHIRLEY. (*Softly.*) Listen, if my glasses are bothering you . . . (*He looks at her, and then puts his face next to hers. They dance for a moment. She closes her eyes again.*) Your face smells very nice . . .
(*The camera holds on them, close, then the scene fades out.*)

DINO's *living room. It is dark.* TONY *stands at the window in the darkness, nervously biting his fingernails. He paces across the room and back to the window. After a moment, the door clicks open.* TONY *whirls.*

TONY. (*Whispering.*) Dino?
DINO. (*Off.*) Yeah.
(DINO *enters the darkened room.* TONY *goes over to him swiftly. All of this scene is done in whispers.*)
TONY. Listen, d'ya know what time it is? We been waitin' on the corner there for an hour. I finally hadda come back here for you. (DINO *walks over to the window and stands there, looking out at the court.* TONY *follows him.*) Willya come on! They're waitin'. (DINO *turns to him, but doesn't move.*) What's a matter with you?
DINO. Nothin'. Go to bed!
TONY. (*Wild.*) Go to bed? What are you, nuts or somethin'? Come on!
DINO. Go to bed, Tony!
TONY. (*Pleading.*) What are you talkin' about? Listen, they're standin' on the corner. (*He tugs at* DINO's *arm.* DINO *turns to him.*) Dino, what're ya doin' here? You act like you're gonna chicken out or somethin'. Are ya comin'? (DINO *slowly shakes his head.* TONY *stares in amazement.*) Of all the guys in the world! My brother!
DINO. Tony, I was cryin' today.
TONY. (*Amazed.*) What?
DINO. Stay here!
TONY. No!
(*He starts for the door.*)
DINO. (*Softly.*) You wanna end up like me?
TONY. (*Fiercely.*) Yes!
(DINO *turns his back on* TONY. TONY *looks at him, and then makes ready again to leave.*)
DINO. (*Loud.*) Hey! (TONY *turns.*) Come 'ere! (TONY *takes a step toward him, and he belts* TONY *once on the chin.* TONY *crumples in a heap on the floor.* DINO *swiftly kneels down next to him. We hear* MR. FALCARO's *angry sleepy voice from inside.*)
MR. FALCARO. (*Off.*) Hey, cut out that noise!

(DINO *looks up, at the sound.*)

DINO. (*Close to tears.*) Okay. (*And then he bends over* TONY *and cradles his head in his arms tenderly. He looks down at* TONY's *face.*) Hey, Tony.

(*Fade out.*)

In MR. SHERIDAN'S *office, the following day. He sits at his desk, working on some papers. The blinds are drawn. We hear the door open. He looks up.* DINO *stands there, still hostile, still angry, but there. He walks into the room and closes the door. He looks* MR. SHERIDAN *over.*

MR. SHERIDAN. Hello, Dino.
(DINO *doesn't answer. He seems now to be searching for something to say. When he finds it finally, his voice is hard, tough, but there is something different about it.*)
DINO. How long does this whole thing take?
(MR. SHERIDAN *waits a moment before he answers.*)

MR. SHERIDAN. (*Gently.*) I can't tell you that, Dino; I don't know. It depends on you. Maybe—three years.

DINO. (*Horrified.*) Three years! (*He turns away from* MR. SHERIDAN *and stalks to the window. He stands in front of the blinds, his face tight, his body tense. Then, suddenly, fiercely, he grabs the Venetian blind cords and violently opens the blinds. Light from the street floods the room. A head goes by, outside the window.* DINO *whirls and faces* MR. SHERIDAN.) What d'ya keep it so dark in her for? (MR. SHERIDAN *doesn't answer.* DINO *slowly walks over to his seat at the desk. He sits down. There is a pause.* MR. SHERIDAN *waits.*) I don't feel like sayin' anything right now.

MR. SHERIDAN. All right. We can just sit for a while if you like.

(*And they do, for just a few moments, until the camera fades out.*)

THE END

Topics for Further Study

1. Why is Dino angry and resentful at the whole world? Is he himself to blame? Are his parents to blame? Is society to blame? Or is no one to blame? Explain your answer.

2. Mr. Sheridan employs an unusual analytical procedure to help Dino. He does not scold, threaten, or judge. How does he help Dino solve his problems and make him understand the reasons for his behavior?

3. There are touches of humor in the play. Mention some of them and discuss why they are included.

4. How do you know that Mr. Mandel, Dino's parole officer, understands juvenile problems?

5. How do you account for the way in which the other young people in the settlement house react to Dino?

6. Many family problems result from a lack of communication among family members. What could Dino have done to improve communication with his father and mother? What could they have done to improve communication with Dino?

7. Italian-American families are usually cohesive; the family members feel a close attachment to one another. Not so in the Falcaro family. Why is the family disunited? Why are the two sons estranged from their parents?

8. "They have their problems, you know," says Mr. Sheridan, referring to Dino's parents. "And just the way their emotional problems helped make you what you are, so did your parents' problems affect them, and theirs them . . . 'way back. This is the way it is, Dino. No one's really to blame." Explain what Mr. Sheridan meant. How was Dino's attitude shaped by his parents' emotional problems?

9. Does the play reveal any difficulties which older generation Italian-Americans experience in a large city? Explain. How might these difficulties be overcome?

10. As the play ends, Dino is on the road to recovery. How did Shirley Wallace, who is shy and somewhat withdrawn, help his adjustment?

11. What do you suppose will happen to Tony, who admires his brother Dino so much? Will any outside influence prevent his deterioration? Explain.

The Jews in the United States

The first Jews to come to America landed in New Amsterdam in 1654—a group of twenty-three refugees fleeing from the Portuguese Inquisition in Brazil, which had been wrested by Portugal from the more tolerant Dutch. The men were of Spanish-Jewish descent, their families before them having fled to Holland to escape the Inquisition in Spain and Portugal. After some hesitation on the part of Peter Stuyvesant, governor of New Amsterdam at the time, this handful was permitted to remain and eventually was granted the liberty to trade, to work, and even to serve in the nightly guard. When the British conquered New Amsterdam and changed its name to New York, the right of public worship was granted to all creeds. Some Jews prospered. Lewis Gomez, for example, became the leading merchant of New York, as well as the leader of the Jewish community. In 1729 the first Jewish house of worship was opened in New York, Congregation Shearith Israel.

Another flourishing group of Jews lived in Rhode Island, whither they had come because of the tolerant views of Roger Williams. Aaron Lopez of Newport was the major shipping merchant of the eastern seaboard. In 1763 the second synagogue in America was opened in Newport. Today it is a national monument and is visited by thousands from all over the world every year.

Jews gradually came to other seaboard settlements—Philadelphia, Charleston, Savannah; by the time of the Revolution they numbered about 2,500, and most were committed to the cause of independence. Jews fought in the Continental army and died for their country's independence. When the government needed funds, Jewish businessmen helped. Some, like Isaac Moses of Philadelphia and Jacob Hart, Sr., of Baltimore, made personal loans to the government. Others furnished the army with uniforms, blankets, guns, and ammunition. Jewish shipowners outfitted their merchant vessels to raid the British on the high seas, to run an armed blockade against British merchandise, and to sink British vessels. Haym Solomon raised almost $200,000 to help finance the Revolution, and became known as "Broker of the Office of Finance" of the United States.

After the Revolution small numbers of Jews continued to come to America. By 1826 there were 6,000. By 1850 the number had risen to 50,000, with seventy-seven Jewish congregations. During the two decades preceding the Civil War, about 200,000 German Jews came to America, fleeing from the reactionary governments resulting from the upheavals all over Europe after 1848. Those Jewish craftsmen who came could easily find employment in their crafts as tailors, shoemakers, tinsmiths, glaziers, goldsmiths, and cabinetmakers. Those who had been merchants in the old country became traveling peddlers and later small shopkeepers. A few of their stores eventually became large establishments such as Gimbels, Macy's, and Abraham and Straus. Levi Strauss, a merchant in San Francisco, produced such a fine product in his trousers and overalls that the name *levis* became associated ever since with those garments.

With the coming of the Civil War, thousands of Jews joined the Union forces and many distinguished themselves in battle. Seven received the Congressional Medal of Honor. Jews in the South gave their lives for the Confederacy. Judah P. Benjamin served as secretary of defense and later secretary of state in the cabinet of Jefferson Davis, having served earlier in the United States Senate. Dr. Simon Baruch served the Confederacy as a leader in the Medical Corps.

The big wave of Jewish immigration began in 1880, however, when Jews fled from the czar's persecutions, arriving at the rate of 100,000 a year. The Jewish community, which totaled 300,000 in 1878, had grown to 3,000,000 by 1914. To assist this flood of immigrants, the Hebrew Immigrant Aid Society was founded in 1881 by the older immigrants and it still performs valuable services to this day. The devastation caused by World War I induced many poverty-stricken Jews from Eastern Europe to flee to America, but the restrictive immigration laws of the early 1920s reduced the flow to a mere trickle. Despite the horrors caused by the Nazis before and during World War II, only a comparative few could escape to America. When the atrocities of the concentration camps became known to Americans, there was such revulsion against the practitioners, and such sympathy for the surviving victims, that the United States was quick to support the United Nations in granting nationhood to Israel.

Although the persecution of Jews in America never approached the overt activities experienced in Europe, there were nevertheless waves of antisemitism at times. To offer some kind of resistance, the German Jews formed B'nai B'rith (Sons of the Covenant), which in 1843 was the first of a number of protective organizations. Later the Anti-Defamation League of this organization was the forerunner in defending the civil, economic, and educational rights of Jews in this country. Other organizations were formed to meet new challenges: the American Jewish Committee in 1906, after the infamous Kishinev massacres in Russia; the American Jewish Congress, led by the distinguished rabbi Stephen S. Wise, in 1917; the Jewish Labor Committee in 1936; and in more recent times the Conference for Soviet Jewry, whose aim is to open the gates of Russia to Jews who wish to emigrate.

Important developments in religious doctrine coincided with Jewish immigration to the United States. The earliest Jews to come to America were of the Spanish Sephardic persuasion, which believed in strict orthodoxy, or adherence to talmudic law. In the middle of the nineteenth century, tens of thousands of German Jews who practised Reform Judaism came, a movement to sever talmudic restriction which had originated in Germany in the eighteenth century. They set about to establish Reform Judaism in this country. Rabbi Isaac Mayer Wise was particularly distinguished in this area. Later in the nineteenth century, an intermediate branch of Judaism was formed, called Conservative Judaism, which tried to preserve most of the traditional aspects of Judaism but adapt them to new circumstances.

In *The Tenth Man* we see a sect of Orthodox Judaism known as Chasidism (or Hasidism), which originally developed in the seventeenth century in central Europe after the massacres by the Ukrainian Cossack leader Chmelnitzki and spread rapidly all over Europe. At a time when many Jews were greatly impoverished and had few material possessions, this sect urged its followers to take joy in communal activities, in prayer, and in personal identification with their God. While the followers might not have much to eat and drink, they could dance and sing the praises of their Lord. Today in certain neighborhoods of New York City and other cities there are Chasidic groups who practice many of the rites of their forefathers in central Europe. They have their own schools and synagogues and live a life almost apart from the rest of the community.

American Jews have played an important role both conceptually and financially in promoting the Zionist ideal—the creation of a homeland for the Jews in Israel. They have supported the new state with tremendous funds. Their contributions have built or heavily endowed such institutions as the Hadassah Hospital and Medical School in Jerusalem, the Weizman Institute, Hebrew University, and the Technion in Haifa. Thousands of American Jews have moved to Israel, and many young Jews have worked on the communal farms known as *kibbutzim* and have studied in Israeli universities.

Jews in America, conscious of the meaning of both oppression and the denial of civil and economic rights, have fought for the welfare of all suppressed minorities in the United States. They were among the founders of the National Association for the Advancement of Colored People, and many on its legal staff are Jews. They have marched in Selma and in Washington, and have pleaded the Negro cause in many courts of the land. They have done much to secure the benefits due all Americans of many minority groups.

Before World War I the majority of American Jews were laborers. Today occupational patterns have changed and most Jews have become middle-class businessmen and professionals. Taking advantage of the educational opportunities which had long been denied to them in their native countries, Jews have assumed positions of eminence and responsibility in all areas. They have been governors (Herbert H. Lehman and Abraham Ribicoff), senators (Jacob Javits), and presidential advisors (Samuel Rosenman, W. W. Rostow, and Henry Kissinger). In science significant contributions have been made by men such as Albert Michaelson and Albert Einstein in physics, Jonas Salk in medicine, and Harold C. Urey in chemistry. In the courts, Justices Felix Frankfurter, Benjamin N. Cardozo, Louis D. Brandeis, and Abe Fortas have been of Jewish extraction. Jews have distinguished themselves in literature as well. George S. Kaufman, Elmer Rice, Clifford Odets, Arthur Miller, and Paddy Chayefsky are but a handful of Jewish playwrights who have helped to make American drama the most significant of the twentieth century. Ben Hecht, Norman Mailer, Bernard Malamud, and Philip Roth have achieved fame as novelists, to mention but a few. In music Leonard Bernstein, Yehudi Menuhin, Isaac Stern, and Mischa Elman are figures of international renown.

Thanks to the opportunities offered to American Jews, the dreams of many who came here have been realized either in their own lifetimes or in the careers of their children and grandchildren. They have contributed to our cultural wealth in greater proportion than their actual numbers, and their contributions continue as the freedom to serve is permitted.

Suggested Reading

Books about the Jews

Buber, Martin. *The Origin and Meaning of Hasidism.* New York: Horizon, 1972. An interesting and lucid explanation of the tenets of this sect and its contemporary significance. Many of the activities in *The Tenth Man* become more meaningful as one reads this study by a master writer.

Handlin, Oscar. *Adventure in Freedom.* New York: McGraw-Hill, 1954. A fascinating chronicle of struggle and achievement, written by the Pulitzer Prize winner to commemorate the tercentenary of Jewish life in America. It contains all the important details, but reads like a good piece of fiction.

Marcus, Jacob Rader. *Memoirs of American Jews.* Philadelphia: Jewish Publication Society, 1955. 3 vols. A remarkable collection of memoirs of well-known and not so well-known Jews that sheds new light on their problems and achievements as they sought to live in freedom with dignity and integrity.

Plays about the Jews

There are literally scores of plays about Jewish life in America. The best reference book is Edward D. Coleman's *The Jew in English Drama*, updated to 1968 by Edgar Rosenberg (New York: The New York Public Library and KTAV Publishing House, 1970).

The following plays were originally published by various firms but can now be obtained in paperback editions from Samuel French, 25 West 45th Street, New York City 10036:

Chayefsky, Paddy. *The Middle of the Night.*
Moll, Elick. *Seidman and Son.*
Regan, Sylvia. *The Fifth Season.*
Rice, Elmer. *Counsellor at Law.*
Spiegelgass, Leonard. *A Majority of One.*
Stein, Joseph. *Enter Laughing.*

Also available in a paperback edition is S. Ansky's *The Dybbuk* (New York: Liveright), an interesting play very popular in the 1920s, which at one time played on Broadway in Hebrew, Yiddish, and English. The play also appears in an anthology entitled *The Dybbuk and Other Great Yiddish Plays*, ed. Joseph C. Landis (New York: Horizon).

The Tenth Man

The Tenth Man, in simplest terms, is a play about the exorcism of a *dybbuk*, a demon or soul of a dead person inhabiting the body of a living person and directing the conduct of that person. Members of the Chasidic sect believed in dybbuks. In the play a dybbuk has apparently entered the body of an attractive and intelligent young girl of eighteen who has been diagnosed as a schizophrenic and who has already been in several mental institutions. Her father wants to commit her again, but her grandfather is against this, believing that, rather than being mentally ill, the girl is possessed of the dybbuk of a Russian prostitute whom he had known in the old country.

To exorcise the dybbuk, a religious ceremony going back hundreds of years in Jewish religious history must be performed. To conduct any ceremony in the Jewish religion, a quorum or *minyan* of ten males over the age of thirteen is needed; it is upon the finding of the tenth man that the play turns.

Out of nowhere, apparently, a stranger to the congregation is found and is practically dragged in to make a *minyan* for the morning services, even before the presence of the dybbuk has been revealed to the congregation. The man has been drinking heavily for three solid days, has been divorced from his wife, has tried to commit suicide numerous times, and is currently undergoing psychoanalysis—a seemingly unlikely match for the possessed girl, who is introduced midway through the play after a delightful series of events, coincidences, and humourous exchanges amongst the members of the congregation. Finally, an old cabalist of the congregation performs the ceremony and exorcises not the young lady's dybbuk, but, surprisingly, that of the young man who had been filled with skepticism and lovelessness. Having fallen deeply in love with the girl in the course of a few hours, he vows that he himself will exorcise her dybbuk by the power of his newly found love for her and faith in life. The play ends as he takes her out of the synagogue to begin their new life, both in a literal and spiritual sense.

Summarized quickly in this way, the story seems like a fairy tale of Chasidic life in the seventeenth or eighteenth century. But Chayefsky's treatment lends verisimilitude to the play's setting, its plot, and its individual characterizations. The author has managed to enchant us and to lead us to a "willing suspension of disbelief," in the words of the great nineteenth-century poet and critic Samuel Taylor Coleridge.

A non-Jewish reader may at first be puzzled by some of the expressions and some of the activities of the Jews as they say their morning prayers and later participate in the rites of exorcism, but one cannot help being caught up in the spirit of the play. As Brooks Atkinson, the dean of New York's theatrical critics, expressed it so well in his review in the *New York Times* on November 6, 1959:

> Some of *The Tenth Man* is like fantasy. Two or three speeches about the reality of faith are sweet and endearing. But the most attractive aspect of this thoroughly original drama is the comic dialogue between the temperamental Jews of middle years who talk with gusto about great subjects—anarchism, communism, materialism, God—always earthy in their choice of words, always restless intellectually, always social in their feeling for one another.

The play is indeed a serious one, but there are moments of humor. Some of the most memorable are: the phone call of the local rabbi with a colleague in Wilmington, Delaware, who has accepted his first pulpit; the wild goose chase on the Long Island Railroad and the Brooklyn subways in search of a special rabbi who can deal with exorcisms; the sexton's unending search for a *minyan* to be able to conduct the daily prayers; the discussions of communism, anarchism, and the personal infidelities of members of the congregation in the old country. In contrast to these moments of humor, there are many serious aspects. At the center is the clash between the faith of the old men and the skepticism of young Arthur, who believes in practically nothing and who apparently wants to end it all. We gain insight not only about the faith of the members of the congregation and the non-faith of a stranger, but about how these Jews look upon the Reform movement, and how to them Judaism is not only a religion but a way of life. Chayefsky has deftly characterized the different members of the congregation, with their weaknesses and inconsistencies, with their splitting of hairs over their faith—each member a living human being. In his delineation of Arthur and the young woman he has given us two very troubled characters, which might to some extent represent the troubles of our present younger generation. It is significant that in the end it is the faith of Arthur in some of the eternal verities—love of life, love of another person, love of God—which gives him the courage both to face his life anew and to help his newly found love to face her own.

PADDY CHAYEFSKY was born in New York City on January 29, 1923. He attended elementary school, DeWitt Clinton High School, and the College of the City of New York before enlisting in the army during World War II. In Germany, while convalescing from a wound, he wrote the book and lyrics for the army musical *No T.O. for Love*. After his discharge he worked briefly in his uncle's print shop, an experience which inspired his television drama *Printer's Measure*.

The writing of his television play *Marty* in 1953 immediately catapulted him into the front rank of television writers. Based on the lives of some of the ordinary people he had known while growing up in the Bronx during the Depression (1929–1939), the play humorously and compassionately tells of a Bronx butcher and a spinster schoolteacher. The 1955 movie version won an Academy Award.

Among his television plays are *The Bachelor Party* (1954), *Printer's Measure* (1954), *The Catered Affair* (1955), *Holiday Song* (1955), and *The Mother* (1955), all of which were reprinted in one volume, entitled *Television Plays* (New York: Simon and Schuster, 1956). The author has provided illuminating postscripts to each of the plays, telling how each developed from the seminal idea to the completed script.

In 1959 Chayefsky turned to the theater with *The Middle of the Night*, a love story about an old manufacturer and an unhappily married girl, starring Edward G. Robinson, who was returning to the legitimate stage after several decades in Hollywood. In 1960 he traveled to Israel for research. Turning to the Bible for inspiration and employing a highly stylized dramatic method, he wrote *Gideon* (1961), an ironic story of man's refusal to accept the assurance of God even after a series of miracles. Among his other endeavors were a not too successful venture into epic theater called *The Passion of Joseph D.* (1964), about Stalin and Lenin, and the satiric *The Latent Heterosexual* (1968), which was more successful. He has written two original movie scripts entitled *The Goddess* and *The Americanization of Emily*, as well as screen adaptions of *Marty*, *The Bachelor Party*, and *The Middle of the Night*.

The Tenth Man

BY

PADDY CHAYEFSKY

CHARACTERS

HIRSCHMAN	EVELYN FOREMAN
SEXTON	ARTHUR BROOKS
SCHLISSEL	HARRIS
ZITORSKY	RABBI
ALPER	KESSLER BOYS
FOREMAN	POLICEMAN

SCENES

The action takes place in an Orthodox Synagogue in Mineola, Long Island.

ACT ONE: Before the Morning Prayers.
ACT TWO: SCENE 1: The Morning Prayers. SCENE 2: Before the Afternoon Prayers.
ACT THREE: The Exorcism.

The Tenth Man by Paddy Chayefsky. Copyright © 1960 by SPD Productions, Inc. Reprinted by permission of Random House, Inc.

CAUTION: Professionals and amateurs are hereby warned that *The Tenth Man*, being fully protected under the Copyright Laws of the United States of America, the British Empire, including the Dominion of Canada, and all other countries of the Copyright Union and Universal Copyright Convention, is subject to royalty. All rights, including professional, amateur, motion picture, recitation, lecturing, public reading, radio and television broadcasting, and the rights of translation into foreign languages, are strictly reserved. Particular emphasis is laid on the question of readings, permission for which must be secured from the author's agent in writing. All inquiries should be addressed to the author's agent, Robert Sanford, 25 West 45th Street, New York, New York.
The amateur acting rights of *The Tenth Man* are controlled exclusively by Samuel French, 25 West 45th Street, New York, N. Y., without whose permission in writing no amateur performance of it may be made.

The Tenth Man

ACT ONE

SCENE: *Interior of the synagogue of the Congregation Ateret-Tifereth Yisroel. It is a poor congregation, and the synagogue is actually a converted shop. A raised platform surrounded by a railing contains the lectern and the Holy Ark. This altar is surrounded by rows of plain wooden folding chairs which constitute the seating accommodations for the congregation. On the far side of the altar is an old desk at which the rabbi presides when teaching Hebrew school. A partitioned area Downstage Right is the rabbi's study, a crowded little cubicle containing a battered mahogany desk and chair, an old leather armchair, a worn leather couch, and piles of black prayer books. On the walls are old framed pictures of bearded patriarchs in desolate obsession over their Talmuds and perhaps a few familiar scenes from the Old Testament. Downstage is a metal heating unit. There is a second heating unit Upstage, and a door leading apparently to a bath-room. The front door is Stage Left.*

TIME: *It is 6:30 A.M. on a cold winter day.*

AT RISE: THE CABALIST *stands in the middle of the synagogue, entirely wrapped in a thick white linen praying shawl with broad black stripes, praying silently from a heavy prayer book that rests on the railing of the altar. Suddenly he pauses in his intense devotions, clutches at the railing as if to hold himself from falling. We have the impression that he is faint, near to swooning. He is a small, bearded man, in his seventies, his face lean and lined, his eyes sunken and hollow. He wears a small black skullcap from beneath which stick out grey forelocks and sidecurls—a testament to his orthodoxy. After a moment, he regains his strength and returns to his prayers. Three men hurry into the synagogue out of the oppressive cold of the street. They are* THE SEXTON, SCHLISSEL *and* ZITORSKY. *They all wear heavy overcoats and grey fedoras.* SCHLISSEL *and* ZITORSKY *are in their early seventies.* THE SEXTON *is a small, nervous, bespectacled man of 48. We know he is a sexton because he carries a huge ring of keys and is always doing something. They rub their hands for warmth and huff and puff and dart quick looks at* THE CABALIST *who is oblivious to their entrance.*

SCHLISSEL. (*Muttering.*) Close the door. (*LIGHT pours down on the synagogue as* THE SEXTON *raises the window curtains.* THE SEXTON *scurries Upstage to fuss with the heater in the rear of the synagogue.* SCHLISSEL *and* ZITORSKY *shuffle Downstage to a small naked radiator and stand silently—indeed a little wearily—for a moment.* SCHLISSEL *sighs.*) So how goes it with a Jew today?

ZITORSKY. How should it go?

SCHLISSEL. Have a pinch of snuff.

ZITORSKY. No, thank you.

168

SCHLISSEL. Davis won't be here this morning. I stopped by his house. He has a cold. His daughter-in-law told me he's still in bed.

ZITORSKY. My daughter-in-law, may she grow rich and buy a hotel with a thousand rooms and be found dead in every one of them.

SCHLISSEL. My daughter-in-law, may she invest heavily in General Motors, and the whole thing should go bankrupt.

ZITORSKY. Sure, go have children.

SCHLISSEL. The devil take them all.

THE SEXTON. (*Scurrying Downstage; to* THE CABALIST *as he passes.*) Hirschman, are you all right? (*He flutters, a small round ball of a man, to the door of the rabbi's office, which he enters.*)

SCHLISSEL. Foreman won't be here today.

ZITORSKY. What's the matter with Foreman?

SCHLISSEL. His granddaughter today. This is the morning.

ZITORSKY. Oh, that's right. Today is the morning.

SCHLISSEL. Listen, it's better for everybody.

ZITORSKY. Sure.

SCHLISSEL. I told Foreman, I said: "Foreman, it's better for everybody." The girl is becoming violent. I spoke to her father. He said to me they live in terror what she'll do to the other children. They came home one night, they found her punching one of the little children.

ZITORSKY. Well, what can you do?

SCHLISSEL. What can you do? You do what they're doing. They're putting her back in the institution.

ZITORSKY. Of course. There she will have the benefit of trained psychiatric personnel.

SCHLISSEL. The girl is incurable. She's been in and out of mental institutions since she was eleven years old. I met the psychiatrist there, you know, when I was up there to visit Foreman last week. I discussed the whole business with him. A fine young fellow. The girl is a schizophrenic with violent tendencies.

ZITORSKY. (*Considers this diagnosis for a moment, then sighs.*) Ah, may my daughter-in-law eat acorns and may branches sprout from her ears.

SCHLISSEL. May my daughter-in-law live to be a hundred and twenty, and may she have to live all her years in *her* daughter-in-law's house.

(*A fourth old Jew now enters from the street, a patrician little man with a Vandyke beard and a black homburg. His name is* ALPER. *He bursts into shrill prayer as he enters.*)

ALPER. (*Chanting.*) As for me in the abundance of Thy loving kindness will I come into Thy house; I will worship toward Thy holy temple in the fear of Thee. How goodly are Thy tents, O Jacob . . . (*As precipitously as the prayer had begun, it now drops into nothing more than a rapid movement of lips.* THE SEXTON'S *acknowledges* ALPER'S *arrival from the rabbi's office, where he plunks himself behind the desk and begins hurriedly to dial the phone.* ALPER'S *voice zooms abruptly up into a shrill incantation again.*) . . . in the truth of Thy salvation. Amen!

SCHLISSEL. Amen!

ZITORSKY. Amen.

(ALPER *joins the other two* OLD MEN *and they stand in silent rueful speculation.*)

THE SEXTON. (*On phone.*) Hello, Harris? This is Bleyer the Sexton. Come on down today, we need you. Foreman won't be here. Davis is sick. We won't have ten men for the morning prayers if you don't come down—Services start in twenty minutes. Hurry up— Wear a sweater under your coat— All right— (*He hangs up, takes a large ledger from the desk and begins to nervously examine the pages.*)

SCHLISSEL. Hirschman slept over in the synagogue again last night. Have you ever seen such pietistic humbug?

ALPER. Well, he is a very devout man. A student of the Cabala. The Rabbi speaks of him with the greatest reverence.

SCHLISSEL. Devout indeed. I assure you this lavish display of orthodoxy is a very profitable business. I was told confidentially just yesterday that his board and food are paid for him by two foolish old women who consider him a saint.

ALPER. It can't cost them very much. He's been fasting the last three days.

SCHLISSEL. And the reason he sleeps in the synagogue so frequently is because his landlady does not give him heat for his own room in the mornings.

ZITORSKY. Ah, go be an old man in the winter.

ALPER. I must say, I really don't know what to do with myself on these cold days.

SCHLISSEL. I'm an atheist. If I had something better to do, would I be here?

ZITORSKY. You know what would be a nice way to kill a day? I think it would be nice to take a trip up to Mount Hope Cemetery and have a look at my burial plot. A lovely cemetery. Like a golf course, actually. By the time one gets there and comes back, the whole day has been used up. Would you like to come? I'll pay both your fares.

ALPER. Why not? I have never been to Mount Hope. I have my burial plot on Mount Zion Cemetery.

ZITORSKY. Oh, that's a beautiful cemetery.

ALPER. Yes, it is. My wife wanted to buy plots in Cedar Lawn because her whole family is buried there, but I wouldn't hear of it.

ZITORSKY. Oh, Cedar Lawn. I wouldn't be buried in Cedar Lawn.

ALPER. It's in such a bad state. The headstones tumble one on top of the other, and everybody walks on the graves.

ZITORSKY. They don't take care in Cedar Lawn. My wife once said, she should rest in peace, that Cedar Lawn was the tenement of cemeteries.

ALPER. A well-turned phrase.

ZITORSKY. She had a way with words, God grant her eternal rest.

ALPER. I'd like you to come to Mount Zion sometime, see my plot.

ZITORSKY. Maybe we could make the trip tomorrow.

SCHLISSEL. Listen to these two idiots, discussing their graves as if they were country estates.

ZITORSKY. Where are you buried, Schlissel?

SCHLISSEL. Cedar Lawn.

ALPER. Well, listen, there are many lovely areas in Cedar Lawn. All my wife's family are buried there.

ZITORSKY. Come with us, Schlissel, and have a look at my grave.

SCHLISSEL. Why not? What else have I got to do?

(ALPER *now slowly goes about the business of donning his praying shawl and phylacteries, which he takes out of a velvet praying bag. Among Jews, prayer is a highly individual matter, and peripatetic to the bargain. The actual ritual of laying on the phylacteries is a colorful one.* ALPER *extracts his left arm from his jacket and re-buttons his jacket so that his shirt sleeved left arm hangs loose. Then, the shirt sleeve is rolled up almost to the shoulders, and the arm phylactery, a long thin black leather thong, is put on by wrapping it around the arm seven times and around the middle finger of the left hand three times. All this is accompanied by rapidly-recited prayers, as is the laying on of the head-phylactery. All the while* ALPER *walks bending and twisting at the knees, raising his voice occasionally in the truly lovely words of incantation. In a far Upstage corner,* THE CABALIST *huddles under his enveloping white praying shawl, his back to everyone else, deeply involved in his personal meditations. The synagogue itself is a shabby little place, the walls yellowed and cracked, and illumined by a fitful overhead bulb. There is indeed at this moment, a sense of agelessness, even of primitive barbarism. During this* THE SEXTON *has dialed a second number.*)

THE SEXTON. Hello? Mr. Arnold Kessler, please— How do you do? This is Mr. Bleyer the Sexton at the synagogue. Perhaps you recall me— Did I wake you up? I'm terribly sorry. As long as you're up, according to my books, your father died one year ago yesterday, on the eleventh day in the month of Schvat, may his soul fly straight to the Heavenly Gates, and how about coming down with your brother and saying a memorial prayer in your father's name— Let me put it this way, Mr. Kessler. You know, we can't have morning prayers without a quorum of ten men. If you and your brother don't come down we won't have a quorum— As a favor to me— Kessler, may your children be such devoted sons, and bring your brother. You are doing a good deed. Peace be with you. Hurry up— (*He hangs up, sits frowning, totaling up on his fingers the number of men he has, scowls.*)

ALPER. (*His voice rises for a brief moment.*) And it shall be to Thee for a sign upon Thy hand, and for a memorial between Thy eyes . . .

THE SEXTON. (*Rises abruptly from his chair and bustles out of the office to the front door of the synagogue. To nobody in particular.*) Listen, I'm going to have to get a tenth Jew off the street somewheres. I'll be right back. Schlissel, will you please fix that bench already, you promised me.

(*He exits,* SCHLISSEL *nods and picks up a hammer. For a moment, only the sing-song murmur of the rapid prayers and the upstage tapping of* SCHLISSEL'S *hammer fill the stage. The front door to the synagogue now opens, and a fifth old Jew peers in. He is a frightened little whisp of a man named* FOREMAN. *He is obviously in a state. He darts terrified looks all about the synagogue, and then abruptly disappears back into the street leaving the synagogue door open. Nobody is yet aware of his brief appearance. A moment later he is back, this time leading a slim young* GIRL *of 18, wearing a topcoat, who is also distracted. The* OLD MAN *herds her quickly across the synagogue to the rabbi's office, pushes her in, and closes the door behind her. She sits in the rabbi's office, almost rigid with terror. Like his friends,* FOREMAN *wears a heavy winter coat and a worn fedora some sizes too small for him. He stands and watches the others apprehensively. At last* ALPER *reaches the end of his laying on of the phylacteries, his voice climbing to a shrill incantation.*)

ALPER. (*To* FOREMAN, *moving slowly as he prays.*) . . . and it shall be for a sign upon Thy hand, and for frontlets between Thy eyes; for by strength of hand the Lord brought us out from Egypt. Amen!

FOREMAN. (*Muttering, his head bobbing nervously.*) Amen!

ALPER. I thought you weren't coming down today, Foreman.

FOREMAN. (*His mouth working without saying anything. Finally says:*) Alper—

ALPER. You seem agitated. Is something wrong?

FOREMAN. (*Staring gauntly at his friend.*) Alper, I have her here.

ALPER. You have who here?

FOREMAN. I have my granddaughter Evelyn here. I have her here in the rabbi's office.

ALPER. What are you talking about?

FOREMAN. I took her out of the house while nobody was looking, and I brought her here. I am faint. Let me sit down. (*He sinks onto a chair.* ALPER *regards him with concern.*)

ALPER. Here, David, let me take your coat.

FOREMAN. Alper, I have seen such a thing and heard words as will place me in my grave before the singing of the evening service. Blessed art Thou, O Lord, King of the Universe, Who hath wrought the wonders of the world. (*Suddenly half-starting from his seat.*) I must speak to Hirschman! This is an affair for Hirschman who has delved into the

Cabala and the forbidden mysteries of numbers.

ALPER. Sit down, Foreman and compose yourself. (FOREMAN *sinks slowly back onto his chair.*) Why did you bring her here? Foreman, you are my oldest friend from our days in the seminary together in Rumni in the Province of Poltava, and I speak to you harshly as only a friend may speak. You are making too much out of this whole matter of the girl. I know how dear she is to you, but the girl is insane, for heaven's sakes! What sort of foolishness is this then to smuggle her out of your son's home? To what purpose? Really, Foreman, a gentle and pious man like you! Your son must be running through the streets at this moment shouting his daughter's name. Call him on the phone and tell him you are bringing her back to him.

FOREMAN. (*Stares at* ALPER, *his pale eyes filled with tears.*) Alper—

ALPER. David, my dear friend, make peace with this situation.

FOREMAN. (*Whispering.*) She is possessed, Alper. She has a dybbuk in her. A demon! It spoke to me. (*He stares down at the floor at his feet, a numb terror settling over his face.*) It spoke to me. I went into my granddaughter this morning to comfort her, and I said: "How are you?" And she seemed quite normal. She has these moments of absolute lucidity. (*He looks gauntly at* ALPER *again.*) She seemed to know she was being taken to the institution again. Then suddenly she fell to the floor in a swoon. I said: "Evelyn, what's the matter?" And she looked up at me, and it was no longer her face, but a face so twisted with rage that my blood froze in my body. And a voice came out of her that was not her own. "Do you know my voice?" And I knew it. I knew the voice. God have mercy on my soul. I stood there like a statue, and my granddaughter lay on the floor with her eyes closed, and the voice came out of her, but her lips never moved. "David Foreman, son of Abram, this is the soul of Hannah Luchinsky, whom you dishonored and weakened in your youth, and the gates of Heaven are closed to me." And my granddaughter began to writhe on the floor as if in the most horrible agony, and she began to laugh so loudly that I was sure my son and daughter-in-law in the living room could hear. I flung the door open in panic, and my son and daughter-in-law were sitting there talking, and they heard nothing. And I tell you shrieks of laughter were coming from this girl on the floor. And I closed the door, and besought God, and finally the dybbuk was silent. May God strike me down on this spot, Alper if every word I tell you is not true.

ALPER. (*Has slowly sat down on an adjacent chair, absolutely enthralled by the story. He stares at* FOREMAN.) A dybbuk?

FOREMAN. (*Nodding.*) A dybbuk. Could you believe such a thing?

ALPER. Who did the dybbuk say she was?

FOREMAN. You should remember her. Hannah Luchinsky.

ALPER. The name is vaguely familiar.

FOREMAN. You remember Luchinsky, the sexton of the Rumni seminary with his three daughters? Hannah was the handsome one, who became pregnant, and they threw stones at her, called her harlot, and drove her out of the city.

ALPER. (*Recognition slowly coming over him.*) Oohhh.

FOREMAN. I was the one who debased her.

ALPER. You? You were such a nose-in-the-books, a gentle and modest fellow. Dear me. A dybbuk. Really! What an extraordinary thing. Schlissel, you want to hear a story?

SCHLISSEL. (*Coming over.*) What?

ALPER. (*To* ZITORSKY *who ambles over.*) Listen to this. Foreman is telling a story here that will turn your blood into water.

SCHLISSEL. What happened?

FOREMAN. What happened, Schlissel, was that I went in to see my granddaughter this morning and discovered that she was possessed by a dybbuk. Now, please, Schlissel, before you go into one of your interminable disputations on the role of superstition in the capitalist economy, let me remind you that I am a follower of Maimonides and—

SCHLISSEL. What are you talking about?

FOREMAN. A dybbuk! A dybbuk! I tell you my granddaughter is possessed by a dybbuk! Oh, my head is just pounding! I do not know which way to turn.

SCHLISSEL. What are you prattling about dybbuks?

ALPER. (*To* SCHLISSEL.) The voice of Hannah Luchinsky spoke to him through the lips of his granddaughter.

ZITORSKY. Oh, a dybbuk.

SCHLISSEL. What nonsense is this?

ALPER. (*To* FOREMAN.) Are you sure?

FOREMAN. (*Angrily.*) Am I sure? Am I a peasant who leaps at every black cat? Have I ever shown a susceptibility to mysticism? Have you not seen me engaging Hirschman over there in violent disputation over the fanatic numerology of the Cabala? Have I not mocked to his very face the murky phantasy of the Gilgul with its wispy souls floating in space? Really! Am I sure! Do you take me for a fool, a prattler of old wives' tales? Really! I tell you I heard that woman's voice as I hear the cold wind outside our doors now and saw my granddaughter writhing in the toils of possession as I see the phylactery on your brow this moment. I was a teacher of biology for thirty-nine years at the Yeshiva High School. A dedicated follower of the great Rambam who scoffed at augurs and sorcerers! For heaven's sakes! Really! I report to you only what I see! (*He strides angrily away, and then his brief flurry of temper flows away as abruptly as it flared.*) My dear Alper, please forgive this burst of temper. I am so distressed by this whole business that I cannot control my wits. I assure you that it is as hard for me to believe my own senses as it is for you.

ZITORSKY. When I was a boy in Lithuania, there was a young boy who worked for the butcher who was possessed by the dybbuk.

SCHLISSEL. (*Scornfully.*) A dybbuk. Sure. Sure. When I was a boy in Poland, I also heard stories about a man who lived in the next town who was possessed by a dybbuk. I was eight years old, and one day after school, my friends and I walked barefoot the six miles to the next town, and we asked everybody, "Where is the man with the dybbuk?" And nobody knew what we were talking about. So I came home and told my mother: "Mama, there is no man with a dybbuk in the next town." And she gave me such a slap across the face that I turned around three times. And she said to me: "Aha! Only eight years old and already an atheist." Foreman, my friend, you talk like my mother who was an ignorant fishwife. I am shocked at you.

FOREMAN. Oh, leave me be, Schlissel. I have no patience with your pontificating this morning.

ALPER. Don't let him upset you, Foreman. The man is a Communist.

FOREMAN. He is not a Communist. He is just disagreeable.

SCHLISSEL. My dear fellow, I have never believed in God. Should I now believe in demons? A dybbuk. This I would like to see.

FOREMAN. (*Furiously.*) Then see! (*He strides to the door of the rabbi's office and wrenches the door open. The* OTHERS *gingerly follow him to the opened doorway and peer in. The girl,* EVELYN, *stares at them, terrified. In a thunderous voice,* FOREMAN *cries out:*) Dybbuk! I direct you to reveal yourself! (THE GIRL *stares at the four patently startled* OLD MEN, *and then suddenly bursts into a bloodcurdling shriek of laughter. The four* OLD MEN *involuntarily take one step back and regard this exhibition wide-eyed.*) What is your name?

THE GIRL. I am Hannah Luchinsky.

FOREMAN. Who are you?

THE GIRL. I am the Whore of Kiev, the companion of sailors.

FOREMAN. How came you to be in my granddaughter's body?

THE GIRL. I was on a yacht in the sea of Odessa, the pleasure of five wealthy merchants. And a storm arose, and all were lost. And my soul rose from the water and flew to the city of Belgorod where my soul appealed to the sages of that city. But since I was debauched they turned their backs on me.

FOREMAN. And then?

THE GIRL. Then my soul entered the body of a cow who became insane and was brought to slaughter and I flew into the body of this girl as if divinely directed.

FOREMAN. What do you want?

THE GIRL. I want the strength of a pure soul so that I may acquire that experience to ascend to heaven.

FOREMAN. I plead with you to leave the body of this girl.

THE GIRL. I have wandered in Gilgul many years, and I want peace. Why do you plague me? There are those among you who have done the same as I and will suffer a similar fate. There is one among you who has lain with whores many times, and his wife died of the knowledge.

ZITORSKY. (*Aghast.*) Oh, my God!

THE GIRL. (*Laughing.*) Am I to answer questions of old men who have nothing to do but visit each other's cemeteries?

ZITORSKY. (*Terrified.*) A dybbuk—a dybbuk—

FOREMAN. Evelyn—Evelyn— She is again in a catatonic state.

(THE GIRL *now sits in the rabbi's chair, sprawling wantonly, apparently finished with the interview. The four* OLD MEN *regard her a little numbly. They are all quite pale as a result of the experience. After a moment,* FOREMAN *closes the door of the rabbi's office, and the four* OLD MEN *shuffle in a silent group Downstage where they stand each reviewing in his own mind the bizarre implications of what they have seen.* FOREMAN *sinks onto a chair and covers his face with his hands. After a long, long moment* ZITORSKY *speaks.*)

ZITORSKY. Well, that's some dybbuk, all right.

SCHLISSEL. The girl is as mad as a hatter and fancies herself a Ukrainian trollop. This is a dybbuk?

ALPER. I found it quite an unnerving experience.

ZITORSKY. She caught me dead to rights. I'll tell you that. I was the one she was talking about there, who trumpeted around with women. Listen, when I was in the garment business, if you didn't have women for the out-of-town-buyers, you couldn't sell a dozen dresses. Oh, I was quite a gamey fellow when I was in business, a madcap really. One day, my wife caught me in the shop with a model— who knew she would be downtown that day?—and from that moment on, my wife was a sick woman and died three years later, cursing my name with her last breath. That was some dybbuk, all right. How she picked me out! It gave me the shivers.

ALPER. Did you notice her use of archaic language and her Russian accent? The whole business had an authentic ring to me.

SCHLISSEL. What nonsense! The last time I was up to Foreman's the girl confided to me in a whisper that she was Susan Hayward. A dybbuk! Ever since she was a child, Foreman has been pumping her head full of the wretched superstitions of the Russian Pale, so she thinks she is a dybbuk. The girl is a lunatic and should be packed off to an asylum immediately.

ALPER. (*He regards* SCHLISSEL *with a disapproving eye; then takes* SCHLISSEL's *arm and leads him a few steps away for a private chat.*) Really, Schlissel, must you always be so argumentative? We are all here agreed that we have a dybbuk in our company, but you always seem intent on being at odds with everyone around you. Really, look at poor Foreman, how distraught he is. Out of simple courtesy, really, for an old friend, can you not affect at least a silence on the matter? And, after all, what else have you got to do today? Ride two and a half hours to look at Zitorsky's tombstone? When you stop and think of it, this dybbuk is quite an exciting affair. Really, nothing like this has happened since Kornblum and Milsky had that fistfight over who would have the seat by the East Wall during the High Holidays.

ZITORSKY. (*Ambling over.*) That's some dybbuk, all right.

SCHLISSEL. (*Frowning.*) All right, so what'll we do with this dybbuk now that we got it?

ALPER. It seems to me, there is some kind of ritual, an exorcism of sorts.

ZITORSKY. Maybe we should tell the rabbi.

SCHLISSEL. A young fellow like that. What does he know of dybbuks? A dybbuk must be exorcised from the body by a rabbi of some standing. You can't just call in some smooth-shaven young fellow fresh from the Seminary for such a formidable matter as a dybbuk. This rabbi has only been here two months. He hardly knows our names.

ALPER. He's right. You have to get a big rabbi for such a business.

SCHLISSEL. What has to be done is we must get in touch with the Korpotchniker rabbi of Williamsburg, who has inherited the mantle of the great Korpotchniker of Lwow, whose fame extends to all the corners of the world.

ZITORSKY. Oh, a sage among sages.

ALPER. I was about to suggest the Bobolovitcher rabbi of Crown Heights.

SCHLISSEL. Where do you come to compare the Bobolovitcher rabbi with the Korpotchniker?

ALPER. I once attended an afternoon service conducted by the Bobolovitcher, and it was an exalting experience. A man truly in the great tradition of Chasidic rabbis.

ZITORSKY. A sage among sages, may his name be blessed for ever and ever.

SCHLISSEL. It shows how much you know. The Bobolovitcher rabbi is a disciple of the Korpotchniker and sat at the Korpotchniker's feet until a matter of only a few years ago.

ALPER. Listen, I'm not going to argue with you. Either one is fine for me.

SCHLISSEL. The Korpotchniker is the number one Chasidic rabbi in the world. If you're going to involve yourself at all, why not go straight to the top?

ALPER. All right, so let it be the Korpotchniker.

ZITORSKY. For that matter, the Lubanower rabbi of Brownsville is a man of great repute.

SCHLISSEL. The Lubanower! Really! He's a young man, for heaven's sakes!

ALPER. Zitorsky, let it be decided then that it will be the Korpotchniker.

ZITORSKY. I only made a suggestion.

SCHLISSEL. The question is how does one get to the Korpotchniker? One does not drop into his home as if it were a public library. One has to solicit his secretary and petition for an audience. It may take weeks.

ALPER. I do think, Schlissel, we shall have to get a more accessible rabbi than that. Ah, here is Hirschman who I am sure can give us excellent counsel in this matter.

(THE CABALIST *has indeed finished his prayers, and is shuffling Downstage, a small, frightened little man.* FOREMAN *leaps from his chair.*)

FOREMAN. Hirschman! (*Everyone crowds around* HIRSCHMAN.)

ZITORSKY. Oh, boy, Hirschman, have we got something to tell you!

ALPER. Zitorsky, please. Hirschman, you are a man versed in the Cabala, a man who prays with all the seventy-two names of the most Ancient of the Ancient Ones.

FOREMAN. (*Blurting out.*) Hirschman, my granddaughter is possessed by a dybbuk!

THE CABALIST. (*Starting back in terror.*) A dybbuk.

ALPER. Foreman, please, one does not announce such a thing as badly as that.

THE CABALIST. Are you sure?

FOREMAN. Hirschman, as a rule, I am not given to whimsy.

THE CABALIST. Was it the soul of a woman wronged in her youth?

FOREMAN. Yes.

THE CABALIST. I heard her cry out last night. I awoke for my midnight devotions, and as I prayed I heard the whimpering of a woman's soul. (*A strange expression of bemused wonder settles over his face.*) I have fasted three days and three nights, and I dismissed the sound of this dybbuk as a phantasy of my weakened state. For only those to whom the Ancient One has raised his veil can hear the traffic of dybbuks. Is this a sign from God that my penitence is over? I have prayed for such a sign. I have felt strange things these past days. Sudden, bursting illuminations have bleached mine eyes, and I have heard the sounds of dead and supernatural things. (*He lifts his worn little face, his eyes wide with wonder. The others are put a little ill-at-ease by this effusive outburst.* FOREMAN, *indeed, is quite overwhelmed.*)

ALPER. Actually, Hirschman, all we want to know is if you knew the telephone number of the Korpotchniker rabbi.

THE CABALIST. (*With some effort, he brings himself back to the moment at hand.*) He is my cousin. I will call him for you. (*He moves slowly off, still obsessed with some private wonder of his own, to the wall phone, Stage Left.*)

ALPER. (*Quite awed.*) Your cousin? You are the Korpotchniker's cousin, Hirschman?

ZITORSKY. (*Hurrying after* THE CABALIST.) You'll need a dime, Hirschman. (*He gives* HIRSCHMAN *the ten cent piece.*)

ALPER. Schlissel, the Korpotchniker's cousin, did you hear? Apparently, he's not such a humbug.

SCHLISSEL. I tell you, he gives me the creeps, that Hirschman.

(HIRSCHMAN *has dialed a number on the wall phone.* FOREMAN *stands hunched with anxiety at his elbow.*)

THE CABALIST. (*To* FOREMAN, *gently.*) Where is she, the dybbuk?

FOREMAN. In the rabbi's office.

THE CABALIST. You are wise to go to the Korpotchniker. He is a Righteous One among the Righteous Ones. We were quite close as children until I abandoned the Rabbinate. (*On the phone, in soft gentle tones.*) Hello? Is this Chaim son of Yosif— This is Israel son of Isaac— And peace be unto you— There is a man here of my congregation who feels his granddaughter is possessed by a dybbuk and would seek counsel from my cousin—He will bless you for your courtesy. Peace be unto you, Chaim son of Yosif. (*He hangs the receiver back in its cradle, turns to* FOREMAN.) Give me a paper and pencil. (*The* OTHERS, *who have crowded around to hear the phone call, all seek in their pockets for a paper and pencil and manage to produce an old envelope and a stub of a pencil between them.*) That was the Korpotchniker's secretary, and you are to go to his home as quickly as you can. I will write the address down for you. It is in Williamsburg in Brooklyn. And you will be received directly after the morning services. (*He sweeps his praying shawl back over his head and retires Upstage again for continued devotions.*)

FOREMAN. Thank you, Hirschman. The eye of the Lord will be open to you in the time of your need.

ZITORSKY. Oh, Williamsburg. That's quite a ride from here.

SCHLISSEL. What are you talking about? Foreman, you take the Long Island Railroad to Atlantic Avenue Station where you go downstairs, and you catch the Brooklyn subway.

ALPER. Maybe I should go along with you, David, because a simple fellow like you will certainly get lost in the Atlantic Avenue Station which is an immense conflux of subways.

SCHLISSEL. What you do, Foreman, is you take the Long Island Railroad to the Atlantic Avenue Station where you take the Double G train on the lower level—

ALPER. Not the Double G train.

SCHLISSEL. What's wrong with the Double G?

ALPER. One takes the Brighton Train.

The Double G Train will take him to Smith Street, which is a good eight blocks walk.

SCHLISSEL. The Brighton Train will take him to Coney Island.

ALPER. Foreman, listen to what I tell you. I will write down the instructions for you because an innocent fellow like you, if they didn't point you in the right direction, you couldn't even find the synagogue in the morning. Where's my pencil? (*He has taken the address paper and pencil from* FOREMAN's *numb fingers and is writing the travelling instructions down.*)

FOREMAN. (*Staring off at the wall of the rabbi's office.*) What shall I do with the girl? I can't leave her here.

ALPER. Don't worry about the girl. She knows me. I'm like a second grandfather to her.

FOREMAN. I don't like to leave her. Did I do right, Alper? Did I do right, kidnapping her this morning and bringing her here? Because the psychiatrist said we must prepare ourselves that she would probably spend the rest of her life in mental institutions. The irrevocability of it! The rest of her life! I was in tears almost the whole night thinking about it. Perhaps, this produced a desperate susceptibility in me so that I clutch even at dybbuks rather than believe she is irretrievably insane. Now, in the sober chill of afterthought, it all seems so unreal and impetuous. And here I am bucketing off to some forbidding rabbi to listen to mystical incantations.

ALPER. The Korpotchniker is not a rogue, Foreman. He is not going to sell you patent medicine. He will advise you quite sensibly, I am sure.

FOREMAN. (*Buttoning his coat.*) Yes, yes, I shall go to see him. You shall have to hide her till I come back. My son has probably called the police by now, and sooner or later they will come here looking for her.

ALPER. Don't worry about it. I won't leave her side for a moment.

FOREMAN. I better tell her I'm going.

She'll be frightened if she looks for me, and I'm not here. Ah, my coat— (*He hurries quickly to the rabbi's office, where he stands a moment, regarding* THE GIRL *with mingled fear and tenderness.* THE GIRL *has sunk into the blank detachment of schizophrenia and stares unseeingly at the floor at her feet.*)

SCHLISSEL. So the girl is a fugitive from the police. The situation is beginning to take on charm.

ALPER. Look at Schlissel. The retired revolutionary. As long as it's against the law, he believes in dybbuks.

SCHLISSEL. I believe in anything that involves a conspiracy.

(*At this point, the front door bursts open, and* THE SEXTON *returns with the announcement.*)

THE SEXTON. I've got a tenth Jew!

ZITORSKY. Sexton, have we got something to tell you!

SCHLISSEL. (*Shushing him abruptly.*) Sha! Idiot! Must you tell everyone?

THE SEXTON. (*He leans back through the open door to the street and says to someone out there.*) Come in, come in— (*A fine-looking, troubled young fellow in his middle thirties, dressed in expensive clothes, albeit a little shabby at the moment, as if he had been on a bender for the last couple of days, enters. His name is* ARTHUR BROOKS. *He stands ill-at-ease and scowling, disturbed in aspect. His Burberry topcoat hangs limply on him.* THE SEXTON *has scooted to the shelf Stage Right from which he takes a black skullcap, nervously talking as he does.*) Harris didn't come in yet?

SCHLISSEL. No.

THE SEXTON. The two Kessler boys, I called them on the phone, they didn't show up yet? (*Thrusts the skullcap on* ARTHUR's *head.*) Here's a skullcap, put it on. (ARTHUR *takes the skullcap absently but makes no move to put it on. He is preoccupied with deep and dark thoughts.* THE SEXTON *heads for the front door.*) The rabbi's not here yet?

SCHLISSEL. He'll be here in a couple of minutes.

THE SEXTON. It's only seven minutes to the services. Listen, I'm going to the

Kesslers'. I'll have to pull them out of their beds, I can see that. I'll be right back. (*To* ARTHUR.) You'll find some phylacteries in the carton there. Alper, give the man a prayer book. Sure, go find ten Jews on a winter morning. (*He exits, closing the front door after himself.*)

FOREMAN. (*As he comes out of the office, adjusting his coat about him.*) All right, I'm going. She didn't eat anything this morning, so see she gets some coffee at least. Let's see. I take the Long Island Railroad to Atlantic Avenue Station. Listen, it has been a number of years since I have been on the subways. Well, wish me luck. Have I got money for carfare? Yes, yes. Well—well—my dear dear friends, peace be with you.

ALPER. And with you, Foreman.

ZITORSKY. Amen.

FOREMAN. (*Opening the door.*) Oh, it's cold out there. (*He exits, closing the door.*)

ALPER. He'll get lost. I'm sure of it.

ZITORSKY. Oh, have you ever seen such excitement? My heart is fairly pounding.

ALPER. Oh, it's just starting. Now comes the exorcism. That should be something to see.

ZITORSKY. Oh, boy.

SCHLISSEL. Oh, I don't know. You've seen one exorcism, you've seen them all.

ZITORSKY. You saw one, Schlissel?

SCHLISSEL. Sure. When I was a boy in Poland, we had more dybbuks than we had pennies. We had a fellow there in my village, a mule driver, a burly chap who reeked from dung and was drunk from morning to night. One day, he lost his wits completely, and it was immediately attributed to a dybbuk. I was a boy of ten, perhaps eleven, and I watched the whole proceedings through a hole in the roof of the synagogue. A miracle-working rabbi who was passing through our district was invited to exorcise the dybbuk. He drew several circles on the ground and stood in the center surrounded by four elders of the community, all dressed in white linen and trembling with terror. The Miracle-Worker bellowed out a series of incantations, and the poor mule driver, who was beside himself with fear, screamed and— Hello, Harris— (*This last is addressed to a very, very old man named* HARRIS, *who is making his halting way into the synagogue at this moment. He barely nods to the others, having all he can do to get into the synagogue and close the door.* SCHLISSEL *continues his blithe story.*)—and fell to the floor. It was a marvelous vaudeville, really. I was so petrified that I fell off the roof and almost broke a leg. The Miracle-Worker wandered off to work other miracles and the mule driver sold his mule and went to America where I assume, because he was a habitual drunkard and an insensitive boor, he achieved considerable success. Our little village had a brief month of notoriety, and we were all quite proud of ourselves.

ALPER. Oh, it sounds like a marvelous ceremony.

SCHLISSEL. Of course, they don't exorcise dybbuks like they used to. Nowadays, the rabbi hangs a small amulet around your neck, intones 'Blessed art Thou, O Lord," and that's an exorcism.

ALPER. Oh, I hope not.

SCHLISSEL. Really, religion has become so pallid recently, it is hardly worthwhile being an atheist.

ZITORSKY. I don't even know if I'll come to see this exorcism. I'm already shivering just hearing about it.

ALPER. Well, you know, we are dealing with the occult here, and it is quite frightening. Hello there, Harris, how are you? (*By now, the* OCTOGENARIAN *has removed his overcoat, under which he wears several layers of sweaters, one of which turns out to be one of his grandson's football jerseys, a striped red garment with the number 63 on it. For the rest of the act, he goes about the business of putting on his phylacteries.* ALPER *claps his hands.*) Well, let me find out if we can help this young Jew here. (*He moves towards* ARTHUR BROOKS, *smiling.*) Can I give you a set of phylacteries?

ARTHUR. (*Scowling, a man who has had a very bad night the night before.*) I'm afraid I wouldn't have the first idea what to do with them.

ALPER. You'll find a praying shawl in one of these velvet bags here.

ARTHUR. No, thank you.

ALPER. (*Offering a small black prayer book.*) Well, here's a prayer book anyway.

ARTHUR. Look, the only reason I'm here is a little man stopped me on the street, asked me if I was Jewish, and gave me the impression he would kill himself if I didn't come in and complete your quorum. I was told all I had to do was stand around for a few minutes wearing a hat. I can't read Hebrew and I have nothing I want to pray about, so there's no sense giving me that book. All I want to know is how long is this going to take because I don't feel very well, and I have a number of things to do.

ALPER. My dear young fellow, you'll be out of here in fifteen or twenty minutes.

ARTHUR. Thank you. (*He absently puts the black skullcap on his head and sits down, scowling. on one of the wooden chairs.* ALPER *regards him for a moment; then turns and goes back to his two colleagues.*)

ALPER. (*To* SCHLISSEL *and* ZITORSKY.) To such a state has modern Jewry fallen. He doesn't know what phylacteries are. He doesn't want a shawl. He can't read Hebrew.

ZITORSKY. I wonder if he's still circumcised.

ARTHUR. (*Abruptly stands.*) I'd like to make a telephone call. (*Nobody hears him. He repeats louder.*) I said, I'd like to make a telephone call.

ALPER. (*Indicating the wall phone.*) Right on the wall there.

ARTHUR. This is rather a personal call.

ALPER. There's a phone in the rabbi's office there. (ARTHUR *crosses to the rabbi's office.*)

SCHLISSEL. Well, look about you, really. Here you have the decline of orthodox Judaism graphically before your eyes. This is a synagogue? A converted grocery store, flanked on one side by a dry cleaner's and on the other by a shoemaker. Really, if it wasn't for the Holy Ark there, this place would look like the local headquarters of the American Labor Party. In Poland, where we were all one step from starvation, we had a synagogue whose shadow had more dignity than this place.

ALPER. It's a shame and a disgrace.

ZITORSKY. A shame and a disgrace.

(*In the rabbi's office* ARTHUR *is regarding the girl,* EVELYN, *with a sour eye.*)

ARTHUR. Excuse me. I'd like to make a rather personal call.

(THE GIRL *stares down at the floor, unhearing, unmoving, off in a phantasmic world of her own distorted creation.* ARTHUR *sits down at the rabbi's desk, turns his shoulder to* THE GIRL, *and begins to dial a number.*)

SCHLISSEL. Where are all the Orthodox Jews? They have apostated to the Reform Jewish temples where they sit around like Episcopalians listening to organ music.

ALPER. Your use of the word "apostasy" in referring to Reform Jews interests me, Schlissel. Is it not written in Sifre on Deuteronomy, "Even if they are foolish, even if they transgress, even if they are full of blemishes, they are still called sons"? So, after all, is it so terrible to be a Reform Jew? Is this not an interesting issue for disputation? Oh, my God!

(*He wheels and starts back for the rabbi's office. The same thought has been entering the other two old fellows' minds, as has been indicated by a growing frown of consternation on each of their faces. They follow* ALPER *to the rabbi's office, where he opens the door quickly and stares in at* ARTHUR BROOKS. *The latter is still seated at the rabbi's desk, waiting for an answer to his phone call, and* THE GIRL *is still in her immobilized state.* ARTHUR *bestows such a baleful eye upon this interruption that the three* OLD MEN *back out of the office and close the door.*)

They remain nervously outside the door of the office. At last, someone answers the phone call.)

ARTHUR. (*On phone, shading his face, and keeping his voice down.*) Hello, Doctor, did I wake you up? This is Arthur Brooks— Yes, I know. Do you think you can find an hour for me this morning?—Oh, I could be in your office in about an hour or so. I'm out in Mineola. My ex-wife lives out here with her parents, you know. And I've been blind drunk for—I just figured it out—three days now. And I just found myself out here at two o'clock in the morning banging on their front door, screaming— (THE GIRL's *presence bothers him. He leans across the desk to her and says:*) Look, this is a very personal call, and I would really appreciate your letting me have the use of this office for just a few minutes.

EVELYN. (*She looks up at him blankly. Hollowly.*) I am the Whore of Kiev, the companion of sailors.

ARTHUR. (*This strikes him as a bizarre comment to make. He considers it for a moment, and then goes back to the phone.*) No, I'm still here. I'm all right. At least, I'm still alive. (*Hides his face in the palm of one hand and rubs his brow nervously.*) I've got to see you, Doc. Don't hang up on me, please. If my analyst hangs up on me, that'll be the end. Just let me talk a couple of minutes— I'm in some damned synagogue. I was on my way to the subway. Oh, my God, I've got to call my office. I was supposed to be in court twice yesterday. I hope somebody had the brains to apply for an adjournment. So it's funny, you know. I'm in this damned synagogue. I'll be down in about an hour, Doctor— Okay. Okay— I'm all right— No, I'm all right— I'll see you in about an hour. (*He hangs up, hides his face in the palms of both hands and slowly pulls himself together. After a moment, he looks up at* THE GIRL, *who is back to staring at the floor. He frowns, stands, goes to the door of the office, opens it, gives one last look at* THE GIRL, *and closes the door again. He finds himself staring at the inquiring faces of the three* OLD MEN.) Listen, I hope you know there's a pretty strange girl in there.

(*The* OLD MEN *bob their heads a little nervously.* ARTHUR *crosses the synagogue, his face dark with his emotions. The three* OLD MEN *regard him anxiously. After a moment,* SCHLISSEL *approaches* ARTHUR.)

SCHLISSEL. A strange girl, you say?

ARTHUR. Yes.

SCHLISSEL. Did she say anything?

ARTHUR. She said: "I am the Whore of Kiev, the companion of sailors."

SCHLISSEL. That was a very piquant statement, wouldn't you say?

ARTHUR. Yes, I think I would call it piquant.

SCHLISSEL. What do you make of it?

ARTHUR. (*Irritably.*) Look, I'm going. I have a hundred things to do. I—

SCHLISSEL. No, no, no, sit down. For heaven's sakes, sit down.

ALPER. (*Hurrying over.*) Don't go. Oh, my, don't go. We need you for a tenth man. We haven't had ten men in the morning in more than a week, I think.

ZITORSKY. (*On* ALPER's *tail.*) Two weeks, at least.

(*At this point,* HARRIS, *who has finally divested himself of his overcoat, muffler, heavy-ribbed button-down sweaters which were over his jacket and is now enwrapt in a praying shawl, bursts into a high, quavering prayer.*)

HARRIS. Blessed art Thou, O Lord, our God, King of the Universe, Who hath sanctified us by his commandments and . . . (*The words dribble off into inaudibility.* ARTHUR BROOKS *darts a startled look at the* OLD MAN, *not being prepared for this method of prayer, and moves a few nervous steps away from the other* OLD MEN, *where he stands rubbing his brow, quite agitated.*)

ALPER. (*Whispering to* SCHLISSEL.) So what happened in there? Did she say anything?

SCHLISSEL. Yes, she said she was the Whore of Kiev, and the companion of sailors.

ALPER. Oh, dear me.

SCHLISSEL. I'm afraid we shall have to get her out of the rabbi's office, because if she keeps telling everybody who walks in there that she is the Whore of Kiev, they will pack us all off to the insane asylum. And let us be quite sensible about this situation. If Foreman has kidnapped the girl, he has kidnapped her, however kindly his motives—not that I expect the police to regard a dybbuk as any kind of sensible explanation. Whatever the case, it would be a good idea to keep the girl a little less accessible. (*The WALL PHONE rings.*) Ah! I'll tell you who that is. That's Foreman's son calling to find out if Foreman and the girl are here. (*The PHONE rings again.*) Well, if you won't answer it, I'll answer it. (*He crosses to the wall phone.*)

ALPER. We could take her to my house. Everybody is still sleeping. We'll put her in the cellar. (*The PHONE rings again. SCHLISSEL picks up the phone.*)

SCHLISSEL. (*On phone.*) Hello. (*He turns to the others, nods his head and makes an expressive face, indicating he was quite right in guessing the caller. The other two OLD MEN move closer to the phone.*) Mr. Foreman, your father isn't here— Listen, I tell you, he isn't here— I wouldn't have the slightest idea—I haven't seen her since I was up to your house last Tuesday. Isn't she home? —If he comes in, I'll tell him— Okay— (*Hangs up, turns to the other two.*) Well, we are in it up to our necks now.

ALPER. (*Stripping off his phylacteries.*) So shall we take her to my house?

SCHLISSEL. All right. Zitorsky, go in and tell her we are going to take her some place else.

ZITORSKY. (*Not exactly inspired by the idea.*) Yeah, sure.

SCHLISSEL. (*To ZITORSKY.*) For heaven's sake, Zitorsky, you don't really believe that's a dybbuk in there.

ZITORSKY. If that's no dybbuk, then you go in and take her.

SCHLISSEL. (*He shuffles slowly to the door of the rabbi's office. Pausing at the closed office door.*) It's getting kind of complicated. Maybe we ought to call Foreman's son and tell him she's here and not get involved.

ZITORSKY. Oh, no!

SCHLISSEL. Ah, well, come on. What can they do to us? They'll call us foolish old men, but then foolishness is the only privilege of old age. So, Alper, you'll deal with her. You know how to talk to her, and we'll hide her in your cellar. So we'll have a little excitement. Listen, Alper, let's get along, you know. Before the Sexton comes back and starts asking us where we're all going.

ALPER. (*He nods apprehensively and takes a few steps into the office. To THE GIRL, who doesn't actually hear him or know of his presence.*) How do you do, my dear Evelyn? This is Alper here. (*She makes no answer. ALPER turns to the other two.*) She's in one of her apathetic states.

ZITORSKY. (*Darting back into the synagogue proper.*) I'll get your coat, Alper.

SCHLISSEL. (*Looking around to see if ARTHUR is paying any attention to what's going on; he is not.*) Well, take her by the arm.

ALPER. Evelyn, your grandfather suggested we take you to my house. You always liked to play with the children's toys in my cellar there, you remember? Come along, and we'll have a good time.

ZITORSKY. (*Giving SCHLISSEL an overcoat.*) Here. Give this to Alper. (*He hurries off to the front door of the synagogue.*)

HARRIS. (*In the process of laying on his phylacteries.*) And from my wisdom, Oh most High God, Thou shalt reserve for me— (*He dribbles off into inaudibility.*)

ALPER. (*Placing a tentative hand on THE GIRL's shoulder.*) Evelyn, dear— (*She looks up startled.*)

ZITORSKY. (*Leaning out the front door, searching up and down the street.*) Oh, it's cold out here.

ALPER. (*To SCHLISSEL, hurriedly, putting on his own overcoat.*) I have a feeling we're going to have trouble here.

SCHLISSEL. I've got your coat here.

ALPER. Evelyn— (*A strange animal-like

grunt escapes THE GIRL, *and she begins to moan softly.*) Evelyn, dear, please don't be alarmed. This is Mr. Alper here who has known you since you were born. (*He is getting a little panicky at the strange sounds coming out of* THE GIRL, *and he tries to grab her arm to help her to her feet. She bursts into a shrill scream, electrifying everybody in the synagogue with the exception of* THE CABALIST, *who is oblivious to everything.* ZITORSKY, *who has just closed the front door, stands frozen with horror.* ARTHUR, *sunk in despondency, looks up startled. The old man,* HARRIS, *pauses briefly as if the sound has been some distant buzzing, and then goes back to his mumbled prayers. Alarmed.*) Evelyn, my dear girl, for heaven's sakes . . .

THE GIRL. (*Screaming out.*) Leave me alone! Leave me alone!

ARTHUR. (*Coming quickly to* SCHLISSEL, *who has shut the office door quickly.*) What's going on in there?

SCHLISSEL. It's nothing, it's nothing.

THE GIRL. (*Screaming.*) They are my seven sons! My seven sons!

ALPER. (*Who is trying earnestly to get out of the office.*) Who closed this door?

ZITORSKY. (*Reaching for the front door.*) I'm getting out of here.

SCHLISSEL. (*To* ZITORSKY.) Where are you going? (*But* ZITORSKY *has already fled into the street.*)

ARTHUR. (*To* SCHLISSEL.) What's all this screaming?

ALPER. (*At last out of the office, he comes scurrying to* SCHLISSEL.) I put my hand on her arm to help her up, and she burst into this fit of screaming.

ARTHUR. (*He strides to the open doorway of the office.* THE GIRL *stares at him, hunched now in terror, frightened and at bay. To* SCHLISSEL.) What have you been doing to this girl?

SCHLISSEL. The girl is possessed by a dybbuk.

ARTHUR. What?

SCHLISSEL. (*To* ALPER.) Zitorsky ran out in the street like a kangaroo.

ALPER. Listen, maybe we should call somebody.

ARTHUR. Listen, what is this?

ALPER. My dear young man, there is no reason to alarm yourself. There is an insane girl in the rabbi's office, but she appears to have quieted down.

ARTHUR. What do you mean, there's an insane girl in the rabbi's office?

ALPER. Yes, she is a catatonic schizophrenic, occasionally violent, but really, go back to your seat. There is no cause for alarm.

ARTHUR. Am I to understand, sir, that it is a practice of yours to keep insane girls in your rabbi's office?

ALPER. No, no. Oh, dear, I suppose we shall have to tell him. But you must promise, my dear fellow, to keep this whole matter between us. (*To* SCHLISSEL.) Zitorsky, you say, took to his heels?

SCHLISSEL. Absolutely flew out of the door.

ALPER. Well, I really can't blame him. It was quite an apprehensive moment. I was a little shaken myself. (*Peeks into the office.*) Yes, she seems to be quite apathetic again. I think we just better leave her alone for the time being.

ARTHUR. Look, what is going on here?

ALPER. My dear fellow, you are, of course, understandably confused. The girl, you see, is possessed by a dybbuk.

ARTHUR. Yes, of course. Well, that explains everything.

ALPER. Well, of course, how would he know what a dybbuk is? A dybbuk is a migratory soul that possesses the body of another human being in order to return to heaven. It is a Lurian doctrine, actually tracing back to the Essenes, I suppose, but popularized during the thirteenth century by the Spanish Cabalists. I wrote several articles on the matter for Yiddish periodicals. My name is Moyshe Alper, and at one time I was a journalist of some repute. (ZITORSKY *appears in the doorway again, peering nervously in.*) Come in, Zitorsky, come in. The girl is quiet again. (ZITORSKY *approaches them warily.*)

ARTHUR. Look, are you trying to tell me you have a girl in there you think is possessed by some demon? Where is her mother or father or somebody who should be responsible for her?

ALPER. If there were someone responsible for her, would she be insane in the first place?

ARTHUR. Of course, this is none of my business—

ALPER. You are a good fellow and let me put you at ease. The girl is in good hands. Nobody is going to hurt her. Her grandfather, who adores her more than his own life, has gone off for a short while.

ZITORSKY. To Williamsburg on the Brighton train.

SCHLISSEL. The Brighton Train takes you to Coney Island.

ZITORSKY. You said the Double G.

ALPER. All right, all right.

ARTHUR. Of course, this is none of my business.

ALPER. (*To* ARTHUR.) I can understand your concern; it shows you are a good fellow, but really the matter is well in hand.

(*The front door opens and there now enter* THE SEXTON *and two young men in their thirties, apparently the* KESSLER BOYS, *who are none too happy about being roused on this cold winter morning. They stand disconsolately around in the back of the synagogue.*)

THE SEXTON. Here are two more, the Kessler boys.

ALPER. Now we'll have ten for a quorum.

ZITORSKY. Kessler? Kessler? Oh, yes, the stationery store. I knew your father.

(*There is a general flurry of movement.* THE SEXTON *hurries about the ritual of baring his left arm, donning the praying shawl and phylacteries, walking nervously about, mumbling his prayers rapidly.* ARTHUR, *quite disturbed again, looks into the rabbi's office at* THE GIRL *again, then moves slowly into the office.* THE GIRL *is again in a world of her own. He closes the door after himself and studies* THE GIRL. SCHLISSEL, ALPER *and* ZITORSKY *watch him warily, taking off their overcoats again and preparing to stay for the impending services.* HARRIS' *shrill quavering voice suddenly leaps up into audibility again.*)

HARRIS. Thou shalt set apart all that openeth the womb of the Lord, and the firstling that cometh of a beast which Thou shalt have, it shall belong to the Lord—

SCHLISSEL. (*To* ALPER.) What are we going to do when the rabbi tries to get into his office? He'll see the girl, and that will be the end of our exorcism. What shall we tell the rabbi?

(*The front door of the synagogue opens, and* THE RABBI *comes striding efficiently in, right on cue. He is a young man in his early thirties, neatly dressed if a little threadbare, and carrying a briefcase.*)

ZITORSKY. Peace be with you, Rabbi.

THE RABBI. Peace be unto you.

ALPER. (*Intercepting* THE RABBI *as he heads for his office.*) How do you do, Rabbi? (THE RABBI *nods as he strides to the door of his office where* SCHLISSEL *blocks the way.*)

SCHLISSEL. We have ten men today, Rabbi.

THE RABBI. Good. (*Reaches for the door to his office.*) I'll just get my phylacteries.

ALPER. (*Seizing* ZITORSKY'S *phylacteries from* ZITORSKY'S *hand.*) Oh, here, use these. It's late, Rabbi.

THE RABBI. (*Taking the phylacteries.*) Fine. Well, let's start the services. (*He turns back to the synagogue proper.*)

(*From all around, each man's voice rises into prayer, as the* CURTAIN *falls.*)

END OF ACT ONE

ACT TWO

SCENE 1

TIME: *Fifteen minutes later.*

AT RISE: ZITORSKY *is reading the prayers. He stands before the lectern on the raised platform singing the primitive chants:*

ZITORSKY. And we beseech Thee according to Thine abundant mercies, Oh, Lord—

THE SEXTON. Young Kessler, come here and open the Ark. (*The* YOUNGER KESSLER *ascends the platform and opens the Ark by drawing the curtains and sliding the doors apart.*)

ZITORSKY. And it came to pass, when the ark set forward, that Moses said, "Rise up, O Lord, and Thine enemies shall be scattered, and they that hate Thee shall flee before Thee. For out of Zion shall go forth the Law, and the word of the Lord from Jerusalem." (*Immediately, the rest of the* QUORUM *plunge into a mumbled response:* "Blessed be Thy name, O Sovereign of the World! Blest by Thy crown, and Thy abiding place!" *Jewish prayers are conducted in a reader and congregation pattern, although frequently the reader's vocalized statements and the congregation's mumbled responses merge and run along simultaneously. In this specific moment of prayer, where the Ark has been opened and the Torah is about to be taken out, the demarcation between reader and congregation is clearcut. The sliding brown wooden doors of the Ark are now open.* THE SEXTON *is reaching in to take out the exquisitely ornamented Torah, which, when its lovely velvet and brocaded cover is taken off, will show itself to be a large parchment scroll divided on two carved rollers. When* THE SEXTON *gets the Torah out, he hands it carefully to* ZITORSKY, *who has been chosen this day for the honor of holding the Torah until it is to be read from.* ZITORSKY, *who, as today's reader, has been reading along with the congregation although more audibly, now allows his voice to ring out clearly, marking the end of this paragraph of prayers.*) . . . May it be Thy gracious will to open my heart in Thy Law, and to grant my heart's desires, and those of all Thy people Israel, for our benefit, throughout a peaceful life. (*Pause.*) Magnify the Lord with me, and let us exalt His name together. (*Again, the* CONGREGATION *leaps into mumbled response.* "Thine, O Lord, is the greatness, and the power, and the glory, and the victory, and the majesty," *etc.* ZITORSKY *marches solemnly to the front of the lectern carrying the Torah before him. Each* MAN *kisses the Torah as it passes him. There is now a ritual of removing the velvet cover, and the Torah is laid upon the lectern.* ZITORSKY, HARRIS *and* THE SEXTON *make a hovering group of three old betallith-ed Jews over it.* THE RABBI *stands rocking slightly back and forth to the Left of the lectern. Off the raised platform, but immediately by the railing stands* THE CABALIST, *rocking back and forth and praying.* ALPER *and* SCHLISSEL *stand at various places, mumbling their responses. The two* KESSLER BOYS *have removed their coats and wear praying shawls but still stand as close to the front door as they can.* ARTHUR BROOKS *stands, leaning against the wall of the rabbi's office, quite intrigued by the solemn prayers and rituals.* THE GIRL *is still in the rabbi's office, but she is standing now, listening as well as she can to the prayers. Her face is peaceful now and quite lovely. Again* ZITORSKY'S *voice rises to indicate the end of a paragraph of prayer.*) Ascribe all of your greatness unto our God, and render honor to the Law.

(*There is now a quick mumbled conference among the three* OLD JEWS *at the lectern, and* THE SEXTON *suddenly leans out and calls to the two* KESSLER BOYS *in the rear.*)

THE SEXTON. Kessler, you want to read from the Torah?

ELDER KESSLER. No, no, no. Get somebody else.

THE SEXTON. Alper? (ALPER *nods and makes his way to the lectern.* THE SEXTON'S *voice, a high, whining incantation, rises*

piercingly into the air, announcing the fact that MOYSHE, *son of Abram, will read from the Torah.*) Rise up, Reb Moses Hia Kohan, son of Abram, and speak the blessing on the Torah. Blessed be He, who in His Holiness gave the Law unto his people Israel, the Law of the Lord is perfect.
CONGREGATION. (*Scattered response.*) And ye that cleave unto the Lord your God are alive every one of you this day.
ALPER. (*Now at the lectern raises his head and recites quickly.*) Blessed is the Lord who is to be blessed for ever and ever.
CONGREGATION. Blessed is the Lord who is to be blessed for ever and ever.
ALPER. Blessed art Thou, O Lord our God, King of the Universe, who has chosen us from all peoples and hast given us Thy Law. Blessed art Thou, O Lord, who givest the Law.
CONGREGATION. Amen!
THE SEXTON. And Moses said . . .
(*There are now four mumbling* OLD JEWS *huddled over the lectern. It all becomes very indistinguishable although* THE SEXTON'S *piercing tenor rises audibly now and then to indicate he is reading.* ALPER *moves into the reader's position and begins to read from the Torah, bending his knees and twisting his body and hunching over the Torah peering at the difficult little Hebrew lettering inscribed therein.* SCHLISSEL *and the* KESSLER BOYS *find seats where they were standing, as does* THE CABALIST. THE RABBI *and* HARRIS *are seated on the raised platform. In the rabbi's office,* THE GIRL *has decided to go out into the synagogue proper. She opens the door and moves a few steps out.* ARTHUR *hears her and turns to her warily.*)
THE GIRL. (*Quite lucidly and amiably.*) Excuse me, sir, are they reading from the Torah now? (*She peers over* ARTHUR'S *shoulder to the* OLD MEN *at the lectern.*)
ARTHUR. Yes, I think so. (*He watches her carefully. She seems all right now. Still there is something excessively ingenuous about her, a tentative, wide-eyed, gently smiling innocence.*)
THE GIRL. Is my grandfather here? (*She peers nervously around the synagogue.*)
ARTHUR. Which one would be your grandfather?
THE GIRL. (*Growing panic.*) No, he's not here. I see Mr. Alper, but I don't see my grandfather.
ARTHUR. I'm sure he will be back soon. (*His calmness reassures her.*)
THE GIRL. (*She studies this strange young man warily.*) I think all synagogues should be shabby because I think of God as being very poor as a child. What do you think of God as?
ARTHUR. I'm afraid I think of God as the Director of Internal Revenue.
THE GIRL. (*She laughs brightly and then immediately smothers her laughter, aware she is in a solemn synagogue.*) You're irreverent. (*She goes frowning again into the rabbi's office and plops down on his swivel chair, and swivels back and forth, very much like a child.* ARTHUR *follows her tentatively, studying her warily yet taken by her ingenuousness. She darts a quick frightened look at him.*) Were you in here just before?
ARTHUR. Well, yes.
THE GIRL. Did I—did I say anything?
ARTHUR. (*Amiably.*) Well, yes.
THE GIRL. (*Sighing.*) I see. Well, I might as well tell you. I've been to several mental institutions. (*She looks quickly at him. He smiles at her.*) You don't seem very disconcerted by that.
ARTHUR. Oh, I expect it might be hard to find somebody who couldn't do with occasional confinement in a mental institution.
(*In the synagogue,* THE SEXTON *now calls* HARRIS *to read from the Torah.*)
THE GIRL. (*She frowns.*) Did my grandfather say when he would be back or where he was going? (*She starts from her seat, frightened again.*)
ARTHUR. I understand he'll be back soon.
THE GIRL. Are you the doctor?
ARTHUR. No. You don't have to be the least bit afraid of me.

THE GIRL. (*She brightens.*) My grandfather and I are very close. I'm much closer to him than I am to my own father. I'd rather not talk about my father, if you don't mind. It's a danger spot for me. You know, when I was nine years old, I shaved all the hair off my head because that is the practice of really orthodox Jewish women. I mean, if you want to be a rabbi's wife, you must shear your hair and wear a wig. That's one of my compulsive dreams. I keep dreaming of myself as the wife of a handsome young rabbi with a fine beard down to his waist and a very stern face and prematurely grey forelocks on his brow. I have discovered through many unsuccessful years of psychiatric treatment that religion has a profound sexual connotation for me. Oh, dear, I'm afraid I'm being tiresome again about my psychiatric history. Really, being insane is like being fat. You can talk about nothing else. Please forgive me. I am sure I am boring you to death.

ARTHUR. No, not at all. It's nice to hear somebody talk with passion about anything, even their insanity.

THE GIRL. (*Staring at him.*) The word doesn't bother you?

ARTHUR. What word?

THE GIRL. Insanity.

ARTHUR. Good heavens, no. I'm a lawyer. Insanity in one form or another is what fills my anteroom. Besides I'm being psychoanalyzed myself and I'm something of a bore about that too. You are a bright young thing. How old are you?

THE GIRL. Eighteen.

ARTHUR. (*Staring at her.*) My God, you're a pretty kid! I can hardly believe you are psychopathic. Are you very advanced?

THE GIRL. Pretty bad. I'm being institutionalized again. Dr. Molineaux's Sanitarium in Long Island. I'm a little paranoid and hallucinate a great deal and have very little sense of reality, except for brief interludes like this, and I might slip off any minute in the middle of a sentence—into some incoherency. If that should happen, you must be very realistic with me. Harsh reality is the most efficacious way to deal with schizophrenics.

ARTHUR. You seem well-read on the matter.

THE GIRL. I'm a voracious reader. I have so little else to do with myself. Will you come and visit me at Dr. Molineaux's Hospital? I am awfully fond of you.

ARTHUR. Yes, of course, I will.

THE GIRL. It won't be as depressing an experience as you might think. If I am not in the violent ward, I will probably be allowed to go to the commissary and have an ice cream soda with you. The worst of an insane asylum is really how poorly dressed the inmates are. They all wear old cable-stitched sweaters. I do like to look pretty. (*A vacuous, atrophied look is beginning to come across her face.*) They ask me to be in a lot of movies, you know, when I have time. Did you see "David and Bathsheba" with Susan Hayward? That was really me. I don't tell anybody that. They don't want me to make movies. My mother, I mean. She doesn't even go to synagogue on Saturday. You're the new rabbi, you know. Sometimes, I'm the rabbi, but they're all afraid of me. The temple is sixty cubits long and made of cypress and overlaid with gold. The burnished Roman legions clank outside the gates, you know. Did you see "The Ten Commandments"? I saw that Tuesday, Wednesday. I was in that. I was the girl who danced. I was in that. Mr. Hirschman is here, too, you know, and my grandfather. Everybody's here. Do you see that boy over there? Go away. Leave us alone. He's insane. He's really Mr. Hirschman the Cabalist. He's making a golem. You ought to come here, Rabbi.

ARTHUR. (*Who has been listening, fascinated, now says firmly.*) I am not the rabbi, Evelyn.

THE GIRL. (*She regards him briefly.*) Well, we're making a golem and—

ARTHUR. You are not making a golem, Evelyn.

THE GIRL. (*She pauses, stares down at the floor at her feet. A grimace of pain winces quickly across her face and then leaves it. After a moment, she mumbles.*) Thank you. (*Suddenly she begins to cry and she throws herself upon* ARTHUR'S *breast, clinging to him, and he holds her gently, caressing her as he would a child.*) Oh, I can't bear being insane.

ARTHUR. (*Gently.*) I always thought that since the insane made their own world it was more pleasurable than this one that is made for us.

THE GIRL. (*Moving away.*) Oh, no, it is unbearably painful. It is the most indescribable desolation. You are all alone in deserted streets. You cannot possibly imagine it.

ARTHUR. I'm afraid I can. I have tried to commit suicide so many times now it has become something of a family joke. Once, before I was divorced, my wife stopped in to tell a neighbor before she went out to shop: "Oh, by the way, if you smell gas, don't worry about it. It's only Arthur killing himself again." Suicides, you know, kill themselves a thousand times, but one day I'll slash my wrists and I will forget to make a last minute telephone call and there will be no stomach pumping samaritans to run up the stairs and smash my bedroom door down and rush me off to Bellevue. I'll make it some day—I assure you of that.

THE GIRL. (*Regarding him with sweet interest.*) You don't look as sad as all that.

ARTHUR. Oh, I have made a profession of ironic detachment. It depresses me to hear that insanity is as forlorn as anything else. I had always hoped to go crazy myself some day since I have apparently no talent for suicide.

THE GIRL. I always thought life would be wonderful if I were only sane.

ARTHUR. Life is merely dreary if you're sane, and unbearable if you are sensitive. I cannot think of a more meaningless sham than my own life. My parents were very poor so I spent the first twenty years of my life condemning the rich for my childhood nightmares. Oh, I was quite a Bernard Barricade when I was in college. I left the Communist Party when I discovered there were easier ways to seduce girls. I turned from reproaching society for my loneliness to reproaching my mother, and stormed out of her house to take a room for myself on the East Side. Then I fell in love—that is to say, I found living alone so unbearable I was willing to marry. She married me because all her friends were marrying somebody. Needless to say, we told each other how deeply in love we were. We wanted very much to be happy. Americans, you know, are frantic about being happy. The American nirvana is a man and his wife watching television amiably and then turning off the lights and effortlessly making the most ardent love to each other. Television unfortunately is a bore and ardent love is an immense drain on one's energy. I began to work day and night at my law office, and besides becoming very successful, I managed to avoid my wife entirely. For this deceit, I was called ambitious and was respected by everyone including my wife who was quite as bored with me as I was with her. We decided to have children because we couldn't possibly believe we were that miserable together. All this while I drove myself mercilessly for fear that if I paused for just one moment, the whole slim, trembling sanity of my life would come crashing down about my feet without the slightest sound. I went to a psychoanalyst who wanted to know about my childhood when I could barely remember whether I took a taxi or a bus to his office that day. I began to drink myself into stupors, pursuing other men's wives, and generally behaving badly. One morning, I stared into the mirror and could barely make out my features. Life is utterly meaningless. I have had everything a man can get out of life—prestige, power, money, women, children, and a handsome home only three blocks from the

Scarsdale Country Club, and all I can think of is I want to get out of this as fast as I can. (*He has become quite upset by now and has to avert his face to hide a sudden welling of tears. He takes a moment to get a good grip on himself, readopts his sardonic air and says.*) As you see, I have quite a theatrical way when I want to.

THE GIRL. (*Brightly.*) Oh, I think you are wonderfully wise.

ARTHUR. Oh, it was said best by your very own King Solomon, the wisest man who ever lived, when he wrote Ecclesiastes.

THE GIRL. Oh, King Solomon didn't write Ecclesiastes. That was written by an anonymous Jewish scholar in Alexandria. I wouldn't put too much stock in it. Weariness was all the rage among the Hellenized Jews.

ARTHUR. (*Staring at her.*) You are an amazing kid.

(*She smiles back at him exuberantly, unabashedly showing her fondness for him. It embarrasses him, and he turns away. He opens the office door, and looks out into the synagogue where the reading of the Torah has come to an end.*)

THE RABBI. (*Singing out.*) Blessed art Thou, O Lord Our God, King of the Universe, who has given us the Law of truth, and has planted everywhere life in our midst. Blessed art Thou O Lord, who givest the Law. (*There is a scattered mumbled response from the* OLD MEN *in the synagogue.*)

ZITORSKY. (*He now takes the Torah and holds it up above his head and chants.*) And this is the Law which Moses set before the children of Israel, according to the commandment of the Lord by the hand of Moses. (*The* FOUR MEN *on the platform form a small group as* ZITORSKY *marches slowly back to the Ark carrying the Torah. A mumble of prayer rustles through the synagogue.* ZITORSKY'S *voice rises out.*) Let them praise the name of the Lord; for His name alone is exalted. (*He carefully places the Torah back into the Ark. A rumble of prayer runs through the synagogue. All the* MEN *in the synagogue are standing now.*)

ARTHUR. (*Turning to* THE GIRL.) They're putting the Torah back. Is the service over?

THE GIRL. No. I have a wonderful book I want to give to you. Mr. Hirschman, our Community Cabalist, gave it to me. It is called "The Book of Splendor," and it is a terribly mystical book. I never met anyone who wanted to know the meaning of life as desperately as you do.

ARTHUR. It sounds very interesting.

THE GIRL. Oh, I'm glad you think so. I have to get it for you.

(SCHLISSEL *pokes his head into the office and indicates to* ARTHUR *that he is needed outside.*)

ARTHUR. I think they need me outside. (*He moves to the door.*)

THE GIRL. Yes, we really shouldn't have been talking during the service.

ARTHUR. (*He goes out of the office, closing the door behind him. He joins* SCHLISSEL, *who is a few steps away, muttering the prayers. Shaking his head.*) What a pity, really. A lovely girl. What a pity. Now, you look like a sensible sort of man. What is all this nonsense about demons? You really should call her father or mother or whoever it is who is responsible for her.

SCHLISSEL. Young man, if we called her father he would come down and take her away.

ARTHUR. Yes. That would be the point, wouldn't it?

SCHLISSEL. Then what happens to our exorcism?

ARTHUR. What exorcism?

SCHLISSEL. Listen, we've got to exorcise the dybbuk.

ARTHUR. (*Aghast.*) Exorcism!

THE SEXTON. (*He leans over the railing of the platform and admonishes them in a heavy whisper.*) Sssshhh!

(SCHLISSEL *promptly turns back to muttering his prayers.* ARTHUR *stares at him in a posture of vague belief.*)

ARTHUR. Are you serious?

ZITORSKY. (*His voice rises up loud and clear.*) . . . And it is said, and the Lord shall be king over all the earth; on that day shall the Lord be One, and His Name One.

(*The* CONGREGATION *which had sat now stands again.* THE SEXTON *leans over the railing and calls to the* KESSLER BOYS.)

THE SEXTON. Kessler, stand up. Now is the time for your memorial prayers.

(*The two* KESSLER BOYS *nod, stand, and look unhappily down at their prayer books.* THE SEXTON *pokes a palsied finger onto a page to show them where to read, and the two* YOUNG MEN *now begin to read painstakingly and with no idea of what they are reading.*)

KESSLER BOYS. Magnified and sanctified by His great Name in the world which He hath created according to His will. May He establish His kingdom in your lifetime and in your days, and in the lifetime of all the house of Israel, speedily and at a near time; and say ye, Amen.

CONGREGATION. Amen. Let His great Name be blessed for ever and ever.

KESSLER BOYS. Blessed, praised, and glorified, exalted, extolled and honored, adored, and lauded, be the Name of the Holy One, blessed be He, beyond, yea, beyond all blessings and hymns, praises and songs, which are uttered in the world, and say ye, Amen.

CONGREGATION. Amen.

(*The front door to the synagogue bursts open and* FOREMAN *thrusts himself in, obviously much distraught, not so distraught, however that he doesn't automatically join in the* "*Amen.*")

KESSLER BOYS. May there be abundant peace from heaven, and life for us and for all Israel; and say ye, Amen.

CONGREGATION. Amen.

KESSLER BOYS. May he who maketh peace in his high places, make peace for us and for all Israel, and say ye, Amen.

CONGREGATION. Amen.

(*The synagogue bursts into a quick mumble of prayers, except for* SCHLISSEL, *who scurries over to* FOREMAN, *who stares back at him white with panic.*)

SCHLISSEL. What happened? You got lost? You took the Long Island Railroad to Atlantic Avenue Station, and you got lost in the Atlantic Avenue Station.

FOREMAN. What Atlantic Avenue Station? I couldn't even find the Long Island Railroad.

SCHLISSEL. Idiot! You are an innocent child! Really! Services are over in a minute, and I'll take you myself. (ALPER *is leaning over the railing of the platform making obvious gestures as if to ask what had happened. Even* ZITORSKY *looks up from his hunched position at the lectern.* SCHLISSEL *announces in a heavy whisper as he starts to put on his coat again.*) He couldn't even find the Long Island Railway Station. (ALPER *clasps his brow.* THE SEXTON *turns around to* SCHLISSEL *and admonishes him with a heavy "Ssshhh!!!"* FOREMAN *has begun walking about, mumbling the prayers by heart, automatically a part of the service again. As he passes* SCHLISSEL, *he indicates with a jerk of his head that he would like to know the well-being of his granddaughter.*) She's all right. Don't worry about her.

(FOREMAN *nods and continues mumbling his prayers. In the rabbi's office,* THE GIRL, *who has been sitting pensively, now stands, goes out of the office, calmly crosses to the rear of the synagogue, and exits out the front door. Absolutely no one is aware she has gone. The* CONGREGATION *now bursts into a loud prayer, obviously the last one of the service, since those* MEN *on the platform begin to meander off, and all those who are still wearing their phylacteries begin to strip them off, even as they say the words of the prayer.*)

CONGREGATION. He is the Lord of the Universe, who reigned ere any creature yet was formed. At the time when all things were made by His desire, then was

His name proclaimed King. And after all things shall have had an end, He alone, the dreadest one shall reign; Who was, who is, and who will be in glory.

(SCHLISSEL, ALPER, ZITORSKY, and FOREMAN *have all rattled quickly through this final paean, impatient to close off the service, while the others continue the slow, clear and ultimate recital. The four* OLD MEN *form a huddled group by the front door.*)

THE FOUR OF THEM. (*Rattling it off.*) And with my spirit, my body also; the Lord is with me, and I will not fear. Amen.

ALPER. Amen, what happened?

SCHLISSEL. I'm taking him myself right away.

ZITORSKY. What happened, you got lost?

FOREMAN. I asked this fellow in the street, I said: "Could you—"

SCHLISSEL. (*To* ALPER.) Listen, keep an eye on that fellow there. He wants to tell the rabbi about the girl. All right, listen. I shall have to lead Foreman by the hand to the Korpotchniker. All right, listen, we're going. Good-bye. Peace be unto you.

ALPER. Take the Long Island Railroad to the Atlantic Avenue Station. Then take the Brighton train.

SCHLISSEL. Oh, for heaven's sakes. Are you presuming to tell me how to get to Williamsburg?

ALPER. All right, go already.

SCHLISSEL. (*Muttering as he leads* FOREMAN *out the door.*) The Brighton train. If we took the Brighton train, we would spend the day in Coney Island. (*He exits with* FOREMAN, *closing the door.*)

(*The rest of the* CONGREGATION *has finally come to the end of the service.*)

CONGREGATION. (*Their scattered voices rising to a coda.*) And with my spirit, my body also; the Lord is with me, and I will not fear. Amen!

SCHLISSEL *and* ALPER. Amen!

(*There is a flurry of dispersion. The two* KESSLER BOYS *mumble "good-byes" and disappear quickly out into the street, buttoning their coats against the cold.* HARRIS, *who is slowly and tremblingly removing his phylacteries, continues slowly to redress himself throughout the rest of the scene.* THE SEXTON *now scurries about gathering the various phylacteries and praying shawls and putting them back into the velvet prayer bags and then putting all the velvet bags and prayer books back into the cardboard carton they were all taken from, an activity he pursues with his usual frenetic desperation. Only* THE RABBI *and* THE CABALIST *continue to say a few prayers, "The Thirteen Principles of Faith," etc.* THE CABALIST *reads them sitting down, hunched over his prayer book.* ALPER *and* ZITORSKY *have genuine cause for alarm concerning* ARTHUR BROOKS, *for he has ambled down to the platform where he stands waiting for* THE RABBI *to finish his prayers. They watch* ARTHUR *warily.* HARRIS *suddenly decides to be communicative. He lifts his old face to* ALPER *and* ZITORSKY.)

HARRIS. Ah, am I thirsty!

ALPER. (*Watching* ARTHUR *carefully.*) Good.

(THE RABBI, *having finished his last prayer, now turns and starts down from the platform.* ARTHUR *steps forward to meet him.*)

ARTHUR. Rabbi—

THE RABBI. (*Walking by him.*) I'll be with you in just a moment. (*He strides directly to his office.* ALPER *leaps to intercept him.*)

ALPER. Rabbi—

THE RABBI. (*Continuing into his office.*) I'll be with you in a minute, Alper. (*He goes into his office and closes the door.* ALPER *clasps his brow and shrugs.* ZITORSKY *mutters an involuntary "Oy." They both nod their heads and wait with the sufferance that is the badge of all their tribe.* ARTHUR *moves a few steps to the rabbi's door and also waits. In the office,* THE RABBI *has sat down, all business, and has dialed a number. On phone.*) I'd like to make a person-to-person call to Rabbi Harry Gersh in Wilmington, Delaware. The number in Wilmington is Kingswood 3–1973— Thank you— (*He hums a snatch of the service.* ALPER *opens the door and comes into the office. He stares just a little openmouthed at the absence of* THE GIRL. *He tugs at his Vandyke beard in contemplation.*) Yes, Alper?

ALPER. Well, I'll tell you, Rabbi— (*He scowls, a little frustrated, then turns and goes out of the office.*) Excuse me.

THE RABBI. (*On phone.*) Locust 6–0932.

ALPER. (*To* ZITORSKY.) She's not there.

ZITORSKY. She's not there?

ALPER. I'll have to go out and look for her. (*Frowning, in contemplation,* ALPER *puts his coat on slowly and exits from the synagogue.*)

THE RABBI. (*His attention is abruptly brought back to the phone. His voice rises into that pitch usually used for long distance calls. On phone.*) Harry, how are you, this is Bernard here, I'm sorry I wasn't in last night, my wife Sylvia said it was wonderful to hear your voice after all those years, how are you, Shirley, and the kids? Oh, that's wonderful. I'm glad to hear it. Harry, my wife tells me you have just gotten your first congregation and you wanted some advice since I have already been fired several times— Good, how much are you getting?—Well, five thousand isn't bad for a first congregation although I always thought out-of-town paid better. And what is it, a one-year contract?— Well, what kind of advice can I give you? Especially you, Harry. You are a saintly, scholarly, and truly pious man, and you have no business being a rabbi. You've got to be a go-getter, Harry, unfortunately. The synagogue I am in now is in an unbelievable state of neglect and I expect to see us in prouder premises within a year. But I've got things moving now. I've started a Youth Group, a Young Married People's Club, a Theatre Club which is putting on its first production next month, "The Man Who Came to Dinner," I'd like you to come, Harry, bring the wife, I'm sure you'll have an entertaining evening. And let me recommend that you organize a little league baseball team. It's a marvelous gimmick. I have sixteen boys in my Sunday School now— Harry, listen, what do I know about baseball?— Harry, let me interrupt you. How in heaven's name are you going to convey an awe of God to boys who will race out of your Hebrew classes to fly model rocket ships five hundred feet in the air exploding in three stages? To my boys, God is a retired mechanic— Well, I'm organizing a bazaar right now. When I hang up on you, I have to rush to the printers to get some raffles printed, and from there I go to the Town Hall for a permit to conduct Bingo games. In fact, I was so busy this morning, I almost forgot to come to the synagogue— (*He says gently.*) Harry, with my first congregation, I also thought I was bringing the word of God. I stood up in my pulpit every Sabbath and carped at them for violating the rituals of their own religion. My congregations dwindled, and one synagogue given to my charge disappeared into a morass of mortgages. Harry, I'm afraid there are times when I don't care if they believe in God as long as they come to Temple. Of course, it's sad— Harry, it's been my pleasure. Have I depressed you?— Come and see us, Harry— Good luck— Of course. Good-bye. (*He hangs up, stands, starts looking around for his briefcase, strides out into the synagogue still searching for it. He is interrupted by* ARTHUR.)

ARTHUR. Rabbi, I have to hurry off, but before I go I would like to talk to you about that girl in your office. These old men tell me she is possessed by a demon and I think they are intending to perform some kind of an exorcism. I must caution you that that girl should be treated only by competent psychiatrists and the most frightful harm might come to her if she is subjected to anything like— Look, do you know about this exorcism, because I cannot believe you would tolerate any—

THE RABBI. (*Who has been trying very hard to follow all this.*) I'm afraid you have me at a disadvantage.

ARTHUR. I'm talking about the girl in your office.

THE RABBI. I'm somewhat new here and don't know everybody yet by name. Please be patient with me. Now I take it you want to get married.

ARTHUR. (*For a moment he briefly considers the possibility he is not really awake. Pensively.*) This whole morning is beginning to seem absolutely— Rabbi, there is a girl in your office, who is insane.

THE RABBI. In my office? (THE RABBI *is suddenly distracted by* ZITORSKY, *who has been wandering around the synagogue, looking up and down between the rows of chairs, and is now looking into the bathroom at the Upstage end of the synagogue.*) Mr. Zitorsky, what are you doing?

ZITORSKY. (*To* ARTHUR, *who is moving quickly to the rabbi's office.*) Well, have you ever seen such a thing? The girl has vanished into thin air. (*He shuffles to* THE RABBI, *absolutely awe-struck by it all.*)

ARTHUR. (*Now examining the interior of the rabbi's office.*) I suspect something more mundane, like simply walking out the door. (*He moves quickly to the front door, which now opens and* ALPER *returns, frowning with thought.*)

ALPER. (*To* ARTHUR.) Well, is that something or isn't it? I looked up and down, I couldn't see her.

(ARTHUR *scowls and goes out into the street, where he stands looking up and down.*)

THE RABBI. Mr. Zitorsky, if you will just tell me what this is all about.

ZITORSKY. (*His eyes wide with awe.*) Rabbi, Mr. Foreman brought his granddaughter down this morning, and he said: "She is possessed by a dybbuk!" Well, what can you say when someone tells you something like that?

THE RABBI. Oh, Mr. Foreman's granddaughter. Yes, of course, I see.

ZITORSKY. So he took us into your office where she was standing, and it spoke to us! What an experience! You cannot imagine! The voice of the dybbuk spoke to us. It was like a hollow echo of eternity, and the girl's whole body was illuminated by a frame of light! Fire flashed from her mouth—all of us were there, ask Alper here, he'll tell you— I swear this on my soul!— The girl began to rise into the air!

ALPER. Actually, Zitorsky is coloring the story a little bit, but—

ZITORSKY. (*Riveted by the marvelousness of the fantasy.*) What are you talking about? You saw it with your own eyes!

ALPER. Well, it was an experience, I must say.

THE RABBI. And the girl has gone now?

ZITORSKY. Into the air about us.

RABBI. And where is Mr. Foreman?

ALPER. He went to Brooklyn.

THE RABBI. What in heaven's name for?

ALPER. To see the Korpotchniker Rabbi.

THE RABBI. (*Quite impressed.*) The Korpotchniker?

ZITORSKY. Certainly! Maybe you don't know this, but Hirschman is his cousin.

THE RABBI. Mr. Hirschman? I have to admit I didn't know that.

ZITORSKY. Oh, sure. Listen, Hirschman is the first-born son of the original Korpotchniker.

ALPER. I am afraid we are drifting from the point.

THE RABBI. (*Frowning.*) The girl probably went home. Why don't you call the girl's home, Mr. Alper, and find out if she's there? I think you are a very close friend of the family.

ARTHUR. (*Who has come back into the synagogue.*) Well, thank God, for the first rational voice I've heard today.

ALPER. (*Nodding his head sadly.*) Yes, I suppose I had better call her father.

ARTHUR. (*Buttoning his coat.*) Fine. (*Glancing at his watch.*) Gentlemen, if you don't need me for anything any more, I would like to get to my analyst. Good morning. (*He strides to the door.*)

THE RABBI. Peace be unto you.

ARTHUR. (*He pauses at the front door, a little amused at the archaic greeting.*) Peace be unto you, Rabbi. (*He opens the door and goes out.*)

THE RABBI. Who was that fellow?

ZITORSKY. Who knows? The Sexton found him on the street.

THE RABBI. (*Buttoning his own coat.*) Well, I have to be down at the printers. A dybbuk. Really. What an unusual thing. Is Mr. Foreman a mystical man? By the way, Mr. Alper—Mr. Zitorsky—you weren't at the meeting of the Brotherhood last night. I think you should take a more active interest in the synagogue. Did you receive an announcement of the meeting? Please come next time. (*Finds his briefcase.*) Ah, there it is, good. (*Heads for the door.*) I would like to know what the Korpotchniker said about this. Will you be here later today? I'll drop in. Let me know what happens. You better call the girl's family right away, Alper. Good morning. Peace be with you.

ALPER *and* ZITORSKY. Peace be with you, Rabbi.

(THE RABBI *exits. The two* OLD MEN *regard each other a little balefully, and then* ALPER *shuffles to the wall phone, where he puts his hand on the phone, resting it on the receiver, quite depressed by the turn of events. In the synagogue,* THE CABALIST *is huddled in prayer, and* THE SEXTON *is sleeping on bench Up Right. A long moment of hushed silence fills the stage.*)

ALPER. (*Hand still on the phone.*) Zitorsky, let us reason this out.

ZITORSKY. Absolutely.

ALPER. (*The Talmudic scholar.*) If I call the girl's home, there are two possibilities. Either she is home or she is not home. If she is home, why call? If she is not home, then there are two possibilities. Either her father has already called the police, or he has not called the police. If he has already called the police, then we are wasting a telephone call. If he has not called the police, he will call them. If he calls the police, then there are two possibilities. Either they will take the matter seriously or they will not. If they don't take the matter seriously, why bother calling them? If they take the matter seriously, they will rush down here to find out what we already know, so what gain will have been made? Nothing. Have I reasoned well, Zitorsky?

ZITORSKY. You have reasoned well.

ALPER. Between you and me, Zitorsky, how many people are there on the streets at this hour that we couldn't spot the girl in a minute? Why should we trouble the immense machinery of the law? We'll go out and find the girl ourselves. (*They are both up in a minute, buttoning their coats, and hurrying to the front door where they pause.*)

ZITORSKY. (*Regarding* ALPER *with awe.*) Alper, what a rogue you are! (ALPER *accepts the compliments graciously, and they both dart out into the street.*)

(*Then, out of the hollow hush of the stage,* THE CABALIST'S *voice rises into a lovely chant as he rocks back and forth, his eyes closed in religious ecstasy.*)

THE CABALIST. (*Singing slowly and with profound conviction.*) I believe with perfect faith in the coming of the Messiah, and though he tarry, I will wait daily for his coming. I believe with perfect faith that there will be a resurrection of the dead at the time when it shall please the Creator, blessed be His name, and exalted the remembrance of him for ever and ever.

(*The front door opens, and* THE GIRL *comes rushing in, holding a beautifully bound leather book. She looks quickly around the synagogue, now empty except for* THE SEXTON, *and then hurries to the rabbi's office, which is, of course, also empty. A kind of panic sweeps over her, and she rushes out into the synagogue again to* THE SEXTON.)

THE GIRL. Mr. Bleyer, the young man that was here, do you know— (*She whirls as the front door behind her again opens and*

ARTHUR *comes back in. We have the feeling he also has been, if not running, at least walking very quickly. He and* THE GIRL *stare at each other for a moment. Then she says to him:*) I went home to get this book for you. I wanted you to have this book I told you about.

ARTHUR. (*Quietly.*) I just simply couldn't go till I knew you were all right. (*For a moment again, they stand poised, staring at each other. Then she sweeps across the stage and flings herself into his arms, crying.*)

THE GIRL. Oh, I love you. I love you. I love you—

(*They stand, locked in embrace.* THE CABALISTS'S *voice rises again in a deeply primitive chant, exquisite in its atavistic ardor.*)

THE CABALIST. For Thy salvation I hope, O Lord! I hope, O Lord, for Thy salvation. O Lord, for Thy salvation I hope! For Thy salvation I hope, O Lord! I hope, O Lord, for Thy salvation! O Lord, for Thy salvation I hope!

(*The CURTAIN quickly falls.*)

END OF SCENE 1

ACT TWO

SCENE 2

TIME: *It is around noon, four hours later.*

AT RISE: *A silent, dozing quiet has settled over the synagogue. Indeed,* THE CABALIST *has dozed off over a thick tome at the Upstage desk on the far side of the altar, his shawl-enshrouded head lying on his book.* THE GIRL, *too, is napping, curled up in the worn leather armchair in the rabbi's office.* THE SEXTON *is sitting like a cobbler on a chair at Right.* ALPER *and* ZITORSKY *sit drowsily on two wooden chairs about Center Stage. Only* ARTHUR *moves restlessly around the synagogue. He looks into the rabbi's office, checking on* THE GIRL, *studies her sleeping sweetness, somehow deeply troubled. All is still, all is quiet. In the synagogue,* THE CABALIST *awakens suddenly and sits bolt upright as if he has just had the most bizarre dream. He stares wide-eyed at the wall ahead of him. He rises, and moves slowly Downstage, his face a study in quiet awe. Apparently, he has had a profoundly moving dream, and he puts his hand to his brow as if to contain his thoughts from tumbling out. An expression of exaltation expounds slowly on his wan, lined, bearded old face. His eyes are wide with terror.*

THE CABALIST. (*Whispering in awe.*) Blessed be the Lord. Blessed be the Lord. Blessed be the Lord. (*He stands staring out over the audience, his face illuminated with ecstasy. Then he cries out.*) Praise ye the Lord! Hallelujah! Praise ye the Lord! Hallelujah! It is good to sing praises unto our God; for it is pleasant and praise is seemly. Praise ye the Lord! Hallelujah! (ALPER *has been watching* THE CABALIST *with drowsy interest.* THE CABALIST *turns and just stares at him.*) My dear friends, my dear, dear friends ... (*Tears fill his old eyes, and his mouth works without saying anything for a moment.*)

ALPER. Are you all right, Hirschman?

THE CABALIST. (*Awed by an inner wonder.*) I was studying the codification of the Law, especially those paragraphs beginning with the letters of my father's name— because today is my father's day of memorial. I have brought some honey cake here, in my father's memory. I have it somewhere in a paper bag. Where did

I put it? I brought it here last night. It is somewhere around—and as I studied, I dozed off and my head fell upon the Book of Mishna.— Oh, my dear friends, I have prayed to the Lord to send me a dream, and He has sent me a dream. I dreamt that I was bathing in a pool of the clearest mountain water. And a man of great posture appeared on the bank, and he said to me: "Rabbi, give me your blessing for I go to make a journey." And I looked closely on the man, and it was the face of my father. And I said unto him: "My father, why do you call me Rabbi? For did I not lustfully throw away the white fringed shawl of the Rabbinate and did I not mock the Lord to thy face? And have I not spent my life in prayer and penitence so that I might cleanse my soul?" And my father smiled upon me, and his bearded face glowed with gentleness, and he said unto me: "Rise from your bath, my son, and put upon you these robes of white linen which I have arrayed for you. For thy soul is cleansed and thou hast found a seat among the righteous. And the countenance of the Lord doth smile upon thee this day. So rise and rejoice and dance in the Holy Place. For thine is eternal peace and thou art among the righteous." Thus was the dream that I dreamt as my head lay on the Book of Mishna. (*He lifts his head and stares upward.*) The Lord shall reign for ever. Thy God, O Zion, unto all generations. Praise ye the Lord. Hallelujah! (*He stares distractedly around him.*) Where is the wine, Sexton? The wine! There was a fine new bottle on Friday! I have been given a seat among the righteous! For this day have I lived and fasted! I have been absolved! Hallelujah! Hallelujah!—Ah, the cakes! Here! Good!— (*He is beginning to laugh.*) I shall dance before the Holy Ark! Sexton! Sexton! Distribute the macaroons that all may share this exalted day! The Lord hath sent me a sign, and the face of my father smiled upon me! (*As abruptly as he had begun to laugh he begins to sob in the effusion of his joy. He sinks onto a chair and cries unashamedly.*)

ALPER. My dear Hirschman, how delighted we are for you.

THE SEXTON. (*Offering some honey cake to* ZITORSKY.) You want some cake there, Zitorsky?

ZITORSKY. I'll have a little wine too as long as we're having a party.

(THE SEXTON *scurries to Offstage Left to get wine.*)

ARTHUR. (*Who has been watching all this, rather taken by it.*) What happened?

ALPER. Mr. Hirschman has received a sign from God. His father has forgiven him, and his soul has been cleansed.

ARTHUR. That's wonderful.

ZITORSKY. (*To* THE SEXTON, *now pouring wine from a decanter.*) I'll tell you, Bleyer, if you have a little whiskey, I prefer that. Wine makes me dizzy.

THE SEXTON. Where would I get whiskey? This is a synagogue, not a saloon.

ZITORSKY. (*Taking his glass of wine.*) Happiness, Hirschman.

ALPER. Some wine for our young friend here. (*To* ARTHUR.) Will you join Mr. Hirschman in his moment of exaltation?

ARTHUR. (*Who is beginning to be quite taken with these old men.*) Yes, of course. (THE SEXTON, *who is pouring the wine and sipping a glass of his own as he pours, has begun to hum a gay Chasidic tune. He hands* ARTHUR *his glass.*)

ZITORSKY. (*Handing his glass back for a refill.*) Oh, will Schlissel eat his heart out when he finds out he is missing a party.

ALPER. (*Making a toast.*) Rabbi Israel, son of Isaac, I think it is fitting we use your rabbinical title—we bow in reverence to you.

THE CABALIST. (*Deeply touched.*) My dear, dear friends, I cannot describe to you my happiness.

ZITORSKY. There hasn't been a party here since that boy's confirmation last month. Wasn't that a skimpy feast for a confirmation— Another glass, please, Sexton. Oh, I'm beginning to sweat. Some confirmation party that was! The boy's father does a nice business in real estate and all he brings down is a few pieces of sponge cake and one bottle of whiskey. One bottle of whiskey for fifty people! As much whiskey as I had couldn't even cure a toothache. Oh boy, am I getting dizzy. When I was a boy, I could drink a whole jar of potato cider. You remember that potato cider we used to have in Europe? It could kill a horse. Oh, boy, what kind of wine is that? My legs are like rubber already. (*Suddenly stamps his foot and executes a few brief Chasidic dance steps.*)

ALPER. This is not a bad wine, you know. A pleasant bouquet.

ZITORSKY. (*Wavering over to* ARTHUR.) Have a piece of cake, young man. What does it say in the Bible? "Go eat your food with gladness and drink your wine with a happy mind?" Give the boy another glass.

ARTHUR. (*Smiling.*) Thank you. I'm still working on this one.

THE CABALIST. (*He suddenly raises his head, bursts into a gay Chasidic chant.*)

> Light is sown,
> sown for the righteous,
> and joy for the upright,
> the upright in heart.
> Oh,
> light is sown,
> sown for the righteous—

ZITORSKY. (*Gaily joining in.*)
> and joy for the upright,
> the upright in heart.
> Oh!

(THE CABALIST *and* ZITORSKY *take each other's shoulders and begin to dance in the formless Chasidic pattern. They are in wonderful spirits.*)
> and joy for the upright—

(THE SEXTON *and* ALPER *join in, clapping their hands and eventually joining the dance so that the four* OLD JEWS *form a small ring, their arms around each other's shoulders, their old feet kicking exuberantly as they stamp about in a sort of circular pattern.*)

ALL.
> The upright in heart.
> Oh!
> Light is sown,
> sown for the righteous,
> and joy for the upright,
> the upright in heart.
> Oh!
> Light is sown,
> sown for the righteous,
> and joy for the upright,
> the upright in heart.

(*Round and round they stomp and shuffle, singing out lustily, sweat forming in beads on their brows. The words are repeated over and over again until they degenerate from shortness of breath into a "Bi-bu-bu-bi-bi—bi-bi-bi-bi-bibibi."* ARTHUR *watches, delighted. Finally,* ALPER, *gasping for breath, breaks out of the ring and staggers to a chair.*)

THE CABALIST. A good sixty years I haven't danced! Oh, enough! Enough! My heart feels as if it will explode! (*He staggers, laughing, from the small ring of dancers and sits down, gasping for air.*)

ALPER. Some more wine, Hirschman?

THE CABALIST. (*Gasping happily.*) Oh!

(ZITORSKY *looks up, noticing* THE GIRL, *who, awakened by the romping, has sidled out into the synagogue and has been watching the gaiety with delight.* ZITORSKY *eyes her wickedly for a moment; then advances on her, his arms outstretched, quite the old cock-of-the-walk.*)

ZITORSKY. Bi-bi-bi-bi-bi-bi-bi— (*He seizes her in his arms and begins to twirl around, much to her delight. She dances with him, her skirt whirling and her feet twinkling, laughing at the sheer physical excitement of it all.* ZITORSKY *supplies the music, a gay chant, the lyrics of which consist of*) Bi-bi-bi-bi-bi-bi-bi—(etc.)—

THE CABALIST. The last time I danced was on the occasion of the last Day of the Holiday of Tabernacles in 1896. I was seventeen years old. (*A sudden frightened frown sweeps across his face. He mutters.*) Take heed for the girl, for the dybbuk will be upon her soon.

ALPER. (*Leaning to him.*) What did you say, Israel son of Isaac?

THE CABALIST. (*He turns to* THE GIRL, *dancing with* ZITORSKY, *and stares at her.*) Let the girl rest, Zitorsky, for she struggles with the dybbuk. Behold. (THE GIRL *has indeed broken away from* ZITORSKY *and has begun an improvised dance of her own. The gaiety is gone from her face and is replaced by a sullen lasciviousness. The dance she does is a patently provocative one, dancing slowly at first, and then with increasing abandon and wantonness.* ZITORSKY *recoils in horror.* THE GIRL *begins to stamp her feet and whirl more and more wildly. Her eyes grow bold and flashing and she begins to shout old gypsy words, a mongrel Russian, Oriental in intonation.* THE CABALIST *slowly moves to* THE GIRL *now, who, when she becomes aware of his coming close, abruptly stops her dance and stands stock still, her face now a mask of extravagant pain.* THE CABALIST *regards her gently and speaks softly to her.*) Lie down, my child, and rest.

THE GIRL. (*At this quiet suggestion, she begins to sway as if she were about to faint. Barely audible.*) I feel so faint, so faint. (*She sinks slowly to the floor, not quite in a swoon, but on the verge.* ARTHUR *races to her side.*)

ARTHUR. Do we have any water here?

ALPER. Wine would be better. Sexton, give her some wine. (THE SEXTON *hurries to her with someone's glass.*)

ARTHUR. (*Holding* THE GIRL'S *head.*) Is she a sickly girl?

ALPER. (*Bending over them.*) She was never sick a day in her life.

THE SEXTON. Here's the wine.

ZITORSKY. (*To* THE SEXTON.) Did I tell you? Did I tell you?

THE GIRL. I feel so faint. I feel so faint.

ARTHUR. (*Bringing the glass of wine to her lips.*) Sip some of this.

THE GIRL. (*Murmuring.*) Save me—save me—

THE CABALIST. The dybbuk weakens her. I have seen this once before.

THE SEXTON. (*To* ZITORSKY.) When you told me about this dybbuk, I didn't believe you.

ZITORSKY. So did I tell you right?

THE SEXTON. Oh, boy.

ARTHUR. Help me get her onto the chair in there.

ALPER. Yes, of course.

THE SEXTON. Here, let me help a little. (*Between the three of them, they manage to get* THE GIRL *up and walk her slowly to the rabbi's office where they gently help her lie down on the leather chair.*)

THE CABALIST. (*To* ZITORSKY.) They haven't heard from Mr. Foreman yet?

ZITORSKY. No, we're waiting.

THE CABALIST. (*Frowning.*) It is not that far to Williamsburg. Well, the girl will sleep now.

(*He walks slowly to the door of the rabbi's office, followed by a wary* ZITORSKY. *In the rabbi's office* ARTHUR *is gently laying* THE GIRL'S *limp sleeping form down on the chair.*)

ARTHUR. (*To the others.*) I think she's fallen asleep.

ALPER. Thank heavens for that.

ARTHUR. (*Straightening.*) Look, I'm going to call her family. She may be quite ill. I think we'd all feel a lot better if she were in the hands of a doctor. If one of you will just give me her home telephone number— (*Just a little annoyed, for nobody answers him.*) Please, gentlemen, I really don't think it's wise to pursue this nonsense any longer.

THE CABALIST. It is not nonsense. I do not speak of dybbuks casually. As a young man, I saw hundreds of people come to my father claiming to be possessed, but, of all these, only two were true dybbuks. Of these two, one was a girl very much like this poor girl, and, even before the black candles and the ram's horn could be brought for the exorcism, she sank down onto the earth and died. I tell you this girl is possessed, and she will die, clutching at her throat and screaming for redemption unless the dybbuk is exorcised. (*He stares at the others, nods his head.*) She will die. Wake the girl. I will take her to the Korpotchniker myself.

ALPER. Zitorsky, wake the girl. I will get her coat. Sexton, call a taxicab for Rabbi Israel. (ALPER, *who had been reaching for the girl's coat, is stayed by* ARTHUR. *He looks up at the young man.*) Young man, what are you doing?

ARTHUR. Mr. Alper, the girl is sick. There may be something seriously wrong with her.

ALPER. Young man, Rabbi Israel says she is dying.

ARTHUR. Well, in that case, certainly let me have her home telephone number.

ALPER. (*Striding into the rabbi's office.*) You are presuming in matters that are no concern of yours.

ARTHUR. (*Following.*) They are as much my concern as they are yours. I have grown quite fond of this girl. I want her returned to the proper authorities, right now. If necessary, I shall call a policeman. Now, let's have no more nonsense.

(ALPER *sinks down behind the desk glowering. A moment of silence fills the room.*)

THE CABALIST. The young man doesn't believe in dybbuks?

ARTHUR. I'm afraid not. I think you are all behaving like madmen.

THE CABALIST. (*He considers this answer for a moment.*) I will tell you an old Chasidic parable. A deaf man passed by a house in which a wedding party was going on. He looked in the window and saw all the people there dancing and cavorting, leaping about and laughing. However, since the man was deaf and could not hear the music of the fiddlers, he said to himself: "Ah, this must be a madhouse." Young man, because you are deaf, must it follow that we are lunatics?

ARTHUR. You are quite right. I did not mean to mock your beliefs, and I apologize for it. However, I am going to call the girl's father, and, if he wants to have the girl exorcised, that's his business. (*He has sat down behind the desk, put his hand on the receiver, and now looks up at* ALPER.) Well?

THE CABALIST. Give him the number, Mr. Alper. (ALPER *fishes an old address book out of his vest pocket, thumbs through the pages, and hands the book opened to* ARTHUR, *who begins to dial.*) There is no one home in the girl's house. Her father, who wishes only to forget about the girl, has gone to his shop in the city, and, at this moment, is overeating at his lunch in a dairy restaurant. The step-mother has taken the younger children to her sister's. The girl's doctor has called the police and has gone about his rounds, and the police are diffidently riding up and down the streets of the community looking for an old Jew and his granddaughter. (ARTHUR *says nothing but simply waits for an answer to his ring.* THE CABALIST *sits down on the arm of the couch and contemplates mildly to himself. At last he says:*) I cannot understand why this young man does not believe in dybbuks.

ALPER. It is symptomatic of the current generation, Rabbi Israel, to be utterly disillusioned. Historically speaking, an era of prosperity following an era of hard times usually produces a number of despairing and quietistic philosophies, for the now prosperous people have found out they are just as unhappy as when they were poor. Thus when an intelligent man of such a generation discovers that two television sets have no more meaning than one or that he gets along no better with his wife in a suburban house than he did in their small city flat, he arrives at the natural assumption that life is utterly meaningless.

THE CABALIST. What an unhappy state of affairs.

ARTHUR. (*Returns the receiver to its cradle, muttering.*) Nobody home.

THE CABALIST. (*To* ARTHUR.) Is that true, young man, that you believe in absolutely nothing?

ARTHUR. Not a damn thing.

THE CABALIST. There is no truth, no beauty, no infinity, no known, no unknown?

ARTHUR. Precisely.

THE CABALIST. Young man, you are a fool.

ARTHUR. Really. I have been reading your book—the Book of Zohar. I am sure it has lost much in the translation, but, sir, any disciple of this abracadabra is presuming when he calls anyone else a fool. (*He produces the book the girl gave him.*)

THE CABALIST. You have been reading The Book of Zohar. Dear young man, one does not read The Book of Zohar, leaf through its pages, and make marginal notes. I have entombed myself in this slim volume for sixty years, raw with vulnerability to its hidden mysteries, and have sensed only a glimpse of its passion. Behind every letter of every word lies a locked image, and behind every image a sparkle of light of the ineffable brilliance of Infinity. But the concept of the Inexpressible Unknown is inconceivable to you. For you are a man possessed by the Tangible. If you cannot touch it with your fingers, it simply does not exist. Indeed, that will be the epithet of your generation —that you took everything for granted and believed in nothing. It is a very little piece of life that we know. How shall I say it? I suggest it is wiser to believe in dybbuks than in nothing at all.

ARTHUR. Mr. Hirschman, a good psychiatrist—even a poor one—could strip your beliefs in ten minutes. You may think of yourself as a man with a God, but I see you as a man obsessed with guilt who has invented a God so he can be forgiven. You have invented it all—the guilt, God, forgiveness, the whole world, dybbuks, love, passion, fulfillment—the whole fantastic mess of pottage—because it is unbearable for you to bear the pain of insignificance. None of these things exist. You've made them all up. The fact is, I have half a mind to let you go through with this exorcism, for, after all the trumpetings of rams' horns and the bellowing of incantations and after the girl falls in a swoon on the floor—I assure you, she will rise up again as demented as she ever was, and I wonder what bizarre rationale and mystique you will expound to explain all that. Now, if the disputation is at an end, I am going to call the police. (*He picks up the receiver again and dials the operator.*)

ALPER. Well, what can one say to such bitterness?

THE CABALIST. (*Shrugs.*) One can only say that the young man has very little regard for psychiatrists.

(*The front door to the synagogue bursts open, and* FOREMAN *and* SCHLISSEL *come hurtling in, breathing heavily and in a state of absolute confusion.* ALPER *darts out into the synagogue proper and stares at them.*)

SCHLISSEL. Oh, thank God, the synagogue is still here!

ALPER. Well?

SCHLISSEL. (*Can hardly talk he is so out of breath.*) Well, what?

ALPER. What did the Korpotchniker say?

SCHLISSEL. Who knows?! Who saw the Korpotchniker?! We've been riding in subways for four hours! Back and forth, in this train, in that train! I am convinced there is no such place as Williamsburg and there is no such person as the Korpotchniker Rabbi! I tell you, twice we got off at two different stations, just to see daylight, and, as God is my witness, both times we were in New Jersey!

FOREMAN. Oh, I tell you, I am sick from driving so much.

ALPER. Idiot! You didn't take the Brighton train!

SCHLISSEL. We took the Brighton train! (*He waves both arms in a gesture of final frustration.*) We took all the trains! I haven't had a bite to eat all morning. Don't tell me about Brighton trains! Don't tell me about anything! Leave me alone, and the devil take your whole capitalist economy! (ZITORSKY, THE SEXTON *and* THE CABALIST *have all come out to see what the noise is all about. Even* ARTHUR *is standing in the office doorway listening to all this.*) We asked this person, we asked that person. This person said that train. That person said this train. We went to a policeman. He puts us on a train. The conductor comes in, says: "Last stop." We get out. As God is my witness, New Jersey. We get back on that train. The conductor says: "Get off next station and take the other train." We get off the next station and take the other train. A man says: "Last stop." We get out. New Jersey!

(*In the rabbi's office,* THE GIRL *suddenly sits bolt upright, her eyes clenched tight in pain, screaming terribly out into the air about her, her voice shrill with anguish.*)

FOREMAN. (*Racing to her side.*) Oh, my God! Evelyn! Evelyn! What is it?!

THE GIRL. (*She clutches at her throat and screams.*) Save me! Save me! Save me!

(ZITORSKY *and* THE SEXTON *begin to mutter rapid prayers under their breath.*)

ALPER. (*Putting his arm around* FOREMAN.) David, she's very ill. We think she may be dying.

ARTHUR. (*He has raced to* THE GIRL, *sits on the couch beside her, takes her into his arms.*) Call a doctor.

FOREMAN. (*In panic to* ALPER *who is standing stock still in the synagogue.*) He says I should call a doctor.

(ARTHUR *puts his hand to his brow and shakes his head as if to clear it of the shock and confusion within it.*)

ALPER. (*Crossing to* THE CABALIST.) Save her, Rabbi Israel. You have had your sign from God. You are among the righteous.

ARTHUR. (*He turns slowly and regards the silent betallithed form of the little* CABALIST. *To* THE CABALIST, *his voice cracking under emotions he was unaware he still had.*) For God's sakes, perform your exorcism or whatever has to be done. I think she's dying.

THE CABALIST. (*He regards* ARTHUR *for a moment with the profoundest gentleness. Then he turns, and with an authoritative voice, instructs* THE SEXTON.) Sexton, we shall need black candles, the ram's horn, praying shawls of white wool, and there shall be ten Jews for a quorum to witness before God this awesome ceremony.

THE SEXTON. Just plain black candles?

THE CABALIST. Just plain black candles.

(ALPER *moves quietly up to* FOREMAN *standing in the office doorway and touches his old friend's shoulder in a gesture of awe and compassion.* FOREMAN, *at the touch, begins to cry and buries his shaking old head on his friend's shoulder.* ALPER *embraces him.*)

ZITORSKY. (*In the synagogue, to* SCHLISSEL.) I am absolutely shaking—shaking.

(ARTHUR, *having somewhat recovered his self-control, sinks down near pulpit, frowning, confused by all that is going on, and moved by a complex of feeling he cannot understand at all.*)

CURTAIN

END OF ACT TWO

ACT THREE

TIME: *Half an hour later.*

AT RISE: THE GIRL *is sitting in the rabbi's office, perched on the couch, nervous, frightened, staring down at her restlessly twisting fingers.* FOREMAN *sits behind the rabbi's desk, wrapped in his own troubled thoughts. He wears over his suit a long, white woolen praying shawl with thick, black stripes, like that worn by* THE CABALIST *from the beginning of the play. Indeed, all the* MEN *now wear these ankle-length white praying shawls, except* ARTHUR, *who at rise is also in the rabbi's office, deep in thought.* THE CABALIST *sits on pulpit, his praying shawl cowled over his head, leafing through a volume, preparing the prayers for the exorcism.* THE SEXTON *is standing by the wall phone, the receiver cradled to his ear, waiting for an answer to a call he has just put in. He is more or less surrounded by* ALPER, SCHLISSEL, *and* ZITORSKY.

ZITORSKY. How about Milsky the butcher?

ALPER. Milsky wouldn't come. Ever since they gave the seat by the East Wall to Kornblum, Milsky said he wouldn't set foot in this synagogue again. Every synagogue I have belonged to, there have always been two kosher butchers who get into a fight over who gets the favored seat by the East Wall during the High Holy Days, and the one who doesn't abandons the congregation in a fury, and the one who does always seems to die before the next High Holy Days.

SCHLISSEL. Kornblum the butcher died? I didn't know Kornblum died.

ALPER. Sure. Kornblum died four years ago.

SCHLISSEL. Well, he had lousy meat, believe me, may his soul rest in peace.

(THE SEXTON *has hung up, recouped his dime, reinserted it, and is dialing again.*)

ZITORSKY. (*To* THE SEXTON.) No answer?

THE SEXTON. (*Shakes his head.*) I'm calling Harris.

SCHLISSEL. Harris? You tell an eighty-two-year-old man to come down and make a tenth for an exorcism, and he'll have a heart attack talking on the phone with you.

THE SEXTON. (*Dialing.*) Well, what else am I to do? It is hard enough to assemble ten Jews under the best of circumstances, but in the middle of the afternoon on a Thursday, it is an absolute nightmare. Aronowitz is in Miami. Klein the Furrier is at his job in Manhattan. It is a workday today. Who shall I call? (*Waiting for someone to answer.*) There are many things that I have to do. The tapestries on the Ark, as you see, are faded and need needlework, and the candelabras and silver goblet for the saying of the Sabbath benediction are tarnished and dull. But every second of my day seems to be taken up with an incessant search for ten Jews— (*On phone.*) Hello, Harris. Harris, this is Bleyer the Sexton. We need you badly down here in the synagogue for a quorum — If I told you why, you wouldn't come— All right, I'll tell you, but, in God's name, don't tell another soul, not even your daughter-in-law—

SCHLISSEL. My daughter-in-law, may she grow like an onion with her head in the ground.

THE SEXTON. (*On phone.*) Hirschman is going to exorcise a dybbuk from Foreman's granddaughter— I said, Hirschman is— A dybbuk. That's right, a dybbuk— Right here in Mineola— That's right. Why should Mineola be exempt from dybbuks?

ALPER. (*Thinking of names.*) There used to be a boy came down here every morning, about eight, nine years ago—a devout boy with forelocks and sidecurls—a pale boy, who was studying to be a Rabbi at the seminary.

THE SEXTON. (*On phone.*) Harris, this is not a joke.

SCHLISSEL. Chwatkin.

ALPER. That's right, Chwatkin. That was the boy's name. Chwatkin. Maybe we could call him. Does he still live in the community?

SCHLISSEL. He's a big television actor. He's on television all the time. Pinky Sims. He's an actor.

ZITORSKY. Pinky Sims? That's a name for a rabbinical student?

THE SEXTON. Put on your sweater and come down.

ALPER. (*To* THE SEXTON, *who has just hung up.*) So Harris is coming?

ZITORSKY. Yes, he's coming. So with Harris, that makes eight, and I am frankly at the end of my resources. I don't know who else to call.

ALPER. This is terrible. Really. God manifests Himself in our little synagogue, and we can't even find ten Jews to say hello.

THE SEXTON. I shall have to go out in the street and get two strangers. (*Putting on his coat.*) Well, I don't look forward to this at all. I will have to stop people on the street, ask them if they are Jewish—which is bad enough—and then explain to them I wish them to attend the exorcism of the dybbuk— I mean, surely you can see the futility of it.

ALPER. We can only get eight. A disgrace. Really. We shall not have the exorcism for lack of two Jews.

THE SEXTON. (*On his way out.*) All right, I'm going. (*He exits.*)

ZITORSKY. (*To* SCHLISSEL.) In those days when I was deceiving my wife, I used to tell her I was entertaining out-of-town buyers. I once told her I was entertaining out-of-town buyers every night for almost three weeks. It was a foolhardy thing to do because even my wife could tell business was not that good. So one night, she came down to my loft on Thirty-Sixth Street and walked in and caught me with —well, I'm sure I've told you this story before.

SCHLISSEL. Many times.

(THE CABALIST *enters the office. Upon his entrance,* THE GIRL *stands abruptly, obviously deeply disturbed and barely in control of herself. She turns from* THE CABALIST *and shades her eyes with her hands to hide her terror.* FOREMAN *looks up briefly. He seems to be in a state of shock.* THE CABALIST *sits down on the couch, lets the cowl of his prayer shawl fall back on his shoulders and contemplates his hands folded patiently between his knees. After a moment, he says:*)

THE CABALIST. (*Quietly.*) Dybbuk, I am Israel son of Isaac. My father was Isaac son of Asher, and I wear his fringed shawl on my shoulders as I talk to you. (*Upon these words,* THE GIRL *suddenly contorts her form as if seized by a violent cramp. She clutches her stomach and bends low and soft sobs begin to come out of her.*) Reveal yourself to me.

THE GIRL. (*In the voice of the dybbuk.*) I am Hannah Luchinsky.

(*In the synagogue,* ALPER, SCHLISSEL *and* ZITORSKY *begin to edge, quite frightened, to the opened office door.* ARTHUR *watches from his seat in the office.*)

THE CABALIST. Why do you possess this girl's body?

THE GIRL. (*Twisting and contorting; in the voice of the dybbuk.*) My soul was lost at sea, and there is no one to say the prayers for the dead over me.

THE CABALIST. I will strike a bargain with you. Leave this girl's body through her smallest finger, doing her no damage, not even a scratch, and I shall sit on wood for you for the First Seven Days of Mourning and shall plead for your soul for the First Thirty Days and shall say the prayers for the dead over you three times a day for the Eleven Months and light the Memorial Lamp each year upon the occasion of your death. I ask you to leave this girl's body.

THE GIRL. (*She laughs quietly. In the voice of the dybbuk.*) You give me short-weight, for you will yourself be dead before the prayers for the new moon.

(*In the office doorway, the three* OLD MEN *shudder.* FOREMAN *looks up slowly.* THE CABALIST *closes his eyes.*)

THE CABALIST. (*Quietly.*) How do you know this?

THE GIRL. (*In the voice of the dybbuk.*) Your soul will fly straight to the Heavenly Gates and you will be embraced by the Archangel Mihoel.

THE CABALIST. Then I enjoin the Angel of Death to speed his way. Dybbuk, I order you to leave the body of this girl.

THE GIRL. (*Her face suddenly flashes with malevolence. In the voice of the dybbuk, shouting.*) No! I seek vengeance for these forty years of limbo! I was betrayed in my youth and driven to the Evil Impulse against my will! I have suffered beyond belief, and my spirit has lived in dunghills and in piles of ashes, and I demand the soul of David son of Abram be cast into Gilgul for the space of forty years times ten to gasp for air in the sea in which I drowned—

FOREMAN. (*Standing in terror.*) No! No!

THE GIRL. (*In the voice of the dybbuk.*) —so that my soul may have peace! A soul for a soul! That is my bargain.

FOREMAN. (*Shouting.*) Let it be then! Leave my granddaughter in peace and I will give my soul in exchange.

THE CABALIST. (*With ringing authority.*) The disposition of David son of Abram's soul will not be decided here. Its fall and ascent has been ordained by the second universe of angels. The bargain cannot be struck! Dybbuk, hear me. I order you to leave the body of this girl through her smallest finger, causing her no pain nor damage, and I give you my word prayers will be said over you in full measure. But if you adjure these words, then must I proceed against you with malediction and anathema.

THE GIRL. (*Laughs.*) Raise not thy mighty arm against me, for it has no fear for me. A soul for a soul. That is my bargain. (*She suddenly begins to sob.*)

THE CABALIST. (*To* ALPER.) We shall have to prepare for the exorcism.

ALPER. I thought that would be the case.

THE GIRL. (*Sitting down on the couch, frightened, in her own voice.*) I am so afraid.

FOREMAN. There is nothing to fear. It will all be over in a minute, like having a tooth pulled, and you will walk out of here a cheerful child.

SCHLISSEL. (*Ambling back into the synagogue proper with* ZITORSKY *and* ALPER.) I tell you, I'd feel a lot better if the Korpotchniker was doing this. If you are going to have a tooth pulled, at least let it be by a qualified dentist.

ZITORSKY. I thought Hirschman handled himself very well with that dybbuk.

SCHLISSEL. (*To* ALPER *and* ZITORSKY.) If I tell you all something, promise you will never throw it back in my face.

ZITORSKY. What?

SCHLISSEL. I am beginning to believe she is really possessed by a dybbuk.

ZITORSKY. I'm beginning to get used to the whole thing.

(THE CABALIST *has stood and moved Upstage to the rear wall of the synagogue where he stands in meditation.* FOREMAN *is sitting again somewhat numbly beside his granddaughter.*)

THE GIRL. (*After a moment.*) I am very frightened, Arthur.

ARTHUR. (*Rises.*) Well, I spoke to my analyst, as you know, and he said he didn't think this exorcism was a bad idea at all. The point is, if you really do believe you are possessed by a dybbuk—

THE GIRL. Oh, I do.

ARTHUR. Well, then, he feels this exorcism might be a good form of shock treatment that will make you more responsive to psychiatric therapy and open the door to an eventual cure. Mr. Hirschman assures me it is a painless ceremony. So you really have nothing to be frightened of.

THE GIRL. Will you be here?

ARTHUR. Of course. Did you think I wouldn't?

(FOREMAN *moves slowly out into the synagogue as if to ask something of* HIRSCHMAN.)

THE GIRL. I always sense flight in you.

ARTHUR. Really.

THE GIRL. You are always taking to your heels, Arthur. Especially in moments like now when you want to be tender. I know that you love me or I couldn't be so happy with you, but the whole idea of love seems to terrify you, and you keep racing off to distant detachments. I feel that if I reached out for your cheek now, you would turn your head or, in some silent way, clang the iron gates shut on me. You have some strange dybbuk all of your own, some sad little turnkey, who drifts about inside of you, locking up all the little doors, and saying, "You are dead. You are dead." You do love me, Arthur. I know that.

ARTHUR. (*Gently.*) I wish you well, Evelyn. We can at least say that.

THE GIRL. I love you. I want so very much to be your wife. (*She stares at him, her face glowing with love. She says quietly.*) I will make you a good home, Arthur. You will be very happy with me. (*He regards her for a moment, caught by her wonder. He reaches forward and lightly touches her cheek. She cannot take her eyes from him.*) I adore you, Arthur.

ARTHUR. (*With deep gentleness.*) You are quite mad. (*They regard each other,* ARTHUR *stands.*)

THE GIRL. You think our getting married is impractical?

ARTHUR. Yes, I would say it was at the least impractical.

THE GIRL. Because I am insane and you are suicidal.

ARTHUR. I do think those are two reasons to give one pause.

THE GIRL. Well, at least we begin with futility. Most marriages takes years to arrive there.

ARTHUR. Don't be saucy, Evelyn.

THE GIRL. (*Earnestly.*) Oh, Arthur, I wouldn't suggest marriage if I thought it was utterly unfeasible. I think we can make a go of it. I really do. I know you have no faith in my exorcism—

ARTHUR. As I say, it may be an effective shock therapy.

THE GIRL. But we could get married this minute, and I still think we could make a go of it. I'm not a dangerous schizophrenic; I just hallucinate. I could keep your house for you. I did for my father very competently before he remarried. I'm a good cook, and you do find me attractive, don't you? I love you, Arthur. You are really very good for me. I retain reality remarkably well with you. I know I could be a good wife. Many schizophrenics function quite well if one has faith in them.

ARTHUR. (*Touched by her earnestness.*) My dear Evelyn—

THE GIRL. I don't ask you to have faith in dybbuks or gods or exorcisms—just in me.

ARTHUR. (*He gently touches her cheek.*) How in heaven's name did we reach this point of talking marriage?

THE GIRL. It is a common point of discussion between people in love.

ARTHUR. (*He kneels before her, takes her hand between his. He loves her.*) I do not love you. Nor do you love me. We met five hours ago and exchanged the elementary courtesy of conversation—the rest is your own ingenuousness.

THE GIRL. I do not remember ever being as happy as I am at this moment. I feel enchanted. (*They are terribly close now. He leans to her, his arms moving to embrace her. And then he stops, and the moment is broken. He turns away, scowls, stands.*) You are in full flight again, aren't you?

ARTHUR. I reserve a certain low level of morality which includes not taking advantage of incompetent minors.

THE GIRL. Why can't you believe that I love you?

ARTHUR. (*Angrily.*) I simply do not believe anybody loves anyone. Let's have an end to this. (*He is abruptly aware that their entire love scene together has been observed by all of the* OLD MEN, *clustered together in the open doorway of the rabbi's office, beaming at them. With a furious sigh, he strides to the door and shuts it in the* OLD MEN's *faces. He turns back to* THE GIRL, *scowling.*) Really, this is all much too fanciful. Really, it is. In an hour, you will be back to your institution, where I may or may not visit you.

THE GIRL. (*She sits slowly down.*) If I were not already insane, the thought that I might not see you again would make me so.

ARTHUR. (*More disturbed than he himself knows.*) I don't know what you want of me.

THE GIRL. (*One step from tears.*) I want you to find the meaning of your life in me.

ARTHUR. But that's insane. How can you ask such an impossible thing?

THE GIRL. Because you love me.

ARTHUR. (*Cries out.*) I don't know what you mean by love! All it means to me is I shall buy you a dinner, take you to the theatre, and then straight to our tryst where I shall reach under your blouse for the sake of tradition while you breathe hotly in my ear in a pretense of passion. We will mutter automatic endearments, nibbling at the sweat on each other's earlobes, all the while gracelessly fumbling with buttons and zippers, cursing under our breath the knots in our shoelaces, and telling ourselves that this whole comical business of stripping off our trousers is an act of nature like the pollination of weeds. Even in that one brief moment when our senses finally obliterate our individual alonenesses, we will hear ringing in our ears the reluctant creaking of mattress springs.

THE GIRL. (*She stares at him, awed by this bitter expostulation.*) You are possessed.

ARTHUR. At your age, I suppose, one still finds theatrical charm in this ultimate of fantasies, but when you have been backstage as often as I have, you will discover love to be an altogether shabby business of cold creams and costumes.

THE GIRL. (*Staring at him.*) You are possessed by a dybbuk that does not allow you to love.

ARTHUR. (*Crying out again in sudden anguish.*) Oh, leave me alone! Let's get on with this wretched exorcism! (*He strides to the door, suddenly turns, confused, disturbed, would say something, but he doesn't know what. He opens the door to find the five* OLD MEN *patiently waiting for him with beaming smiles. This disconcerts him and he turns to* THE GIRL *again, and is again at a loss for words. She stares at the floor.*)

THE GIRL. We could be very happy if you would have faith in me.

ARTHUR. (*He turns and shuffles out of the office. To the* OLD MEN.) It was tasteless of you to gawk at us. (*He continues into the synagogue trailed by the* OLD MEN. *He sits and is immediately surrounded by the* OLD MEN.)

FOREMAN. Are you interested in this girl, young man, because my son is not a rich man, by any means, but he will give you a fine wedding, catered by good people, with a cantor—

ZITORSKY. And a choir.

FOREMAN. —Possibly, and a dowry perhaps in the amount of five hundred dollars—which, believe me, is more than he can afford. However, I am told you are a professional man, a lawyer, and the father of the bride must lay out good money for such a catch.

ALPER *and* ZITORSKY. Sure— Absolutely.

FOREMAN. Of course, the girl is an incompetent and you will have to apply to the courts to be appointed the committee of her person—

ALPER. —a formality, I assure you, once you have married her.

FOREMAN. As for the girl, I can tell you first hand, she is a fine Jewish girl—

ZITORSKY. Modest—

ALPER. Devout—

FOREMAN. —and she bakes first-rate pastries.

ARTHUR. (*Staring at the gay* OLD MEN *with disbelief.*) You are all mad, madder than the girl, and if I don't get out of here soon, I shall be as mad as the rest.

ZITORSKY. A beauty, young man. Listen, it is said—better a full-bosomed wife than to marry a Rothschild.

SCHLISSEL. Leave the man alone. We have all been miserably married for half a century ourselves. How can you in good faith recommend the institution?

ALPER. The girl is so obviously taken with him. It would be a good match.

FOREMAN. (*Anxiously.*) Perhaps he is married already.

ALPER. (*To* ARTHUR.) My dear fellow, how wonderful to be in love.

ARTHUR. I love nothing!

THE CABALIST. Yes. The girl is quite right. He is possessed. He loves nothing. Love is an act of faith, and yours is a faithless generation. That is your dybbuk.

(*The front door of the synagogue opens, and* THE SEXTON *slips quickly in, quietly closing the door after himself.*)

ARTHUR. (*To* THE CABALIST.) Don't you think it's time to get on with this exorcism?

THE CABALIST. Yes. (*He stands, moves to the pulpit, sits.*)

ALPER. (*To* THE SEXTON.) Did you get anybody?

THE SEXTON. (*He moves in his nervous way down into the synagogue. He has obviously been on the go since he left; sweat beads his brow, and he is breathing heavily. Unbuttoning his coat and wiping his brow.*) Gentlemen, we are in the soup.

SCHLISSEL. You couldn't find anybody?

THE SEXTON. Actually, we have nine now, but the issue of a quorum has become an academic one. Oh, let me catch my breath. The rabbi will be here in a few minutes.

ALPER. The rabbi.

THE SEXTON. I saw him on Woodhaven Boulevard, and he said he would join us. Harris is on his way already. I saw him coming down the hill from his house. But the whole matter is academic.

ALPER. You told the rabbi we need him to exorcise the girl's dybbuk?

THE SEXTON. Well, what else was I to say? He asked me what I needed a quorum for at one o'clock in the afternoon, and I told him, and he thought for a moment, and he said: "All right, I'll be there in a few minutes." He is quite a nice fellow, something of a press agent perhaps, but with good intentions. Oh, I am perspiring like an animal. I shall surely have the ague tomorrow. I have been running all over looking for Jews. I even went to Friedman the Tailor. He wasn't even in town. So let me tell you. I was running back here. I turned the corner on Thirty-Third Road there, and I see parked right in front of the synagogue a police patrol car. (*The* OTHERS *start.*)

ALPER. (*Looking up.*) Oh?

THE SEXTON. That's what I mean when I say we are in the soup.

SCHLISSEL. Did they say something to you?

THE SEXTON. Sure they said something. I tell you, my heart gave such a turn when I saw that police car there. They were sitting there, those two policemen, big strapping cossacks with dark faces like avenging angels, smoking cigarettes, and with their revolvers bulging through their blue overcoats. As I walked across the street to the synagogue, my knees were knocking.

ALPER. When was this? It was just now?

THE SEXTON. Just this second. Just before I came in the door— Hello, Harris, how are you?

(*This last to the octogenarian of the first act,* HARRIS, *who, bundled in his heavy overcoat, muffler, and with his hat pulled down on his head, has just entered the synagogue.*)

ZITORSKY. (*To* THE SEXTON.) So what happened?

HARRIS. (*In his high shrill voice, as he unbuttons his overcoat.*) Gentlemen! Have you heard about this dybbuk?

SCHLISSEL. Harris, we were all here at the time he called you.

THE SEXTON. Harris, did you see the police car outside?

SCHLISSEL. So what did the policeman say?

THE SEXTON. (*Unbuttoning his collar and wiping his neck with a handkerchief.*) This big strapping fellow with his uniform full of buttons looks up, he says: "You know a man named David Foreman? We're looking for him and his granddaughter, a girl, eighteen years old." Well?! Eh! Well, are we in the soup or not?

(SCHLISSEL *goes to the front door, opens it a conspiratorial crack, looks out.*)

ARTHUR. I don't think the police will bother you if you get your exorcism started right away. They won't interrupt a religious ceremony, especially if they don't know what it is.

THE CABALIST. (*Who has made his own mind up.*) Sexton, fetch the black candles, one for each man.

(THE SEXTON *scurries to the rabbi's office where the black candles are lying on the desk, wrapped in brown grocery paper.*)

ARTHUR. (*Moving to the front door.*) I'll stand by the door and talk to the police if they come in.

SCHLISSEL. (*Closing the front door.*) They're out there, all right.

THE CABALIST. (*He looks about the little synagogue, immensely dignified now, almost beautified in his authority. The* OTHERS *wait on his words.*) I shall want to perform the ablutions of the Cohanim. Is there a Levite among you?

SCHLISSEL. I am a Levite.

THE CABALIST. You shall pour the water on my hands.

(THE SEXTON *scoots across the synagogue carrying black candles to everyone.*)

HARRIS. (*Looking distractedly about.*) What are we doing now? Where is the dybbuk?

ALPER. Harris, put on a praying shawl.

HARRIS. (*Moving nervously to the office door.*) Is this actually a serious business then? Where is the dybbuk? Tell me because Bleyer the Sexton told me nothing—

THE CABALIST. There is nothing in the Book of Codes which gives the procedure for exorcism, so I have selected those passages to read that I thought most apt. For the purpose of cleansing our souls, we shall recite the Alchait, and we shall recite that prayer of atonement which begins: "Sons of man such as sit in darkness." As you pray these prayers, let the image of God in any of His seventy-two faces rise before you.

ALPER. (*Crossing into rabbi's office.*) I'll get the books.

THE SEXTON. (*Giving* SCHLISSEL *a metal bowl.*) Fill it with water.

SCHLISSEL. I'm an atheist. Why am I mixed up in all this?

ALPER. We do not have a quorum. Will this be valid?

THE CABALIST. We will let God decide.

THE SEXTON. When shall I blow the ram's horn?

THE CABALIST. I shall instruct you when.

HARRIS. (*Putting on his shawl.*) What shall I do? Where shall I stand?

ZITORSKY. (*To* HARRIS.) Stand here, and do not be afraid.

FOREMAN. (*He comes out of the rabbi's office, carrying a long white woolen praying shawl which he gives to* ARTHUR.) I will show you how to put it on. (*He helps* ARTHUR *enshroud himself in the prayer shawl.*)

(SCHLISSEL *comes out of the washroom carefully carrying his brass bowl now filled with water. He goes to* THE CABALIST, *who holds his white hands over the basin.* SCHLISSEL *carefully pours the water over them.* THE CABALIST *says with great distinctness.*)

THE CABALIST. Blessed art Thou, O Lord our God, King of the Universe, Who hath sanctified us by His commandments, and has commanded us to cleanse our hands.

ALL. Amen.

(*The* OTHERS *watch until the last of the water has been poured over his hands. A sudden silence settles over the synagogue. They are all standing about now,* SEVEN MEN, *cloaked in white, holding their prayer books.* THE CABALIST *dries his hands on a towel handed to him by* SCHLISSEL. *He puts the towel down, rolls his sleeves down, takes his long shawl and with a sweep of his arms cowls it over his head, lifts his face, and cries out.*)

THE CABALIST. Thou knowest the secrets of eternity and the most hidden mysteries of all living. Thou searchest the innermost recesses, and tryest the reins and the heart. Nought is concealed from Thee, or hidden from Thine eyes. May it then be Thy will, O Lord our God and God of our fathers, to forgive us for all our sins, to pardon us for all our iniquities, and to grant us remission for all our transgressions.

(*As one, the other* OLD MEN *sweep their shawls over their heads and begin the ancient, primitive recital of their sins. They* ALL *face towards the Ark, standing in their place, bending and twisting at the knees and beating upon their breasts with the clenched fist of their right hand. They* EACH *pray individually, lifting up their voices in a wailing of the spirit.*)

ALL OF THEM. For the sin which we have committed before Thee under compulsion, or of our own will; And for the sin which we have committed before Thee in hardening of the heart! For the sin which we have committed before Thee unknowingly:

ZITORSKY. And for the sin which we have committed before Thee with utterance of the lips.

FOREMAN. For the sin which we have committed before Thee by unchastity.

SCHLISSEL. For the sin which we have committed before Thee by scoffing;

HARRIS. For the sin which we have committed before Thee by slander; And for the sin which we have committed before Thee by the stretched-forth neck of pride: (*It is a deadly serious business, this gaunt confessional. The spectacle of the* SEVEN MEN, *cloaked in white, crying out into the air the long series of their sins and their pleas for remission, has a suggestion of the fearsome barbarism of the early Hebrews. They stand, eyes closed, and in the fervor of communication with God, their faces pained with penitence. The last of the old men,* HARRIS, *finally cries out the last lines of supplication, his thin voice all alone in the hush of the synagogue.*) And also for the sins for which we are liable to any of the four death penalties inflicted by the Court—stoning, burning, beheading, and strangling; for Thou art the Forgiver of Israel and the Pardoner of the tribes of Jeshurun in every generation and besides Thee we have no King, who pardoneth and forgiveth.

(*Again, the silence falls over the stage.*)

THE CABALIST. Children of men, such as sit in darkness and in the shadow of death, being bound in affliction and iron, He brought them out of darkness, and the shadow of death.

THE OTHERS. Children of men, such as sit in darkness and in the shadow of death, being bound in affliction and iron, He brought them out of darkness, and the shadow of death.

(*The repetition of these lines has its accumulative effect on* ARTHUR. *His lips begin to move involuntarily, and soon he has joined the* OTHERS, *quietly muttering the words.*)

THE CABALIST. Fools because of their transgressions, and because of their iniquities are afflicted.

ARTHUR *and* THE OTHERS. Fools because of their transgressions and because of their iniquities are afflicted.

THE CABALIST. They cry unto The Lord in their trouble, and He saveth them out of their distress.

ARTHUR *and* THE OTHERS. They cry unto The Lord in their trouble, and He saveth them out of their distress.

THE CABALIST. Then He is gracious unto him and saith:

ARTHUR *and* THE OTHERS. Then He is gracious unto him and saith:

THE CABALIST. Deliver him from going down to the pit; I have found a ransom.

ARTHUR *and* THE OTHERS. Deliver him from going down to the pit; I have found a ransom.

THE CABALIST. Amen.

THE OTHERS. Amen.

THE CABALIST. Bring the girl in, Mr. Foreman. (FOREMAN *nods and goes into the rabbi's office.*)

ALPER. (*To* SCHLISSEL.) I don't like it. Even if the Rabbi comes, there will only be nine of us. I am a traditionalist. Without a quorum of ten, it won't work.

SCHLISSEL. (*Muttering.*) So what do you want me to do?

(*In the rabbi's office,* FOREMAN *touches* THE GIRL's *shoulder, and she starts from the coma-like state she was in, and looks at him.*)

FOREMAN. Come. It is time.

THE GIRL. (*She nods nervously and sits up. There is a vacuous look about her, the vague distracted look of the insane. Quite numbly.*) Where are you taking me? My mother is in Rome. They put the torch to her seven sons, and they hold her hostage. (*She rises in obedience to her* GRANDFATHER's *arm; he gently escorts her out of the office into the synagogue proper. All the while she maintains a steady drone of rattling gibberish.*) Where were you yesterday? I asked everybody about you. You should have been here. We had a lot of fun. We had a party, and there were thousands of people, Jerobites and Bedouins, dancing like gypsies. (*She suddenly lapses into a sullen silence, staring at the ground, her shoulders jerking involuntarily. The* OTHERS *regard her uneasily.*)

THE SEXTON. Shall I take the ram's horn out?

THE CABALIST. Yes.

(THE SEXTON *produces the horn-shaped trumpet from the base of the pulpit. The front door of the synagogue now opens, and a tall, strapping young* POLICEMAN, *heavy with the authority of his thick blue overcoat, steps one step into the synagogue. He stands in the opened doorway, one hand on the latch of the door, his attitude quite brusque as if he could not possibly get his work done if he had to be polite.*)

THE POLICEMAN. Is Rabbi Marks here? (ALPER *throws up his arms in despair. The* OTHERS *alternately stare woodenly at the* POLICEMAN *or down at the floor.* ARTHUR, *still deeply disturbed, rubs his brow.* THE CABALIST *begins to pray silently, only his lips moving in rapid supplication.*)

THE SEXTON. No, he's not.

THE POLICEMAN. I'm looking for a girl named Evelyn Foreman. Is that the girl? (*He indicates* THE GIRL.)

ALPER. (*Moving away, muttering.*) Is there any need, officer, to be so brusque or to stand in an open doorway so that we all chill to our bones?

THE POLICEMAN. (*Closing the door behind him.*) Sorry.

SCHLISSEL. (*To* ZITORSKY.) A real cossack, eh? What a brute. He will take us all to the station house and beat us with night sticks.

THE POLICEMAN. (*A little more courteously.*) A girl named Evelyn Foreman. Her father has put out a call for her. She's missing from her home. He said she might be here with her grandfather. Is there a Mr. David Foreman here? (NOBODY *says anything.*)

ALPER. You are interrupting a service, Officer.

THE POLICEMAN. I'm sorry. Just tell me, is that the girl? I'll call in and tell them we found her.

SCHLISSEL. (*He suddenly advances on* THE POLICEMAN.) First of all, where do you come to walk in here like you were raiding a poolroom? This is a synagogue, you animal. Have a little respect.

THE POLICEMAN. All right, all right, I'm sorry. I happen to be Jewish myself.

ALPER. (*He looks up quickly.*) You're Jewish? (*Turns slowly to* THE SEXTON.) Sexton, our tenth man.

THE SEXTON. Alper, are you crazy?

ALPER. A fine, strapping Jewish boy. (*To* THE POLICEMAN.) Listen, we need a tenth. You'll help us out, won't you?

SCHLISSEL. (*Strolling nervously past* ALPER.) Alper, what are you doing, for God's sakes?

ALPER. We have to have ten men.

SCHLISSEL. What kind of prank is this? You are an impossible rogue, do you know that?

ALPER. (*Taking* SCHLISSEL *aside.*) What are you getting so excited about? He doesn't have to know what it is. We'll tell him it's a wedding. I think it's funny.

SCHLISSEL. Well, we will see how funny it is when they take us to the basement of the police station and beat us with their night sticks.

ALPER. Night sticks. Really, Schlissel,

you are a romantic. (*Advancing on* THE POLICEMAN.) I tell you, officer, it would really help us out if you would stay ten or fifteen minutes. This girl—if you really want to know—is about to be married, and what is going on here is the Ritual of Shriving.

ZITORSKY. Shriving?

ALPER. A sort of ceremony of purification. It is a ritual not too commonly practiced any more, and I suggest you will find it quite interesting.

HARRIS. (*To* SCHLISSEL.) What is he talking about?

SCHLISSEL. Who knows?

THE POLICEMAN. (*He opens the door* ZITORSKY *had shut and calls out to his colleague outside.*) I'll be out in about ten minutes, Tommy, all right? (*He opens the door further to allow the entrance of* THE RABBI, *who now comes hurrying into the synagogue, still carrying his briefcase.*) Hello, Rabbi, how are you?

THE RABBI. (*He frowns, a little confused at* THE POLICEMAN'S *presence.*) Hello, officer, what are you doing here? (*He moves quickly to his office, taking stock of everything as he goes, the* SEVEN OLD MEN *and* ARTHUR *in their white shawls—* THE GIRL *standing woodenly in the center of the synagogue.* ALPER *and* ZITORSKY *greet him with helloes, which he nods back.*)

THE POLICEMAN. They've asked me to make a tenth for the shriving.

THE RABBI. (*Frowning as he darts into his office.*) Shriving? (*He opens his desk to get out his own large white shawl, unbuttoning his coat as he does. He notes* ALPER *who has followed him to the doorway.*) What is the policeman doing here?

ALPER. We needed a tenth.

THE POLICEMAN. (*Amiably to* ZITORSKY.) This is the girl, isn't it? (ZITORSKY *nods his head a little bleakly.*) What's really going on here?

(*In his office,* THE RABBI *sweeps his large shawl over his shoulders.*)

ALPER. We have said Al-chait and a prayer of atonement, and we are waiting now just for you.

(THE RABBI *frowns in troubled thought, slips his skullcap on as he clips his fedora off. In the synagogue,* ZITORSKY *shuffles to* SCHLISSEL.)

ZITORSKY. (*Indicating* THE POLICEMAN *with his head, he mutters.*) He knows, he knows.

SCHLISSEL. Of course. Did Alper expect to get away with such a collegiate prank?

THE RABBI. (*In his office, he has finished a rapid, silent prayer he has been saying, standing with his eyes closed. He looks up at* ALPER *now.*) I would rather not take any active role in this exorcism. I am not quite sure of my rabbinical position. But it would please me a great deal to believe once again in a God of dybbuks. (*He walks quickly past* ALPER *out into the synagogue.* ALPER *follows.*) Well, we are ten.

(*A silence falls upon the gathered men.*)

FOREMAN. May God look upon us with the eye of mercy and understanding and may He forgive us if we sin in our earnestness.

THE OTHERS. Amen.

THE CABALIST. Sexton, light the candles. (THE SEXTON *lights each man's candle.* THE CABALIST *advances slowly to* THE GIRL, *who stands slackly, her body making small occasional jerking movements, apparently in a schizophrenic state.* THE CABALIST *slowly draws a line before* THE GIRL *with the flat of his toe. Quietly.*) Dybbuk, I draw this line beyond which you may not come. You may not do harm to anyone in this room. (*The* OLD MEN *shift nervously in their various positions around the synagogue. To* THE SEXTON.) Open the Ark. (THE SEXTON *moves quickly up to the altar and opens the brown sliding doors of the Ark, exposing the several scrolls within, standing in their handsomely covered velvet coverings.* THE CABALIST *moves slowly back to his original position; he says quietly:*) Dybbuk, you are in the presence of God and His Holy Scrolls. (THE GIRL *gasps.*) I plead with you one last time to leave the body of this girl. (*There is no answer.*) Then I will invoke the curse of excommunication upon your pitiable soul. Sexton, blow Tekiah. (THE

SEXTON *raises the ram's horn to his lips, and the eerie, frightening tones shrill out into the hushed air.*) Sexton, blow Shevurim. (*Again,* THE SEXTON *raises the ram's horn and blows a variation of the first hollow tones.*) Sexton, blow Teruah. (*A third time,* THE SEXTON *blows a variation of the original tones.*) Sexton, blow the Great Tekiah and, upon the sound of these tones, dybbuk, you will be wrenched from the girl's body and there will be cast upon you the final anathema of excommunication from all the world of the living and from all the world of the dead. Sexton, blow the great Tekiah.

(*For the fourth time,* THE SEXTON *raises the ram's horn to his lips and blows a quick succession of loud blasts. A silence falls heavily on the gathered* MEN, *the notes fading into the air. Nothing happens.* THE GIRL *remains as she was, standing slackly, her hands making involuntary little movements.* FOREMAN'S *head sinks slowly on his chest, and a deep expression of pain covers his face.* THE CABALIST *stares steadily at* THE GIRL. *Then, suddenly,* ARTHUR *begins to moan softly, and then with swift violence, a horrible atavistic scream tears out of his throat. He staggers one brief step forward. At the peak of his scream, he falls heavily down on the floor of the synagogue in a complete faint. The echoes of his scream tingle momentarily in the high corners of the air in the synagogue. The* OTHERS *stand petrified for a moment, staring at his slack body on the floor.*)

ALPER. My God. I think what has happened is that we have exorcised the wrong dybbuk.

THE POLICEMAN. (*He starts towards* ARTHUR'S *limp body.*) All right, don't crowd around. Let him breathe.

THE CABALIST. He will be all right in a moment.

ZITORSKY. If I didn't see this with my own eyes, I wouldn't believe it.

THE RABBI. Mr. Hirschman, will he be all right?

THE CABALIST. Yes.

SCHLISSEL. (*With simple devoutness.*) Praise be to the Lord, for His compassion is everywhere.

(THE RABBI *moves slowly down and stares at* ARTHUR *as* SCHLISSEL, ZITORSKY *and* ALPER *help him to a chair.*)

ALPER. How are you, my dear fellow?

ARTHUR. (*Still in a state of bemused shock.*) I don't know.

THE SEXTON. (*Coming forward with some wine.*) Would you like a sip of wine?

ARTHUR. (*Taking the goblet.*) Yes, thank you very much. (*Turning to look at* THE GIRL.) How is she? (*Her schizophrenic state is quite obvious.* ARTHUR *turns back, his face furrowed and his eyes closed now in a mask of pain.*)

SCHLISSEL. Was it a painful experience, my friend?

ARTHUR. I don't know. I feel beyond pain. (*Indeed his hands are visibly trembling as if from cold, and the very rigidity of his masklike face is a frozen thing. Words become more difficult to say.*) I feel as if I have been reduced to the moment of birth, as if the universe has become one hunger. (*He seems to be almost on the verge of collapse.*)

ALPER. A hunger for what?

ARTHUR. (*Gauntly.*) I don't know.

THE CABALIST. For life.

ARTHUR. (*At these words he sinks back onto his chair exhausted.*) Yes, for life. I want to live. (*He opens his eyes and begins to pray quietly.*) God of my fathers, You have exorcised all truth as I knew it out of me. You have taken away my reason and definition. Give me then a desire to wake in the morning, a passion for the things of life, a pleasure in work, a purpose to sorrow— (*He slowly stands, for a reason unknown even to himself, and turns to regard the slouched figure of* THE GIRL.) Give me all these things in one—give me the ability to love. (*In a hush of the scene, he moves slowly to* THE GIRL *and stands before her crouched slack figure.*) Dybbuk, hear me. I will cherish this girl, and give her a home. I will tend to her needs and hold her in my arms when she screams out with your voice. Her soul is mine now—her soul, her charm, her beauty—even you, her insanity, are mine. If God will not exorcise you, dybbuk, I will. (*To* THE GIRL) Evelyn, I will get your coat. We have a lot of things to do this afternoon. (*He turns to the* OTHERS.) It is not a simple matter to get somebody released from an institution in New York. (*He starts briskly across to the rabbi's office, pauses at the door.*) Officer, why don't you just call in and say you have located the girl and she is being brought to her father? (*To* FOREMAN.) You'd better come along with us. Would somebody get my coat? We will need her father's approval. We shall have to stop off at my office and have my secretary draw some papers.

(MR. FOREMAN *has hurriedly gotten* THE GIRL'S *coat,* ARTHUR'S *coat, and his own. In this rather enchanted state, these* THREE *drift to the exit door.*)

THE POLICEMAN. Rabbi, is this all right?
THE RABBI. Yes, quite all right.
ARTHUR. (*Pausing at the door, bemused, enchanted.*) Oh—thank you all. Good-bye.
ALL. Good-bye.
ZITORSKY. Go in good health.
ALPER. Come back and make a tenth for us sometime.

(ARTHUR *smiles and herds* THE GIRL *and* FOREMAN *out of the synagogue. The door closes behind them.*)

SCHLISSEL. (*Sitting with a deep sigh.*) Well, what is one to say? An hour ago, he didn't believe in God; now he's exorcising dybbuks.

ALPER. (*Pulling up a chair.*) He still doesn't believe in God. He simply wants to love. (ZITORSKY *joins the other two.*) And when you stop and think about it, gentlemen, is there any difference? Let us make a supposition . . .

(*As the* CURTAIN *falls, life as it was slowly returns to the synagogue. The three* OLD MEN *engage in disputation,* THE CABALIST *returns to his isolated studies,* THE RABBI *moves off into his office,* THE SEXTON *finds a chore for himself, and* THE POLICEMAN *begins to button his coat.*)

END OF THE PLAY

Topics for Further Study

1. For a better understanding of the significance of the rites of exorcism, consult any modern dictionary under the words *dybbuk, exorcise, caballa (kaballa, kabbala)*, and Chasidism (Hasidism).
2. In what respects is this play realistic? In what respects is it imaginative?
3. Paddy Chayefsky has been both praised highly and condemned for his realistic dialogue. Discuss examples that seem realistic, others that seem out of place, others that are witty.
4. How has the play relevance for our times? Are many of our young people possessed of a "dybbuk" of lack of faith in living?
5. Arthur Brooks, drunk, suicidal, cynical, and without faith, changes markedly in the course of the play. Were you convinced? Why or why not?
6. The great English dramatist John Galsworthy said that "character is the best plot there is." Point out how the characters of Evelyn and Arthur move the plot along.

   Discuss in writing any one of the following topics:
   (*a*) Modern Miracles
   (*b*) Can Faith Move Mountains?
   (*c*) The Meaning of Chasidism (or the cabala) for Our Own Time
   (*d*) Coincidences in *The Tenth Man*.

7. Discuss the young rabbi's advice to his fellow rabbi in Baltimore. Is Chayefsky being satirical or factual? Do you find any objection to the activities engaged in by the young rabbi with his parishioners?
8. Are you prepared for the sudden falling in love of Evelyn and Arthur? Is this part of the miraculous element in the play?
9. How has Chayefsky managed to characterize so brilliantly and distinctly each of the ten men in the *minyan*?

The Blacks in the United States

Blacks are the largest minority ethnic group in America, comprising about one-tenth the total population. They were brought here as captives from Africa beginning about 1660 and for two hundred years thereafter were imported and sold as field hands for the vast Southern cotton and tobacco plantations. The conditions under which they were transported were cruel and inhuman. The "slavers," as the ships were called, were fetid, insanitary, and infested with rats. The captive Blacks were manacled in pairs, chained to the decks, and sometimes packed so close together that they could not turn around. Thousands died during the voyage from starvation, disease, and terror, and many that survived were broken in spirit.

Profit was the basis of slavery. Plantation owners could operate their vast tracts of land at little cost and make huge profits because they did not have to pay for labor. The adult slaves and their offspring were the owner's property. Families were at the mercy of their masters; if the owners wished to sell their slaves, they could separate husbands from wives and children from their parents, for the slaves had no legal rights. Under the complete control of their masters, the Blacks were denied education, property, and the freedom to move about; they were not allowed to vote nor could they seek redress in the courts for injustices committed against them.

All slaves were emancipated by law after the Civil War, but whites, particularly in the South, established customs and laws which kept them in subjection. They were obliged to attend segregated schools, travel in separate trains, and sit in the rear of buses; they could not walk in parks restricted to whites, eat in white restaurants, or be admitted to white hospitals. They were excluded from juries and denied the right to vote unless their father or grandfather had voted in 1866 or unless they could pass an exacting literacy test. There were separate toilets for whites and Blacks in public places, separate waiting rooms at railroad stations, separate drinking fountains, and separate swimming pools.

The doctrine of separate but equal facilities was legitimized by a Supreme Court decision in 1896. It was not until 1954 that the high court reversed itself in the case of *Brown* v. *the Board of Education of Topeka, Kansas*, ruling that separate schools were inherently unequal. The effects of this decision and related decisions were far-reaching and are still being felt.

Most Blacks now living in the United States were born here. A relatively small number come from the West Indies and very few from Africa. Until 1910 most Blacks lived in the state in which they were born. Between 1910 and 1945 there was a trickle of migration northward; and after World War II the migration accelerated rapidly. In 1910 70 percent of the Black population lived in the South. Today about 75 percent of the Black population lives in the North, chiefly in California, Illinois, Michigan, New York, Ohio, and Pennsylvania.

Discriminatory practices in Southern hotels, restaurants, and stores; the denial of their civil rights; and poor living conditions impelled many Blacks to migrate to the North in search of better opportunities. The North offered more jobs, higher wages, and better schools. No longer restricted to working on farms or doing menial labor for minimal compensation, many were drawn by the prospect of learning new skills on the job or in training programs provided by employers or set up by state or federal governments.

Today northern Blacks are congregated in cities, particularly in New York City, Chicago, Los Angeles, Detroit, Philadelphia, Washington, D.C., and Baltimore. Some of these cities are now predominantly Black. Within the cities Blacks gather in ghettoes, such as Harlem in New York City or Watts in Los Angeles, where living conditions are deplorable, although probably a cut above those in the rural South. The ghettoes are overcrowded, rents are high, housing is often wretched, crime and drug addiction are common, and tensions are acute.

Despite great handicaps the Black has made and continues to make great strides forward. He is entering occupations and professions hitherto closed to him, such as law, medicine, government, education, and banking, and is gradually reaching economic equality with whites. The 1970 census shows that the number of black families with annual incomes of more than $10,000 jumped from 11 percent in 1960 to 28 percent in 1970, while the comparable figures for white families rose at a somewhat slower rate, from 31 percent to 52 percent. Organizations such as the National Association for the Advancement of Colored People (NAACP), the Congress of Racial Equality, and the Urban League are working continually to promote the welfare and safeguard the civil rights of Blacks.

During the 1960s these and other civil rights organizations conducted sit-ins, marches, and demonstrations to establish the constitutional rights of Blacks and to free them from the indignities of segregation. Although these activities were non-violent in intent, violence sometimes erupted when white segregationists attacked the demonstrators, and law enforcement officers arrested and imprisoned the leaders of the demonstrations. Contemporary leaders of the civil rights movement include Roy Wilkins, former executive secretary of the NAACP, and the Reverend Ralph Abernathy, who, replacing the late Martin Luther King, served as head of the Southern Christian Leadership Conference for several years until resigning in July 1973.

Still quoted are the teachings of Malcolm X, who broke away from the Black Muslim movement in the 1950s and became an orthodox Muslim. He urged the establishment of a separate Black nation and called upon his followers not to smoke or drink, to support Black business organizations, to work hard, and to improve themselves by education. Malcolm X was assassinated in 1965.

Black leaders with extremist views have limited rather than national followings. Among them are Stokely Carmichael, H. Rap Brown, Huey Newton, and Floyd McKissick. The lack of wide support given to these revolutionists suggests that American Blacks prefer to use constitutional means to effect reforms.

All these leaders, from the most conservative to the most radical, are trying to develop in their followers a sense of identity, a pride in Black tradition and culture, a vision of a better life, and the acceptance of a responsibility for their emergence to equal status with other Americans.

Individual Blacks have distinguished themselves in many fields. In government, Thurgood Marshall is an associate justice of the Supreme Court, Robert C. Weaver was U.S. Secretary for Urban Affairs, and Ralph Bunche was for many years a high ranking official in the United Nations. Labor leader A. Phillip Randolph, civic leader Mary McLeod Bethune, and General Benjamin O. Davis are Blacks, as was the first surgeon to operate on the human heart.

Black writers are expressing the conscience, problems, and aspirations of their people. In novels, plays, poems, and articles they portray Black mores and culture, show where their people have been, where they are now, and where they should advance to. Their contributions have adrenalized American literature, strengthening it by their vigor and originality. Novelist James Baldwin and poets Countee Cullen, Paul Lawrence Dunbar, Langston Hughes, and James Weldon Johnson are among the notable writers of our time, and the plays of Ossie Davis, Lonnie Elder, Lorraine Hansberry, LeRoi Jones, and Louis Peterson have been successfully presented on Broadway and on stages throughout the world.

America's musical heritage has been greatly enriched by Black elements. Negro spirituals have a universal appeal because of their simplicity, religious fervor, and musical excellence. Folk songs and ballads composed by anonymous Negroes in the old South, like *Carry Me Back to Ole Virginny*, and the plantation songs of Stephen Foster, a white man who was influenced by the Black tradition, are deeply moving. Blacks created ragtime, blues, and jazz, distinctive musical forms which became internationally popular. George Gershwin's "Rhapsody in Blue," which has become a modern classic, is rooted in blues music. Among the great Black jazz musicians are Louis Armstrong, Count Basie, Ray Charles, Nat "King" Cole, Duke Ellington, and Thomas "Fats" Waller.

In the ranks of great singers of the concert stage are Marian Anderson, Roland Hayes, Mahalia Jackson, Leontyne Price, Paul Robeson, and William Warfield. Singers of popular songs include Pearl Bailey, Harry Belafonte, Sammy Davis, Ella Fitzgerald, and Aretha Franklin. Sidney Poitier has played many starring roles in films, Bill Cosby is a TV star, and James Earl Jones has starred in several Broadway plays.

Sports are one means by which Blacks have achieved economic and social status. In their athletic activities many emphasize their ethnicity and refuse to divorce it from their accomplishments, demanding to be recognized not only as athletes but as Black athletes. In her autobiography, *I Always Wanted to Be Somebody*, Althea Gibson, high-ranking tennis star, points out that Jackie Robinson "thrived on his role as a Negro battling for equality."

Black stars and superstars dominate almost every sport. Jesse Owens, in the 1936 Olympics, was the first man ever to win four gold medals in a single Olympics competition. When Jackie Robinson was admitted to professional baseball in 1947, he broke the color barrier. Hank Aaron, Roy Campanella, Bob Gibson, Willie Mays, John Milner, and Frank Robinson are among the many outstanding Black players who followed Robinson. Basketball without Wilt Chamberlain, Walt Frazier, Kareem Abdul-Jabbar (Lou Alcindor), Willis Reed, Oscar Robertson, and Jo-Jo White would be tame, but these and other superb Black athletes have made it an exciting and increasingly popular sport. In football, Jimmy Brown, who retired from the Cleveland Browns in 1966, Emerson Boozer, Bob Hayes, Ron Johnson, and Gene Washington are among the top professionals; and Arthur Ashe is a top-seeded tennis player.

Boxing, too, has been dominated by Blacks for many decades. Professional boxing offered a quick road to wealth to those who suffered discrimination in other fields. Moreover, it always had a symbolic importance for minority groups: witness Jewish boxers like Barney Ross and Benny Leonard, Italian-Americans like "Rocky" Marciano, and Irish-Americans like John L. Sullivan and John J. Corbett. Blacks quickly rose to the top of almost every weight class. With two exceptions every heavyweight champion since 1937 has been a Black: Joe Louis (1937–1949), Ezzard Charles (1949–1951), Jersey Joe Walcott (1951–1952), Floyd Patterson (1956–1959 and 1960–1962), Sonny Liston (1962–1964), Muhammad Ali (Cassius Clay, 1964–1970), Joe Frazier (1970–1973), and George Foreman, who became champion in 1973. Other Blacks among the boxing greats are Henry Armstrong, "Sugar Ray" Robinson, Dick Tiger, and Emile Griffith.

Perhaps the best-known contemporary Black is the late Reverend Martin Luther King, Jr., the Nobel Prize winner and civil rights leader whose eloquence stirred thousands and whose life is an inspiration to all, regardless of race. Dr. King led the "March on Washington" in the summer of 1963 at which 250,000 Americans, whites as well as Blacks, demonstrated their determination to end discrimination and second-class citizenship and to make Blacks full partners in the American way of life. His moving "I have a dream" oration delivered that day is an acknowledged masterpiece. That dream was cut short by his assassination on April 3, 1968, a deed that shocked the world; but the civil rights movement which he espoused and the non-violent policies he advocated are still very much alive today.

Suggested Reading

Books about the Blacks

Butcher, Margaret Just. *The Negro in American Culture.* New York: Signet, 1971. A scholarly and readable record of what America has done to the Black people—and what Blacks have accomplished in and for America.

Hughes, Langston and Meltzer, Milton. *Pictorial History of the Negro in America.* Third revised edition. New York: Crown, 1969. Contains more than 1,200 illustrations of events and personalities in the dramatic and turbulent course of Black history, and examines the social, political, artistic, and economic aspects of Black development.

Leinwand, Gerald. *The Negro in the City.* New York: Washington Square Press, 1968. Attempts to portray the problems of the Blacks who have migrated from the South to the large urban centers of the North. Contains selections from the writings of James Baldwin, Dick Gregory, Booker T. Washington, Malcolm X, Martin Luther King, Jr., and others.

Ploski, Harry A. and Kaier, Ernest, editors. *The Negro Almanac.* New York: The Bellwether Company, 1971. A one-volume repository on Black life and culture as seen within the framework of three basic categories: history, biography, and statistics. The enormous amount of factual material is organized within a framework of almost instant accessibility.

Plays about the Blacks

D'Usseau, Arnaud and Gow, James. *Deep Are the Roots.* New York: Charles Scribner's Sons, 1946.

McCullers, Carson. *Member of the Wedding.* New York: New Directions, 1951.

Peterson, Louis. *Take a Giant Step.* New York: Samuel French, 1954.

A Raisin in the Sun

A Raisin in the Sun touches on issues that are still current and troublesome. It is concerned with the problems of the Younger family, which is the Black race in microcosm, struggling to advance against tremendous odds but never losing hope. The aspirations of the Youngers are seriously challenged when they attempt to move from their slum tenement into a better neighborhood. They encounter opposition from the white residents and are told, obliquely but firmly, that they are not welcome.

The Youngers have dreams of lifting themselves from lower-class to middle-class status. They seek better education for their children and entrance into professional occupations. One member, Beneatha, wants to return to Africa to assist in the Black nationalist movement. The family's efforts to realize their dreams are the focus of the play. In spite of difficulties they retain their dignity and persevere in their determination. In certain ways they carry on as Blacks, proud of their race and its accomplishments; in other ways they behave as any other Americans would in the same circumstances.

A Raisin in the Sun won the Drama Circle Critics Award for 1958–1959, competing with Tennessee Williams' *Sweet Bird of Youth,* Eugene O'Neill's *A Touch of the Poet,* and Archibald McLeish's *J.B.* The play's appeal is universal because it deals with real people—their aspirations, frustrations, joys, and angers. Despite the fact that it undeniably skirts the edge of tragedy as troubles increase and tension rises among the family members, the author called the play a comedy, and rightly so, for it ends on a hopeful note and a promise of a brighter day for the Younger family.

Brooks Atkinson, drama critic for the *New York Times,* said it had "vigor as well as veracity." Frank Ashton of the *New York World-Telegram and Sun* declared: "It is honest drama, catching up real people . . . It will make you proud of human beings." Clive Barnes described it as "a quiet black cry in a white wilderness." After its success on the stage the play was made into a popular film and, more recently, it has been made into a highly successful musical. Of *A Raisin in the Sun* Miss Hansberry said: "The thing I tried to show was the many gradations of even one Negro family, the clash of the old and the new, but most of all, the unbelievable courage of the Negro people." This is what she has done—and done admirably.

LORRAINE HANSBERRY was born in Chicago in 1930 of well-to-do parents. Her father was a real estate investor and banker who battled in the courts against restrictive housing covenants. This background is interesting since one of the themes of *A Raisin in the Sun* is the efforts of a Black family to move from a ghetto into the suburbs.

Miss Hansberry's first ambition was to be an artist and to that end she studied art at the University of Chicago, the Chicago Art Institute, and the University of Guadalajara in Mexico. Abandoning art as a career, she came to New York City and worked at various jobs. While on the staff of a Harlem publication, she wrote *A Raisin in the Sun*, which opened in New York in 1959 to unanimous critical approval. In addition to *A Raisin in the Sun* she wrote *The Sign in Sidney Brustein's Window* and *To Be Young, Beautiful and Black*, a posthumous compilation of unproduced works. Her untimely death at the age of thirty-five cut short a promising career.

A Raisin in the Sun

BY

LORRAINE HANSBERRY

CHARACTERS

RUTH YOUNGER
TRAVIS YOUNGER
WALTER LEE YOUNGER (BROTHER)
BENEATHA YOUNGER
LENA YOUNGER (MAMA)

JOSEPH ASAGAI
GEORGE MURCHISON
KARL LINDNER
BOBO
MOVING MEN

A Raisin in the Sun by Lorraine Hansberry. Copyright © 1958, 1959 by Robert Nemiroff as the Executor of the Estate of Lorraine Hansberry. Reprinted by permission of Random House, Inc.

CAUTION: Professionals and amateurs are hereby warned that *A Raisin in the Sun*, being fully protected under the Copyright Laws of the United States of America, the British Empire, including the Dominion of Canada, and all other countries of the Universal Copyright and Berne Conventions, is subject to royalty. All rights, including professional, amateur, motion picture, recitation, lecturing, public reading, radio and television broadcasting, and the rights of translation into foreign languages, are strictly reserved. Particular emphasis is laid on the question of readings, permission for which must be secured in writing. All inquiries should be addressed to the publisher.

A Raisin in the Sun

What happens to a dream deferred?
Does it dry up
Like a raisin in the sun?
Or fester like a sore—
And then run?
Does it stink like rotten meat?
Or crust and sugar over—
Like a syrupy sweet?

Maybe it just sags
Like a heavy load.

Or does it explode?

—Langston Hughes

ACT ONE

SCENE 1

The YOUNGER *living room would be a comfortable and well-ordered room if it were not for a number of indestructible contradictions to this state of being. Its furnishings are typical and undistinguished and their primary feature now is that they have clearly had to accommodate the living of too many people for too many years—and they are tired. Still, we can see that at some time, a time probably no longer remembered by the family (except perhaps for* MAMA*) the furnishings of this room were actually selected with care and love and even hope—and brought to this apartment and arranged with taste and pride.*

That was a long time ago. Now the once loved pattern of the couch upholstery has to fight to show itself from under acres of crocheted doilies and couch covers which have themselves finally come to be more important than the upholstery. And here a table or a chair has been moved to disguise the worn places in the carpet; but the carpet has fought back by showing its weariness, with depressing uniformity, elsewhere on its surface.

Weariness has, in fact, won in this room. Everything has been polished, washed, sat on, used, scrubbed too often. All pretenses but living itself have long since vanished from the very atmosphere of this room.

Moreover, a section of this room, for it is not really a room unto itself, though the landlord's lease would make it seem so, slopes backward to provide a small kitchen area, where the family prepares the meals that are eaten in the living room proper, which must also serve as dining room. The single window that has been provided for these "two" rooms is located in this kitchen area. The sole natural light the family may enjoy in the course of a day is only that which fights its way through this little window.

At left, a door leads to a bedroom which is shared by MAMA and her daughter, BENEATHA. At right, opposite, is a second room (which in the beginning of the life of this apartment was probably a breakfast room) which serves as a bedroom for WALTER and his wife, RUTH.

TIME: *Sometime between World War II and the present.*

PLACE: *Chicago's Southside.*

AT RISE: *It is morning dark in the living room.* TRAVIS *is asleep on the make-down bed at center. An alarm clock sounds from within the bedroom at right, and presently* RUTH *enters from that room and closes the door behind her. She crosses sleepily toward the window. As she passes her sleeping son she reaches down and shakes him a little. At the window she raises the shade and a dusky Southside morning light comes in feebly. She fills a pot with water and puts it on to boil. She calls to the boy, between yawns, in a slightly muffled voice.*

RUTH *is about thirty. We can see that she was a pretty girl, even exceptionally so, but now it is apparent that life has been little that she expected, and disappointment has already begun to hang in her face. In a few years, before thirty-five even, she will be known among her people as a "settled woman."*

She crosses to her son and gives him a good, final, rousing shake.

RUTH. Come on now, boy, it's seven thirty! (*Her son sits up at last, in a stupor of sleepiness.*) I say hurry up, Travis! You ain't the only person in the world got to use a bathroom! (*The child, a sturdy, handsome little boy of ten or eleven, drags himself out of the bed and almost blindly takes his towels and "today's clothes" from drawers and a closet and goes out to the bathroom, which is in an outside hall and which is shared by another family or families on the same floor.* RUTH *crosses to the bedroom door at right and opens it and calls in to her husband.*) Walter Lee! . . . It's after seven thirty! Lemme see you do some waking up in there now! (*She waits.*) You better get up from there, man! It's after seven thirty I tell you. (*She waits again.*) All right, you just go ahead and lay there and next thing you know Travis be finished and Mr. Johnson'll be in there and you'll be fussing and cussing round here like a mad man! And be late too! (*She waits, at the end of patience.*) Walter Lee—it's time for you to get up!

(*She waits another second and then starts to go into the bedroom, but is apparently satisfied that her husband has begun to get up. She stops, pulls the door to, and returns to the kitchen area. She wipes her face with a moist cloth and runs her fingers through her sleep-disheveled hair in a vain effort and ties an apron around her housecoat. The bedroom door at right opens and her husband stands in the doorway in his pajamas, which are rumpled and mismated. He is a lean, intense young man in his middle thirties, inclined to quick nervous movements and erratic speech habits— and always in his voice there is a quality of indictment.*)

WALTER. Is he out yet?

RUTH. What you mean *out*? He ain't hardly got in there good yet.

WALTER. (*Wandering in, still more oriented to sleep than to a new day.*) Well, what was you doing all that yelling for if I can't even get in there yet? (*Stopping and thinking.*) Check coming today?

RUTH. They *said* Saturday and this is just Friday and I hopes to God you ain't going to get up here first thing this morning and start talking to me 'bout no money—'cause I 'bout don't want to hear it.

WALTER. Something the matter with you this morning?

RUTH. No—I'm just sleepy as the devil. What kind of eggs you want?

WALTER. Not scrambled. (RUTH *starts to scramble eggs.*) Paper come? (RUTH *points impatiently to the rolled up* Tribune *on the table, and he gets it and spreads it out and vaguely reads the front page.*) Set off another bomb yesterday.

RUTH. (*Maximum indifference.*) Did they?

WALTER. (*Looking up.*) What's the matter with you?

RUTH. Ain't nothing the matter with me. And don't keep asking me that this morning.

WALTER. Ain't nobody bothering you. (*Reading the news of the day absently again.*) Say Colonel McCormick is sick.

RUTH. (*Affecting tea-party interest.*) Is he now? Poor thing.

WALTER. (*Sighing and looking at his watch.*) Oh, me. (*He waits.*) Now what is that boy doing in that bathroom all this time? He just going to have to start getting up earlier. I can't be being late to work on account of him fooling around in there.

RUTH. (*Turning on him.*) Oh, no he ain't going to be getting up no earlier no such thing! It ain't his fault that he can't get to bed no earlier nights 'cause he got a bunch of crazy good-for-nothing clowns sitting up running their mouths in what is supposed to be his bedroom after ten o'clock at night . . .

WALTER. That's what you mad about, ain't it? The things I want to talk about with my friends just couldn't be important in your mind, could they?

(*He rises and finds a cigarette in her handbag on the table and crosses to the little window and looks out, smoking and deeply enjoying this first one.*)

RUTH. (*Almost matter of factly, a complaint too automatic to deserve emphasis.*) Why you always got to smoke before you eat in the morning?

WALTER. (*At the window.*) Just look at 'em down there . . . Running and racing to work . . . (*He turns and faces his wife and watches her a moment at the stove, and then, suddenly.*) You look young this morning, baby.

RUTH. (*Indifferently.*) Yeah?

WALTER. Just for a second—stirring them eggs. It's gone now—just for a second it was—you looked real young again. (*Then, drily.*) It's gone now—you look like yourself again.

RUTH. Man, if you don't shut up and leave me alone.

WALTER. (*Looking out to the street again.*) First thing a man ought to learn in life is not to make love to no colored woman first thing in the morning. You all some evil people at eight o'clock in the morning.

(TRAVIS *appears in the hall doorway, almost fully dressed and quite wide awake now, his towels and pajamas across his shoulders. He opens the door and signals for his father to make the bathroom in a hurry.*)

TRAVIS. (*Watching the bathroom.*) Daddy, come on!

(WALTER *gets his bathroom utensils and flies out to the bathroom.*)

RUTH. Sit down and have your breakfast, Travis.

TRAVIS. Mama, this is Friday. (*Gleefully.*) Check coming tomorrow, huh?

RUTH. You get your mind off money and eat your breakfast.

TRAVIS. (*Eating.*) This is the morning we supposed to bring the fifty cents to school.

RUTH. Well, I ain't got no fifty cents this morning.

TRAVIS. Teacher say we have to.

RUTH. I don't care what teacher say. I ain't got it. Eat your breakfast, Travis.

TRAVIS. I *am* eating.

RUTH. Hush up now and just eat!

(*The boy gives her an exasperated look for her lack of understanding, and eats grudgingly.*)

TRAVIS. You think Grandmama would have it?

RUTH. No! And I want you to stop asking your grandmother for money, you hear me?

TRAVIS. (*Outraged.*) Gaaaleee! I don't ask her, she just gimme it sometimes!

RUTH. Travis Willard Younger—I got too much on me this morning to be—

TRAVIS. Maybe Daddy—

RUTH. *Travis!*

(*The boy hushes abruptly. They are both quiet and tense for several seconds.*)

TRAVIS. (*Presently.*) Could I maybe go carry some groceries in front of the supermarket for a little while after school then?

RUTH. Just hush, I said. (*Travis jabs his spoon into his cereal bowl viciously, and rests his head in anger upon his fists.*) If you through eating, you can get over there and make up your bed.

(*The boy obeys stiffly and crosses the room, almost mechanically, to the bed and more or less carefully folds the covering. He carries the bedding into his mother's room and returns with his books and cap.*)

TRAVIS. (*Sulking and standing apart from her unnaturally.*) I'm gone.

RUTH. (*Looking up from the stove to inspect him automatically.*) Come here. (*He crosses to her and she studies his head.*) If you don't take this comb and fix this here head, you better! (TRAVIS *puts down his books with a great sigh of oppression, and crosses to the mirror. His mother mutters under her breath about his "slubbornness."*) 'Bout to march out of here with that head looking just like chickens slept in it! I just don't know where you get your slubborn ways . . . And get your jacket, too. Looks chilly out this morning.

TRAVIS. (*With conspicuously brushed hair and jacket.*) I'm gone.

RUTH. Get carfare and milk money—(*Waving one finger.*)—and not a single penny for no caps, you hear me?

TRAVIS. (*With sullen politeness.*) Yes'm.

(*He turns in outrage to leave. His mother watches after him as in his frustration he approaches the door almost comically. When she speaks to him, her voice has become a very gentle tease.*)

RUTH. (*Mocking; as she thinks he would say it.*) Oh, Mama makes me so mad sometimes, I don't know what to do! (*She waits and continues to his back as he stands stock-still in front of the door.*) I wouldn't kiss that woman good-bye for nothing in this world this morning! (*The boy finally turns around and rolls his eyes at her, knowing the mood has changed and he is vindicated; he does not, however, move toward her yet.*) Not for nothing in this world! (*She finally laughs aloud at him and holds out her arms to him and we see that it is a way between them, very old and practised. He crosses to her and allows her to embrace him warmly but keeps his face fixed with masculine rigidity. She holds him back from her presently and looks at him and runs her fingers over the features of his face. With utter gentleness—*) Now—whose little old angry man are you?

TRAVIS. (*The masculinity and gruffness start to fade at last.*) Aw gaalee—Mama . . .

RUTH. (*Mimicking.*) Aw—gaaaaalleeeee, Mama! (*She pushes him, with rough playfulness and finality, toward the door.*) Get on out of here or you going to be late.

TRAVIS. (*In the face of love, new aggressiveness.*) Mama, could I *please* go carry groceries?

RUTH. Honey, it's starting to get so cold evenings.

WALTER. (*Coming in from the bathroom and drawing a make-believe gun from a make-believe holster and shooting at his son.*) What is it he wants to do?

RUTH. Go carry groceries after school at the supermarket.

WALTER. Well, let him go . . .

TRAVIS. (*Quickly, to the ally.*) I *have* to—she won't gimme the fifty cents . . .

WALTER. (*To his wife only.*) Why not?

RUTH. (*Simply, and with flavor.*) 'Cause we don't have it.

WALTER. (*To* RUTH *only.*) What you tell the boy things like that for? (*Reaching down*

into his pants with a rather important gesture.) Here, son—
> (*He hands the boy the coin, but his eyes are directed to his wife's.* TRAVIS *takes the money happily.*)

TRAVIS. Thanks, Daddy.
> (*He starts out.* RUTH *watches both of them with murder in her eyes.* WALTER *stands and stares back at her with defiance, and suddenly reaches into his pocket again on an afterthought.*)

WALTER. (*Without even looking at his son, still staring hard at his wife.*) In fact, here's another fifty cents . . . Buy yourself some fruit today—or take a taxicab to school or something!

TRAVIS. Whoopee—
> (*He leaps up and clasps his father around the middle with his legs, and they face each other in mutual appreciation; slowly* WALTER LEE *peeks around the boy to catch the violent rays from his wife's eyes and draws his head back as if shot.*)

WALTER. You better get down now—and get to school, man.

TRAVIS. (*At the door.*) O.K. Good-bye.
> (*He exits.*)

WALTER. (*After him, pointing with pride.*) That's *my* boy. (*She looks at him in disgust and turns back to her work.*) You know what I was thinking 'bout in the bathroom this morning?

RUTH. No.

WALTER. How come you always try to be so pleasant!

RUTH. What is there to be pleasant 'bout!

WALTER. You want to know what I was thinking 'bout in the bathroom or not!

RUTH. I know what you thinking 'bout.

WALTER. (*Ignoring her.*) 'Bout what me and Willy Harris was talking about last night.

RUTH. (*Immediately—a refrain.*) Willy Harris is a good-for-nothing loud mouth.

WALTER. Anybody who talks to me has got to be a good-for-nothing loud mouth, ain't he? And what you know about who is just a good-for-nothing loud mouth? Charlie Atkins was just a "good-for-nothing loud mouth" too, wasn't he! When he wanted me to go in the dry-cleaning business with him. And now—he's grossing a hundred thousand a year. A hundred thousand dollars a year! You still call *him* a loud mouth!

RUTH. (*Bitterly.*) Oh, Walter Lee . . .
> (*She folds her head on her arms over the table.*)

WALTER. (*Rising and coming to her and standing over her.*) You tired, ain't you? Tired of everything. Me, the boy, the way we live—this beat-up hole—everything. Ain't you? (*She doesn't look up, doesn't answer.*) So tired—moaning and groaning all the time, but you wouldn't do nothing to help, would you? You couldn't be on my side that long for nothing, could you?

RUTH. Walter, please leave me alone.

WALTER. A man needs for a woman to back him up . . .

RUTH. Walter—

WALTER. Mama would listen to you. You know she listen to you more than she do me and Bennie. She think more of you. All you have to do is just sit down with her when you drinking your coffee one morning and talking 'bout things like you do and—(*He sits down beside her and demonstrates graphically what he thinks her methods and tone should be.*)—you just sip your coffee, see, and say easy like that you been thinking 'bout that deal Walter Lee is so interested in, 'bout the store and all, and sip some more coffee, like what you saying ain't really that important to you—And the next thing you know, she be listening good and asking you questions and when I come home—I can tell her the details. This ain't no fly-by-night proposition, baby. I mean we figured it out, me and Willy and Bobo.

RUTH. (*With a frown.*) Bobo?

WALTER. Yeah. You see, this little liquor store we got in mind cost seventy-five thousand and we figured the initial investment on the place be 'bout thirty thousand, see. That be ten thousand each. Course, there's a couple of hundred you got to pay so's you don't spend your life just waiting for them clowns to let your license get approved—

RUTH. You mean graft?

WALTER. (*Frowning impatiently.*) Don't call it that. See there, that just goes to show you what women understand about the world. Baby, don't *nothing* happen for you in this world 'less you pay *somebody* off!

RUTH. Walter, leave me alone! (*She raises her head and stares at him vigorously—then says, more quietly.*) *Eat* your eggs, they gonna be cold.

WALTER. (*Straightening up from her and looking off.*) That's it. There you are. Man say to his woman: I got me a dream. His woman say: Eat your eggs. (*Sadly, but gaining in power.*) Man say: I got to take hold of this here world, baby! And a woman will say: Eat your eggs and go to work. (*Passionately now.*) Man say: I got to change my life, I'm choking to death, baby! And his woman say—(*In utter anguish as he brings his fists down on his thighs.*)—Your eggs is getting cold!

RUTH. (*Softly.*) Walter, that ain't none of our money.

WALTER. (*Not listening at all or even looking at her.*) This morning, I was lookin' in the mirror and thinking about it . . . I'm thirty-five years old; I been married eleven years and I got a boy who sleeps in the living room—(*Very, very quietly.*)—and all I got to give him is stories about how rich white people live . . .

RUTH. Eat your eggs, Walter.

WALTER. *Damn* my eggs . . . damn all the eggs that ever was!

RUTH. Then go to work.

WALTER. (*Looking up at her.*) See—I'm trying to talk to you 'bout myself—(*Shaking his head with the repetition.*)—and all you can say is eat them eggs and go to work.

RUTH. (*Wearily.*) Honey, you never say nothing new. I listen to you every day, every night and every morning, and you never say nothing new. (*Shrugging.*) So you would rather *be* Mr. Arnold than be his chauffeur. So—I would *rather* be living in Buckingham Palace.

WALTER. That is just what is wrong with the colored woman in this world . . . Don't understand about building their men up and making 'em feel like they somebody. Like they can do something.

RUTH. (*Drily, but to hurt.*) There *are* colored men who do things.

WALTER. No thanks to the colored woman.

RUTH. Well, being a colored woman, I guess I can't help myself none.

(*She rises and gets the ironing board and sets it up and attacks a huge pile of rough-dried clothes, sprinkling them in preparation for the ironing and then rolling them into tight fat balls.*)

WALTER. (*Mumbling.*) We one group of men tied to a race of women with small minds.

(*His sister* BENEATHA *enters. She is about twenty, as slim and intense as her brother. She is not as pretty as her sister-in-law, but her lean, almost intellectual face has a handsomeness of its own. She wears a bright-red flannel nightie, and her thick hair stands wildly about her head. Her speech is a mixture of many things; it is different from the rest of the family's insofar as education has permeated her sense of English—and perhaps the Midwest rather than the South has finally—at last—won out in her inflection; but not altogether, because over all of it is a soft slurring and transformed use of vowels which is the decided influence of the Southside. She passes through the room without looking at either* RUTH *or* WALTER *and goes to the outside door and looks, a little blindly, out to the bathroom. She sees that it has been lost to the Johnsons. She closes the door with a sleepy vengeance and crosses to the table and sits down a little defeated.*)

BENEATHA. I am going to start timing those people.

WALTER. You should get up earlier.

BENEATHA. (*Her face in her hands. She is still fighting the urge to go back to bed.*) Really—would you suggest dawn? Where's the paper?

WALTER. (*Pushing the paper across the table to her as he studies her almost clinically, as though he has never seen her before.*) You a horrible-looking chick at this hour.

BENEATHA. (*Drily.*) Good morning, everybody.

WALTER. (*Senselessly.*) How is school coming?

BENEATHA. (*In the same spirit.*) Lovely. Lovely. And you know, biology is the greatest. (*Looking up at him.*) I dissected something that looked just like you yesterday.

WALTER. I just wondered if you've made up your mind and everything.

BENEATHA. (*Gaining in sharpness and impatience.*) And what did I answer yesterday morning—and the day before that?

RUTH. (*From the ironing board, like someone disinterested and old.*) Don't be so nasty, Bennie.

BENEATHA. (*Still to her brother.*) And the day before that and the day before that!

WALTER. (*Defensively.*) I'm interested in you. Something wrong with that? Ain't many girls who decide—

WALTER and BENEATHA. (*In unison.*) —"to be a doctor."

(*Silence.*)

WALTER. Have we figured out yet just exactly how much medical school is going to cost?

RUTH. Walter Lee, why don't you leave that girl alone and get out of here to work?

BENEATHA. (*Exits to the bathroom and bangs on the door.*) Come on out of there, please!

(*She comes back into the room.*)

WALTER. (*Looking at his sister intently.*) You know the check is coming tomorrow.

BENEATHA. (*Turning on him with a sharpness all her own.*) That money belongs to Mama, Walter, and it's for her to decide how she wants to use it. I don't care if she wants to buy a house or a rocket ship or just nail it up somewhere and look at it. It's hers. Not ours—*hers*.

WALTER. (*Bitterly.*) Now ain't that fine! You just got your mother's interest at heart, ain't you, girl? You such a nice girl—but if Mama got that money she can always take a few thousand and help you through school too—can't she?

BENEATHA. I have never asked anyone around here to do anything for me!

WALTER. No! And the line between asking and just accepting when the time comes is big and wide—ain't it!

BENEATHA. (*With fury.*) What do you want from me, Brother—that I quit school or just drop dead, which!

WALTER. I don't want nothing but for you to stop acting holy 'round here. Me and Ruth done made some sacrifices for you—why can't you do something for the family?

RUTH. Walter, don't be dragging me in it.

WALTER. You are in it—Don't you get up and go work in somebody's kitchen for the last three years to help put clothes on her back?

RUTH. Oh, Walter—that's not fair . . .

WALTER. It ain't that nobody expects you to get on your knees and say thank you, Brother; thank you, Ruth; thank you, Mama—and thank you, Travis, for wearing the same pair of shoes for two semesters—

BENEATHA. (*Dropping to her knees.*) Well—I *do*—all right?—thank everybody . . . and forgive me for ever wanting to be anything at all . . . forgive me, forgive me!

RUTH. Please stop it! Your mama'll hear you.

WALTER. Who the hell told you you had to be a doctor? If you so crazy 'bout messing 'round with sick people—then go be a nurse like other women—or just get married and be quiet . . .

BENEATHA. Well—you finally got it said . . . It took you three years but you finally got it said. Walter, give up; leave me alone—it's Mama's money.

WALTER. *He was my father, too!*

BENEATHA. So what? He was mine, too—and Travis' grandfather—but the insurance money belongs to Mama. Picking on me is not going to make her give it to you to invest in any liquor stores— (*Underbreath, dropping into a chair.*)—and I for one say, God bless Mama for that!

WALTER (*To* RUTH.) See—did you hear? Did you hear!

RUTH. Honey, please go to work.

WALTER. Nobody in this house is ever going to understand me.

BENEATHA. Because you're a nut.

WALTER. Who's a nut?

BENEATHA. You—you are a nut. Thee is mad, boy.

WALTER. (*Looking at his wife and his sister from the door, very sadly.*) The world's most backward race of people, and that's a fact.

BENEATHA. (*Turning slowly in her chair.*) And then there are all those prophets who would lead us out of the wilderness— (WALTER *slams out of the house.*)—into the swamps!

RUTH. Bennie, why you always gotta be pickin' on your brother? Can't you be a little sweeter sometimes? (*Door opens.* WALTER *walks in.*)

WALTER (*To Ruth.*) I need some money for carfare.

RUTH. (*Looks at him, then warms; teasing, but tenderly.*) Fifty cents? (*She goes to her bag and gets money.*) Here, take a taxi.

(WALTER *exits.* MAMA *enters. She is a woman in her early sixties, full-bodied and strong. She is one of those women of a certain grace and beauty who wear it so unobtrusively that it takes a while to notice. Her dark-brown face is surrounded by the total whiteness of her hair, and, being a woman who has adjusted to many things in life and overcome many more, her face is full of strength. She has, we can see, wit and faith of a kind that keep her eyes lit and full of interest and expectancy. She is, in a word, a beautiful woman. Her bearing is perhaps most like the noble bearing of the women of the Hereros of Southwest Africa—rather as if she imagines that as she walks she still bears a basket or a vessel upon her head. Her speech, on the other hand, is as careless as her carriage is precise—she is inclined to slur everything—but her voice is perhaps not so much quiet as simply soft.*)

MAMA. Who that 'round here slamming doors at this hour?

(*She crosses through the room, goes to the window, opens it, and brings in a feeble little plant growing doggedly in a small pot on the window sill. She feels the dirt and puts it back out.*)

RUTH. That was Walter Lee. He and Bennie was at it again.

MAMA. My children and they tempers. Lord, if this little old plant don't get more sun than it's been getting it ain't never going to see spring again. (*She turns from the window.*) What's the matter with you this morning, Ruth? You looks right peaked. You aiming to iron all them things? Leave some for me. I'll get to 'em this afternoon. Bennie honey, it's too drafty for you to be sitting 'round half dressed. Where's your robe?

BENEATHA. In the cleaners.

MAMA. Well, go get mine and put it on.

BENEATHA. I'm not cold, Mama, honest.

MAMA. I know—but you so thin . . .

BENEATHA. (*Irritably.*) Mama, I'm not cold.

MAMA. (*Seeing the make-down bed as* TRAVIS *has left it.*) Lord have mercy, look at that poor bed. Bless his heart—he tries, don't he?

(*She moves to the bed* TRAVIS *has sloppily made up.*)

RUTH. No—he don't half try at all 'cause he knows you going to come along behind him and fix everything. That's just how come he don't know how to do nothing right now—you done spoiled that boy so.

MAMA. Well—he's a little boy. Ain't supposed to know 'bout housekeeping. My baby, that's what he is. What you fix for his breakfast this morning?

RUTH. (*Angrily.*) I feed my son, Lena!

MAMA. I ain't meddling—(*Underbreath; busy-bodyish.*) I just noticed all last week he had cold cereal, and when it starts getting this chilly in the fall a child ought to have some hot grits or something when he goes out in the cold—

RUTH. (*Furious.*) I gave him hot oats—is that all right!

MAMA. I ain't meddling. (*Pause.*) Put a lot of nice butter on it? (RUTH *shoots her an angry look and does not reply.*) He likes lots of butter.

RUTH. (*Exasperated.*) Lena—

MAMA. (*To* BEANEATHA. MAMA *is inclined to wander conversationally sometimes.*) What was you and your brother fussing 'bout this morning?

BENEATHA. It's not important, Mama. (*She gets up and goes to look out at the bathroom, which is apparently free, and she picks up her towels and rushes out.*)

MAMA. What was they fighting about?

RUTH. Now you know as well as I do.

MAMA. (*Shaking her head.*) Brother still worrying hisself sick about that money?

RUTH. You know he is.

MAMA. You had breakfast?

RUTH. Some coffee.

MAMA. Girl, you better start eating and looking after yourself better. You almost thin as Travis.

RUTH. Lena—

MAMA. Un-hunh?

RUTH. What are you going to do with it?

MAMA. Now don't you start, child. It's too early in the morning to be talking about money. It ain't Christian.

RUTH. It's just that he got his heart set on that store—

MAMA. You mean that liquor store that Willy Harris want him to invest in?

RUTH. Yes—

MAMA. We ain't no business people, Ruth. We just plain working folks.

RUTH. Ain't nobody business people till they go into business. Walter Lee say colored people ain't never going to start getting ahead till they start gambling on some different kinds of things in the world—investments and things.

MAMA. What done got into you, girl? Walter Lee done finally sold you on investing.

RUTH. No. Mama, something is happening between Walter and me. I don't know what it is—but he needs something—something I can't give him any more. He needs this chance, Lena.

MAMA. (*Frowning deeply.*) But liquor, honey—

RUTH. Well—like Walter say—I spec people going to always be drinking themselves some liquor.

MAMA. Well—whether they drinks it or not ain't none of my business. But whether I go into business selling it to 'em *is*, and I don't want that on my ledger this late in life. (*Stopping suddenly and studying her daughter-in-law.*) Ruth Younger, what's the matter with you today? You look like you could fall over right there.

RUTH. I'm tired.

MAMA. Then you better stay home from work today.

RUTH. I can't stay home. She'd be calling up the agency and screaming at them, "My girl didn't come in today—send me somebody! My girl didn't come in!" Oh, she just have a fit . . .

MAMA. Well, let her have it. I'll just call her up and say you got the flu—

RUTH. (*Laughing.*) Why the flu?

MAMA. 'Cause it sounds respectable to 'em. Something white people get, too. They know 'bout the flu. Otherwise they think you been cut up or something when you tell 'em you sick.

RUTH. I got to go in. We need the money.

MAMA. Somebody would of thought my children done all but starved to death the way they talk about money here late. Child, we got a great big old check coming tomorrow.

RUTH. (*Sincerely, but also self-righteously.*) Now that's your money. It ain't got nothing to do with me. We all feel like that—Walter and Bennie and me—even Travis.

MAMA. (*Thoughtfully, and suddenly very far away.*) Ten thousand dollars—

RUTH. Sure is wonderful.

MAMA. Ten thousand dollars.

RUTH. You know what you should do, Miss Lena? You should take yourself a trip somewhere. To Europe or South America or someplace—

MAMA. (*Throwing up her hands at the thought.*) Oh, child!

RUTH. I'm serious. Just pack up and leave! Go on away and enjoy yourself some. Forget about the family and have yourself a ball for once in your life—

MAMA. (*Drily.*) You sound like I'm just about ready to die. Who'd go with me? What I look like wandering 'round Europe by myself?

RUTH. Shoot—these here rich white women do it all the time. They don't think nothing of packing up they suitcases and piling on one of them big steamships and —swoosh!—they gone, child.

MAMA. Something always told me I wasn't no rich white woman.

RUTH. Well—what are you going to do with it then?

MAMA. I ain't rightly decided. (*Thinking. She speaks now with emphasis.*) Some of it got to be put away for Beneatha and her schoolin'—and ain't nothing going to touch that part of it. Nothing. (*She waits several seconds, trying to make up her mind about something, and looks at* RUTH *a little tentatively before going on.*) Been thinking that we maybe could meet the notes on a little old two-story somewhere, with a yard where Travis could play in the summertime, if we use part of the insurance for a down payment and everybody kind of pitch in. I could maybe take on a little day work again, few days a week—

RUTH. (*Studying her mother-in-law furtively and concentrating on her ironing, anxious to encourage without seeming to.*) Well, Lord knows, we've put enough rent into this here rat trap to pay for four houses by now . . .

MAMA. (*Looking up at the words "rat trap" and then looking around and leaning back and sighing—in a suddenly reflective mood—*) "Rat trap"—yes, that's all it is. (*Smiling.*) I remember just as well the day me and Big Walter moved in here. Hadn't been married but two weeks and wasn't planning on living here no more than a year. (*She shakes her head at the dissolved dream.*) We was going to set away, little by little, don't you know, and buy a little place out in Morgan Park. We had even picked out the house. (*Chuckling a little.*) Looks right dumpy today. But Lord, child, you should know all the dreams I had 'bout buying that house and fixing it up and making me a little garden in the back— (*She waits and stops smiling.*) And didn't none of it happen.

(*Dropping her hands in a futile gesture.*)

RUTH. (*Keeps her head down, ironing.*) Yes, life can be a barrel of disappointments, sometimes.

MAMA. Honey, Big Walter would come in here some nights back then and slump down on that couch there and just look at the rug, and look at me and look at the rug and then back at me—and I'd know he was down then . . . really down. (*After a second very long and thoughtful pause; she is seeing back to times that only she can see.*) And then, Lord, when I lost that baby—little Claude—I almost thought I was going to lose Big Walter too. Oh, that man grieved hisself! He was one man to love his children.

RUTH. Ain't nothin' can tear at you like losin' your baby.

MAMA. I guess that's how come that man finally worked hisself to death like he done. Like he was fighting his own war with this here world that took his baby from him.

RUTH. He sure was a fine man, all right. I always liked Mr. Younger.

MAMA. Crazy 'bout his children! God knows there was plenty wrong with Walter Younger—hard-headed, mean, kind of wild with women—plenty wrong with him. But he sure loved his children. Always wanted them to have something—be something. That's where Brother gets all these notions, I reckon. Big Walter used to say, he'd get right wet in the eyes sometimes, lean his head back with the water standing in his eyes and say, "Seem like God didn't see fit to give the black man nothing but dreams—but He did give us children to make them dreams seem worth while." (*She smiles.*) He could talk like that, don't you know.

RUTH. Yes, he sure could. He was a good man, Mr. Younger.

MAMA. Yes, a fine man—just couldn't never catch up with his dreams, that's all.

(BENEATHA *comes in, brushing her hair and looking up to the ceiling, where the sound of a vacuum cleaner has started up.*)

BENEATHA. What could be so dirty on that woman's rugs that she has to vacuum them every single day?

RUTH. I wish certain young women 'round here who I could name would take inspiration about certain rugs in a certain apartment I could also mention.

BENEATHA. (*Shrugging.*) How much cleaning can a house need, for Christ's sakes.

MAMA. (*Not liking the Lord's name used thus.*) Bennie!

RUTH. Just listen to her—just listen!

BENEATHA. Oh, God!

MAMA. If you use the Lord's name just one more time—

BENEATHA. (*A bit of a whine.*) Oh, Mama—

RUTH. Fresh—just fresh as salt, this girl!

BENEATHA. (*Drily.*) Well—if the salt loses its savor—

MAMA. Now that will do. I just ain't going to have you 'round here reciting the scriptures in vain—you hear me?

BENEATHA. How did I manage to get on everybody's wrong side by just walking into a room?

RUTH. If you weren't so fresh—

BENEATHA. Ruth, I'm twenty years old.

MAMA. What time you be home from school today?

BENEATHA. Kind of late. (*With enthusiasm.*) Madeline is going to start my guitar lessons today.

(MAMA *and* RUTH *look up with the same expression.*)

MAMA. Your *what* kind of lessons?

BENEATHA. Guitar.

RUTH. Oh, Father!

MAMA. How come you done taken it in your mind to learn to play the guitar?

BENEATHA. I just want to, that's all.

MAMA. (*Smiling.*) Lord, child, don't you know what to do with yourself? How long it going to be before you get tired of this now—like you got tired of that little play-acting group you joined last year? (*Looking at Ruth.*) And what was it the year before that?

RUTH. The horseback-riding club for which she bought that fifty-five-dollar riding habit that's been hanging in the closet ever since!

MAMA. (*To* BENEATHA.) Why you got to flit so from one thing to another, baby?

BENEATHA. (*Sharply.*) I just want to learn to play the guitar. Is there anything wrong with that?

MAMA. Ain't nobody trying to stop you. I just wonders sometimes why you has to flit so from one thing to another all the time. You ain't never done nothing with all that camera equipment you brought home—

BENEATHA. I don't flit! I—I experiment with different forms of expression—

RUTH. Like riding a horse?

BENEATHA. —People have to express themselves one way or another.

MAMA. What is it you want to express?

BENEATHA. (*Angrily.*) Me! (MAMA *and* RUTH *look at each other and burst into raucous laughter.*) Don't worry—I don't expect you to understand.

MAMA. (*To change the subject.*) Who you going out with tomorrow night?

BENEATHA. (*With displeasure.*) George Murchison again.

MAMA. (*Pleased.*) Oh—you getting a little sweet on him?

RUTH. You ask me, this child ain't sweet on nobody but herself—(*Underbreath.*) Express herself!

(*They laugh.*)

BENEATHA. Oh—I like George all right, Mama. I mean I like him enough to go out with him and stuff, but—

RUTH. (*For devilment.*) What does *and stuff* mean?

BENEATHA. Mind your own business.

MAMA. Stop picking at her now, Ruth. (*A thoughtful pause, and then a suspicious sudden look at her daughter as she turns in her chair for emphasis.*) What *does* it mean?

BENEATHA. (*Wearily.*) Oh, I just mean I couldn't ever really be serious about George. He's—he's so shallow.

RUTH. Shallow—what do you mean he's shallow? He's *Rich!*

MAMA. Hush, Ruth.

BENEATHA. I know he's rich. He knows he's rich, too.

RUTH. Well—what other qualities a man got to have to satisfy you, little girl?

BENEATHA. You wouldn't even begin to understand. Anybody who married Walter could not possibly understand.

MAMA. (*Outraged.*) What kind of way is that to talk about your brother?

BENEATHA. Brother is a flip—let's face it.

MAMA. (*To* RUTH, *helplessly.*) What's a flip?

RUTH. (*Glad to add kindling.*) She's saying he's crazy.

BENEATHA. Not crazy. Brother isn't really crazy yet—he—he's an elaborate neurotic.

MAMA. Hush your mouth!

BENEATHA. As for George. Well. George looks good—he's got a beautiful car and he takes me to nice places and, as my sister-in-law says, he is probably the richest boy I will ever get to know and I even like him sometimes—but if the Youngers are sitting around waiting to see if their little Bennie is going to tie up the family with the Murchisons, they are wasting their time.

RUTH. You mean you wouldn't marry George Murchison if he asked you someday? That pretty, rich thing? Honey, I knew you was odd—

BENEATHA. No I would not marry him if all I felt for him was what I feel now. Besides, George's family wouldn't really like it.

MAMA. Why not?

BENEATHA. Oh, Mama—The Murchisons are honest-to-God-real-*live*-rich colored people, and the only people in the world who are more snobbish than rich white people are rich colored people. I thought everybody knew that. I've met Mrs. Murchison. She's a scene!

MAMA. You must not dislike people 'cause they well off, honey.

BENEATHA. Why not? It makes just as much sense as disliking people 'cause they are poor, and lots of people do that.

RUTH. (*A wisdom-of-the-ages manner. To* MAMA.) Well, she'll get over some of this—

BENEATHA. Get over it? What are you talking about, Ruth? Listen, I'm going to be a doctor. I'm not worried about who I'm going to marry yet—if I ever get married.

MAMA *and* RUTH. *If!*

MAMA. Now, Bennie—

BENEATHA. Oh, I probably will . . . but first I'm going to be a doctor, and George, for one, still thinks that's pretty funny. I couldn't be bothered with that. I am going to be a doctor and everybody around here better understand that!

MAMA. (*Kindly.*) 'Course you going to be a doctor, honey, God willing.

BENEATHA. (*Drily.*) God hasn't got a thing to do with it.

MAMA. Beneatha—that just wasn't necessary.

BENEATHA. Well—neither is God. I get sick of hearing about God.

MAMA. Beneatha!

BENEATHA. I mean it! I'm just tired of

hearing about God all the time. What has He got to do with anything? Does he pay tuition?

MAMA. You 'bout to get your fresh little jaw slapped!

RUTH. That's just what she needs, all right!

BENEATHA. Why? Why can't I say what I want to around here, like everybody else?

MAMA. It don't sound nice for a young girl to say things like that—you wasn't brought up that way. Me and your father went to trouble to get you and Brother to church every Sunday.

BENEATHA. Mama, you don't understand. It's all a matter of ideas, and God is just one idea I don't accept. It's not important. I am not going out and be immoral or commit crimes because I don't believe in God. I don't even think about it. It's just that I get tired of Him getting credit for all the things the human race achieves through its own stubborn effort. There simply is no blasted God—there is only man and it is he who makes miracles!

(MAMA *absorbs this speech, studies her daughter and rises slowly and cross to* BENEATHA *and slaps her powerfully across the face. After, there is only silence and the daughter drops her eyes from her mother's face, and* MAMA *is very tall before her.*)

MAMA. Now—you say after me, in my mother's house there is still God. (*There is a long pause and* BENEATHA *stares at the floor wordlessly.* MAMA *repeats the phrase with precision and cool emotion.*) In my mother's house there is still God.

BENEATHA. In my mother's house there is still God.

(*A long pause.*)

MAMA. (*Walking away from* BENEATHA, *too disturbed for triumphant posture. Stopping and turning back to her daughter.*) There are some ideas we ain't going to have in this house. Not long as I am at the head of this family.

BENEATHA. Yes, ma'am.

(MAMA *walks out of the room.*)

RUTH. (*Almost gently, with profound understanding.*) You think you a woman, Bennie—but you still a little girl. What you did was childish—so you got treated like a child.

BENEATHA. I see. (*Quietly.*) I also see that everybody thinks it's all right for Mama to be a tyrant. But all the tyranny in the world will never put a God in the heavens!

(*She picks up her books and goes out.*)

RUTH. (*Goes to* MAMA's *door.*) She said she was sorry.

MAMA. (*Coming out, going to her plant.*) They frightens me, Ruth. My children.

RUTH. You got good children, Lena. They just a little off sometimes—but they're good.

MAMA. No—there's something come down between me and them that don't let us understand each other and I don't know what it is. One done almost lost his mind thinking 'bout money all the time and the other done commence to talk about things I can't seem to understand in no form or fashion. What is it that's changing, Ruth?

RUTH. (*Soothingly, older than her years.*) Now . . . you taking it all too seriously. You just got strong-willed children and it takes a strong woman like you to keep 'em in hand.

MAMA. (*Looking at her plant and sprinkling a little water on it.*) They spirited all right, my children. Got to admit they got spirit—Bennie and Walter. Like this little old plant that ain't never had enough sunshine or nothing—and look at it . . .

(*She has her back to* RUTH, *who has had to stop ironing and lean against something and put the back of her hand to her forehead.*)

RUTH. (*Trying to keep* MAMA *from noticing.*) You . . . sure . . . loves that little old thing, don't you? . . .

MAMA. Well, I always wanted me a garden like I used to see sometimes at the back of the houses down home. This plant is close as I ever got to having one. (*She looks out of the window as she replaces the plant.*) Lord, ain't nothing as dreary as the view from this window on a dreary day, is there? Why ain't you singing this morning, Ruth? Sing that "No Ways Tired." That song always lifts me up so— (*She turns at last to see that* RUTH *has slipped quietly into a chair, in a state of semiconsciousness.*) Ruth! Ruth honey—what's the matter with you . . . Ruth!

CURTAIN

SCENE 2

It is the following morning, a Saturday morning, and house cleaning is in progress at the YOUNGERS. *Furniture has been shoved hither and yon and* MAMA *is giving the kitchen-area walls a washing down.* BENEATHA, *in dungarees, with a handkerchief tied around her face, is spraying insecticide into the cracks in the walls. As they work, the radio is on and a Southside disk-jockey program is inappropriately filling the house with a rather exotic saxophone blues.* TRAVIS, *the sole idle one, is leaning on his arms, looking out of the window.*

TRAVIS. Grandmama, that stuff Bennie is using smells awful. Can I go downstairs, please?

MAMA. Did you get all them chores done already? I ain't seen you doing much.

TRAVIS. Yes'm—finished early. Where did Mama go this morning?

MAMA. (*Looking at* BENEATHA.) She had to go on a little errand.

TRAVIS. Where?

MAMA. To tend to her business.

TRAVIS. Can I go outside then?

MAMA. Oh, I guess so. You better stay right in front of the house, though . . . and keep a good lookout for the postman.

TRAVIS. Yes'm. (*He starts out and decides to give his* AUNT BENEATHA *a good swat on the legs as he passes her.*) Leave them poor little old cockroaches alone, they ain't bothering you none.

(*He runs as she swings the spray gun at him both viciously and playfully.* WALTER *enters from the bedroom and goes to the phone.*)

MAMA. Look out there, girl, before you be spilling some of that stuff on that child!

TRAVIS. (*Teasing.*) That's right—look out now!

(*He exits.*)

BENEATHA. (*Drily.*) I can't imagine that it would hurt him—it has never hurt the roaches.

MAMA. Well, little boys' hides ain't as tough as Southside roaches.

WALTER. (*Into phone.*) Hello—Let me talk to Willy Harris.

MAMA. You better get over there behind the bureau. I seen one marching out of there like Napoleon yesterday.

WALTER. Hello, Willy? It ain't come yet. It'll be here in a few minutes. Did the lawyer give you the papers?

BENEATHA. There's really only one way to get rid of them, Mama—

MAMA. How?

BENEATHA. Set fire to this building.

WALTER. Good. Good. I'll be right over.

BENEATHA. Where did Ruth go, Walter?

WALTER. I don't know.

(*He exits abruptly.*)

BENEATHA. Mama, where did Ruth go?

MAMA. (*Looking at her with meaning.*) To the doctor, I think.

BENEATHA. The doctor? What's the matter? (*They exchange glances.*) You don't think—

MAMA. (*With her sense of drama.*) Now I ain't saying what I think. But I ain't never been wrong 'bout a woman neither.

(*The phone rings.*)

BENEATHA. (*At the phone.*) Hay-lo . . . (*Pause, and a moment of recognition.*) Well—when did you get back! . . . And how was it? . . . Of course I've missed you—in my way . . . This morning? No . . . house cleaning and all that and Mama hates it if I let people come over when the house is like this . . . You *have*? Well, that's different . . . What is it— Oh, what the hell, come on over . . . Right, see you then.

(*She hangs up.*)

MAMA. (*Who has listened vigorously, as is her habit.*) Who is that you inviting over here with this house looking like this? You ain't got the pride you was born with!

BENEATHA. Asagai doesn't care how houses look, Mama—he's an intellectual.

MAMA. *Who?*

BENEATHA. Asagai—Joseph Asagai. He's an African boy I met on campus. He's been studying in Canada all summer.

MAMA. What's his name?

BENEATHA. Asagai, Joseph. Ah-sah-guy . . . He's from Nigeria.

MAMA. Oh, that's the little country that was founded by slaves way back . . .

BENEATHA. No, Mama—that's Liberia.

MAMA. I don't think I never met no African before.

BENEATHA. Well, do me a favor and don't ask him a whole lot of ignorant questions about Africans. I mean, do they wear clothes and all that—

MAMA. Well, now, I guess if you think we so ignorant 'round here maybe you shouldn't bring your friends here—

BENEATHA. It's just that people ask such crazy things. All anyone seems to know about when it comes to Africa is Tarzan—

MAMA. (*Indignantly.*) Why should I know anything about Africa?

BENEATHA. Why do you give money at church for the missionary work?

MAMA. Well, that's to help save people.

BENEATHA. You mean save them from *heathenism*—

MAMA. (*Innocently.*) Yes.

BENEATHA. I'm afraid they need more salvation from the British and the French.

(RUTH *comes in forlornly and pulls off her coat with dejection. They both turn to look at her.*)

RUTH. (*Dispiritedly.*) Well, I guess from all the happy faces—everybody knows.

BENEATHA. You pregnant?

MAMA. Lord have mercy, I sure hope it's a little old girl. Travis ought to have a sister.

(BENEATHA *and* RUTH *giver her a hopeless look for this grandmotherly enthusiasm.*)

BENEATHA. How far along are you?

RUTH. Two months.

BENEATHA. Did you mean to? I mean did you plan it or was it an accident?

MAMA. What do you know about planning or not planning?

BENEATHA. Oh, Mama.

RUTH. (*Wearily.*) She's twenty years old, Lena.

BENEATHA. Did you plan it, Ruth?

RUTH. Mind your own business.

BENEATHA. It is my business—where is he going to live, on the *roof*? (*There is silence following the remark as the three women react to the sense of it.*) Gee—I didn't mean that, Ruth, honest. Gee, I don't feel like that at all. I—I think it is wonderful.

RUTH. (*Dully.*) Wonderful.

BENEATHA. Yes—really.

MAMA. (*Looking at* RUTH, *worried.*) Doctor say everything going to be all right?

RUTH. (*Far away.*) Yes—she says everything is going to be fine . . .

MAMA. (*Immediately suspicious.*) "She"— What doctor you went to?

(RUTH *folds over, near hysteria.*)

MAMA. (*Worriedly hovering over* RUTH.) Ruth honey—what's the matter with you—you sick?

(RUTH *has her fists clenched on her thighs and is fighting hard to suppress a scream that seems to be rising in her.*)

BENEATHA. What's the matter with her, Mama?

MAMA. (*Working her fingers in* RUTH's *shoulder to relax her.*) She be all right. Women gets right depressed sometimes when they get her way. (*Speaking softly, expertly, rapidly.*) Now you just relax. That's right . . . just lean back, don't think 'bout nothing at all . . . nothing at all—

RUTH. I'm all right . . .
(*The glassy-eyed look melts and then she collapses into a fit of heavy sobbing. The bell rings.*)

BENEATHA. Oh, my God—that must be Asagai.

MAMA. (*To* RUTH.) Come on now, honey. You need to lie down and rest awhile . . . then have some nice hot food. (*They exit,* RUTH's *weight on her mother-in-law.* BENEATHA, *herself profoundly disturbed, opens the door to admit a rather dramatic-looking young man with a large package.*)

ASAGAI. Hello, Alaiyo—

BENEATHA. (*Holding the door open and regarding him with pleasure.*) Hello . . . (*Long pause.*) Well—come in. And please excuse everything. My mother was very upset about my letting anyone come here with the place like this.

ASAGAI. (*Coming into the room.*) You look disturbed too . . . Is something wrong?

BENEATHA. (*Still at the door, absently.*) Yes . . . we've all got acute ghetto-itus. (*She smiles and comes toward him, finding a cigarette and sitting.*) So—sit down! How was Canada?

ASAGAI. (*A sophisticate.*) Canadian.

BENEATHA. (*Looking at him.*) I'm very glad you are back.

ASAGAI. (*Looking back at her in turn.*) Are you really?

BENEATHA. Yes—very.

ASAGAI. Why—you were quite glad when I went away. What happened?

BENEATHA. You went away.

ASAGAI. Ahhhhhhhh.

BENEATHA. Before—you wanted to be so serious before there was time.

ASAGAI. How much time must there be before one knows what one feels?

BENEATHA. (*Stalling this particular conversation. Her hands pressed together, in a deliberately childish gesture.*) What did you bring me?

ASAGAI. (*Handing her the package.*) Open it and see.

BENEATHA. (*Eagerly opening the package and drawing out some records and the colorful robes of a Nigerian woman.*) Oh, Asagai! . . . You got them for me! . . . How beautiful . . . and the records too! (*She lifts out the robes and runs to the mirror with them and holds the drapery up in front of herself.*)

ASAGAI. (*Coming to her at the mirror.*) I shall have to teach you how to drape it properly. (*He flings the material about her for the moment and stands back to look at her.*) Ah—*Oh-pay-gay-day, oh-gbah-mu-shay*. (*A Yoruba exclamation for admiration.*) You wear it well . . . very well . . . mutilated hair and all.

BENEATHA. (*Turning suddenly.*) My hair—what's wrong with my hair?

ASAGAI. (*Shrugging.*) Were you born with it like that?

BENEATHA. (*Reaching up to touch it.*) No . . . of course not.
(*She looks back to the mirror, disturbed.*)

ASAGAI. (*Smiling.*) How then?

BENEATHA. You know perfectly well how . . . as crinkly as yours . . . that's how.

ASAGAI. And it is ugly to you that way?

BENEATHA. (*Quickly.*) Oh, no—not ugly . . . (*More slowly, apologetically.*) But it's so hard to manage when it's, well—raw.

ASAGAI. And so to accommodate that—you mutilate it every week?

BENEATHA. It's not mutilation!

ASAGAI. (*Laughing aloud at her seriousness.*) Oh . . . please! I am only teasing you because you are so very serious about these things. (*He stands back from her and folds his arms across his chest as he watches her pulling at her hair and frowning in the mirror.*) Do you remember the first time you met me at school? . . . (*He laughs.*) You came up to me and you said—and I thought you were the most serious little thing I had ever seen—you said: (*He imitates her.*) "Mr. Asagai—I want very much to talk with you. About Africa. You see, Mr. Asagai, I am looking for my *identity!*"
(*He laughs.*)

BENEATHA. (*Turning to him, not laughing.*) Yes—

(*Her face is quizzical, profoundly disturbed.*)

ASAGAI. (*Still teasing and reaching out and taking her face in his hands and turning her profile to him.*) Well . . . it is true that this is not so much a profile of a Hollywood queen as perhaps a queen of the Nile— (*A mock dismissal of the importance of the question.*) But what does it matter? Assimilationism is so popular in your country.

BENEATHA. (*Wheeling, passionately, sharply.*) I am not an assimilationist!

ASAGAI. (*The protest hangs in the room for a moment and* ASAGAI *studies her, his laughter fading.*) Such a serious one. (*There is a pause.*) So—you like the robes? You must take excellent care of them—they are from my sister's personal wardrobe.

BENEATHA. (*With incredulity.*) You—you sent all the way home—for me?

ASAGAI (*With charm.*) For you—I would do much more . . . Well, that is what I came for. I must go.

BENEATHA. Will you call me Monday?

ASAGAI. Yes . . . We have a great deal to talk about. I mean about identity and time and all that.

BENEATHA. Time?

ASAGAI. Yes. About how much time one needs to know what one feels.

BENEATHA. You never understood that there is more than one kind of feeling which can exist between a man and a woman—or, at least, there should be.

ASAGAI. (*Shaking his head negatively but gently.*) No. Between a man and a woman there need be only one kind of feeling. I have that for you . . . Now even . . . right this moment . . .

BENEATHA. I know—and by itself—it won't do. I can find that anywhere.

ASAGAI. For a woman it should be enough.

BENEATHA. I know—because that's what it says in all the novels that men write. But it isn't. Go ahead and laugh—but I'm not interested in being someone's little episode in America or—(*With feminine vengeance.*)—one of them! (ASAGAI *has burst into laughter again.*) That's funny as hell, huh!

ASAGAI. It's just that every American girl I have known has said that to me. White—black—in this you are all the same. And the same speech, too!

BENEATHA. (*Angrily.*) Yuk, yuk, yuk!

ASAGAI. It's how you can be sure that the world's most liberated women are not liberated at all. You all talk about it too much!

(MAMA *enters and is immediately all social charm because of the presence of a guest.*)

BENEATHA. Oh—Mama—this is Mr. Asagai.

MAMA. How do you do?

ASAGAI. (*Total politeness to an elder.*) How do you do, Mrs. Younger. Please forgive me for coming at such an outrageous hour on a Saturday.

MAMA. Well, you are quite welcome. I just hope you understand that our house don't always look like this. (*Chatterish.*) You must come again. I would love to hear all about—(*Not sure of the name.*)—your country. I think it's so sad the way our American Negroes don't know nothing about Africa 'cept Tarzan and all that. And all that money they pour into these churches when they ought to be helping you people over there drive out them French and Englishmen done taken away your land.

(*The mother flashes a slightly superior look at her daughter upon completion of the recitation.*)

ASAGAI. (*Taken aback by this sudden and acutely unrelated expression of sympathy.*) Yes . . . yes . . .

MAMA. (*Smiling at him suddenly and relaxing and looking him over.*) How many miles is it from here to where you come from?

ASAGAI. Many thousands.

MAMA. (*Looking at him as she would* WALTER.) I bet you don't half look after yourself, being away from your mama either. I spec you better come 'round here from time to time and get yourself some decent home-cooked meals . . .

ASAGAI. (*Moved.*) Thank you. Thank you very much. (*They are all quiet, then—*) Well . . . I must go. I will call you Monday, Alaiyo.

MAMA. What's that he call you?

ASAGAI. Oh—"Alaiyo." I hope you don't mind. It is what you would call a nickname, I think. It is a Yoruba word. I am a Yoruba.

MAMA. (*Looking at* BENEATHA.) I—I thought he was from—

ASAGAI. (*Understanding.*) Nigeria is my country. Yoruba is my tribal origin—

BENEATHA. You didn't tell us what Alaiyo means . . . for all I know, you might be calling me Little Idiot or something . . .

ASAGAI. Well . . . let me see . . . I do not know how just to explain it . . . The sense of a thing can be so different when it changes languages.

BENEATHA. You're evading.

ASAGAI. No—really it is difficult . . . (*Thinking.*) It means . . . it means One for Whom Bread—Food—Is Not Enough. (*He looks at her.*) Is that all right?

BENEATHA. (*Understanding, softly.*) Thank you.

MAMA. (*Looking from one to the other and not understanding any of it.*) Well . . . that's nice . . . You must come see us again— Mr.—

ASAGAI. Ah-sah-guy . . .

MAMA. Yes . . . Do come again.

ASAGAI. Good-bye.

(*He exits.*)

MAMA. (*After him.*) Lord, that's a pretty thing just went out here! (*Insinuatingly, to her daughter.*) Yes, I guess I see why we done commence to get so interested in Africa 'round here. Missionaries my aunt Jenny!

(*She exits.*)

BENEATHA. Oh, Mama! . . .

(*She picks up the Nigerian dress and holds it up to her in front of the mirror again. She sets the headdress on haphazardly and then notices her hair again and clutches at it and then replaces the headdress and frowns at herself. Then she starts to wriggle in front of the mirror as she thinks a Nigerian woman might.* TRAVIS *enters and regards her.*)

TRAVIS. You cracking up?

BENEATHA. Shut up.

(*She pulls the headdress off and looks at herself in the mirror and clutches at her hair again and squinches her eyes as if trying to imagine something. Then, suddenly, she gets her raincoat and kerchief and hurriedly prepares for going out.*)

MAMA. (*Coming back into the room.*) She's resting now. Travis, baby, run next door and ask Miss Johnson to please let me have a little kitchen cleanser. This here can is empty as Jacob's kettle.

TRAVIS. I just came in.

MAMA. Do as you told. (*He exits and she looks at her daughter.*) Where you going?

BENEATHA. (*Halting at the door.*) To become a queen of the Nile!

(*She exits in a breathless blaze of glory.* RUTH *appears in the bedroom doorway.*)

MAMA. Who told you to get up?

RUTH. Ain't nothing wrong with me to be lying in no bed for. Where did Bennie go?

MAMA. (*Drumming her fingers.*) Far as I could make out—to Egypt. (RUTH *just looks at her.*) What time is it getting to?

RUTH. Ten twenty. And the mailman going to ring that bell this morning just like he done every morning for the last umpteen years.

(TRAVIS *comes in with the cleanser can.*)

TRAVIS. She say to tell you that she don't have much.

MAMA. (*Angrily.*) Lord, some people I could name sure is tight-fisted! (*Directing her grandson.*) Mark two cans of cleanser down on the list there. If she that hard up for kitchen cleanser, I sure don't want to forget to get her none!

RUTH. Lena—maybe the woman is just short on cleanser—

MAMA. (*Not listening.*) —Much baking powder as she done borrowed from me all these years, she could of done gone into the baking business!

(*The bell sounds suddenly and sharply and all three are stunned—serious and silent—mid-speech. In spite of all the other conversations and distractions of the morning, this is what they have been waiting for, even* TRAVIS, *who looks helplessly from his mother to his grandmother.* RUTH *is the first to come to life again.*)

RUTH. (*To* TRAVIS.) Get down them steps, boy!

(TRAVIS *snaps to life and flies out to get the mail.*)

MAMA. (*Her eyes wide, her hand to her breast.*) You mean it done really come?

RUTH. (*Excited.*) Oh, Miss Lena!

MAMA. (*Collecting herself.*) Well . . . I don't know what we all so excited about 'round here for. We known it was coming for months.

RUTH. That's a whole lot different from having it come and being able to hold it in your hands . . . a piece of paper worth ten thousand dollars . . . (TRAVIS *bursts back into the room. He holds the envelope high above his head, like a little dancer, his face is radiant and he is breathless. He moves to his grandmother with sudden slow ceremony and puts the envelope into her hands. She accepts it, and then merely holds it and looks at it.*) Come on! Open it . . . Lord have mercy, I wish Walter Lee was here!

TRAVIS. Open it, Grandmama!

MAMA. (*Staring at it.*) Now you all be quiet. It's just a check.

RUTH. Open it . . .

MAMA. (*Still staring at it.*) Now don't act silly . . . We ain't never been no people to act silly 'bout no money—

RUTH. (*Swiftly.*) We ain't never had none before—*open it!*

(MAMA *finally makes a good strong tear and pulls out the thin blue slice of paper and inspects it closely. The boy and his mother study it raptly over* MAMA's *shoulders.*)

MAMA. Travis! (*She is counting off with doubt.*) Is that the right number of zeros.

TRAVIS. Yes'm . . . ten thousand dollars. Gaalee, Grandmama, you rich.

MAMA. (*She holds the check away from her, still looking at it. Slowly her face sobers into a mask of unhappiness.*) Ten thousand dollars. (*She hands it to* RUTH.) Put it away somewhere, Ruth. (*She does not look at* RUTH; *her eyes seem to be seeing something somewhere very far off.*) Ten thousand dollars they give you. Ten thousand dollars.

TRAVIS. (*To his mother, sincerely.*) What's the matter with Grandmama—don't she want to be rich?

RUTH. (*Distractedly.*) You go on out and play now, baby. (TRAVIS *exits.* MAMA *starts wiping dishes absently, humming intently to herself.* RUTH *turns to her, with kind exasperation.*) You've gone and got yourself upset.

MAMA. (*Not looking at her.*) I spec if it wasn't for you all . . . I would just put that money away or give it to the church or something.

RUTH. Now what kind of talk is that. Mr. Younger would be just plain mad if he could hear you talking foolish like that.

MAMA. (*Stopping and staring off.*) Yes . . . he sure would. (*Sighing.*) We got enough to do with that money, all right. (*She halts then, and turns and looks at her daughter-in-law hard;* RUTH *avoids her eyes and* MAMA *wipes her hands with finality and starts to speak firmly to* RUTH.) Where did you go today, girl?

RUTH. To the doctor.

MAMA. (*Impatiently.*) Now, Ruth . . . you know better than that. Old Doctor Jones is strange enough in his way but there ain't nothing 'bout him make somebody slip and call him "she"—like you done this morning.

RUTH. Well, that's what happened—my tongue slipped.

MAMA. You went to see that woman, didn't you?

RUTH. (*Defensively, giving herself away.*) What woman you talking about?

MAMA. (*Angrily.*) That woman who—

(WALTER *enters in great excitement.*)

WALTER. Did it come?

MAMA. (*Quietly.*) Can't you give people a Christian greeting before you start asking about money?

WALTER. (*To* RUTH.) Did it come? (RUTH *unfolds the check and lays it quietly before him, watching him intently with thoughts of her own.* WALTER *sits down and grasps it close and counts off the zeros.*) Ten thousand dollars— (*He turns suddenly, frantically to his mother and draws some papers out of his breast pocket.*) Mama—look. Old Willy Harris put everything on paper—

MAMA. Son—I think you ought to talk to your wife . . . I'll go on out and leave you alone if you want—

WALTER. I can talk to her later—Mama, look—

MAMA. Son—

WALTER. WILL SOMEBODY PLEASE LISTEN TO ME TODAY!

MAMA. (*Quietly.*) I don't 'low no yellin' in this house, Walter Lee, and you know it— (WALTER *stares at them in frustration and starts to speak several times.*) And there ain't going to be no investing in no liquor stores. I don't aim to have to speak on that again.

(*A long pause.*)

WALTER. Oh—so you don't aim to have to speak on that again? So *you* have decided . . . (*Crumpling his papers.*) Well, *you* tell that to my boy tonight when you put him to sleep on the living-room couch . . . (*Turning to* MAMA *and speaking directly to her.*) Yeah—and tell it to my wife, Mama, tomorrow when she has to go out of here to look after somebody else's kids. And tell it to *me*, Mama, every time we need a new pair of curtains and I have to watch *you* go out and work in somebody's kitchen. Yeah, you tell me then!

(WALTER *starts out.*)

RUTH. Where you going?

WALTER. I'm going out!

RUTH. Where?

WALTER. Just out of this house somewhere—

RUTH. (*Getting her coat.*) I'll come too.

WALTER. I don't want you to come!

RUTH. I got something to talk to you about, Walter.

WALTER. That's too bad.

MAMA. (*Still quietly.*) Walter Lee— (*She waits and he finally turns and looks at her.*) Sit down.

WALTER. I'm a grown man, Mama.

MAMA. Ain't nobody said you wasn't grown. But you still in my house and my presence. And as long as you are—you'll talk to your wife civil. Now sit down.

RUTH. (*Suddenly.*) Oh, let him go on out and drink himself to death! He makes me sick to my stomach! (*She flings her coat against him.*)

WALTER. (*Violently.*) And you turn mine too, baby! (RUTH *goes into their bedroom and slams the door behind her.*) That was my greatest mistake—

MAMA. (*Still quietly.*) Walter, what is the matter with you?

WALTER. Matter with me? Ain't nothing the matter with *me!*

MAMA. Yes there is. Something eating you up like a crazy man. Something more than me not giving you this money. The past few years I been watching it happen to you. You get all nervous acting and kind of wild in the eyes— (WALTER *jumps up impatiently at her words.*) I said sit there now, I'm talking to you!

WALTER. Mama—I don't need no nagging at me today.

MAMA. Seem like you getting to a place where you always tied up in some kind of knot about something. But if anybody ask you 'bout it you just yell at 'em and bust out the house and go out and drink somewheres. Walter Lee, people can't live with that. Ruth's a good, patient girl in her way—but you getting to be too much. Boy, don't make the mistake of driving that girl away from you.

WALTER. Why—what she do for me?

MAMA. She loves you.

WALTER. Mama—I'm going out. I want

to go off somewhere and be by myself for a while.

MAMA. I'm sorry 'bout your liquor store, son. It just wasn't the thing for us to do. That's what I want to tell you about—

WALTER. I got to go out, Mama— (*He rises.*)

MAMA. It's dangerous, son.

WALTER. What's dangerous?

MAMA. When a man goes outside his home to look for peace.

WALTER. (*Beseechingly.*) Then why can't there never be no peace in this house then?

MAMA. You done found it in some other house?

WALTER. No—there ain't no woman! Why do women always think there's a woman somewhere when a man gets restless. (*Coming to her.*) Mama—Mama—I want so many things . . .

MAMA. Yes, son—

WALTER. I want so many things that they are driving me kind of crazy . . . Mama—look at me.

MAMA. I'm looking at you. You a good-looking boy. You got a job, a nice wife, a fine boy and—

WALTER. A job. (*Looks at her.*) Mama, a job? I open and close car doors all day long. I drive a man around in his limousine and I say, "Yes, sir; no, sir; very good, sir; shall I take the Drive, sir?" Mama, that ain't no kind of job . . . that ain't nothing at all. (*Very quietly.*) Mama, I don't know if I can make you understand.

MAMA. Understand what, baby?

WALTER. (*Quietly.*) Sometimes it's like I can see the future stretched out in front of me—just plain as day. The future, Mama. Hanging over there at the edge of my days. Just waiting for me—a big, looming blank space—full of *nothing*. Just waiting for *me*. (*Pause.*) Mama—sometimes when I'm downtown and I pass them cool, quiet-looking restaurants where them white boys are sitting back and talking 'bout things . . . sitting there turning deals worth millions of dollars . . . sometimes I see guys don't look much older than me—

MAMA. Son—how come you talk so much 'bout money?

WALTER. (*With immense passion.*) Because it is life, Mama!

MAMA. (*Quietly.*) Oh— (*Very quietly.*) So now it's life. Money is life. Once upon a time freedom used to be life—now it's money. I guess the world really do change . . .

WALTER. No—it was always money, Mama. We just didn't know about it.

MAMA. No . . . something has changed. (*She looks at him.*) You something new, boy. In my time we was worried about not being lynched and getting to the North if we could and how to stay alive and still have a pinch of dignity too . . . Now here come you and Beneatha—talking 'bout things we ain't never even thought about hardly, me and your daddy. You ain't satisfied or proud of nothing we done. I mean that you had a home; that we kept you out of trouble till you was grown; that you don't have to ride to work on the back of nobody's streetcar— You my children— but how different we done become.

WALTER. You just don't understand, Mama, you just don't understand.

MAMA. Son—do you know your wife is expecting another baby? (WALTER *stands, stunned, and absorbs what his mother has said.*) That's what she wanted to talk to you about. (WALTER *sinks down into a chair.*) This ain't for me to be telling—but you ought to know. (*She waits.*) I think Ruth is thinking 'bout getting rid of that child.

WALTER. (*Slowly understanding.*) No—no —Ruth wouldn't do that.

MAMA. When the world gets ugly enough—a woman will do anything for her family. *The part that's already living.*

WALTER. You don't know Ruth, Mama, if you think she would do that.

(RUTH *opens the bedroom door and stands there a little limp.*)

RUTH. (*Beaten.*) Yes I would too, Walter. (*Pause.*) I gave her a five-dollar down payment.

(*There is total silence as the man stares at his wife and the mother stares at her son.*)

MAMA. (*Presently.*) Well— (*Tightly.*) Well—son, I'm waiting to hear you say something . . . I'm waiting to hear how you be your father's son. Be the man he was . . . (*Pause.*) Your wife say she going to destroy your child. And I'm waiting to hear you talk like him and say we a people who give children life, not who destroys them— (*She rises.*) I'm waiting to see you stand up and look like your daddy and say we done give up one baby to poverty and that we ain't going to give up nary another one . . . I'm waiting.

WALTER. Ruth—

MAMA. If you a son of mine, tell her! (WALTER *turns, looks at her and can say nothing. She continues, bitterly.*) You . . . you are a disgrace to your father's memory. Somebody get me my hat.

CURTAIN

ACT TWO

SCENE 1

TIME: *Later the same day.*

AT RISE: RUTH *is ironing again. She has the radio going. Presently* BENEATHA'S *bedroom door opens and* RUTH'S *mouth falls and she puts down the iron in fascination.*

RUTH. What have we got on tonight!

BENEATHA. (*Emerging grandly from the doorway so that we can see her thoroughly robed in the costume Asagai brought.*) You are looking at what a well-dressed Nigerian woman wears— (*She parades for* RUTH, *her hair completely hidden by the headdress; she is coquettishly fanning herself with an ornate oriental fan, mistakenly more like Butterfly than any Nigerian that ever was.*) Isn't it beautiful? (*She promenades to the radio and, with an arrogant flourish, turns off the good loud blues that is playing.*) Enough of this assimilationist junk! (RUTH *follows her with her eyes as she goes to the phonograph and puts on a record and turns and waits ceremoniously for the music to come up. Then, with a shout—*) OCOMOGOSIAY!

(RUTH *jumps. The music comes up, a lovely Nigerian melody.* BENEATHA *listens, enraptured, her eyes far away—"back to the past." She begins to dance.* RUTH *is dumbfounded.*)

RUTH. What kind of dance is that?

BENEATHA. A folk dance.

RUTH. (*Pearl Bailey.*) What kind of folks do that, honey?

BENEATHA. It's from Nigeria. It's a dance of welcome.

RUTH. Who you welcoming?

BENEATHA. The men back to the village.

RUTH. Where they been?

BENEATHA. How should I know—out hunting or something. Anyway, they are coming back now . . .

RUTH. Well, that's good.

BENEATHA. (*With the record.*)
    Alundi, alundi
    Alundi alunya
    Jop pu a jeepua
    Ang gu sooooooooo
    Ai yai yae . . .
    Ayehaye—alundi . . .

(WALTER *comes in during this performance; he has obviously been drinking. He leans against the door heavily and watches his sister, at first with distaste. Then his eyes look off—"back to the past"—as he lifts both his fists to the roof, screaming.*)

WALTER. YEAH ... AND ETHIOPIA STRETCH FORTH HER HANDS AGAIN! ...

RUTH. (*Drily, looking at him.*) Yes—and Africa sure is claiming her own tonight. (*She gives them both up and starts ironing again.*)

WALTER. (*All in a drunken, dramatic shout.*) Shut up! ... I'm digging them drums ... them drums move me! ... (*He makes his weaving way to his wife's face and leans in close to her.*) In my *heart of hearts*— (*He thumps his chest.*)—I am much warrior!

RUTH. (*Without even looking up.*) In your heart of hearts you are much drunkard.

WALTER. (*Coming away from her and starting to wander around the room, shouting.*) Me and Jomo ... (*Intently, in his sister's face. She has stopped dancing to watch him in this unknown mood.*) That's my man, Kenyatta. (*Shouting and thumping his chest.*) FLAMING SPEAR! HOT DAMN! (*He is suddenly in possession of an imaginary spear and actively spearing enemies all over the room.*) OCOMOGOSIAY ... THE LION IS WAKING ... OWIMOWEH! (*He pulls his shirt open and leaps up on a table and gestures with his spear. The bell rings.* RUTH *goes to answer.*)

BENEATHA. (*To encourage* WALTER, *thoroughly caught up with this side of him.*) OCOMOGOSIAY, FLAMING SPEAR!

WALTER. (*On the table, very far gone, his eyes pure glass sheets. He sees what we cannot, that he is a leader of his people, a great chief, a descendant of Chaka, and that the hour to march has come.*) Listen, my black brothers—

BENEATHA. OCOMOGOSIAY!

WALTER. —Do you hear the waters rushing against the shores of the coastlands—

BENEATHA. OCOMOGOSIAY!

WALTER. —Do you hear the screeching of the cocks in yonder hills beyond where the chiefs meet in council for the coming of the mighty war—

BENEATHA. OCOMOGOSIAY!

WALTER. —Do you hear the beating of the wings of the birds flying low over the mountains and the low places of our land—

(RUTH *opens the door.* GEORGE MURCHISON *enters.*)

BENEATHA. OCOMOGOSIAY!

WALTER. —Do you hear the singing of the women, singing the war songs of our fathers to the babies in the great houses ... singing the sweet war songs? OH, DO YOU HEAR, MY BLACK BROTHERS!

BENEATHA. (*Completely gone.*) We hear you, Flaming Spear—

WALTER. Telling us to prepare for the greatness of the time— (*To* GEORGE.) Black Brother!

(*He extends his hand for the fraternal clasp.*)

GEORGE. Black Brother, hell!

RUTH. (*Having had enough, and embarrassed for the family.*) Beneatha, you got company—what's the matter with you? Walter Lee Younger, get down off that table and stop acting like a fool ...

(WALTER *comes down off the table suddenly and makes a quick exit to the bathroom.*)

RUTH. He's had a little to drink ... I don't know what her excuse is.

GEORGE. (*To* BENEATHA.) Look honey, we're going *to* the theatre—we're not going to be *in* it ... so go change, huh?

RUTH. You expect this boy to go out with you looking like that?

BENEATHA. (*Looking at* GEORGE.) That's up to George. If he's ashamed of his heritage—

GEORGE. Oh, don't be so proud of yourself, Bennie—just because you look eccentric.

BENEATHA. How can something that's natural be eccentric?

GEORGE. That's what being eccentric means—being natural. Get dressed.

BENEATHA. I don't like that, George.

RUTH. Why must you and your brother make an argument out of everything people say?

BENEATHA. Because I hate assimilationist Negroes!

RUTH. Will somebody please tell me what assimila-who-ever means!

GEORGE. Oh, it's just a college girl's way of calling people Uncle Toms—but that isn't what it means at all.

RUTH. Well, what does it mean?

BENEATHA. (*Cutting* GEORGE *off and staring at him as she replies to* RUTH.) It means someone who is willing to give up his own culture and submerge himself completely in the dominant, and in this case, *oppressive* culture!

GEORGE. Oh, dear, dear, dear! Here we go! A lecture on the African past! On our Great West African Heritage! In one second we will hear all about the great Ashanti empires; the great Songhay civilizations; and the great sculpture of Bénin—and then some poetry in the Bantu—and the whole monologue will end with the word *heritage!* (*Nastily.*) Let's face it, baby, your heritage is nothing but a bunch of raggedy-assed spirituals and some grass huts!

BENEATHA. *Grass huts!* (RUTH *crosses to her and forcibly pushes her toward the bedroom.*) See there . . . you are standing there in your splendid ignorance talking about people who were the first to smelt iron on the face of the earth! (RUTH *is pushing her through the door.*) The Ashanti were performing surgical operations when the English—(RUTH *pulls the door to, with* BENEATHA *on the other side, and smiles graciously at* GEORGE. BENEATHA *opens the door and shouts the end of the sentence defiantly at* GEORGE)—were still tatooing themselves with blue dragons . . . (*She goes back inside.*)

RUTH. Have a seat, George. (*They both sit.* RUTH *folds her hands rather primly on her lap, determined to demonstrate the civilization of the family.*) Warm, ain't it? I mean for September. (*Pause.*) Just like they always say about Chicago weather: If it's too hot or cold for you, just wait a minute and it'll change. (*She smiles happily at this cliché of clichés.*) Everybody say it's got to do with them bombs and things they keep setting off. (*Pause.*) Would you like a nice cold beer?

GEORGE. No, thank you. I don't care for beer. (*He looks at his watch.*) I hope she hurries up.

RUTH. What time is the show?

GEORGE. It's an eight-thirty curtain. That's just Chicago, though. In New York standard curtain time is eight forty.

(*He is rather proud of this knowledge.*)

RUTH. (*Properly appreciating it.*) You get to New York a lot?

GEORGE. (*Offhand.*) Few times a year.

RUTH. Oh—that's nice. I've never been to New York.

(WALTER *enters. We feel he has relieved himself, but the edge of unreality is still with him.*)

WALTER. New York ain't got nothing Chicago ain't. Just a bunch of hustling people all squeezed up together—being "Eastern."

(*He turns his face into a screw of displeasure.*)

GEORGE. Oh—you've been?

WALTER. *Plenty* of times.

RUTH. (*Shocked at the lie.*) Walter Lee Younger!

WALTER. (*Staring her down.*) Plenty! (*Pause.*) What we got to drink in this house? Why don't you offer this man some refreshment. (*To* GEORGE.) They don't know how to entertain people in this house, man.

GEORGE. Thank you—I don't really care for anything.

WALTER. (*Feeling his head; sobriety coming.*) Where's Mama?

RUTH. She ain't come back yet.

WALTER. (*Looking* MURCHISON *over from head to toe, scrutinizing his carefully casual tweed sports jacket over cashmere V-neck sweater over soft eyelet shirt and tie, and soft slacks, finished off with white buckskin shoes.*) Why all you college boys wear them fairyish-looking white shoes?

RUTH. Walter Lee!

(GEORGE MURCHISON *ignores the remark.*)

WALTER. (*To* RUTH.) Well, they look crazy as hell—white shoes, cold as it is.

RUTH. (*Crushed.*) You have to excuse him—

WALTER. No he don't! Excuse me for what? What you always excusing me for! I'll excuse myself when I needs to be excused! (*A pause.*) They look as funny as them black knee socks Beneatha wears out of here all the time.

RUTH. It's the college *style*, Walter.

WALTER. Style, hell. She looks like she got burnt legs or something!

RUTH. Oh, Walter—

WALTER. (*An irritable mimic.*) Oh, Walter! Oh, Walter! (*To* MURCHISON.) How's your old man making out? I understand you all going to buy that big hotel on the Drive? (*He finds a beer in the refrigerator, wanders over to* MURCHISON, *sipping and wiping his lips with the back of his hand, and straddling a chair backwards to talk to the other man.*) Shrewd move. Your old man is all right, man. (*Tapping his head and half winking for emphasis.*) I mean he knows how to operate. I mean he thinks *big*, you know what I mean, I mean for a *home*, you know? But I think he's kind of running out of ideas now. I'd like to talk to him. Listen, man, I got some plans that could turn this city upside down. I mean I think like he does. *Big.* Invest big, gamble big, hell, lose *big* if you have to, you know what I mean. It's hard to find a man on this whole Southside who understands my kind of thinking—you dig? (*He scrutinizes* MURCHISON *again, drinks his beer, squints his eyes and leans in close, confidential, man to man.*) Me and you ought to sit down and talk sometimes, man. Man, I got me some ideas . . .

MURCHISON. (*With boredom.*) Yeah—sometimes we'll have to do that, Walter.

WALTER. (*Understanding the indifference, and offended.*) Yeah—well, when you get the time, man. I know you a busy little boy.

RUTH. Walter, please—

WALTER. (*Bitterly, hurt.*) I know ain't nothing in this world as busy as you colored college boys with your fraternity pins and white shoes . . .

RUTH. (*Covering her face with humiliation.*) Oh, Walter Lee—

WALTER. I see you all all the time—with the books tucked under your arms—going to your (*British A—a mimic.*) "clahsses." And for what! What the hell you learning over there? Filling up your heads—(*Counting off on his fingers.*)—with the sociology and the psychology—but they teaching you how to be a man? How to take over and run the world? They teaching you how to run a rubber plantation or a steel mill? Naw—just to talk proper and read books and wear white shoes . . .

GEORGE. (*Looking at him with distaste, a little above it all.*) You're all wacked up with bitterness, man.

WALTER. (*Intently, almost quietly, between the teeth, glaring at the boy.*) And you—ain't you bitter, man? Ain't you just about had it yet? Don't you see no stars gleaming that you can't reach out and grab? You happy?—You contented son-of-a-bitch—you happy? You got it made? Bitter? Man, I'm a volcano. Bitter? Here I am a giant—surrounded by ants! Ants who can't even understand what it is the giant is talking about.

RUTH. (*Passionately and suddenly.*) Oh, Walter—ain't you with nobody!

WALTER. (*Violently.*) No! 'Cause ain't nobody with me! Not even my own mother!

RUTH. Walter, that's a terrible thing to say!

(BENEATHA *enters, dressed for the evening in a cocktail dress and earrings.*)

GEORGE. Well—hey, you look great.

BENEATHA. Let's go, George. See you all later.

RUTH. Have a nice time.

GEORGE. Thanks. Good night. (*To* WALTER, *sarcastically.*) Good night, *Prometheus.*

(BENEATHA *and* GEORGE *exit.*)

WALTER. (*To* RUTH.) Who is Prometheus?

RUTH. I don't know. Don't worry about it.

WALTER. (*In fury, pointing after* GEORGE.) See there—they get to a point where they can't insult you man to man—they got to go talk about something ain't nobody never heard of!

RUTH. How do you know it was an insult? (*To humor him.*) Maybe Prometheus is a nice fellow.

WALTER. Prometheus! I bet there ain't even no such thing! I bet that simple-minded clown—

RUTH. Walter—
(*She stops what she is doing and looks at him.*)

WALTER. (*Yelling.*) Don't start!

RUTH. Start what?

WALTER. Your nagging! Where was I? Who was I with? How much money did I spend?

RUTH. (*Plaintively.*) Walter Lee—why don't we just try to talk about it . . .

WALTER. (*Not listening.*) I been out talking with people who understand me. People who care about the things I got on my mind.

RUTH. (*Wearily.*) I guess that means people like Willy Harris.

WALTER. Yes, people like Willy Harris.

RUTH. (*With a sudden flash of impatience.*) Why don't you all just hurry up and go into the banking business and stop talking about it!

WALTER. Why? You want to know why? 'Cause we all tied up in a race of people that don't know how to do nothing but moan, pray and have babies!
(*The line is too bitter even for him and he looks at her and sits down.*)

RUTH. Oh, Walter . . . (*Softly.*) Honey, why can't you stop fighting me?

WALTER. (*Without thinking.*) Who's fighting you? Who even cares about you?
(*This line begins the retardation of his mood.*)

RUTH. Well— (*She waits a long time, and then with resignation starts to put away her things.*) I guess I might as well go on to bed . . . (*More or less to herself.*) I don't know where we lost it . . . but we have . . . (*Then, to him.*) I—I'm sorry about this new baby, Walter. I guess maybe I better go on and do what I started . . . I guess I just didn't realize how bad things was with us . . . I guess I just didn't really realize— (*She starts out to the bedroom and stops.*) You want some hot milk?

WALTER. Hot milk?

RUTH. Yes—hot milk.

WALTER. Why hot milk?

RUTH. 'Cause after all that liquor you come home with you ought to have something hot in your stomach.

WALTER. I don't want no milk.

RUTH. You want some coffee then?

WALTER. No, I don't want no coffee. I don't want nothing hot to drink. (*Almost plaintively.*) Why you always trying to give me something to eat?

RUTH. (*Standing and looking at him helplessly.*) What else can I give you, Walter Lee Younger?
(*She stands and looks at him and presently turns to go out again. He lifts his head and watches her going away from him in a new mood which began to emerge when he asked her "Who cares about you?"*)

WALTER. It's been rough, ain't it, baby? (*She hears and stops but does not turn around and he continues to her back.*) I guess between two people there ain't never as much understood as folks generally thinks there is. I mean like between me and you— (*She turns to face him.*) How we gets to the place where we scared to talk softness to each other. (*He waits, thinking hard himself.*) Why you think it got to be like that? (*He is thoughtful, almost as a child would be.*) Ruth, what is it gets into people ought to be close?

RUTH. I don't know, honey. I think about it a lot.

WALTER. On account of you and me, you mean? The way things are with us. The way something done come down between us.

RUTH. There ain't so much between us, Walter . . . Not when you come to me and try to talk to me. Try to be with me . . . a little even.

WALTER. (*Total honesty.*) Sometimes ... sometimes ... I don't even know how to try.

RUTH. Walter—

WALTER. Yes?

RUTH. (*Coming to him, gently and with misgiving, but coming to him.*) Honey ... life don't have to be like this. I mean sometimes people can do things so that things are better... You remember how we used to talk when Travis was born ... about the way we were going to live ... the kind of house ... (*She is stroking his head.*) Well, it's all starting to slip away from us ...

(MAMA *enters, and* WALTER *jumps up and shouts at her.*)

WALTER. Mama, where have you been?

MAMA. My—them steps is longer than they used to be. Whew! (*She sits down and ignores him.*) How you feeling this evening, Ruth?

(RUTH *shrugs, disturbed some at having been prematurely interrupted and watching her husband knowingly.*)

WALTER. Mama, where have you been all day?

MAMA. (*Still ignoring him and leaning on the table and changing to more comfortable shoes.*) Where's Travis?

RUTH. I let him go out earlier and he ain't come back yet. Boy, is he going to get it!

WALTER. Mama!

MAMA. (*As if she has heard him for the first time.*) Yes, son?

WALTER. Where did you go this afternoon?

MAMA. I went downtown to tend to some business that I had to tend to.

WALTER. What kind of business?

MAMA. You know better than to question me like a child, Brother.

WALTER. (*Rising and bending over the table.*) Where were you, Mama? (*Bringing his fists down and shouting.*) Mama, you didn't go do something with that insurance money, something crazy?

(*The front door opens slowly, interrupting him, and* TRAVIS *peeks his head in, less than hopefully.*)

TRAVIS. (*To his mother.*) Mama, I—

RUTH. "Mama I" nothing! You're going to get it, boy! Get on in that bedroom and get yourself ready!

TRAVIS. But I—

MAMA. Why don't you all never let the child explain hisself.

RUTH. Keep out of it now, Lena.

(MAMA *clamps her lips together, and* RUTH *advances toward her son menacingly.*)

RUTH. A thousand times I have told you not to go off like that—

MAMA. (*Holding out her arms to her grandson.*) Well—at least let me tell him something. I want him to be the first one to hear... Come here, Travis. (*The boy obeys, gladly.*) Travis—(*She takes him by the shoulder and looks into his face*)—you know that money we got in the mail this morning?

TRAVIS. Yes'm—

MAMA. Well—what you think your grandmama gone and done with that money?

TRAVIS. I don't know, Grandmama.

MAMA. (*Putting her finger on his nose for emphasis.*) She went out and she bought you a house! (*The explosion comes from* WALTER *at the end of the revelation and he jumps up and turns away from all of them in a fury.* MAMA *continues, to* TRAVIS.) You glad about the house? It's going to be yours when you get to be a man.

TRAVIS. Yeah—I always wanted to live in a house.

MAMA. All right, gimme some sugar then— (TRAVIS *puts his arms around her neck as she watches her son over the boy's shoulder. Then, to* TRAVIS, *after the embrace.*) Now when you say your prayers tonight, you thank God and your grandfather—'cause it was him who give you the house—in his way.

RUTH. (*Taking the boy from* MAMA *and pushing him toward the bedroom.*) Now you get out of here and get ready for your beating.

TRAVIS. Aw, Mama—

RUTH. Get on in there—(*Closing the door behind him and turning radiantly to her mother-in-law.*) So you went and did it!

MAMA. (*Quietly, looking at her son with pain.*) Yes, I did.

RUTH. (*Raising both arms classically.*) Praise God! (*Looks at* WALTER *a moment, who says nothing. She crosses rapidly to her husband.*) Please, honey—let me be glad . . . you be glad too. (*She has laid her hands on his shoulders, but he shakes himself free of her roughly, without turning to face her.*) Oh, Walter . . . a home . . . a home. (*She comes back to* MAMA.) Well—where is it? How big is it? How much it going to cost?

MAMA. Well—

RUTH. When we moving?

MAMA. (*Smiling at her.*) First of the month.

RUTH. (*Throwing back her head with jubilance.*) Praise God!

MAMA. (*Tentatively, still looking at her son's back turned against her and* RUTH.) It's—it's a nice house too . . . (*She cannot help speaking directly to him. An imploring quality in her voice, her manner, makes her almost like a girl now.*) Three bedrooms—nice big one for you and Ruth. . . . Me and Beneatha still have to share our room, but Travis have one of his own—and (*With difficulty.*) I figure if the—new baby—is a boy, we could get one of them double-decker outfits . . . And there's a yard with a little patch of dirt where I could may be get to grow me a few flowers . . . And a nice big basement . . .

RUTH. Walter honey, be glad—

MAMA. (*Still to his back, fingering things on the table.*) 'Course I don't want to make it sound fancier than it is . . It's just a plain little old house—but it's made good and solid—and it will be *ours.* Walter Lee—it makes a difference in a man when he can walk on floors that belong to *him* . . .

RUTH. Where is it?

MAMA. (*Frightened at this telling.*) Well—well—it's out there in Clybourne Park—

(RUTH'S *radiance fades abruptly, and* WALTER *finally turns slowly to face his mother with incredulity and hostility.*)

RUTH. Where?

MAMA. (*Matter-of-factly.*) Four o six Clybourne Street, Clybourne Park.

RUTH. Clybourne Park? Mama, there ain't no colored people living in Clybourne Park.

MAMA. (*Almost idiotically.*) Well, I guess there's going to be some now.

WALTER. (*Bitterly.*) So that's the peace and comfort you went out and bought for us today!

MAMA. (*Raising her eyes to meet his finally.*) Son—I just tried to find the nicest place for the least amount of money for my family.

RUTH. (*Trying to recover from the shock.*) Well—well—'course I ain't one never been 'fraid of no crackers, mind you— but—well, wasn't there no other houses nowhere?

MAMA. Them houses they put up for colored in them areas way out all seem to cost twice as much as other houses. I did the best I could.

RUTH. (*Struck senseless with the news, in its various degrees of goodness and trouble, she sits a moment, her fists propping her chin in thought, and then she starts to rise, bringing her fists down with vigor, the radiance spreading from cheek to cheek again.*) Well—well!—All I can say is—if this is my time in life—*my time*—to say good-bye—(*And she builds with momentum as she starts to circle the room with an exuberant, almost tearfully happy release*)—to these Goddamned cracking walls!—(*She pounds the walls.*)—and these marching roaches!—(*She wipes at an imaginary army of marching roaches.*)—and this cramped little closet which ain't now or never was no kitchen! . . . then I say it loud and good, *Hallelujah! and good-bye misery . . . I don't never want to see your ugly face again!* (*She laughs joyously, having practically destroyed the apartment, and flings her arms up and lets them come down happily, slowly, reflectively, over her abdomen, aware for the first time perhaps that the life therein pulses with happiness and not despair.*) Lena?

MAMA. (*Moved, watching her happiness.*) Yes, honey?
RUTH. (*Looking off.*) Is there—is there a whole lot of sunlight?
MAMA. (*Understanding.*) Yes, child, there's a whole lot of sunlight.
(*Long pause.*)
RUTH. (*Collecting herself and going to the door of the room* TRAVIS *is in.*) Well—I guess I better see 'bout Travis. (*To* MAMA.) Lord, I sure don't feel like whipping nobody today!
(*She exits.*)
MAMA. (*The mother and son are left alone now and the mother waits a long time, considering deeply, before she speaks.*) Son—you—you understand what I done, don't you? (WALTER *is silent and sullen.*) I—I just seen my family falling apart today . . . just falling to pieces in front of my eyes . . . We couldn't of gone on like we was today. We was going backwards 'stead of forwards—talking 'bout killing babies and wishing each other was dead . . . When it gets like that in life—you just got to do something different, push on out and do something bigger . . . (*She waits.*) I wish you say something, son . . . I wish you'd say how deep inside you you think I done the right thing—
WALTER. (*Crossing slowly to his bedroom door and finally turning there and speaking measuredly.*) What you need me to say you done right for? *You* the head of this family. You run our lives like you want to. It was your money and you did what you wanted with it. So what you need for me to say it was all right for? (*Bitterly, to hurt her as deeply as he knows is possible.*) So you butchered up a dream of mine—you—who always talking 'bout your children's dreams . . .
MAMA. Walter Lee—
(*He just closes the door behind him.* MAMA *sits alone, thinking heavily.*)
CURTAIN

SCENE 2

TIME: *Friday night. A few weeks later.*
AT RISE: *Packing crates mark the intention of the family to move.* BENEATHA *and* GEORGE *come in, presumably from an evening out again.*

GEORGE. O.K. . . . O.K., whatever you say . . . (*They both sit on the couch. He tries to kiss her. She moves away.*) Look, we've had a nice evening; let's not spoil it, huh? . . .
(*He again turns her head and tries to nuzzle in and she turns away from him, not with distaste but with momentary lack of interest; in a mood to pursue what they were talking about.*)
BENEATHA. I'm *trying* to talk to you.
GEORGE. We always talk.
BENEATHA. Yes—and I love to talk.
GEORGE. (*Exasperated; rising.*) I know it and I don't mind it sometimes . . . I want you to cut it out, see— The moody stuff, I mean. I don't like it. You're a nice-looking girl . . . all over. That's all you need, honey, forget the atmosphere. Guys aren't going to go for the atmosphere—they're going to go for what they see. Be glad for that. Drop the Garbo routine. It doesn't go with you. As for myself, I want a nice—(*Groping.*)—simple(*Thoughtfully.*)—sophisticated girl . . . not a poet—O.K.?
(*She rebuffs him again and he starts to leave.*)
BENEATHA. Why are you angry?
GEORGE. Because this is stupid! I don't go out with you to discuss the nature of "quiet desperation" or to hear all about your thoughts—because the world will go on thinking what it thinks regardless—

BENEATHA. Then why read books? Why go to school?

GEORGE. (*With artificial patience, counting on his fingers.*) It's simple. You read books —to learn facts—to get grades—to pass the course—to get a degree. That's all— it has nothing to do with thoughts.

(*A long pause.*)

BENEATHA. I see. (*A longer pause as she looks at him.*) Good night, George.

(GEORGE *looks at her a little oddly, and starts to exit. He meets* MAMA *coming in.*)

GEORGE. Oh—hello, Mrs. Younger.

MAMA. Hello, George, how you feeling?

GEORGE. Fine—fine, how are you?

MAMA. Oh, a little tired. You know them steps can get you after a day's work. You all have a nice time tonight?

GEORGE. Yes—a fine time. Well, good night.

MAMA. Good night. (*He exits.* MAMA *closes the door behind her.*) Hello, honey. What you sitting like that for?

BENEATHA. I'm just sitting.

MAMA. Didn't you have a nice time?

BENEATHA. No.

MAMA. No? What's the matter?

BENEATHA. Mama, George is a fool— honest. (*She rises.*)

MAMA. (*Hustling around unloading the packages she has entered with. She stops.*) Is he, baby?

BENEATHA. Yes.

(BENEATHA *makes up* TRAVIS's *bed as she talks.*)

MAMA. You sure?

BENEATHA. Yes.

MAMA. Well—I guess you better not waste your time with no fools.

(BENEATHA *looks up at her mother, watching her put groceries in the refrigerator. Finally she gathers up her things and starts into the bedroom. At the door she stops and looks back at her mother.*)

BENEATHA. Mama—

MAMA. Yes, baby—

BENEATHA. Thank you.

MAMA. For what?

BENEATHA. For understanding me this time.

(*She exits quickly and the mother stands, smiling a little, looking at the place where* BENEATHA *just stood.* RUTH *enters.*)

RUTH. Now don't you fool with any of this stuff, Lena—

MAMA. Oh, I just thought I'd sort a few things out.

(*The phone rings.* RUTH *answers.*)

RUTH. (*At the phone.*) Hello—Just a minute. (*Goes to door.*) Walter, it's Mrs. Arnold. (*Waits. Goes back to the phone. Tense.*) Hello. Yes, this is his wife speaking . . . He's lying down now. Yes . . . well, he'll be in tomorrow. He's been very sick. Yes—I know we should have called, but we were so sure he'd be able to come in today. Yes—yes, I'm very sorry. Yes . . . Thank you very much. (*She hangs up.* WALTER *is standing in the doorway of the bedroom behind her.*) That was Mrs. Arnold.

WALTER. (*Indifferently.*) Was it?

RUTH. She said if you don't come in tomorrow that they are getting a new man . . .

WALTER. Ain't that sad—ain't that crying sad.

RUTH. She said Mr. Arnold has had to take a cab for three days . . . Walter, you ain't been to work for three days! (*This is a revelation to her.*) Where you been, Walter Lee Younger? (WALTER *looks at her and starts to laugh.*) You're going to lose your job.

WALTER. That's right . . .

RUTH. Oh, Walter, and with your mother working like a dog every day—

WALTER. That's sad too— Everything is sad.

MAMA. What you been doing for these three days, son?

WALTER. Mama—you don't know all the things a man what got leisure can find to do in this city . . . What's this—Friday night? Well—Wednesday I borrowed Willy Harris' car and I went for a drive . . . just me and myself and I drove and drove . . . Way out . . . way past South

Chicago, and I parked the car and I sat and looked at the steel mills all day long. I just sat in the car and looked at them big black chimneys for hours. Then I drove back and I went to the Green Hat. (*Pause.*) And Thursday—Thursday I borrowed the car again and I got in it and I pointed it the other way and I drove the other way—for hours—way, way up to Wisconsin, and I looked at the farms. I just drove and looked at the farms. Then I drove back and I went to the Green Hat. (*Pause.*) And today—today I didn't get the car. Today I just walked. All over the Southside. And I looked at the Negroes and they looked at me and finally I just sat down on the curb at Thirty-ninth and South Parkway and I just sat there and watched the Negroes go by. And then I went to the Green Hat. You all sad? You all depressed? And you know where I am going right now—

(RUTH *goes out quietly.*)

MAMA. Oh, Big Walter, is this the harvest of our days?

WALTER. You know what I like about the Green Hat? (*He turns the radio on and a steamy, deep blues pours into the room.*) I like this little cat they got there who blows a sax . . . He blows. He talks to me. He ain't but 'bout five feet tall and he's got a conked head and his eyes is always closed and he's all music—

MAMA. (*Rising and getting some papers out of her handbag.*) Walter—

WALTER. And there's this other guy who plays the piano . . . and they got a sound. I mean they can work on some music . . . They got the best little combo in the world in the Green Hat . . . You can just sit there and drink and listen to them three men play and you realize that don't nothing matter worth a damn, but just being there—

MAMA. I've helped do it to you, haven't I, son? Walter, I been wrong.

WALTER. Naw—you ain't never been wrong about nothing, Mama.

MAMA. Listen to me, now. I say I been wrong, son. That I been doing to you what the rest of the world been doing to you. (*She stops and he looks up slowly at her and she meets his eyes pleadingly.*) Walter—what you ain't never understood is that I ain't got nothing, don't own nothing, ain't never really wanted nothing that wasn't for you. There ain't nothing as precious to me . . . There ain't nothing worth holding on to, money, dreams, nothing else—if it means —if it means it's going to destroy my boy. (*She puts her papers in front of him and he watches her without speaking or moving.*) I paid the man thirty-five hundred dollars down on the house. That leaves sixty-five hundred dollars. Monday morning I want you to take this money and take three thousand dollars and put it in a savings account for Beneatha's medical schooling. The rest you put in a checking account— with your name on it. And from now on any penny that come out of it or that go in it is for you to look after. For you to decide. (*She drops her hands a little helplessly.*) It ain't much, but it's all I got in the world and I'm putting it in your hands. I'm telling you to be the head of this family from now on like you supposed to be.

WALTER. (*Stares at the money.*) You trust me like that, Mama?

MAMA. I ain't never stop trusting you. Like I ain't never stop loving you.

(*She goes out, and* WALTER *sits looking at the money on the table as the music continues in its idiom, pulsing in the room. Finally, in a decisive gesture, he gets up, and, in mingled joy and desperation, picks up the money. At the same moment,* TRAVIS *enters for bed.*)

TRAVIS. What's the matter, Daddy? You drunk?

WALTER. (*Sweetly, more sweetly than we have ever known him.*) No, Daddy ain't drunk. Daddy ain't going to never be drunk again . . .

TRAVIS. Well, good night, Daddy.

(*The* FATHER *has come from behind the couch and leans over, embracing his son.*)

WALTER. Son, I feel like talking to you tonight.

TRAVIS. About what?

WALTER. Oh, about a lot of things. About you and what kind of man you going to be when you grow up ... Son— son, what do you want to be when you grow up?

TRAVIS. A bus driver.

WALTER. (*Laughing a little.*) A what? Man, that ain't nothing to want to be!

TRAVIS. Why not?

WALTER. 'Cause, man—it ain't big enough—you know what I mean.

TRAVIS. I don't know then. I can't make up my mind. Sometimes Mama asks me that too. And sometimes when I tell you I just want to be like you—she says she don't want me to be like that and sometimes she says she does ...

WALTER. (*Gathering him up in his arms.*) You know what, Travis? In seven years you going to be seventeen years old. And things is going to be very different with us in seven years, Travis ... One day when you are seventeen I'll come home—home from my office downtown somewhere—

TRAVIS. You don't work in no office, Daddy.

WALTER. No—but after tonight. After what your daddy gonna do tonight, there's going to be offices—a whole lot of offices ...

TRAVIS. What you gonna do tonight, Daddy?

WALTER. You wouldn't understand yet, son, but your daddy's gonna make a transaction ... a business transaction that's going to change our lives ... That's how come one day when you 'bout seventeen years old I'll come home and I'll be pretty tired, you know what I mean, after a day of conferences and secretaries getting things wrong the way they do ... 'cause an executive's life is hell, man— (*The more he talks the farther away he gets.*) And I'll pull the car up on the driveway ... just a plain black Chrysler, I think, with white walls —no—black tires. More elegant. Rich people don't have to be flashy ... though I'll have to get something a little sportier for Ruth—maybe a Cadillac convertible to do her shopping in ... And I'll come up the steps to the house and the gardener will be clipping away at the hedges and he'll say, "Good evening, Mr. Younger." And I'll say, "Hello, Jefferson, how are you this evening?" And I'll go inside and Ruth will come downstairs and meet me at the door and we'll kiss each other and she'll take my arm and we'll go up to your room to see you sitting on the floor with the catalogues of all the great schools in America around you. .... All the great schools in the world! And—and I'll say, all right son—it's your seventeenth birthday, what is it you've decided? ... Just tell me where you want to go to school and you'll *go*. Just tell me, what it is you want to be—and you'll *be* it. .... Whatever you want to be—Yessir! (*He holds his arms open for* TRAVIS.) You just name it, son ... (TRAVIS *leaps into them.*) and I hand you the world!

(WALTER's *voice has risen in pitch and hysterical promise and on the last line he lifts* TRAVIS *high.*)

(*BLACKOUT*)

SCENE 3

TIME: *Saturday, moving day, one week later.*

Before the curtain rises, RUTH'S *voice, a strident, dramatic church alto, cuts through the silence.*

It is, in the darkness, a triumphant surge, a penetrating statement of expectation: "Oh, Lord, I don't feel no ways tired! Children, oh, glory hallelujah!"

As the curtain rises we see that RUTH *is alone in the living room, finishing up the family's packing. It is moving day. She is nailing crates and tying cartons.* BENEATHA *enters, carrying a guitar case, and watches her exuberant sister-in-law.*

RUTH. Hey!
BENEATHA. (*Putting away the case.*) Hi.
RUTH. (*Pointing at a package.*) Honey—look in that package there and see what I found on sale this morning at the South Center. (RUTH *gets up and moves to the package and draws out some curtains.*) Lookahere—hand-turned hems!
BENEATHA. How do you know the window size out there?
RUTH. (*Who hadn't thought of that.*) Oh—Well, they bound to fit something in the whole house. Anyhow, they was too good a bargain to pass up. (RUTH *slaps her head, suddenly remembering something.*) Oh, Bennie—I meant to put a special note on that carton over there. That's your mama's good china and she wants 'em to be very careful with it.
BENEATHA. I'll do it.

(BENEATHA *finds a piece of paper and starts to draw large letters on it.*)

RUTH. You know what I'm going to do soon as I get in that new house?
BENEATHA. What?
RUTH. Honey—I'm going to run me a tub of water up to here . . . (*With her fingers practically up to her nostrils.*) And I'm going to get in it—and I am going to sit . . . and sit . . . and sit in that hot water and the first person who knocks to tell *me* to hurry up and come out—
BENEATHA. Gets shot at sunrise.
RUTH. (*Laughing happily.*) You said it, sister! (*Noticing how large* BENEATHA *is absent-mindedly making the note.*) Honey, they ain't going to read that from no airplane.
BENEATHA. (*Laughing herself.*) I guess I always think things have more emphasis if they are big, somehow.
RUTH. (*Looking up at her and smiling.*) You and your brother seem to have that as a philosophy of life. Lord, that man—done changed so 'round here. You know—you know what we did last night? Me and Walter Lee?
BENEATHA. What?
RUTH. (*Smiling to herself.*) We went to the movies. (*Looking at* BENEATHA *to see if she understands.*) We went to the movies. You know the last time me and Walter went to the movies together?
BENEATHA. No.
RUTH. Me neither. That's how long it been. (*Smiling again.*) But we went last night. The picture wasn't much good, but that didn't seem to matter. We went—and we held hands.
BENEATHA. Oh, Lord!
RUTH. We held hands—and you know what?
BENEATHA. What?
RUTH. When we come out of the show it was late and dark and all the stores and things was closed up . . . and it was kind of chilly and there wasn't many people on the streets . . . and we was still holding hands, me and Walter.
BENEATHA. You're killing me.

(WALTER *enters with a large package. His happiness is deep in him; he cannot keep still with his new-found exuberance. He is singing and wiggling and snapping his fingers. He puts his package in a corner and puts a phonograph record, which he has brought in with him, on the record player. As the music comes up he dances over to* RUTH *and tries to get her to dance with him. She gives in at last to his raunchiness and in a fit of giggling allows herself to be drawn into his mood and together they deliberately burlesque an old social dance of their youth.*)

BENEATHA. (*Regarding them a long time as they dance, then drawing in her breath for a deeply exaggerated comment which she does not particularly mean.*) Talk about—

oldddddddddd-fashionedddddddd—Negroes!

WALTER. (*Stopping momentarily.*) What kind of Negroes?

(*He says this in fun. He is not angry with her today, nor with anyone. He starts to dance with his wife again.*)

BENEATHA. Old-fashioned.

WALTER. (*As he dances with* RUTH.) You know, when these *New Negroes* have their convention—(*Pointing at his sister.*)—that is going to be the chairman of the Committee on Unending Agitation. (*He goes on dancing, then stops.*) Race, race, race! . . . Girl, I do believe you are the first person in the history of the entire human race to successfully brainwash yourself. (BENEATHA *breaks up and goes on dancing. He stops again, enjoying his tease.*) Damn, even the N double A C P takes a holiday sometimes! (BENEATHA *and* RUTH *laugh. He dances with* RUTH *some more and starts to laugh and stops and pantomimes someone over an operating table.*) I can just see that chick someday looking down at some poor cat on an operating table before she starts to slice him, saying . . . (*Pulling his sleeves back maliciously.*) "By the way, what are your views on civil rights down there? . . ."

(*He laughs at her again and starts to dance happily. The bell sounds.*)

BENEATHA. Sticks and stones may break my bones but . . . words will never hurt me!

(BENEATHA *goes to the door and opens it as* WALTER *and* RUTH *go on with the clowning.* BENEATHA *is somewhat surprised to see a quiet-looking middle-aged white man in a business suit holding his hat and a briefcase in his hand and consulting a small piece of paper.*)

MAN. Uh—how do you do, miss. I am looking for a Mrs.— (*He looks at the slip of paper.*) Mrs. Lena Younger?

BENEATHA. (*Smoothing her hair with slight embarrassment.*) Oh—yes, that's my mother. Excuse me. (*She closes the door and turns to quiet the other two.*) Ruth! Brother! Somebody's here. (*Then she opens the door. The man casts a curious quick glance at all of them.*) Uh—come in please.

MAN. (*Coming in.*) Thank you.

BENEATHA. My mother isn't here just now. Is it business?

MAN. Yes . . . well, of a sort.

WALTER. (*Freely, the Man of the House.*) Have a seat. I'm Mrs. Younger's son. I look after most of her business matters.

(RUTH *and* BENEATHA *exchange amused glances.*)

MAN. (*Regarding* WALTER, *and sitting.*) Well— My name is Karl Lindner . . .

WALTER. (*Stretching out his hand.*) Walter Younger. This is my wife—(RUTH *nods politely.*)—and my sister.

LINDNER. How do you do.

WALTER. (*Amiably, as he sits himself easily on a chair, leaning with interest forward on his knees and looking expectantly into the newcomer's face.*) What can we do for you, Mr. Lindner.

LINDNER. (*Some minor shuffling of the hat and briefcase on his knees.*) Well—I am a representative of the Clybourne Park Improvement Association—

WALTER. (*Pointing.*) Why don't you sit your things on the floor?

LINDER. Oh—yes. Thank you. (*He slides the briefcase and hat under the chair.*) And as I was saying—I am from the Clybourne Park Improvement Association and we have had it brought to our attention at the last meeting that you people—or at least your mother—has bought a piece of residential property at—(*He digs for the slip of paper again.*)—four o six Clybourne Street . . .

WALTER. That's right. Care for something to drink? Ruth, get Mr. Lindner a beer.

LINDNER. (*Upset for some reason.*) Oh—no, really. I mean thank you very much, but no thank you.

RUTH. (*Innocently.*) Some coffee?

LINDNER. Thank you, nothing at all.

(BENEATHA *is watching the man carefully.*)

LINDNER. Well, I don't know how much you folks know about our organization.

(*He is a gentle man; thoughtful and somewhat labored in his manner.*) It is one of these community organizations set up to look after—oh, you know, things like block upkeep and special projects and we also have what we call our New Neighbors Orientation Committee . . .

BENEATHA. (*Drily.*) Yes—and what do they do?

LINDNER. (*Turning a little to her and then returning the main force to* WALTER.) Well—it's what you might call a sort of welcoming committee, I guess. I mean they, we, I'm the chairman of the committee—go around and see the new people who move into the neighborhood and sort of give them the lowdown on the way we do things out in Clybourne Park.

BENEATHA. (*With appreciation of the two meanings, which escape* RUTH *and* WALTER.) Un-huh.

LINDNER. And we also have the category of what the association calls—(*He looks elsewhere.*)—uh—special community problems . . .

BENEATHA. Yes—and what are some of those?

WALTER. Girl, let the man talk.

LINDNER. (*With understated relief.*) Thank you. I would sort of like to explain this thing in my own way. I mean I want to explain to you in a certain way.

WALTER. Go ahead.

LINDNER. Yes. Well. I'm going to try to get right to the point. I'm sure we'll all appreciate that in the long run.

BENEATHA. Yes.

WALTER. Be still now!

LINDNER. Well—

RUTH. (*Still innocently.*) Would you like another chair—you don't look comfortable.

LINDNER. (*More frustrated than annoyed.*) No, thank you very much. Please. Well—to get right to the point I— (*A great breath, and he is off at last.*) I am sure you people must be aware of some of the incidents which have happened in various parts of the city when colored people have moved into certain areas— (BEATHA *exhales* heavily and starts tossing a piece of fruit up and down in the air.*) Well—because we have what I think is going to be a unique type of organization in American community life—not only do we deplore that kind of thing—but we are trying to do something about it. (BENEATHA *stops tossing and turns with a new and quizzical interest to the man.*) We feel—(*gaining confidence in his mission because of the interest in the faces of the people he is talking to*)—we feel that most of the trouble in this world, when you come right down to it—(*He hits his knee for emphasis.*)—most of the trouble exists because people just don't sit down and talk to each other.

RUTH. (*Nodding as she might in church, pleased with the remark.*) You can say that again, mister.

LINDNER. (*More encouraged by such affirmation.*) That we don't try hard enough in this world to understand the other fellow's problem. The other guy's point of view.

RUTH. Now that's right.

(BENEATHA *and* WALTER *merely watch and listen with genuine interest.*)

LINDNER. Yes—that's the way we feel out in Clybourne Park. And that's why I was elected to come here this afternoon and talk to you people. Friendly like, you know, the way people should talk to each other and see if we couldn't find some way to work this thing out. As I say, the whole business is a matter of *caring* about the other fellow. Anybody can see that you are a nice family of folks, hard working and honest I'm sure. (BENEATHA *frowns slightly, quizzically, her head tilted regarding him.*) Today everybody knows what it means to be on the outside of *something*. And of course, there is always somebody who is out to take the advantage of people who don't always understand.

WALTER. What do you mean?

LINDNER. Well—you see our community is made up of people who've worked hard as the dickens for years to build up that little community. They're not rich and fancy people; just hard-working, honest people who don't really have much but those little homes and a dream of the kind of community they want to raise their children in. Now, I don't say we are perfect and there is a lot wrong in some of the things they want. But you've got to admit that a man, right or wrong, has the right to want to have the neighborhood he lives in a certain kind of way. And at the moment the overwhelming majority of our people out there feel that people get along better, take more of a common interest in the life of the community, when they share a common background. I want you to believe me when I tell you that race prejudice simply doesn't enter into it. It is a matter of the people of Clybourne Park believing, rightly or wrongly, as I say, that for the happiness of all concerned that our Negro families are happier when they lived in their *own* communities.

BENEATHA. (*With a grand and bitter gesture.*) This, friends, is the Welcoming Committee!

WALTER. (*Dumbfounded, looking at* LINDNER.) Is this what you came marching all the way over here to tell us?

LINDNER. Well, now we've been having a fine conversation. I hope you'll hear me all the way through.

WALTER. (*Tightly.*) Go ahead, man.

LINDNER. You see—in the face of all things I have said, we are prepared to make your family a very generous offer . . .

BENEATHA. Thirty pieces and not a coin less!

WALTER. Yeah?

LINDNER. (*Putting on his glasses and drawing a form out of the briefcase.*) Our association is prepared, through the collective effort of our people, to buy the house from you at a financial gain to your family.

RUTH. Lord have mercy, ain't this the living gall!

WALTER. All right, you through?

LINDNER. Well, I want to give you the exact terms of the financial arrangement—

WALTER. We don't want to hear no exact terms of no arrangements. I want to know if you got any more to tell us 'bout getting together?

LINDNER. (*Taking off his glasses.*) Well—I don't suppose that you feel . . .

WALTER. Never mind how I feel—you got any more to say 'bout how people ought to sit down and talk to each other? . . . Get out of my house, man.

(*He turns his back and walks to the door.*)

LINDNER. (*Looking around at the hostile faces and reaching and assembling his hat and briefcase.*) Well—I don't understand why you people are reacting this way. What do you think you are going to gain by moving into a neighborhood where you just aren't wanted and where some elements—well —people can get awful worked up when they feel that their whole way of life and everything they've ever worked for is threatened.

WALTER. Get out.

LINDNER. (*At the door, holding a small card.*) Well—I'm sorry it went like this.

WALTER. Get out.

LINDNER. (*Almost sadly regarding* WALTER.) You just can't force people to change their hearts, son.

(*He turns and puts his card on a table and exits.* WALTER *pushes the door to with stinging hatred, and stands looking at it.* RUTH *just sits and* BENEATHA *just stands. They say nothing.* MAMA *and* TRAVIS *enter.*)

MAMA. Well—this all the packing got done since I left out of here this morning. I testify before God that my children got all the energy of the dead. What time the moving men due?

BENEATHA. Four o'clock. You had a caller, Mama.

(*She is smiling, teasingly.*)

MAMA. Sure enough—who?

BENEATHA. (*Her arms folded saucily.*) The Welcoming Committee.

(WALTER *and* RUTH *giggle.*)

MAMA. (*Innocently.*) Who?

BENEATHA. The Welcoming Committee. They said they're sure going to be glad to see you when you get there.

WALTER. (*Devilishly.*) Yeah, they said they can't hardly wait to see your face.

(*Laughter.*)

MAMA. (*Sensing their facetiousness.*) What's the matter with you all?

WALTER. Ain't nothing the matter with us. We just telling you 'bout the gentleman who came to see you this afternoon. From the Clybourne Park Improvement Association.

MAMA. What he want?

RUTH. (*In the same mood as* BENEATHA *and* WALTER.) To welcome you, honey.

WALTER. He said they can't hardly wait. He said the one thing they don't have, that they just *dying* to have out there is a fine family of colored people! (*To* RUTH *and* BENEATHA.) Ain't that right!

RUTH *and* BENEATHA. (*Mockingly.*) Yeah! He left his card in case—

(*They indicate the card, and* MAMA *picks it up and throws it on the floor—understanding and looking off as she draws her chair up to the table on which she has put her plant and some sticks and some cord.*)

MAMA. Father, give us strength. (*Knowingly—and without fun.*) Did he threaten us?

BENEATHA. Oh—Mama—they don't do it like that any more. He talked Brotherhood. He said everybody ought to learn how to sit down and hate each other with good Christian fellowship.

(*She and* WALTER *shake hands to ridicule the remark.*)

MAMA. (*Sadly.*) Lord, protect us . . .

RUTH. You should hear the money those folks raised to buy the house from us. All we paid and then some.

BENEATHA. What they think we going to do—eat 'em?

RUTH. No, honey, marry 'em.

MAMA. (*Shaking her head.*) Lord, Lord, Lord . . .

RUTH. Well—that's the way the crackers crumble. Joke.

BENEATHA. (*Laughingly noticing what her mother is doing.*) Mama, what are you doing?

MAMA. Fixing my plant so it won't get hurt none on the way . . .

BENEATHA. Mama, you going to take *that* to the new house?

MAMA. Un-huh—

BENEATHA. That raggedy-looking old thing?

MAMA. (*Stopping and looking at her.*) It expresses *me.*

RUTH. (*With delight, to* BENEATHA.) So there, Miss Thing!

(WALTER *comes to* MAMA *suddenly and bends down behind her and squeezes her in his arms with all his strength. She is overwhelmed by the suddenness of it and, though delighted, her manner is like that of* RUTH *with* TRAVIS.)

MAMA. Look out now, boy! You make me mess up my thing here!

WALTER. (*His face lit, he slips down on his knees beside her, his arms still about her.*) Mama . . . you know what it means to climb up in the chariot?

MAMA. (*Gruffly, very happy.*) Get on away from me now . . .

RUTH. (*Near the gift-wrapped package, trying to catch* WALTER'S *eye.*) Psst—

WALTER. What the old song say, Mama . . .

RUTH. Walter—Now?

(*She is pointing at the package.*)

WALTER. (*Speaking the lines, sweetly, playfully, in his mother's face.*)

I got wings . . . you got wings . . .
All God's Children got wings . . .

MAMA. Boy—get out of my face and do some work . . .

WALTER.

When I get to heaven gonna put on my wings,
Gonna fly all over God's heaven . . .

BENEATHA. (*Teasingly, from across the room.*) Everybody talking 'bout heaven ain't going there!

WALTER. (*To* RUTH, *who is carrying the box across to them.*) I don't know, you think we ought to give her that . . . Seems to me she ain't been very appreciative around here.

MAMA. (*Eying the box, which is obviously a gift.*) What is that?

WALTER. (*Taking it from* RUTH *and putting it on the table in front of* MAMA.) Well—what you all think? Should we give it to her?

RUTH. Oh—she was pretty good today.

MAMA. I'll good you—

(*She turns her eyes to the box again.*)

BENEATHA. Open it, Mama.

(*She stands up, looks at it, turns and looks at all of them, and then presses her hands together and does not open the package.*)

WALTER. (*Sweetly.*) Open it, Mama. It's for you. (MAMA *looks in his eyes. It is the first present in her life without its being Christmas. Slowly she opens her package and lifts out, one by one, a brand-new sparkling set of gardening tools.* WALTER *continues, prodding.*) Ruth made up the note—read it . . .

MAMA. (*Picking up the card and adjusting her glasses.*) "To our own Mrs. Miniver—Love from Brother, Ruth and Beneatha." Ain't that lovely . . .

TRAVIS. (*Tugging at his father's sleeve.*) Daddy, can I give her mine now?

WALTER. All right, son. (TRAVIS *flies to get his gift.*) Travis didn't want to go in with the rest of us, Mama. He got his own. (*Somewhat amused.*) We don't know what it is . . .

TRAVIS. (*Racing back in the room with a large hatbox and putting it in front of his grandmother.*) Here!

MAMA. Lord have mercy, baby. You done gone and bought your grandmother a hat?

TRAVIS. (*Very proud.*) Open it!

(*She does and lifts out an elaborate, but very elaborate, wide gardening hat, and all the adults break up at the sight of it.*)

RUTH. Travis, honey, what is that?

TRAVIS. (*Who thinks it is beautiful and appropriate.*) It's a gardening hat! Like the ladies always have on in the magazines when they work in their gardens.

BENEATHA. (*Giggling fiercely.*) Travis—we were trying to make Mama Mrs. Miniver—not Scarlett O'Hara!

MAMA. (*Indignantly.*) What's the matter with you all! This here is a beautiful hat! (*Absurdly.*) I always wanted me one just like it!

(*She pops it on her head to prove it to her grandson, and the hat is ludicrous and considerably oversized.*)

RUTH. Hot dog! Go, Mama!

WALTER. (*Doubled over with laughter.*) I'm sorry, Mama—but you look like you ready to go out and chop you some cotton sure enough!

(*They all laugh except* MAMA, *out of deference to* TRAVIS's *feelings.*)

MAMA. (*Gathering the boy up to her.*) Bless your heart—this is the prettiest hat I ever owned— (WALTER, RUTH *and* BENEATHA *chime in—noisily, festively and insincerely congratulating* TRAVIS *on his gift.*) What are we all standing around here for? We ain't finished packin' yet. Bennie, you ain't packed one book.

(*The bell rings.*)

BENEATHA. That couldn't be the movers . . . it's not hardly two good yet—

(BENEATHA *goes into her room.* MAMA *starts for door.*)

WALTER. (*Turning, stiffening.*) Wait—wait—I'll get it.

(*He stands and looks at the door.*)

MAMA. You expecting company, son?

WALTER. (*Just looking at the door.*) Yeah—yeah . . .

(MAMA *looks at* RUTH, *and they exchange innocent and unfrightened glances.*)

MAMA. (*Not understanding.*) Well, let them in, son.

BENEATHA. (*From her room.*) We need some more string.

MAMA. Travis—you run to the hardware and get me some string cord.

(MAMA *goes out and* WALTER *turns and looks at* RUTH. TRAVIS *goes to a dish for money.*)

RUTH. Why don't you answer the door, man?

WALTER. (*Suddenly bounding across the floor*

to her.) 'Cause sometimes it hard to let the future begin! (*Stooping down in her face.*)
   I got wings! You got wings!
   All God's children got wings!
(*He crosses to the door and throws it open. Standing there is a very slight little man in a not too prosperous business suit and with haunted frightened eyes and a hat pulled down tightly, brim up, around his forehead.* TRAVIS *passes between the men and exits.* WALTER *leans deep in the man's face, still in his jubilance.*)
   When I get to heaven gonna put on my
      wings,
   Gonna fly all over God's heaven . . .
(*The little man just stares at him.*)
   Heaven—
(*Suddenly he stops and looks past the little man into the empty hallway.*) Where's Willy, man?
   BOBO. He ain't with me.
   WALTER. (*Not disturbed.*) Oh—come on in. You know my wife.
   BOBO. (*Dumbly, taking off his hat.*) Yes—h'you, Miss Ruth.
   RUTH. (*Quietly, a mood apart from her husband already, seeing* BOBO.) Hello, Bobo.
   WALTER. You right on time today . . . Right on time. That's the way! (*He slaps* BOBO *on his back.*) Sit down . . . lemme hear.
      (RUTH *stands stiffly and quietly in back of them, as though somehow she senses death, her eyes fixed on her husband.*)
   BOBO. (*His frightened eyes on the floor, his hat in his hands.*) Could I please get a drink of water, before I tell you about it, Walter Lee?
      (WALTER *does not take his eyes off the man.* RUTH *goes blindly to the tap and gets a glass of water and brings it to* BOBO.)
   WALTER. There ain't nothing wrong, is there?
   BOBO. Lemme tell you—
   WALTER. Man—didn't nothing go wrong?
   BOBO. Lemme tell you—Walter Lee. (*Looking at* RUTH *and talking to her more than to* WALTER.) You know how it was. I got to tell you how it was. I mean first I got to tell you how it was all the way . . . I mean about the money I put in, Walter Lee . . .
   WALTER. (*With taut agitation now.*) What about the money you put in?
   BOBO. Well—it wasn't much as we told you—me and Willy— (*He stops.*) I'm sorry, Walter. I got a bad feeling about it. I got a real bad feeling about it . . .
   WALTER. Man, what you telling me about all this for? . . . Tell me what happened in Springfield . . .
   BOBO. Springfield.
   RUTH. (*Like a dead woman.*) What was supposed to happen in Springfield?
   BOBO. (*To her.*) This deal that me and Walter went into with Willy— Me and Willy was going to go down to Springfield and spread some money 'round so's we wouldn't have to wait so long for the liquor license . . . That's what we were going to do. Everybody said that was the way you had to do, you understand, Miss Ruth?
   WALTER. Man—what happened down there?
   BOBO. (*A pitiful man, near tears.*) I'm trying to tell you, Walter.
   WALTER. (*Screaming at him suddenly.*) THEN TELL ME, GODDAMMIT . . . WHAT'S THE MATTER WITH YOU?
   BOBO. Man . . . I didn't go to no Springfield, yesterday.
   WALTER. (*Halted, life hanging in the moment.*) Why not?
   BOBO. (*The long way, the hard way to tell.*) 'Cause I didn't have no reasons to . . .
   WALTER. Man, what are you talking about!
   BOBO. I'm talking about the fact that when I got to the train station yesterday morning—eight o'clock like we planned . . . Man—*Willy didn't never show up.*
   WALTER. Why . . . where was he . . . where is he?
   BOBO. That's what I'm trying to tell you . . . I don't know . . . I waited six hours . . . I called his house . . . and I waited . . . six hours . . . I waited in that train station six hours . . . (*Breaking*

into tears.) That was all the extra money I had in the world... (*Looking up at* WALTER *with the tears running down his face.*) Man, Willy is gone.

WALTER. Gone, what you mean Willy is gone? Gone where? You mean he went by himself. You mean he went off to Springfield by himself—to take care of getting the license— (*Turns and looks anxiously at* RUTH.) You mean maybe he didn't want too many people in on the business down there? (*Looks to* RUTH *again, as before.*) You know Willy got his own ways. (*Looks back to* BOBO.) Maybe you was late yesterday and he just went on down there without you. Maybe—maybe—he's been callin' you at home tryin' to tell you what happened or something. Maybe—maybe—he just got sick. He's somewhere—he's got to be somewhere. We just got to find him—me and you got to find him. (*Grabs* BOBO *senselessly by the collar and starts to shake him.*) We got to!

BOBO. (*In sudden angry, frightened agony.*) What's the matter with you, Walter! When a cat take off with your money he don't leave you no maps!

WALTER. (*Turning madly, as though he is looking for* WILLY *in the very room.*) Willy!... Willy... don't do it... Please don't do it... Man, not with that money... Man, please, not with that money... Oh, God... Don't let it be true... (*He is wandering around, crying out for* WILLY *and looking for him or perhaps for help from God.*) Man... I trusted you... Man, I put my life in your hands... (*He starts to crumple down on the floor as* RUTH *just covers her face in horror.* MAMA *opens the door and comes into the room, with* BENEATHA *behind her.*) Man... (*He starts to pound the floor with his fists, sobbing wildly.*) That money is made out of my father's flesh...

BOBO. (*Standing over him helplessly.*) I'm sorry, Walter... (*Only* WALTER's *sobs reply.* BOBO *puts on his hat.*) I had my life staked on this deal, too...

(*He exits.*)

MAMA. (*To* WALTER.) Son— (*She goes to him, bends down to him, talks to his bent head.*) Son... Is it gone? Son, I gave you sixty-five hundred dollars. Is it gone? All of it? Beneatha's money too?

WALTER. (*Lifting his head slowly.*) Mama... I never... went to the bank at all...

MAMA. (*Not wanting to believe him.*) You mean... your sister's school money... you used that too... Walter?...

WALTER. Yessss!... All of it... It's all gone...

(*There is total silence.* RUTH *stands with her face covered with her hands;* BENEATHA *leans forlornly against a wall, fingering a piece of red ribbon from the mother's gift.* MAMA *stops and looks at her son without recognition and then, quite without thinking about it, starts to beat him senselessly in the face.* BENEATHA *goes to them and stops it.*)

BENEATHA. Mama!

(MAMA *stops and looks at both of her children and rises slowly and wanders vaguely, aimlessly away from them.*)

MAMA. I seen... him... night after night... come in... and look at that rug... and then look at me... the red showing in his eyes... the veins moving in his head... I seen him grow thin and old before he was forty... working and working and working like somebody's old horse... killing himself... and you—you give it all away in a day...

BENEATHA. Mama—

MAMA. Oh, God... (*She looks up to Him.*) Look down here—and show me the strength.

BENEATHA. Mama—

MAMA. (*Folding over.*) Strength...

BENEATHA. (*Plaintively.*) Mama...

MAMA. Strength!

CURTAIN

ACT THREE

An hour later.

At curtain, there is a sullen light of gloom in the living room, gray light not unlike that which began the first scene of Act One. At left we can see WALTER *within his room, alone with himself. He is stretched out on the bed, his shirt out and open, his arms under his head. He does not smoke, he does not cry out, he merely lies there, looking up at the ceiling, much as if he were alone in the world.*

In the living room BENEATHA *sits at the table, still surrounded by the now almost ominous packing crates. She sits looking off. We feel that this is a mood struck perhaps an hour before, and it lingers now, full of the empty sound of profound disappointment. We see on a line from her brother's bedroom the sameness of their attitudes. Presently the bell rings and* BENEATHA *rises without ambition or interest in answering. It is* ASAGAI, *smiling broadly, striding into the room with energy and happy expectation and conversation.*

ASAGAI. I came over . . . I had some free time. I thought I might help with the packing. Ah, I like the look of packing crates! A household in preparation for a journey! It depresses some people . . . but for me . . . it is another feeling. Something full of the flow of life, do you understand? Movement, progress . . . It makes me think of Africa.

BENEATHA. Africa!

ASAGAI. What kind of a mood is this? Have I told you how deeply you move me?

BENEATHA. He gave away the money, Asagai . . .

ASAGAI. Who gave away what money?

BENEATHA. The insurance money. My brother gave it away.

ASAGAI. Gave it away?

BENEATHA. He made an investment! With a man even Travis wouldn't have trusted.

ASAGAI. And it's gone?

BENEATHA. Gone!

ASAGAI. I'm very sorry . . . And you, now?

BENEATHA. Me? . . . Me? . . . Me I'm nothing . . . Me. When I was very small . . . we used to take our sleds out in the wintertime and the only hills we had were the ice-covered stone steps of some houses down the street. And we used to fill them in with snow and make them smooth and slide down them all day . . . and it was very dangerous you know . . . far too steep . . . and sure enough one day a kid named Rufus came down too fast and hit the sidewalk . . . and we saw his face just split open right there in front of us . . . And I remember standing there looking at his bloody open face thinking that was the end of Rufus. But the ambulance came and they took him to the hospital and they fixed the broken bones and they sewed it all up . . . and the next time I saw Rufus he just had a little line down the middle of his face . . . I never got over that . . .

(WALTER *sits up, listening on the bed. Throughout this scene it is important that we feel his reaction at all times, that he visibly respond to the words of his sister and* ASAGAI.)

ASAGAI. What?

BENEATHA. That that was what one person could do for another, fix him up—sew up the problem, make him all right again. That was the most marvelous thing in the world . . . I wanted to do that. I always thought it was the one concrete thing in the world that a human being could do. Fix up the sick, you know—and make them whole again. This was truly being God . . .

ASAGAI. You wanted to be God?

BENEATHA. No—I wanted to cure. It used to be so important to me. I wanted to cure. It used to matter. I used to care.

I mean about people and how their bodies hurt . . .

ASAGAI. And you've stopped caring?

BENEATHA. Yes—I think so.

ASAGAI. Why?

(WALTER *rises, goes to the door of his room and is about to open it, then stops and stands listening, leaning on the door jamb.*)

BENEATHA. Because it doesn't seem deep enough, close enough to what ails mankind—I mean this thing of sewing up bodies or administering drugs. Don't you understand? It was a child's reaction to the world. I thought that doctors had the secret to all the hurts . . . That's the way a child sees things—or an idealist.

ASAGAI. Children see things very well sometimes—and idealists even better.

BENEATHA. I know that's what you think. Because you are still where I left off—you still care. This is what you see for the world, for Africa. You with the dreams of the future will patch up all Africa—you are going to cure the Great Sore of colonialism with Independence——

ASAGAI. Yes!

BENEATHA. Yes—and you think that one word is the penicillin of the human spirit: "Independence!" But then what?

ASAGAI. That will be the problem for another time. First we must get there.

BENEATHA. And where does it end?

ASAGAI. End? Who even spoke of an end? To life? To living?

BENEATHA. An end to misery!

ASAGAI. (*Smiling.*) You sound like a French intellectual.

BENEATHA. No! I sound like a human being who just had her future taken right out of her hands! While I was sleeping in my bed in there, things were happening in this world that directly concerned me—and nobody asked me, consulted me—they just went out and did things—and changed my life. Don't you see there isn't any real progress, Asagai, there is only one large circle that we march in, around and around, each of us with our own little picture—in front of us—our own little mirage that we think is the future.

ASAGAI. That is the mistake.

BENEATHA. What?

ASAGAI. What you just said—about the circle. It isn't a circle—it is simply a long line—as in geometry, you know, one that reaches into infinity. And because we cannot see the end—we also cannot see how it changes. And it is very odd but those who see the changes are called "idealists"—and those who cannot, or refuse to think, they are the "realists." It is very strange, and amusing too, I think.

BENEATHA. You—you are almost religious.

ASAGAI. Yes . . . I think I have the religion of doing what is necessary in the world—and of worshipping man—because he is so marvelous, you see.

BENEATHA. Man is foul! And the human race deserves its misery!

ASAGAI. You see: *you* have become the religious one in the old sense. Already, and after such a small defeat, you are worshipping despair.

BENEATHA. From now on, I worship the truth—and the truth is that people are puny, small and selfish. . . .

ASAGAI. Truth? Why is it that you despairing ones always think that only you have the truth? I never thought to see *you* like that. You! Your brother made a stupid, childish mistake—and you are grateful to him. So that now you can give up the ailing human race on account of it. You talk about what good is struggle; what good is anything? Where are we all going? And why are we bothering?

BENEATHA. *And you cannot answer it!* All your talk and dreams about Africa and Independence. Independence and then what? What about all the crooks and petty thieves and just plain idiots who will come into power to steal and plunder the same as before—only now they will be black and do it in the name of the new Independence— You cannot answer that.

ASAGAI. (*Shouting over her.*) *I live the answer!* (*Pause.*) In my village at home it is the exceptional man who can even read a newspaper . . . or who ever *sees* a book at all. I will go home and much of what I will have to say will seem strange to the people of my village . . . But I will teach and work and things will happen, slowly and swiftly. At times it will seem that nothing changes at all . . . and then again . . . the sudden dramatic events which make history leap into the future. And then quiet again. Retrogression even. Guns, murder, revolution. And I even will have moments when I wonder if the quiet was not better than all that death and hatred. But I will look about my village at the illiteracy and disease and ignorance and I will not wonder long. And perhaps . . . perhaps I will be a great man . . . I mean perhaps I will hold on to the substance of truth and find my way always with the right course . . . and perhaps for it I will be butchered in my bed some night by the servants of empire . . .

BENEATHA. *The martyr!*

ASAGAI. . . . or perhaps I shall live to be a very old man, respected and esteemed in my new nation . . . And perhaps I shall hold office and this is what I'm trying to tell you, Alaiyo; perhaps the things I believe now for my country will be wrong and outmoded, and I will not understand and do terrible things to have things my way or merely to keep my power. Don't you see that there will be young men and women, not British soldiers then, but my own black countrymen . . . to step out of the shadows some evening and slit my then useless throat? Don't you see they have always been there . . . that they always will be. And that such a thing as my own death will be an advance? They who might kill me even . . . actually replenish me!

BENEATHA. Oh, Asagai, I know all that.

ASAGAI. Good! Then stop moaning and groaning and tell me what you plan to do.

BENEATHA. Do?

ASAGAI. I have a bit of a suggestion.

BENEATHA. What?

ASAGAI. (*Rather quietly for him.*) That when it is all over—that you come home with me—

BENEATHA. (*Slapping herself on the forehead with exasperation born of misunderstanding.*) Oh—Asagai—at this moment you decide to be romantic!

ASAGAI. (*Quickly understanding the misunderstanding.*) My dear, young creature of the New World—I do not mean across the city—I mean across the ocean; home—to Africa.

BENEATHA. (*Slowly understanding and turning to him with murmured amazement.*) To—to Nigeria?

ASAGAI. Yes! . . . (*Smiling and lifting his arms playfully.*) Three hundred years later the African Prince rose up out of the seas and swept the maiden back across the middle passage over which her ancestors had come—

BENEATHA. (*Unable to play.*) Nigeria?

ASAGAI. Nigeria. Home. (*Coming to her with genuine romantic flippancy.*) I will show you our mountains and our stars; and give you cool drinks from gourds and teach you the old songs and the ways of our people—and, in time, we will pretend that—(*Very softly.*)—you have only been away for a day—

(*She turns her back to him, thinking. He swings her around and takes her full in his arms in a long embrace which proceeds to passion.*)

BENEATHA. (*Pulling away.*) You're getting me all mixed up—

ASAGAI. Why?

BENEATHA. Too many things—too many things have happened today. I must sit down and think. I don't know what I feel about anything right this minute.

(*She promptly sits down and props her chin on her fist.*)

ASAGAI. (*Charmed.*) All right, I shall leave you. No—don't get up. (*Touching her, gently, sweetly.*) Just sit awhile and think . . . Never be afraid to sit awhile and think. (*He goes to door and looks at her.*) How often I have looked at you and said, "Ah—so this is what the New World hath finally wrought . . ."

(*He exits.* BENEATHA *sits on alone. Presently* WALTER *enters from his room and starts to rummage through things, feverishly looking for something. She looks up and turns in her seat.*)

BENEATHA. (*Hissingly.*) Yes—just look at what the New World hath wrought! . . . Just look! (*She gestures with bitter disgust.*) There he is! *Monsieur le petit bourgeois noir*—himself! There he is—Symbol of a Rising Class! Entrepreneur! Titan of the system! (WALTER *ignores her completely and continues frantically and destructively looking for something and hurling things to floor and tearing things out of their place in his search.* BENEATHA *ignores the eccentricity of his actions and goes on with the monologue of insult.*) Did you dream of yachts on Lake Michigan, Brother? Did you see yourself on that Great Day sitting down at the Conference Table, surrounded by all the mighty bald-headed men in America? All halted, waiting, breathless, waiting for your pronouncements on industry? Waiting for you—Chairman of the Board? (WALTER *finds what he is looking for—a small piece of white paper—and pushes it in his pocket and puts on his coat and rushes out without ever having looked at her. She shouts after him.*) I look at you and I see the final triumph of stupidity in the world!

(*The door slams and she returns to just sitting again.* RUTH *comes quickly out of* MAMA'*s room.*)

RUTH. Who was that?

BENEATHA. Your husband.

RUTH. Where did he go?

BENEATHA. Who knows—maybe he has an appointment at U.S. Steel.

RUTH. (*Anxiously, with frightened eyes.*) You didn't say nothing bad to him, did you?

BENEATHA. Bad? Say anything bad to him? No—I told him he was a sweet boy and full of dreams and everything is strictly peachy keen, as the ofay kids say!

(MAMA *enters from her bedroom. She is lost, vague, trying to catch hold, to make some sense of her former command of the world, but it still eludes her. A sense of waste overwhelms her gait; a measure of apology rides on her shoulders. She goes to her plant, which has remained on the table, looks at it, picks it up and takes it to the window sill and sits it outside, and she stands and looks at it a long moment. Then she closes the window, straightens her body with effort and turns around to her children.*)

MAMA. Well—ain't it a mess in here, though? (*A false cheerfulness, a beginning of something.*) I guess we all better stop moping around and get some work done. All this unpacking and everything we got to do. (RUTH *raises her head slowly in response to the sense of the line; and* BENEATHA *in similar manner turns very slowly to look at her mother.*) One of you all better call the moving people and tell 'em not to come.

RUTH. Tell 'em not to come?

MAMA. Of course, baby. Ain't no need in 'em coming all the way here and having to go back. They charges for that too. (*She sits down, fingers to her brow, thinking.*) Lord, ever since I was a little girl, I always remembers people saying, "Lena—Lena Eggleston, you aims too high all the time. You needs to slow down and see life a little more like it is. Just slow down some." That's what they always used to say down home—"Lord, that Lena Eggleston is a high-minded thing. She'll get her due one day!"

RUTH. No, Lena . . .

MAMA. Me and Big Walter just didn't never learn right.

RUTH. Lena, no! We gotta go. Bennie—tell her . . . (*She rises and crosses to* BENEATHA *with her arms outstretched.* BENEATHA *doesn't respond.*) Tell her we can still move . . . the notes ain't but a hundred and twenty-five a month. We got four grown people in this house—we can work . . .

MAMA. (*To herself.*) Just aimed too high all the time—

RUTH. (*Turning and going to* MAMA *fast—the words pouring out with urgency and desperation.*) Lena—I'll work . . . I'll work twenty hours a day in all the kitchens in Chicago . . . I'll strap my baby on my back if I have to and scrub all the floors in America and wash all the sheets in America if I have to—but we got to move . . . We got to get out of here . . .

(MAMA *reaches out absently and pats* RUTH's *hand.*)

MAMA. No—I sees things differently now. Been thinking 'bout some of the things we could do to fix this place up some. I seen a second-hand bureau over on Maxwell Street just the other day that could fit right there. (*She points to where the new furniture might go.* RUTH *wanders away from her.*) Would need some new handles on it and then a little varnish and then it look like something brand-new. And—we can put up them new curtains in the kitchen . . . Why this place be looking fine. Cheer us all up so that we forget trouble ever came . . . (*To* RUTH.) And you could get some nice screens to put up in your room round the baby's bassinet . . . (*She looks at both of them, pleadingly.*) Sometimes you just got to know when to give up some things . . . and hold on to what you got.

(WALTER *enters from the outside, looking spent and leaning against the door, his coat hanging from him.*)

MAMA. Where you been, son?
WALTER. (*Breathing hard.*) Made a call.
MAMA. To who, son?
WALTER. To The Man.
MAMA. What man, baby?
WALTER. The Man, Mama. Don't you know who The Man is?
RUTH. Walter Lee?
WALTER. *The Man.* Like the guys in the streets say—The Man. Captain Boss—Mistuh Charley . . . Old Captain Please Mr. Bossman . . .
BENEATHA. (*Suddenly.*) Lindner!
WALTER. That's right! That's good. I told him to come right over.
BENEATHA. (*Fiercely, understanding.*) For what? What do you want to see him for!
WALTER. (*Looking at his sister.*) We going to do business with him.

MAMA. What you talking 'bout, son?
WALTER. Talking 'bout life, Mama. You all always telling me to see life like it is. Well—I laid in there on my back today . . . and I figured it out. Life just like it is. Who gets and who don't get. (*He sits down with his coat on and laughs.*) Mama, you know it's all divided up. Life is. Sure enough. Between the takers and the "tooken." (*He laughs.*) I've figured it out finally. (*He looks around at them.*) Yeah. Some of us always getting "tooken." (*He laughs.*) People like Willy Harris, they don't never get "tooken." And you know why the rest of us do? 'Cause we all mixed up. Mixed up bad. We get to looking 'round for the right and the wrong; and we worry about it and cry about it and stay up nights trying to figure out 'bout the wrong and the right of things all the time . . . And all the time, man, them takers is out there operating, just taking and taking. Willy Harris? Shoot—Willy Harris don't even count. He don't even count in the big scheme of things. But I'll say one thing for old Willy Harris . . . he's taught me something. He's taught me to keep my eye on what counts in this world. Yeah— (*Shouting a little.*) Thanks, Willy!
RUTH. What did you call that man for, Walter Lee?
WALTER. Called him to tell him to come on over to the show. Gonna put on a show for the man. Just what he wants to see. You see, Mama, the man came here today and he told us that them people out there where you want us to move—well they so upset they willing to pay us not to move out there. (*He laughs again.*) And—and oh, Mama—you would of been proud of the way me and Ruth and Bennie acted. We told him to get out . . . Lord have mercy! We told the man to get out. Oh, we was some proud folks this afternoon, yeah. (*He lights a cigarette.*) We were still full of that old-time stuff . . .
RUTH. (*Coming toward him slowly.*) You talking 'bout taking them people's money to keep us from moving in that house?
WALTER. I ain't just talking 'bout it,

baby—I'm telling you that's what's going to happen.

BENEATHA. Oh, God! Where is the bottom! Where is the real honest-to-God bottom so he can't go any farther!

WALTER. See—that's the old stuff. You and that boy that was here today. You all want everybody to carry a flag and a spear and sing some marching songs, huh? You wanna spend your life looking into things and trying to find the right and the wrong part, huh? Yeah. You know what's going to happen to that boy someday—he'll find himself sitting in a dungeon, locked in forever—and the takers will have the key! Forget it, baby! There ain't no causes—there ain't nothing but taking in this world, and he who takes most is smartest—and it don't make a damn bit of difference *how*.

MAMA. You making something inside me cry, son. Some awful pain inside me.

WALTER. Don't cry, Mama. Understand. That white man is going to walk in that door able to write checks for more money than we ever had. It's important to him and I'm going to help him . . . I'm going to put on the show, Mama.

MAMA. Son—I come from five generations of people who was slaves and sharecroppers—but ain't nobody in my family never let nobody pay 'em no money that was a way of telling us we wasn't fit to walk the earth. We ain't never been that poor. *(Raising her eyes and looking at him.)* We ain't never been that dead inside.

BENEATHA. Well—we are dead now. All the talk about dreams and sunlight that goes on in this house. All dead.

WALTER. What's the matter with you all! I didn't make this world! It was give to me this way! Hell, yes, I want me some yachts someday! Yes, I want to hang some real pearls 'round my wife's neck. Ain't she supposed to wear no pearls? Somebody tell me—tell me, who decides which women is suppose to wear pearls in this world. I tell you I am a *man*—and I think my wife should wear some pearls in this world!

(This last line hangs a good while and WALTER *begins to move about the room. The word "Man" has penetrated his consciousness; he mumbles it to himself repeatedly between strange agitated pauses as he moves about.)*

MAMA. Baby, how you going to feel on the inside?

WALTER. Fine! . . . Going to feel fine . . . a man . . .

MAMA. You won't have nothing left then, Walter Lee.

WALTER. *(Coming to her.)* I'm going to feel fine, Mama. I'm going to look that son-of-a-bitch in the eyes and say—*(He falters.)*—and say, "All right, Mr. Lindner.—*(He falters even more.)*—that's your neighborhood out there. You got the right to keep it like you want. You got the right to have it like you want. Just write the check and—the house is yours." And, and I am going to say— *(His voice almost breaks.)* And you—you people just put the money in my hand and you won't have to live next to this bunch of stinking niggers! . . . *(He straightens up and moves away from his mother, walking around the room.)* Maybe—maybe I'll just get down on my black knees . . . *(He does so;* RUTH *and* BENNIE *and* MAMA *watch him in frozen horror.)* Captain, Mistuh, Bossman. *(He starts crying.)* A-hee-hee-hee! *(Wringing his hands in profoundly anguished imitation.)* Yasssssuh! Great White Father, just gi' ussen de money, fo' God's sake, and we's ain't gwine come out deh and dirty up yo' white folks neighborhood . . .

(He breaks down completely, then gets up and goes into the bedroom.)

BENEATHA. That is not a man. That is nothing but a toothless rat.

MAMA. Yes—death done come in this here house. *(She is nodding, slowly, reflectively.)* Done come walking in my house. On the lips of my children. You what supposed to be my beginning again. You—what supposed to be my harvest. *(To* BENEATHA.*)* You—you mourning your brother?

BENEATHA. He's no brother of mine.

MAMA. What you say?

BENEATHA. I said that that individual in that room is no brother of mine.

MAMA. That's what I thought you said. You feeling like you better than he is today? (BENEATHA *does not answer.*) Yes? What you tell him a minute ago? That he wasn't a man? Yes? You give him up for me? You done wrote his epitaph too—like the rest of the world? Well, who give you the privilege?

BENEATHA. Be on my side for once! You saw what he just did, Mama! You saw him—down on his knees. Wasn't it you who taught me—to despise any man who would do that. Do what he's going to do.

MAMA. Yes—I taught you that. Me and your daddy. But I thought I taught you something else too . . . I thought I taught you to love him.

BENEATHA. Love him? There is nothing left to love.

MAMA. There is always something left to love. And if you ain't learned that, you ain't learned nothing. (*Looking at her.*) Have you cried for that boy today? I don't mean for yourself and for the family 'cause we lost the money. I mean for him; what he been through and what it done to him. Child, when do you think is the time to love somebody the most; when they done good and made things easy for everybody? Well then, you ain't through learning—because that ain't the time at all. It's when he's at his lowest and can't believe in hisself 'cause the world done whipped him so. When you starts measuring somebody, measure him right, child, measure him right. Make sure you done taken into account what hills and valleys he come through before he got to wherever he is.

(TRAVIS *burst into the room at the end of the speech, leaving the door open.*)

TRAVIS. Grandmama—the moving men are downstairs! The truck just pulled up.

MAMA. (*Turning and looking at him.*) Are they, baby? They downstairs?

(*She sighs and sits.* LINDNER *appears in the doorway. He peers in and knocks lightly, to gain attention, and comes in. All turn to look at him.*)

LINDNER. (*Hat and briefcase in hand.*) Uh—hello . . .

(RUTH *crosses mechanically to the bedroom door and opens it and lets it swing open freely and slowly as the lights come up on* WALTER *within, still in his coat, sitting at the far corner of the room. He looks up and out through the room to* LINDNER.)

RUTH. He's here.

(*A long minute passes and* WALTER *slowly gets up.*)

LINDNER. (*Coming to the table with efficiency, putting his briefcase on the table and starting to unfold papers and unscrew fountain pens.*) Well, I certainly was glad to hear from you people. (WALTER *has begun the trek out of the room, slowly and awkwardly, rather like a small boy, passing the back of his sleeve across his mouth from time to time.*) Life can really be so much simpler than people let it be most of the time. Well—with whom do I negotiate? You, Mrs. Younger, or your son here? (MAMA *sits with her hands folded on her lap and her eyes closed as* WALTER *advances.* TRAVIS *goes close to* LINDNER *and looks at the papers curiously.*) Just some official papers, sonny.

RUTH. Travis, you go downstairs.

MAMA. (*Opening her eyes and looking into* WALTER'S.) No. Travis, you stay right here. And you make him understand what you doing, Walter Lee. You teach him good. Like Willy Harris taught you. You show where our five generations done come to. Go ahead, son—

WALTER. (*Looks down into his boy's eyes.* TRAVIS *grins at him merrily and* WALTER *draws him beside him with his arm lightly around his shoulders.*) Well, Mr. Lindner. (BENEATHA *turns away.*) We called you— (*There is a profound, simple groping quality in his speech.*)—because, well, me and my family (*He looks around and shifts from one foot to the other.*) Well—we are very plain people . . .

LINDNER. Yes—

WALTER. I mean—I have worked as a

chauffeur most of my life—and my wife here, she does domestic work in people's kitchens. So does my mother. I mean—we are plain people . . .

LINDNER. Yes, Mr. Younger—

WALTER. (*Really like a small boy, looking down at his shoes and then up at the man.*) And —uh—well, my father, well, he was a laborer most of his life.

LINDNER. (*Absolutely confused.*) Uh, yes—

WALTER. (*Looking down at his toes once again.*) My father almost beat a man to death once because this man called him a bad name or something, you know what I mean?

LINDNER. No, I'm afraid I don't.

WALTER. (*Finally straightening up.*) Well, what I mean is that we come from people who had a lot of pride. I mean—we are very proud people. And that's my sister over there and she's going to be a doctor— and we are very proud—

LINDNER. Well—I am sure that is very nice, but—

WALTER. (*Starting to cry and facing the man eye to eye.*) What I am telling you is that we called you over here to tell you that we are very proud and that this is—this is my son, who makes the sixth generation of our family in this country, and that we have all thought about your offer and we have decided to move into our house because my father—my father—he earned it. (MAMA *has her eyes closed and is rocking back and forth as though she were in church, with her head nodding the amen yes.*) We don't want to make no trouble for nobody or fight no causes—but we will try to be good neighbors. That's all we got to say. (*He looks the man absolutely in the eyes.*) We don't want your money.

(*He turns and walks away from the man.*)

LINDNER. (*Looking around at all of them.*) I take it then that you have decided to occupy.

BENEATHA. That's what the man said.

LINDNER. (*To* MAMA *in her reverie.*) Then I would like to appeal to you, Mrs. Younger. You are older and wiser and understand things better I am sure . . .

MAMA. (*Rising.*) I am afraid you don't understand. My son said we was going to move and there ain't nothing left for me to say. (*Shaking her head with double meaning.*) You know how these young folks is nowadays, mister. Can't do a thing with 'em. Good-bye.

LINDNER. (*Folding up his materials.*) Well —if you are that final about it . . . There is nothing left for me to say. (*He finishes. He is almost ignored by the family, who are concentrating on* WALTER LEE. *At the door* LINDNER *halts and looks around.*) I sure hope you people know what you're doing.

(*He shakes his head and exits.*)

RUTH. (*Looking around and coming to life.*) Well, for God's sake—if the moving men are here—LET'S GET THE HELL OUT OF HERE!

MAMA. (*Into action.*) Ain't it the truth! Look at all this here mess. Ruth, put Travis' good jacket on him . . . Walter Lee, fix your tie and tuck your shirt in, you look just like somebody's hoodlum. Lord have mercy, where is my plant? (*She flies to get it amid the general bustling of the family, who are deliberately trying to ignore the nobility of the past moment.*) You all start on down . . . Travis child, don't go empty-handed . . . Ruth, where did I put that box with my skillets in it? I want to be in charge of it myself . . . I'm going to make us the biggest dinner we ever ate tonight . . . Beneatha, what's the matter with them stockings? Pull them things up, girl . . .

(*The family starts to file out as two moving men appear and begin to carry out the heavier pieces of furniture, bumping into the family as they move about.*)

BENEATHA. Mama, Asagai—asked me to marry him today and go to Africa—

MAMA. (*In the middle of her getting-ready activity.*) He did? You ain't old enough to marry nobody— (*Seeing the moving men lifting one of her chairs precariously.*) Darling, that ain't no bale of cotton, please handle it so we can sit in it again. I had that chair twenty-five years . . .

(*The movers sigh with exasperation and go on with their work.*)

BENEATHA. (*Girlishly and unreasonably trying to pursue the conversation.*) To go to Africa, Mama—be a doctor in Africa . . .

MAMA. (*Distracted.*) Yes, baby—

WALTER. Africa! What he want you to go to Africa for?

BENEATHA. To practice there . . .

WALTER. Girl, if you don't get all them silly ideas out your head! You better marry yourself a man with some loot. . .

BENEATHA. (*Angrily, precisely as in the first scene of the play.*) What have you got to do with who I marry!

WALTER. Plenty. Now I think George Murchison—

(*He and* BENEATHA *go out yelling at each other vigorously;* BENEATHA *is heard saying that she would not marry* GEORGE MURCHISON *if he were Adam and she were Eve, etc. The anger is loud and real till their voices diminish.* RUTH *stands at the door and turns to* MAMA *and smiles knowingly.*)

MAMA. (*Fixing her hat at last.*) Yeah—they something all right, my children . . .

RUTH. Yeah—they're something. Let's go, Lena.

MAMA. (*Stalling, starting to look around at the house.*) Yes—I'm coming. Ruth—

RUTH. Yes?

MAMA. (*Quietly, woman to woman.*) He finally come into his manhood today, didn't he? Kind of like a rainbow after the rain . . .

RUTH. (*Biting her lip lest her own pride explode in front of* MAMA.) Yes, Lena.

(WALTER's *voice calls for them raucously.*)

MAMA. (*Waving* RUTH *out vaguely.*) All right, honey—go on down. I be down directly.

(RUTH *hesitates, then exits.* MAMA *stands, at last alone in the living room, her plant on the table before her as the lights start to come down. She looks around at all the walls and ceilings and suddenly, despite herself, while the children call below, a great heaving thing rises in her and she puts her fist to her mouth, takes a final desperate look, pulls her coat about her, pats her hat and goes out. The lights dim down. The door opens and she comes back in, grabs her plant, and goes out for the last time.*)

CURTAIN

Topics for Further Study

1. The Youngers had been slaves and sharecroppers for five generations. Why did they decide to move North?
2. Why did Mama refuse to give Walter Lee the insurance money to purchase a share of the liquor store? Why did she decide later to turn over the bulk of the insurance money to him?
3. Why did Ruth also oppose Walter Lee's get-rich-quick plan?
4. All the Youngers have dreams—Walter Lee, Ruth, Beneatha, and Mama. What was each one's dream? At the end of the play at least one dream is on the way to realization. Which one?
5. Why did Walter Lee inform Mr. Lindner that the Youngers had decided to move into their new home despite his attempt to persuade them not to? Did Walter Lee make the right decision?
6. What is the outlook for Travis, who represents the sixth generation?
7. If Beneatha stayed in the United States, she would probably earn more money and live under better conditions, yet she seriously considers marrying Asagai and practicing medicine in Africa. Why?
8. Why is the title of the play appropriate?
9. Darwin T. Turner, a Black critic, said that *A Raisin in the Sun* is "one of the most perceptive presentations of Afro-Americans in the history of the American professional theatre." How is it perceptive? Cite instances.
10. One critic likened *A Raisin in the Sun* to Chekhov's *The Cherry Orchard*. Another likened it to Sean O'Casey's *Juno and the Paycock*. Read *The Cherry Orchard* or *Juno and the Paycock*, or both, and point out resemblances to *A Raisin in the Sun*.

Day of Absence

Day of Absence is a comedy—but it is a comedy with a sting. Although there is plenty of laughter, for the situation is funny and the characters absurd, the play has a serious message and a sharp thrust. It is a drama of social protest.

The action starts early in the morning of a hot day in a small Southern town when Clem and Luke, two white shop owners, discover that all the Blacks have suddenly and mysteriously disappeared, leaving no trace of their whereabouts. There is consternation among the whites. The whole town goes to pieces. The whites cannot run their homes, business, or town government without the Blacks. Factories are paralyzed, stores cannot sell their goods, garbage remains uncollected, and transportation comes to a standstill. In the course of the excitement it is reported that certain town officials—including the vice-mayor, several city council members, and the chairman of the Junior Chamber of Commerce—have also disappeared, suggesting to the whites that these officials had "Nigra" blood in them, something they had never before suspected. In an atmosphere of hysteria the mayor mobilizes the police, emergency committees, and vigilante squads to track down the missing "nigras" and bring them back.

The rest of the play is devoted to the town's frantic search, the mayor's desperate pleading over national television for the return of the departed Blacks, and the town's descent into total chaos and darkness. In the final scene, when the lights rise again, Clem and Luke slowly awake as if from a trance. They are fascinated to see Rastus, a Black, shuffle on stage. Rastus is the Stepin Fetchit movie stereotype of the lazy, dull Black who has no recollection of missing a day. The concluding lines strike a prophetic note:

LUKE. (*Eyes sweeping around in all directions.*) Well . . . There's the others, Clem . . . Back just like they useta be . . . Everything's same as always . . .

CLEM. ??? . . . . Is it . . . Luke . . . !

The method by which the author drives home his satirical thrusts is expressionism, a dramatic technique which originated in Germany during the 1920s and soon spread to other countries. Expressionism is antirealistic. It makes use of short scenes and staccato dialogue, and often seeks to convey a sense of the bizarre and grotesque. *Day of Absence*, for example, is intended for an all-Black cast, except for the role of Announcer. The players use white facial make-up and blond wigs, reversing the tradition of the minstrel show in which white actors wore Black make-up and Black wigs. Characters are not real; instead of being distinctive personalities they are representatives of a class. For example, the Club Woman stands for a type of wealthy snob whose sole occupation seems to be attending meetings of feminine organizations. The Industrialist stands for all crass employers interested only in profits. Other figures such as Mr. Council Clan, Reb Pious, and Mrs. Handy Anna Aide represent forces greater than themselves and their names suggest their affiliations. They always use opprobrious terms to refer to Blacks: coon, darky, dinge, jigaboo, and nigra. All are stereotypes drawn with an acid pen. Their absurd clichés and prejudices make them ludicrous.

In expressionist plays lighting effects are often substituted for realistic scenery. The author, for instance, gives the following directions for the lighting in *Day of Absence*:

> This is a red-white-and-blue play—meaning the whole production should be designed around the basic color scheme of our patriotic trinity. Lighting should illustrate, highlight, and detail time, action, and mood. Opening scenes stage-lit with white rays of morning, transforming to panic reds of afternoon, flowing into ominous blues of evening.

The action takes place on an almost bare stage with almost no props.

The author, Douglas Turner Ward, is an angry man, sarcastically surveying the exploitation of Blacks by whites. His wit is biting and his bitterness shows up in every line of the play—even in the stage directions, as when he advises directors to "Go 'long wit' the Blacks—besides all else they need the work more." *Day of Absence* is a satire, that is, it holds up human shortcomings to reprobation by means of derision. White discrimination is revealed and attacked by sharp and caustic laughter, instead of by reasoned argument. By wit, sarcasm, and exaggeration, the play exposes the bigotry and selfishness of whites in their relations with Blacks.

DOUGLAS TURNER WARD was born in 1931 on a Louisiana sugarcane and rice plantation where his parents worked as field hands. As a boy he experienced discrimination because of his color, and the memory of the indignities he suffered is still vivid. After graduating from high school in New Orleans, he spent a year at Wilberforce University, Ohio, and another at the University of Michigan.

Deciding that he was not profiting from college, he set out for New York where he worked as a journalist on a Black newspaper and joined an actors' workshop to study acting and playwriting. After some minor roles in off-Broadway and Broadway plays, he became an understudy to Sidney Poitier in *A Raisin in the Sun* and assumed the leading role in the play when it went on a national tour. He is familiar to viewers because of his many TV appearances.

When *Day of Absence* was presented together with *Happy Ending* for the first time in 1965, Mr. Ward played a leading role in each play. Subsequently, he won the Vernon Rice Drama Award for playwriting and an Obie Award for acting. Another play, *The Reckoning*, was presented in 1969. He is the founder and codirector of the Negro Ensemble Company, a New York repertory group.

Writes Mr. Ward: "Even with its uneven quality, the overall Black theatre movement is the most vital and muscular development in the theatre today. The non-Black writer has to consciously arrive at an intellectual perception of the underlying conflicts of his society. But for Blacks, the conflicts, contradictions and absurdities are all right on the surface."

Mr. Ward's plays show a first-hand acquaintance with these "conflicts, contradictions, and absurdities." He knows whereof he writes, and his plays therefore have insights often missing from plays about Blacks by white authors.

Day of Absence

BY

DOUGLAS TURNER WARD

CHARACTERS

CLEM	INDUSTRIALIST
LUKE	BUSINESSWOMAN
JOHN	CLUBWOMAN
MARY	COURIER
FIRST OPERATOR	ANNOUNCER
SECOND OPERATOR	CLAN
THIRD OPERATOR	AIDE
SUPERVISOR	PIOUS
JACKSON	DOLL WOMAN
MAYOR	BRUSH WOMAN
FIRST CITIZEN	MOP MAN
SECOND CITIZEN	RASTUS
THIRD CITIZEN	

The time is now. Play opens in unnamed Southern town of medium population on a somnolent cracker morning—meaning no matter the early temperature, it's gonna get hot. The hamlet is just beginning to rouse itself from the sleepy lassitude of night.

NOTES ON PRODUCTION

No scenery is necessary—only actors shifting in and out on an almost bare stage and freezing into immobility as focuses change or blackouts occur.

Play is conceived for performance by a Negro cast, a reverse minstrel show done in white-face. Logically, it might also be performed by

---

Day of Absence by Douglas Turner Ward. Copyright © 1966 by Douglas Turner Ward. Reprinted by permission of the author and of the Dramatists Play Service, Inc.

CAUTION: *Day of Absence*, being duly copyrighted, is subject to a royalty. The amateur acting rights in the play are controlled exclusively by the Dramatists Play Service, Inc., 440 Park Avenue South, New York, New York 10016. No amateur performance of the play may be given without obtaining in advance the written permission of the Dramatists Play Service, Inc., and paying the requisite fee.

whites—at their own risk. If any producer is faced with choosing between opposite hues, author strongly suggests: "Go 'long wit' the blacks—besides all else, they need the work more."

If acted by the latter, race members are urged to go for broke, yet cautioned not to ham it up too broadly. In fact—it just might be more effective if they aspire for serious tragedy. Only qualification needed for Caucasian casting is that the company fit a uniform pattern—insipid white; also played in white-face.

Before any horrifying discrimination doubts arise, I hasten to add that a bonafide white actor should be cast as the Announcer in all productions, likewise a Negro thespian in pure native black as Rastus. This will truly subvert any charge that the production is unintegrated.

All props, except essential items (chairs, brooms, rags, mop, debris) should be imaginary (phones, switchboard, mikes, eating utensils, food, etc.). Actors should indicate their presence through mime.

The cast of characters develops as the play progresses. In the interest of economical casting, actors should double or triple in roles wherever possible.

PRODUCTION CONCEPT

This is a red-white-and-blue play—meaning the entire production should be designed around the basic color scheme of our patriotic trinity. *Lighting* should illustrate, highlight and detail time, action and mood. Opening scenes stage-lit with white rays of morning, transforming to panic reds of afternoon, flowing into ominous blues of evening. *Costuming* should be orchestrated around the same color scheme. In addition, subsidiary usage of grays, khakis, yellows, pinks, and combinative patterns of stars-and-bars should be employed. Some actors (Announcer and Rastus excepted, of course) might wear white shoes or sneakers, and some women characters clothed in knee-length frocks might wear white stockings. Blonde wigs, both for males and females, can be used in selected instances. *Makeup* should have uniform consistency, with individual touches thrown in to enhance personal identity.

SAMPLE MODELS OF MAKEUP AND COSTUMING

Mary: Kewpie-doll face, ruby-red lips painted to valentine-pursing, moon-shaped rouge circles implanted on each cheek, blond wig of fat-flowing ringlets, dazzling ankle-length snow-white nightie.

Mayor: Seersucker white ensemble, ten-gallon hat, red string-tie and blue belt.

Clem: Khaki pants, bareheaded and blond.

Luke: Blue work-jeans, strawhatted.

Club Woman: Yellow dress patterned with *symbols of Dixie*, gray hat.

Clan: A veritable, riotous advertisement of red-white-and-blue combinations with stars-and-bars tossed in.

Pious: White ministerial garb with *black* cleric's collar topping his snow-white shirt.

Operators: All in red with different color wigs.

All other characters should be carefully defined through costuming which typify their identity.

DAY OF ABSENCE

SCENE: *Street.*
TIME: *Early morning.*

CLEM. (*Sitting under a sign suspended by invisible wires and bold-printed with the lettering: "STORE."*) 'Morning, Luke . . .

LUKE. (*Sitting a few paces away under an identical sign.*) 'Morning, Clem. . . .

CLEM. Go'n' be a hot day.

LUKE. Looks that way. . . .

CLEM. Might rain though. . . .

LUKE. Might.

CLEM. Hope it does. . . .

LUKE. Me, too. . . .

CLEM. Farmers could use a little wet spell for a change. . . . How's the Missis?

LUKE. Same.

CLEM. 'N' the kids?

LUKE. Them, too. . . . How's yourns?

CLEM. Fine, thank you. . . . (*They both lapse into drowsy silence waving lethargically from time to time at imaginary passersby.*) Hi, Joe. . . .

LUKE. Joe. . . .

CLEM. . . . How'd it go yesterday, Luke?

LUKE. Fair.

CLEM. Same wit' me. . . . Business don't seem to git no better or no worse. Guess we in a rut, Luke, don't it 'pear that way to you?—Morning, ma'am.

LUKE. Morning. . . .

CLEM. Tried display, sales, advertisement, stamps—everything, yet merchandising stumbles 'round in the same old groove. . . . But—that's better than plunging downwards, I reckon.

LUKE. Guess it is.

CLEM. Morning, Bret. How's the family? . . . That's good.

LUKE. Bret—

CLEM. Morning, Sue.

LUKE. How do, Sue.

CLEM. (*Staring after her.*) . . . Fine hunk of woman.

LUKE. Sure is.

CLEM. Wonder if it's any good?

LUKE. Bet it is.

CLEM. Sure like to find out!

LUKE. So would I.

CLEM. You ever try?

LUKE. Never did. . . .

CLEM. Morning, Gus. . . .

LUKE. Howdy, Gus.

CLEM. Fine, thank you. (*They lapse into silence again.* CLEM *rouses himself slowly, begins to look around quizzically.*) Luke . . . ?

LUKE. Huh?

CLEM. Do you . . . er, er—feel anything —funny . . . ?

LUKE. Like what?

CLEM. Like . . . er—something—strange?

LUKE. I dunno . . . haven't thought about it.

CLEM. I mean . . . like something's wrong—outta place, unusual?

LUKE. I don't know. . . . What you got in mind?

CLEM. Nothing . . . just that—just that —like somp'ums outta kilter. I got a funny feeling somp'ums not up to snuff. Can't figger out what it is . . .

LUKE. Maybe it's in your haid?

CLEM. No, not like that. . . . Like somp'ums happened—or happening— gone haywire, loony.

LUKE. Well, don't worry 'bout it, it'll pass.

CLEM. Guess you right. (*Attempts return to somnolence but doesn't succeed.*) . . . I'm sorry, Luke, but you sure you don't feel nothing peculiar . . . ?

LUKE. (*Slightly irked.*) Toss it out your mind, Clem! We got a long day ahead of us. If something's wrong, you'll know 'bout it in due time. No use worrying about it 'till it comes and if it's coming, it will. Now, relax!

CLEM. All right, you right. . . . Hi, Margie. . . .

LUKE. Marge.

CLEM. (*Unable to control himself.*) Luke, I don't give a damn what you say. Somp'ums topsy-turvy, I just know it!

LUKE. (*Increasingly irritated.*) Now look here, Clem—it's a bright day, it looks like it's go'n git hotter. You say the wife and kids are fine and the business is no better or no worse? Well, what else could be wrong? ... If somp'ums go'n' happen, it's go'n' happen anyway and there ain't a damn fool thing you kin do to stop it! So you ain't helping me, yourself or nobody else by thinking 'bout it. It's not go'n' be no better or no worse when it gits here. It'll come to you when it gits ready to come and it's go'n' be the same whether you worry about it or not. So stop letting it upset you! (LUKE *settles back in his chair.* CLEM *does likewise.* LUKE *shuts his eyes. After a few moments, they reopen. He forces them shut again. They reopen in greater curiosity. Finally, he rises slowly to an upright position in the chair, looks around frowningly. Turns slowly to* CLEM.) ... Clem? ... You know something? ... Somp'um is peculiar ...

CLEM. (*Vindicated.*) I knew it, Luke! I just knew it! Ever since we been sitting here, I been having that feeling!

(*Scene is blacked out abruptly. Lights rise on another section of the stage where a young couple lie in bed under an invisible-wire-suspension-sign lettered: "HOME." Loud insistent sounds of baby yells are heard.* JOHN, *the husband, turns over trying to ignore the cries,* MARY, *the wife, is undisturbed.* JOHN's *efforts are futile, the cries continue until they cannot be denied. He bolts upright, jumps out of bed and disappears off-stage. Returns quickly and tries to rouse* MARY.)

JOHN. Mary ... (*Nudges her, pushes her, yells into her ear, but she fails to respond.*) Mary, get up ... Get up!

MARY. Ummm ... (*Shrugs away, still sleeping.*)

JOHN. GET UP!

MARY. UMMMMMMMMM!

JOHN. Don't you hear the baby bawling! ... NOW GET UP!

MARY. (*Mumbling drowsily.*) ... What baby ... whose baby ... ?

JOHN. Yours!

MARY. Mine? That's ridiculous ... what'd you say ... ? Somebody's baby bawling? ... How could that be so? (*Hearing screams.*) Who's crying? Somebody's crying! ... What's crying? ... WHERE'S LULA?!

JOHN. I don't know. You better get up.

MARY. That's outrageous! ... What time is it?

JOHN. Late 'nuff! Now rise up!

MARY. You must be joking. ... I'm sure I still have four or five hours sleep in store —even more after that head-splittin' blow-out last night ... (*Tumbles back under covers.*)

JOHN. Nobody told you to gulp those last six bourbons—

MARY. Don't tell me how many bourbons to swallow, not after you guzzled the whole stinking bar! ... Get up? ... You must be cracked. ... Where's Lula? She must be here, she always is ...

JOHN. Well, she ain't here yet, so get up and muzzle that brat before she does drive me cuckoo!

MARY. (*Springing upright, finally realizing gravity of situation.*) Whaddaya mean Lula's not here? She's always here, she must be here. ... Where else kin she be? She supposed to be. ... She just can't *not* be here—CALL HER!

(*Blackout as* JOHN *rushes offstage. Scene shifts to a trio of Telephone Operators perched on stools before imaginary switchboards. Chaos and bedlam are taking place to the sound of buzzes.* PRODUCTION NOTE: *Effect of following dialogue should simulate rising pandemonium.*)

FIRST OPERATOR. The line is busy—

SECOND OPERATOR. Line is busy—

THIRD OPERATOR. Is busy—

FIRST OPERATOR. Doing best we can—

SECOND OPERATOR. Having difficulty—

THIRD OPERATOR. Soon as possible—

FIRST OPERATOR. Just one moment—

SECOND OPERATOR. Would you hold on—

THIRD OPERATOR. Awful sorry, madam—

FIRST OPERATOR. Would you hold on, please—

SECOND OPERATOR. Just a second, please—
THIRD OPERATOR. Please hold on, please—
FIRST OPERATOR. The line is busy—
SECOND OPERATOR. The line is busy—
THIRD OPERATOR. The line is busy—
FIRST OPERATOR. Doing best we can—
SECOND OPERATOR. Hold on please—
THIRD OPERATOR. Can't make connections—
FIRST OPERATOR. Unable to put it in—
SECOND OPERATOR. Won't plug through—
THIRD OPERATOR. Sorry madam—
FIRST OPERATOR. If you wait a moment—
SECOND OPERATOR. Doing best we can—
THIRD OPERATOR. Sorry—
FIRST OPERATOR. One moment—
SECOND OPERATOR. Just a second—
THIRD OPERATOR. Hold on—
FIRST OPERATOR. Yes—
SECOND OPERATOR. STOP IT!—
THIRD OPERATOR. HOW DO I KNOW—
FIRST OPERATOR. YOU ANOTHER ONE!
SECOND OPERATOR. HOLD ON DAMMIT!
THIRD OPERATOR. UP YOURS, TOO!
FIRST OPERATOR. THE LINE IS BUSY—
SECOND OPERATOR. THE LINE IS BUSY—
THIRD OPERATOR. THE LINE IS BUSY—

(*The switchboard clamors a cacophony of buzzes as* OPERATORS *plug connections with the frenzy of a Chaplin movie. Their replies degenerate into a babble of gibberish. At the height of frenzy, the* SUPERVISOR *appears.*)
SUPERVISOR. WHAT'S THE SNARL-UP???!!!
FIRST OPERATOR. Everybody calling at the same time, ma'am!
SECOND OPERATOR. Board can't handle it!

THIRD OPERATOR. Like everybody in big New York City is trying to squeeze a call through to li'l' ole us!
SUPERVISOR. God!... Somp'um terrible musta happened!... Buzz the emergency frequency hookup to the Mayor's office and find out what the hell's going on!
(*Scene blacks out quickly to* CLEM *and* LUKE.)
CLEM. (*Something slowly dawning on him.*) Luke...?
LUKE. Yes, Clem?
CLEM. (*Eyes roving around in puzzlement.*) Luke...?
LUKE. (*Irked.*) I said what, Clem!
CLEM. Luke...? Where—where is—the—the—?
LUKE. THE WHAT?!
CLEM. Nigras...?
LUKE. ????? What...?
CLEM. Nigras.... Where is the Nigras, where is they, Luke...? ALL THE NIGRAS!... I don't see no Nigras...?!
LUKE. Whatcha mean...?
CLEM. (*Agitatedly.*) Luke, there ain't a darky in sight.... And if you remember, we ain't spied a nappy hair all morning.... The Nigras, Luke! We ain't laid eyes on nary a coon this whole morning!!!
LUKE. You must be crazy or something, Clem!
CLEM. Think about it, Luke, we been sitting here for an hour or more—try and recollect if you remember seeing jist *one* go by?!!!
LUKE. (*Confused.*) ... I don't recall ... But ... but there musta been some.... The heat musta got you, Clem! How in hell could that be so?!!!
CLEM. (*Triumphantly.*) Just think, Luke! ... Look around ya.... Now, every morning mosta people walkin' 'long this street is colored. They's strolling by going to work, they's waiting for the buses, they's sweeping sidewalks, cleaning stores, starting to shine shoes and wetting the mops—right?!... Well, look around you, Luke—where is they? (*Luke paces up and down, checking.*) I told you, Luke, they ain't nowheres to be seen.

LUKE. ???? . . . This . . . this . . . some kind of holiday for 'em—or something?

CLEM. I don't know, Luke . . . but . . . but what I do know is they ain't here 'n' we haven't seen a solitary one. . . . It's scaryfying. Luke . . . !

LUKE. Well . . . maybe they's jist standing 'n' walking and shining on other streets.—Let's go look!

(*Scene blacks out to* JOHN *and* MARY. *Baby cries are as insistent as ever.*)

MARY. (*At end of patience.*) SMOTHER IT!

JOHN. (*Beyond his.*) That's a hell of a thing to say 'bout your own child! You should know what to do to hush her up!

MARY. Why don't you try?!

JOHN. You had her!

MARY. You shared in borning her?!

JOHN. Possibly not!

MARY. Why, you lousy—!

JOHN. What good is a mother who can't shut up her own daughter?!

MARY. I told you she yells louder every time I try to lay hands on her.— Where's Lula? Didn't you call her?!

JOHN. I told you I can't get the call through!

MARY. Try ag'in—

JOHN. It's no use! I tried numerous times and can't even git through to the switchboard. You've got to quiet her down yourself. (*Firmly.*) Now, go in there and clam her up 'fore I lose my patience! (MARY *exits. Soon, we hear the yells increase. She rushes back in.*)

MARY. She won't let me touch her, just screams louder!

JOHN. Probably wet 'n' soppy!

MARY. Yes! Stinks something awful! Phooooey! I can't stand that filth and odor!

JOHN. That's why she's screaming! Needs her didee changed—Go change it!

MARY. How you 'spect me to when I don't know how?! Suppose I faint?!

JOHN. Well let her blast away. I'm getting outta here.

MARY. You can't leave me here like this!

JOHN. Just watch me! . . . See this nice split-level cottage, peachy furniture, multi-colored teevee, hi-fi set 'n' the rest? . . . Well, how you think I scraped 'em together while you curled up on your fat li'l' fanny? . . . By gitting outta here— not only *on time* . . . but EARLIER!— Beating a frantic crew of nice young executives to the punch—gitting there fustest with the mostest brown-nosing you ever saw! Now if I goof one day—just ONE DAY!—You reckon I'd stay ahead? NO! . . . There'd be a wolf-pack trampling over my prostrate body, racing to replace my smiling face against the boss' left rump! . . . NO, MAM! I'm zooming outta here on time, just as I always have and what's more—you go'n' fix me some breakfast, I'M HUNGRY!

MARY. But—

JOHN. No buts about it! (*Flash blackout as he gags on a mouthful of coffee.*) What you trying to do, STRANGLE ME!!! (*Jumps up and starts putting on jacket.*)

MARY. (*Sarcastically.*) What did you expect?

JOHN. (*In biting fury.*) That you could possibly boil a pot of water, toast a few slices of bread and fry a coupler eggs! . . . It was a mistaken assumption!

MARY. So they aren't as good as Lula's!

JOHN. That is an overstatement. Your efforts don't result in anything that could possibly be digested by man, mammal, or insect! . . . When I married you, I thought I was fairly acquainted with your faults and weaknesses—I chalked 'em up to human imperfection. . . . But now I know I was being extremely generous, over-optimistic and phenomenally deluded!—You have no idea how useless you really are!

MARY. Then why'd you marry me?!

JOHN. Decoration!

MARY. You shoulda married Lula!

JOHN. I might've if it wasn't 'gainst the segregation law! . . . But for the sake of my home, my child and my sanity, I will even take a chance in sacrificing my slippery grip on the status pole and drive by her shanty to find out whether she or someone like her kin come over here and prevent some ultimate disaster. (*Storms toward door, stopping abruptly at exit.*) Are you sure you kin make it to the bathroom wit'out Lula backing you up?!!!

(*Blackout. Scene shifts to Mayor's office where a cluttered desk stands center amid papered debris.*)

MAYOR. (*Striding determinedly toward desk, stopping midways, bellowing.*) WOODFENCE! . . . WOODFENCE! . . . WOODFENCE! (*Receiving no reply, completes distance to desk.*) JACKSON! . . . JACKSON!

JACKSON. (*Entering worriedly.*) Yes, sir . . . ?

MAYOR. Where's Vice-Mayor Woodfence, that no-good brother-in-law of mine?!

JACKSON. Hasn't come in yet, sir.

MAYOR. HASN'T COME IN?!!! . . . Damn bastard! Knows we have a crucial conference. Soon as he staggers through that door, tell him to shoot in here! (*Angrily focusing on his disorderly desk and littered surroundings.*) And git Mandy here to straighten up this mess—Rufus too! You know he shoulda been waiting to knock dust off my shoes soon as I step in. Get 'em in here! . . . What's the matter wit' them lazy Nigras? . . . Already had to dress myself because of JC, fix my own coffee without MayBelle, drive myself to work 'counta Bubber, feel my old Hag's tits after Sapphi—NEVER MIND!— Git 'em in here—QUICK!

JACKSON. (*Meekly.*) They aren't . . . they aren't here, sir . . .

MAYOR. Whaddaya mean they aren't here? Find out where they at. We got important business, man! You can't run a town wit' laxity like this. Can't allow things to git snafued jist because a bunch of lazy Nigras been out gitting drunk and living it up all night! Discipline, man, discipline!

JACKSON. That's what I'm trying to tell you, sir . . . they didn't come in, can't be found . . . none of 'em.

MAYOR. Ridiculous, boy! Scare 'em up and tell 'em scoot here in a hurry befo' I git mad and fire the whole goddamn lot of 'em.

JACKSON. But we can't find 'em, sir.

MAYOR. Hogwash! Can't nobody in this office do anything right?! Do I hafta handle every piddling little matter myself?! Git me their numbers, I'll have 'em here befo' you kin shout to—

(*Three men burst into room in various states of undress.*)

ONE. Henry—they vanished!

TWO. Disappeared into thin air!

THREE. Gone wit' out a trace!

TWO. Not a one on the street!

THREE. In the house!

ONE. On the job!

MAYOR. Wait a minute!! . . . Hold your water! Calm down—!

ONE. But they've gone, Henry—GONE! all of them!

MAYOR. What the hell you talking 'bout? Who's gone—?

ONE. The Nigras, Henry! They gone!

MAYOR. Gone? . . . Gone where?

TWO. That's what we trying to tell ya— they just disappeared! The Nigras have disappeared, swallowed up, vanished! All of 'em! Every last one!

MAYOR. Have everybody 'round here gone batty? . . . That's impossible, how could the Nigras vanish?

THREE. Beats me, but it's happened!

MAYOR. You mean a whole town of Nigras just evaporate like this—poof!— Overnight?

ONE. Right!

MAYOR. Y'all must be drunk! Why, half this town is colored. How could they just sneak out!

TWO. Don't ask me, but there ain't one in sight!

MAYOR. Simmer down 'n' put it to me easy-like.

ONE. Well . . . I first suspected somp'um smelly when Sarah Jo didn't show up this morning and I couldn't reach her—

TWO. Dorothy Jane didn't 'rive at my house—

THREE. Georgia Mae wasn't at mine neither—and SHE sleeps in!

ONE. When I reached the office, I realized I hadn't seen nary one Nigra all morning! Nobody else had either—wait a minute—Henry, have you?!

MAYOR. ??? Now that you mention it... no, I haven't...

ONE. They gone, Henry. ... Not a one on the street, not a one in our homes, not a single, last living one to be found nowheres in town. What we gon' do?!

MAYOR. (*Thinking.*) Keep heads on your shoulders 'n' put clothes on your back.... They can't be far. ... Must be 'round somewheres.... Probably playing hide 'n' seek, that's it! ... JACKSON!

JACKSON. Yessir?

MAYOR. Immediately mobilize our Citizens Emergency Distress Committee!—Order a fleet of sound trucks to patrol streets urging the population to remain calm—situation's not as bad as it looks—everything's under control! Then have another squadron of squawk buggies drive slowly through all Nigra alleys, ordering them to come out wherever they are. If that don't git 'em organize a vigilante search-squad to flush 'em outta hiding! But most important of all, track down that lazy goldbricker, Woodfence and tell him to git on top of the situation! By God, we'll find 'em even if we hafta dig 'em outta the ground!

(*Blackout. Scene shifts back to* JOHN *and* MARY *a few hours later. A funeral solemnity pervades their mood.* JOHN *stands behind* MARY *who sits, in a scene duplicating the famous "American Gothic" painting.*)

JOHN. ... Walked up to the shack, knocked on door, didn't git no answer. Hollered "LULA? LULA ... ?—Not a thing. Went 'round the side, peeped in window—nobody stirred. Next door—nobody there. Crossed other side of street and banged on five or six other doors—not a colored person could be found! Not a man, neither woman or child— not even a little black dog could be seen, smelt or heard for blocks around. ... They've gone, Mary.

MARY. What does it all mean, John?

JOHN. I don't know, Mary ...

MARY. I always had Lula, John. She never missed a day at my side. ... That's why I couldn't accept your wedding proposal until I was sure you'd welcome me and her together as a package. How am I gonna git through the day? My baby don't know *me*, I ain't acquainted wit' *it*. I've never lifted cover off pot, swung a mop or broom, dunked a dish or even pushed a dustrag. I'm lost wit'out Lula, I need her, John, I need her.

(*Begins to weep softly.* JOHN *pats her consolingly.*)

JOHN. Courage, honey. ... Everybody in town is facing the same dilemma. We mustn't crack up ...

(*Blackout. Scene shifts back to* MAYOR's *office later in day. Atmosphere and tone resembles a wartime headquarters at the front.* MAYOR *is poring over huge map.*)

INDUSTRIALIST. Half the town is gone already, Henry. On behalf of the factory owners of this town, you've got to bail us out! Seventy-five per cent of all production is paralyzed. With the Nigras absent, men are waiting for machines to be cleaned, floors to be swept, crates lifted, equipment delivered and bathrooms to be deodorized. Why, restrooms and toilets are so filthy until they not only cannot be sat in, but it's virtually impossible to get within hailing distance because of the stench!

MAYOR. Keep your shirt on, Jeb—

BUSINESSMAN. Business is even in worse condition, Henry. The volume of goods moving 'cross counters has slowed down to a trickle—almost negligible. Customers are not only not purchasing—but the absence of handymen, porters, sweepers, stock-movers, deliverers and miscellaneous dirty-work doers is disrupting the smooth harmony of marketing!

CLUB WOMAN. Food poisoning, severe indigestitis, chronic diarrhea, advanced diaper chafings and a plethora of unsanitary household disasters dangerous to life, limb and property! . . . As a representative of the Federation of Ladies' Clubs, I must sadly report that unless the trend is reversed, a complete breakdown in family unity is imminent. . . . Just as homosexuality and debauchery signalled the fall of Greece and Rome, the downgrading of Southern Bellesdom might very well prophesy the collapse of our indigenous institutions. . . . Remember—it has always been pure, delicate, lily-white images of Dixie femininity which provided backbone, inspiration and ideology for our male warriors in their defense against the on-rushing black horde. If our gallant men are drained of this worship and idolatry—God knows! The cause won't be worth a Confederate nickel!

MAYOR. Stop this panicky defeatism, y'all hear me! All machinery at my disposal is being utilized. I assure you wit' great confidence the damage will soon repair itself.—Cheerful progress reports are expected any moment now.—Wait! See, here's Jackson. . . . Well, Jackson?

JACKSON. (*Entering.*) As of now, sir, all efforts are fruitless. Neither hide nor hair of them has been located. We have not unearthed a single one in our shack-to-shack search. Not a single one has heeded our appeal. Scoured every crick and cranny inside their hovels, turning furniture upside down and inside out, breaking down walls and tearing through ceilings. We made determined efforts to discover where 'bouts of our faithful uncle Toms and informers—but even they have vanished without a trace. . . . Searching squads are on the verge of panic and hysteria, sir, wit' hotheads among 'em campaigning for scorched earth policies. Nigras on a whole lack cellars, but there's rising sentiment favoring burning to find out whether they're underground—DUG IN!

MAYOR. Absolutely counter such foolhardy suggestions! Suppose they are tombed in? We'd only accelerate the gravity of the situation using incendiary tactics! Besides, when they're rounded up where will we put 'em if we've already burned up their shacks—IN OUR OWN BEDROOMS?!!!

JACKSON. I agree, sir, but the mood of the crowd is becoming irrational. In anger and frustration, they's forgetting their original purpose was to FIND the Nigras!

MAYOR. At all costs! Stamp out all burning proposals! Must prevent extremist notions from gaining ascendancy. Git wit' it. . . . Wait—'n' for Jehovah's sake, find out where the hell is that trifling slacker, WOODFENCE!

COURIER. (*Rushing in.*) Mr. Mayor! Mr. Mayor! . . . We've found some! We've found some!

MAYOR. (*Excitedly.*) Where?!

COURIER. In the—in the— (*Can't catch breath.*)

MAYOR. (*Impatiently.*) Where, man? Where?!!!

COURIER. In the colored wing of the city hospital!

MAYOR. The hos—? The hospital! I shoulda known! How could those helpless, crippled, cut and shot Nigras disappear from a hospital! Shoulda thought of that! . . . Tell me more, man!

COURIER. I—I didn't wait, sir. . . . I—I ran in to report soon as I heard—

MAYOR. WELL GIT BACK ON THE PHONE, YOU IDIOT, DON'T YOU KNOW WHAT THIS MEANS!

COURIER. Yes, sir.

(*Races out.*)

MAYOR. Now we gitting somewhere! . . . Gentlemen, if one sole Nigra is among us, we're well on the road to rehabilitation! Those Nigras in the hospital must know somp'um 'bout the others where'bouts. . . . Scat back to your colleagues, boost up their morale and inform 'em that things will zip back to normal in a jiffy! (*They start to file out, then pause to observe the* COURIER *reentering dazedly.*) Well . . . ? Well, man . . . ? WHAT'S THE MATTER WIT' YOU, NINNY, TELL ME WHAT ELSE WAS SAID?!

COURIER. They all . . . they all . . . they all in a—in a—a coma, sir . . .

MAYOR. They all in a what . . . ?

COURIER. In a coma, sir . . .

MAYOR. Talk sense, man! . . . Whaddaya mean, they all in a coma?

COURIER. Doctor says every last one of the Nigras are jist laying in bed . . . STILL . . . not moving . . . neither live or dead . . . laying up there in a coma . . . every last one of 'em . . .

MAYOR. (*Splutters, then grabs phone.*) Get me Confederate Memorial. . . . Put me through to the Staff Chief. . . . YES, this is the Mayor. . . . Sam? . . . What's this I hear? . . . But how could they be in a coma, Sam? . . . You don't know! Well, what the hell you think the city's paying you for! . . . You've got 'nuff damn hacks and quacks there to find out! . . . How could it be somp'um unknown? You mean Nigras know somp'um 'bout drugs your damn butchers don't?! . . . Well, what the crap good are they! . . . All right, all right, I'll be calm. . . . Now, tell me. . . . Uh huh, uh huh. . . . Well, can't you give 'em some injections or somp'um . . . ?— You did . . . uh huh . . . DID YOU TRY A LI'L' ROUGH TREATMENT?— that too, huh. . . . All right, Sam, keep trying. . . . (*Puts phone down delicately, continuing absently.*) Can't wake 'em up. Just lay there. Them that's sick won't git no sicker, them that's half-well won't git no better, babies that's due won't be born and them that's come won't show no life. Nigras wit' cuts won't bleed and them which need blood won't be transfused . . . He say dying Nigras is even refusing to pass away! (*Is silently perplexed for a moment, then suddenly breaks into action.*) JACKSON?! . . . Call up the police—THE JAIL! Find out what's going on there! Them Nigras are captives! If there's one place we got darkies under control, it's there! Them sonsabitches too onery to act right either for colored or white! (JACKSON *exits. The* COURIER *follows.*) Keep your fingers crossed, citizens, them Nigras in jail are the most important Nigras we got!

(*All hands are raised conspicuously aloft, fingers prominently ex-ed. Seconds tick by. Soon* JACKSON *returns crestfallen.*)

JACKSON. Sheriff Bull says they don't know whether they still on premises or not. When they went to rouse Nigra jailbirds this morning, cell-block doors refused to swing open. Tried everything— even exploded dynamite charges—but it just wouldn't budge. . . . Then they hoisted guards up to peep through barred windows, but couldn't see good 'nuff to tell whether Nigras was inside or not. Finally, gitting desperate, they power-hosed the cells wit' water but had to cease 'cause Sheriff Bull said he didn't wanta jeopardize drowning the Nigras since it might spoil his chance of shipping a record load of cotton pickers to the State Penitentiary for cotton-snatching jubilee. . . . Anyway —they ain't heard a Nigra-squeak all day.

MAYOR. ??? That so . . . ? WHAT 'BOUT TRAINS 'N' BUSSES PASSING THROUGH? There must be some dinges riding through?

JACKSON. We checked . . . not a one on board.

MAYOR. Did you hear whether any other towns lost their Nigras?

JACKSON. Things are status-quo everywhere else.

MAYOR. (*Angrily.*) Then what the hell they picking on us for!

COURIER. (*Rushing in.*) MR. MAYOR! Your sister jist called—HYSTERICAL! She says Vice-Mayor Woodfence went to bed wit her last night, but when she woke up this morning he was gone! Been missing all day!

MAYOR. ??? Could Nigras be holding brother-in-law Woodfence hostage?!

COURIER. No, sir. Besides him—investigations reveal that dozens of more prominent citizens—two City Council members, the chairman of the Junior Chamber of Commerce, our City College All-Southern half-back, the chairlady of the Daughters of the Confederate Rebellion, Miss Cotton-Sack Festival of the Year and numerous other miscellaneous nobodies—are all absent wit'out leave. Dangerous evidence points to the conclusion that they have been infiltrating!

MAYOR. Infiltrating???
COURIER. Passing all along!
MAYOR. ? ? ? PASSING ALL ALONG???
COURIER. Secret Nigras all the while!
MAYOR. NAW!

(CLUB WOMAN *keels over in faint.* JACKSON, BUSINESSMAN *and* INDUSTRIALIST *begin to eye each other suspiciously.*)

COURIER. Yessir!
MAYOR. PASSING???
COURIER. Yessir!
MAYOR. SECRET NIG—!???
COURIER. Yessir!
MAYOR. (*Momentarily stunned to silence.*) The dirty mongrelizers! . . . Gentlemen, this is a grave predicament indeed. . . . It pains me to surrender priority to our states' right credo, but it is my solemn task and frightening duty to inform you that we have no other recourse but to seek outside help for deliverance.

(*Blackout. Lights re-rise on Huntley-Brinkley-Murrow-Sevareid-Cronkite-Reasoner-type* ANNOUNCER *grasping a hand-held microphone [imaginary] a few hours later. He is vigorously, excitedly mouthing his commentary, but no sound escapes his lips. . . . During this dumb, wordless section of his broadcast, a bedraggled assortment of figures marching with picket signs occupy his attention. On their picket signs are inscribed various appeals and slogans.* "CINDY LOU UNFAIR TO BABY JOE" . . . "CAP'N SAM MISS BIG BOY" . . . "RETURN LI'L' BLUE TO MARSE JIM" . . . "INFORMATION REQUESTED 'BOUT MAMMY GAIL" . . . "BOSS NATHAN PROTEST TO FAST LEROY." *Trailing behind the marchers, forcibly isolated, is a woman dressed in widow-black holding a placard which reads:* "WHY DIDN'T YOU TELL US—YOUR DEFILED WIFE AND TWO ABSENT MONGRELS.")

ANNOUNCER. (*Who has been silently mouthing his delivery during the picketing procession, is suddenly heard as if caught in the midst of commentary.*) . . . Factories standing idle from the loss of non-essential workers. Stores shuttered from the absconding of uncrucial personnel. Uncollected garbage threatening pestilence and pollution. . . . Also, each second somewheres in this former utopia below the Mason and Dixon, dozens of decrepit old men and women usually tended by faithful nurses and servants are popping off like flies—abandoned by sons, daughters and grandchildren whose refusal to provide their doddering relatives with bedpans and other soothing necessities result in their hasty, nasty, messy corpus delicties. . . . But most crucially affected of all by this complete drought of Afro-American resources are policemen and other public safety guardians denied their daily quota of Negro arrests. One officer known affectionately as "TWO-A-DAY-PETE" because of his unblemished record of TWO Negro headwhippings per day has already been carted off to the County Insane Asylum—straight-jacketed, screaming and biting, unable to withstand the shock of having his spotless slate sullied by interruption. . . . It is feared that similar attacks are soon expected among municipal judges prevented for the first time in years of distinguished bench-sitting from sentencing one simple Negro to a hoosegow or pokey. . . . Ladies and gentlemen, as you trudge in from the joys and headaches of workday chores and dusk begins to descend on this sleepy Southern hamlet, we REPEAT—today—before early morning dew had dried upon magnolia blossoms, your comrade citizens of this lovely Dixie village awoke to the realization that some—pardon me! Not some—but ALL OF THEIR NEGROES were missing.... Absent, vamoosed, departed, at bay, fugitive, away, gone and so-far unretrieved.... In order to dispel your incredulity, gauge the temper of your suffering compatriots and just possibly prepare you for the likelihood of an equally nightmarish eventuality, we have gathered a cross-section of this city's most distinguished leaders for exclusive interviews.... First, Mr. Council Clan, grand-dragoon of this area's most active civic organizations and staunch bellwether of the political opposition.... Mr. Clan, how do you ACCOUNT for this incredible disappearance?

CLAN. A PLOT, plain and simple, that's what it is, as plain as the corns on your feet!

ANNOUNCER. Whom would you consider responsible?

CLAN. I could go on all night.

ANNOUNCER. Cite a few?

CLAN. Too numerous.

ANNOUNCER. Just one?

CLAN. Name names when time comes.

ANNOUNCER. Could you be referring to native Negroes?

CLAN. Ever try quaranteening lepers from their spots?

ANNOUNCER. Their organizations?

CLAN. Could you slice a nose off a mouth and still keep a face?

ANNOUNCER. Commies?

CLAN. Would you lop off a titty from a chest and still have a breast?

ANNOUNCER. Your city government?

CLAN. Now you talkin'!

ANNOUNCER. State administration?

CLAN. Warming up!

ANNOUNCER. Federal?

CLAN. Kin a blind man see?!

ANNOUNCER. The Court?

CLAN. Is a pig clean?!

ANNOUNCER. Clergy?

CLAN. Do a polecat stink?!

ANNOUNCER. Well, Mr. Clan, with this massive complicity, how do you think the plot could've been prevented from succeeding?

CLAN. If I'da been in office, it never woulda happened.

ANNOUNCER. Then you're laying major blame at the doorstep of the present administration?

CLAN. Damn tooting!

ANNOUNCER. But from your oft-expressed views, Mr. Clan, shouldn't you and your followers be delighted at the turn of events? After all—isn't it one of the main policies of your society to *drive* Negroes away? *Drive* 'em back where they came from?

CLAN. DRIVVVE, BOY! DRIIIVVVE! That's right!... When we say so and not befo'. Ain't supposed to do nothing 'til we tell 'em. Got to stay put until we exercise our God-given right to tell 'em when to git!

ANNOUNCER. But why argue if they've merely jumped the gun? Why not rejoice at this premature purging of undesirables?

CLAN. The time ain't ripe yet, boy.... The time ain't ripe yet.

ANNOUNCER. Thank you for being so informative, Mr. Clan—Mrs. Aide? Mrs. Aide? Over here, Mrs. Aide.... Ladies and gentlemen, this city's Social Welfare Commissioner, Mrs. Handy Anna Aide. ... Mrs. Aide, with all your Negroes *AWOL*, haven't developments alleviated the staggering demands made upon your Welfare Department? Reduction of relief requests, elimination of case loads, removal of chronic welfare dependents, et cetera?

AIDE. Quite the contrary. Disruption of our pilot projects among Nigras saddles our white community with extreme hardship.... You see, historically, our agencies have always been foremost contributors to the Nigra Git-A-Job movement. We pioneered in enforcing social welfare theories which oppose coddling the fakers. We strenuously believe in helping Nigras help themselves by participating in meaningful labor. "Relief is Out, Work is In," is our motto. We place them as maids, cooks, butlers, and breast-feeders, cesspool-diggers, wash-basin maintainers, shoe-shine boys, and so on—mostly on a volunteer self-work basis.

ANNOUNCER. Hired at prevailing salaried rates, of course?

AIDE. God forbid! Money is unimportant. Would only make 'em worse. Our main goal is to improve their ethical behavior. "Rehabilitation Through Positive Participation" is another motto of ours. All unwed mothers, loose-living malingering fathers, bastard children and shiftless grandparents are kept occupied through constructive muscle-therapy. This provides the Nigra with less opportunity to indulge his pleasure-loving amoral inclinations.

ANNOUNCER. They volunteer to participate in these pilot projects?

AIDE. Heavens no! They're notorious shirkers. When I said the program is voluntary, I meant white citizens in overwhelming majorities do the volunteering. Placing their homes, offices, appliances and persons at our disposal for use in "Operation Uplift." . . . We would never dare place such a decision in the hands of the Nigra. It would never get off the ground! . . . No, they have no choice in the matter. "Work or Starve" is the slogan we use to stimulate Nigra awareness of what's good for survival.

ANNOUNCER. Thank you, Mrs. Aide, and good luck . . . Rev? . . . Rev? . . . Ladies and gentlemen, this city's foremost spiritual guidance counselor, Reverend Reb Pious. . . . How does it look to you, Reb Pious?

PIOUS. (*Continuing to gaze skyward.*) It's in *His* hands, son, it's in *His* hand.

ANNOUNCER. How would you assess the disappearance, from a moral standpoint?

PIOUS. An immoral act, son, morally wrong and ethically indefensible. A perversion of Christian principles to be condemned from every pulpit of this nation.

ANNOUNCER. Can you account for its occurrence after the many decades of the Church's missionary activity among them?

PIOUS. It's basically a reversion of the Nigra to his deep-rooted primitivism. . . . Now, at last, you can understand the difficulties of the Church in attempting to anchor God's kingdom among ungratefuls. It's a constant, unrelenting, no-holds-barred struggle against Satan to wrestle away souls locked in his possession for countless centuries! Despite all our aid, guidance, solace and protection, Old BeezleBub still retains tenacious grips upon the Nigras' childish loyalty—comparable to the lure of bright flames to an infant.

ANNOUNCER. But actual physical departure, Reb Pious? How do you explain that?

PIOUS. Voodoo, my son, voodoo. . . . With Satan's assist, they have probably employed some heathen magic which we cultivated, sophisticated Christians know absolutely nothing about. However, before long we are confident about counteracting this evil witch-doctory and triumphing in our Holy Savior's name. At this perilous juncture, true believers of all denominations are participating in joint, 'round-the-clock observances, offering prayers for our Master's swiftest intercession. I'm optimistic about the outcome of his intervention. . . . Which prompts me—if I may, sir—to offer these words of counsel to our delinquent Nigras. . . . I say to you without rancor or vengeance, quoting a phrase of one of your greatest prophets, Booker T. Washington: "Return your buckets to where they lay and all will be forgiven."

ANNOUNCER. A very inspirational appeal, Reb Pious. I'm certain they will find the tug of its magnetic sincerity irresistible. Thank you, Reb Pious. . . . All in all—as you have witnessed, ladies and gentlemen—this town symbolizes the face of disaster. Suffering as severe a prostration as any city wrecked, ravaged, and devastated by the holocaust of war. A vital, lively, throbbing organism brought to a screeching halt by the strange enigma of the missing Negroes. . . . We take you now to offices of the one man into whose hands has been thrust the final responsibility of rescuing this shuddering metropolis from the precipice of destruction. . . . We give you the honorable Mayor, Henry R. E. Lee . . . Hello, Mayor Lee.

MAYOR. (*Jovially.*) Hello, Jack.

ANNOUNCER. Mayor Lee, we have just concluded interviews with some of your city's leading spokesmen. If I may say so, sir, they don't sound too encouraging about the situation.

MAYOR. Nonsense, Jack! The situation's well-in-hand as it could be under the circumstances. Couldn't be better in hand. Underneath every dark cloud, Jack, there's always a ray of sunlight, ha, ha, ha.

ANNOUNCER. Have you discovered one, sir?

MAYOR. Well, Jack, I'll tell you. . . . Of course we've been faced wit' a little crisis, but look at it like this—we've faced 'em befo': Sherman marched through Georgia—ONCE! Lincoln freed the slaves—MOMENTARILY! Carpetbaggers even put Nigras in the Governor's mansion, state legislature, Congress and the Senate of the United States. But what happened?—Ole Dixie bounced right on back up. . . . At this moment the Supreme Court's trying to put Nigras in our schools and the Nigra has got it in his haid to put hisself everywhere. . . . But what you 'spect go 'n' happen?—Ole Dixie will kangaroo back even higher. Southern courage, fortitude, chivalry and superiority always wins out. . . . SHUCKS! We'll have us some Nigras befo' daylight is gone!

ANNOUNCER. Mr. Mayor, I hate to introduce this note, but in an earlier interview, one of your chief opponents, Mr. Clan, hinted at your own complicity in the affair—

MAYOR. A LOT OF POPPYCOCK! Clan is politicking! I've beaten him four times outta four and I'll beat him four more times outta four! This is no time for partisan politics! What we need now is level-headedness and across-the-board unity. This typical, rash, mealy-mouth, shooting-off-at-the-lip of Clan and his ilk proves their insincerity and voters will remember that in the next election! Won't you, voters?! (*Has risen to the height of his campaign oratory.*)

ANNOUNCER. Mr. Mayor! . . . Mr. Mayor! . . . Please—

MAYOR. . . . I tell you, I promise you—

ANNOUNCER. PLEASE, MR. MAYOR!

MAYOR. Huh? . . . Oh—yes, carry on.

ANNOUNCER. Mr. Mayor, your cheerfulness and infectious good spirits lead me to conclude that startling new developments warrant fresh-found optimism. What concrete, declassified information do you have to support your claim that Negroes will reappear before nightfall?

MAYOR. Because we are presently awaiting the pay-off of a masterful five-point supra-recovery program which can't help but reap us a bonanza of Nigras 'fore sundown! . . . First: Exhaustive efforts to pinpoint the where'bouts of our own missing darkies continue to zero in on the bullseye. . . . Second: The President of the United States, following an emergency cabinet meeting, has designated us the prime disaster area of the century—National Guard is already on the way. . . . Third: In an unusual, but bold maneuver, we have appealed to the NAACP 'n' all other Nigra conspirators to help us git to the bottom of the vanishing act. . . . Fourth: We have exercised our non-reciprocal option and requested that all fraternal southern states express their solidarity by lending us some of their Nigras temporarily on credit. . . . Fifth and foremost: We have already gotten consent of the Governor to round up all stray, excess and incorrigible Nigras to be shipped to us under escort of the State Militia. . . . That's why we've stifled pessimism and are brimming wit' confidence that this full-scale concerted mobilization will ring down a jackpot of jigaboos 'fore light vanishes from sky!—

ANNOUNCER. Congratulations! What happens if it fails?

MAYOR. Don't even think THAT! Absolutely no reason to suspect it will.... (*Peers over shoulder, then whispers confidentially while placing hand over mouth by* ANNOUNCER's *imaginary mike.*) ... But speculating on the dark side of your question—if we don't turn up some by nightfall, it may be all over. The harm has already been done. You see the South has always been glued together by the uninterrupted presence of its darkies. No telling how unstuck we might git if things keep on like they have.—Wait a minute, it musta paid off already! Mission accomplished 'cause here's Jackson head a time wit' the word.... Well, Jackson, what's new?

JACKSON. Situation on the home front remains static, sir—can't uncover scent or shadow. The NAACP and all other Nigra front groups 'n' plotters deny any knowledge or connection wit' the missing Nigras. Maintained this even after appearing befo' a Senate Emergency Investigating Committee which subpoenaed 'em to Washington post haste and threw 'em in jail for contempt. A handful of Nigras who agreed to make spectacular appeals for ours to come back to us, have themselves mysteriously disappeared. But, worst news of all, sir, is our sister cities and counties, inside and outside the state, have changed their minds, fallen back on their promises and refused to lend us any Nigras, claiming they don't have 'nuff for themselves.

MAYOR. What 'bout Nigras promised by the Governor?!

JACKSON. Jailbirds and vagrants escorted here from chain-gangs and other reservations either revolted and escaped enroute or else vanished mysteriously on approaching our city limits.... Deterioration rapidly escalates, sir. Estimates predict we kin hold out only one more hour before overtaken by anarchistic turmoil.... Some citizens seeking haven elsewheres have already fled, but on last report were being forcibly turned back by armed sentinels in other cities who wanted no parts of 'em—claiming they carried a jinx.

MAYOR. That bad, huh?

JACKSON. Worse, sir... we've received at least five reports of plots on your life.

MAYOR. What?!—We've gotta act quickly then!

JACKSON. Run out of ideas, sir.

MAYOR. Think harder, boy! ˙

JACKSON. Don't have much time, sir. One measly hour, then all hell go'n' break loose.

MAYOR. Gotta think of something drastic, Jackson!

JACKSON. I'm dry, sir.

MAYOR. Jackson! Is there any planes outta here in the next hour?

JACKSON. All transportation's been knocked out, sir.

MAYOR. I thought so!

JACKSON. What were you contemplating, sir?

MAYOR. Don't ask me what I was contemplating! I'm still boss 'round here! Don't forgit it!

JACKSON. Sorry, sir.

MAYOR. . . . Hold the wire! . . . Wait a minute . . . ! Waaaaait a minute—GODAMNIT! All this time crapping 'round, diddling and fotsing wit' puny li'l' solutions—all the while neglecting our ace in the hole, our trump card! Most potent weapon for digging Nigras outta the woodpile!!! All the while right befo' our eyes! . . . Ass! Why didn't you remind me?!!!

JACKSON. What is it, sir?

MAYOR. . . . ME—THAT'S WHAT! ME! A personal appeal from ME! *Directly to them!* . . . Although we wouldn't let 'em march to the polls and express their affection for me through the ballot box, we've always known I'm held highest in their esteem. A direct address from their beloved Mayor! . . . If they's anywheres close within the sound of my voice, they'll shape up! Or let us know by a sign they's ready to!

JACKSON. You sure *that'll* turn the trick, sir?

MAYOR. As sure as my ancestors befo' me who knew that when they puckered their lips to whistle, ole Sambo was gonna come a-lickety-splitting to answer the call! ... That same chips-down blood courses through these Confederate gray veins of Henry R. E. Lee!!!

ANNOUNCER. I'm delighted to offer our network's facilities for such a crucial public interest address, sir. We'll arrange immediately for your appearance on an international hookup, placing you in the widest proximity to contact them wherever they may be.

MAYOR. Thank you, I'm very grateful. ...Jackson, re-grease the machinery and set wheels in motion. Inform townspeople what's being done. Tell 'em we're all in this together. The next hour is countdown. I demand absolute cooperation, city-wide silence and inactivity. I don't want the Nigras frightened if they're nearby. This is the most important hour in town's history. Tell 'em if one single Nigra shows up during hour of decision, victory is within sight. I'm gonna git 'em that one— maybe all! Hurry and crack to it! (ANNOUNCER *rushes out, followed by* JACKSON. *Blackout. Scene re-opens, with* MAYOR *seated, eyes front, spotlight illuminating him in semi-darkness. Shadowy figures stand in the background, prepared to answer phones or aid in any other manner.* MAYOR *waits patiently until "GO!" signal is given. Then begins, his voice combining elements of confidence, tremolo and gravity.*) Good evening.... Despite the fact that millions of you wonderful people throughout the nation are viewing and listening to this momentous broadcast— and I thank you for your concern and sympathy in this hour of our peril—I primarily want to concentrate my attention and address these remarks solely for the benefit of our departed Nigra friends who may be listening somewhere in our far-flung land to the sound of my voice.... If you are—it is with heart-felt emotion and fond memories of our happy association that I ask—"Where are you ... ?" Your absence has left a void in the bosom of every single man, woman and child of our great city. I tell you— you don't know what it means for us to wake up in the morning and discover that your cheerful, grinning, happy-go-lucky faces are missing!... From the depths of my heart, I can only meekly, humbly suggest what it means to me personally.... You see—the one face I will never be able to erase from my memory is the face— not of my Ma, not of Pa, neither wife or child—but the image of the first woman I came to love so well when just a wee lad—the vision of the first human I laid clear sight on at childbirth—the profile— better yet, the full face of my dear old ... Jemimah—God rest her soul.... Yes! My dear ole mammy, wit' her round ebony moonbeam gleaming down upon me in the crib, teeth shining, blood-red bandana standing starched, peaked and proud, gazing down upon me affectionately as she crooned me a Southern lullaby.... OH! It's a memorable picture I will eternally cherish in permanent treasure chambers of my heart, now and forever always.... Well, if this radiant image can remain so infinitely vivid to me all these many years after her unfortunate demise in the Po' folks home—THINK of the misery the rest of us must be suffering after being *freshly* denied your soothing presence?! We need ya. If you kin hear me, just contact this station 'n' I will welcome you back personally. Let me just tell you that since you eloped, nothing has been the same. How could it? You're part of us, you belong to us. Just give us a sign and we'll be contented that all is well.... Now if you've skipped away on a little fun-fest, we understand, ha, ha. We know you like a good time and we don't begrudge it to ya. Hell—er, er, we like a good time ourselves—who doesn't? ... In fact, think of all the good times we've had together, huh? We've had some real fun, you and us, yesiree!... Nobody knows better than you and I what fun we've had together. You singing us those old Southern coon songs and dancing those Nigra jigs and us clapping, prodding 'n' spurring you on! Lots of fun, huh?! . . . OH BOY! The times we've had together. . . . If you've snucked away for a bit of fun by yourself, we'll go 'long wit' ya—long as you let us know where you at so we won't be worried about you. . . . We'll go 'long wit' you long as you don't take the joke too far. I'll admit a joke is a joke and you've played a LULU! . . . I'm warning you, we can't stand much more horsing 'round from you! Business is business 'n' fun is fun! You've had your fun so now let's get down to business! Come on back, YOU HEAR ME!!! . . . If you been hoodwinked by agents of some foreign government, I've been authorized by the President of these United States to inform you that this liberty-loving Republic is prepared to rescue you from their clutches. Don't pay no 'tention to their sireen songs and atheistic promises! You better off under our control and you know it! . . . If you been bamboozled by rabble-rousing nonsense of your own so-called leaders, we prepared to offer same protection. Just call us up! Just give us a sign! . . . Come on, give us a sign . . . give us a sign— even a teeny-weeny one . . . ??!! (*Glances around checking on possible communications. A bevy of headshakes indicate no success.* MAYOR *returns to address with desperate fervor.*) Now look—you don't know what you doing! If you persist in this disobedience, you know all too well the consequences! We'll track you to the end of the earth, beyond the galaxy, across the stars! We'll capture you and chastise you with all the vengeance we command! 'N' you know only too well how stern we kin be when doublecrossed! The city, the state and the entire nation will crucify you for this unpardonable defiance! (*Checks again.*) No call . . . ? No sign . . . ? Time is running out! Deadline slipping past! They gotta respond! They gotta! (*Resuming.*) Listen to me! I'm begging y'all, you've gotta come back . . . ! LOOK GEORGE! (*Waves dirty rag aloft.*) I brought the rag you wax the car wit'. . . . Don't this bring back memories, George, of all the days you spent shining that automobile to shimmering perfection . . . ? And you, Rufus?! . . . Here's the shoe polisher and the brush! . . . 'Member, Rufus? . . . Remember the happy mornings you spent popping this rag and whisking this brush so furiously 'till it created music that was sympho-nee to the ear . . . ? And you—MANDY? . . . Here's the wastebasket you didn't dump this morning. I saved it just for you! . . . LOOK, all y'all out there . . . ?

(*Signals and a three-person procession parades one after the other before the imaginary camera.*)

DOLL WOMAN. (*Brandishing a crying baby [doll] as she strolls past and exits.*) She's been crying ever since you left, Caldonia . . .

MOP MAN. (*Flashing mop.*) It's been waiting in the same corner, Buster . . .

BRUSH MAN. (*Flagging toilet brush in one hand and toilet plunger in other.*) It's been dry ever since you left, Washington . . .

MAYOR. (*Jumping in on the heels of the last exit.*) Don't these things mean anything to y'all? By God! Are your memories so short?! Is there nothing sacred to ya? . . . Please come back, for my sake, please! All of you—even you questionable ones! I promise no harm will be done to you! Revenge is disallowed! We'll forgive everything! Just come on back and I'll git down on my knees— (*Immediately drops to knees.*) I'll be kneeling in the middle of Dixie Avenue to kiss the first shoe of the first one 'a you to show up. . . . *I'll smooch any other spot you request.* . . . Erase this nightmare 'n' we'll concede any demand you make, just come on back—please???!! . . . PLEEEEEEEZE?!!!

VOICE. (*Shouting.*) TIME!!!

MAYOR. (*Remaining on knees, frozen in a pose of supplication. After a brief, deadly silence, he whispers almost inaudibly.*) They wouldn't answer . . . they wouldn't answer . . .

(*Blackout as bedlam erupts offstage. Total blackness holds during a sufficient interval where offstage sound-effects create the illusion of complete pandemonium, followed by a diminution which trails off into an expressionistic simulation of a city coming to a strickened standstill: industrial machinery clanks to halt, traffic blares to silence, etc.* . . . *The stage remains dark and silent for a long moment, then lights re-arise on the* ANNOUNCER.)

ANNOUNCER. A pitiful sight, ladies and gentlemen. Soon after his unsuccessful appeal Mayor Lee suffered a vicious pummeling from the mob and barely escaped with his life. National Guardsmen and State Militia were impotent in quelling the fury of a town venting its frustration in an orgy of destruction—a frenzy of rioting, looting and all other aberrations of a town gone berserk. . . . Then—suddenly—as if a magic wand had been waved, madness evaporated and something more frightening replaced it: Submission. . . . Even whimperings ceased. The city: exhausted, benumbed.—Slowly its occupants slinked off into shadows, and by midnight, the town was occupied exclusively by zombies. The fight and life had been drained out. . . . Pooped. . . . Hope ebbed away as completely as the beloved, absent Negroes. . . . As our crew packed gear and crept away silently, we treaded softly—as if we were stealing away from a mausoleum. . . . The Face Of A Defeated City.

(*Blackout. Lights rise slowly at the sound of a rooster-crowing, signalling the approach of a new day, the next morning. Scene is same as opening of play.* CLEM *and* LUKE *are huddled over dazedly, trancelike. They remain so for a long count. Finally, a figure drifts on stage, shuffling slowly.*)

LUKE. (*Gazing in silent fascination at the approaching figure.*) . . . Clem . . . ? Do you see what I see or am I dreaming . . . ?

CLEM. It's a . . a Nigra, ain't it, Luke . . . ?

LUKE. Sure looks like one, Clem—but we better make sure—eyes could be playing tricks on us. . . . Does he still look like one to you, Clem?

CLEM. He still does, Luke—but I'm scared to believe—

LUKE. . . . Why . . . ? It looks like Rastus, Clem!

CLEM. Sure does, Luke . . . but we better not jump to no hasty conclusion . . .

LUKE. (*In timid softness.*) That you, Rastus . . . ?

RASTUS. (*Stepin Fetchit, Willie Best, Nicodemus, B. McQueen and all the rest rolled into one.*) Why . . . howdy . . . Mr. Luke . . . Mr. Clem . . .

CLEM. It is him, Luke! It is him!

LUKE. Rastus?

RASTUS. Yas . . . sah?

LUKE. Where was you yesterday?

RASTUS. (*Very, very puzzled.*) Yes . . . ter . . . day? . . . Yester . . . day . . . ? Why . . . right . . . here . . . Mr. Luke . . .

LUKE. No you warn't, Rastus, don't lie to me! Where was you yestiddy?

RASTUS. Why . . . I'm sure I was . . . Mr. Luke . . . Remember . . . I made . . . that . . . delivery for you . . .

LUKE. That was MONDAY, Rastus, yestiddy was TUESDAY.

RASTUS. Tues . . . day . . . ? You don't say . . . Well . . . well . . . well . . .

LUKE. Where was you 'n' all the other Nigras yesterday, Rastus?

RASTUS. I . . . thought . . . yestiddy . . . was Monday, Mr. Luke—I coulda swore it . . . ! . . . See how . . . things . . . kin git all mixed up? . . . I coulda swore it . . .

LUKE. TODAY is WEDNESDAY, Rastus. Where was you TUESDAY?

RASTUS. Tuesday . . . huh? That's somp'um . . . I . . . don't . . . remember . . . missing . . . a day . . . Mr. Luke . . . but I guess you right . . .

LUKE. Then where was you!!!???

RASTUS. Don't rightly know, Mr. Luke. I didn't know I had skipped a day—But that jist goes to show you how time kin fly, don't it, Mr. Luke . . . Uuh, uuh, uuh . . . (*He starts shuffling off, scratching head, a flicker of a smile playing across his lips.* CLEM *and* LUKE *gaze dumbfoundedly as he disappears.*)

LUKE. (*Eyes sweeping around in all directions.*) Well. . . . There's the others, Clem. . . . Back jist like they useta be. . . . Everything's same as always . . .

CLEM. ??? . . . . Is it . . . Luke . . . ! (*Slow fade.*)

CURTAIN

Topics for Further Study

1. The author of *Day of Absence* gets a message across to all who read or see the play. What message does he convey?

2. The play is a satirical fantasy. Would it have been more effective if it had been a serious, realistic drama?

3. The author recommends that the actors be Black and that they play their roles with white facial make-up and blond wigs. Why?

4. *Day of Absence* is an expressionistic drama. Expressionism has six distinguishing characteristics:

   (*a*) anti-realism;
   (*b*) abrupt, jerky dialogue;
   (*c*) short scenes;
   (*d*) characters representative of a class;
   (*e*) absence of realistic scenery, and the substitution of special lighting effects;
   (*f*) frequent use of mass effects.

By referring to incidents and stage directions, show that *Day of Absence* fulfills these distinguishing marks of expressionism.

5. What is the significance of the last two lines of the play?

6. Admittedly *Day of Absence* is a one-sided presentation. Would it be equally effective if both sides were presented?

7. Mr. Ward does not write in an expressionistic vein only. *Happy Ending*, which he also wrote and which premiered with *Day of Absence* in 1965, is a realistic comedy of social criticism which examines Black-white relations. Read and contrast it with *Day of Absence*.

8. Read an expressionistic drama and compare it to *Day of Absence*. Suggestions:

   R.U.R. by Karel Capek
   Red Roses for Me by Sean O'Casey
   The Emperor Jones by Eugene O'Neill
   The Adding Machine by Elmer Rice
   The Skin of Our Teeth by Thornton Wilder.

The Puerto Ricans in the United States

Spanish colonization of Puerto Rico began in 1508 under the leadership of Ponce de Leon, who was appointed governor. The native Indians whom the Spaniards encountered, members of the peaceful Taino tribe, were practically enslaved by the colonists to work in the gold mines and at other menial tasks. Many of the natives died, committed suicide, or fled to other islands. Remnants of their civilization, however, left a lasting, if minor, influence on the Puerto Rican culture that was to develop. It was the Indians, for example, who first introduced Europeans to products like corn, tobacco, and yucca, and many Taino words, such as *canoa*, *tabaco*, and *maiz*, were incorporated into both Spanish and English. Later, when large-scale agriculture was introduced, African slaves were imported to cultivate sugar cane, and they too became an important influence on the emerging culture.

By the eighteenth century virtually all Puerto Rico's military and commercial affairs were controlled by a handful of Spanish rulers. During the nineteenth century, when most of the Spanish colonies gained their independence, Puerto Rico remained under Spain's control. It was not until the conclusion of the Spanish-American War in 1898 that Spain finally gave up the island, ceding it to the United States.

The Jones-Shafforth Act in 1917 gave American citizenship to Puerto Ricans and made them subject to the draft. In 1950 President Truman signed the Puerto Rican Commonwealth Bill, giving Puerto Ricans the right to choose between commonwealth or colonial status. They voted for a commonwealth in June 1951, and Puerto Rico became a Free Associated State of the United States.

It was about 1910 that large numbers of Puerto Ricans began moving to the continent. At that time a little over 1,500 had come to New York City. By 1920 the number had risen to 12,000. Most came from Puerto Rico's rural areas, where mechanization of agricultural techniques had caused wide-scale unemployment. Crop failures also contributed to the exodus. Overpopulation, attractive stories about better opportunities in America, and ease in entering the United States because of United States citizenship were among the factors which led to the presence of 1,500,000 Puerto Ricans on the mainland by 1970. Whereas the early migrants worked almost exclusively as farm laborers, they now hold occupations in such areas as the garment industry, food trades, and building and service trades. About 60 percent of the Puerto Rican migrants live in New York City and its environs; other large communities are found in Philadelphia, Chicago, Los Angeles, and San Francisco.

When Puerto Ricans came to the mainland, they brought their own cultural heritage and social values. But whereas on the Spanish-speaking island they were the majority, on the mainland they have become one of the minority groups to whom English is a second language. Some do not, unlike many other immigrant groups who came to America to improve their lot, intend to remain on mainland United States for the rest of their lives. Many Puerto Ricans have come to make a better living than on the island, but they hope eventually to return there, to buy some property, and to live out their years where they were born. Their children have had a greater problem because only until recently they had to attend schools where only English was spoken. In recent years, however, federal funds under Title V11 ESA have been used for bilingual and bicultural education. Pilot experiments are taking place in many communities in which communication skills, arithmetic, science, and other subjects are being taught in both English and Spanish.

Gradually Puerto Ricans are assuming roles of leadership and contributing to the Puerto Rican community as well as to the entire citizenry. Herman Badillo served as borough president of the Bronx, is currently in Congress, and ran for mayor of the City of New York in 1973. Roberto Clemente, a star of the Pittsburgh Pirates, was killed in a plane crash while on a mercy mission to Managua, bearing aid to those stricken by the earthquake there in 1972.

The Puerto Ricans have a rich cultural background, essentially Spanish in origin. A Puerto Rican theater has existed in New York City for several years where plays have been performed in both English and Spanish before tens of thousands of spectators in city parks and elsewhere. The annual Puerto Rican Day provides an opportunity for a rich cultural display including national music, dancing, costumes, and cooking. Actresses like Miriam Colon have won great praise for their performances on both the English- and Spanish-speaking stage.

Since Spanish is the first language in *El Barrio*, as the area in Spanish Harlem in New York City is called, it is natural that we find some Puerto Rican authors in New York writing in Spanish, such as Thomas Martinez Ruiz, who wrote *Primavera en Nueva York* (Spring in New York), a volume of poems written in Spanish with occasional attempts at English.

There is also a group of writers in Puerto Rico who write in their native Spanish about Puerto Ricans in America. Among them are Isabel Cuchi Coll, whose three-act play, *La Familia de Justo Malgeno*, published in Spain in 1963, deals with the trials and tribulations of a Puerto Rican family in New York. Francisco Arrivi, director of the theater program of the Instituto de Cultura Puertorriquena of San Juan, has written *El Murciélago* (The Bat), which takes place in New York, with a flashback to Puerto Rico, and *Medusas en la Bahia*, which takes place in San Juan, with a flashback to Washington.

The Puerto Ricans have been the subject of numerous sociological and economic studies. Some of the important ones worth reading are *The Puerto Rican Journey: New York's Newest Immigrants* by C. Wright Mills; *The Newcomers: Negroes and Puerto Ricans in a Changing Metropolis* by Clarence Senior and Rose Golden; and *La Vida* by Oscar Handlin and Oscar Lewis. An excellent pamphlet which is rich in detail and interestingly written is *The Puerto Ricans: A Resource Unit for Teachers*, published in 1972 by the Anti-Defamation League of B'nai B'rith in New York City. It contains one of the most complete bibliographies on Puerto Ricans in America, and is required reading for all those interested in the many facets of their personalities, ideals, and aspirations.

Suggested Reading

Books about the Puerto Ricans

Fitzpatrick, Joseph P. *Puerto Rican Americans.* Englewood Cliffs, New Jersey: Prentice-Hall, 1971. A scholarly work about the Puerto Ricans on the mainland, with a special focus on New York City. It concerns the island's background, the impact on the mainland, and the people's process of adjustment.

Handlin, Oscar. *The Newcomers.* Cambridge, Mass.: Harvard University Press, 1959. An illuminating comparison of the experience of Blacks and Puerto Ricans, as the newest migrants to New York City, with earlier immigrant groups.

Wagenheim, Kal. *Puerto Rico: A Profile.* New York: Praeger, 1971. A study of the geographical, cultural, social, and economic features of Puerto Rico. It recounts the history of the island from its discovery in the sixteenth century to the present day, with emphasis on the influences of Spanish and American domination and the movement for self-government and independence.

Plays about the Puerto Ricans

Anderson, Walt. *Me Candido!* in Oakes, Theresa and Weiss, M. Jerry, eds. *The Unfinished Journey.* New York: McGraw-Hill, 1967.

Laurents, Arthur; Bernstein, Leonard; and Sondheim, Stephen. *West Side Story.* New York: Random House, 1958. Also in paperback with William Shakespeare's *Romeo and Juliet.* New York: Dell, 1965.

The Oxcart

In *The Oxcart* René Marqués portrays many of the hopes and aspirations of Puerto Ricans preparing to come to the mainland, and the heartaches and disappointments they suffer when they arrive here. The play captures many poignant aspects of the total spectrum of the Puerto Rican experience. There are excellent portraits of natives who have a strong attachment for the land; of those who seek a better life away from the land in a large city; and of those whose main hope is that this better life is to be found on the mainland, a hope that is only to be dashed by the squalor and discrimination facing them when they arrive. Finally, there is represented the renewed vision of hope in those who ultimately choose to return to the island, a difficult decision faced by many thousands who come to the mainland filled with hope, but find only despair.

René Marqués wrote *The Oxcart* in Spanish in 1951 and it was performed in that language in 1953 both in Puerto Rico and in New York. When the English version opened in New York at the Greenwich Mews Theater on December 19, 1966, the well-known Puerto Rican actress, Miriam Colon, who had created the part of Juanita in the 1953 Spanish production in New York, was again in that role. Another of Puerto Rico's foremost actresses, Lucy Boscana, played the role of Doña Gabriela, as she had done in the Spanish production in San Juan.

The Oxcart was both a critical and popular success. With a run of eighty-nine performances, it was the fifth longest-running off-Broadway play of the 1966-1967 season. In August 1967, through the efforts of Miss Colon, *The Oxcart* was revived by the newly created Puerto Rican Traveling Theater. Free outdoor performances were given in various parks and playgrounds throughout New York City, giving thousands of people who had never seen a live play an opportunity to see a drama that had much significance for them.

RENÉ MARQUÉS was born on October 4, 1919, in the city of Arecibo on the north coast of Puerto Rico. He studied agronomy at the College of Agriculture in Mayaguez and later worked for two years in the Department of Agriculture in San Juan. Having developed an interest in literature, he left his position and in 1946 traveled to Madrid, where he studied classical and contemporary theater at the university. Upon returning to Puerto Rico, he founded and directed a small theater group in his native city of Arecibo. The Rockefeller Foundation gave him a grant in 1948 which enabled him to come to New York to study playwriting at Columbia University.

In 1950 Marqués returned to Puerto Rico, where he wrote educational materials, including films for the government. The following year he helped found The Experimental Theater of the Ateneo in San Juan and was its director for three years. That same year he wrote *The Oxcart*, which was performed two years later in San Juan and in New York. He won a Guggenheim grant in 1957 and spent that year in New York writing his first novel, *La vispera del hombre* (The Eve of Man).

A number of themes are predominant in the writings of Marqués. The importance of the land as opposed to the mechanized society of the city is well represented in *The Oxcart*. *Los soles truncos* (The Truncated Suns, 1958) reflects his concern for the difficult task of preserving the desirable elements of the Spanish heritage from the onslaughts of foreign contemporary values and ways of living. This concern often manifests itself in Marqués's work in terms of the guilt feelings he portrays in many of his characters. Many of them—Luis, for example, in *The Oxcart*—feel guilty because they are torn between the values of their own largely rural and Spanish-influenced culture and the conflicting ones of another civilization to which they are tied by political and economic necessity, but from whose crass commercialism they instinctively withdraw. This guilt feeling is most clearly portrayed in *El apartamiento* (The Apartment, 1964), a play written in the style of the Theater of the Absurd, which represents the paradoxical situation which many nationalist thinkers believe the island occupies.

Another major theme is his strong belief in complete political independence for Puerto Rico. Marqués was the first Puerto Rican author to utilize the revolutionary activities of the Nationalist movement as material for his plays and stories. In three of his plays—*Palm Sunday* (the only play he has written in English, 1959), *La muerte no entrara en palacio* (Death Shall Not Enter the Palace, 1956), and *Un nino azul para esa sombra* (A Blue Child for That Shadow, 1960)— the Nationalist movement received serious attention. He has treated it comically in *La casa sin reloj* (The House without a Clock, 1961). In his historical drama *Mariana o el alba* (Mariana or the Dawn, 1965) he uses an actual abortive revolt against Spain in the nineteenth century to draw a parallel with the fight for complete independence from the United States today.

The Oxcart

BY

RENÉ MARQUÉS

CHARACTERS

CHAGUITO
DOÑA GABRIELA
JUANITA
DON CHAGO
LUIS
GERMANA
LITO
MATILDE
DOÑA ISABEL
PACO
LIDIA
MR. PARKINGTON

SCENES

ACT ONE: A rural district in the mountains outside of San Juan, Puerto Rico.
ACT TWO: "La Perla," slum district beside the ancient fortress of El Morro in San Juan, Puerto Rico.
ACT THREE: Spanish District in the Bronx, New York City, U.S.A.

The time is the present.

The Oxcart by René Marqués, translated by Charles Pilditch, is used by permission of Charles Scribner's Sons. Copyright © 1969 René Marqués.

CAUTION: Professionals and amateurs are hereby warned that *The Oxcart* being fully protected under the copyright laws of the United States of America, the British Empire, including the Dominion of Canada, and all other countries of the Copyright Union, is subject to a royalty. All inquiries regarding professional, amateur, motion picture, recitation, public reading, radio and television broadcasting rights should be addressed to René Marqués, in care of Charles Scribner's Sons.

The Oxcart

ACT ONE

Interior of a little house belonging to country folk. The main room serves as living room, dining room, and bedroom at night for those members of the family who can not be accommodated in the only bedroom of the house. The little house, made from good, native wood left over from more prosperous times, has been repaired with tarpaper and cheap, imported boards. The roof is made of beaver board and thatch. The rafters are of mangrove wood.

At the rear, a dividing wall with a door in the middle leading to the bedroom. This bedroom has an open window, invisible to the audience, the light from which comes into the main room. At the left, the main door is open onto the front yard. At the right, foreground, a low door leads to the shed where the kitchen is. The walls are unpainted, darkened by mildew and time.

When the curtain rises, no furniture or persons are in sight. To the right, near the door to the kitchen, there is an old, broken-down table. The only thing that keeps it standing is the support it gets from the wall. This is the only piece of furniture in the house. On the table and scattered about the floor in a disorderly fashion are boxes, packages, bundles, some packed, others half packed. Together they give the impression of someone moving. We don't know if the tenants are arriving or leaving, but the house has the sad appearance of unoccupied dwellings. On the walls are religious scenes taken chiefly from Catholic almanacs. The characters will sit on the floor or on the boxes and bundles, or simply will squat down on their heels.

The road crosses behind the house, parallel to it.

It is five o'clock on a September afternoon.

Right and left, that of the spectator.

CHAGUITO *enters from the left, barefoot, carrying a cardboard carton. The carton has a cover, and several holes have been punched in its sides.* CHAGUITO *enters cautiously, looks distrustingly toward the rear and toward the kitchen door. Then he tiptoes across the stage, puts the box on the floor beside the table, mixing it in with the other boxes. He carefully puts a sack over the box and starts to leave, still on tiptoe. From the kitchen* DOÑA GABRIELA'S *voice is heard calling:*

DA. GABRIELA. (*In a bad mood.*) Chaguito! (CHAGUITO *stops abruptly and then reacts by running out and disappearing through the door at the left.* DA. GABRIELA *enters through the door at the right. She carries some small kitchen utensils which she puts in one of the boxes. She is muttering to herself, angrily.*) Is there no end to all this! And that devilish kid, where's he off to now? (*Calling.*) Chaguitooo! (*Goes to the door at left.*) Chaguitooo! Look at him out there! Answer when I call you! Leave that damn top alone, and come wash your face! Come on, now, it's getting late. (*Coming back.*) Oh, that boy!

JUANITA. (*Her voice coming from the back-*

room.) Mamá, where are my pink panties?

DA. GABRIELA. On the nail in the wall where the bed was.

JUANITA. (*From the backroom, still invisible.*) And my high-heeled shoes? I can't find them.

DA. GABRIELA. (*Placing several old books in a box.*) In the trunk, in the trunk. What's got into you today? You're running around in there like a crazy cockroach. Now hurry up and get dressed. (*Muttering.*) Anyway, I dunno why you wanna wear high heels. We gotta walk more than two miles over all those stones to get to the highway. You'll wear 'em out!

JUANITA. (*Still invisible in the backroom.*) Don't be silly. If Cico's going to take our things in his oxcart, we can go along with 'em, in the cart.

DA. GABRIELA. All right, all right, lazy. Come along now, and don't worry about the oxcart. There's still a lot to do. (*Goes back to the door at the left.*) Chaguitoo! Chaguitoo!

JUANITA. (*Entering from the rear, combing her hair briskly.*) Ay, mamá, not so loud. You'll break my eardrums.

DA. GABRIELA. (*Annoyed.*) I'll break 'em for you all right if you don't go get that brat for me. Luis'll be here any minute, and nothing's ready. (*Impatiently.*) Leave your hair alone, and do as I say!

JUANITA. All right, I'm going. (*Shouting as loud as her mother, or louder.*) Chaguitooo! Chaguitoo!

(*Goes out left.*)

DA. GABRIELA. (*Packing and talking out loud.*) What a mess! Your kids get a bright idea and then you get stuck with all the work! Luis will have my head if he don't find everything ready to go when he gets here. Oh, that one. He's the most trouble of all. (*Sorry.*) God forgive me, I'm always complaining. Poor Luis! he tries so hard. He's the best one of all. I hope to God he's found that damn rooster. Now, where's my saint's statue? I don't remember packing it already.

DON CHAGO. (*Entering from the left with a bundle of clothes.*) Lose something, girl?

DA. GABRIELA. (*Answering automatically.*) My wooden saint. (*Reacting.*) Oh, it's you! I thought you were up in Río Arriba, at Tomás' place. I'm glad you came back. Have you changed your mind?

DON CHAGO. No, daughter.

(*Squats on his heels beside the door.*)

DA. GABRIELA. (*Recovering her bad humor.*) Oh, father, you're still as stubborn as a mule.

DON CHAGO. Well, what d'you expect? Like they say, you can't teach an old dog new tricks. Anyhow, old people like me are always in the way.

DA. GABRIELA. Maybe *now*. 'Cause when you lived with us, you were never in the way.

DON CHAGO. I wasn't in the way *here*. But *there*, where you people're going, God only knows.

DA. GABRIELA. You think I'm so dumb I don't know what's wrong with you?

DON CHAGO. Well, maybe you . . .

DA. GABRIELA. You don't wanna leave this little piece o' land.

DON CHAGO. It's just that I kin always find somethin' to do here. Up there, an empty old man like me couldn't do anything.

DA. GABRIELA. Oh, don't be silly, father. You're just a softhearted, spoiled old man. That's what's the matter with you. You're afraid of a change.

DON CHAGO. (*Always pleasant.*) Afraid? Maybe so. The years make us afraid.

DA. GABRIELA. And what did my brother Tomás say?

DON CHAGO. What could he say! That it was all right, of course.

DA. GABRIELA. Then everything's settled? You're going to live with them?

DON CHAGO. Yes.

DA. GABRIELA. I don't get it. You left day before yesterday, and here you are back again. Why come back if you're not comin' with us?

DON CHAGO. Eh, no reason. Just to be with you today.

DA. GABRIELA. And so just for that you walked almost ten miles with your asthma.

DON CHAGO. I don't walk with my asthma. I've got strong legs.

DA. GABRIELA. (*Pointing to his bundle of clothes.*) And to come see us off you brought your clothes along.

DON CHAGO. (*Pretending.*) What clothes? Oh, yeah. I didn't want to leave 'em up there while I was gone. I don't like people goin' through my things.

DA. GABRIELA. Do you think for a minute they're goin' to put up with all your nonsense? Tomás' wife won't stand for anything. How did she treat you?

DON CHAGO. Good enough.

DA. GABRIELA. She couldn't stand you before.

DON CHAGO. Well, I suppose by now she's used to bein' my daughter-in-law.

DA. GABRIELA. Hmmf.

DON CHAGO. What's that?

DA. GABRIELA. Nothing. But there's somethin' funny here. (*Interrupting herself.*) Oh, look! Here's my saint. Must've been Juanita who put it in this box. Stupid! She puts it in with the pots and pans to get broke.

DON CHAGO. And what's the difference if it gets broke?

DA. GABRIELA. What d'you mean what's the difference?

DON CHAGO. (*Shrugging his shoulders.*) Well, anyway, I dunno why you wanna lug that piece o' junk around with you.

DA. GABRIELA. How can you dare talk like that about mother's St. Anthony statue?

DON CHAGO. Yes, I know. It's the one that helped your mother land me.

DA. GABRIELA. Aha. As if you weren't glad she did.

DON CHAGO. (*Slyly.*) That could be. I don't remember any more.

DA. GABRIELA. Yeah, yeah. You forget very easy when you want to.

DON CHAGO. That's one of the few advantages of bein' old. Now, I'd like to know what your husband'd say about that old statue.

DA. GABRIELA. He wouldn't say anything. He was my husband, may he rest in peace, the one who "landed" me. Ha. I gave him a hard enough time to convince me.

DON CHAGO. (*Laughing.*) That night I caught you both under the mango tree—you were pretty convinced then.

DA. GABRIELA. (*Furious.*) Now don't talk fresh, old man. Have respect for the dead.

DON CHAGO. And the living. After all, the dead can't feel or suffer.

DA. GABRIELA. All right, that's enough. You always had it in for my poor dead husband.

DON CHAGO. I had it in for him *before* he was dead; afterwards, no. While he was alive we had to help him out by mortgaging the farm, acre by acre. And now that he's dead, look what he's left your kids. Plenty of problems but not a piece o' land big enough to plant potatoes in.

DA. GABRIELA. He had a hard time, that's all. First the hurricane destroyed the coffee crop. Then the sugar cane spread up to the mountains. And he never understood sugar cane. He didn't like it. He always dreamed about coffee. He didn't get along so good with people, neither. Things were changing in the mountains, but he didn't realize it in time. And he was so unlucky in politics—always on the losing side. He never had a district commissioner to protect him. Some people are born lame or crippled or hunchbacked. My husband was born under the wrong star. And that's as bad as a hunchback—no one can cure it.

DON CHAGO. Ah, daughter. It's very easy to blame the stars for man's misfortunes. But the God's truth is that on account o' him, you people are bein' kicked out today.

DA. GABRIELA. What d'you want us to do? The mortgage came due. Where are we supposed to get the money from?

DON CHAGO. The farm was so pretty. And the well has the best water in these parts. Thirty acres it was. I always had the best sweet potato patch on the side of the hill. Where's Luis?

DA. GABRIELA. He's out lookin' for that big rooster. He was goin' to sell it this morning, and when he went to look for it, it wasn't there. It seems like the earth just swallowed it up.

DON CHAGO. The earth don't swallow up roosters. More likely some neighbor used it for soup.

DA. GABRIELA. We don't have thieves around here. No one could've taken it. And Luis is fit to be tied.

DON CHAGO. Chaguito's the one who oughta be mad. He loved that old rooster like it was a girl.

DA. GABRIELA. Yes, the poor kid wanted to take it with us. But Luis said we couldn't keep it down there, that it was better to sell it here. So now Chaguito's happy, but Luis is the one who's fuming.

DON CHAGO. Luis is young and strong. He could've managed.

DA. GABRIELA. I just told you he went to look for the rooster.

DON CHAGO. I'm not talkin' about the rooster. I mean the farm.

DA. GABRIELA. Well, he tried hard enough. But he wants to leave. He says it's not right to be a peasant all your life. (*Interrupting herself.*) Look how he's got that shirt all torn! Where'd I put my needle and thread?

(*Looks, finds needle and thread, begins to mend shirt.*)

DON CHAGO. You can say what you like, but we're all just farm people. I've been a farmer all my life: before I got married, then on your mother's farm, then on the part that was left to you. And now I'm still a farmer wherever I can make a dime. What's wrong with bein' a farmer? It's the only way to be close to the land.

DA. GABRIELA. (*Mending.*) That's all right for you. You can't live if your hands aren't full of earth. But Luis wants more than that.

DON CHAGO. And you?

DA. GABRIELA. I have to go wherever he goes.

DON CHAGO. You really love that boy.

DA. GABRIELA. I don't know what you're talking about. I've loved him almost from the day he was born.

DON CHAGO. Yes, like he was your own son.

DA. GABRIELA. (*Stops mending.*) Quiet. You know we don't talk about that in this house.

DON CHAGO. Oh, daughter, you can't hide the whole sky with one hand. As far as I'm concerned, everybody knows about it.

DA. GABRIELA. (*Starting her work again.*) As long as *he* doesn't find out . . .

(*Shouts are heard from* CHAGUITO *and* JUANITA. *They enter from the left, shouting and fighting.*)

CHAGUITO. No, damn it! Let me go, fresh, let me go!

JUANITA. You're gonna learn to mind me. The way you made me chase you! Ay! You dog, don't you bite me! Mamá, make him stop!

DA. GABRIELA. (*Separating them and grabbing* CHAGUITO *by an ear.*) Damn brat! Be still! Just look at you! (*Smacks him on the head.*) Get out in the kitchen and scrub that dirty face.

JUANITA. (*Taking advantage of her mother's protection.*) Take that, you stinker! Pimple puss!

(*Hits him with her hand.*)

CHAGUITO. (*Twisting furiously in his mother's arms and kicking out at* JUANITA, *who easily avoids him.*) I know what's the matter with you. You're mad at me 'cause I caught you makin' out the other day with that sick lookin' friend o' yours.

JUANITA. Liar. Gossip.

DA. GABRIELA. (*Pushing* CHAGUITO *to the right.*) To the kitchen, I said.

(CHAGUITO *disappears through the door at the right.*)

JUANITA. You see, mamá? Nobody can do anything with that kid. He's got no respect for anyone. I had to chase him all the way to the cave.

DON CHAGO. (*Suddenly somber.*) The cave!

JUANITA. Yes, he went in there 'cause

he knows I'm afraid of the bats. And then he started to throw stones at me. 'Till I finally grabbed one of his feet. Look at the way I look!

DON CHAGO. He's right, though. The Indian Cave makes a good shelter.

DA. GABRIELA. (*Dryly.*) What sick lookin' friend?

JUANITA. (*With an innocent face.*) Who d'you mean?

DA. GABRIELA. Don't play dumb. The one Chaguito saw you with.

JUANITO. Oh, I don't know . . .

(CHAQUITO *sticks his wet face through the kitchen door.*)

CHAQUITO. Miguel, the one who works for Don Tello.

(*Disappears.*)

DA. GABRIELA. Oh, so that's the one? And how long has this been goin' on?

JUANITA. He's lying. Don't listen to that shameless brat. It's all lies!

DA. GABRIELA. (*Dryly, with a hint of a threat.*) Since when . . . ?

JUANITA. Well . . . For about a month. But don't get the wrong idea. He had his eye on me for a long time. Then one day he spoke to me.

DA. GABRIELA. And what about that "makin' out"?

JUANITA. (*Sincerely indignant.*) More of that brat's lies. Just lies. What happened was that one day Miguel took my hand and Chaquito saw us. Since then that pimple puss spends all his time bothering me and saying he's gonna tell you.

DA. GABRIELA. And what else?

JUANITA. That's all.

DA. GABRIELA. (*Hitting her.*) So you let the first man who passes take you by the hand, eh?

JUANITA. (*Crying.*) That's not true. Miguel has good intentions. He said he was gonna talk to you.

DA. GABRIELA. (*Changing her tone.*) He said that?

JUANITA. Yes. And that we were going to live on Don Tello's farm.

DA. GABRIELA. But married, right?

JUANITA. Well, sure. I suppose so.

DA. GABRIELA. Supposing won't get you anywhere. If he really wants to marry you, let him get the license. But this one's probably as shameless as the rest of them. Nowadays the young people around here don't get married according to the law of God.

DON CHAGO. And who's gonna marry them? They say the priest'd rather play ball in town than climb up here. In my day priests were really priests.

DA. GABRIELA. Thank God we're gettin' out of this place.

DON CHAGO. And do you think people get married more in the towns than here?

DA. GABRIELA. At least there the priest is always at hand. And if he's not, I'll be there to fetch him.

DON CHAGO. In my time you didn't have to fetch him. The priest was always into everything, even your dinner. I remember Don Hilario. When you least expected him, there he was, riding on his old donkey. But he worked hard, Don Hilario, fighting with the Devil. Sometimes the Devil even tempted him. But as a priest, he was a hard-working man. They say today's priests use perfume and even wear silk underwear.

(*Laughs.*)

DA. GABRIELA. Don't talk like that, father. God'll punish you.

DON CHAGO. *I'm* not the one who says it. That popular song says it, don't you remember? (*Starts to sing.*) "The bishop is . . ."

DA. GABRIELA. (*Trying not to laugh, trying to be strict.*) Cut that out, old man, cut that out. I won't let you get us all condemned. You know that song's been forbidden.

DON CHAGO. That's right, my girl, they forbid everything. Even music. In my day the government didn't bother about forbidding things. We had a lot of fun then, letting off steam and criticizing with music. Today nobody would take the chance. Those "misters" in the government are more dead than alive and don't even know how to laugh. And since they don't know

how to, they don't want us to have any fun. They want us to be as spineless and dull as they are. But I'm too old now to start gettin' so serious.
(*Laughs.*)
JUANITA. Heavens, grandpa, you're just like a kid!
DON CHAGO. Yes, ma'am, the world is upside down. They say us old folks are like kids, but it's the kids today who seem like old fogies.
DA. GABRIELA. I wonder what's happened to Luis? He should've been back by now.
DON CHAGO. Now there's a perfect example for you, that Luis of yours. Have you ever seen a more serious kid? He's old before his time. I've never seen him have a real good laugh.
DA. GABRIELA. He just don't like to talk too much. But he's a good boy.
DON CHAGO. I didn't say he wasn't. But I can't understand people who don't laugh. There must be something wrong with their souls. Something that makes them as sorrowful as the dead. And that's against the law of God. God is very wise. He gives us life to enjoy it and then, when He gets tired, He cuts us short with death so we'll keep quiet. That's how it goes, daughter, so I'm gonna keep waggin' my tongue and showin' my old, toothless mouth 'till He shuts it for me.
DA. GABRIELA. Times change, father. Boys today got more worries than we had. And they got ambitions.
DON CHAGO. Non-conformity—that's what they got. Before, the man worked and the woman got married. And nobody complained.
DA. GABRIELA. But it's not so easy to work today. (*Looking slyly at* JUANITA.) Or to get married.
DON CHAGO. Oh, I don't know; you still have that statue . . .
DA. GABRIELA. That's enough about my St. Anthony. Where'd you get the idea he's not good for anythin' but catchin' a husband? (*To* JUANITA.) And you, what'd you put him in there for, with all the pots and pans? What're you doin' there in the doorway lookin' outside anyway? You dumb or somethin'? Get busy packing. You got all your clothes ready?
JUANITA. (*Shrugging her shoulders.*) Bah. I'm coming. For all the clothes I've got . . .
(*Enters the backroom.*)
DA. GABRIELA. Hah. Who d'you think you are? The governor's wife? (*To* DON CHAGO.) Nowadays people don't even know how to be poor.
DON CHAGO. (*Laughing.*) We'll have to teach them!
DA. GABRIELA. No. What they need to be taught is pride.
DON CHAGO. There's very little o' that left. And the little there is, I dunno where they've hid it.
CHAGUITO. (*His voice from the kitchen.*) Gimme a five dollar bill and you'll see how fast I get you some, old man.
DA. GABRIELA. Shut up, you.
DON CHAGO. Leave him alone. It's the God's honest truth. (*Raising his voice and speaking to* CHAGUITO, *who is in the kitchen.*) You're only repeating more or less what you hear all over. It's the same thing on the radio in the bar, and in the newspapers, and from the schoolteachers, and the politicians in the capital.
DA. GABRIELA. And what's all this got to do with pride?
DON CHAGO. Well, just that everybody's preachin' the dollar, daughter. To have pride today you gotta have money. That's as clear as daylight. Before, you could be poor and still have dignity. And you know why? 'Cause the poor had somethin' to believe in. Some believed in God, others believed in the land, others believed in men. Today they don't let us believe in anythin'. Today they just teach your kids to believe in money . . . and what they call science. They say they kin see all our ills now through that tube they call a microscope. And all the good things they promise us are supposed to be in that piece o' green paper called a dollar. But never anythin' about the heart. Nobody remembers the heart. And the heart dries

up like an old bean. Oh, daughter, you can't have dignity or pride with your heart shriveled up like a bean!

DA. GABRIELA. Look who's talkin'! A man who makes fun even of the saints. You don't believe in anythin'.

DON CHAGO. I believe in the land. Once I believed in men. But now I only believe in the land.

DA. GABRIELA. Well, the land's not gonna help you none, old man. Especially when it's not yours.

DON CHAGO. Maybe so. The truth is I get along okay. And the land, whether it's mine or somebody else's, is still the land. It's got the same color, and the same smell when it rains, and it lets you work it like a humble woman. And it's better than a woman 'cause it gives birth without a lotta noise and fuss. And what's more, it bears what you want it to.

(LUIS *enters from the left*.)

LUIS. Well, is everything ready? Hi, grandpa; your blessing.

DON CHAGO. May God bless you, my son.

LUIS. (*To* DA. GABRIELA.) Did you put my books with my clothes?

DA. GABRIELA. Yes. Everything's about ready, Luis. And the oxcart?

LUIS. It'll be here any minute. Come on now, old girl, hurry up. (*To* DON CHAGO.) Weren't you up at Uncle Tomás' place?

DON CHAGO. Yes, I was up there.

LUIS. And what happened? Have you decided to come with us?

DON CHAGO. No . . . I'll stay out here in the country.

LUIS. I don't see why. But if that's what you want, it's okay with me.

DON CHAGO. What happened to that rooster? Your mother tells me you lost it.

LUIS. Oh, don't mention that. I couldn't find it. And just my luck. Miguel, Don Tello's helper, came to buy it just now. He was gonna give me three dollars for it. He's still waitin', there in the bar. He says if I find it before five o'clock I should take it to him and he'll still buy it. But I can't find it.

DA. GABRIELA. Three dollars is a good price.

(JUANITA *hears the name* "*Miguel*" *and sticks her head through the door*.)

JUANITA. Where'd you say Don Tello's helper was waiting?

DA. GABRIELA. (*Sharply*.) Where it don't matter to you.

(JUANITA *disappears quickly*.)

LUIS. (*Disturbed*.) A rooster can't just disappear like that, in thin air.

CHAGUITO. (*Sticking his head through the kitchen door*.) That's what I say. It sounds like witchcraft. Somebody probably put a spell on that rooster.

(*Disappears*.)

DA. GABRIELA. Listen, Luis. Did you know that helper of Don Tello's, that Miguel, had his eye on Juanita?

LUIS. I thought I smelt somethin' goin' on there.

DA. GABRIELA. You've got a better nose than me. Why didn't you tell me?

LUIS. Well, I didn't want to be too hasty. (*Alarmed*.) Why? Did anythin' happen?

DA. GABRIELA. No, not yet, it seems. But if we weren't gettin' out o' here now, somethin' could've happened.

LUIS. Don't exaggerate, mother. The fellow seems serious. Besides, Juanita's old enough to get engaged.

DA. GABRIELA. Engaged, yes. Even married. But not anythin' else.

LUIS. Don't worry. That's why I'm here. To watch out for my sister. Not Miguel or anybody's gonna try anythin' funny with her if they know they've gotta answer to me.

(CHAGUITO *enters from the kitchen. He has washed his feet, arms, and face. He is still wet*.)

LUIS. And you? You haven't changed your clothes yet?

CHAGUITO. The women spend all their time pushin' me around. And you never know what they want. When're we goin'?

LUIS. Right away. We're still waitin' for the cart.

CHAGUITO. (*Alarmed.*) The cart? (*Offended.*) We're goin' to San Juan in an oxcart? (*Rebelling.*) Well, I won't go!

LUIS. No, stupid. We're goin' in the cart as far as the highway. From there we can catch a public cab for San Juan.

CHAGUITO. Oh, that's better! 'Cause I'm not gonna let the city folks make a monkey outta me. Ha. A fine sight we'd make in an oxcart, like old-fashioned peasants.

DON CHAGO. No, we all know you're one o' them modern peasants who rides around in a fancy car.

DA. GABRIELA. All right, get dressed, boy, get dressed. Move!

CHAGUITO. Fancy car or not, at least I've been to the city more times than you.

DON CHAGO. Right you are, kid. (*Laughs.*) I don't deny it.

DA. GABRIELA. Well, now. I'm gonna make you some coffee.

(*Exits to kitchen.*)

DON CHAGO. It'll be the last we'll have here. I'm gonna miss it. So, Luis, tell me about the new house. What's it like?

LUIS. Well, it's nothin' outta this world. It's pretty small and run down. But it's got a lotta advantages.

DON CHAGO. (*Jesting.*) Really!

LUIS. Right! There's a spigot almost right next to the house. You don't have to bother goin' so far for water like here.

DON CHAGO. Does it have a garden?

LUIS. No, no garden.

DON CHAGO. Aha! A house without land. I knew it. And the street's probably right on top o' you.

LUIS. No, the street's far enough away.

DON CHAGO. Well, then it's gotta have some land, even if it's only enough to plant a row o' beans.

LUIS. No, the house isn't on land.

DON CHAGO. You don't say! So they build houses in the air now?

LUIS. No, grandpa, it's just that it's all stones and rock, understand? Since it's right next to the sea. . . . And the houses are real close together 'cause there's not much space.

DON CHAGO. It must get awful hot.

LUIS. Not a bit! It's real windy. Didn't I tell you it was right next to the sea? The street I told you about is much higher. A real good street called a boulevard. To get in or out of the neighborhood, we gotta use that street called a boulevard.

DON CHAGO. Aren't there any roads in the neighborhood itself?

LUIS. Well, they're more like alleys. Real steep, see? 'Cause the neighborhood is all downhill.

DON CHAGO. And whatta they call that damn neighborhood?

LUIS. It's called—La Perla.

DON CHAGO. La Perla? (*Laughs.*) Ah, jees! A pearl that goes downhill. That's a good one!

LUIS. (*Enthusiastically.*) What's the difference what it's called! Who cares if it's uphill or down! It's in San Juan, in the capital. Where there's opportunity for everybody. Where you don't have to live like a miserable peasant. Where there's good schools for Chaguito. Where there's work for me and Juanita. Where life'll be easier for the old lady. I told you already she won't have to break her back cartin' water. And there's electricity.

DON CHAGO. That don't have to be paid for, I suppose.

LUIS. And we'll live real close to the sea.

DON CHAGO. Bah, the sea, the sea. Salt water that's good for nothin'.

LUIS. Well, it's good for swimmin'. And it's good for takin' and bringin' ships. From the bedroom window you can see the ships headin' north. You know what I mean, grandpa? Ships that take you to other lands. And airplanes too. Big birds that come and go. That'd be good, wouldn't it? To go far away, real far . . . To New York, maybe . . .

DON CHAGO. Good God, you are in a hurry, boy! You're not even to San Juan yet and you're already on your way to New York.

LUIS. Naah, I was only talkin'.

DON CHAGO. Yeah, yeah. Anybody'd think you're tryin' to get away from somethin'... Such a big hurry to forget the land!

LUIS. Bah, land. If it had only given us somethin'.

DON CHAGO. Give and take, son, give and take. What've you given to the land?

LUIS. Work.

DON CHAGO. Out of duty. That's not enough. You've gotta love the land.

LUIS. Aah, that's your idea. You love *people*. The land's a *thing*, and you can't love *things*.

DON CHAGO. That's what *you* say. When people do you wrong, the land'll still be there for you to love. (*Approaching* LUIS.) C'mon now son. What's wrong?

LUIS. Nothin'. What could be wrong?

DON CHAGO. There must be somethin'. Nobody walks around like a soul in hell without feelin' some little sting in their heart.

LUIS. Bah, you and your ideas.

DON CHAGO. You had a piece o' land and a house and you let 'em slip right through your fingers. You're strong and you're not afraid of hard work, but you spend all your time daydreaming about foolish things.

LUIS. They're not "foolish things" to me.

DON CHAGO. You're young and you oughta like to raise a little hell, but you look like you're always in mourning. Now you make the family go off to the city. Why?

LUIS. To live, grandpa, to live.

DON CHAGO. Ah, hell, you think we're all dead here?

LUIS. Worse than dead. Here we're nothin'.

DON CHAGO. I'll never understand you, my boy.

LUIS. I'm only thinkin' about the future, grandpa. The land isn't worth anythin' anymore unless you got a lot of it. Every day there's more machines in the fields and less work. Now the land is only profitable for the government and the big corporations. For a little guy like me to try and live from a tiny piece o' land—that's not livin' at all. And now that we don't even have our own land—it's even worse. I'm not gonna be just another peasant. The future's not in the land anymore; it's in industry. You gotta go to the cities.

DON CHAGO. If everybody thinks like you, what's gonna become of the land?

LUIS. Let the sugar corporations and the government work it.

DON CHAGO. Poor land!

LUIS. Poor us, if we stay here.

DON CHAGO. I dunno where you get them ideas.

LUIS. From myself. And everything around me. I'm not blind.

DON CHAGO. In my day...

LUIS. Times change, grandpa. What was good for you isn't good for me anymore. My father was right. If he had moved to the city, we wouldn't be in the mess we're in.

DON CHAGO. If your father had worked the land like he should've, you wouldn't be in the mess you're in. That's true.

LUIS. Others have left and been lucky. Look at our friend Moncho. He got set up in town. And Cirilo, Marta's husband, he went to New York and stayed.

DON CHAGO. God knows how!

LUIS. No matter. It's gotta be better than here.

DON CHAGO. You *are* stubborn.

LUIS. No more than you. And anyway, I've got a debt to pay.

DON CHAGO. You couldn't pay the one you got already.

LUIS. No, I don't mean the mortgage. I mean the old lady.

DON CHAGO. What debt is that?

LUIS. I owe her more than the others do.

DON CHAGO. What d'you mean?

LUIS. Well, she's been *too* good to me.

DON CHAGO. It's only natural, you're her son.

LUIS. Well, okay, her son. But I've gotta show her I'm worth more than the others. And I can't do it here. I dunno why, but I can't. I'm suffocating here on this land. The land my father mortgaged. The same land I couldn't save. And I couldn't 'cause I don't believe in it. I tell you there's no future here; it's dead. And I'm not gonna spend the rest o' my life with the dead, like all our neighbors around here. I look at them and they're so hopeless and resigned, it burns me up. And I don't know if it's because they are what they are or because I'm different from them. Why do I feel different, grandpa? Why don't I feel that I belong here like the rest o' them?

DON CHAGO. I don't know, son. Your thoughts are as tangled as an eggplant patch, and I don't get it. I think you put too many ideas in that skull o' yours. A man who works the land can't afford to have a lot of ideas. The only thought that makes him happy is the thought of the land. The rest sooner or later make him a little soft in the head.

LUIS. Yeah. Only the stupid peasants are happy.

DON CHAGO. It all depends what you call stupid.

LUIS. I know what I mean.

DON CHAGO. All right, so where're you gonna work, there in the capital?

LUIS. In a factory. I start next week.

DON CHAGO. Farm-worker here. Factory-worker there. It's all the same.

LUIS. No, it's not the same. I believe in that. There's where the future is.

DA. GABRIELA. (*From the kitchen.*) Luis. Luis. Come bring this coffee to your grandfather.

(LUIS *goes out to the kitchen. Brief pause.* JUANITA *enters from the backroom. She looks toward the kitchen with an air of mystery, then goes and kneels beside* DON CHAGO.)

JUANITA. Grandpa. Tell Miguel to come see me. I'm gonna be waiting for him all the time.

DON CHAGO. Hnnh?

JUANITA. Will you tell him?

DON CHAGO. Maybe. I suppose I will.

JUANITA. Don't be like that, grandpa. Don't make me go away mad. Tell him.

DON CHAGO. Listen, tell me something. You heard your brother Luis. Where does he get such notions if he's hardly ever been away from here?

JUANITA. How do I know? Unless it's from books and the papers. You know he's always reading.

CHAGUITO. (*From the backroom.*) It's from the talks he has with Chinto, the driver of the public cab. Every afternoon they talk and talk like two old ladies. And they always talk about the same thing.

DON CHAGO. And who asked you?

CHAGUITO. (*From the backroom.*) Aah, don't get smart, old man. Damn this shoe!

JUANITA. Please, grandpa, remember what I told you. You will tell Miguel?

(LUIS *enters from right with a cup of coffee.*)

LUIS. Here you are, grandpa. (*To* JUANITA.) Are you ready?

JUANITA. Yes.

DON CHAGO. This coffee's good. My daughter's always made the best coffee.

LUIS. Chaguito. Hurry up.

CHAGUITO. (*Out of sight in the backroom.*) I'm comin'. Don't rush me.

LUIS. Are you glad we're moving?

JUANITA. (*Shrugging her shoulders.*) I don't care one way or another.

DON CHAGO. Maybe she's leavin' somethin' behind.

JUANITA. Grandpa!

LUIS. Anything she leaves here can go to San Juan if it wants to. It knows where we're gonna live.

(CHAGUITO *enters from the rear. He carries a bundle of clothes under one arm. Under the other arm he carries a shoe. His other shoe is half on his left foot, and he struggles to get it on without dropping the bundle or losing his balance.*)

CHAGUITO. Damn it anyway! These shoes are no damn good. I dunno why the hell I gotta wear these brogues.

(*Sits on floor and keeps struggling.*)

LUIS. So you can get civilized.

CHAGUITO. Damn it anyway . . .

LUIS. And learn to talk better. You're goin' to live in the city.

CHAGUITO. You don't say. And whatta

they talk there, Spanish or Chinese? Got it. Uf.

(*Starts to put on the other shoe.*)

LUIS. You'll learn to talk better in school.

CHAGUITO. Oh, yeah? You think I'm such a sucker I'm goin' to school in town instead of earnin' some dough?

LUIS. Don't be a dope. You're going to school so you can learn to make more money. The dumb ones never get ahead.

CHAGUITO. Right, if you're born dumb. But I know enough.

JUANITA. Yeah. With your three years of school.

CHAGUITO. You shut up. Women speak when spoken to.

DON CHAGO. (*Laughing.*) Hah, hah! If I could've said that to my wife!

JUANITA. That's it. Laugh and encourage this fresh thing.

(*At this moment the muffled crow of a rooster is heard. It comes from the box that Chaguito placed near the table at the beginning of the act, but it is difficult for those on stage to locate the sound, which seems to come from the bowels of the earth.*)

LUIS. What was that?

CHAGUITO. (*Pretending.*) What?

LUIS. That rooster.

CHAGUITO. What rooster?

LUIS. That sounds like the big rooster.

(*Looks in the backroom.*)

CHAGUITO. (*Naively.*) I didn't hear nothin'.

JUANITA. Well I did. Sounds like it came from the rafters.

DA. GABRIELA. (*Sticking her head in from the kitchen.*) Did you hear that? Luis, sounds like the rooster's under the house.

(*Disappears.*)

LUIS. (*Undecided.*) It sounded to me like it was in here.

CHAGUITO. How could it be in here? Didn't you hear what the old lady said? It's under the house. Let's go look.

(LUIS, JUANITA, *and* CHAGUITO *leave rapidly through the left.* DON CHAGO *silently approaches the box hidden under the sack. The clucking of the rooster can be heard.* DON CHAGO *lifts the sack, squats down, and partially opens the lid. He shuts it quickly, laughing to himself.* CHAGUITO *appears timidly at the door to the left.*)

CHAGUITO. (*Getting* DON CHAGO's *attention.*) Pst. Pst. (*Softly.*) Grandpa, please. Don't tell on me.

DON CHAGO. (*In the same tone as* CHAGUITO.) So the rooster disappeared, eh?

CHAGUITO. (*Entering.*) Aw, jees, grandpa. Don't say nothin'. If you do, Luis'll sell the rooster on me. You heard what he said. Miguel is waitin' for it.

DON CHAGO. What the hell, he'll give him three whole dollars for the damn rooster. You think you can get more in town?

CHAGUITO. No, I don't wanna sell it. I wanna keep it.

DON CHAGO. And what good is keepin' it? It's not a fighting cock. It don't lay eggs. You wanna keep it for a Christmas stew?

CHAGUITO. No, I just wanna keep it. It's mine. I don't have nothin' else. But the rooster's mine. I raised him. And he knows me. Here they come. (*Anguished.*) Are you gonna tell on me?

(LUIS *and* JUANITA *enter from the left.*)

LUIS. I sure don't get it.

JUANITA. It's not under the house. (*Looking up.*) I told you I thought it was in the rafters.

DON CHAGO. Don't be silly. The rooster's not in the rafters and it's not under the house.

LUIS. So where is it?

(CHAGUITO *makes desperate faces at* DON CHAGO *begging him not to tell.*)

DON CHAGO. 'Till what time did you say Miguel was gonna wait to buy the rooster?

LUIS. Till four thirty.

DON CHAGO. I'm sure he got tired by now. (*Looking through the door at the sun.*) It's already five o'clock.

LUIS. Okay, okay. You know somethin' about the rooster?

DON CHAGO. (*Laughing.*) I should say I do. (CHAGUITO *tears his hair with rage.*) What you heard wasn't the big rooster.

JUANITA. No? It sure sounded like it.

DON CHAGO. That's right, 'cause it was the ghost of the rooster.

(*Laughs.*)

JUANITA. C'mon.

LUIS. Seems funny, you talkin' like that, grandpa.

CHAGUITO. (*Now over his fright.*) What's so strange about that? Why can't roosters have ghosts? Anyway I think you and Juanita imagined the whole thing. I didn't hear nothin'. What about you, grandpa?

DON CHAGO. Well, I don't pay much attention to what I hear. My ears are pretty old now.

(DA. GABRIELA *enters with two cups of coffee. She gives one to* LUIS *and offers the remaining one to* JUANITA.)

DA. GABRIELA. (*To* JUANITA.) You want some coffee?

JUANITA. No.

CHAGUITO. (*Finally getting the other shoe on.*) *I* want some.

DA. GABRIELA. Well, go get it.

(*Sits and drinks from the cup.*)

CHAGUITO. (*Gets up in a bad mood and goes toward the kitchen.*) That's what I get for bein' born last, the runt o' the family. (*Limping.*) Damn shoes.

(*Exits.*)

LUIS. Mamá, some day I've gotta teach that kid a thing or two.

DA. GABRIELA. Whenever you want.

LUIS. But you oughta straighten him out.

DA. GABRIELA. I'm sick and tired of hittin' him.

JUANITA. Tryin' to hit him, maybe. 'Cause he's so hard to catch.

DON CHAGO. Too many beatin's don't mean a thing. In my day we got fewer beatin's, but they did more good.

LUIS. (*Slightly ironic.*) Yes, grandpa, we all know everything was done better in your day.

DON CHAGO. Those were good times, my boy. There were less people, it's true, but they were better. Life was long, and nobody was in a hurry. If you didn't finish a thing today, you finished it tomorrow. The important thing wasn't *when* you finished it. The important thing was to do a good job. Today everythin's done any old way. And nothin' turns out any good. Nobody gives a damn. Nobody wants to do anythin'. Before, no matter how poor a person was, he had his own little piece of earth, his pride, his dignity. Nowadays there's not enough room for everybody. And there's no room for pride. And there's no place in the heart for dignity.

LUIS. (*Gently.*) There's dignity today too, grandpa.

DA. GABRIELA. Maybe it's just not the same as you knew it, father.

DON CHAGO. Yeah, maybe they've changed its name so's I don't recognize it no more. (*Pause.*)

(CHAGUITO *enters from the left with a cup of coffee. He sits down. He senses that the mood has changed. During his absence, at the grandfather's evocation, something impalpable, like a shadow of nostalgia, an undefined fear of the future, an awareness of the uncertainty of the present has taken hold of those on stage. They speak slowly, sipping their coffee, savoring in each swallow something of the past which is slipping away from them.*)

CHAGUITO. Why so quiet? You'd think it was a wake.

DON CHAGO. The times that died were good, son.

(*Pause.*)

JUANITA. We won't hear the cocks crow at dawn any more. Or the coquís at dusk.

LUIS. But we'll hear the sea.

DA. GABRIELA. I'm goin' to miss the smell of patchouli.

LUIS. The smell of salt air is more healthy.

JUANITA. Was it here where I was born, mamá?

DA. GABRIELA. No. You were born in the big, old house. Just Chaguito was born here.

CHAGUITO. It figgers. I had to be born in this dump.

LUIS. You remember the chestnut pony, ma?

DA. GABRIELA. Yes, your father's pony. We sold it after the hurricane.

LUIS. I learned to ride on that pony. You don't see them like that any more.

CHAGUITO. Today they got cars that're faster.

DON CHAGO. The little farm was like a well-kept orchard. It gave us a lotta pleasure.

DA. GABRIELA. Just like my husband. Remember, father? When he put on his Sunday clothes he looked just like somebody from the capital.

DON CHAGO. Yeah, he liked to show off. To give the local girls a thrill.

JUANITA. A man shouldn't be like a rooster. Were you jealous, mamá?

DA. GABRIELA. Who, me? They were just his little pleasures, may he rest in peace.

CHAGUITO. And what about you, ma? Didn't you like to give the boys a thrill?

DA. GABRIELA. Oh, I guess so, but not on purpose. I couldn't help it if God made me pretty. (*Pointing to a beam.*) We never got around to fixing that beam, Luis. Well, so much the better. It would've been a waste of time. Let the new owner fix it.

DON CHAGO. (*Laughing.*) I'll never forget the day you hit your brother Tomás with that rock. Your mother was so mad, you could see the sparks fly.

DA. GABRIELA. It was on Candlemas Day. You hid me 'till she got over it. I was a real little tomboy, huh, father?

(DON CHAGO *laughs quietly. Pause.*)

CHAGUITO. Yeah, when they're little they say women are more eager than men. What did you do, grandpa, the first time a girl kissed you?

DON CHAGO. Me? Ha, ha. Well, that was a long time ago. I can't even remember. (*Laughing.*) I suppose I just let her do it so she'd do it again.

CHAGUITO. Well not me. Last year at Christmas when Tomás' daughter came here, she kissed me. I went after her with a rock . . .

DA. GABRIELA. What'd you say?

JUANITA. It doesn't matter. This kid's nuts about throwin' rocks.

LUIS. A stoning for a kiss? Too bad for your cousin!

CHAGUITO. So what. That's filthy. She slobbered all over my face.

(*They all laugh.*)

LUIS. Isn't that cart coming yet? (*Looks out the door.*)

DA. GABRIELA. The later the better. (LUIS *looks at her questioningly.*) It'll be darker. Then they won't see us when we get there.

LUIS. Are you ashamed, ma?

DA. GABRIELA. I don't know. But I don't wanna be seen arriving in a new neighborhood.

(*Short pause.*)

JUANITA. (*Softly, as if talking to herself.*) The sun is just going down behind the tops of the trees.

DA. GABRIELA. I hope they take good care of the house. We should've fixed that beam, Luis. If the new owner came today, I'd tell him. Couldn't we send him word to be sure and fix it?

LUIS. Let him manage the best he can.

DA. GABRIELA. It's a good little house. And well kept. Remember? It was one of the few that survived the last hurricane. The kitchen floor needs two or three new boards. The rest is all right. (*Barely perceptible change in her voice.*) The bed and chair you took yesterday, are you sure they're safe in . . . the new house?

LUIS. Yes, the house has a padlock and key.

DA. GABRIELA. If Tomás had only lent us a few dollars we could've at least saved the house and the last three acres.

JUANITA. (*Absorbed, as if to herself.*) In

the red currant bush there are two nightingales fighting over a female.

LUIS. Uncle said he had no money. It's probably true. Times are hard.

DON CHAGO. But he wanted to take over the mortgage from the new owner.

LUIS. He did?

DA. GABRIELA. So my own brother wanted to take over our house and land from us?

DON CHAGO. Well, if he paid off the mortgage he had a right. And he wasn't really takin' anythin' from us. He was buyin' from the new owner. But the owner didn't wanna sell.

CHAGUITO. I bet you're on that mangy Tomás' side. Since you're gonna eat his beans now . . .

LUIS. (*Indignant, turning to* CHAGUITO *and intending to hit him.*) Shut up, you little animal. You don't know what you're saying.

CHAGUITO. (*Furious.*) Don't you dare hit me. You got no right.

LUIS. What d'you mean?

CHAGUITO. Don't make me talk. I know a lot you don't know.

LUIS. (*Stopping suddenly.*) What do you know?

CHAGUITO. That you got no right in this house . . .

DA. GABRIELA. (*Going rapidly toward* CHAGUITO.) He doesn't know anything. All he knows is how to be fresh and inconsiderate.

CHAGUITO. Don't you hit me, ma.

(LUIS *intervenes and saves* CHAGUITO *from the mother's fury.*)

LUIS. Leave him alone, ma. You're hurting him. It's not worth it.

DA. GABRIELA. I think it's worth it.

JUANITA. (*Who hasn't moved, calmly.*) He's been asking for it for a long time.

(*Looks outside again and forgets the others.* CHAGUITO *writhes on the floor behind* LUIS, *who stays between him and the mother.*)

LUIS. Look at the state he's in, ma. You're hurting him.

DA. GABRIELA. (*Withdrawing.*) It hurts me more to have a son I'm ashamed of.

CHAGUITO. Yeah, now it seems I'm the . . .

DON CHAGO. Quiet, boy, you're askin' for another beatin'. And stop cryin'. Tattle-tales should at least learn not to cry when they get their hides tanned for 'em.

LUIS. Why all the fuss? All the other times Chaguito's acted up, nobody tried to correct him.

DON CHAGO. It all depends on the mood you're in, son. And that one, she's thickheaded. Takes after her mother.

DA. GABRIELA. (*Evading* LUIS' *inquisitive look.*) He's not gonna be disrespectful to his . . . grandfather.

DON CHAGO. All right, all right. Listen, Luis, why don't you make one last effort to save the farm?

LUIS. An effort?

DON CHAGO. Well, then, a loan. There's still time. Ask for an extension.

LUIS. And who's gonna loan *me* money?

DON CHAGO. The bank.

LUIS. In whose name?

DON CHAGO. In Don Tello's. If I talk to him . . . maybe . . . he might just . . . We were good friends once. He owed me a lotta favours.

JUANITA. (*Hopefully.*) What d'you say, Luis? He might!

LUIS. (*After a brief pause.*) You think so? (*Worried.*) Well . . . Maybe Chaguito's right. Maybe I don't have the right . . .

DA. GABRIELA. (*Authoritatively.*) Don't say that!

LUIS. Why not. Maybe I don't have the right to change your lives like this. I'm the only one who wants to go. The rest of you don't think the way I do. Maybe I dunno how to fight for something. If I could get that loan . . .

DA. GABRIELA. (*Interrupting him.*) No! No loans. We're going. We're leaving this accursed place for good today. If the rest of you want to stay, you can. I'm going. And you are too, Luis.

LUIS. But, ma, you never liked the idea of leaving.

DA. GABRIELA. Who says so? I never said that. And now I say we're going. Now I'm the one who says let's go. No loans. I don't want Luis to be in debt all his life. We wouldn't be able to pay in the long run, and it'd be the same story. It's better to get out now, while Luis is still young and can make a new start someplace else.

LUIS. (*Approaching the mother, very moved.*) Honest, ma? You're really glad to go?

DA. GABRIELA. Yes, I'm glad. (LUIS *hugs her.*) It's better this way.

DON CHAGO. Yes, it probably is.

JUANITA. So what's the difference? That's what we decided anyhow. But for a minute you made me think . . . (*Shrugs her shoulders, sighs.*) Grandpa, will you promise me something?

DON CHAGO. What, my child?

JUANITA. Will you get me a nightingale?

DON CHAGO. (*Laughing.*) A nightingale? What for?

JUANITA. To have in the city.

DON CHAGO. (*Joking.*) I'll get it right this minute.

JUANITA. No, I don't mean this minute. You can bring it to me there, in a cage.

DON CHAGO. Hmmm . . . A nightingale in a cage . . .

CHAGUITO. (*Forgetting his recent beating and displeasure.*) Yesterday I killed one with a stone.

JUANITA. What a little brute you are!

DON CHAGO. A cage is worse than getting killed by a stone. A nightingale is too proud to live locked up. It'd die of rage. No, my child, no. Leave the nightingales free.

JUANITA. I don't think I can get used to it. I'm afraid of the sea.

CHAGUITO. What a dope! The water's heavier in the sea and you can swim better'n in the river. (*Making up.*) Right, Luis?

LUIS. Yes, that's right. It's so long since I went swimmin' in the river! Is it still deep, Chaguito?

CHAGUITO. Naah . . . Real shallow. You can't even dive.

DA. GABRIELA. It's true that at night the sea can scare you. When my husband's mother died, we had to go up to the north coast. She had gone to live there with a daughter. We stayed two nights in Hatillo, in my sister-in-law's house. The sea spent both nights crying like a sick child. It was like a moan from the next world. Every time I think about those nights, I tremble like a reed.

JUANITA. Did you remember the little clump of mint?

DA. GABRIELA. Yes. It's there, beside that box. I planted it in a tin can to take it along with me.

LUIS. Everything's goin' to be all right. You'll see.

(GERMANA *enters from the left.*)

GERMANA. Anybody home?

LUIS. Hi.

DON CHAGO. Look who's here! Germana!

DA. GABRIELA. Oooh . . . (*This "Oooh" said in the tone of "Hi, what's new?"*) How's your husband?

GERMANA. Still there, poor thing. Flat on his back. I thought you'd already gone.

DA. GABRIELA. We'll be going any minute now.

GERMANA. My, what a lotta packages! And the furniture?

LUIS. I took it yesterday.

GERMANA. You're not leaving anythin' you can't use? What about this table? You gonna give it to somebody?

CHAGUITO. (*Joking.*) Yeah, we're gonna give it to the mayor.

GERMANA. (*Examining the table closely.*) Heavens, it's no good for anythin'. Except for firewood. I wouldn't want it even as a gift.

CHAGUITO. Don't worry. Nobody's givin' it to you.

DA. GABRIELA. Take it if you want it.

GERMANA. Really? (*Pretending.*) Well, I'll take it as a favor to the new owner. So he won't have the trouble o' throwin' it out. It's a mess o' splinters. (*Snooping in the backroom.*) Can I help with anythin'? I like to be helpful. Especially for such nice people like you. You don't know how sorry I am you're movin'. Just like I said to my husband. You don't have such good neighbors every day. That piece o' wood in the bedroom? You gonna throw it away?

CHAGUITO. It's the lock for the window.

GERMANA. Ha. Poor people's windows don't need a lock. (*To* LUIS.) Did you say good-bye to Chinta?

LUIS. No. I haven't seen her.

GERMANA. (*Snooping among the packages.*) She spent the whole night crying. If you ask me, the damn kid's in love with you. (*Confronting him.*) What's the matter, you don't like her?

LUIS. (*Disconcerted, evasive.*) Well . . .

GERMANA. (*Snooping again.*) Well if you like her, take her. Neither her father or me's gonna stand in your way. I don't say this 'cause she's my daughter, but the girl's good and she works hard. We know she'd be in good hands with you.

DA. GABRIELA. My son's not one to run off with girls.

GERMANA. No?

DA. GABRIELA. Listen, loudmouth, don't go too far. My son's as manly as the rest. But when he wants a woman, it'll be to get married.

GERMANA. That's fine if he can afford to get married. (*To* LUIS.) It's your loss, stupid. Chinta couldn't be better. All the boys in the neighborhood are crazy 'bout my daughter.

DON CHAGO. If they're so crazy about her, she wouldn't need all the publicity you give her.

LUIS. Don't worry, lady, 'cause when I want a woman, I'll pick her myself. And if I picked Chinta, I wouldn't need your recommendation.

DON CHAGO. Well said. A mother's recommendation is a trap set by the devil to snare you into marriage.

GERMANA. (*Going towards the kitchen.*) Bah, the man always gets caught, with a trap or without. (*Looking into the kitchen.*) Oh, you've just made coffee! Got any left?

CHAGUITO. Yeah, the grounds.

GERMANA. What about the strainer? You gonna take it?
(*Exits right.*)

DA. GABRIELA. Yes, I'm gonna take it. (*To* JUANITA.) Go wash it and bring it here. That one'll clean out the house if you let her.
(JUANITA *exits.*)

DON CHAGO. You know somethin'? I'm really sorry to see you all go.
(*Pause. They all look at one another.*)

LUIS. Why don't you come with us?

DON CHAGO. Leave here?
(*Pause.*)
(*The creaking of an approaching cart begins to be heard. The four characters raise their heads expectantly. Then they look at each other.* LUIS *is the first to get up.*)

LUIS. The oxcart!
(*Goes to door at left.*)

DA. GABRIELA. (*Getting up.*) Is it the cart?

LUIS. Yes.

DON CHAGO. The cart!
(LUIS *turns and looks at* DON CHAGO.)
(JUANITA *enters from the kitchen with the clean strainer in her hand. She realizes what is happening and remains standing beside the kitchen door.*)

JUANITA. (*Anguished.*) Now?
(*There is a moment of immobility among the characters. A great shadow of anguish passes over them, a mute interrogation of the future, a fear of tomorrow, a desire not to act, to remain fixed and allow the fascination of the cart to pass by. The creaking of the cart is heard as it advances slowly but inexorably. Then the oxdriver's voice breaks the silence:* "Ooois . . . ooois . . . Pull, Lucero." LUIS *breaks away from the general feeling. He turns toward the door.*)

LUIS. (*Waving his hand.*) Hey, Cico! We're all ready.

DON CHAGO. Okay. C'mon, hurry up. We gotta load all this junk.

DA. GABRIELA. Oh, that's right. Chaguito, the trunk. Bring the trunk. Juanita, put the strainer in that box.

LUIS. Hurry up. Let's go.

(*There is a moment of confusion.* CHAGUITO *goes to the backroom and comes out dragging a small, old, dirty trunk.* JUANITA *puts the strainer in a box.* DON CHAGO *and* DA. GABRIELA *keep piling boxes and bundles next to the door.* LUIS *carries them from the door to the cart.*)

DA. GABRIELA. Careful with the little pot of mint. Don't break it on me.

JUANITA. Where's my bundle of clothes?

CHAGUITO. I didn't touch it.

JUANITA. Oh, my God, I can't find it!

DON CHAGO. Luis took it out already, girl.

CHAGUITO. (*To* JUANITA, *shouting wildly.*) Don't touch that box, damn you! Don't touch it! It's mine.

JUANITA. Heavens, you scared me. If it's yours, take it. But don't shout at me again or I'll pull your ears off!

LUIS. (*Coming to the door and taking a package.*) C'mon, it's getting dark. (*Goes out.*)

(GERMANA *appears in the kitchen door with an empty kerosene can.*)

GERMANA. Listen, what about this can, eh?

DA. GABRIELA. What can?

DON CHAGO. (*To* JUANITA.) No, not that bundle.

JUANITA. Gee, you can't touch anything here. So I won't bother helping. Bye.

GERMANA. This can that was in the kitchen?

DA. GABRIELA. I don't know. Take it. Take it and don't ask. Take whatever junk you find.

GERMANA. Well, I only asked 'cause I'm not one to take things that belong to other people.

(*Exits again to kitchen.*)

LUIS. (*From outside.*) Chaguito, c'mon out here, boy, and help load these bundles.

CHAGUITO. (*Carefully carrying the box with the rooster.*) God, I hope he don't start to crow now.

(*Exits left.*)

DA. GABRIELA. (*Glancing in the backroom.*) Everything outta here? (*Looking at the empty living room.*) Nothing left here? (*Looking into the kitchen.*) Nothing left out there?

GERMANA. (*From the kitchen.*) Not a thing, kid, not even a splinter!

LUIS. (*From outside.*) Let's go. Let's go.

DA. GABRIELA. We're coming!

(DA. GABRIELA *and* JUANITA *look at* DON CHAGO *in silence.*)

CHAGUITO. (*From outside.*) C'mon!

DON CHAGO. Well, well, get going. Don't just stand there like two sticks.

LUIS. (*Coming to the door.*) Cico can't wait any longer. Grandpa, you staying?

DON CHAGO. I'm staying.

LUIS. Well, give me your blessing.

DON CHAGO. God bless you, my boy. Take care of the family for me.

LUIS. Don't worry, grandpa, I'll take care o' them. Let's go.

(*Exits.*)

DA. GABRIELA. (*Approaching* DON CHAGO.) Stubborn old man! Take care of yourself, father.

(*She embraces him. It is a long, tight embrace, full of emotion, but without tears.*)

DON CHAGO. Bah, I've weathered many a storm.

DA. GABRIELA. I know you're strong. But you're old, father. And you'll be alone. Don't be foolish. Take care.

DON CHAGO. You see that the little family gets ahead. And give 'em the back o' your hand when they need it. C'mon now, they're waiting.

DA. GABRIELA. (*Leaving* DON CHAGO'S *arms, going toward the door at the left, but stopping now and then to look at her father.*) Remind Tomás' wife about the poultice for your asthma. And don't get too tired. (*Takes a last look at the house as if to engrave it forever in her memory.*) Close up the house for me before you go. Your blessing.

(*Exits quickly to the left.*)

DON CHAGO. God bless you.
(JUANITA *sobs, leaning against the wall.*)
CHAGUITO. (*From outside.*) Juanita! Don't keep us waitin', damn it!
(DON CHAGO *approaches* JUANITA.)
DON CHAGO. Let's go, miss. You got no reason to cry. You're a young lady now.
JUANITA. (*Between sobs.*) I don't wanna go.
DON CHAGO. Why not? Wait'll you see how beautiful the city is! So many pretty things! And the sea's not frightening. It's just water, salt water. It can't swallow up the land. Don't you know the land breaks the waves on the shore, and that holds back the sea? C'mon, little lady.
(*Tries to lead her but she resists by holding on to a beam in the wall.*)
JUANITA. I don't wanna go. I don't wanna go!
LUIS. (*From outside.*) Juanitaaaa . . .
DON CHAGO. You know what I'm gonna do? I'm gonna tell some young fella I know that Juanita's waitin' for him in the city. (JUANITA *lets go of the beam and begins to look at* DON CHAGO *as she wipes her nose with the back of her hand.*) And I'm gonna tell him he can go visit her in that pretty little house by the sea.
JUANITA. Honest, grandpa?
DON CHAGO. (*Leading her to the door.*) Yes, child, honest. Boy, that Miguel's gonna be so happy when I tell him! (*Laughs.*) Now, good-bye, girl. May God go with you. Oh, wait. I almost forgot. (*Searches in his pocket. Takes out a dirty handkerchief. Carefully unties a knot and takes out a half dollar.*) Take this. A half dollar. For you.
JUANITA. (*Moved.*) Oh, grandpa, no.
DON CHAGO. Yes, c'mon. What do I want it for?
JUANITA. You might need it.
DON CHAGO. My son Tomás'll give me all I need from now on.
JUANITA. Good-bye, grandpa. Thanks.
(*Kisses him and exits left.*)
CHAGUITO. (*From outside.*) Hurry up, hurry up, sick lookin' devil!

(GERMANA *enters from the right. She carries a few small pieces of wood, a dish made from a hollowed-out gourd, and an empty oat container.*)
GERMANA. So that's it! They've gone off without even sayin' good-bye to me. (*Puts the odds and ends on the table.*) That's what you call consideration! Bunch of peasants! (*Approaches the door where* DON CHAGO *is.*) Thankless lot!
(*When she gets next to* DON CHAGO, *she changes her tone.*)
CHAGUITO. (*From outside.*) So long, old man! Don't let Tomás' wife get away with anythin'. And give a shot in the head to that little brat who kissed me last year.
(*The creaking of the cart is heard as it begins to move away. Now and then the driver's "Ooo ooo iis" is heard.*)
GERMANA. (*With much arm-waving.*) G'bye! G'bye! God bless you! May the Virgin protect you! Oh, that Gabriela's been like a sister to me! Good luck! Oh, how I'm gonna miss you! Have a good trip! Luis, don't forget you can have Chinta if you want her. May the Lord be good and send you lots o' money! (*Between* GERMANA'S *remarks, "Good-byes" are heard from those in the cart.* GERMANA, *her comedy of leave-taking finished, suddenly changes her tone, turns to* DON CHAGO, *and asks realistically.*) Well, what're you gonna do now? You gonna stay here?
DON CHAGO. I'm going to close up the house.
(*Goes to the backroom to shut the window.*)
GERMANA. I dunno why you need that bolt on the window. I could use it on my front door.
DON CHAGO. (*Returning.*) Poor people's doors don't need bolts.
GERMANA. Okay. You gonna go back to Rio Arriba now, to Tomás' place?
DON CHAGO. No.
GERMANA. That's good. 'Cause it's night already. But you got no place to sleep here.

(GERMANA *begins to collect her junk and place it near the door.*)

DON CHAGO. (*Looking into the kitchen.*) Who said I was gonna sleep in this cemetery?

GERMANA. (*Goes to the right.*) The kitchen's all shut now. Well, come over to my place. I can put up a hammock for you in the shed. (*Takes the table out through the door at left. Leaves it outside and re-enters.* DON CHAGO *lovingly examines the house, caressing the walls.*) That daughter o' yours and those kids! Look at 'em leavin' you here like this! Well, I suppose they say it's one less mouth to feed. That's all right for me with my poor husband flat on his back and not able to work.

DON CHAGO. (*Absorbed.*) They wanted me to go to the city. I'm the one who didn't want to go.

GERMANA. Is that right? I thought . . . Well, the way things are with us it'd be better if Chinta went off. I'd still have the other little belly to feed. I never saw a kid hungry all the time like that one. Your family's different. You may be under water, but you're not drowned yet. You got a son with money. When you're up at Tomás' place, don't forget us. I've always been good to you and yours. Well, c'mon.

DON CHAGO. I appreciate it, woman. But I'm goin' to my new house.

GERMANA. What d'you mean? I thought you said you weren't goin' to Tomás' tonight?

DON CHAGO. I did. And I'll say it again. I'm not goin' to Tomás' tonight or ever again.

GERMANA. Well I'll be . . . I don't get it.

DON CHAGO. His wife don't want me. And Tomàs says I'm too old now to help him on the farm, that I'm not good for anythin' no more.

GERMANA. But what're you gonna do?

DON CHAGO. Go on livin'.

GERMANA. So the rich son . . . (*Suddenly thinking it best to get out of her offer.*) Oh, wait a minute, now I remember! We don't have a hammock at our place. We lent it to my husband's brother-in-law. I almost forgot.

DON CHAGO. (*Smiling understandingly.*) Don't worry, old girl. I'm not gonna sleep at your place.

GERMANA. And just where're you gonna live?

DON CHAGO. (*Putting his bundle of clothes on his shoulder.*) In the Indian Cave.

GERMANA. My God, you're nuts!

DON CHAGO. (*Signaling her to leave.*) C'mon . . .

GERMANA. What good'll it do you to stay here? You gonna go begging? Look, run after the cart. Go to the city.

DON CHAGO. C'mon, c'mon. I gotta close up.

GERMANA. (*Collecting her things: kerosene can, wood, etc.*) How you gonna live in that cave? (*Goes out to the left. Her voice continues without interruption from outside.*) Nobody can live in a cave. Look, at least go over to Don Tello's place. They'll let you sleep in the shed.

DON CHAGO. (*Going out.*) What for? When people give you a kick in the pants, the land'll always take you back.

(*He shuts the door. The scene is empty and dark except for the dim light of nightfall which finds its way in between several poorly joined boards.*)

GERMANA. (*From outside, in the distance.*) Boy, is he a nut! My God, who'd have thought that old man was so crazy? He looked so healthy and happy . . .

(*As* GERMANA's *voice fades away, the creaking of the departing oxcart can still be heard in the distance.*)

THE CURTAIN SLOWLY FALLS

ACT TWO

Interior of a shack in La Perla. The layout of the house is similar to the country house of Act One. The entrance to the house is at the left foreground. At the rear, a partition with a door in the middle leading to the only bedroom. In the doorway there is a single curtain made of cretonne that was once brightly colored, but which is now faded and dirty. Light comes over the partition from a small, open window in the bedroom. In the center of the right side wall there is an open window. In the right foreground, the door to the kitchen. The ceiling is low. The doors and windows are smaller than normal size. Obviously the house has been built from scraps of leftover materials such as tarpaper, tin, roofing, boards from crates, etc.

Rear left, a small, iron folding bed. Left foreground, next to the door, a broken-down chair. Between the kitchen door and the window on the right, a square table covered with cheap, worn-out oilcloth showing bunches of exotic fruits, chiefly apples and cherries. Next to the table, a chair and a bench. On the table, an oil-lamp with its chimney blackened from the smoke. In the rear right corner, rolled up and hanging on a nail, a hammock of white sackcloth, dirty from use, with hemp fastenings. Almost in the center of the room, there is a rocking chair, one of those small, low chairs so loved by our grandmothers. Wood, painted black, with back and seat of yellowish, deteriorated straw. The scarcely-hinted-at arms of the chair are very low, thus giving more freedom to the hands for sewing and embroidering. The chair shows off its age with great dignity. It is alone, isolated from the other furniture, foreign to the grime of the walls, to the narrowness of the room, to the gaudy oilcloth on the table. The old rocker, a memento of better times, does not belong to this world which surrounds it. Therefore in its dignified isolation there is a certain air of resigned bitterness. Precisely over the chair, hanging from the ceiling, there is a dirty electric cord. On the end of the cord there is a socket. There is no bulb in the socket. On the back wall, to the right, there is a small, empty shelf. On the same wall, near the rear door, there is an old black rosary hanging on a nail. On the back wall, to the left, there is a picture of the Virgin of Carmen, probably taken from some Catholic calendar. It is a reproduction of some painting by a well-know artist. Its colors are now faded. Under the picture there is a small branch of blessed palm, now dry.

The shack is on a gentle incline running from left to right. The structure is made level by long pilings on the right side, which faces the beach. The kitchen, out of sight, sticks out over the sand and rocks washed by the waves when the Atlantic is angry. The ocean, in its peacefulness or its fury, can be seen from the window on the right. It can also be seen from the window that we do not see in the bedroom. The light that enters in torrents through the window on the right and that which comes in over the partition at the rear is a diffuse light; the particles of sea water in the atmosphere give this clarity an appearance of luminous and floating gauze. The door at the left opens onto a narrow, damp alley. The light that comes from there is cold, poor. Except for the right side, the house is surrounded by other dwellings. At the end of the alley on the left, out of sight, there is a tiny bar with a jukebox.

Left and right, that of the spectator.

The tempo and atmosphere of this act contrast severely with those of the first act. It is not so much the slum life seen *by the spectator as that* felt *by the still unadapted rural person, like a vertigo of unknown origin which he does not know how to combat.*

It is three-thirty in the afternoon. At this hour the slum is relatively peaceful.

From time to time arguing voices, the jukebox in the bar, and the bawling of some child are heard. Then we are again enveloped in the silence of the slum composed of small noises and the constant beating of the waves on the rocks.

When the curtain rises, no one is on stage. A savage rhumba can be heard on the jukebox in the bar. Bongos and kettledrums predominate in the orchestration. The furious rhythm of the music contrasts abruptly with the calmness and silence of the house.

LITO *sticks his head in through the door at the left. He is an eight- or nine-year-old kid, but looks no more than seven, lively and happy-go-lucky, but with eyes that are prematurely sad. He is the only character who says "Grabiela" instead of "Gabriela".*

LITO. Doña Grabiela! (*Pause.*) Doña Grabiela! (*He enters and raises his voice.*) Doña Grabiela!

DA. GABRIELA. (*From the kitchen.*) I'm coming! Who is it?

LITO. It's me.

(DA. GABRIELA *enters from the right, drying her arms and hands on an old petticoat which she has put around her waist in place of an apron. She has two sage leaves stuck to her temples with soft wax to relieve her headache.*)

DA. GABRIELA. And who is "me"? Oh, it's you. That damn jukebox! It's gonna drive me crazy. (*Going to the left, muttering.*) They got no consideration for the next one. (*Shouting out the door at the left.*) For God's sake, lower that jukebox. I can't hear myself think!

DRUNKEN MAN'S VOICE. (*Shouting from afar, to the left.*) Whatsa matter, lady, don't you like music?

DA. GABRIELA. (*Grumbling.*) Music! Ha! Music! (*Goes away from the door. The volume of the jukebox is lowered and the music continues in the background until the record ends.*) What d'you want, boy?

LITO. Don Severo, the owner o' the bar, wants Luis to go see him.

DA. GABRIELA. What's he want him for?

LITO. Well . . .

DA. GABRIELA. To try an' collect?

LITO. Well . . . I dunno.

DA. GABRIELA. Yes. Yes. You never know. Come here. (LITO *slowly obeys.*) Look at me. What did Don Severo tell you?

LITO. For Luis to go there.

DA. GABRIELA. What for?

LITO. (*Sincerely.*) To play dominoes. (*Protesting.*) But if Don Severo finds out I told you, he won't gimme any more nickels to go to the movies.

DA. GABRIELA. Ah, what a stupid old man. He wants Luis to pay what he owes him, and he takes him off to the bar to teach him lazy men's games. How's Luis gonna pay him if he don't have a job? And how's he gonna get a job if he's always playin' in the bar?

LITO. (*Mischievously.*) Well . . . prob'ly he won't have to pay nothin'.

DA. GABRIELA. (*Ironically, more to herself than to Lito.*) Don't tell me Don Severo's gone into the relief business?

LITO. I dunno. But I know one thing . . .

DA. GABRIELA. What?

LITO. Well, that Don Severo's wife is in love with Luis.

DA. GABRIELA. (*Grabbing Lito by one arm.*) What'd you say, boy?

LITO. Well . . . just that.

DA. GABRIELA. You mean the niece. Martita, right?

LITO. No, not Martita. Doña Isa, Don Severo's wife.

DA. GABRIELA. (*Shaking him.*) You're a shameless liar.

LITO. Ay, don't get mad, Doña Grabiela. Everybody knows it.

DA. GABRIELA. And Don Severo?

LITO. (*Laughing.*) Ah, well, *he* don't know it!

DA. GABRIELA. And Luis? You don't know if Luis . . . ? (*Ashamed, interrupting* herself, letting go of LITO.) No! You don't know nothin'. You don't even know what you're talkin' about. (*Brief pause. She turns to him with vigor.*) And you're gonna stop tellin' stories. If you keep sayin' those awful things to people, I'm gonna . . . (*Her threatening gesture vanishes. She leans on the rocker. Almost to herself.*) People are bad. Bad! (*Reacting.*) What're you standin' there for? What d'you want? I got no nickels to give you. (LITO *looks at her with his big, sad eyes, smiling a little, without being impressed by the abruptness of* DA. GABRIELA'S *words.*) Look how dirty you are, boy! (*She holds his face with one hand and with the other takes a corner of her improvised apron and wipes a smudge from his cheek.*) How long since you had a bath?

LITO. (*Lying gently.*) Yesterday.

DA. GABRIELA. Yesterday? Last week, maybe. You look like a little pig. And that hair hasn't seen a comb for a week. (*She messes his hair with a rough kindness.*) Go in the bedroom and bring me the comb. (*She sits in the rocker as* LITO *goes in the bedroom.*) Did your father find a job?

LITO. (*From within.*) Yeah, he got somethin'. Where's the comb?

DA. GABRIELA. On the shelf, beside the mirror. At least your stepmother's probably happy now.

LITO. (*Appearing from the rear with a large black comb lacking several teeth.*) Hah, that's a laugh! You never know when that one's happy. Last night she got drunk again. (*Gives the comb to* DA. GABRIELA.) What a big comb!

DA. GABRIELA. Oh, she got drunk? (*Ironically, as she begins combing.*) Probably to celebrate your father's new job.

(LITO *opens the only button on his shirt and, with an abrupt gesture, uncovers his back, showing it to* DA. GABRIELA.)

LITO. Yeah, look how she celebrated it.

DA. GABRIELA. (*Letting out an exclamation of sad surprise.*) Poor little boy! (*She passes her fingers gently over his bruised back, but reacts suddenly, closing his shirt and buttoning it.*) Hmmh. You must've done somethin' bad.

LITO. I didn't do nothin'. The old man brought me a top and she got mad 'cause she said it was a waste o' money. I hadda go sleep behind the bar.

DA. GABRIELA. (*Combing his hair.*) And why didn't you come over here?

LITO. It was real late. You had everythin' shut. Luis says I should come live with you. But that damn wife o' my old man . . .

DA. GABRIELA. I know. She's like the dog that never ate or let anybody else eat.

LITO. Can I stay here again, tonight?

DA. GABRIELA. Sure, you can. Aah, look at that! You got lice! Sit down here, boy, sit down here. (LITO *sits on the floor.*) Good heavens, but you're crawlin' with 'em.

(*She begins to delouse him.*)

LITO. (*His head leaning on* DA. GABRIELA'S *lap.*) I'm no trouble, am I? I'll sleep there, on the floor. And I don't eat much.

DA. GABRIELA. Nobody here eats much. (*She kills a louse between her fingernails.*) Except the lice.

(JUANITA *enters from the left. She is thin and pale. There is something somber in her look. She has lost some of the girlish spontaneity she had in Act One.*)

LITO. Hi, Juanita. Did you know my father brought me a top?

DA. GABRIELA. (*To* LITO.) Sit still. (*To* JUANITA, *but without interrupting her task.*) Where were you? You didn't fetch the water. I hadda climb all the way up to that other spigot to get it.

JUANITA. (*Shrugging her shoulders.*) You must like to do extra work. There's a spigot right there outside.

DA. GABRIELA. I never like to do extra work. The spigot outside there is broke. If you did what you're supposed to, you'd know it.

JUANITA. All right. All right.

DA. GABRIELA. And you still haven't answered my question. Where you been?

JUANITA. At Matilde's house.

DA. GABRIELA. I don't like that Matilde.

LITO. I do. Sometimes she gives me nickels.

DA. GABRIELA. What were you doin' in that house?

JUANITA. Listenin' to the radio.

LITO. The adventures of Dick Tracy?

JUANITA. (*Very dignified.*) I don't listen to that silly kid stuff.

DA. GABRIELA. And just what silly stuff do you listen to?

JUANITA. It's not silly. It's a story, a real good story, "Tormented Love."

LITO. (*With contempt.*) Bah! Those stupid love stories!

JUANITA. It was so pretty. They were saying romantic things and the marquise had already fallen on the sofa. The lover, who was just an engineer and not a nobleman like her husband, knelt down on the floor and took the marquise's shoes off. Then he took her stockings off and kissed her feet...

LITO. Ugh! How punky!

JUANITA. (*Furious.*) Animal! A marquise's feet never smell!

DA. GABRIELA. (*Getting up indignantly.*) Oh yes they do. And you stink too when you tell about such stupid things. (*The jukebox is heard again full blast.*) And that house stinks where you go to hear them. (*Turning toward the door at the left.*) And that damn stuff they call music stinks. (*Shouting.*) Lower that! Lower that!

LITO. (*Also shouting.*) I'll go to the bar an' lower it, Doña Grabiela.

(*Exits rapidly through the left.*)

DA. GABRIELA. (*Covering her ears with her hands.*) God Almighty! God Almighty!

(*The music becomes almost imperceptible. Pause.* DA. GABRIELA *moves slowly to the center.*)

JUANITA. What's the matter, mamá? You feel sick?

DA. GABRIELA. (*In a low voice.*) My head! I got a headache... (*Goes to the window on the right.*) The smells! The noises! Not even the sea can wash them away. Damn sea. The air gets dirty and harmful. What good is so much water if it can't clean all this filth? (*Sighing.*) The air in the mountains was clean.

JUANITA. Everything was clean in the mountains.

DA. GABRIELA. And us too. We were clean, clean inside... (*Turning with sudden force.*) You're not goin' back any more to that Matilde's house.

JUANITA. But mamá, I don't do anythin' bad. If we had a radio...

DA. GABRIELA. (*Bitter.*) There's hardly enough money to buy food and there's gonna be no money for a radio. (*Furious.*) And even if there was! D'you think I'm gonna have a contraption in my house that talks about women who deceive their husbands?

JUANITA. Mamá, she's a marquise.

DA. GABRIELA. Marquise or princess, I don't want no filthy things in my house. I don't wanna hear no indecent talk in my family.

JUANITA. (*Ironically.*) Well, then, we'll have to go live in the swanky part o' town.

DA. GABRIELA. My house'll be decent, here or anyplace else. We might be poor, but we come from a good family. And I don't want none o' you to forget that. If I have to beat it into you, you're gonna remember you're from a good family. Things are like they oughta be. As long as I'm alive my family will be *my family*. A family with dignity and pride. (*She stops suddenly, looking at a small shelf on the wall.*) Where is it? Where's my St. Anthony statue? (*Goes to the wall and touches the empty shelf in anguished surprise.*) Where's my wooden saint?

JUANITA. It was there this morning.

DA. GABRIELA. (*Turning around.*) Yes, it was here. But it's not there now. Who took it?

JUANITA. I didn't take anythin'.

DA. GABRIELA. Well help me look for it. (*They both look.*) That's all I needed. For them to take my saint. Look in the bedroom. (JUANITA *exits through the rear door.* DA. GABRIELA *keeps searching.*) Ay, Blessed St. Anthony, help me to find you!

(*Shouts and running are heard outside to the left. A man's voice shouts, "Animal, watch where you're goin'."*)

JUANITA. (*Entering from the rear.*) It's not in the bedroom, mamá.

CHAGUITO. (*From outside, left.*) Get outta my way, you creep.

(CHAGUITO *enters through the left in one leap. The force of his running carries him almost to the middle of the room.*)

CHAGUITO. (*On the floor, breathless.*) Shut the door! Shut that door!

(*The two women, startled by* CHAGUITO's *noisy and meteoric entrance, look at him in surprise.*)

DA. GABRIELA. What is this? What the devil's the matter with you?

(CHAGUITO *gets up quickly without answering. He runs to the left and shuts the door. The youngest child in the family now wears shoes every day. He is dirty and has the unmistakable look of an urban petty thief. He goes to the rear, left, quickly removes his shoes, gets into bed, and pulls the covers up to his neck.*)

DA. GABRIELA. What's wrong with you, eh? You gone crazy?

CHAGUITO. I'm sick. If anybody asks about me, I'm sick.

JUANITA. You look more scared than sick.

CHAGUITO. Shut up, you.

DA. GABRIELA. (*Going to the door at the left.*) Scared or sick, I'm gonna find out right now what's goin' on.

(*Just as* DA. GABRIELA *goes to open the door,* CHAGUITO *sits up in bed and screams hysterically.*)

CHAGUITO. Don't open that door, ma! Don't open it!

(DA. GABRIELA *stops. She quickly goes to the bed, throws back the cover, makes* CHAGUITO *get up, and furiously shaking him, asks.*)

DA. GABRIELA. What's goin' on? Who're you runnin' away from? Answer! What've you done, you devil, what've you done?

CHAGUITO. I didn't do nothin'. Lemme go.

DA. GABRIELA. Why aren't you in school?

CHAGUITO. (*Lying.*) 'Cause one o' the teachers was absent and they let us out early.

DA. GABRIELA. And why were you runnin' like that, eh?

CHAGUITO. (*Lying.*) I had a fight.

DA. GABRIELA. Why did you fight? Why?

CHAGUITO. (*Still lying.*) 'Cause . . . they called you a name.

DA. GABRIELA. And what did you do to make 'em call me a name? Answer me!

(*Knock at the door.* CHAGUITO *is terrified.*)

CHAGUITO. (*In a low voice, crying.*) Lemme go! They're out there! Can't you hear? Lemme get out the window. Lemme go!

(*Another knock at the door.*)

DA. GABRIELA. Juanita, open that door.

CHAGUITO. (*Twisting helplessly in his mother's strong arms.*) No! No! Lemme go! No!

(*He finally stops, out of breath, watching fearfully as* JUANITA *opens the door.* JUANITA *opens it and* LITO *appears.*)

LITO. Why'd you shut the door?

(DA. GABRIELA *lets go of* CHAGUITO, *who falls exhausted on the bed.* JUANITA *begins to laugh as she caresses* LITO's *head.*)

JUANITA. Don't tell me you're the one who was chasin' Chaguito?

LITO. Chaguito? (*Seeing* CHAGUITO *for the first time, he takes the top out of his pocket and happily approaches the bed.*) Hey, Chaguito, I didn't see you! Look, look how nice! My father brought it for me last night. (*Sits beside* CHAGUITO.) You like it? Spin it, if you want. Here's the cord.

CHAGUITO. (*In a bad mood.*) Leave me alone.

(LITO *looks at him surprised. Then he looks at the top. He gets up and goes to* DA. GABRIELA.)

LITO. What's the matter with Chaguito?

DA. GABRIELA. (*Distracted.*) He's sick . . .

JUANITA. (*Joking.*) From fright.

CHAGUITO. Shut up!

JUANITA. Don't pay any attention to that dope, Lito. Come, show me your top.

LITO. (*Getting excited.*) You wanna spin it?

JUANITA. Me? Well, sure. Of course! I'm a great top spinner.

(DA. GABRIELA *sits in the rocker, leans her head back, closes her eyes, and begins to rock. The chair creaks rhythmically. Meanwhile* JUANITA *has been winding the cord around the top rather clumsily. Obviously she has never practiced this sport.*)

JUANITA. All set.

LITO. (*Excitedly.*) Spin it! Spin it!

JUANITA. (*Not very sure of herself.*) Sure, right away . . . Here goes . . . (*Shuts her eyes and throws the top. It bounces without spinning.*)

LITO. (*Laughing loudly.*) You don't know how to spin a top, Juanita.

JUANITA. (*Abashed.*) Who says so?

LITO. I say so. You're clumsy. (*Singing.*) You don't know how. You don't know how.

JUANITA. (*Chasing him.*) Come here, you little scamp. If I catch you, I'll pull off one o' your ears.

(*Laughing and shouting,* JUANITA *chases* LITO *around* DA. GABRIELA'S *chair. A slight smile comes to the mother's lips as she continues rocking with her eyes shut. What a world of memories are awakened in her by the simple happiness of this family scene! Finally* JUANITA *catches* LITO. *They both roll on the floor, laughing.*)

JUANITA. I got you, you buggy kid, I got you.

(*They roll on the floor, hitting each other with their hands. Suddenly* JUANITA *becomes pale and puts her hand to her forehead.* LITO *takes advantage of this to get away, still laughing, and seek refuge in* DA. GABRIELA'S *lap. She hugs him protectively and kisses him as she places him on her bosom as though he were a baby.*)

LITO. She's after me, Doña Grabiela! Don't let her catch me!

DA. GABRIELA. No. Nobody'll catch you here.

(JUANITA *gets up with difficulty and goes toward the rear. She leans against the bedroom doorway.*)

CHAGUITO. What's the matter with you?

(JUANITA *doesn't answer and enters the bedroom.* DA. GABRIELA *and* LITO *are not aware of the incident.*)

LITO. (*Nestled in* DA. GABRIELA'S *lap.*) You smell like my mother, Doña Grabiela. I remember her from when I was real little.

(LUIS *enters from the left. He carries a paper bag with groceries and another crudely wrapped package. He stops in the doorway.*)

LUIS. (*In a happy tone, after looking around.*) What a life the men in this house have! One in bed and the other in the lap of the best mother in the world.

LITO. (*Getting up, happily.*) Luis! (*He runs to* LUIS *and jumps into his arms.*) Where you been? Don Severo wanted you to go to the bar to play dominoes. What d'you got there? I bet you don't know what my father brought me? (*He jumps down and looks for his top.*) Look!

LUIS. Oh, boy, a top! You know how to spin it?

LITO. Sure I do. But Juanita don't.

DA. GABRIELA. Luis . . .

LUIS. (*Coming forward.*) Stay there nice and quiet now, ma. I got somethin' for you.

DA. GABRIELA. (*Her voice trembles from emotion and uncertainty.*) Luis . . . you're . . . You're happy . . . !

(*We don't know if it's a question or an exclamation.*)

LUIS. (*Squatting down beside her chair.*) That's right, ma. Look. (*He keeps taking things from the bag and putting them in* DA. GABRIELA's *lap.*) Plantains. Yellow yautías. Sweet potatoes. Yams. Green bananas. And codfish!

DA. GABRIELA. Good heavens! Where'd you get all that?

LUIS. You'll find out. We're gonna have a real feast of fruits, vegetables, and fish. None o' that rice or canned stuff. Fresh vegetables and codfish. Remember how you used to fix it when grandpa was alive, back there in the country? And somethin' else. Sweet coconut.

(*Takes out a small bag with the delicacy.*)

(CHAGUITO *and* LITO *have approached and watch with eager eyes.*)

CHAGUITO. I want some o' that candy.

LITO. Me too.

DA. GABRIELA. No, sir. Not now. I'll give you some after we eat.

LUIS. It won't be as good as you used to make, ma. But it'll taste good anyway if we remember grandpa.

DA. GABRIELA. Luis . . . where'd you get all this?

LUIS. (*Replacing the things in the paper bag.*) In the market place at Río Piedras. And just my luck. Right after buying . . .

DA. GABRIELA. But the money . . . Where'd you . . .

LUIS. Hold on. Right after buyin' all this, I ran into Miguel . . .

LITO. Who's Miguel?

CHAGUITO. Juanita's sick lookin' boy friend.

LITO. And why's he sick lookin'?

CHAGUITO. 'Cause he's from the hills, where they're all sick lookin'.

LUIS. (*Getting up with the packages.*) If you look at yourself in the mirror you'll see that's the truest thing you ever said.

DA. GABRIELA. Don't pay no attention to this snob. Go on.

LUIS. Where's Juanita?

CHAGUITO. She's in the bedroom. Now she goes around faintin' like a movie star.

(LUIS *puts the packages on the table.*)

DA. GABRIELA. All right. Go on. What happened then?

LUIS. Well, just that Miguel had gone there to sell vegetables and he could've let me have 'em cheaper.

DA. GABRIELA. (*Getting up.*) Did he ask about Juanita?

LUIS. Yes, and he sent her somethin'. I brought it along. He said he was gonna bring it, but as long as he met me there, it was better for me to bring it.

DA. GABRIELA. I would've been more pleased if he brought it himself.

LITO. (*Shouting.*) Juanita, your sweetheart sent you a present.

CHAGUITO. (*Hitting him on the head.*) Shhh! Loudmouth!

LUIS. Chaguito, go on outside and play with Lito.

LITO. Yeah, yeah. Let's go play with the top.

CHAGUITO. (*Offended.*) I don't play with little kids.

LUIS. Go on outside.

CHAGUITO. I don't feel like goin' out.

DA. GABRIELA. Maybe not now you don't. 'Cause you live more in the street than in this house.

CHAGUITO. Okay. But I'm goin' to the movies.

DA. GABRIELA. With whose money?

CHAGUITO. With mine.

DA. GABRIELA. And where'd you get it from?

CHAGUITO. Aw, don't worry, I know how to get it.

LITO. Take me to the movies, huh?

CHAGUITO. No. C'mon. You go out first.

(LITO *exits left.* CHAGUITO *cautiously approaches the door, glances outside, then looks at* LUIS, *and finally goes out.*)

DA. GABRIELA. (*After quickly glancing toward the backroom, in a low voice.*) Listen, Luis, you think Miguel would've come if he didn't meet you?

LUIS. I dunno. Probably. The truth is since Juanita don't want anythin' to do with him . . .

DA. GABRIELA. That's what I don't understand. What's the matter with your sister, Luis? She didn't wanna come to the city 'cause she was in love with that fella. And now that he came here and wants to get married and take her back to the country, she don't wanna hear from him.

LUIS. I dunno, ma. I suppose women are like that . . .

DA. GABRIELA. No . . . Women aren't like that 'less somethin's wrong. Juanita hasn't worked for two months. She quit 'cause she says she had a fight with the boss. She don't wanna go out to work any more. She don't work in the house. All she wants to do is listen to stories on the radio at that Matilde's place. And look at Chaguito. He don't go to school, he don't work. He's always stuck in the movies watchin' some cops and robbers story. The other day I caught him smoking. He says he runs errands. But he's got more than he could make doin' that. Where's he get the money? We don't have money for coffee, and he's got money to go to the damn movies and to buy cigarettes.

LUIS. Ma, I gotta tell you somethin'. Somethin' bad.

DA. GABRIELA. (*Looking fixedly at* LUIS.) Bad? Let's have it, boy. I'm used to it by now.

LUIS. Last month Chaguito was arrested.

DA. GABRIELA. Arrested?

LUIS. Yes. When I told you that Chinto, the cab driver, had taken Chaguito to spend a few days in the country, Chaguito was in jail. They tried him and thanks to Don Severo, the owner of the bar, they suspended the sentence. The judge said since it was his first time she'd excuse him. But if it happened again, she wouldn't show any mercy.

DA. GABRIELA. But what did Chaguito do? Why'd they arrest him?

LUIS. For stealing a wrist watch from a peddler. When he tried to sell it down by the docks, a cop caught him.

DA. GABRIELA. A thief! (*Brief pause. Turning her back to* LUIS.) A thief! I should've known. A thief! (*Puts her hand to her forehead, in a low voice which, as she speaks, increases until it becomes a cry of rebellion and sorrow.*) What's happening to my family? What's happening to my children? Oh, Blessed St. Anthony! What sins am I paying for? What did I do wrong? Work, sweat, tears, love . . . and sometimes beatings to make 'em grow up right. But none o' that's any good. What a world this is where a mother can't make her own kids good any more!

LUIS. C'mon, ma.

DA. GABRIELA. Your grandfather used to say the poor were saved by their dignity. (*Desperately.*) Oh, old man, you did the right thing by dyin'! You did the right thing by gettin' out o' this world where the poor's got no more dignity to save 'em.

(*Falls sobbing in her chair.*)

LUIS. (*Moved.*) Ma, don't be like this. Don't cry. I can't take it.

DA. GABRIELA. (*After a pause, quickly raising her head.*) Can it be that God has forgotten us? Today my St. Anthony disappeared on me. Luis, what's happening to us? I don't understand. If your grandfather was here, he could explain it. Why is God forgetting us?

LUIS. Ma, don't worry so. God don't forget the poor.

DA. GABRIELA. You're right. Forgive me, God. Forgive me, Blessed St. Anthony. I'm gettin' old. That's the matter. I'm gettin' scared o' life. And I can't let that happen. God gave me a family. (*Getting up and turning sharply to* LUIS, *recovering her strength.*) Where's Chaguito? Where's that damn kid? I'm gonna beat him within an inch o' his life! I'm gonna make him honest if I have to kill him!

LUIS. No, ma. Listen to me. Chaguito's not to blame.

DA. GABRIELA. What d'you mean not to blame?

LUIS. I'm the one to blame. For bringin' you to the city. And then for havin' such bad luck at work. Five jobs in a year. And so many weeks outta work. If I had a good job, Chaguito'd have money for the movies . . .

DA. GABRIELA. And what's he gotta go

to the movies for? You never went to the movies when you were his age.

LUIS. But here it's different. In the country there's the river to swim in, trees to climb, birds to hunt, slingshots for target practice, animals to run after. Here the kids got no way to have a good time. And then the rooster Chaguito brought from the country, I hadda sell it on him 'cause we needed the money. What's the kid gonna do if he don't go to the movies?

DA. GABRIELA. He could get a job.

LUIS. Right. That's just what I wanted to tell you. (*Animated.*) But, ma! So much talk and I still haven't told you the most important thing. (*Deliberate pause to make it important.*) I found a job!

DA. GABRIELA. (*Approaching him, half unbelieving, half happy.*) Really, Luis?

LUIS. Really. How else could I buy all that food?

DA. GABRIELA. That's right! That's what I was gonna ask you a while back. Where the money came from. (*Unbelieving.*) But . . . They paid you . . . already?

LUIS. They gave me an advance.

DA. GABRIELA. (*All doubt and misgivings gone.*) Luis, you found a job! Thank you, Blessed St. Anthony! So that's why you were so happy when you came in. That's why you bought the sweet coconut. And I didn't give you a chance to tell me. And I made you sad talkin' so much. How awful I am! Well, tell me all about it. What kind o' work is it? How'd you get it?

LUIS. (*Laughing.*) You won't believe it. It's like in the movies.

DA. GABRIELA. I dunno what movies are like. But whatever you tell me, I'll believe you, Luis. I'll believe you. Now tell me.

LUIS. Well, I was comin' from a construction job in Hato Rey. I couldn't find anythin' there, so then I started walkin' without anythin' special in mind. Just walkin' along the sidewalk lookin' at the houses and the gardens. Then I passed by this house that had almost two acres o' land. The house was like a palace. And there was this lady with shorts on, in the garden. She was bendin' over weedin' some rose bushes.

DA. GABRIELA. With shorts? You don't mean panties, Luis?

LUIS. (*Laughing.*) No, ma. With shorts, like the tourists.

DA. GABRIELA. Heavens! And you could see her from the street?

LUIS. Of course!

DA. GABRIELA. And she knew you could?

LUIS. She had to. So then I stopped to watch . . .

DA. GABRIELA. (*Reproaching him.*) Luis!

LUIS. No, ma, not that. She had real thin, hairy legs. And thighs like a chicken. They were nothin' to look at. But it made me laugh 'cause the lady was wearin' gloves. And she didn't know how to weed. She had a trowel and what she was doin' was breakin' the roots o' the rose bushes. So I put on a straight face and said to her: "Hey, lady, you want a hand with that?"

DA. GABRIELA. (*Laughing.*) And what did she say?

LUIS. Well, she said to me: (*Pronouncing with affected correctness.*) "What do you want?" Then I said to her: "I don't want anythin' lady. But the weeds beside the trunk can only be pulled out by hand. And you won't be able to do it with gloves on. And if you're gonna weed with a trowel you shouldn't dig so deep, 'cause you'll just break the roots o' the bushes."

DA. GABRIELA. That probably made her mad, right?

LUIS. Not a bit. She got up, not too easy, more like she was splittin' around the waist, and said to me: (*Pronouncing with affected correctness.*) "Do you know about gardening?" Then I told her: "I'm from the country, lady. And I know the land." So we began talkin'. I went in the garden and started to weed the rose bushes. The lady was lookin' for a gardener 'cause the one she had left. And she gave me the job.

DA. GABRIELA. You don't say! And how much is she gonna pay you?

LUIS. Ten dollars a week, lunch every

day, and Sundays off. To tell the truth it's not much . . .

DA. GABRIELA. Well it's enough for weedin' rose bushes. What else grows on all that land?

LUIS. Flowers, and grass, and trees . . .

DA. GABRIELA. Nothin' to eat?

LUIS. Nope, not a thing.

DA. GABRIELA. (*Shaking her head.*) What next! More than an acre o' land and they don't plant anythin' to eat!

LUIS. Probably 'cause they don't need it. But, gee, it's pretty, ma. I told the lady we could plant a little vegetable garden in back. She said it was all right as long as it didn't bring bugs. The poor thing says she has a fit every time she sees a bug. Oh, and on Saturdays I have to wash the family car. A real beaut'. With a motor that purrs like a kitten. One o' those big Cadillacs. And I can bring Chaguito along every day to help me. 'Cause I told the lady all about us. And she was real nice. She gave me three dollars in advance. She says I can bring Chaguito to help me as long as she don't have to pay him. That way Chaguito can learn the job and take over as gardener when I get somethin' better.

DA. GABRIELA. That's a good idea, Luis.

LUIS. Sure, ma! Now you'll see everythin's gonna be all right. Chaguito'll be with me so he won't bother you no more, an' he won't get in any more trouble. And another thing, ma. Now that I got a job, I'm gonna talk to Martita, Doña Isa and Don Severo's niece. So as soon as I find a good job we can get married.

DA. GABRIELA. I'm glad you decided on that, Luis. A man isn't complete 'till he's got his own woman. (*In a good mood, taking the bag of groceries.*) Well, if we're gonna have that feast, I better start boilin' the vegetables. (*Goes to the right. Stops at the kitchen door and turns around laughing.*) You know somethin', Luis? You came to the city to get away from the land. And now the land helps you out right here in the city.

LUIS. What d'you mean by that, ma?

DA. GABRIELA. That one acre o' land in Hato Rey gives you what all your industries couldn't.

(*Exits right.*)

LUIS. (*With a forced laugh.*) It's true, ma. The mountain goat always heads back to the hills.

(LUIS *suddenly becomes somber and serious. He looks at the floor while biting his nails. An airplane is heard approaching over the shack.* LUIS *slowly raises his head and then goes to the window at the right. His eyes follow the Pan American "Constellation" heading for New York.* JUANITA *appears in the doorway at the rear. She is pale and her hair is disheveled. She looks at* LUIS *in silence. Then she says:*)

JUANITA. You still thinkin' about goin' away?

(LUIS *turns around, startled.*)

LUIS. Oh, it's you. (*He slowly moves away from the window with his head down.*) I found a job.

JUANITA. (*Without taking her eyes off him.*) Yeah, as a farmer.

LUIS. Times are bad.

JUANITA. Times are always bad for people like us. You should've known that when you brought us here. (*Bitter.*) So it's the same old story. Farmer-boy there, farmer-boy here.

LUIS. Okay. You said it once already.

JUANITA. So what? Don't you like to hear it? Ha! The country was no good for a peasant like you. The city! The future was in the capital. Everything good. Good jobs, good schools, electric light . . . (*Looking sarcastically at the light cord.*) You forgot they didn't give electricity free. And the beach was beautiful, and you could go swimmin'! But the beach is filthy and anyone who goes near those damn waves is a goner. And the air was so healthy! But here everything stinks of filth and garbage. This is the dream you were lookin' for! This is the future that was gonna save us all!

LUIS. All right. All right. Things didn't

work out the way I thought. But instead o' criticizing, why don't you help me? (*Strongly.*) It's not right to blame me 'cause we're poor. We've always been poor. (*Shouting, in helpless protest.*) What d'you want me to do? What can a man do to stop bein' poor?

JUANITA. (*Recovering her tone of younger sister, in passionate supplication.*) What does it matter to be poor as long as you're clean inside! But it's impossible here. Let's get outta here, Luis. Let's get outta here!

LUIS. Go away?

JUANITA. Yes.

LUIS. But where?

JUANITA. To New York, to Hell, to anyplace! Just now you were thinkin' about leavin'. Don't deny it! You were at that window watchin' a plane goin' north, wishin' you had wings to get away from here.

LUIS. (*Somber.*) But men don't have wings.

JUANITA. Don Severo said he'd loan you the money for the tickets if you went north to work with his brother.

LUIS. Yeah, but . . . I can't. I don't wanna owe Don Severo any more money. I don't want any more worries for the old lady. I got work here now. I'll get somethin' even better. (*Looking at the window, beginning to feel the fascination of the horizon.*) Of course, it'd be easier up there. They say there's plenty o' work. They pay good. An' the poor man's as good as the rich. (*He keeps approaching the window.*) It must be pretty, huh? A country where a man can do somethin' to stop bein' poor . . .

JUANITA. And where a woman can be respected by the men.

LUIS. Where all the machines in the world come from, and all the money in the world, and the good things that make all the people in the world happy.

JUANITA. (*She has approached the window and is behind* LUIS.) Where the air isn't dirty from noise and filth. 'Cause they say the snow is white and clean like cotton.

LUIS. Clean and white . . .

JUANITA. Like the fairyland that grandpa used to tell us about when we were little. It must be pretty, Luis.

LUIS. Yes, the land of dreams. (*Coming back to reality and turning away from the window.*) No! No, Juanita, it can't be. A man can't spend his life running away. Anyway . . . the old lady don't like the cold.

JUANITA. (*Clinging to* LUIS' *arm, in a deafening voice.*) Who cares about the cold! Let's get outta here, Luis. I can't go on livin' here. Don't you understand? I can't I can't!

LUIS. (*Pulling away.*) I'll get a job in another factory. There's still a future here. And you'll marry Miguel.

JUANITA. No!

LUIS. Of course. Look, I forgot. Miguel sent you that over there. I met him in the market place. He was sellin' vegetables. He told me he'd come over some other day.

JUANITA. No! Don't let him come!

LUIS. And why not? What's the matter with you? (*Goes to hand her the package.*) Here, take this.

(*In the distance are heard a policeman's whistle, a crowd of voices, and* LITO's *voice calling,* "LUIS.")

JUANITA. Nothin's the matter. But I don't wanna see him. (*Hysterical.*) I don't want him to come here. Not that. I don't wanna see him.

LITO. (*Approaching from the left.*) Luis! Luis! They're takin' him away! Luis!

(LITO *appears in the door at the left. He stops, out of breath.*)

LITO. Luis, c'mere, hurry. A cop caught Chaguito.

(DA. GABRIELA *appears in the kitchen door.*)

DA. GABRIELA. What did you say?

LUIS. (*Approaching* LITO.) What did he do now?

LITO. The cop says he's been lookin' for him. That Chaguito sold a wooden saint to some tourists for two dollars. That the tourists gave him a ten-dollar-bill to change and that Chaguito ran off with it and never came back.

(*Before* LITO *finishes,* LUIS *has already rushed out to the left.*)

DA. GABRIELA. My saint! Did you hear, Juanita? It was him! It was him! (*Rushes out to the left. Her heart-rending voice is heard in the distance.*) Chaguito! Chaguito!

LITO. Aren't you comin', Juanita? (JUANITA *doesn't answer.* LITO *disappears shouting.*) Not that way, Doña Grabiela. Through the alley by the bar!

(JUANITA, *who had remained aloof from what has happened, stares at the package on the table. She approaches it slowly and opens it. There appears before her eyes a roughly carved model of the oxcart in which she left her native district to go to the capital. She takes it gently and raises it to eye level. As she does this, we hear very soft, bucolic music, the creaking of an oxcart, and the driver's voice calling in the distance, as in a dream,* "Oooois, Lucero, oooiiis." *Suddenly an airplane is heard approaching. As it passes over the house, it drowns out the other sounds.* JUANITA *sinks down on the bench by the table, leans her forehead on her arm, and sobs convulsively.*)

MATILDE *enters from the left. She is thirty-five years old and rather plump, but she still conserves her very feminine and provocative shape. Her serious voice has a certain trace of tiredness which contrasts with her energetic movements. She quickly glances around the house and then looks compassionately at* JUANITA.)

MATILDE. It's great to have a good little cry all by yourself. (JUANITA *is startled and tries to cover up her tears.*) Take it easy. It's only me. I came to find out what's goin' on with the cops. I heard they arrested your brother Luis.

JUANITA. (*Rising.*) No. It was Chaguito.

MATILDE. Oh, that one? So what're you cryin' for, kid? As long as they don't make off with the one who brings home the beans . . . (*Approaching the table.*) Hey, what's this? (JUANITA *has tried to hide the model of the cart, but it is too late.*) An oxcart! (*Laughing.*) Don't tell me you still play with toys. Who brought it to you? Luis?

JUANITA. Well, in a way. A friend from the country sent it.

MATILDE. A friend? Hmm, I bet he's more than a friend and his name is Miguel, right? (*Shrugging her shoulders.*) An oxcart! Why didn't he send you a bunch o' bananas?

JUANITA. (*Pensive, more to herself than to* MATILDE.) It's just like Cico's oxcart.

MATILDE. And what one is that?

JUANITA. (*Coming back to reality.*) The one we left the country in.

MATILDE. Hah. So he sends you this one so's you can go back the same way you left, eh?

JUANITA. Don't laugh at me, Matilde.

MATILDE. I'm not laughin' at you kid. I'm laughin' at the men who only know how to talk in circles. What the hell, an oxcart!

MAN'S VOICE. (*Coming from a house to the left.*) Matilde! Matilde!

JUANITA. Listen, somebody's callin' you.

MAN'S VOICE. Matilde!

JUANITA. Isn't that your husband?

MATILDE. (*With disgust.*) That's him all right. (*Goes to the left. Leaning out the door, shouting.*) Whatsa matter? Did my little dear lose somethin'?

MAN'S VOICE. Where are you? C'mon, I just got home.

MATILDE. (*Winking at* JUANITA, *with a voice like honey, but shouting.*) You don't say so, my saint! So you just got home! Isn't that nice! (*With sudden dryness.*) Well, if you just got in, you can wait. I'm busy.

MAN'S VOICE. But, baby, come an' get me some clean clothes.

MATILDE. (*To* JUANITA.) Clean clothes, he says! Didn't I tell you that they talk in circles? That's not what he wants. I know him like I was his mother! (*Shouting outside.*) Stay dirty a little while longer, sweetie. You know I like you better that way.

MAN'S VOICE. But, my little saint . . .

MATILDE. Just hold out a little longer . . .

for the clean clothes. (*Conclusively.*) And don't bother me again. (*Goes away from the door, sighing.*) Sometimes I get fed up! The worst thing is we don't learn from experience. But who can get along without a husband? Who, huh kid? (*Stopping suddenly.*) Whatsa matter? You embarrassed by what I'm sayin'?

JUANITA. (*Somewhat restrained.*) Matilde, mamá don't want me goin' over to your house any more.

MATILDE. (*Unaffected by the news.*) That so? Poor old thing! She's lost here. In the long run she'll probably get used to it. We all do. But at her age it's more of an effort. (*Pointing to the rocker, laughing.*) Look at that chair. Who'd ever think o' sittin' in one o' them things today? That's somethin' from our grandmothers' times. Mine had a rockin' chair too, back there in the country. And would you believe it, she used to spend the whole damn day rockin'. Back and forth, back and forth. Just imagine! Moving without moving. Movin' without gettin' anywheres. Stayin' in the same place! Like a car that don't run. Like a bus that don't leave the bus stop. How nutty! People sure were stupid in them days.

JUANITA. Mamá's not a bit stupid, eh?

MATILDE. Okay, okay. I don't mean her. But times change. There must be some reason why the Americans came to bring us up to date. That's right, kid. You take an American, an' he won't lift a finger 'less it's to get somethin' he can see and touch. You tell an American to waste his time in a rockin' chair, and he'll tell you to go to hell. O' course he'll tell you in English, but he'll tell you. (*With an air of superiority.*) Last year I met an American and I learned a lot, kid, a lot. Look, I came here to talk about you, not about men. You're my friend and I wanna help you. I came to let you know I talked to Doña Celinda. Everything's all set. You can go to her place right this afternoon.

JUANITA. (*Terrified.*) This afternoon? (*Retreating.*) No!

MATILDE. Why not, kid? Sure, right now. I thought we had it all settled yesterday. That's what you wanted.

JUANITA. No, I can't.

MATILDE. Yes, you can. (*Approaches* JUANITA, *convincingly.*) If you don't do that, what're you gonna do, eh?

JUANITA. I dunno. I dunno what to do. It's drivin' me crazy.

MATILDE. Now there's an idea. Wouldn't it be great to go crazy whenever you wanted to. But it's not that easy, kid. Only the ones who don't wanna go crazy end up in the nuthouse. C'mon. Let's go.

JUANITA. (*Clinging to part of the wall.*) No!

MATILDE. So, you gonna tell Miguel then what's goin' on?

JUANITA. No, no. I'd die o' shame.

MATILDE. Bah, nobody dies from that. So? You gonna marry him without sayin' nothin?

JUANITA. No. I wouldn't do that.

MATILDE. So what would you do, I'd like to know.

JUANITA. It's just that I don't want anyone to find out. Matilde, help me!

MATILDE. (*Annoyed.*) And how d' you want me to help you, if you won't help yourself? What's this about goin' crazy? What's this about dyin'? What's this about shame? Where you been livin', kid? You think you're the only one it ever happened to? And anyway, what did happen? One day after work you stay for supper at a girl friend's house? You get back late to La Perla and in some dark alley some guy grabs you and . . .

JUANITA. Stop!

MATILDE. You don't even know who the shameless guy is.

JUANITA. Shut up!

MATILDE. (JUANITA *sobs.* MATILDE *goes toward her in a motherly way.*) C'mon kid! It's no use cryin'! You can't help bein' born a woman.

JUANITA. Wouldn't it be better to let it go . . . 'till tomorrow?

MATILDE. What for? The longer you let these things go, the worse it is. C'mon, let's go; don't be afraid.

JUANITA. (*Now beside the door at the left.*) Will you go with me?

MATILDE. (*Going out left, keeping hold of* JUANITA's *hand.*) Of course, kid, of course. C'mon. Let's go.

(*Exits.*)

JUANITA. How rough the sea is! You hear it?

MATILDE. (*From outside.*) Yeah, don't bother 'bout the sea now. C'mon.

JUANITA. I'm . . . coming.

(*In spite of her words,* JUANITA *resists and lets go of* MATILDE's *hand. She looks around in anguish, as if expecting that a sudden call might keep her in the house.*)

MATILDE. (*From outside.*) C'mon, kid, get goin'!

(JUANITA *makes the sign of the cross and exits left. During the last part of this scene the sound of the waves beating against the foundation on the right side of the shack has become more intense. Now the sea is clearly heard as a menacing force. The stage remains empty for a few seconds. Then* LUIS *enters from the left. He is deeply disturbed. He sees the cart on the table. He approaches. Then he looks toward the rear and calls softly.*)

LUIS. Juanita! (*Goes to the door at the rear. Loudly.*) Juanita! (*Turns around.*)

(*At this moment* DOÑA ISABEL *enters from the left.* DOÑA ISA, *as* DON SEVERO's *wife is called by her neighbors, belongs to what might be called the "bourgeoisie" of the slum. She dresses better than the other women, wears nylon stockings, and keeps her hair well-combed. She is about forty-four years old, tall and slender. Her speech shows urban influence and schooling. She tends to pronounce final letters instead of dropping them. Nevertheless, she often does omit them. In her speech, correct forms such as "nothing" and "of" fight tenaciously with the more popular forms of "nothin'" and "o'".*)

DA. ISA. Juanita was going down the alley with Matilde. Do you want me to call her?

LUIS. (*Disturbed by* DA. ISA's *presence.*) No . . . no thanks.

DA. ISA. Your mother's probably going through hell now. The worst part is that Chaguito'll surely go to jail. Severo told me he wouldn't be able to do anything this time.

LUIS. I know, Doña Isa.

DA. ISA. And what about you? What will you do?

LUIS. I got a job today.

DA. ISA. Really? That'll tie you down here even more, won't it?

LUIS. (*Ignoring her remark.*) Oh, I wanted to tell you I'll soon be able to pay the bill I owe Don Severo.

DA. ISA. (*Smiling.*) There's no hurry.

LUIS. Maybe not for you, but for me there is. I'm ashamed o' owin' Don Severo money.

DA. ISA. (*Approaching* LUIS.) Why? Everybody lives in debt.

LUIS. (*Uneasy.*) Yeah, but Don Severo . . . He's been so good to us.

DA. ISA. (*Putting her head gently on* LUIS' *arm.*) Are you sure it's on account of Severo that you feel ashamed?

LUIS. (*Motionless from the touch of her hand, without looking at her.*) Why . . . why d'you ask that?

DA. ISA. (*Drawing closer.*) Couldn't it be because people are talking? Couldn't it be because everybody says that I'm . . . your mistress?

LUIS. (*Drawing away suddenly.*) Lies! Gossip!

DA. ISA. That's what they say.

LUIS. But you know they're just lies.

DA. ISA. It all depends. (*Moving away from him.*) The truth is that people are blind. I've got a niece at home who may not be what you'd call beautiful, but at least she's very cute. Nobody can deny that you like Martita. Nobody can deny that you've been courting her. But people don't see that. It's much tastier to imagine that you're chasing after the aunt. Because the aunt is married and so much older. And that's really a spicy thought.

LUIS. You shouldn't pay no attention to those things.

DA. ISA. Of course not! Until one night you go to see Martita. But before you go you have a few drinks. To give you courage. Because you finally realize you need a woman. And you're going to propose. With a few drinks gone to your head.

LUIS. Stop it, Doña Isa!

DA. ISA. But Martita's not home. Severo's taken her to the movies. 'Cause you just don't know how much Severo loves that niece of mine! So you find me alone. Me, the old, married aunt. The one the neighbors say is your mistress.

LUIS. I know. There's no forgivin' what I did.

DA. ISA. No, Luis, you weren't to blame.

LUIS. Yes, I was. For havin' drank. Why'd I have to drink all that rum?

DA. ISA. But Luis, all the rum in the world wouldn't mean a thing if I didn't want it to happen. At my age a woman knows when *not* to want. But I wanted it to happen.

LUIS. Doña Isa!

DA. ISA. It's true, Luis. I wanted it. And I'm not ashamed of it. You probably wouldn't understand. You have your family. You don't know what it is like to live alone. Yes, I know. I have a husband and a niece. But it's not the same. Tell me, haven't you ever wanted anything with all your heart, with all the strength of your soul?

LUIS. Yes . . .

DA. ISA. You're good, Luis. From the first time I saw you, I knew you were good. So good, that sometime's it's hard for me to think of you as a man. It seems more as though you're a little boy looking for a mother's caresses. And I never know if the desire I have to caress you is for the man or the little boy.

LUIS. Don't say that . . . Don't talk like that. It makes me feel sorry for you.

DA. ISA. It shouldn't. I don't need your pity. What I need is for you to go away from here.

LUIS. Go away?

DA. ISA. Yes.

LUIS. But I just found a job.

DA. ISA. It doesn't matter.

LUIS. Go away! You're the one who oughta go away.

DA. ISA. It's been so many years since we came to live here. This was just a tiny area then. Poor, but decent. I was the teacher at the little schoolhouse. And Severo opened the bar. You won't believe it, but this didn't look anything like it does today. It was even pretty with the old Spanish walls, the lighthouse, the sentry boxes, the sea. Then, almost without our even realizing it, this horrible thing started creeping in on us. More and more kept on arriving. And this little piece of land didn't get any bigger. The people changed, the sea changed, even the air changed. I left the school. Severo and I had also changed. You see? If a change like this came all of a sudden, you'd get frightened and have time to get away. But when the change comes little by little, you get accustomed to it, you change too, and then there's no escape. But you can get away, Luis. You still have time.

LUIS. I couldn't take a cent from your husband for that trip.

DA. ISA. *I'll* give you the money. And you can send it to me when you're able.

LUIS. No. Even less from you. I can't take money from a woman.

DA. ISA. It's a loan, Luis. You'll pay me back.

LUIS. No. I have to get outta this by myself. I can't give up. This is my country. New things are bein' done here, big things. These are new times. The era of machines. And I have faith in that. The rest is all dead. I gotta fit into this new life. I gotta fight.

DA. ISA. Fight what?

LUIS. If only they hadn't closed the factory. I dunno. Some things I just don't get. They send us factories an' all that from the States to help us out. But if the ones right up there order 'em to raise our salaries, then they shut down the factories and send 'em back up there 'cause it's not to their advantage no more. So the deal is for us to earn less than the ones up there. And why should that be? Tell me. Aren't we all equal, us down here an' them up there?

DA. ISA. I don't know, Luis.

LUIS. I don't get the jobs I want. I like machines. 'Cause there's somethin' great an' mysterious-like in a machine. They're just pieces of iron and steel, but you'd almost say they were alive. Almost like they had souls.

DA. ISA. You are a little boy, Luis. How's a piece of iron gonna have a soul? For me a machine is only . . . a machine.

LUIS. But it's more than that! Before, a man used to own other men called slaves. But today a man owns a machine an' it's his friend, not his slave.

DA. ISA. You do say some strange things! I don't like machines. I don't understand them. They make me afraid.

LUIS. The future is in machines.

DA. ISA. Yes, but yours, your future. What're you going to do?

LUIS. I dunno, Doña Isa. I don't have any roots. I can't seem to get settled. I don't fit anywhere.

DA. ISA. Well, be careful, Luis. Be careful you don't grow roots here 'cause they'll only rot on you. Look what's happened to the rest of us. Look what's happening to your own family. Look inside yourself and find out what's happening to you. (*Approaching him, her voice broken from emotion.*) All this is like a lottery where the numbers have gone mad. (*She gently clings to both his arms, leans her cheek on his broad shoulder in timid possession, and murmurs:*) Go away from here, Luis, go away.

(DA. GABRIELA *enters from the left. In spite of her distress, she is wounded by the scene before her. She pulls herself together and says firmly:*)

DA. GABRIELA. Not this too! (LUIS *and* DA. ISA *are startled.* DA. ISA *quickly moves away from him. To* LUIS.) So you were gonna get married! To the niece! And for that you gotta snuggle up to the aunt! (*To* DA. ISA.) Aren't you ashamed? Here, in my own house? A married woman? A woman of your age?

LUIS. Mamá . . .

DA. GABRIELA. Don't call me mamá! (*To* DA. ISA.) I always thought the women who had the gall to take a lover would at least know where to meet him. But no, you gotta come here lookin' for him. To carry on right under my nose.

(DA. ISA *exits rapidly through the left.*)

LUIS. (*Lowering his head, defeated.*) You wouldn't understand.

DA. GABRIELA. You're right. I only understand things the way God wants 'em.

LUIS. She's not a bad woman.

DA. GABRIELA. I don't say she is. But at least you see I haven't made a big stink.

LUIS. She's an unfortunate woman who suffers a lot.

DA. GABRIELA. We all have to suffer. But that doesn't stop us from actin' with dignity. (*Interrupting* LUIS, *who tries to speak.*) Don't say another thing. I don't want no more explanations. You're a man and can have your affairs. But I never thought it'd be with a married woman. I figgered it was with the niece. But that's your business. If you don't wanna get married, it's up to you. The only thing I ask is for you not to bring your women to this house. Juanita's got enough bad examples 'round here already. Where is she anyway?

LUIS. I think she went out.

DA. GABRIELA. I told her not to. (*Looking around.*) She don't care about the house. Look at this mess! My house was never so upset. (*Starts to pick things up.*) I gotta do it all. You people think I got twenty hands. (*Seeing the cart.*) Is that what Miguel sent Juanita? (*Picking it up.*) What good work, isn't it? It looks just like Cico's oxcart. (*Sighing.*) Ay, these kids! When'll they finally get married! (*Puts the* cart on the shelf where the saint used to be. Picks up the paper the cart was wrapped in.) It makes me mad to think that them heretics might be laughin' at my St. Anthony. Nobody's got the right to make fun o' my wooden saint.

LUIS. They're prob'ly not makin' fun of it, ma. They prob'ly just wanted to take it back for a souvenir.

DA. GABRIELA. Yeah, just like they take castanets or maracas. And I'm left without my saint. That's the sad part. (*Arranges the blanket on the bed.*) You think they'll throw the book at that kid?

LUIS. I dunno. They'll prob'ly send him to reform school 'till he's of age.

DA. GABRIELA. (*Interrupting her work.*) All that time?

LUIS. Could be . . .

DA. GABRIELA. Then he won't be goin' to school.

LUIS. They say they teach 'em a trade there.

DA. GABRIELA. What kind o' trade?

LUIS. Well, I dunno. Whatever one he likes.

DA. GABRIELA. An' if what he likes is stealin'?

LUIS. Well, they'll teach him to be honest.

DA. GABRIELA. (*Starting her work again as she moves her head in doubt.*) I hope to God they can. I know I can't. (*Suddenly crying out.*) Oh, my God, the vegetables! They'll get all dried up in me. (*Exits quickly through the right. We hear her from the kitchen.*) Look at that! Another minute they would've been all burned.

LUIS. Don't let that food get ruined on me, ma.

(*Far-away shouts of "Help," "Save her" are heard. Then a confused sound of voices that increases in volume during the following scene.*)

DA. GABRIELA. (*Coming to the kitchen door.*) Don't worry. They're all right. But we're gonna need some olive oil. What's that?

LUIS. I dunno. Sounds like a fight.

DA. GABRIELA. At least I don't have to worry that Chaguito's mixed up in some fight now. (*Presses a hand to her eyes as if to keep the tears from forming.*) God must know what He's doin'. But it's hard to lose a son.

LUIS. C'mon, don't say that. Chaguito's alive. You haven't lost him.

DA. GABRIELA. I started to lose him a long time ago. You sure that's a fight?

(*The voices approach the house. Some comments are clearly heard: "Make way," "Is she alive?" "Get outta the way," "Let us through."*)

LUIS. (*Going to the left.*) Looks like they're carryin' someone . . .

LITO. (*Outside, from the left.*) Luis! Doña Grabiela! Luis!

LUIS. (*Looking out the door.*) What's goin' on . . . ? (*Stops.*) Oh God!

(*Rushes out.* DA. GABRIELA *has remained still, looking toward the door. As the noise outside gets closer, her hand slowly goes to her breast and finally is clenched over her heart. At that moment* LUIS *enters with* JUANITA *in his arms. Her body is limp and wet.* LITO *and* MATILDE *follow after* LUIS.)

DA. GABRIELA. (*Taking a step toward* LUIS *and stopping.*) Is she . . . dead?

MATILDE. No, ma'am, no.

LUIS. An accident, ma. They say she fell into the sea.

(DA. GABRIELA *reacts calmly and diligently.*)

DA. GABRIELA. Take her in the bedroom. Hurry up! Put her to bed. (*To* MATILDE.) You, get me hot water. (MATILDE *exits quickly to the right. To* LITO.) You, go to the store and get a bottle o' rubbing alcohol . . . Run! (LUIS *exits through the rear door with* JUANITA *in his arms.* LITO *runs out through the left.* DA. GABRIELA *leans out, left.*) Thank you for bringin' her. Now please go away. I don't want nobody else in here. (*Shuts the door.*) Luis, get me the khaki blanket outta the trunk. (*Goes to the bed, rear left, takes the blanket she had smoothed out earlier, and goes toward the rear door.*) Blessed St. Anthony, help us! (*Stops in the*

rear doorway and calls to MATILDE.) As soon as the water's hot, bring it here!
(*Exits rear.*)
LUIS. (*From within.*) Is this the blanket?
DA. GABRIELA. (*From within.*) Yes, bring it here. Shut that window. (*The light that enters through the window in the backroom goes out.*) Now leave. (LITO *enters from the left, out of breath, with a bottle of cheap rubbing alcohol.*)
LITO. Here it is.
LUIS. Gimme it. Go get a quarter pound o' coffee. Run! Wait. (*Takes some coins from his pocket.*) Pay Don Severo for the alcohol and the coffee.
LITO. How's Juanita?
LUIS. She's all right. Go on.
LITO. She didn't fall, you know? I saw her jump.
(LITO *rushes out, left, like a shot.* LUIS *goes to the rear door.*)
LUIS. Here's the alcohol.
(*Puts the bottle through the curtain without looking in.* MATILDE *enters from the right with a pan of hot water.*)
MATILDE. (*Going to the rear.*) The water's ready, Doña Gabriela.
(*Exits rear.*)
DA. GABRIELA. (*From within.*) Put it here.
MATILDE. (*From within.*) You want me to help you?
DA. GABRIELA. (*Within.*) No, thanks. Go heat more water for coffee.
(MATILDE *enters from the rear. She hurries toward the kitchen. Before she gets to the door,* LUIS *grabs her by the arm.*)
LUIS. (*In a low, forceful voice.*) What happened?
MATILDE. I dunno. Lemme go. I got things to do.
LUIS. (*Not letting go.*) Tell me what it was that happened.
MATILDE. You know already. Juanita fell into the water.
LUIS. She didn't fall. Somebody saw her jump. Why?
MATILDE. How do I know?

LUIS. (*Shaking her.*) You know. You were with her. What happened?
MATILDE. Okay. I suppose you oughta know anyway. Juanita was pregnant.
LUIS. (*Shaking her furiously.*) It's a lie! A lie!
MATILDE. Lemme go. Lemme go if you don't want me to shout it so's everybody finds out. (LUIS *lets her go.*) Yeah, she was pregnant.
LUIS. (*After a pause.*) Who was it?
MATILDE. I dunno.
LUIS. Who was it? Miguel?
MATILDE. No.
LUIS. (*Grabbing her wrist.*) Tell me who it was. Right now. Tell me who it was.
MATILDE. I dunno. I dunno, I tell you.
LUIS. Well then, she'll have to tell me.
(*Starts to go to the rear.*)
MATILDE. (*Stopping him.*) She can't tell you. Don't be stupid. Leave her be.
LUIS. If she don't tell me, I'll kill her!
(*Gets away from* MATILDE *and goes in a blind rage toward the rear.*)
MATILDE. Think of Doña Gabriela! She don't know!
(*As* LUIS *is about to arrive at the bedroom door,* DA. GABRIELA *appears in it. Her arms hang inertly beside her body. In one hand she holds the bottle of alcohol.* LUIS *remains still. Their eyes meet. The bottle of alcohol falls to the floor. There is a terrible silence broken only by the beating of the waves on the rocks.* MATILDE *rushes out through the left.*)
LUIS. Mamá!
(DA. GABRIELA *doesn't answer. She takes a few uncertain steps and finally says in a hoarse voice.*)
DA. GABRIELA. And I threw a woman outta my house 'cause she sinned against God. And God punishes me by makin' my daughter commit the most horrible sin a woman can commit. But He saved her from the other sin. He didn't let her die. So's we can pay for it together.
LUIS. I'll find him, ma. I'll make him marry her.
DA. GABRIELA. Luis, those with my

blood are cursed. My father died on the land, in a cave, like a dog without an owner. My son is in jail. My daughter is dishonored . . . Only you've been saved. 'Cause you're not . . .

LUIS. (*Almost shouting.*) No, ma, no! The curse is on all of us. And I'm glad it's on me too. So I can suffer with you. So you won't be alone.

DA. GABRIELA. No, Luis, not you.

LUIS. You think I'm not cursed too? The curse o' havin' taken all o' you away from the country? The curse o' havin' stuck you in this here hell? The curse o' always bein' poor? The curse o' never bein' good for anythin'?

DA. GABRIELA. And why should that be, Luis? Why? It's all well an' good if somethin' happens to you and you say: "God's will be done." And another time if somethin' happens to you and you say: "Let it be how God wants it." But God can't always be wantin' what's bad. His will can't be to always hurt us where it's most painful. 'Cause then God'd be bad. And God can't be bad, Luis. God can't be bad.

LUIS. If He's not bad, there's somebody bad. There's *somethin'* bad. And we don't know what it is. We can't see it. We can't strike out at it or kill it.

DA. GABRIELA. No, you can't. If you could, you might feel better. A man who strikes and kills gets rid of hate and suffering from his heart like that. But a mother whose soul has been all dried up, a mother whose heart has suddenly been eaten away by termites, can't be consoled by blows or death.

LUIS. Well then, what're we gonna do, ma?

DA. GABRIELA. Nothin', Luis, nothin'. (*Takes the rosary down from the nail.*) I'm gonna pray.

(*Kisses the cross on the rosary and crosses herself with it.*)

LUIS. (*In an anguished cry.*) Ma, let's get outta here! (*Goes to her and shakes her by the shoulders.*) Let's go! Don't start prayin'. Shout, say somethin'. Hit me! Tell me to do whatever you want, but don't just stand there so quiet like, thinkin' about God. Let's do somethin'. Let's shake off this curse from on top of us. Let's go away from here. Far away. Make another life. Where people are different. Speak to me, ma. Tell me we're alive, that we can still fight!

DA. GABRIELA. I feel old, Luis.

LUIS. I'll be young for the two of us. We'll go far away. Real far.

DA. GABRIELA. What for, Luis, what for?

LUIS. To start again. To fight some more . . .

(*Pause.*)

DA. GABRIELA. Yes, you're a man. You need to fight. You need to fight to feel alive, don't you, Luis? (*Goes toward the rocker.*) You're the man o' the house. Whatever you decide, that's what we'll do, Luis. Whatever you decide. (*Sits down. The same rhumba from the beginning of the act is heard from the jukebox in the bar.* DA. GABRIELA *sighs.*) I'll pray a little.

LUIS. That damn noise!

(*Exits left.*)

DA. GABRIELA. It don't matter Luis. Noises aren't important any more.

(*She rocks with her eyes shut, passing the beads of the rosary between her fingers.* LITO *enters through the left crying and carrying the small package of coffee. He sees* DA. GABRIELA *and slowly approaches her. He sits at her feet. Snivelling, he says:*

LITO. Some tough kid stole my top, Doña Grabiela. (*Cries inconsolably.*)

(*With one hand* DA. GABRIELA *caresses* LITO's *head as he leans it against her knees. With her other hand she continues saying the rosary. The rhumba on the jukebox is heard even more wildly.*)

THE CURTAIN FALLS

ACT THREE

One year later. A small apartment in Morrisania, Puerto Rican area in the Bronx, New York. Sixth floor of an old, run-down building. In the foreground, extreme right, main door of the apartment. Occupying a little less than one-fourth of the stage, three feet behind the curtain line, there is a wall five feet long that runs parallel to the proscenium, starting almost at the frame of the front door. Along this wall there is a closed door leading to the small bathroom. In the wall to the right of the bathroom door there are three hooks for hanging up clothes. There are two woolen jackets on two of the hooks. There is a felt hat on the third. To the left of this door there is a framed print showing an ornate snowscape. This wall forms a passageway that goes from the front door to the living room. The latter occupies the rest of the stage.

In the right background of the living room there is a small window that looks out on a dark, inside courtyard. From the outside of the window frame to a point unseen by the audience, there extends over the courtyard a pulley line for hanging up clothes when the weather is good. At the rear, to the left of the window and next to it, there is an open door leading to the kitchen. A table and three chairs can be seen in the kitchen. The table is covered with an imitation embroidered tablecloth made of white plastic. A green pitcher, a black coffee can, and a yellow sugar bowl are on the table. On the part of the rear wall that runs from the kitchen door to the wall on the left there is a frame print of the Sacred Heart of Jesus. On the wall on each side of this print there is a small, gaudy flower holder with faded and dirty artificial flowers. Beneath the print there is an old studio couch covered with cretonne. To the left of the couch, in the corner formed by the two walls, there is a small table with a shiny, aggressive radio of the latest style, in direct contrast to the rest of the furniture. On the radio is the wooden oxcart that Miguel gave to JUANITA. *In the left wall of the living room there is a wide doorway covered with a curtain of flowered cretonne leading to the only bedroom.*

In the left foreground, an upholstered chair showing unmistakable signs of age and dirt. Next to the right wall of the living room, between the rear window and the entrance passageway, another armchair similar to the one at the left. To the right of the chair there is a floor lamp with a parchment shade covered with printed flowers. To the left of the chair there is an old, rusty kerosene heater that doesn't work.

The living room floor is covered with worn, flowered linoleum. The passageway and the living room were painted years ago with a bright, rose colored paint. Dampness and time have faded the original color, and large whitish stains can be seen in several places. The visible part of the kitchen is painted a light green. There, too, dampness and time have faded the paint.

The bedroom to the left, the door to which is visible, faces the street. The noise of an electric drill can be heard tearing up the pavement. At regular intervals an elevated train can be heard passing in the distance.

Left and right, that of the audience.

It is a cold, gray autumn day with a threat of snow.

DOÑA GABRIELA *enters from the kitchen with a plastic shopping bag. She leaves the bag on the divan. She takes a woolen scarf and puts it around her head tying it under her chin. She opens a small black purse and examines its contents as she goes to the door at the left. She stops in front of the door and says:*

DA. GABRIELA. Luis, I left your breakfast ready. All you have to do is heat the milk. (*Shuts her purse and goes to the couch. The doorbell rings.* DA. GABRIELA *hesitates. She goes to the right. The bell rings again and then the rapping of knuckles is heard on the door.* DA. GABRIELA *opens the door.* JUANITA *enters wearing a woolen coat. She wears a silk kerchief on her head, the ends tied under her chin. She has woolen gloves and a leather handbag. For the first time we see her heavily made-up. She carries a package under one arm.*) Oh, it's you, child.

JUANITA. How's everythin', mamá? (*Kisses her.*) Blessing . . .

DA. GABRIELA. God bless you. (*Shutting the door.*) My heavens, what cold air comes in from those damn stairs!

JUANITA. (*Taking off her coat.*) And Luis?

DA. GABRIELA. He hasn't got up yet. Oh, is that a new coat? (*She helps* JUANITA *take off her coat and hangs it on a hook near the door as she examines it.*) Expensive. Must've cost you a lot, huh?

(JUANITA *pretends not to hear her mother's question. She takes off her kerchief, exposing her hair now curled with a permanent wave.*)

JUANITA. Are you goin' out?

DA. GABRIELA. Yes, I'm goin' to the market. (*Noticing for the first time* JUANITA's *curled hair.*) Listen, what'd you do to your hair?

JUANITA. A permanent. Look, I brought you somethin' that I bought yesterday in the grocery.

DA. GABRIELA. How strange it makes you look! (*Takes the package and carries it to the kitchen.*) You had such pretty hair. (*Exits rear.*)

JUANITA. I brought you canned meat pies. Wait'll you see how good they are.

DA. GABRIELA. (*From the kitchen, out of sight.*) Ay, you're right. Luis'll go out o' his mind for 'em. Just think Puerto Rican meat pies in a can! What next! (*Short pause.*) Listen, is it expensive that thing you had done to your hair?

JUANITA. (*Laughing as she finishes removing her gloves.*) Why, you thinkin' o' gettin' a permanent?

DA. GABRIELA. (*From the kitchen.*) Ha! They could kill me before I'd let 'em touch my hair. Not to have hair is worse than bein' naked. I said it 'cause you're spendin' a lot, you know?

JUANITA. Don't worry. A dollar more or less never made anybody rich. (*Rubbing her arms.*) What's the matter with the heat?

DA. GABRIELA. (*Entering from the rear.*) That piece o' junk don't work.

JUANITA. Why don't you complain?

DA. GABRIELA. You were prettier with long hair.

(*The noise from a passing elevated train is heard.*)

JUANITA. I dunno how you put up with that noise from the elevated.

DA. GABRIELA. I don't even hear it no more. What bothers me is the noise from them machines they got fixin' the street. When you pass by 'em you think they're drillin' your brains out.

JUANITA. And Lidia? Does she know I was comin' today?

DA. GABRIELA. (*Taking the shopping bag from the sofa.*) Yes, I told her. She'll prob'ly be up here any minute. You're gonna stay for lunch, aren't you?

JUANITA. Sure. Oh, I told a friend he could come see me here.

DA. GABRIELA. A friend? Well, I'll be right back. (*Passing the right rear window and looking out.*) What a day! What an ugly day! (*Goes toward the passageway at the right.*) If it gets too cold, go in the kitchen and light the oven.

JUANITA. Put my coat on, mamá.

DA. GABRIELA. No, child, no. (*Takes a woolen sweater from a hook near the door and puts it on while observing* JUANITA.) I dunno if it's your hair, but you look older today.

JUANITA. (*With a forced laugh.*) People cut their hair to look younger, mamá.

(DA. GABRIELA *goes to open the door, then stops. She turns to* JUANITA.)

DA. GABRIELA. Juanita, you oughta come live with us.

(*Opens the door and leaves.* JUANITA *remains looking pensively toward the door. Then she goes to the sofa and sits down in the right corner, doubling her legs under her. She turns on the radio. Reaches out with her arm, takes her pocketbook, takes out a cigarette and lights it. The music of a "blues" is heard.* JUANITA *takes a deep puff on the cigarette and notices the oxcart. She looks at it, stretches out her hand and takes it. She examines it and puts it back on the radio. Her fingers are still caressing the rough form when* LUIS *enters from the left. He now appears nervous and taciturn. There is something terribly disturbing gnawing at the soul of this transplanted country-boy. He is shirtless and shoeless. He doesn't see* JUANITA *and crosses rapidly to the right.*)

JUANITA. (*Without moving.*) Hello!

LUIS. (*Stopping and turning around.*) Oh, you're here.

JUANITA. Yes, like you see.

LUIS. And the old lady?

JUANITA. At the market. (LUIS *makes a gesture of impatience.*) What's the matter, am I botherin' you?

LUIS. Heat me the milk for the coffee. (*Enters the bathroom and shuts the door.* JUANITA *gets up indolently. Exits rear. We hear* JUANITA'S *movements in the kitchen, the water running in the bathroom basin, and the sleepy "blues" on the radio.*)

LUIS' VOICE. Change that music!

JUANITA. (*Coming to the kitchen door.*) What'd you say?

LUIS' VOICE. (*From the bathroom.*) Change that music!

JUANITA. Why? It's pretty.

LUIS' VOICE. It makes you wanna cry. Sounds like a funeral. Turn it off!

(JUANITA *shrugs her shoulders, goes to the radio and changes the station.* The "*danza*" Margarita *by Tavárez is heard.*)

JUANITA. There's the Spanish station for you.

(JUANITA *goes to the kitchen. We see her putting* LUIS' *breakfast on the table.* LUIS *comes out of the bathroom, crosses rapidly and exits through the door on the left. A few seconds later he returns with his shirt half on and his shoes in his hand. He sits on the sofa and begins to put on his shoes. He stops to turn off the radio, then returns to his task.*)

JUANITA. (*From the kitchen.*) Your breakfast's ready. (*Comes to the rear door.*) What happened?

LUIS. Nothin'.

JUANITA. You shut off the radio?

LUIS. Yeah.

JUANITA. What d'you got a radio for if you don't listen to it?

LUIS. (*Getting up and tucking his shirt in his pants.*) So's I can listen to it when I feel like it.

JUANITA. (*Joking.*) And you don't feel like it now?

LUIS. Nope.

JUANITA. The milk's gettin' cold.

(LUIS *enters the kitchen, sits at the table with his back to the living room, and begins to eat.* JUANITA *takes a newspaper and sits down in the armchair on the right. She glances indifferently at the front page, then looks toward the kitchen.*)

JUANITA. You need anythin'? (*She awaits an answer from* LUIS, *who pretends not to hear.*) How's your job goin'? (LUIS *continues eating and doesn't answer.* JUANITA *gets up.*) That new radio must've cost you a pretty penny. (*Pause.*) Looks like you're really makin' progress. (*Pause.*) Of course, mamá would rather have had a new armchair. (*Approaching the rear door, changing her tone.*) Have you noticed how old she seems? (*In a low voice, full of emotion.*) Her days are numbered, Luis.

LUIS. (*Turning half-way round.*) Shut up!

JUANITA. (*Turns around.*) She used to be as strong as the trunk of an ausubo tree. The hurricanes couldn't blow her over. But up here she's gettin' all bent over like a dry stalk o' sugar cane. She's wrinklin' up on us like a dried fig.

LUIS. (*Getting up violently.*) Shut up! She's better than ever.

JUANITA. Her hair is turnin' the same color as this gray, American sky. And her hands . . . you remember her hands? When she used to grab the handle of the millstone and turn it, her hands looked like a giant's hands. And when the corn came out as yellow flour, it seemed like a miracle from her own hands and not the work of the handle and the stones. I was a little girl then and her hands were big and strong. I saw her hands today. And they were so small, and they shook so when she tried to button her sweater!

LUIS. She's strong. She's better than ever. She's strong, I tell you!

JUANITA. And she doesn't scold us anymore. Have you noticed how she doesn't scold us anymore? But she looks at me. She looks at me in such a way! And it's worse than a scolding.

LUIS. She don't need nothin'. She's got everythin'. Everythin'.

JUANITA. Are you sure, Luis?

LUIS. I've given her what I've always wanted to give her, a decent life. She's got clothes and she's got food. And a real good bed. And she can rest whenever she wants to. And she's got all the money she needs. And I've given her all that. That's why I've been workin' so hard. That's why I work overtime. So she can live right.

JUANITA. I know now you've gotten what you wanted.

LUIS. And I brought her to this neighborhood from Harlem. So she can live better here. And we don't owe nothin' to nobody. Two months ago I sent Doña Isa the last cent she lent us for the plane fare. When have we ever been better off? Never!

JUANITA. Yeah, you're makin' money all right.

LUIS. And I'll keep on makin' it. More and more. Money. Not to be poor, understand? That's what's important.

JUANITA. But mamá . . .

LUIS. What d'you have to worry about the old lady for? She's all right. She don't need a thing. And I'm the one who gave it all to her! You went off to live someplace else . . .

JUANITA. I work in Brooklyn. It's too far . . .

LUIS. Others from here work in Long Island. And that's even further. But they live here, in their homes. Except that in their homes you can't do certain things . . .

JUANITA. Shut up!

LUIS. Don't make me talk, then.

JUANITA. Okay. Talk. I'm not afraid o' what you'll say.

LUIS. 'Cause you don't have any shame.

JUANITA. Aren't you lucky to have so much! But listen close. Those certain things you mentioned can be done anyplace. All you need is to want to do 'em. Whether it's Bronx, Brooklyn, or Long Island. If I left this house, it was for the good of all of us. 'Cause you and mamá were drivin' me crazy. You watchin' me, spyin' on me all the time like I was some criminal. And mamá lookin' at me, always lookin' at me, like she didn't know me. Like she wanted to get to know me and she couldn't.

LUIS. It was like a stab with a dagger, you goin' away from here.

JUANITA. Stabs can be cured. If I stayed here, it would've been like a knife always stuck in her heart. And that can't be cured. Besides, you wouldn't have gotten what you have if I stayed. I earn my own living and I don't cost you a cent. And for your information, if you've been able to pay back Doña Isa, it's 'cause I've been givin' mamá somethin' every month.

LUIS. It's a lie! She never told me . . .

JUANITA. What for? If you don't even hear what people tell you any more.

LUIS. But where does the money go?

JUANITA. Where does it go? You oughta know that. You buy a fancy radio and mamá has to go out in the street with a sweater.

LUIS. I bought her a good coat. But she don't wanna wear it. She's got it put away in the closet. She says it's better to keep it like new in case somethin' happens and she has to sell it. Don't blame me for her crazy ideas.

JUANITA. No, I know we all got our own crazy ideas. (*Indicating Luis' wristwatch.*) Like that gold watch. How much do you still owe on it?

LUIS. (*Furious.*) What's it to you? Do I ask you how much you owe on that necklace, or that permanent, or all that junk you smear on your face?

JUANITA. No, you don't ask me 'cause you know what I'll tell you. You know that *I* don't owe anythin' on all that. *Others* owe on it.

LUIS. Well, I forbid you to give another cent o' that money to the old lady.

JUANITA. Really? Why?

LUIS. 'Cause it's dirty money.

JUANITA. There's no such thing as dirty money or clean money. There's just money. And in that sweatshop I earn barely enough to keep alive. Whatever else I can get to help the old lady or for the things I want, it's nobody's business what kind o' money it is.

LUIS. Well, it does matter to me.

JUANITA. But not to me. That's the advantage o' bein' a woman, right? We don't have to be as decent as you men.

LUIS. (*Advancing menacingly.*) I oughta smash your face.

JUANITA. (*Without moving.*) Go ahead. (*Pause.*) But you wouldn't dare.

LUIS. (*Turning his back.*) It's not that I wouldn't dare. It's just that you're a woman. And you're my sister. (*Pause.*) Why don't you come live with us? What d'you have to work for? I can work for all of us. (*Turning to her.*) You won't have to do without a thing. I work overtime. I'm gonna earn more. I'll have more money. Leave all that. Come back here, Juanita, so you can take care o' the old lady.

JUANITA. If it was for that . . . But it's

not. I know that line. Mamá'd be the one who'd be takin' care o' me. And you'd start spyin' on me again.

LUIS. No, I promise . . . If you behave right . . .

JUANITA. Ah, you see? If I behave right! The thing is I don't feel like behavin' right any more. And just what does behave right mean? One day we left our little farm in an oxcart 'cause we were goin' in search of freedom. The mountains were closing in on us, and we fled to the sea. But the sea closed in on us too, and we fled from the sea. Now we're closed in by buildings that look like mountains and seas of people who push us and shove us. If this is freedom, I wanna enjoy it alone. Without answerin' to anybody. You got that? I'm gonna drive my own cart and lead the oxen wherever I want.

(*The doorbell rings.*)

LUIS. Shut up! There's the old lady.

JUANITA. Mamá's got a key. She don't have to ring. What's the matter with you? Why don't you open the door?

(*She goes to the right and opens the door.* PACO *enters. He is thirty years old. He is well dressed and well groomed, like the majority of the frustrated writers from the Puerto Rican colony in New York. He is the blond type of country person descended from Canary Islanders. His voice has the unmistakable metallic, polished sound of a radio announcer. The nostalgia of his homeland in this frustrated writer has marked romantic characteristics.*)

PACO. Hi, how are you, Juanita?

JUANITA. Hi, Paco!

PACO. Caramba! I forgot your number. I though I wasn't going to find the house.

JUANITA. Especially since here all the buildin's are the same. Come in. Come in.

(PACO *proceeds to enter and stops on seeing* LUIS.)

PACO. Hello.

JUANITA. Oh, this is my brother Luis. Luis, a friend.

PACO. (*Extending his hand, warmly.*) Pleased to meet you.
(LUIS, *with wry face, shakes hands. There is a moment of embarrassing silence.*)
JUANITA. Sit down. Mamá went out. She'll be right back. When you meet her, you'll know the rest o' the family.
(*Pause.* PACO *sits down.*)
PACO. (*For the sake of saying something.*) It's a pleasant neighborhood, isn't it?
JUANITA. At least it's better than Harlem. That's what Luis says.
(JUANITA *and* PACO *look at* LUIS *to get him to agree.* LUIS *pays no attention.*)
JUANITA. (*Insisting.*) Right, Luis?
LUIS. Huh . . . ?
JUANITA. Weren't you goin' out?
LUIS. No.
JUANITA. Oh, it seemed to me . . .
LUIS. No.
(*Annoying pause.*)
JUANITA. Why don't you bring Paco a beer?
LUIS. There isn't any beer.
JUANITA. Yes, there is. I brought some. Well, I'll go get it.
(*Gets up.*)
PACO. Please, don't bother.
JUANITA. It's no bother. But I don't think it's very cold.
(*Exits rear.* LUIS *and* PACO *look at each other out of the corners of their eyes.* PACO *takes out his cigarettes. He gets up and offers one to* LUIS.)
LUIS. Thanks, but I don't smoke.
(PACO *sits down and lights a cigarette.*)
PACO. You're lucky not to have any minor vices.
LUIS. (*Agreeing.*) Hunh . . .
PACO. What kind of work do you do?
LUIS. Factory work.
PACO. Nearby?
LUIS. Almost next door.
PACO. What kind of factory?
LUIS. Boilers.
PACO. Oh . . . !
LUIS. What about you, do you work?

PACO. (*Laughing.*) Sure! What else!
LUIS. What d'you do?
PACO. Announcer.
LUIS. What?
PACO. Radio announcer.
LUIS. Ah . . . !
PACO. (*Pointing to the radio.*) That's a nice set.
LUIS. Yeah.
PACO. Do you listen to the Spanish station?
LUIS. Sometimes.
PACO. I have my programs from 8 to 11 in the mornings and from 2 to 5 in the afternoons. You've probably heard me.
LUIS. (*Emphasizing the fact.*) I'm workin' at those times.
PACO. (*Laughing.*) Well so am I.
LUIS. You get paid for that?
PACO. Yes, of course.
JUANITA. (*From the kitchen.*) I can't find the opener, Luis.
LUIS. It's in the little drawer. (*To* PACO.) Where'd you meet Juanita?
PACO. At my brother's house.
LUIS. Your brother?
PACO. Yes. My sister-in-law works with Juanita.
LUIS. Your brother's wife?
PACO. Naturally.
LUIS. Do you have any more relatives?
PACO. Not here. In Puerto Rico. (*Pause.*) So? How do you like it here?
LUIS. And your wife?
PACO. My wife? Ah no, I'm a bachelor.
(JUANITO *enters with two glasses of beer on a plate. She offers one to* PACO.)
JUANITA. I don't know if you like it with a head on it.
PACO. That's all right, thanks.
JUANITA. (*Giving the other glass to* LUIS.) You're really not goin' to work?
PACO. Work today? But it's a holiday!
JUANITA. My brother works overtime. He just lives for that. For his work.
LUIS. My shift begins at eleven. I'm not in any hurry.
PACO. Aren't you having anything to drink?

JUANITA. I don't like beer.

LUIS. How long have you known each other?

PACO. Two weeks, more or less. Isn't that so?

JUANITA. This is the fourth time we've seen each other.

(*Pause. The men drink.*)

LUIS. The old lady's late.

JUANITA. Yes. (*Pause.*)

LUIS. I have to get goin'.

(*He doesn't move.*)

PACO. You do? (*Lying.*) I'm so sorry! (*Pause.*)

LUIS. (*Getting up.*) Well . . .

PACO. (*Getting up.*) Well . . .

JUANITA. Don't forget your jacket.

(*Takes the glass from his hand.*)

LUIS. I don't need a jacket. I'm not goin' outside. Have you seen the dominoes?

JUANITA. No. You probably have 'em in your room.

(LUIS *exits left.*)

PACO. (*With comic disconcertedness.*) Is he going to invite me to play dominoes?

JUANITA. No. He's going' to play with a neighbor. That's the only fun he has.

PACO. He seems worried, doesn't he?

JUANITA. (*Shrugging her shoulders.*) He's gotten ugly. He don't even know how to treat people any more.

PACO. Bah! It's not important. We all have our bad days.

JUANITA. Bad days? No, it's not that. You want more beer?

PACO. I still have some.

JUANITA. Ah, so you do.

(LUIS *enters from the left with a box of dominoes.*)

JUANITA. Well, are you goin' or not?

LUIS. This is my house.

JUANITA. So you oughta be more polite to company then.

LUIS. He's your company, not mine. (*Facing up to* PACO.) You were born in the city, right? Probably in San Juan. You talk good and have a rich boy's face. We're country folk. We come from the mountains. We used to eat bananas and roots. But here we're as good as anybody else. And we live well. And we got a radio. And we're gonna have TV. 'Cause I earn enough for all that.

JUANITA. Have you gone crazy? What does he care what you eat or what you earn?

PACO. It doesn't matter. Leave him alone. He asked me a question. No, I wasn't born in the city. I was born in the country near Morovis. What you call my good speech is just a means of earning a living. We all do what we can.

JUANITA. And that business about bein' as good as anybody else here is a big joke. Ha! My side's splittin' from laughin' so hard. The way we get kicked around all the time. Yeah, yeah, we're all equal. Except that everybody else here's worth more than us. But that don't bother you. You just worry about money and machines. Go on, go wait for your shift at work. Go play dominoes. But while you're playin' you'll be thinkin' about your machines. And you won't be able to enjoy yourself. 'Cause machines are eatin' your life away. They're your friends, and your family. Machines are your wife and your kids. Go on, fill yourself with 'em 'till you bust. But leave us be.

LUIS. What're you carryin' on so about machines for? What would we do if it wasn't for them, eh? Machines give us life.

JUANITA. God gives us life.

LUIS. I'm not talkin' about God. (*Brusquely, turning to* PACO.) What d'you think?

PACO. I don't know . . . For me, machines are just a good means of work. But, of course, there was work before there were machines.

LUIS. But do you know what a machine really is? No, you don't know nothin'. A machine is a tremendous thing. It's like a miracle. There's somethin' you can never completely understand in a machine. Any day it's apt to do somethin' unexpected. But people think that by knowin' about the nuts and screws it's got inside, they know what it is. But they don't know;

they don't know nothin'. You really never can get to know it. You see why I say it's such a marvellous thing?

PACO. Yes . . . It seems as though you think a machine has . . . life and brains . . . a soul and a will of its own.

JUANITA. Are you goin' or stayin'? 'Cause if you stay to talk about machines, I'm the one who's goin'.

LUIS. Whenever I go in the subway, I keep thinkin': "What'll it do now? What's it gonna do now?" Yesterday a subway train in Brooklyn turned over. I bet you didn't know that!

PACO. Yes, I knew it. Those accidents aren't so rare.

LUIS. And the noise in the factory! The oven! Do you know what it's like, that enormous belly with a hunger for things you can't even guess? Like the sea. Only better . . . or worse. It's a marvel. It's a mystery you can't understand. But someday I'll find out . . . I have to find out.

(*Exits right. Pause.*)

JUANITA. Oh, please excuse all this! That brother o' mine loses his head whenever he talks about machines.

PACO. He's a strange fellow.

JUANITA. An idiot!

PACO. No. Your brother's not happy.

JUANITA. Hah, what a discovery! Do you know anyone who is happy?

PACO. Yes . . . relatively.

JUANITA. Well, either I'm happy or I'm not happy. I don't get that stuff about "relatively".

PACO. And . . . are you happy?

JUANITA. Well, the truth is I don't know if I'm happy. There was a time when I was happy. And I thought I was gonna be even more happy. But instead I was really disgraced more than ever. Now I don't know. I'm not sufferin', but I'm not content. I feel hollow like a gourd.

PACO. It's the emptiness of New York...

JUANITA. (*Laughing bitterly.*) Yeah. Emptiness. Eight million hollow gourds.

PACO. For that reason it's all the more terrible.

JUANITA. (*Approaching the window.*) And the summer is so short. It seems like this sky is ashamed o' bein' seen blue.

PACO. You miss your little island, don't you?

JUANITA. Although it's hard enough anyway to see the sky. Those mountains o' buildin's have no pity on anybody.

PACO. There's no room for pity when the sky is so far away.

JUANITA. It must be that the cold oppresses a person's heart. (*Moving away from the window.*) Grandpa used to say that the heart can dry up like an old bean. But here it don't dry up. It freezes. It freezes up like ice. And that's even worse.

PACO. They say that love can melt hearts of ice.

JUANITA. Yeah, in the soap operas. And in the movies.

PACO. Why did you invite me to come here?

JUANITA. I don't know. You make me sad. Maybe you'd better go.

PACO. Why?

JUANITA. I told you you make me sad.

PACO. You don't live here, do you?

JUANITA. No.

PACO. And why didn't you invite me to your house?

JUANITA. This is my house.

PACO. And the other?

JUANITA. A boarding house.

PACO. But do you receive visitors there?

JUANITA. Visitors? Yes.

PACO. But me, on the other hand . . .

JUANITA. Are you sorry you came?

PACO. No. I'd like to be your friend.

JUANITA. I know.

PACO. And you?

JUANITA. I don't have friends. They're just eight million hollow gourds.

PACO. I also feel lonely.

JUANITA. Lonely? Speakin' good English? With that light face? You could even pass for an American.

PACO. I'm Puerto Rican. And I feel the loneliness the way you do.

JUANITA. An American probably wouldn't feel what you feel. But there are other things an American would understand and you wouldn't.

PACO. What things?

JUANITA. I'll bring you another beer.

PACO. I thought you wanted me to go.

JUANITA. You can drink it before you go. (*Exits rear.*)

PACO. (*After a pause, looking towards the rear.*) How about having lunch together someplace and then going to Radio City?

JUANITA. (*From the kitchen.*) Do you intend to go into debt on my account?

PACO. Don't worry. I got paid yesterday.

JUANITA. Wouldn't a neighborhood movie be better?

PACO. Well, whatever you want.

JUANITA. (*Coming in with the beer.*) I was just talkin'. I don't plan on goin' out. (*Hands him the glass of beer.*)

PACO. What are you up to, Juanita? What kind of game is this?

JUANITA. Game?

PACO. Why don't you answer my question?

JUANITA. You make me sad. I don't know who you are.

PACO. A man who offers to share his loneliness with you.

JUANITA. (*Disturbed.*) How?

PACO. By marrying you.

JUANITA. (*Pale, evading him.*) You're mad.

PACO. I'm not going to lie and say I'm madly in love. But since I met you, I knew we needed each other.

JUANITA. You've only seen me four times.

PACO. I see women 365 times a year. And they don't interest me.

JUANITA. And so why do I?

PACO. It must be because there's something in you that doesn't belong to this world of New York. Because there's something fresh in you like the fields near Morovis. Maybe a certain flavor of the land . . .

JUANITA. The land is bitter . . .

PACO. But it gives life. And I haven't been able to erase the sight of my land.

JUANITA. Why did you leave it, then?

PACO. For the same reason we all leave it. Because we believe we can only be successful away from it.

JUANITA. Did you also have illusions?

PACO. Yes. I wanted to be a writer.

JUANITA. A writer? You gotta study a lot for that.

PACO. Not really. Anyway I couldn't. I had hardly gotten to Rio Piedras to study at the University when my parents died. I couldn't continue.

JUANITA. What did you do?

PACO. I was a janitor in a government building. Then assistant linotypist at a printer's. I got a few minor parts in some soap operas on the radio. The main thing was just to earn something to live on. But what mattered to me were the stories I was writing and nobody wanted to publish. I did everything imaginable to get a job as a journalist, but it was impossible. In the government newspaper my ideas were too much pro-independence. In the papers backed by big business what I wrote sounded like communism. And a communist magazine rejected some articles of mine because they thought they were too bourgeois.

JUANITA. Why was that?

PACO. I don't know. They all made a special effort to fit me into some neat little political pigeon-hole. I couldn't think for myself. I had to belong to some group where others would think for me. That way, the others felt more at ease.

JUANITA. I don't get it. I've always thought what I've wanted to.

PACO. No, Juanita. You don't realize it, but the thing is others do think for you. And I got fed up with it. I decided to tell them all to go to hell. And I came here, to look for my liberty.

JUANITA. And did you find it?

PACO. (*Laughing.*) Yeah. At the entrance to the harbor, with a torch in one hand and a book in the other. But the torch and the book are just reinforced concrete.

JUANITA. Ah, I've seen that too!

PACO. Sure, that's why they have it

there, so we all see it. But for me everything was the same, if not worse. Ten years ago I arrived in New York to write a novel. A hack novel that would make me famous. Then I could go back to Puerto Rico and all those who had turned me down would have to accept me and recognize their stupid mistake.

JUANITA. What's the name o' the novel?

PACO. I never wrote it.

JUANITA. For God's sake! That's a fine thing!

PACO. It's true. New York didn't give my any freedom, but it did dry up my enthusiasm. But I don't care any more! I probably would never be any good as a writer.

JUANITA. You're an animal! Just think, if I could write I sure wouldn't give up so easy! Never! With the tremendous things I'd have to say! I'd never let anythin' get the best o' me!

PACO. Probably what I need is your help.

JUANITA. My help?

PACO. Marry me, and make me write.

JUANITA. Who, me? Hah, that's enough o' that. Nobody can make anybody do anythin'. Besides, I got no intention o' marryin' you. I don't understand you at all.

PACO. All you have to understand is my loneliness.

JUANITA. Don't be an idiot. If your loneliness was joined to mine, we'd just have a bigger loneliness. What do we gain by that?

PACO. Two lonelinesses together stop being loneliness.

JUANITA. You're talkin' now like in the soap operas. But for a long time now I don't believe in the radio. Look, you've let your beer get warm.

LIDIA'S VOICE. (*Coming from the right.*) Juanita! Telephone!

PACO. Sounds like you're being called.

LIDIA. (*Knocking at the door at the right and calling.*) Juanita! Come to the janitor's phone!

JUANITA. (*Shouting.*) Coming. (*To* PACO.) Well, you can go now.

PACO. You're throwing me out now?

JUANITA. We agreed you'd go as soon as you finished your beer. And since you're not gonna drink it . . .

PACO. But we also agreed that you were going to invite me to lunch or that I was going to invite you.

JUANITA. Yes, but I didn't really know you then. (*Gives him his hat.*) Good-bye, Paco.

PACO. I haven't met your mother.

JUANITA. I'll tell her about you. It'll be the same thing.

PACO. When will I see you again?

JUANITA. Someday. I dunno. Good-bye.

(PACO *opens the door and confronts* LIDIA. *She is twenty-six years old, slender and tall, with very dull hair down to her shoulders and a bang over her forehead à la Claudette Colbert. Her prominent dark eyes glow against her olive complexion, giving her the look of a gypsy.* PACO *greets her rapidly and leaves.* LIDIA *enters, looks back, and gives an admiring whistle.*)

LIDIA. What a good-lookin' fellow! Where'd you find him?

JUANITA. Do you know who's callin' me?

LIDIA. Nobody. The janitor's wife told me some real handsome guy had come up here after you arrived. And I wanted to see that treasure with my own eyes.

JUANITA. Nosey!

LIDIA. Is he Latin?

JUANITA. From Morovis. Well, how's everything with you?

LIDIA. Don't change the subject. We're talkin' about your life, not mine. How come you brought him here?

JUANITA. How do I know! Maybe 'cause he seemed different. And 'cause I liked him. But I don't like him now. And I don't like him for that reason, 'cause he is different.

LIDIA. I don't follow you.

JUANITA. Neither do I. But that's how it

is. I just realized it here, a minute ago, while he was talkin'.

LIDIA. (*Shrugging her shoulders.*) When we women feel like complicatin' a thing, we can't even understand ourselves. (*Examining the glass left by* PACO.) You got beer?

JUANITA. Yeah, there's some in the icebox.

LIDIA. (*Going to the rear door.*) I'm gonna take one. Your brother and my husband stayed down there playin' dominoes and drinkin' all I had left.

(*Exits rear.*)

JUANITA. How's your husband?

LIDIA. (*Out of sight, in the kitchen.*) Okay. Still mixed up in the same business.

JUANITA. That's dangerous. Don't your husband realize that?

LIDIA. (*Appearing with a glass of beer.*) He knows. He knows. But he don't care.

JUANITA. Sure, since he's a man.

LIDIA. I'm tired o' tellin' him: "Look, Juan, with my widow's relief and a few honest bucks you could earn, we'd make out all right." But he says he'd rather go to jail than work for an American.

JUANITA. Well just think that any day, when you least expect it . . .

LIDIA. You think I dunno that? I don't have any kind o' life. Every time I see a cop, my heart gets stuck in my throat. I have nightmares. I hear shots, horrible shots, and then I see Juan stretched out on the floor bleedin'. Then I wake up shoutin' for him. And he gets mad 'cause I don't let him sleep in peace. No, I tell you, this is no kind o' life.

JUANITA. I would've left him if I were you.

LIDIA. Yeah, it's easy to say it like that. But I can't do it. And the worst part is the kid. Every day she gets more like my last husband. And every day she likes this one less. The house is gettin' to be like hell for me. If it wasn't for that poor little girl, I'd . . .

JUANITA. Careful, Lidia. There are some things you shouldn't even think about.

LIDIA. Well you thought about it, and you almost did it.

JUANITA. For that reason, Lidia, for that very reason. Look how I've paid for what I did. That's why I say: don't even think about it.

LIDIA. Damn it anyway! Why should I have to have this kind o' luck? Just look at the disgrace! My first husband, the one I brought from Puerto Rico, was so honest, so honest, that just 'cause he was a month without findin' work and he couldn't stand it, he threw himself off the roof. He was too proud. But he left me in the street with a kid to support. This one, on the other hand, has so little, so little shame, that he don't know how to be honest.

JUANITA. Cowards!

LIDIA. No, definitely not! My Juan is a real man.

JUANITA. A real man when it's convenient for him. But at heart, a coward. Like all o' them. Like all o' them who come fleein' from Puerto Rico 'cause they think everythin's easier here. 'Cause they don't know how to face up to life there, in their own land. Yeah, yeah, my brother works. Your husband don't work. But they're both the same. They're our men. The manliest men in the world! The most cowardly!

(DA. GABRIELA *enters through the door at the right in time to hear* JUANITA's *last words.*)

DA. GABRIELLA. Sometimes you need a lotta courage to be a coward. Hello, Lidia!

LIDIA. How are you, Doña Gabriela? (*Takes the bag of groceries from her and carries it to the kitchen.*)

DA. GABRIELA. How's your little girl? She hasn't been here for days.

LIDIA. She started to come down with the flu.

DA. GABRIELA. You do right by takin' care o' her. These days can be fatal. (*Takes a letter from her pocket.*) Ah, look, Juanita. We got a letter. Read it to me.

(JUANITA *takes the letter.*)

LIDIA. Oh, how nice! A letter from Puerto Rico!

JUANITA. It's from Uncle Tomás. (*Tears open the envelope.*)

DA. GABRIELA. He hasn't written for days . . .

LIDIA. If you want, I can go.

DA. GABRIELA. What for, child? A letter from home is no secret for anybody. Sit down. (*To* JUANITA.) Let's see. What does he say? What does that uncle o' yours say?

JUANITA. (*Reading.*) "Dear Sister: I hope this letter finds you all well there. Here, thank God, all are well, except the wife, who still has her aches and pains."

DA. GABRIELA. Poor thing! She always was delicate. And I always said so to my brother. "That wife o' yours is gonna be flat on her back after your first kid. She's too narrow in the hips." And I was right.

JUANITA. (*Reading.*) "About Tomasita I can tell you she has good grades in school, but since she's a young lady now, there's no livin' with her." (*Interrupting her reading.*) She's quite a girl! Remember the time Tomasita kissed Chaguito and he got so mad?

DA. GABRIELA. Yes, 'cause she slobbered all over him. I suppose now she's given up that habit o' kissin' boys. (*Laughs.*) Go on. Go on.

JUANITA. (*Reading.*) "Yesterday I sent you a few pounds of coffee from the farm and some sweet potato preserve. I was gonna send you some oranges too from the tree that the old man planted beside the well, but the post office wouldn't let me 'cause they say the oranges from here can contaminate the American oranges. I must tell you that I intend to buy four more acres of land. They belong to Miguel, Don Tello's helper." (*Interrupting herself.*) Miguel!

DA. GABRIELA. Must be his father's little piece o' land.

JUANITA. (*Eagerly reading again.*) "He inherited them from his father, who died two weeks ago . . ."

DA. GABRIELA. Don't tell me he died! Poor Simon! (*Makes the sign of the cross.*) May God have him in His Glory.

JUANITA. (*Reading.*) "Miguel wants to sell the four acres and go to New York." (*Interrupting her reading.*) No! Don't let him do that!

DA. GABRIELA. Go on! Go on!

JUANITA. (*Reading very slowly, with an unsteady voice.*) "For a long time Miguel has been talkin' about goin' up north to work. But he wants to go to New York, not to Michigan. I think that fellow hasn't been able to forget Juanita . . ."

DA. GABRIELA. Thank you, Blessed St. Anthony!

LIDIA. That Miguel, isn't he the one who gave you the model oxcart?

DA. GABRIELA. That's him, all right. But go on. What else does the letter say?

JUANITA. (*Reading with difficulty, her voice trembling from emotion.*) "He still has to straighten out a mess of papers about the inheritance . . ."

(JUANITA *interrupts herself and stands up.*)

LIDIA. What's the matter?

JUANITA. I can't read any more. My throat's dry.

DA. GABRIELA. Go get some water. Go on. (JUANITA *exits rapidly through the rear.*) You go on readin', Lidia.

LIDIA. (*Taking the letter.*) Lemme see where she was . . . (*Looks. Reads to herself.*) ". . . mess o' papers about the inheritance . . ." (*Out loud.*) Yeah, here it is. (*Reads.*) "So I won't be able to buy the four acres from him for about a month. And I've been thinkin' if you people have in mind to come back, I could let you work that little plot I'm gonna buy and we could share the crops . . ."

DA. GABRIELA. (*Laughing.*) Half! Oh boy, that brother o' mine is too smart! You hear that, Juanita? Seems like they're runnin' out o' share croppers back there in the country.

LIDIA. (*Reading.*) ". . . and maybe later Luis could buy those four little acres that really are worth while."

DA. GABRIELA. Oh, well, now that's more reasonable!

LIDIA. (*Reading.*) "If you decide, let me know. Miguel asked me for your address. So when he gets to New York, he'll look you up and you can all talk about everything and everybody back here." (*Interrupts herself, looks to the rear, and then, approaching* DA. GABRIELA, *asks in a low voice.*) Listen, that Miguel, is he good-lookin?

DA. GABRIELA. (*In a low voice.*) Good-lookin'! (*Laughing to herself.*) He's thinner than a rail and he's got a face as serious as one carved on an Indian stone. (*In a serious tone.*) But he's very good, you know? And a hard worker. And Juanita likes him. (*Looking to the rear, in a loud voice, pretending.*) Well, what's the matter? Go on reading, go on.

LIDIA. (*Reading.*) "I hope you receive the coffee and the sweet potato preserve all right. My wife sends you her best wishes. Greetings from me to all of you, and may you receive best regards from your brother who loves you, Tomás."

(LUIS *enters through the door at the right.*)

DA. GABRIELA. That's all? He don't say any more?

LIDIA. No . . .

LUIS. (*Advancing rapidly toward the living room.*) Juanita, my lunch box, I'm goin' now! (*Entering the living room and seeing* DA. GABRIELA.) Oh, you're back. (*Looking around.*) And the other one?

DA. GABRIELA. What other one?

LUIS. The one who came to see Juanita.

LIDIA. He left a while ago.

LUIS. Oh, listen, your husband wants you to go take care o' the kid. She's havin' another coughin' spell.

LIDIA. (*Going to the right.*) Oh, Holy Mother! Again?

DA. GABRIELA. Wait. Wait a minute. I'm gonna get you somethin' for her.

(*Exits through the left.*)

LIDIA. Here, a letter from your uncle. (LUIS *takes the letter and sits down in the chair at the left to read it.* LIDIA *looks at him, and finally approaches him timidly.*) Luis . . . Juan didn't say anythin' to you about lookin' for work?

LUIS. Eh? (*Momentarily raising his eyes from the letter.*) Your husband? No, he didn't tell me anythin'.

(*Becomes absorbed again in his reading.*)

LIDIA. I'm afraid for Juan. Every day I'm more afraid, Luis.

(DA. GABRIELA *enters from the left with a bottle of rubbing alcohol and a small jar.*)

DA. GABRIELA. Here, child. Give her a good rub-down with warm alcohol. Then rub her little chest and throat good with mentholatum. And then cover her all up good and don't let her get outta bed or get cold. You'll see it'll do her good! God willing, she'll be all better in the morning.

LIDIA. Oh, thanks a lot, Doña Gabriela! May God pay you back.

(*From the stairs are heard confused shouts and the sound of running.*)

FIRST VOICE. The police! The police!

SECOND VOICE. Run, here they come! Run!

VOICE OF POLICEMAN. Stop him! Stop him!

SECOND VOICE. Let him escape. Don't be such cowards!

POLICEMAN. That damned Porto Rican!

THIRD VOICE. (*Dominating the other voices, urgently, desperately.*) Run, man, or they'll kill you!

(LIDIA *and* DA. GABRIELA, *who were heading towards the right, stop.*)

DA. GABRIELA. What's goin' on? What are they shoutin' for? What are those people sayin'?

LIDIA. (*In anguish.*) The police! (*Frightened.*) Good God, the police! (*Then shouting.*) Juan!

(*Simultaneously with* LIDIA'S *scream, six terrible, deafening pistol shots which shake the building are heard.* JUANITA *appears at the rear.* LUIS *jumps up.* LIDIA *escapes from* DA. GABRIELA'S *arms and gets as far as the door at the right.* DA. GABRIELA,

LUIS, *and* JUANITA *run to stop her.*)
LIDIA. Juan! Juan! Juan!
(LUIS *arrives in time to lean against the door to keep it shut while* DA. GABRIELA *and* JUANITA *grab* LIDIA *and pull her back to the living room.*)
LIDIA. Lemme go! Lemme go!
DA. GABRIELA. You can't go out now, child.
JUANITA. Take it easy, Lidia, for God's sake, take it easy.
LIDIA. Juan! They've killed him on me! I told him. Don't do it, Juan, don't do it! Oh my God! They've killed him on me!
LUIS. I'll go see what's happenin'.
LIDIA. Yes, Luis, go and see. Go and see. (LUIS *exits.* LIDIA *screams.*) The kid, Luis, the kid! (DA. GABRIELA *and* JUANITA *lead her to the sofa.*) Just like my dreams! Noises and blood! What good is a man's body if it's full o' holes and bleeding? What good is a woman if she can't save her man's body? (*Rebelling.*) But nobody had the right to kill him. He only wanted the things that everybody wants. (*They seat her on the sofa.* DA. GABRIELA *sits down at her right.*) Nobody had the right to leave me alone again!
(*She sobs noisily, hiding her face in* DA. GABRIELA's *lap.* DA. GABRIELA *caresses her in a motherly way.*)
DA. GABRIELA. You don't know what's happened. Why would they kill your husband? You're just scared from the noise o' the shots. That's all that's the matter. You've just been over frightened. C'mon now. You'll see it wasn't anythin'. Juanita, bring me the rubbin' alcohol.
(JUANITA *brings the bottle of alcohol that* LIDIA *has dropped in the hall.* DA. GABRIELA *rubs some on* LIDIA's *neck.*)
LIDIA. (*Between sobs.*) He wasn't bad, Doña Gabriela, Juan wasn't bad at all.
(LUIS *enters through the right. He appears somber. He advances to the living room and stops.* DA. GABRIELA *and* JUANITA *straighten up instinctively and question him with anguished looks.* LIDIA *feels the weight of the anxious silence and slowly raises her head from* DA. GABRIELA's *lap. With an automatic gesture she pushes away from her face the strands of hair that cover her eyes. She begins to get up, at the same time turning her face very slowly towards* LUIS. *She looks at him for an instant. Then she throws herself at him and shakes him by the shoulders.*)
LIDIA. Say it! What're you waitin' for? Say it!
LUIS. (*Slowly.*) No. It wasn't him.
LIDIA. (*Petrified.*) What?
LUIS. (*Always somber. Without intending to console her.*) It wasn't your husband.
LIDIA. (*Not understanding.*) No? No? It wasn't him? (*Finally realizing all the joy the news implies for her.*) It wasn't Juan! (*Moves away from* LUIS *and goes shakily to the right.*) Juan! (*At last giving free rein to her emotions, she begins to run and exits shouting; her voice is a tremor of wild happiness.*) Juan! Juan! Juan!
DA. GABRIELA. Who was it, Luis?
LUIS. I dunno. Some guy who stole a pocketbook from an American lady in the street.
DA. GABRIELA. But... did they kill him?
LUIS. He was runnin' away and he ducked into this buildin'. They filled him full o' lead on the floor upstairs.
DA. GABRIELA. May God pardon him. (*Makes the sign of the cross and mutters a prayer as she exits through the left.*)
JUANITA. Was he... Puerto Rican?
LUIS. Yes.
JUANITA. The scum! To kill a man like that for stealin' ...!
LUIS. A five-dollar bill, a lipstick, and a dirty handkerchief. That's what was in the pocketbook he robbed from the yankee. But they didn't find neither a gun or a knife on him. Only a medal of the Virgin of the Carmen. And a letter from his mother postmarked in Lares, Puerto Rico. "I'm glad God has helped you and you're getting ahead," the letter said. He was just a kid, but they put six bullets in his chest.

To kill him for real! To kill him once and for all!

JUANITA. And you say it so calmly!

LUIS. (*Abruptly.*) I'm not calm. I'm not calm inside!

JUANITA. (*Furious.*) But you *look* like you're calm. And it's the same as if you were. 'Cause a person shows what he feels. And if he don't show it, he's a coward!

LUIS. So what the hell do you want me to do?

JUANITA. Show you got blood in your veins. If you feel the same rage I feel, instead o' keepin' it inside, shout it out loud. This way, like me. (*Open the window and shouts.*) Scum! Murderers!

LUIS. Shut up!

(*Goes to her, pushes her brusquely away, and shuts the window.*)

JUANITA. And if you feel like breakin' somethin', show it by breakin' it. This way, like I do. (*Takes the glass that* LIDIA *had left and smashes it against the heater.*) 'Cause a person's gotta protest some way. Somehow you gotta say you don't agree with the things that are goin' on. Somehow you gotta show you got guts and a heart, dignity and pride.

(DA. GABRIELA *enters from the left.*)

DA. GABRIELA. What's goin' on here, Juanita? What's all this racket?

LUIS. (*Gathering the pieces of glass together with his foot.*) So now you shouted and you broke somethin'. What good did it do you?

JUANITA. No good, no good at all. I raise a rumpus and that's it. 'Cause upstairs there they've killed a guy from Lares and it shocks me. It don't matter to anybody else. But it does to me. And I want them to *know* that it matters to me.

DA. GABRIELA. It matters to all of us, child. He was a human bein'. And besides, he was one of us. But some things just can't be helped. Especially by a woman. And even less by a hysterical woman. 'Cause this is a man's world . . .

JUANITA. (*Interrupting her.*) Well, let 'em show that it is! If it's theirs, why don't they make it any better? But they don't dare. Don't you see, ma, they're a bunch o' cowards.

LUIS. Talk. Talk. That's all you know how to do. But it's not enough.

DA. GABRIELA. It's hard to be a man, Juanita, it's hard!

JUANITA. (*Turning to* LUIS.) Of course it's not enough just to talk! But at least it's better than bein' quiet and still like you were dead.

DA. GABRIELA. All right, all right, that's enough. It can't be helped. What can be helped is this mess. Juanita, get the dustpan and pick up those pieces of glass. And the next time you come here, you bring me another glass just like the one you broke. (JUANITA *exits rear.*) The next time it occurs to you to shout like a carzy woman or to start breakin' things, I'm gonna beat you silly. You're both gonna see I've still got a ready hand. And you won't forget you're still my kids. My kids will always be my kids, even when their beards reach down to their belly buttons! (*To* LUIS.) What's wrong with you? Why're you lookin' at me like that?

LUIS. (*Smiling.*) You haven't scolded us for so long.

DA. GABRIELA. And since you forgot how it used to be, now you don't like it.

LUIS. On the contrary. I like it. I like it better than seein' you sad.

DA. GABRIELA. (*Grumbling.*) Sad! Sad! Who's sad? You think to be happy I gotta spend my life dancin' a cha-cha-cha? That'd sure be sad! At my age to have to be smilin' all the time like some little fifteen-year-old chicken. No, boy, no. Those things should be left for silly teenagers like Tomás' daughter. (*Interrupts herself.*) Oh, now that I mention Tomás. I didn't tell you we got a letter from that brother o' mine. (*Searching.*) Where's that letter? Where'd Lidia put it?

(LUIS' *face grows somber again.*)

LUIS. I have it.

DA. GABRIELA. Did you read it already?

LUIS. Yes.

(*Sits down in the chair at the left.*)

DA. GABRIELA. (*Trying to hide her anxiety.*) What did you think of it?

LUIS. Well . . . !

DA. GABRIELA. Four acres to share.

LUIS. Bah! Who can live from four acres?

DA. GABRIELA. Yes, that's what I say . . . But it all depends. It's Miguel's father's farm. Good land.

LUIS. Hnnh.

(JUANITA *enters from the rear and begins to pick up the glass from the floor.*)

DA. GABRIELA. And it's got a good well.

LUIS. Yeah . . .

DA. GABRIELA. The best well in the district. The water is sweeter and purer than from Tomás' well. (*Short pause.*) A well right on your own farm is a great advantage.

LUIS. Half a farm . . .

DA. GABRIELA. It's true. (*Pretending indignation.*) No, if that's the best Tomás can think of. He's a sly one, that brother o' mine. (*Transition.*) Of course, he's givin' us the chance to buy the land . . . And meanwhile he'd have to supply us with seeds, and the oxen . . . and the plow . . . (*Unable to hide her enthusiasm.*) Tomatoes grow good there. And they bring a good price. What d'you think? It'd be a business. (*Sitting on the floor at* LUIS' *feet.*) Naturally I'd help you with the sowing. And you could even find somethin' you like better to do . . . I'd take care o' the farm. Chaguito gets outta reform school soon. Between him and me we could make somethin' outta that plot o' land. The last time he wrote he said he was in charge o' the vegetable garden. So he's got experience now.

(JUANITA *has finished and has stood up. She watches, moved by her mother's enthusiasm.*)

LUIS. (*Bending down toward* DA. GABRIELA *and staring at her, unable to hide a slight trembling in his voice.*) Mamá, are you happy?

DA. GABRIELA. (*Taken by surprise.*) Eh? Me? Yes . . . Well of course I'm happy!

(JUANITA *looks sharply at* LUIS *and exits rapidly through the rear.*)

LUIS. Do you need anythin'?

DA. GABRIELA. Who me? Heavens, no! (*Getting up.*) What am I gonna need!

LUIS. (*Getting up, taking* DA. GABRIELA *by the shoulders and forcing her to look him in the eye.*) Are you sure?

DA. GABRIELA. Of course! Since . . . you give me everythin'. You give me all I could need.

LUIS. (*Smiling.*) I'm glad. Then get my lunch box ready, 'cause it's gettin' late and my shift at the factory starts in a little while.

DA. GABRIELA. Oh, that's right! (*Moves away from him and goes to the rear.*) How stupid o' me! Talkin', talkin' and forgettin' what time it is. But don't worry, I'll bring you your lunch box right away, right away.

(*Exits rapidly through the rear.* LUIS *goes to the hooks near the door, takes down a wool plaid hunting jacket and puts it on. Buttoning it, he returns to the living room.* JUANITA *enters from the rear.*)

LUIS. (*Seeing* JUANITA.) I'm glad Miguel's comin'. It's the best thing he could do.

JUANITA. (*Dryly.*) Best for who?

LUIS. For him, of course! And probably for you. I'll send Chaguito his ticket as soon as he gets out . . .

JUANITA. What are you anyway? The Department of Emigration or the Department of Tourism?

LUIS. (*Brusquely.*) I don't care about Emigration or Tourism! What I care about is my family.

JUANITA. (*Ironically.*) And machines! Machines that give life!

LUIS. Yes, I care about that, too.

JUANITA. More than the family. Don't deny it. 'Cause we don't have the mystery that machines have. That mysterious thing you're lookin' for and can't ever find.

LUIS. I'll find it . . .

JUANITA. Yeah, you'll find it. Like the

treasure hidden by Juan Bobo in the belly o' the iron kettle! In the belly o' the machine! The life-givin' machine! And what is a machine? The pistols that fired six shots upstairs a little while ago are machines. Didn't that ever occur to you? They're machines all right. And where's the life they gave?

LUIS. That's different. You don't understand my machines.

JUANITA. No, I don't understand 'em. Thank God I don't. And I hope Miguel and Chaguito never understand 'em either!

(DA. GABRIELA *enters from the rear with the lunch box.*)

DA. GABRIELA. All ready, Luis. Here it is.

(*Hands* LUIS *the lunch box.*)

LUIS. (*Going to the right.*) Okay. See you this afternoon.

DA. GABRIELA. The coffee's already got sugar in. Oh, and I put in one o' them canned meat pies for you that Juanita brought.

(LUIS *takes the felt hat that's hanging on the wall and puts it on. He opens the door and is about to go out, but he stops. He hesitates, then turns and goes toward* DA. GABRIELA. *He stops in front of her.*)

LUIS. (*With humble gentleness.*) Blessing, ma.

DA. GABRIELA. (*Kissing him tenderly.*) God bless you, my son. (LUIS *hugs her tightly and exits rapidly through the right.*) My poor boy! We shouldn't fight with him, Juanita.

JUANITA. If I fight with him, it's for his own good, mamá.

DA. GABRIELA. (*Returning slowly to the living room.*) We have to take care o' him. We have to take good care o' him. He's sick.

JUANITA. (*Approaching* DA. GABRIELA.) Sick?

DA. GABRIELA. He's sick inside.

JUANITA. What d' you mean?

DA. GABRIELA. Somethin' bad is happenin' to him. Haven't you noticed it?

JUANITA. Well, I know he's changed.

DA. GABRIELA. Some little worm of sorrow is eatin' away at his heart.

JUANITA. I'd say it was his mind . . .

DA. GABRIELA. No, his heart. My son is like a little orphan that's all alone, all alone. And he don't know which way to turn. Like a motherless lamb on the side of a steep rock. He can't go up. And it's a long, long way down . . .

JUANITA. (*Cautiously, with tenderness.*) Mamá, Luis is . . . an orphan, right? He's not your son . . .

DA. GABRIELA. (*Straightening up, indignant, as if she had been struck.*) Luis is my son! He's my son!

JUANITA. Yes, mamá, I know. It's as if he was your son. But he's the son of my father and of . . .

DA. GABRIELA. (*Violent.*) Quiet!

JUANITA. Mamá, you can't hide the whole sky with one hand. Those things always get found out . . .

DA. GABRIELA. And how did you find it out?

JUANITA. People were talkin' back in the country . . .

DA. GABRIELA. And they hadda tell you. People are bad, bad!

JUANITA. What's the difference? I'm a woman, mamá. I understand these things. Anyway it doesn't matter. Luis is my brother. He's always been my brother. Even if he don't know it, I . . .

DA. GABRIELA. But he does know! (*Falls into a chair.*) That's what's so awful, he knows it!

JUANITA. (*Astonished.*) He knows it?

DA. GABRIELA. Yes. He's never told me. Some things don't have to be said. But he knows. And for that reason he loves me more. He loves me from gratitude. And that's no good. A child's love for his parents should come from his soul, not from gratitude. And Luis has been too concerned with gratitude. Why do you think he loaded us into the oxcart to take us to La Perla? Why do you think he brought us here? Why do you think he's killin' himself workin' like an animal?

'Cause he wants me to be happy. 'Cause he wants to make me happy whether I want to or not. 'Cause he thinks I'll be happy if I have things I didn't have before. My poor son! How little he knows about happiness!

JUANITA. Mamá, you're a saint!

DA. GABRIELA. (*Getting up, indignant.*) A saint! A saint! If I was a saint I could've made a miracle and given happiness to that son o' mine. I could've made him not feel the need for a mother. But Luis has always been an orphan. Don't you see he's lost in a world where he don't belong? Don't you realize he's always searchin', like a lost lamb that can't find its mother?

JUANITA. (*Pensively.*) Can that be what he's lookin' for? Can that be what he's lookin' for in machines, mamá?

DA. GABRIELA. I dunno. I dunno. I only know it's drivin' him crazy. Crazy from sorrow 'cause he don't find what he's lookin' for.

(*Sobs.*)

JUANITA. Mamá, mamá, don't cry. We'll take care o' him, mamá. We'll be like two mothers for him.

DA. GABRIELA. That's why I told you to come live with us. 'Cause I feel so helpless now. 'Cause I can't make him happy.

JUANITA. Yes, mamá, I'll come and live with you. First thing tomorrow I'll bring my stuff. But now, why don't you lay down a little while and rest? I'll get lunch ready.

(*Knock at the door.* DA. GABRIELA *quickly dries her tears.*)

DA. GABRIELA. There's somebody there.

JUANITA. You go in the bedroom. I'll open the door.

DA. GABRIELA. No, no. You go get the lunch. I'll see who it is.

(DA. GABRIELA *goes to the entrance hall.* JUANITA *hesitates a moment, then exits rear.* DA. GABRIELA *opens the door and* MR. PARKINGTON *enters. He is a tall, thin American about forty years old. He is dressed in black and carries a fall overcoat on his arm. He has a leather briefcase in his hand and an extremely friendly smile on his face.*)

PARKINGTON. Good day!

DA. GABRIELA. Good . . .

PARKINGTON. The lady of the house, no doubt?

DA. GABRIELA. Can I help you?

PARKINGTON. If it's no trouble, I'd like very much to talk to you about the Lord.

DA. GABRIELA. What lord . . . ? The landlord?

PARKINGTON. The Lord Creator of Heaven and Earth. I have named Jehovah, my dear sister! May I come in? (*Enters without waiting for an answer.*) Thank you. You're very kind. (DA. GABRIELA *looks at him in amazement, shuts the door, and follows him to the living room.*)

(*With a friendly smile.*) May I sit down, madam? (*Sits down before* DA. GABRIELA *can indicate for him to do so.*) Thank you.

JUANITA. (*Out of sight in the kitchen.*) Who is it, mamá?

DA. GABRIELA. I dunno. Some American . . .

PARKINGTON. My name is Parkington, sister.

JUANITA. (*Appearing in the rear doorway with a can of chopped ham in one hand and the opener in the other.*) What does he want?

DA. GABRIELA. I'm still waitin' for him to tell me.

PARKINGTON. (*Rising politely on seeing* JUANITA.) Pleased to meet you, miss.

JUANITA. (*Giving him the once over as she speaks to* DA. GABRIELA.) Mamá, I've told you not to open the door here to people you don't know.

DA. GABRIELA. The door o' my house has always been open. If I shut it here it's on account o' the cold. Well, mister, say what you have to say.

(JUANITA *exits rear.*)

PARKINGTON. Thank you, madam. The hospitality of you Latins is marvellous. I've always said so. Well then, here's my card (*Hands it to her and sits down again.*) As you can see, I represent the Church of God, Incorporated.

DA. GABRIELA. (*Surprised.*) God incorporated? Incorporated to what?

PARKINGTON. No, no. God is not incorporated. What's incorporated is the Church.

DA. GABRIELA. And what does that mean?

PARKINGTON. (*In a tight spot.*) It means ... Let's see ... Incorporated is ... a corporation.

JUANITA. (*Out of sight in the kitchen.*) Like the sugar mills, mamá! Like the sugar mills in Puerto Rico!

DA. GABRIELA. I don't understand. But go on ...

PARKINGTON. Well, you must've read about it in the papers ... it's had magnificent publicity, front page publicity ... the creation of the Municipal Committee for the Betterment of the Puerto Ricans. The mayor of this great democratic city of New York is terribly interested in you people. (JUANITA *appears in the doorway and listens sceptically.*) The mayor, following the doctrine of Jehovah, makes no discriminations between Negroes or whites, rich or poor, Puerto Ricans or Americans.

JUANITA. Since when?

PARKINGTON. (*Interrupted.*) What did you say, miss?

JUANITA. The miss says since when don't the mayor make distinctions.

PARKINGTON. (*In another tight spot.*) Well ... Since always. Of course, errors have been made in the past ... Errors that we all lament ... It won't happen again! It'll be different from now on.

JUANITA. How different?

PARKINGTON. What?

JUANITA. I said, how will it be different from now on?

PARKINGTON. Well ... the betterment of the Puerto Rican colony, miss. So it can be on the same level ... (*Realizes he is putting his foot in it.*) I mean, so it can be equal ... (*Bites his tongue in time.*) Well ... so it won't be an object of discrimination.

JUANITA. (*Leaning in the kitchen doorway.*) So they're gonna make us better. They're gonna make us good as the Americans. That means that we're not any good now, that we're not equal to the rest o' you.

PARKINGTON. Please, miss! You misunderstand me.

JUANITA. (*Taking a step forward.*) Look, mister, what you're sayin' I'd understand even in Chinese. It's as clear as daylight. (*Looks toward the window and corrects herself.*) Like the daylight in my country, of course. (*Exits rear.*)

PARKINGTON. Oh, what a shame! The girl doesn't understand. But the thing is that the Church of God, Incorporated, is going to cooperate fully with the Municipal Committee for the Betterment of the Puerto Ricans. It's a titanic job, my sister. But we'll do it! You can be sure we'll do it. (*Takes out some leaflets and keeps handing them to* DA. GABRIELA.) Our mission is not only religious. It's also social ...

DA. GABRIELA. (*Wanting to be pleasant and show an interest in something the visitor proposes.*) Oh, you're gonna hold dances!

PARKINGTON. (*Jumping back.*) Dances?

DA. GABRIELA. But didn't you say ... ?

PARKINGTON. We are part of the Committee for the Betterment of the Puerto Ricans. And we don't solve social problems with dances. What we hold are meetings. And problems are discussed. And orientation work is performed. (*Takes out another series of folders.*) The Puerto Ricans must become orientated to this mechanized civilization. They must give up superstitions and idolatry. They must become familiar with the world of machines. Look, here are some very useful folders. They're in Spanish, very well translated. (*Keeps handing folders to* DA. GABRIELA.) The Puerto Rican workers must recognize their responsibilities and yield the maximum labor. We orient them. In that way difficulties are avoided. And accidents are prevented. Like the one that just happened there in the boiler factory.

DA. GABRIELA. In the boiler factory?

PARKINGTON. Yes, madam, yes. I ran into all the commotion just minutes before coming here. (JUANITA *appears in the door-*

way.) And all because of carelessness and clumsiness on the part of a Puerto Rican worker. That's why I say . . .

JUANITA. (*Coming forward.*) A Puerto Rican worker?

PARKINGTON. Yes, miss. That's why I say the orientation of the workers is essential in a highly mechanized society.

DA. GABRIELA. What happened in the boiler factory?

PARKINGTON. The accident I mention. Because New York, as our democratic mayor strongly affirms, opens its arms to the Puerto Ricans. But . . .

JUANITA. What accident! What accident?

PARKINGTON. (*Annoyed by the interruptions.*) But haven't I told you already?

DA. GABRIELA. (*Terribly upset.*) No, you haven't said a thing! For the love o' God, tell us what happened!

PARKINGTON. Well, one of those frequent accidents when you're dealing with people not accustomed . . .

JUANITA. (*Going to him, violently.*) Cut out the stupid talk and tell us once and for all what happened! What happened in the boiler factory?

PARKINGTON. But, miss, you won't let me get a word in. It seems that a worker was examining the inside of one of the machines. The machine began to work and the man was trapped among the many steel parts that kept going full speed. The unfortunate fellow's body . . .

(*Violent knocking is heard on the door, and at the same time* LIDIA'*s voice is heard calling urgently: "Juanita! Juanita! Juanita, open the door! Juanita!"* JUANITA *runs to the door at the right and opens it.* LIDIA *enters, her expression changed. She tries to speak softly to* JUANITA. DA. GABRIELA *takes a step toward the hall but stops in the living room, her eyes wide open, the fingers of both hands pressed against her lips as if she wanted to prevent something vital from escaping from her body.*)

LIDIA. (*Out of breath, in a low voice.*) Juanita! Telephone. In the janitor's office. It's urgent! Come right away. It's urgent!

(JUANITA *and* LIDIA *exit rapidly through the right.* DA. GABRIELA *goes slowly to the sofa. She stops in front of it, before the image of the Sacred Heart. She falls to her knees and sinks her face in the sofa cushion. We see only her bent back, which moves in rhythm to her difficult breathing.* MR. PARKINGTON, *disconcerted, doesn't know what to do. He finally collects his things quietly. Then he takes a step toward* DA. GABRIELA. *He stops, turns slowly, and exits through the right. Interval. Immobility. Silence.* JUANITA *enters through the right. Then* LIDIA. JUANITA *is very pale, and her movements give the impression of a momentary somnambulism. She slowly enters the living room.* LIDIA, *crying quietly, follows a short distance behind her. When she gets to the end of the hall and sees* DA. GABRIELA *kneeling,* LIDIA *stops and puts both hands to her mouth to drown her sobs. Leaning against the wall, her face between her hands, she cries silently.* JUANITA *keeps going forward. She stops beside* DA. GABRIELA, *and with a look lost in space, says:*)

JUANITA. The orphan found what he was looking for, mother. Luis finally discovered the mystery of the machines that gave life.

(DA. GABRIELA *remains still.* JUANITA *slowly lowers her eyes toward the kneeling figure.*) Did you hear what I said, mamá?

(DA. GABRIELA *slowly raises her head and looks at the Sacred Heart.*)

DA. GABRIELA. Take him to your bosom, Lord. Be a good father to my son!

JUANITA. They'll take him from the hospital to the nearest funeral parlor. Within an hour we can go and see him.

(DA. GABRIELA *gets up.*)

DA. GABRIELA. I don't want them to bury him in this land of no sunshine. Will it cost much to take him to Puerto Rico?

JUANITA. It doesn't matter what it costs. We'll do whatever you say.

DA. GABRIELA. (*Noting* LIDIA's *presence.*) How's your little girl, Lidia? (LIDIA *runs and throws herself in* DA. GABRIELA's *arms and sobs convulsively on her shoulder.* DA. GABRIELA *caresses her in a motherly fashion.*) There. There. Don't cry. My son is happy now. The land where he was born will always be the mother who lets him sleep without toil or sorrow. (LIDIA *leaves* DA. GABRIELA's *arms, goes more calmly to the hall, drying her tears, and exits right.* DA. GABRIELA *speaks in an illumined tone.*) Because now I know what was happening to us all. The curse of the land! The land is sacred. The land can not be abandoned. We must go back to what we left behind so that the curse of the land won't pursue us any more. And I'll return with my son to the land from where we came. And I'll sink my hands in the red earth of my village just as my father sunk his to plant the seeds. And my hands will be strong again. And my house will smell once more of patchouli and peppermint. And there'll be land outside. Four acres to share. Even though that's all! It's good land. It's land that gives life. Only four acres. Even if they're not ours!

JUANITA. They will be ours. They'll be yours, mamá! 'Cause I'm goin' back with you to my village.

DA. GABRIELA. (*Gently, as if waking from a dream.*) You? You too? But you always said that from now on you were gonna drive the oxcart of your life wherever you wanted.

JUANITA. For that very reason, mamá, for that very reason! 'Cause I do drive it wherever I want. And we'll get back before Miguel sells those acres. And if it's true that he wants me, I'll be his wife and the land will be ours. And we'll save Miguel from comin' here in search o' the mystery that killed my brother. And we'll save Chaguito. 'Cause it's not a question o' going back to the land to live like we were dead. Now we know the world don't change by itself. We're the ones who change the world. And we're gonna help change it. We're gonna go like people with dignity, like grandpa used to say. With our heads high. Knowin' there are things to fight for. Knowin' that all God's children are equal. And my children will learn things I didn't learn, things they don't teach in school. That's how we'll go back home! You and I, mamá, as firm as ausubo trees above our land, and Luis resting beneath it!

DA. GABRIELA. Yes, just like you say. Like ausubos. As firm as ausubos. (*Her voice begins to break.*) Like ausubos that machines can never cut down! (*Sobs. Her crying, so long held back, breaks forth noisily until her entire body shakes and begins to bend. Little by little* DA. GABRIELA *slips to the floor, beside* JUANITA, *and remains kneeling, then seated on her heels, then bent over herself like a small, insignificant ball, shaken by sobs and pierced by sorrow, at the feet of her daughter who stands firm and decided.*)

CURTAIN

Topics for Further Study

1. Discuss on the basis of this play, the following statement:
   "The sense of the Puerto Rican family permeates the culture of the island and extends beyond its shores. The cohesiveness of the family unit is the backbone of Puerto Rico."
2. René Marqués studied agronomy and worked in the Puerto Rican Department of Agriculture for two years. Show evidences in *The Oxcart* of his love of the land and of his belief in its importance for meaningful living.
3. Compare and contrast Doña Gabriela with Mrs. Hansen in *I Remember Mama* and Mrs. Younger in *A Raisin in the Sun*. Which of these mothers most appeals to you? What are the differences and similarities in the religious faith of these three characters? Do you know mothers who share their character traits?
4. Chaguito is a juvenile delinquent. What, if anything, could have been done to prevent his behavior? What would you suggest for reducing juvenile delinquency in your own neighborhood?
5. Were you satisfied with the ending of *The Oxcart*? How would you have ended it?
6. With the aid of *Reader's Guide to Periodical Literature* and *New York Theater Critics Reviews* for 1966–1967, investigate the reviews of this play when it first appeared in New York City and report to the class either orally or in writing on the critical reaction.
7. Read René Marqués's English play *Palm Sunday* and report to the class orally or in writing.
8. Read one of the books about Puerto Rico listed after the essay on the Puerto Ricans and report either orally or in writing to the class.
9. Hold a panel discussion on one of the following topics:
   (*a*) The country vs. the city as a place for raising a family.
   (*b*) Assimilation vs. cultural differentiation as a means of promoting the advancement of an ethnic group.
   (*c*) Should young Puerto Rican students be taught bilingually on the continent?

The Mexicans in the United States

Today there are about 5,000,000 Mexican-Americans in the United States, the second largest minority after the Blacks. Their origin dates back to the Spanish conquistadores who entered the Southwest in the 1500s before British Jamestown was built. Some of them were of pure Spanish blood; others (known as *mestizos*) were of mixed Spanish and Indian blood. They contributed much to this area of our country, introducing such domesticated animals as horses, cattle, sheep, and goats, as well as the fruits and most of the vegetables that are such an important part of the agriculture of the region. They knew how to extract minerals from the earth, began the livestock industry, and established irrigation systems.

The first encounters between traders from the United States and frontiersmen from New Spain took place in the early years of the nineteenth century. A new relationship began in 1824 after Mexico achieved its independence from Spain. The United States acquired the Louisiana Territory, which stretched from the Gulf of Mexico to the Pacific Ocean. Expansionist-minded Americans immigrated into Mexican territory in the Southwest, where the liberal Mexican laws encouraged development. But eventually Texas broke away to form the Lone Star State in 1836. After the United States annexed Texas in 1845, it was obvious that war between Mexico and the United States was inevitable. The Mexican-American War (1846–1848) was not popular among many in the United States, but when it was over the treaty of Guadaloupe Hidalgo gave the United States California and New Mexico (which included Arizona).

After 1848 and the victory of United States forces over Mexico, conditions were not favorable to Mexican-Americans. They appeared as a former enemy to many and as a dangerous element that had to be watched and contained. Gradually many of them began to occupy a place of economic, social, and political inferiority. Despite contributions to agriculture, mining, transportation and industry, their inferior status continued. One of the reasons was the legal system and the bureaucratic institutions that preserved their inferior status.

From 1910 to 1922 when Mexico was undergoing a revolution, there was a mass migration of Mexicans to the United States. Some of them managed to escape with some material wealth; but most who came were unskilled workers or farm laborers. With the coming of World War I and the curtailment of

European and Oriental immigrant labor, the Mexican border was opened to workers from the farming areas of Mexico. It was they who established the great agricultural industry of the San Joaquin, Imperial, Salt River, Merella, and lower Rio Grande Valleys.

The migration came to a halt during the Great Depression. To alleviate the pressures created by unemployment, the government adopted the policy of simply deporting thousands of Mexican laborers, many of whom were bona fide American citizens. In 1940, again to meet agricultural needs, the United States and Mexico instituted the *Los Braceros Program*, which permitted thousands of Mexican laborers to come here to do seasonal work and return when the jobs were completed. In addition to the workers who entered legally, many thousands without proper credentials waded across the Rio Grande; these "wetbacks," as they were called, were constantly being rounded up and returned home. This program was terminated in 1964.

Mexican-Americans have resisted acculturation more tenaciously than most other minority groups. Because they felt discriminated against, they clung to their native Spanish language and their customs. In the large cities they lived together in *barrios*, similar to the ghettoes of other minorities. Here they felt more at home because they did not have to learn a new language, and because in unity there was a certain degree of strength. Some managed to emerge from the *barrio* by dint of hard work and educational opportunities, but for the vast majority of Mexican-Americans it was to be their home throughout their lives. Many felt that the education they were getting was inferior to that of the Anglos. The drop-out rate of Mexican-American students was far higher than that of the Anglos because many felt that their education was meaningless and irrelevant. They were discriminated against in industry and business.

Nevertheless, despite so many handicaps, Mexican-Americans have distinguished themselves in many walks of life and have become national figures: for example, Senator Joseph Montoya of New Mexico, Congressmen Henry B. Gonzalez and Eligio de la Garza from Texas, and Lee Trevino, the great golf pro. Scores of Mexican-American teachers in colleges across the land as well as doctors and scientists have demonstrated qualities of leadership in their respective fields of endeavor.

President Lyndon B. Johnson, who grew up with many Mexican-Americans and who taught for a time in one of their schools, tried more than any other president before him to give recognition and support to this minority. In 1967 he formed the Inter-Agency Committee on Mexican Affairs and appointed Vincente Jiminez as the director. The highlight of the committee's activity was the Cabinet Committee hearings on Mexican Affairs held in El Paso in October 1967. President Nixon continued the Inter-Agency Committee under the direction of Martin Castillo. In an effort to assist Mexican-Americans in the field of industry, commerce, and finance, he appointed Hilary Sandoval as head of the Small Business Administration.

In the past few years many young Mexican-Americans have organized themselves to fight for a better way of life. Representing themselves by the term *Chicano* (an abbreviated form of Mexicano, which was heretofore a pejorative term), they have militantly demanded better working conditions for agricultural laborers and better educational career opporunitities—civil rights that every American should be entitled to. They have published a magazine, *El Grito* (*The Shout*), which serves as an outlet for much Chicano literature, in both Spanish and English. The Chicano Press Association now coordinates the affairs of twelve newspapers in the Southwest states, Illinois, and Wisconsin. New writers have been published in the Anglo magazines and by Anglo book publishers. A Chicano Teachers Association has been formed with a membership of several hundred who teach in both English and foreign language departments in colleges. To meet the needs of students participating in Hispanic Studies departments on many college campuses, a spate of anthologies has appeared in recent years, some of which are listed in the "Suggested Reading."

It is safe to say that while discrimination against Mexican-Americans still exists, and will probably exist for a long time to come, there have been many significant changes, some because of the natural diminution of prejudice resulting from the many civil rights laws that have been passed in recent years. In other instances, as in the strikes by the grape pickers and lettuce pickers led by Cesar Chavez, it was actual confrontation that led to social and economic improvement. Finally, as the majority of the population has learned more about the culture and the ideas of their Mexican-American neighbors, greater understanding has resulted as well as greater tolerance and a reduction of prejudice.

Suggested Reading

Books about the Mexican-Americans

Galarza, Ernesto; Gallegos, Herman; and Samora, Julian. *Mexican Americans in the Southwest*. Santa Barbara: McNally and Loftin, 1970. Studies in the evolution of the Mexican-American community in Arizona, California, Colorado, New Mexico, and Texas since 1900. It describes the survival of the Mexican-American's underlying cultural heritage.

Grebler, Leo; Moore, Joan W.; and Guzman, Ralph C. *The Mexican American People: the Nation's Second Largest Minority*. New York: The Free Press-Macmillan, 1970. A broad analysis of the Mexican-American in the Southwest, focusing on problems of the urban population. The study includes a thorough analysis of data obtained from community surveys.

Robinson, Cecil. *With the Ears of Strangers: The Mexican American in American Literature*. Tucson: University of Arizona Press, 1963. Presents an illuminating summary of portrayals of Mexicans and Mexican-Americans, ranging from impressions of early settlers to the more solid portrayals in contemporary fiction.

Steiner, Stan. *La Raza: The Mexican Americans*. New York: Harper and Row, 1970. A vividly written, dramatic account of the author's investigation of Mexican-Americans, focusing on their economic status, cultural inheritance, and growing political sophistication.

Anthologies of Mexican-American Literature

Ortega, Philip D. *We Are Chicanos*. New York: Washington Square Press, 1973.
Paredes, Americo and Paredes, Raymond. *Mexican-American Authors*. Boston: Houghton Mifflin, 1972.
Valdez, Luis and Steiner, Sam. *Aztlan: An Anthology of Mexican American Literature*. New York: Knopf, 1972.

Collections of Chicano Plays

De Leon, Nephtheli. *5 Plays*. Denver: Totinem Publications, 1972.
Valdez, Luis. *Actos: El Teatro Campesino*. San Juan Bautista, California: Cucuracha Press.

Wetback Run

Theodore Apstein has taken an experience shared by thousands of Mexican farm laborers and turned it into a stimulating and moving work of art. The play provides insight into the motivations that lead these workers to leave their homes and families behind and run the risk of being caught in their illegal attempts to enter the United States in search of a better living. Jacinto Sandoval is a hard worker who cannot farm his bit of land profitably and hopes to improve his lot by crossing into the United States over the International Bridge and securing employment. The innocent laborer is stopped at the bridge, made aware of the legal complications, and advised to return in the summer, when American contractors will come to Mexico seeking his labor.

He is approached by Torres, a labor racketeer, who has been living like a leech on the backs of those whom he has helped to cross over illegally. So eager is Jacinto to get work to support his wife and sons that he even risks swimming across the river when his rowboat and its occupants are spotted by the searchlights of the border policemen. Once safe on American soil he obtains a job, picking grapefruit at a salary much larger than he has ever earned before. In fact, he is even able to send money to his wife. But the racketeer Torres finds him and threatens to expose him to the border police unless protection money is paid every week. Jacinto agrees to this demand, but balks when he learns that Torres has planned to smuggle his wife and sons over the same way that he came. This is too much for him and he walks away from both Torres and the more understanding Ramirez, the grower, to give himself up to the border police and return to his family. We see demonstrated in the play the hostility that is shown by older Mexican-American workers who resent the presence of the wetbacks because they will work for lower wages and thus cause unemployment for older workers. The racketeer Torres cannot understand Jacinto's action in surrendering to the border police, but Ramirez does understand and admire a man who can hold his head up and face the facts of life.

THEODORE APSTEIN is uniquely qualified to write about Mexican-Americans. Born in Kiev, Russia, on July 3, 1918, he moved to Mexico at an early age, where he received most of his early education. His experience there helped him to develop the sympathy and compassion for Mexicans so evident in *Wetback Run*. He has also resided in Argentina, Chile, and Colombia.

Among his writings are eight long plays, one of which, *Paradise Inn*, was performed on Broadway, and many short plays. In addition to *Wetback Run* he has written *Fortunata Writes a Letter*, *Making the Bear*, *The Beans of Our House*, and *Before the Bullfight*.

Mr. Apstein has written scripts for the CBS Sunday morning series *Lamp unto My Feet* and *Theater Guild on the Air*. With the aid of a grant from the Rockefeller Foundation, he made a two-year study of Latin-American theaters.

His folk plays are well known for their humorous and sympathetic treatment of the problems of the poor people in South and Central America.

Wetback Run

BY

THEODORE APSTEIN

CHARACTERS

JACINTO SANDOVAL
IMMIGRATION INSPECTOR
GOVERNMENT OFFICIAL
TORRES
FIRST MAN
RAMIREZ
ANTONIO
ADOLFO
MOLLY
CHARLIE
OLD MAN
OLD WOMAN
FERNANDO
FIRST PATROLMAN
SECOND PATROLMAN
CARLOS

TIME: In the 1950s.
PLACE: The border line between Mexico and the United States.

Wetback Run by Theodore Apstein. Copyright © 1961 by Theodore Apstein. Reprinted by permission of Theodore Apstein.

CAUTION: All rights reserved. This play, in its printed form, is designed for the reading public only. All dramatic, motion-picture, radio, television and other rights in it are fully protected by copyright in the United States, the British Empire, including the Dominion of Canada, and all other countries of the Copyright Union. No performance, professional or amateur, nor any broadcast, nor any public reading or recitation, may be given without the written permission, in advance, of the author, Theodore Apstein, 623 North Walden Drive, Beverly Hills, Calif. 90210.

Wetback Run

SCENE 1

Fade in: Close shot of a boy of six swinging on a very rudimentary wooden gate, which is part of a fence. The boy is dressed in the white duck suiting of Mexican country people. We pull back and see JACINTO SANDOVAL, *in his mid-twenties, appear in the yard.* JACINTO *is also dressed in white, wears a straw hat and sandals, and is carrying a cardboard suitcase.*

JACINTO. Fernando! (*The boy turns, sees him, jumps off the gate.*) I am leaving now. (*The boy looks down at the ground. He is sad, but doesn't know what to say. He wiggles his toes in the sand.*) Fernando, I will come back. (*The boy nods, but he is having a hard time trying not to cry.* JACINTO *puts down his suitcase, takes an orange out of his pocket.*) Fernando . . . (*The boy looks up.* JACINTO *throws the orange to him. The boy catches it.*) Very good, Fernando. (*He opens his hands, asking* FERNANDO *to throw it back to him.* FERNANDO *does.* JACINTO *catches it.*) When I come back, we will have not only this (*Meaning the orange.*) but meat and rice and enough milk, like the mother and sister of my friend, Pascual. (*The game continues during the following exchange.*) There is always meat on their table since Pascual went to the north.

FERNANDO. Is my mother still crying?

JACINTO. Yes, but she will stop soon, if *you* do not cry.

FERNANDO. (*Shakes his head. He will not cry.*) Then . . . you are not scared?

JACINTO. I will not lie to you, my son. I *am* a little scared. It is the first time I leave Santa Teresa. But there is no work for a man in these fields. The earth is so dry—not enough food to give to my three good sons and wife. (*He drops the orange and opens his arms to* FERNANDO. *The boy rushes to him.*

JACINTO *holds him tightly, caresses him, kisses him.*) Look, Fernando—there—far—it is only a little piece of blue sky. But there is more—and I must find it. (*He pulls himself away, picks up the suitcase and goes to the gate.*)

FERNANDO. Father! (*There is anguish in his cry, but when* JACINTO *turns to him, the boy is smiling. He has the orange in his hand. He shows* JACINTO *that he wants to throw it to him.*)

JACINTO. No, it is for you.

FERNANDO. Please—take it. (JACINTO, *moved by the boy's faith and trust, holds his hand open. The boy throws him the orange.*)

(*Dissolve to: Close shot of a passport being stamped. Pull back to show a Mexican* IMMIGRATION INSPECTOR *behind a window.*)

INSPECTOR. Terminated, with you. Walk across the bridge! Show your passport to the American immigration inspector on the other side! (*The woman standing in front of the window awaits further instructions. He hands her the passport.*) That is all. Goodbye. Next?

(*The woman leaves and a man approaches the window. We pull further back to see the sign* "Oficina de Migración" *over the window. And we pan to the waiting room with benches, water fountain, and other windows.* JACINTO *comes in with his cardboard suitcase. He looks around curiously and approaches the person nearest to him on the bench, an* OLD WOMAN.)

OLD WOMAN. Sit down. Here! I am next.

JACINTO. Thank you. (*Sits down.*) They told me to come here. 'I wanted to walk across the bridge, but they said to come here first.

OLD WOMAN. Always the same thing. Hours. You have to wait hours. Who wants to cross the Big River anyway? Better to eat a few beans and stay in your own land.

(TORRES, *a man with a sly smile on his lips, comes in, walks through the room, examining the faces of the immigrants.*)

INSPECTOR. Next? (*The* OLD WOMAN *jumps up, picks up her bundles.*) No—not you! You have to wait until the lawyer comes with your papers. Next! (JACINTO *crosses to the window.*) Next!

JACINTO. But the señora was here before me.

INSPECTOR. No politeness here. She has to wait. Come here!

JACINTO. Good day, Señor Inspector.

INSPECTOR. Good day, Señor . . .

JACINTO. Sandoval. Jacinto Sandoval.

INSPECTOR. Now may I see your border-crossing card?

JACINTO. No.

INSPECTOR. What do you mean, no?

JACINTO. I have no card.

INSPECTOR. But you wish to cross the border?

JACINTO. Yes, Señor Inspector. I wish to work.

INSPECTOR. I see. (*Extends his hand.*) Passport? Your passport! The document you were given at the government office.

JACINTO. I did not go to any office. Pascual told me this was the place to come.

INSPECTOR. Pascual?

JACINTO. Pascual Flores. He crossed the bridge last year.

INSPECTOR. (*Impatient.*) You can't just cross the bridge! Look, Señor . . .

JACINTO. Sandoval.

INSPECTOR. Señor Sandoval. This bridge: it is not simply a bridge over the Big River. It is the line between two countries—the border, the frontier.

JACINTO. Yes, yes, I know. I wish to go to the other country.

INSPECTOR. There are laws! American laws. Mexican laws. And you, Señor Jacinto Sandoval, you must comply with the laws of both countries!

JACINTO. You know, Señor Inspector, you remind me a little of Amparo.

INSPECTOR. And who is Amparo?

JACINTO. (*Laughs.*) My wife.

INSPECTOR. Get out of here! Get out!

JACINTO. No—no, please, Señor Inspector, do not be so angry. There is something I do not understand . . .

INSPECTOR. Something!

JACINTO. Santa Teresa is only a very small village and I do not know—I do not know about bridges that are between two countries—or lines, or borders. Please tell me what I must do. I will do anything! Anything, Señor Inspector. But I must cross the Big River!

(*Several people have gathered around the window.*)

INSPECTOR. Very well! Go back and sit down. All of you! And well, you need a passport. You go there—(*Points to another window.*)—they will give you your passport. But you will need six photographs of your face.

JACINTO. Six. So many?

INSPECTOR. The law says six. Good luck to you, Señor Jacinto Sandoval! Next?

(*We come up on a sign which reads* "Oficina de Pasaportes" *and see the* GOVERNMENT OFFICIAL *at the window.*)

OFFICIAL. A passport, huh? There are many requirements to obtain a passport.

(*We pull back to see* JACINTO *on the other side of the window.*)

JACINTO. I already have them. (*Shows him the photographs.*) Please, señor, I only have enough to eat today. I think I can get work before today is finished if only . . .

OFFICIAL. Naturally you have your permit from the Ministry of the Interior? And your labor permit? And the contract?

JACINTO. No.

OFFICIAL. Who are you going to work for?

JACINTO. How do I know? I am going to *look* for work.

OFFICIAL. On the other side of the Big River? It is not permitted. You come back next summer. Then the recruiting committee is here.

JACINTO. Who?

OFFICIAL. The men who come to hire Mexicans for work in the north. Come next summer, señor! Maybe they will select you. I am very sorry. (*He closes the shutters of his window.* JACINTO, *disheartened, turns away from the window.* TORRES, *who is nearby, approaches him.*)

TORRES. Señor, I see you are having difficulties. It is not necessary to have so many difficulties only to cross a bridge, eh? Perhaps I may be of help. Permit me to invite you to have a little something . . .

(*Dissolve to: The counter of a hole-in-the-wall eating place, as* TORRES *and* JACINTO *appear.*)

TORRES. (*To the* WAITER.) Pancho, pulque—two. (*The* WAITER *fills two tall glasses with a milky liquid from a barrel labeled* "pulque," *and serves them.*) Pulque is the best drink of any.

JACINTO. (*Toasting him.*) Health!

TORRES. (*After taking a drink.*) So . . . naturally now you will have to return to your village?

JACINTO. To go back to Santa Teresa, like this—with my tail between my legs. . . .

TORRES. I understand, Señor Sandoval. You are not the first to leave a home looking for fortune.

JACINTO. Amparo, my wife, she thinks it is wrong to be a stranger in another land. So she always says to me: put out the dream, Jacinto. But always there is the scorched earth—and every day I saw more of my sons' bones through the skin. I cannot put out the dream. I do not wish to. (*Pause.*) My friend Pascual never told me that only in the summer they hire men for the north.

TORRES. Even then it is difficult. Many want to go. Few are taken. Often it is a question of money, like this: (*Indicates money passing under the counter.*) You understand? (*A pause.*) I have a border crossing card. (*Shows it to* JACINTO.) I have business, on both sides of the Big River.

JACINTO. But if you have business on the other side, also, is it possible that you can give me a contract? I will take any kind of work.

TORRES. I cannot give you a contract. However—

JACINTO. Yes?

TORRES. You have muscle, señor. Do you also have what makes a man?

JACINTO. I will prove it to you any way you wish.

TORRES. Every month men *row* across the river.

JACINTO. Without the permit? But then if they are caught . . .

TORRES. I ask if you have what makes a man. Forget it señor! (*Rising.*) Go home, Señor Sandoval! It is much safer there. With your wife—what is her name—Amparo?

JACINTO. Señor, I would like to go.

TORRES. Ah? Then I will see if we can make arrangements. (JACINTO *takes out his little sack of money, which he carries on a string around his neck.*) Please, señor, we will not talk of such things now. The important matter is to get you to the other side of the Big River. (*Dissolve to: Riverbank on the Mexican side. It is night. We hear the sound of the water. There is an occasional reflection from a shaft of light that is thrown on the river from a lighthouse tower. Otherwise the place is quite dark. Two* MEN *squat against a piece of driftwood. One lights a cigarette. The* OLD MAN *munches on a piece of bread.* TORRES *enters with* JACINTO.) It will be tonight. We have to wait until they stop throwing light on the river. You can sit there with the others.

FIRST MAN. Your first time to go across?

JACINTO. Yes, yes, the first time. You

have been there before? (TORRES *smiles, and leaves.*)

FIRST MAN. (*To the* OLD MAN.) Did you hear, Señor? Have I been there? So . . . the first time, eh! We have an apprentice with us. Apprentice wetback, we welcome you.

JACINTO. Apprentice, I understand. But the other word . . .

FIRST MAN. The señor has never heard of men who wet their backs. Sometimes there has to be a little swimming to arrive at the other shore. And that is the name they have for us there—wetbacks.

JACINTO. I do not care about the name. But if you have been there before, why did you not get a contract to come again? If you have a contract, you can walk across the bridge.

FIRST MAN. (*Sarcastically.*) The Inspector does not like my face.

OLD MAN. Wetbacks get no contracts.

JACINTO. Why did you not stay?

FIRST MAN. I? I was caught. If you are caught one time, you can never get a permit—or a passport. He—(*Pointing to the* OLD MAN.)—he was never caught, but he got homesick for his village. Still you always try again. The dollars are there.

OLD MAN. Tell him everything! They pay less to wetbacks. Then, after you pay for the privilege of crossing, there is not much left.

FIRST MAN. So, señor, still you want to go?

JACINTO. Yes. Señor, the difficulties you tell me about—to me they are very small.

TORRES. (*Returning with* PEPE, *the boatman.*) Pepe, have the boat ready in a half hour! Then it will be safe. Well, and I wish you good fortune.

JACINTO. You are not going with us?

TORRES. There is no need. *I* can walk across the bridge. But I'll see you, Jacinto Sandoval. Don't worry; I'll see you on the other side.

(*Dissolve to: The boat on the river.*

The three MEN *and* PEPE *are in it. We hear the sound of oars striking the water.*)

FIRST MAN. You look to the other side with hope, apprentice?

JACINTO. Yes, yes!

(*A shaft of light hits the boat. They all duck.*)

FIRST MAN. They saw us.

OLD MAN. Back! We must return!

JACINTO. But we are already in the middle of the River. (*In the distance, they hear the screeching of the border patrol cars.*) What?

OLD MAN. The border patrols. Row back!

JACINTO. No! Please . . .

OLD MAN. Fool! We are still closer to the Mexican bank. Tomorrow night we can try again.

JACINTO. No. Tonight! A few more minutes.

OLD MAN. We are going back.

JACINTO. I will not go back. I must cross!

FIRST MAN. Sit down, idiot! (*The screeching sound is heard again.*) Row back! (JACINTO *jumps into the river.*)

OLD MAN. Fool! Come back to the boat! He risks his life. So big is his need to go to the other side . . .

FIRST MAN. Row quickly! (*A shaft of light hits them again.*) Quickly!

(*Dissolve to: Underbrush on the U.S. side,* JACINTO *pulls himself out of the river onto land. He is thoroughly drenched. He hears the sound of a mocking bird and other night noises. Nearby, a car passes by on the highway.* JACINTO *picks up a handful of soil, looks at it, smiles, then sits down and stretches out, relaxed. Suddenly, he hears the terrifying screech of a patrol car. He sits up, tense and frightened.*)

SCENE 2

Fade in: The underbrush, early in the morning, JACINTO *is still asleep, and the soil he held in his hand when he went to sleep has spilled around him. He awakens. He sits up. He collects the soil, sifts it through his fingers. He listens carefully— not a sound. But he feels the intense heat and wipes his face with his sleeve. He lifts his head over the bushes. There is nothing in sight. He stands up, erect, strong, a man looking into the distance with hope.*

Dissolve to: A diner, sound of cars whizzing by. On the counter, there is a display of sandwiches wrapped in wax paper; cookies and pies. The COUNTERMAN *is pouring hot water into the coffee urn.* JACINTO *enters, several coins in his hand. He reaches for a sandwich. The* COUNTERMAN *proceeds to put it on a plate.*

JACINTO. Also coffee, please.

(*Just as the* COUNTERMAN *sets the cup of coffee on the counter, we hear the screeching of the patrol cars.* JACINTO *turns and runs to a nearby farmhouse. We see a gate and a pump with a dipper.* JACINTO *appears. He sees the well. He pushes the gate open, approaches the pump, and is about to reach for the water. Suddenly, a big, comfortable man appears. This is* RAMIREZ.)

RAMIREZ. Where did *you* come from? You're thirsty. Help yourself! (JACINTO *stands frozen, wondering whether he should run once more.*) What's the matter with you? You haven't eaten?

JACINTO. I—I only want a little water.

RAMIREZ. Wait! (*Hands him the dipper.*) You can't drink with your hands.

JACINTO. Thank you.

RAMIREZ. How long have you been on this side?

JACINTO. Oh, I . . .

RAMIREZ. You do not have to answer. My father came from Mexico, but I was born in Texas. My name is still Ramirez, and I like it. Have you picked grapefruit before? (JACINTO *shakes his head.*) But you look strong. Want to work? (JACINTO *nods.*) I ask no questions. The boss doesn't ask me questions—if the work is done. The money is thirty cents an hour. The work is hard. You want it, you can have it.

JACINTO. Can I start now?

RAMIREZ. After you eat . . .

JACINTO. It is like a miracle . . .

RAMIREZ. What?

JACINTO. The earth is dry here also, but you have a harvest, a good harvest.

RAMIREZ. Ah, we have brought water here; we worked with this earth and we forced it to be a valley.

JACINTO. In Santa Teresa . . .

RAMIREZ. No, do not tell me where you are from. Do I have to ask a man where he comes from? No! I am only the foreman. I am not the Department of Immigration.

JACINTO. Yes—thank you.

RAMIREZ. Go to the bunkhouse. (*Calls.*) Antonio! Fix up something to eat! I've hired a new man.

(*Dissolve to: The bunkhouse.* JACINTO *is soon at a table, devouring a dish of beans and a mug of coffee.* ANTONIO, *a nice-looking man in his late twenties, sits on his bunk, drinking coffee.*)

ANTONIO. First I came across seven years ago. Maybe it is eight. I do not know. First I came here. Ramirez hired me. Then came brrr, brrr, brrr, the border patrols with their noise machines. I ran. I went more north. Later they caught me. They sent me back to Mexico. But I came across again. Because—there is Molly. She is a woman.

JACINTO. Naturally.

ANTONIO. Her name is Maria de los Angeles, but she came here when she was a baby, so she is Molly. She's a citizen and

I am not, so I cannot marry her. I have no rights. The food is good, eh?

JACINTO. Excellent.

ANTONIO. What can be better than beans, eh?

JACINTO. Do you have paper—to write a letter?

ANTONIO. To Mexico? That is dangerous.

JACINTO. It is already more than a week. And it is hard to live without my wife, Amparo, and the boys. I have three sons.

ANTONIO. Three, eh? You are so young.

JACINTO. I was married when I was eighteen.

ANTONIO. You told your wife you were coming here?

JACINTO. Yes.

ANTONIO. She was not afraid—to know her man is a wetback?

JACINTO. That, she did not know. (*Wanting to shake off this thought.*) I must get to work.

(*The scene shifts to the bunkhouse.* TORRES *is sitting at the table, peeling a grapefruit.* RAMIREZ *is pacing the floor.*)

RAMIREZ. I do not know what you want. How can I tell where he comes from? I hire new men all the time. They come, they go. And you have no right to ask me . . .

TORRES. You would prefer to have the border patrol question you?

(JACINTO *and* ANTONIO *come in.* JACINTO *rushes to* TORRES, *shakes his hand heartily.*)

JACINTO. Señor Torres!

RAMIREZ. You act like long-lost brothers.

TORRES. Well, and we almost are.

RAMIREZ. Okay. (*He shrugs and goes out.*)

TORRES. So. You are happy here, Jacinto?

JACINTO. Oh, yes. So much money, Señor Torres! Last Saturday I sent to Amparo ten dollars. Ten dollars. Do you know that is one hundred twenty-five pesos, and thirty centavos? But—how did you find me?

TORRES. I have my ways. (*Pointing to* ANTONIO.) And who is he?

JACINTO. Oh, forgive me. My friend, Antonio Lisna! Señor Torres!

TORRES. I am pleased to meet a friend of Jacinto Sandoval's. How did you enter this country?

ANTONIO. Without your help.

JACINTO. (*Surprised by* ANTONIO's *rudeness.*) Antonio . . .

TORRES. You would like to prove you entered without my help? Jacinto, your friend owes me something, I believe.

JACINTO. Antonio owes you . . . ? You know Señor Torres?

ANTONIO. No. But when I saw him, I knew. I owe him—whatever he asks for. How much?

TORRES. For now, five dollars.

JACINTO. But how can you take his money for nothing?

TORRES. He does not object.

ANTONIO. Jacinto does not understand yet that if I do not give you money, you will alert the patrols.

JACINTO. No! He helps men to cross the River.

TORRES. I have to be paid for my services—(*As* ANTONIO *pays him.*)—even when they are not performed. I provide for your friend something most valuable—protection. (*To* ANTONIO.) Thank you, señor. You will not need a receipt. And you, Jacinto, perhaps you think you owe me nothing because you jumped out of the boat so bravely?

JACINTO. Do not laugh at me! I understand I have to pay. (*He digs into his shoes.*) Very well. Five dollars.

TORRES. Ten.

JACINTO. But if I pay you ten, what will I send Amparo this week?

TORRES. Next week I will only take five. (*He takes* JACINTO's *money and starts to go.*)

JACINTO. Torres! Do you have a letter for me? From Amparo? I wrote her to send letters to your address, like you told me.

TORRES. Not this time. Maybe next

Saturday. Work hard, señores. (*He leaves.*)

JACINTO. I am sorry. It is because of me that you had to pay.

ANTONIO. There is always a Torres—if not this one, another—selling us a cent of protection for a dollar.

JACINTO. A man like that—they permit him to cross the border when he wishes—but you and I who want to work—it is not right . . . (*The screeching of the patrol car is heard, a haunting sound.*) Antonio . . .

ANTONIO. I hear. No. They are only passing by.

JACINTO. Every time I hear them, I tremble. I do not like to be afraid. How long will it take to save one thousand pesos?

ANTONIO. It depends on how much Torres takes every week.

JACINTO. It is not right.

ANTONIO. No? And was it right for you to come here?

JACINTO. (*The question of right has never entered his mind before.*) Right—for me . . . ?

ANTONIO. Yes, was it?

JACINTO. I do not understand. You—you think it is not right—and you stay here?

ANTONIO. I told you why. I love Molly. I love her, Jacinto. (*Embarrassed by his confession, he goes to his bunk and lies down.*)

JACINTO. She is probably very nice . . . Molly.

ANTONIO. Yes. But she does not wish to live in Mexico.

JACINTO. When—when do you see her? Does she live in the town?

ANTONIO. No, on the road, not far from here. Sometimes, when it is dark, I go there.

JACINTO. And you are fortunate; you see her. Every night before I close my eyes, I see the face of Amparo. (*He lies down on his bunk.*) It is almost December—the time for the *posadas*. Amparo puts on her green dress. Do you remember the *posadas*, Antonio? Twelve days of feasts! Twelve days of rejoicing! People dancing and singing; the whole village is together! And I think: this year my son, Fernando, is old enough to play with the other children. They will have gifts. And he—he will have nothing from me.

ANTONIO. Your wife will have a gift for him, from the money you send.

JACINTO. It is not the same. No . . .

ANTONIO. You are lonely, Jacinto. I know. Maybe it would not be so hard if sometimes you could see people sing, dance . . .

JACINTO. You mean in the town? Do you ever go?

ANTONIO. A long time ago. Before I knew Molly. But, no, it is too dangerous.

JACINTO. Maybe only one night . . .

ANTONIO. No, Jacinto!

JACINTO. I wish to see the people here: how they laugh, and talk, and dance—only one time.

ANTONIO. I do not know . . .

JACINTO. On Saturday. Next Saturday, yes? Come with me! Please! (*Dissolve to: Exterior of a saloon with the sign* "The Rose of the Valley." *We see two men walk in. A drunken man with a guitar comes rolling out.* JACINTO *and* ANTONIO *are seen on the street. They run around the back alley, to the entrance. Inside a jukebox is playing. A lot of men are at the bar, drinking, talking.* JACINTO *and* ANTONIO *come in, and* ANTONIO *points out an empty spot at the bar.* JACINTO *suddenly notices the* OLD MAN, *starts to greet him.*) Señor . . . ? (*The* OLD MAN *turns away.* JACINTO *is surprised by this, and as he turns, he jostles another man,* ADOLFO, *spilling his drink.*) Forgive me. (ADOLFO *gives him a resentful look.*)

ADOLFO. (*To his friend,* CARLOS.) I can smell them.

CARLOS. Ah, how can you know?

ADOLFO. Fear in his eyes. The way he said forgive me. More of them here—and we get less pay. Fewer jobs. The wetbacks take anything. It is always more than they made at home.

CARLOS. The patrols pick them up all the time. I have no envy—never to know where you will be the next day—it is no life.

ADOLFO. All right, but still they are competition for us.

CARLOS. And still you cannot be sure they are wetbacks.
(JACINTO *and* ANTONIO *have moved to the empty place at the bar.*)
ANTONIO. Beer.
JACINTO. No! Pulque!
ANTONIO. (*Insistently.*) Beer.
ADOLFO. You hear that? He asked for pulque. Come, Carlos!
CARLOS. Wait! Why start anything?
ANTONIO. Do not ask for pulque here! And anyway, they do not have it.
JACINTO. It is a pity. Pulque cured with almonds—it is the sweetest taste of any drink.
(*The* BARTENDER *brings them two beers and* ANTONIO *pays him.* ADOLFO *approaches them.*)
ADOLFO. Pulque is the sweetest taste, eh?
JACINTO. Yes. I remember it is . . . yes.
ADOLFO. You had pulque very recently, eh?
ANTONIO. What do you wish with my friend?
ADOLFO. I do not like him. Or you, either. (CARLOS *tries to pull* ADOLFO *away anxious to avoid a brawl.*)
ANTONIO. Drink your beer, Jacinto! (*Forcibly he takes* JACINTO *by the arm and turns him towards the bar, away from* ADOLFO.)
ADOLFO. Yes, turn your back to me, coward wetback! (JACINTO *starts to swing at* ADOLFO, *but* ANTONIO *stops him.*) Let him, let him . . .
ANTONIO. Leave us alone! We are not bothering you.
JACINTO. He insulted me!
ANTONIO. He did not speak to you.
ADOLFO. I spoke to him all right—to both of you. Why do you come to take my work away from me?
ANTONIO. There is enough work for every man.
JACINTO. Antonio, why do you permit him to . . .
ADOLFO. Permit me, eh? Listen to this, wetback! It is not only work you take away from us; it is our honor. Yes, our honor! Carlos and I—we were born in this country. We belong here. But we look like you. Our names sound like yours. So now they see us and they think *we* do not belong.
(*The* BARTENDER *comes to help* CARLOS *pull* ADOLFO *away, pushing back the men who have gathered around them.* JACINTO *glances around and sees hostility everywhere. He turns to* ANTONIO.)
JACINTO. It is true?
ANTONIO. Do not worry about him.
JACINTO. But if because of me . . . I do not know . . .
ANTONIO. That is best: not to know. Drink your beer!
JACINTO. They do not like us, Antonio. I see it in the face of every man. Maybe we should go.
(*A sound is heard. It is like a whistling noise, but as it gradually comes nearer, we recognize it as the sound of the patrol cars. There is total silence in the saloon. Then the* OLD MAN *darts out.* JACINTO *wants to go, but* ANTONIO *grabs his arm to stop him.*)
ANTONIO. No! There is no time.
JACINTO. But he . . .
ANTONIO. Beer!
(*Two* PATROLMEN *come in. A man starts the jukebox again, and the crowd resumes talking and drinking.*)
FIRST PATROLMAN. (*Approaching* ADOLFO.) Where d'you come from?
ADOLFO. I work in the big citrus grove.
FIRST PATROLMAN. I mean where d'you come from: where're you born?
ADOLFO. San Marcos, Texas.
FIRST PATROLMAN. Got you birth certificate? (ADOLFO *resentfully reaches for his wallet, takes it out and extracts the certificate to show the* PATROLMAN.) Adolfo Sanchez . . . ?
ADOLFO. Yes. Sanchez!
(*The* PATROLMAN *returns the certificate to him.* ADOLFO *glares at* JACINTO. *The* PATROLMAN *turns to look at him.* JACINTO *looks back at him, picks up his bottle and drinks his beer. He drains the bottle, puts it*

down, wipes his mouth with his sleeves still keeping his eyes on the PATROLMAN.)
SECOND PATROLMAN. Come on; let's blow.
(*They go out. Silence. Then the jukebox starts again. A sound of a car driving off.*)
ANTONIO. That was very brave, Jacinto!
JACINTO. You do not know how scared I was. (*Walks over to* ADOLFO.) God bless you, señor. (*He and* ANTONIO *go out.*) You told me it is not right . . . It isn't.
ANTONIO. What can you do? Go home?
JACINTO. No, but it is better that I understand, if I do something that is wrong. Yes, it is better . . .
(*Suddenly* TORRES *comes running down the street.*)
TORRES. What are you doing here—on the street where the patrols can see you?
ANTONIO. They were here.
JACINTO. They did not bother us.
TORRES. They are going to the grove. It is a complete inspection. It is better that you disappear for one or two days.
JACINTO. Disappear? Where do we go?
ANTONIO. Come, Jacinto! You and I— we will go to Molly's house.
TORRES. Go! (*He pushes* ANTONIO, *who in turn starts to pull* JACINTO *away. The sound of sirens in the distance is growing louder.*) Hurry! The patrols are all over town tonight. (*He pushes* JACINTO.)
JACINTO. Do not push me! I am not an animal.
TORRES. Listen to him—listen!
JACINTO. Yes, listen! You have no right to push me! Maybe what I do is wrong, but what you do is wrong, also.
TORRES. Stop arguing with me and run! (*The screeching becomes louder.*) Do you want them to catch you, to send you back to Santa Teresa?
JACINTO. That does not seem so bad, Torres—now.
TORRES. No? Who will you go to, eh? To your wife, Amparo? Your sons? They have already left Santa Teresa.
JACINTO. (*Stunned.*) What?
TORRES. They are coming here, to you.
JACINTO. Amparo is . . .
ANTONIO. Jacinto, quickly!
JACINTO. (*To* TORRES.) Why?
(ADOLFO *comes out of the saloon and watches.*)
TORRES. Run! There is no time!
JACINTO. Amparo . . . (*He hears the cars stop.* ANTONIO *runs off.* JACINTO *hesitates for a second, and then follows him.*)
TORRES. (*Turns to* ADOLFO.) I knew he would run. Always, they run.

SCENE 3

MOLLY's *kitchen.* JACINTO *is at the window, looking out.* MOLLY *is stirring a pot of* pozole *on the stove.* ANTONIO *is seated at the table.*

MOLLY. (*To* JACINTO.) What's the matter? Don't you like my *pozole*?
JACINTO. Oh, yes. The *pozole* is truly good. The corn is strong, the pork is fresh, and the seasoning . . .
MOLLY. Is hot!
JACINTO. Is good!
MOLLY. It's too hot for me, but Antonio likes it this way. All right, Jacinto, eat!
ANTONIO. You did not sleep for three nights. Now you do not eat.
JACINTO. I do not understand why Amparo and my sons are gone from Santa Teresa. I did not write her to come.
MOLLY. Eat! When you're worried, the best is to fill your stomach with good food.
(JACINTO *sits down and starts eating.* ANTONIO *takes* MOLLY's *hand. She's embarrassed to have him do this in front of* JACINTO, *and moves away.*)
JACINTO. No, please! I like to see you— like this . . .

ANTONIO. It makes you homesick. I am sorry.

JACINTO. Do not be sorry. It is good to see love between you and Maria de los Angeles.

MOLLY. I can't even pronounce that. Call me Molly. That's my name: Molly.

ANTONIO. All right, all right, Molly.

JACINTO. Are you ashamed that you were born in Mexico?

MOLLY. I'm only ashamed that I'm twenty-eight years old, and not married. (*This is meant as an accusation against* ANTONIO.)

JACINTO. (*Slowly.*) I am ashamed . . .

ANTONIO. You?

JACINTO. Yes. I was never ashamed until I became a wetback. When I have to run, when I have to hide . . .

MOLLY. Oh, Jacinto, I don't mind hiding you. (*A knock at the door.* MOLLY *glances out the window.*) It's only Torres. (*She opens the door.*)

TORRES. (*Coming in.*) The inspection is finished. You men can return to the grove. Ramirez wants you to hurry; he has to make up for lost time.

JACINTO. Torres, where is my family?

TORRES. (*Ignores him, going to the table.*) Pozole, eh? Why did you not invite me? (MOLLY *picks up another plate.*) Thank you, I will. (*He takes a napkin and sits down.*)

JACINTO. I asked you a question.

TORRES. And I hear. I have something for you. (*He takes out a letter.* MOLLY *motions to* ANTONIO *to come out with her and they leave.* JACINTO *tears the letter open and starts reading, while* TORRES *eats his stew.*) Your wife explains? I have always said I am your friend. Now I bring to you your family.

JACINTO. I did not ask you . . .

TORRES. I know when a man is lonely. And well, when I spoke to your Amparo . . .

JACINTO. You—you were in Santa Teresa? (TORRES *nods.*) What did she say?

TORRES. She is anxious to come here. She wishes to be with you. And your sons are eager to see you again. I could not say no to them, eh? The baby: he is already crawling.

JACINTO. Yes? He was only . . . But they cannot come here! They do not have papers. Torres, I do not want them to cross like I . . .

TORRES. They will not bother a woman —or little boys.

JACINTO. Fernando starts in school next month.

TORRES. He can start here. Very good schools. I will fix the papers for him, and he can say he was born on this side.

JACINTO. Lies!

TORRES. One little lie.

JACINTO. No. No. I want them to go back—to Santa Teresa.

TORRES. It is too late for that. They are already on the way to the border. Do you not wish to see them?

JACINTO. You know that I do. It is not life to be here without them. But it is wrong, it is wrong . . .

TORRES. Well, and there is nothing you can do about it. Except to pay me a small advance.

(*The scene is the exterior of the farm. A little boy is swinging on the gate, in the same way* FERNANDO *was in Mexico.* JACINTO *comes out of the bunkhouse, on his way to the pump, with a coffeepot in his hand. Suddenly he sees the boy, and stops.*)

JACINTO. Fernando! (*The boy swings around to face* JACINTO, *looks surprised, and jumps off the gate.*) I am sorry.

CHARLIE. (*Going to* JACINTO, *with a grapefruit in his hand.*) My name's Charlie. Charlie Ramirez.

JACINTO. Oh, yes—naturally—you are Ramirez' son.

CHARLIE. What did you call me?

JACINTO. Fernando. It is the name of my oldest son. He is five years—no, he is already six years old.

CHARLIE. I'm nine. Where is your son?

JACINTO. In Santa Teresa. That is in Mexico.

CHARLIE. My grandfather was born in Mexico.

JACINTO. But you—you were born here?

CHARLIE. Oh, sure.

JACINTO. It is good to be on the soil where you were born, huh?

CHARLIE. What? Catch! (*He throws him the grapefruit.* JACINTO *catches it. They take each other in—the beginning of a friendship.* JACINTO *throws the grapefruit back to him.*) You haven't been around here very long, have you?

JACINTO. No

CHARLIE. You're not one of those wetbacks?

JACINTO. (*Hesitates. Then, as he throws the grapefruit back to* CHARLIE.) No.

CHARLIE. I didn't really think you were.

JACINTO. No? Why not?

CHARLIE. Well—you're all right.

JACINTO. (*While the grapefruit game continues.*) Charlie . . .

CHARLIE. Yes?

JACINTO. I am one.

CHARLIE. One what?

JACINTO. Wetback. I had to swim. My back was truly wet.

CHARLIE. But that's sneaking in. (*In a whisper.*) You can tell me: are you a bandit?

JACINTO. No, no, Charlie; I am an honest man. (CHARLIE *goes to the pump.*) You cannot believe, eh, that a man can be honest, and still sneak in?

CHARLIE. Well, I don't know. In school they tell me . . . well, I don't know; they might be wrong.

JACINTO. No. No, Charlie. They are not wrong. (*He turns to go.*)

CHARLIE. Hey . . .

JACINTO. I will see you later. (CHARLIE *looks after him, as* JACINTO *goes into the bunkhouse, to* ANTONIO'S *bunk.*) Antonio, I must go . . .

ANTONIO. Eh? Where?

JACINTO. I cannot sit here and let them cross the river—Amparo and my sons—I have to stop them.

ANTONIO. How? How will you stop them?

JACINTO. I will go to the border.

ANTONIO. Jacinto, the border is a very big place.

JACINTO. I know. But what can I do? I cannot write a letter. I do not know where . . . if I go, maybe . . . maybe . . . I have to!

ANTONIO. The patrols will catch you before you find Amparo, and then what?

JACINTO. I do not want my sons to hide, to run, to sneak in!

(*He puts on his hat, and goes to the door.* ANTONIO *grabs him by the arm.*)

ANTONIO. Do you not see it is too late? You will not find them. Wait! When they are here, then . . .

JACINTO. Then it will be too late for them, also. No, I must go!

ANTONIO. Please, Jacinto! (*The screeching of the patrols is heard in the distance. This shocks* JACINTO *into the reality of the situation.* ANTONIO *lets go of him, and* JACINTO *slowly retreats to his bunk, like an imprisoned man.*)

JACINTO. I had a home in Santa Teresa, a family. Now there is no one there, and I am here, and I cannot move.

(TORRES *enters, follwed by two Mexicans.*)

TORRES. Quick! Quick! (*He pushes the men towards their bunks, where they start packing.*) When you reach McAlister, Oklahoma, you go to a diner named "The Bowl of Chili" and you ask for Paco. He will tell you where to go. (*To* JACINTO.) Why do you sit here? The patrols will be here in five minutes. (ANTONIO *starts gathering his clothes, but* JACINTO *just sits there.*) Jacinto, you hear what I say?

RAMIREZ. (*Rushing into the bunkhouse.*) Why does this always happen at the most busy time? Do you have better work for them in the north?

TORRES. Please, Ramirez, the men must go north for their protection. I tell you this business gets more difficult every month.

RAMIREZ. My heart bleeds for you.

TORRES. What are you so arrogant about? You hire them, no?

RAMIREZ. It does not matter to me what men I hire.

TORRES. No? You pay these as much as others? So . . . do not throw stones!

(*One of the men starts for the door with his things.*)

TORRES. Very well, and be careful! (*The man leaves.* TORRES *turns and sees that* JACINTO *hasn't moved.*) What is the matter with you? This time you need your things, you will not come back here.

ANTONIO. I will help him. (*He gets* JACINTO's *clothes, throws them on the bunk.*)

JACINTO. Where this time? You say north?

TORRES. Yes. Oklahoma is the name.

MOLLY. (*Off.*) Antonio! Antonio! (*She comes in, very upset.*) Antonio, is it true what they tell me? You're leaving?

ANTONIO. I will come back.

MOLLY. One day I will be an old woman and you will say this to me.

TORRES. He does not have time now for your crying. Go! Go! (*He pushes them out of the bunkhouse.*)

JACINTO. Do not talk to her like this! Why do you always push others?

TORRES. You have to hurry, also!

JACINTO. Where is Amparo? Where are my sons?

TORRES. They will catch up with you. The arrangements are made. Your wife has already given me the money . . .

JACINTO. You took money from her, also? The money that I send to her! There is no decency in you, Torres! (*He hits* TORRES. RAMIREZ *tries to hold him back.*) No! You will tell me where they are! (*To* RAMIREZ.) Let me alone! (*He pins* TORRES *against the bunk.*) Where is Amparo?

TORRES. In my shack, on the other side of the River.

JACINTO. The place where I took the boat?

TORRES. Yes. They are waiting—for a night without much moon—to cross.

(*The sirens of the patrol cars are approaching. The man who was still packing rushes out.*)

RAMIREZ. You must go quickly!

JACINTO. No. Let him run. Let them all run. They run so many times . . . now they cannot stop. I will not run!

RAMIREZ. Jacinto; you will be safe in the north.

TORRES. (*Frightened.*) If you do not wish for your wife to come up, I will tell her to wait—or to return to Santa Teresa.

JACINTO. Who are you to tell my wife what to do? Eh? I will tell her myself when I see her. I *will* see her! You know, *that* seems like a dream.

RAMIREZ. Jacinto, you are angry. But listen, it is always better not to be caught.

JACINTO. Do not worry, Ramirez. I do not wish you to have trouble because of me. I will walk to the road, until I meet the patrol cars.

TORRES. Fool! You forget how it was in Santa Teresa. With your dry earth! With always bad harvests!

JACINTO. I do not forget, Torres. But a man can fight against a bad harvest. I see it here.

RAMIREZ. It's the work of many years, Jacinto.

JACINTO. I have many years. (TORREZ *sinks into a chair.* JACINTO *shakes* RAMIREZ' *hand. The sirens are very near.*) If some day I wish to come back, I will walk across the bridge with Amparo and my sons, and I will say: Señor Inspector, here are the papers for Jacinto Sandoval and his family.

RAMIREZ. Why—why did you wish to come in the first place?

JACINTO. I did not know, Ramirez, how much it means to hold up my head. It is nice here, but it is still only one little piece of blue sky. And for me—for me it looks better from Santa Teresa. (*He goes out.*)

TORRES. He will ruin both of us.

RAMIREZ. I like him. A man who holds his head up—how often do you find one like that?

(JACINTO *walks down the road with his bundle. The screeching of the cars is getting louder.* JACINTO *looks determined. We hear the brakes as the cars stop. So does the screeching.* JACINTO *smiles and goes towards the patrolmen, ready and eager to face them.*)

CURTAIN

Topics for Further Study

1. Write a sequel to *Wetback Run*, showing how Jacinto gets back to his wife and children across the border and what plans they make for a living in Mexico.

2. For a complete treatment of the *bracero* farm laborers, read Ernesto Galarza's *Merchants of Labor: The Mexican Bracero Story* (Santa Barbara: McNally and Loftin, 1965) and give an oral or written report.

3. Discuss the morality of committing illegal acts in order to provide for one's family. Are people justified at any time to ignore the law because of economic difficulties? Discuss pro and con.

4. Theodore Apstein has taken an occurrence that probably has happened thousands of times and made it into an artistic piece of work. How has he done it? What appeals most to you: the plot, the characterization, the idea behind the play?

5. From your study of American history, were other immigrants viewed with suspicion by immigrants who had arrived on these shores earlier? Are such fears present today? What can be done to remove such fears and prejudices?

6. Does Apstein reveal his own attitude toward Jacinto and his fellow wetbacks, or does he let the story convey its own meaning? How might a Chicano playwright have handled this story differently?

7. Write an ending to the play that differs from the one by Apstein, in which Jacinto makes a decision other than to return home.

Dassel-Cokato Jr. Sr. High School Library
Independent District 466